The Invention of Greek Ethnography

GREEKS OVERSEAS

Series Editors
Carla Antonaccio and Nino Luraghi

This series presents a forum for new interpretations of Greek settlement in the ancient Mediterranean in its cultural and political aspects. Focusing on the period from the Iron Age until the advent of Alexander, it seeks to undermine the divide between colonial and metropolitan Greeks. It welcomes new scholarly work from archaeological, historical, and literary perspectives, and invites interventions on the history of scholarship about the Greeks in the Mediterranean.

A Small Greek World
Networks in the Ancient Mediterranean
Irad Malkin

Italy's Lost Greece
Magna Graecia and the Making of Modern Archaeology
Giovanna Ceserani

The Invention of Greek Ethnography
From Homer to Herodotus
Joseph E. Skinner

Pindar and the Construction of Syracusian Monarchy in the Fifth Century B.C.
Kathryn A. Morgan

The Poetics of Victory in the Greek West
Epinician, Oral Tradition, and the Deinomenid Empire
Nigel Nicholson

The Invention of Greek Ethnography

From Homer to Herodotus

JOSEPH E. SKINNER

OXFORD
UNIVERSITY PRESS

OXFORD
UNIVERSITY PRESS

Oxford University Press is a department of the University of Oxford.
It furthers the University's objective of excellence in research, scholarship,
and education by publishing worldwide.

Oxford   New York
Auckland   Cape Town   Dar es Salaam   Hong Kong   Karachi
Kuala Lumpur   Madrid   Melbourne   Mexico City   Nairobi
New Delhi   Shanghai   Taipei   Toronto

With offices in
Argentina   Austria   Brazil   Chile   Czech Republic   France   Greece
Guatemala   Hungary   Italy   Japan   Poland   Portugal   Singapore
South Korea   Switzerland   Thailand   Turkey   Ukraine   Vietnam

Oxford is a registered trade mark of Oxford University Press
in the UK and certain other countries.

Published in the United States of America by
Oxford University Press
198 Madison Avenue, New York, NY 10016

© Oxford University Press 2012

First issued as an Oxford University Press paperback, 2016

Library of Congress Cataloging-in-Publication Data
Skinner, Joseph (Joseph Edward)
The invention of Greek ethnography : ethnography and history from Homer to Herodotus / Joseph Skinner.
p.   cm. — (Greeks overseas)
Includes bibliographical references.
ISBN 978-0-19-979360-0 (hardcover); 978-0-19-022918-4 (paperback)
1. Ethnology—Greece—History. 2. Historiography—Greece—History. 3. History, Ancient—Historiography.
4. National characteristics, Greek. 5. Greece—Civilization—To 146 B.C. I. Title.
DF135.S55   2012
305.800938—dc23   2011017482

1 3 5 7 9 8 6 4 2

Printed in the United States of America
on acid-free paper

CONTENTS

Figure 0.1 Map of the ancient Mediterranean with principal sites mentioned in the text. Map by the author.

Figure 1.1 Statuette of mounted Amazon from the rim of a cinerary urn (see also cover illustration), height approximately 11 cm. About 480 B.C., Campanian Bronze, British Museum 560, from S. Maria di Capua Vetere. Drawn from photo: S. Haynes, 1965, *Etruscan Bronze Utensils*, pls. 3-4. Drawing by the author.

Figure 2.1 Sculpture of a kneeling archer, thought to represent Paris, Temple of Aphaia, west pediment, c.490-480 BC © Stiftung Archäologie, Munich. Reproduced with kind permission of Prof. Dr. Vinzenz Brinkmann.

Figure 2.2 Photo: Seated Amazon. Fragment of an Attic red-figure cup, height 5.75cm, 5th century B.C. Liverpool, Garstang Museum C671. Reproduced with kind permission of the Garstang Museum of Archaeology, University of Liverpool. Photograph: J. R. Petersen.

Figure 2.3 Head of Bousiris. Attic black-figure sherd, Siana cup, ca.565 B.C., attributed to the Heidelberg Painter. Palermo, Museo Archaeologico Regionale 1986. Redrawn from *LIMC* III pl. 131, Bousiris no.29. Drawing by the author.

Figure 3.1 Silver tetradrachm of Cyrene, AR 15.46g c.525-480 B.C., recovered from Naucratis. Obv. Cyrene seated, facing left; left field, silphium bearing fruit; test cut, rev., type effaced (BM1886, o802.12). Reproduced with kind permission of the Trustees of the British Museum.

Figure 3.2 The blinding of Polyphemus. Aristonothos Krater (side B). ca. 650 B.C., from Caere. Rome, Musei Capitolini 6. Drawn from photo. Drawing by the author.

Figure 4.1 Regional map of Northern Pontic Region. Redrawn from Bresson, A. et al., eds., 2007, *Une koinè pontique: cités grecques, sociétés indiginès et empires mondiaux sur le littoral nord de la mer noire (VIIe s.a.C.- IIIe s. a.C.)*, 18, fig. 1. Map by the author.

Figure 4.2 Map of Olbia. Redrawn from S. D. Kryzhitskiy, "Excavations at Olbia in the past three decades," in D. Braund and S. D. Kryzhitskiy, eds., 2007, *Classical Olbia and the Scythian World: From the Sixth century BC to the second century AD*, 8, fig. 2. Map by the author.

Figure 4.3 *Stele of Leoxos*. Drawn from photo: M. F. Vos, 1963, *Scythian Archers in Archaic Attic Vase-Painting*, pl. XV. Drawing by the author.

Figure 4.4 Southern Calabria. Regional map showing major sites and topography. Map by the author.

Figure 4.5 Photo: Kore alabastron from San Salvatore, mid-sixth century B.C. Reproduced with kind permission of Prof. Lin Foxhall, Bova Marina Archaeological Project. Photograph: Lin Foxhall.

Figure 4.6 The imagined centre: Delphi and Olympia. Map by the author.

Figure 4.7 The Sanctuary of Zeus at Olympia. Redrawn from A. Mallwitz, 1988, "Cult and competition locations at Olympia," in W. J. Raschke, ed., *The Archaeology of the Olympics: The Olympics and Other Festivals in Antiquity*, 82, fig. 6.2. Map by the author.

Figure 4.8 Delphi, The Sanctuary of Apollo. Redrawn from C. Morgan, 1990, *Athletes and Oracles*, 128, fig. 19. Map by the author.

Figure 4.9 Bronze sphyrelaton from Olympia. Olympia Museum: Height ca.1.2m. Redrawn from B. Borell and D. Rittig, 1998, *Ol-Forsch* 26, pls. 57, 54. Drawing by the author.

ACKNOWLEDGMENTS

While the eclectic nature of this book renders ellipses and solecisms all but inevitable, the remainder bears witness to the enduring patience and unswerving generosity of one individual in particular. Thomas Harrison first introduced me to Greek ethnography—and Herodotus—during my undergraduate studies at the University of St. Andrews. Then, as now, his passion for his subject was both infectious and inspiring, but this has been more than matched by the kindness and wisdom that he has subsequently displayed in his capacity as teacher, supervisor, and friend. I have also benefited from the help and support of a veritable cohort of benefactors who gave freely of their time and knowledge, whether by reading chapter sections or inspiring conversation. Christopher Tuplin, Zosia Archibald, Robin Osborne, Kostas Vlassopoulos, Catherine Morgan, Eran Almagor, Theodora Hadjimichael, Amy Coker, Sean Gurd, and Lin Foxhall have all read and commented on chapter sections; it goes without saying that they bear no responsibility for any errors that remain. I am particularly indebted to Lin for years of help and support in her capacity as "archaeological mentor" and remain deeply grateful for both the initial opportunity to participate in the Bova Marina Archaeological Project (BMAP) and permission to publish data from the site at San Salvatore. Participation in BMAP brought with it a chance to consider broad-brush questions of identity and difference in a regional setting in the company of scholars who have all influenced my outlook and approach in one way or another (notably John Robb, Jonathan Prag, Hamish Forbes, and David Yoon). Discussions with Irad Malkin, Ian Jenkins, John Davies, Matthew Fitzjohn, Andrew Meadows, and Renee Hirschon have been a great source of help and inspiration, while Michael Sommer provided advice and support at the drop of a hat. Graham Oliver and Phiroze

Vasunia provided invaluable feedback in their capacity as examiners; in drawing my attention to the numerous ways in which my arguments might be developed or sharpened they have done much to improve the end result. The same is equally true of Oxford University Press's anonymous readers and Simon Hornblower, who kindly drew attention to a number of editorial lapses that would have otherwise escaped detection. Their insightful and supportive comments are all gratefully acknowledged. If the reader encounters anything remiss in this volume it will be my fault and mine alone. When it comes to the book itself, my intellectual debts are obvious and too numerous to mention—this being, after all, a work of synthesis. I respectfully acknowledge the generations of scholarship upon which this study is predicated and remain ever conscious of standing, however precariously, on the shoulders of giants. Of these, special mention should go to the indefatigable Felix Jacoby, who both framed many of the problems here discussed and created that monument to erudition and diligence, *Die Fragmente der Griechischen Historiker* (*FGrHist*).

While support for this research came primarily in the form of a bursary from the University of Liverpool—supplemented by a graduate teaching fellowship—I have also benefited from the generosity of other institutions whose support I gratefully acknowledge. Special thanks are due to first the Classical Association and subsequently the Fondation Hardt pour l'étude de l'Antiquité classique for grants that permitted me to pursue my studies at the oasis of peace and tranquility that is "La Chandoleine"—an extraordinary place of refuge and inspiration where I met many good friends. Following the completion of my doctorate I had the privilege of spending a year as School Student at the British School at Athens (2009–2010). I am delighted to have this opportunity to express my gratitude to the staff at both institutions for their unstinting help and support, together with the steady stream of visiting scholars who did so much to enrich my time in Geneva/Athens en passant. In the case of Athens, special thanks must go to Catherine Morgan and Robert Pitt for their unstinting attempts to pass on their knowledge and expertise and the School's librarians for their utter brilliance, patience, and resourcefulness. For assistance with matters technical I am variously indebted to Andrew Wilson, Jennifer Mirdamadi, George Bruseker, and John Robert Peterson.

My debt to my friends remains incalculable: a collection of often bemused and long-suffering individuals without whose companionship this project would have seemed overwhelmingly daunting. For support and camaraderie in the face of adversity, including much needed excursions for cake and coffee and acts of kindness and hospitality too numerous to mention, special thanks go to Rosie Fletcher, John Gait, Jo Kyffin, Jo Paul, Tom Loughlin, Angelos Papadopoulos, Stephen Flett, ElTayeb Abass, Nai One Lai, Jordan Rockford, Maggi and David Creese, Davide Salvo, Michael Iliakis, and Jean-Sébastien Balzat. Tim Gore, Alan Patterson, and Peter Mann provided (what might loosely be termed as) encouragement from afar and welcome bolt-holes in Winchester, Edinburgh, and Eton.

Warmest thanks are due to Vinzenz Brinkmann and Munich's Stiftung Archäologie, the Trustees of the British Museum, and the Garstang Museum of Archaeology, University of Liverpool for permission to reproduce images. I am equally grateful to Oxford University Press's senior editor, Stefan Vranka, together with the series editors, Carla Antonaccio and Nino Luraghi, for their encouragement and support. At a more practical level, I would have been all at sea on more than one occasion without the help of first Deirdre Brady and then Sarah Pirovitz, editorial assistants both at OUP.

Lastly to my beloved family: Benj and Kat, but especially my parents, who taught me the measure of happiness.

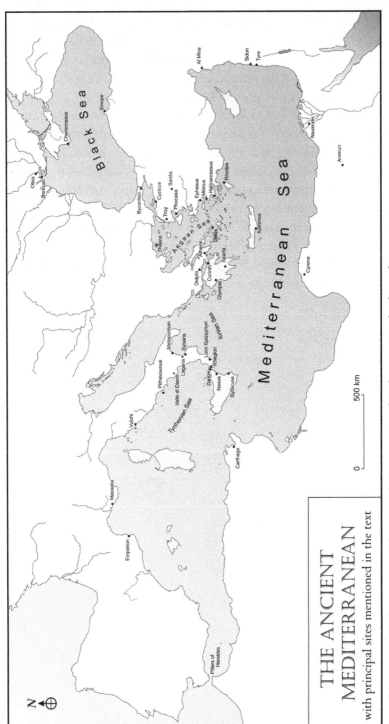

Map of the ancient Mediterranean with principal sites mentioned in the text. Map by the author.

The Invention of Greek Ethnography

CHAPTER 1 | Ethnography before Ethnography

GREEK ETHNOGRAPHY IS CONVENTIONALLY defined as the self-conscious prose study of non-Greek peoples. A study of its origins and function might at first appear relatively straightforward. Greek ethnographic interests are widely assumed to have developed in tandem with the wider sense of (Greek) identity from which they took their cue. This collective sense of identity is generally thought to have remained hazy and loosely organized until the fifth-century war with Persia whereupon it rapidly crystallized into a diametric opposition between "Hellene" and "barbarian."[1] In providing the basis for a series of prose accounts in which the habits and customs of non-Greeks might be held up to scrutiny, this new sense of cultural identity brought clarity and focus to previously diffuse imaginings. The inspiration for this genre has been variously explained in terms of an innate curiosity toward foreign lands and peoples characteristic of enlightened and "scientific" Hellenes,[2] a profound sense of culture shock engendered by an encounter with an entirely alien polity, and direct experience of Persian

---

[1] For this model (discussed further below): E. Hall 1989 (on ethnography in particular) and J. Hall 1997, 2002. For earlier approaches to ancient ethnography, see Trüdinger 1918; Norden 1920; K. E. Müller 1972; Thomas 1982. While the emergence of Panhellenic sentiments and an associated Greek–barbarian antithesis has recently been down-dated to the late sixth–early fifth century B.C., a period of mounting tension between Ionian Greeks and Achaemenid Persia, the latter still marks the watershed between hazy and oppositional identities; see L. Mitchell 2007 (for Panhellenism/chronology) and H. J. Kim 2009.

[2] E.g., Fornara 1983, 12–13 (an idealized and somewhat contestable view very much at variance with that of recent commentators who see Ionia as the locus of the Greek–barbarian antithesis): "Early ethnography is marked by a scientific objectivity and unprejudiced characterization of alien modes of life that are a pleasure to behold. It has been asserted that a condition for such detachment was the relative amity of Greek and barbarian in Ionia until the time of Croesus . . . [b]ut the scientific perspective was maintained in spite of the Ionian Revolt and the Persian Wars. No explanation of this impressive Hellenic mental trait is required." (The author is responding to Schwabl 1962, 23.)

imperial practices.[3] The "invention" of Greek ethnography is widely agreed to have paved the way for yet another great invention, however, a momentous development first conceived and expounded by the great German philologist and historian Felix Jacoby (1876–1959).[4] Inspired by recent events, an accomplished exponent of the genre underwent a dramatic conversion: Herodotus the ethnographer gave way to Herodotus the historian, and an entirely new genre emerged in the form of so-called Great Historiography.[5]

While widely subscribed to and beguiling in its simplicity, this thesis is open to critique. What appears at first sight to be an entirely convincing narrative of an evolution from archaic to classical periods turns out, on closer inspection, to contain many glosses and elisions—some comparatively minor and subtle, others less so. It might be argued, for instance, that the neat periodization, which sees "archaic" and "classical" identities—and therefore ethnographies—as separate and distinct, possesses a dubious perspicuity.[6] Did the explosion of ethnography that occurred during the fifth-century b.c. really arise as the result of a specific historical event, or was it rather the product of a long-running interest in the foreign or alien, the signs of which had long been evident?[7] Was ethnography, like the barbarian, "invented" in response to the unprecedented levels of intercultural contact that accompanied Persian incursions into Ionia and mainland Greece and what role did it play overall in the emergence of any common sense of "Greek" identity?[8] How should the textualization of ethnographic knowledge be interpreted in the light of a vast array of material evidence attesting to the *longue durée* of intercultural contact and exchange?[9] As questions multiply, the study of Greek ethnography appears far less simple and straightforward—and perhaps more interesting as a result.

---

[3] H. J. Kim 2009, 24 and passim. See further below.

[4] Based on a paper presented a year earlier in Berlin at the International Congress for Historical Studies, "Über die Entwicklung der griechischen Historiographie und den Plan einer neuen Sammlung der griechischen Historikerfragmente" was published in the journal *Klio* in 1909. See further below.

[5] I.e., narrative history. For overview and discussion of the nature and origins of ancient historiography, see Marincola 1997, 1–3; 2001, 1–3. For revolutions/inventions in general, see R. Osborne 2006.

[6] See Gruen 2011; Gunter 2009 for recent discussion and critique. For identities in the ancient Mediterranean see now van Dommelen and Knapp 2011a, 1: "[B]ounded cultures and well-defined populations with readily distinct identities may have been far less common than usually assumed."

[7] See, in particular, Malkin 1998a; Dougherty 2001.

[8] See Bentley 1993 for a historical account of the processes of intercultural contact and exchange but not without S. Hall 1990; Bhabha 1994; Sewell 1999; Antonaccio 2003 on culture theory.

[9] See Sourvinou-Inwood 2005; 1991 on preconceptions/"perceptual filters." For "structuring," see Humphreys 1978; 2004. Cf. Siapkas 2003 on ethnicity in particular.

1.1 Framing the Problem: Defining Ethnography

Before we proceed further we should consider some of the factors that have shaped the way in which ethnography is conceived as both discipline and practice.[10] The gap separating modern and ancient ethnographies should not be underestimated, there being no (ancient) term to denote ethnography per se.[11] The word that Herodotus used to describe his work encompasses a wide variety of fields of which ethnography—if defined simply in the modern sense of writing about foreign peoples—forms only a component part. A term rooted in the Ionian tradition of investigative enquiry, *historiê* means simply "research" or "enquiry," with other authors elsewhere being referred to simply as *logopoioi* ("writers of *logoi*").[12] Indeed, while it would later become standard practice to refer to early ethnographic works using an adjective derived from the lands/peoples upon which they were based (*Persika, Aigyptiaka, Lydiaka*), it is uncertain whether this reflects specific knowledge of individual works to which such titles were assigned, at or around the time of composition, or the assumption that fragmentary material on Persia, Egypt, or Lydia could *only* have had its origins in an independent prose study of a specific tribe or people.[13] In contrast, the historic link with imperialism means that modern conceptions of ethnography remain largely associated with the description of "primitive" peoples and colonial subjects, a ready breeding ground of neocolonialist and Orientalist attitudes. Ethnography is therefore "imagined" as a science in which the habits and customs of remote or exotic peoples are conscientiously documented by intrepid Europeans.[14]

---

[10] Cf. Hammersley and Atkinson 1983; Clifford and Marcus 1986. The (English) term "ethnography" is first attested in 1834 (*Penny Cyclopaedia* II 97; *Oxford English Dictionary* (Compact Edition) (1971) s.v. Ethnography) and was subsequently defined by the ninth edition of the *Encyclopaedia Britannica* as embracing "the descriptive details . . . of the human aggregates and organizations" (*Encyclopaedia Britannica* VIII (1878) 613 s.v. Ethnography).

[11] Jacoby 1909, 88. In fact, Jacoby found it impossible to establish a definition of ethnography that was compatible with his theory postulating a linear development for Greek historiography. For detailed discussion of the problems and their consequences, see Andrea Zambrini's "Aspetti dell'etnografia in Jacoby" (Zambrini 2006) and chapter 5.

[12] Cf. Herodotus *Histories* V 36.6 (hereafter referred to as "Hdt."). See Fornara 1983; Fowler 1996; Schepens 1997; Clarke 1999. For related discussion of this prediisciplinary world, see Thomas 2000.

[13] Schepens 1997; Clarke 1999. See, however, Fraser 2009, 5 together with Jacoby 1949, 100–101: "What we know about the great work of cataloguing and . . . what we know about the conditions under which Greek prose literature developed . . . does not justify extensive scepticism in regard either to the authenticity of books accepted in the library or to the independence of works which the librarians regarded as distinct."

[14] Asad 1973; Comaroff and Comaroff 1992; Lidchi 1997; Penny 2002. On Orientalism: Said 1978; 1993 with notable responses from Clifford 1988 and Bhabha 1994 ("The other question"). Cf. Marcus 2001.

Ethnographic studies, however, have undergone something of a revolution in recent years following a profound shift in attitudes that marked the gradual stagnation and ultimate disintegration of "old world" colonial empires.[15] In fact, traditional definitions of ethnography do little justice to a field of enquiry whose theories and methodologies now find application in disciplines ranging from history and human geography to sociology and cultural studies.[16] Modern ethnography is now defined by its practitioners in far broader terms as approaches to lived culture: "the disciplined and deliberate witness-cum-recording of human events,"[17] whose ultimate goal is nothing less than a reflexive understanding of contemporary society. When viewed in its broadest sense, ethnography, to quote James Clifford, is simply a collection of "diverse ways of thinking and writing about culture" from an outsider's perspective.[18]

Largely immune to such paradigm shifts, classicists and historians remain firmly wedded to the idea of ethnography as a specifically "Greek" invention, one of many revolutions in thought and practice that provided the foundation for "Western civilisation."[19] The contrast could not be greater with the more reflexive and theoretically refined postcolonial, postmodern conception of ethnography as *practice*.[20] When we apply this idea to the study of ancient ethnography as a whole, questions immediately arise concerning the way in which early ethnographies are variously identified and defined. This is, in short, a topic ripe for reappraisal. Although Herodotean "reflexivity"

---

[15] See Asad 1973. For effects: Clifford 1988.

[16] Angrosino 2007 discusses ethnography's response to this "changing research context": technology, globalization, transnational communities, and virtual worlds (see chap. 9 and *passim*). Cf. Atkinson et al. 2001; Coffey 1999; and more traditional field manuals, e.g., Agar 1980; Ellen 1984. For a similar shift in relation to geography: McDowell 1997. Cf. Driver 2001; Mansvelt 2005.

[17] Willis and Trondman 2000, 5. For a bibliographic survey/overview of currents in cultural fieldwork, see Faubion 2001. For current approaches, see Angrosino 2007.

[18] Clifford 1988, 9. Although Clifford is quite explicit in stating that modern ethnography exists in both traditional and innovative forms (Clifford 1988, 9), the two schools of thought make for unhappy bedfellows. For a vigorous rebuttal of the assertion that ethnography is inseparable from anthropology, see Ingold 2008. Robust critique of recent trends in anthropological studies can be found in Forbes 2007, xvi–vii, chap. 2. For the significance of "writing," see below. Maintaining an outsider's perspective is not always easily achieved as (modern) Greek ethnographers have recently discovered: "Greek ethnographers of Greece—like all native ethnographers—have to deal with the problem of achieving cognitive distance: the given socio-cultural and linguistic contiguity with the subjects of their research does not only work to their advantage, but may also blind them to the most obvious and self-evident, yet most important, aspects of life in the 'field'" (Papataxiarchis 2010, 424). (Cognitive distance—or rather the lack of it—had not hitherto been a problem since the ethnographic study of modern Greece was largely pioneered by practitioners working in British, American, and French schools of social and cultural anthropology.)

[19] See Goldhill 2002.

[20] For notions of practice, see Bourdieu 1977; 1990.

has received much attention in recent years, encouraging the suspicion that both Herodotus and perhaps ancient ethnography as a whole are a little more "modern" than we thought, the nature and origins of early ethnographic enquiry have yet to be explored in any detail.[21]

Herodotus has certainly been very much in vogue of late. The veritable avalanche of monographs and conference proceedings devoted to the painstaking analysis of his output and ideas must rank among one of the most impressive literary comebacks of the late twentieth/early twenty-first centuries—at least where Classics is concerned.[22] This aside, the study of Greek ethnography has remained largely static in recent years.[23] It follows, therefore, that while modern anthropologists now concern themselves with recounting ethnographies of television, popular literature, and inner-city youth culture, Greek ethnographers are still restricted—by and large—to studying the ancient equivalents of the Ik, San, or Yanamamo in what amounts to a relatively unimaginative exercise in self-definition.[24] Ethnographic asides on Athens, Spartan kingship, and, perhaps most famously, the Aetolian Eurytanians, notorious for their unintelligible speech and taste for raw flesh (ἀγνωστότατοι δὲ γλῶσσαν καὶ ὠμοφάγοι), receive little more than cursory attention as a result.[25]

Classicists are, in other words, inherently selective when it comes to defining ancient ethnographies, while the criteria upon which such definitions are based are rarely discussed.[26] There remains a very clear tension, therefore, between James Clifford's broader definition of ethnography and the

---

[21] For valuable insights, however, see Kim 2009; Dougherty 2001; Malkin 1998a; Murray 1988–1989.

[22] A selection includes: Hartog 1988 [1980]; one Hardt Entretien (vol. 35); Harrison 2000a; Thomas 2000; Bichler 2001; Munson 2001; Luraghi 2001c; Derow and Parker 2003; Karageorghis and Taifacos 2004; Irwin and Greenwood 2007; and *Companions* by both Bakker et al. (2002) and Dewald and Marincola (2006).

[23] Compare this to Greg Woolf's recent (and altogether innovative) study tracing the relationship between ethnography and empire in the Roman West and valuable comparative work on ethnographic and geographical knowledge in premodern societies (Woolf 2010; Raaflaub and Talbert 2010; Kim 2009).

[24] Cf. Turnbull 1972 (Ik); Thomas 1969; Lee 1979 (San); Chagnon 1997 (Yanamamo); and current issues of *Ethnography*.

[25] Thucydides III 94. Cf. Hdt. V 78; VI 56–60 cf. I 65–8. The latter is particularly notable in the light of recent debate surrounding the nature and extent of Spartan particularism for which see Hodkinson 2009a. Harman's decision to approach Xenophon's fourth-century *Lakedaimoniōn Politeia* as ethnography first and foremost stands out amid a more general tendency to explain ethnographic description of Sparta (often described as *barbarization*) as ideologically driven and historically contingent (cf. Harman 2009; Hodkinson 2009b; Millender 2002). For Spartan kingship, see Millender 2002; 2009.

[26] E.g., G. E. R. Lloyd 2002, 17 citing Aristotle's *Poetics*: "It was, to be sure, perfectly possible . . . to distinguish historiography from other forms of *historia*, zoology, psychology, geography or whatever, viz. by their subject matter."

sort we instinctively set out to find in antiquity. "Thinking about culture" in a reflexive fashion does not obviously equate to simple bipolar oppositions between "Greek" and "barbarian" nor, for that matter, a prose genre rigidly constrained to the study of the same.[27] It follows that in order to study ancient *historiê* for evidence of an interest in the manners and customs of peoples, foreign or otherwise, we need first to divest ourselves of a great deal of conceptual baggage as to what ethnography "proper" entails. Once any distorting influences or preconceptions have been stripped away we will be better placed to comprehend the manner in which questions of identity were discursively explored both prior to the emergence of a prose genre and outwith its (somewhat limited) boundaries.[28]

Signs of an "ethnographic interest" are arguably far more widespread than is conventionally allowed—although this is not, in itself, surprising given the overall severity of the criteria employed in its definition. Although material expressions of an interest in foreign peoples are both comparatively widespread *and* well documented, they have been largely neglected as a body of evidence relating to ethnographic thought.[29] One of the aims of this study, therefore, is to incorporate material evidence for an interest in foreign lands and peoples into a wider discussion of the nature and purpose of "ethnographic" discourse. Such interests were by no means restricted to "Greeks" alone, however, as we shall see.

1.2 "Other" Ethnographies

At a time when increasing emphasis is being placed on the permeability of cultural boundaries separating "Greek" and "Etruscan," how should we interpret, for example, the statuettes of four prancing horses, ridden by archers, which adorn the rim of a cinerary urn of supposedly Etrusco-Campanian

---

[27] Cf. Thomas 1982 where this rigidity of style and subject matter is seen as characteristic of the genre as a whole. For related discussion see now Gruen 2011a. The decision to focus solely on prose is hard to justify when the actual mode of delivery would have retained a significant oral component. Amid a vast bibliography, see Evans 2008; Thomas 2000. See now Malkin 2011, 218, emphasizing the importance of "Greeks looking at each other across the sea."

[28] See, however, Woolf 2009 for recent critique of "extreme cultural constructionist readings of ancient ethnography" (211) and an alternative, prose-orientated approach highlighting the importance of the middle ground as a source of ethnographic data.

[29] When acknowledged it is primarily as an ancillary to the textual evidence and/or issues pertaining to one group in particular: e.g., Scythian archers (see below) or attitudes toward skin color (Snowden 1970, 1991; Isaac 2004). For recent, albeit limited discussion, see Mitchell 2007; Kim 2009. Cf. studies of religious, artistic, and literary interaction between the Greek world and the Ancient Near East from the late second millennium B.C. onward, where Greek interest in foreign things and ideas can at times seem all-consuming. (See further below.)

FIGURE 1.1 Statuette of mounted Amazon from the rim of a
cinerary urn (inset, see also cover illustration), height approximately 11 cm. About 480 B.C., Campanian Bronze, British Museum
560, from S. Maria di Capua Vetere. Drawn from photo: S. Haynes,
1965, *Etruscan Bronze Utensils*, pls. 3–4. Drawing by the author.

design?[30] (See fig. 1.1.) The figures in question wear pointed caps and are, in a
number of cases, depicted delivering what would later be referred to as a
"Parthian shot"—turning in the saddle to loose an arrow while still at the
gallop. Surely such attention to detail places it on a par with material such as
Herodotus's excursus on Scythia, insofar as it is indicative of a certain degree
of knowledge and interest in the exotic/alien on behalf of both artist and audience.[31] While the manner in which individuals "engaged," whether singly

[30] Cf. a similar group from adorning an Etrusco-Campanian urn from Capua, ca. 510–490 B.C.,
GR1856. 12–26, 796 and 800; GR1964 12–21.1; GR1973.3–1.1. See Lubtchansky 2005, 95–99, figs.
18–24. On Etruscan identity, see Spivey 2007, 232; cf. Torelli 1996. For a terracotta antefix from
Capua's Fondo Patturelli sanctuary depicting an Amazon/Scythian facing outward, wearing a
pointed cap, see Lubtchansky 2005, 108 fig. 34 (with references); and Koch 1912, pl. X.1. Cf.
Megaw and Megaw 1990 for Etruscan goods in a Scythian context.
[31] See Dench 2007, 493 for the extent to which "the ethnographic gaze" is predicated upon a certain
level of knowledge being present among the target audience(s). The processes underpinning the
production, trade, and subsequent use and reception of such objects and imagery will be explored in
greater length below in contexts ranging from monumental sculpture to devices stamped upon coins.

or collectively, with such an object cannot be gauged with any degree of certainty, the suggestion that it would have prompted self-conscious reflection concerning one or more points of cultural difference does not seem overly far-fetched. Relating such material imaginings to the ethnographic enquiries of early Greek prose authors is far from straightforward, however, and raises a very important question: to what extent were both Greek ethnography and any associated discourse regarding the habits and cultures of foreign peoples a specifically *Greek* invention? While the recovery of such artifacts in a south Italian context suggests that an interest in the habits and customs of steppe nomads—be they Scythians or, as interpreted in this case, Amazons—was in fact widespread throughout the region, further evidence is arguably required if we are to gain an impression of the nature and content of these "other ethnographies."[32] Rather than embarking on a lengthy trawl of textual and iconographic evidence stretching back several millennia, I should like merely to highlight a few examples for the purposes of comparison before moving on to more detailed discussion of the Greek milieu.

If we extend our gaze further afield, evidence for ancient ethnographic interests can easily be discerned. The brightly painted frescoes depicting gold-bearing Nubians and "Asiatics" that once adorned the tomb of Sobekhotep at Thebes (Luxor), now displayed in the British Museum, are a notable case in point. Dated to the reign of Thutmose IV (ca. 1400 B.C.), they in all likelihood allude to duties that Sobekhotep was required to undertake during his lifetime in his capacity as a high-ranking treasury official. As such, they follow established (and widely documented) conventions for depicting foreign lands and peoples, the ideological bases of which can be traced back to as early as the third millennium B.C.[33] According to these conventions, Egypt's neighbors were almost invariably represented in one of two guises: subject nations rendering tribute to pharaoh or the vanquished barbarian—either dead or dying under the onslaught of pharaoh and his armies (a theme encapsulated in the "smiting pharaoh" motif) or bound and taken captive. Although rigorously subordinated to royal ideology and a dualistic mode of thought that saw Egypt as the center of the cosmos amid a sea of barbarians, empirical knowledge of foreign lands and peoples did, therefore, find (albeit

---

[32] It being no longer acceptable to dismiss the Etruscans as wealthy yet tasteless magpies: avid consumers of Greek pottery but fundamentally lacking in knowledge or refinement. Cf. Boardman 1999, 199–200. For an interest in Greek myth in Etruscan art and society, see Dench 1995, 39ff.; Spivey 1997. See, however, Osborne 2004b, 42 (re)emphasizing the connection between Athenian vase-painters and their (Athenian) public.
[33] Moers 2010, 178. BM 1869, 1025.3–4 (Nubians); BM 1869, 1025.5; BM 1852, 0223.1 (Lydians/"Asiatics"). See Dziobek and Raziq 1990; Moers 2010, esp. 178–179 for discussion and references.

limited) expression as part of a wider discourse that portrayed foreigners as unremittingly inferior.[34]

Our next example of early ethnographic interest is rather more exceptional: the unusually detailed and somewhat enigmatic description of the people of Urartu offered in Sargon II's *Letter to the God Aššur* (714 B.C.):

> The people who live in the district are without equal in all of Urartu in their knowledge of riding horses. For years they had been catching the young colts of (wild) horses, native to this wide land, and raising them for the royal army [or Urartu]. But they are not caught as far over as Sŭbi, a district which the people of Urartu call Mannean country, nor are their herds seen there. They do not saddle them, but (whether) going forward, turning to one side, or turning around, (as the tactics) of battle require, they are (never) seen to break the yoke (i.e. to become separated from their team).[35]

It should be emphasized that the level of ethnographic detail preserved in Sargon's *Letter to the God Aššur* makes it highly atypical when compared to the vast majority of textual sources now extant. Interpreted by A. Leo Oppenheim as a document intended for recital during public ceremonies, composed with a view to eliciting a particular set of responses from its target audience (the priests and citizens of Assur), it invites the conclusion that the Assyrian empire was in fact far more interested in the manners and customs of its subjects than might otherwise be supposed.[36] It should be no surprise, therefore, that the unusually "Herodotean" nature of Sargon's *Letter* has prompted comparisons with the intellectual and cultural milieu that prevailed in Ionia during the sixth century B.C.[37] While this analogy may appear somewhat rose-tinted (Sargon's subjects were, after all, being regaled with an account of the subjugation, humiliation, and defeat of Assyria's neighbors), signs of ethnographic interest are readily apparent—even if it is merely an adjunct to Assyrian imperial ideology.[38]

---

[34] See Moers 2010 for further discussion and examples.

[35] Luckenbill, *ARAB* 2.84. For early Mesopotamian views of the world, see Michalowski 2010.

[36] Oppenheim 1960, 146. Cf. Sparks 1998, 31: "[T]he text suggests that other ethnographic materials probably existed in the Neo-Assyrian libraries, despite the fact that so few examples have come our way." For discussion of the means by which foreigners were identified in Neo-Assyrian palace reliefs and royal inscriptions, the ideological messages they conveyed, and target audience(s), see Zaccagnini 1982; Reade 1979.

[37] See Oppenheim 1960, 146: "[T]he text addresses itself to an audience really interested in hearing about foreign peoples, their way of life, their religion and customs. In fact, one feels tempted to draw a parallel between the priests and citizens of Assur of 714 B.C. and the audience which listened to the *logoi* of the predecessors of the Ionian logographers only a century or so later in Asia Minor. In that light we have . . . what Herodotus would have called an 'Urartean logos.'" See Dalley 2005; Kravitz 2003; and Sparks 1998 for further discussion and references.

[38] Cf. Megan Cifarelli's discussion of the cultural ideology underpinning the visual propaganda of the Assyrian empire (Cifarelli 1998).

Further signs of ethnographic interest can likewise be found in the Apadana reliefs from Persepolis.[39] Designed to illustrate the immense power and wealth of the Achaemenid empire, the reliefs depict twenty-three tribute-bearing delegations from regions as far-flung as Lydia and Arachosia, together with ushers in Persian and Median dress. Originally brightly painted, the figures are depicted at approximately a quarter-life- size in three registers, converging on the centrally aligned double-staircases that provided access to the terrace on its northern and eastern sides. The result is a lively pastiche of ethnographic data in which items of dress, exotic commodities, and practices variously considered to be emblematic of a particular population are reproduced in meticulous detail, with cypress trees marking the break between individual delegations.[40] Even in their present-day state, devoid of paint and variously battered and mutilated, they form a stark contrast to the serried ranks of Persians and Medes—guards and members of the nobility—depicted on the opposing side of the facade. While it might be unwise, in this instance, to infer a desire to record ethnographic data for its own sake, the King's sculptors appear to have singled out traits capable of conjuring a notion of "Gandahara," "Arabia," and "Egypt" to an audience of dignitaries, petitioners, and whoever else had cause to climb the staircases leading to the Apadana.[41]

---

[39] See Root 1979; Schmidt 1953; Kim 2009, 24, where the Apadana stairway is described as "a veritable ethnographic museum." For related discussion concerning both the nature of Persian imperial ideology and a resulting penchant for depicting foreign peoples, see Harrison 2010, 96–97.

[40] See Ma 2008 for discussion of "the specificity of ethnic definition in Achaemenid art" (247). The manner in which Persians divided their empire into administrative units (satrapies) based on ethnic and cultural criteria has recently been linked to the earliest glimmerings of Greek ethnographic thought: an "oppositional" worldview that distinguished between an emergent community of Hellenes and a monolithic "barbarian" entity that could be subdivided into culturally differentiated "others" (Kim 2009, 24–25, 144). This original and engaging model stands in need of further refinement, however, since it both underestimates the extent to which ethnographic and geographical knowledge played a role in the ideologies and power structures of earlier Near Eastern empires and presents Ionian Greeks as lacking the imagination or originality necessary to devise systems of thought and understanding capable of accommodating a wide variety of cultural difference—while simultaneously highlighting the active role that individual Greeks played in Persian imperial practices.

[41] For the difficulties in distinguishing between certain categories of foreign people, see Illiakis 2009, 150–152; Henkelman and Stolper 2009; Briant 2002, 175ff. For wider discussion see Kurht 2007; Curtis and Razmjou 2005, 65–85; Roaf 1983; 1974; Root 1979; Schmidt 1953. The desire to single out particular populations is equally apparent in the rock-cut reliefs adorning Darius I's tomb at Naqsh-i-Rustam, some 6 km from Persepolis on the royal road to Susa, and the monument at Bisitun (Bhagasthana) overlooking the route from Ecbatana to Babylon. At Naqsh-i-Rustam, the king's subjects are depicted holding the throne platform aloft with individual labels proclaiming "Behold the Ionian who wears the Petasus," "Behold the Libyan" together with trilingual inscriptions in Old Persian, Elamite, and Babylonian (DNa; DNb). See Kurht 2007, 500, fig. 11.14; Brosius 2000, 42–43, 64–65; Schmidt 1970. In this case, however, the audience is primarily divine as the inscriptions are displayed at a height that would render them illegible to onlookers on the ground (the tomb itself is positioned some 15m above the ground with the facade rising to a further 22m).

Such attention to detail is equally prevalent on a much smaller scale, however. Take, for example, the images inscribed on Achaemenid cylinder seals depicting the Persian royal hero in combat with one or more foes[42] or the Achaemenid-era wood paintings from the tumulus at Tatarli in Phrygia.[43] Recently restored by conservators working for the Bavarian Archäologische Staatssammlung, the painted timbers from Tatarli provide a dazzling display of "ethnic types": Persian riders and their commander, horse nomads, and what might reasonably be assumed to be Phrygian warriors.[44] Like Sargon's *Letter*, these paintings represent something of an anomaly insofar as they are both one of the very few examples of wood-based painting (of any kind) to have survived from antiquity and the only known case in which a wood-lined chamber tomb has survived with its decoration intact. It can, however, be linked to a tradition of monumental painting—of which this is unlikely to be the most accomplished example[45]—that was comparatively widespread throughout the ancient world, raising questions as to whether viewing, reading, and ultimately "consuming" such imagery would in fact have been a familiar experience for contemporary audiences. A lot more could be said about the images from Tatarli but it is the interest in, and evident ability to signal, cultural specificity via details of physiognomy, costume, and matériel that are most relevant in this context.

What does this brief overview tell us, however, aside from the fact that ethnographic interests were (as one might expect) by no means limited to Greeks alone? Although evidence for ethnographic imaginings can be found in the art and literature of the Ancient Near East, the self-conscious prose study of foreign peoples remains something of a rarity and, as such, a comparatively unique response to the experience of intercultural contact. Explaining this apparent singularity is rather more difficult, however. So-called anomalies such as Sargon's *Letter* highlight the dangers of resorting to essentialist categorizations or generalizing statements when the dataset in question is manifestly incomplete. Whether we can distinguish, in the words of Emma Dench, between different "ways of seeing that can sometimes be

---

[42] E.g., the nomadic Saka or "pointed hat Scythians," warriors riding camels (thought to be Arab tribesmen), and heroically naked Greek hoplites bearing their distinctive arms and armor. For which see, Tallis 2005, 228–231, pls. 413–414 (opponents in nomad-style dress), 423–424 (Greeks, naked or otherwise); Speleers 1948, 182n1458; Boardman 2001, 456n365 (camel riders in flight); Ma 2008.

[43] For discussion and further references, see Summerer 2007, 2009; Draycott 2010a; Tuplin 2010. For related discussion regarding the dynamics of political and cultural interaction within the Achaemenid empire, see Tuplin 2007, 2011; Brosius 2011; Miller 2011.

[44] See Draycott 2010a for discussion of the various "identities" portrayed.

[45] Achaemenid specialists have highlighted certain errors in depicting Persian royal iconography and clothing, see Tuplin 2010; Summerer 2007.

identified as specific not just to individual artistic or literary contexts but also . . .
to individual cultures and societies" is something of a moot point.[46] It might
ultimately be argued that the juxtaposition of categories such as "Egyptian,"
"Persian," and "Greek" is far too brittle and subjective a process to provide a
useful basis for discussion.[47] Although the similarities and differences separating campaign narratives, monumental sculpture, and epic poetry must
certainly be acknowledged and if possible explained, an attempt to catalogue
them with a view to identifying qualities intrinsic to one group in particular would take us far beyond the remit of the present volume.[48] Instead of
emphasizing the apparent singularity of Greek ethnography as a literary
phenomenon that emerged during the fifth century B.C., this study sets out
to emphasize the role that ethnographic interests played in a wider discursive process—a process through which Greek culture and identity were both
invented and defined.[49]

1.3 Ethnography (re) Defined.

If we turn our attention again to the ancient Mediterranean world, a lively
and wide-ranging interest in foreign lands and peoples is apparent not only
in the material representations and iconographic evidence but also in a varied corpus of literary and subliterary allusions and fragments to which the
label "ethnography" is rarely, if ever, applied.[50] These range from cases in

---

[46] Dench 2007, 493. While comparison of such attitudes and interests has, for example, been a
feature of scholarly discussion of the ethnographic interests of the Neo-Assyrian empire compared to that of "the Greeks," the latter tells us relatively little about how such information was
gathered, read, and interpreted on a day-to-day basis. E.g., Sparks 1998, 31n19 (stressing the
uniqueness of Herodotus) and 72: "In a few isolated cases, the Assyrian materials do exhibit a
degree of scholarly ethnographic interest . . . [however] . . . because much of Assyria's scribal
activity took place in a monarchic context, the monarchic concerns precluded the development
of a full-blown ethnographic genre in Mesopotamia." Cf. Dubovsky 2006, 122ff.; Zaccagnini
1982 for detailed discussion of ethnographic knowledge and its uses under the Neo-Assyrian
empire.
[47] For similar arguments regarding cultural interaction within the eastern Mediterranean world
from the late second millennium B.C. onward, see Gunter 2009.
[48] For concepts of otherness and the portrayal of foreigners in general, see Moers 2010; Kamal
forthcoming (Egypt), Weigui 2001; Kim 2009; di Cosmo 2010 (China), Pu 2005 (the Ancient
Near East). Cf. Gruen 2005a for Jewish perceptions of Persia. For perceptions of Greeks, see
Sancisi-Weerdenberg 2001; Ma 2008; Malkin 2011, 219.
[49] The question as to how and why Greek ethnography emerged as a prose genre is one to which
we shall return in the final chapter.
[50] Although see Norden 1920, 13: "[D]ie Keime der darunter begriffenen Wissenschaft besch-
reibender Länder- und Völkerkunde liegen eingebettet in ältestem hellenischen Erdreiche"
([T]he seeds of the nascent science of describing lands and peoples lie embedded in the soil of
ancient Hellas).

which the nomadic Scythians are held up as a paradigmatic "other," such as in the poetry of Anacreon, to their incorporation into catalogue poetry together with Ethiopians, Libyans, and Pygmies.[51] A trawl through the Fragmentary Greek Historians also reveals evidence that "ethnographic concerns" were all but ubiquitous. Examples of an interest in questions of identity and difference include Xanthus the Lydian's assertion that it was King Adramytes of Lydia who initiated the practice of sterilizing women and employing them in the place of male eunuchs, or the (equally colorful) allegation that the Magi routinely indulged in incestuous practices with their mothers and daughters.[52] Perhaps one of the most celebrated (and intriguing) "snapshots" indicative of both wider interests in identity and difference and the systems of knowledge and understanding through which they found expression can be found in a fragmentary paean attributed to Pindar:

Νόμος ὁ πάντων βασιλεύς
θνατῶν τε καὶ ἀθανάτων
ἄγει δικαιῶν τὸ βιαιότατον
ὑπερτάτᾳ χειρί.
Law, the king of all,
of mortals and immortals,
guides them as it justifies utmost violence
with a sovereign hand.[53]

This passage occurs in the context of Herodotus's celebrated anecdote concerning an experiment, allegedly undertaken by Darius, to discover whether he could persuade two peoples from the furthest extremes of his empire to swap ancestral customs. However, the king's enquiry as to how much money it would take before they were willing to either eat or cremate

---

[51] Anac. Fr. 356b (Scythians); Hes. Fr. 150, 17–19 (Ethiopians, Libyans, Pygmies).

[52] FGrHist 765 F 19, 28. Cf. the later writings of Hellanicus of Lesbos incorporating topics as diverse as an etymology for the Chaldaeans, the Amazonian custom of cutting off one breast, and the foundation myth of Thebes (FGrHist 4 F 59, 16, 1).

[53] Fr. 169a 1–4 cf. Hdt. III 38. 4. Exactly how Νόμος ὁ πάντων Βασιλεύς should be interpreted remains the subject of debate. It is unclear whether Herodotus's citation referred to this paean in particular or another espousing similar sentiments: "ἄλλα δ' ἄλλοισιν νόμιμα, σφετέραν δ' αἰνεῖ δίκαν ἀνδρῶν ἕκαστος" (Customs vary among men, and each man praises his own way) (Fr. 215a) on which see: Rutherford 2001, 387–389; Ferrari 1992; Heinimann 1945. It is cited in Scholia to Il. II. 400; Erbse 1969–83, i. 270 also AG iii. 154; Artemidorus, Oneirocritica, 4. 2, 243. The fact that Fr. 169a—as preserved in Plato's Gorgias 484b—forms the basis for the argument that "might is right," a prelude to the cataloguing of Herakles' labors (τεκμαίρομαι ἔργοισιν Ἡρακλέος [Pindar Fr. 169a 4–5]) suggests that this may indeed be the case. Ferrari 1991, 77 adopts the view that Herodotus was mistaken in citing Pindar's Fr. 169a for a relativistic view of νόμος and meant to cite Fr. 125a instead. Regardless of whether Herodotus was mistaken or not, the fragment appears to have attained the status of a proverb.

the corpses of their fathers was in each case met with outright refusal, thereby demonstrating that Cambyses was completely mad (ἐμάνη μεγάλως) when he set about abusing Egyptian religion and tradition. Discussion of the fragment and the anecdote in which it is embedded has focused predominantly on the extent to which it reflects a relativistic view of νόμος (law/custom) as espoused by the fifth-century sophists—whether on the part of Pindar or Herodotus.[54] It is, however, equally if not more important (from the point of view of the present study) that Pindar uttered such sentiments at all, and that Herodotus felt moved to cite him as an authority. Does this make Pindar too an ethnographer of sorts, or at least someone whose experience of cultural difference was sufficiently wide-ranging for him to be sensitive to such issues?[55] How did Pindar obtain what knowledge he had about foreign peoples and customs? Might the statement implicitly extend to encompass "foreign" Greeks, with epinicia suddenly transformed into a potential mine of information relating to all kinds of laws and customs? Just as a recent comparison of Thucydides and Pindar has successfully demonstrated that both poet and historian drew on similar materials, it seems highly likely that Herodotus and Pindar shared common interests and sources.[56] While in no way remarkable on one level, this has far-reaching implications when it comes to gauging the pervasiveness of ethnographic themes and interests.

This study adopts an altogether different approach to identifying ancient ethnography from the scholarly mainstream. "Thinking about culture from the point of view of an outsider" envisages representations of peoples, customs, products, and places as all being in some way "ethnographic"—no matter whom they relate to and regardless of whether they figure in myth-poetry, iconography, or prose. Conventional *historiê*/enquiries are ranked alongside material, subliterary, and iconographic evidence, attesting to the wealth of ideas and information in circulation at any one time throughout the emerging cultural *koiné* we now call "Greek."[57] While the use of comparatively broad-based criteria to define "ethnography" might appear unorthodox, or perhaps even to

---

[54] On Pindar: Rutherford 2001, 388 explicitly disagrees with Heinimann (Heinimann 1945, 71ff.) that such statements should not be seen in the context of a doctrine of relativity: "Prima facie, this is a statement of a relativistic theory of νόμος of the sort that one would associate with the sophists." Cf. Thomas 2000, 124–129 for a similar argument for Herodotus while Romm 1998, 98–99 discusses some of the problems associated with divining Herodotus's views.

[55] The text as it stands makes no further allusion to νόμος but is understood as an opening statement in some way related to the eulogy that followed. Little more can be achieved by way of reconstruction beyond that already achieved by Rutherford and others.

[56] Hornblower 2004, 56–58 and *passim*. For knowledge of Pindar among fifth-century authors, see Irigoin 1952, 11–20.

[57] As opposed to the more restricted, logocentric, definition in which prose accounts are held to be preeminent. Cf. E. Hall 1989; Thomas 2000; J. Hall 1997, 2002. For similarly broad-based discussion relating to geography and exploration see McDowell 1997; Driver 2001.

extend the term beyond all reasonable bounds, it at least captures something of the thought-world from which early prose accounts emerged. When viewed holistically, the fragmentary collections of stray references, proverbs, and visual allusions collated in the following chapters indicate that knowledge relating to a variety of foreign peoples was far more widespread than has been suggested, for instance, by Edith Hall.[58] "Enquiries" of this sort are not simply indicative of the musings of some erudite theoretician or wordsmith, whose creative output would have been entirely inaccessible to contemporaries, or the obscure tinkering of an artisan divorced from his intellectual and cultural milieu. We are not simply dealing, therefore, with ethnography as "text." Instead, ethnographies would primarily have been encountered either aurally or visually, during public spectacles, or as some passing quip in the agora or symposium. The status of such knowledge might at times lend itself to elite discourses and the processes of self-fashioning (a point to which we shall return below), but this remains a far cry from the idea of an elevated, rational, or scientific discourse (nascent or otherwise) of the kind attributed to the Ionian logographers in general, and individuals like Hecataeus and Herodotus in particular—largely divorced from both their immediate (literary) contemporaries and a wider social context.[59]

We shall return to the problem of context in due course, but what were the wider effects of this supposed ferment of ethnographic interests and activity? Acts of empirical representation are never "value-free"—a fact now widely acknowledged in ethnographic studies—but discursive practices through which identities may actively be constructed.[60] Far from being mere epiphenomena, discourses of identity and difference are in fact *constitutive* of identity.[61] This is not simply a matter of "writing culture," however, as we shall

---

[58] For recent discussion of "thought worlds"/"lived experience": Malkin 1998a; Vlassopoulos 2007b, 236.

[59] This is, somewhat paradoxically, one of the drawbacks of Rosalind Thomas's treatment of Herodotean discourse stressing links with philosophical and medical writers, argument, and the language of proof (Thomas 2000). See Fowler 1996 on Herodotus. Cf. Erskine 2005, 130.

[60] Clifford and Marcus 1986.

[61] Literary works exploring colonial difference have similarly been interpreted—to great effect—as a mechanism for critical self-reflection. Cf. Gikandi 1996. Cf. S. Hall 2003 [1996], 91: "[W]hile not wanting to expand the territorial claims of the discursive infinitely, how things are represented and the 'machineries' and regimes of representation in a culture do play a *constitutive*, and not merely a reflexive, after-the-event, role . . . in the constitution of social and political life." Cf. Malkin 2011, 218 where knowledge (and representation?) of foreign peoples and customs are assumed to have played a role in a "Hellenic convergence": "Greek-Barbarian 'difference' consists . . . in the multi-polar differences *among* barbarians that Greeks could observe which seems to have been contrasted with what was recognizable, acceptable, and commonly Greek. . . . [B]ecause of the intensive time-frame and the great number of settlements and sub-settlements across widening geographical horizons, connectivity and network dynamics speeded up the spread of mutual patterns and the awareness of their common significance, as well as perhaps their overall coherent similarity in relation to the varied and distinct identities of non-Greeks" (author's italics).

see. When divorced from the material evidence, questions of practice and the politics of knowledge, literary-led approaches can only provide us with an at-best partial appreciation of the manner in which identities were constructed. Instead, we need to adopt a more synthetic approach, extending our discussion to encompass diverse media and genres, stressing their interconnectedness and daring to *imagine* scenarios in which such material and ideas would have been alternately experienced and actively employed.[62]

When writing what is essentially a history of ideas, we must also allow for a "play" of meaning—both temporal and spatial—as groups and individuals as far-flung as Olbia and Cyrene, Massalia and Miletus "read" images, heard or relayed stories, and experienced difference in sequences that both played out and varied over time and space. In order to write a history of ethnographic activity and thought we will need to encompass multiple readings and perspectives, framing the problem in a very different manner from standard techniques of historical reconstruction and interpretation. This is not simply a question, however, of adopting novel methodological approaches for their own sake. Instead, highlighting this "play" of meaning is a vital precursor to any attempt to conceptualize—and on some levels explain—complex historical processes and the overarching narratives through which they are interpreted.[63]

The comparative ease with which Greek ethnography is defined as a genre is a direct result of the manner in which Greek identity is traditionally conceptualized as ethnography, written by Greeks.[64] Who or what is *Greek*, however, when and, most importantly, why? In opening up both Greek ethnography and identity for discussion, this study questions not only the functional status of "Greek" ethnography as *practice* but also the essential coherence of any sense of Greek identity upon which it was supposedly predicated.[65] This in turn will have far-reaching implications for the (still widely subscribed-to) theory devised and expounded by Felix Jacoby charting the origins of the historical consciousness: the way in which Great Historiography came into being.[66] While undoubtedly groundbreaking, Jacoby's thesis was founded on the (tacit) assumption that Greek identity already existed as a coherent and homogenous entity. Although endemic at the time, such

---

[62] See Vlassopoulos 2007b for spirited discussion of a perceived malaise afflicting historical scholarship on the ancient world (especially 221ff. on the various solutions proposed).

[63] For narratives (past/present) see Walbank 1951; Humphreys 1978; Erskine 2005; Vlassopoulos 2007b.

[64] See Vlassopoulos 2007b for trenchant discussion. Cf. (variously) Walbank 1951; J. Hall 1997; Konstan 2001; Lomas 2004a.

[65] For notions of practice see Bourdieu 1990.

[66] Jacoby 1909.

assumptions appear less robust in the light of more than a generation of scholarship indicating both the inherent complexity of individual and group identities and the vast fields of difference manifest throughout the Greek world in its entirety.[67] Before we move on to examine the extent to which Jacoby's definition of ethnography can be said to bear the hallmarks of a contemporary colonial episteme, we should first take a closer look at the way in which we both think and write about Greek identity.

1.4 Approaches to (Greek) Identity

The product of an intellectual climate shaped by global systems of commerce, near-instantaneous electronic communication, the Internet, and an anxious multiculturalism, this study is very much "a child of its times," with all the strengths and weaknesses that this implies. Its selective use of critical approaches to consumption and reception, culture theory, social networks, and postcolonial studies reflects contemporary mindsets and preoccupations both within and outside academia.[68] Instead of adopting an Athenocentric focus or stressing the primary importance of frontiers and marginal locations in the formation of identities, this study adopts a perspective that encompasses *both* the "old" world of central Greece *and* regions situated "on the fringes," where Greek and non-Greek met—mindful of the fact that the disinterested ancient observer may, in many cases, have been hard-pressed to tell them apart.[69] Socially constructed and historically contingent, poleis, *ethnê*, local, and regional identities are all equally "within the frame but as discursive constructs subject to continual processes of contestation and reaffirmation, rather than essentialist categories that remained forever static and fixed.

The concept of identity is often articulated in a vague and contradictory manner, reflecting a variety of opinions as to how such questions should be addressed (if at all).[70] Attempts to identify the point at which the ethnogenesis of "the community of the Hellenes" actually occurred have provoked

---

[67] On "Greek difference": Brock and Hodkinson 2000; Redfield 2003; Morgan 2003; Hornblower 2008; Zacharia 2008; Malkin 2011.

[68] E.g., Glennie 1995; Foxhall 1998, 2005; Mansvelt 2005 (consumption); Graziosi 2002 (reception); Malkin 2003a, 2003b, 2011 (networks); S. Hall 1990; Bhabha 1994 (culture); Butler 1990, 1997, 2004 (performatives).

[69] Cf. Burgers 2004.

[70] See Siapkas 2003 for a good overview/critique plus various responses to Jonathan Hall's *Hellenicity*, esp. Mitchell 2005. On approaches: J. Hall 1997, 2002; Siapkas 2003 (ethnicity); Foxhall and Salmon 1998; Brulé 2003 (gender); Vlassopoulos 2007b (subaltern voices). For wide-ranging discussion of Mediterranean identities see now van Dommelen and Knapp 2011b.

considerable controversy. Great stress has been placed upon the extent to which putative kinship and, to a lesser extent, territory provided the bases for conceptualizing archaic Greek identity. Intercultural contact, whether through settlement overseas from circa eighth century B.C. onward or as a result of contact with Persia during the late sixth to early fifth centuries B.C., has likewise been singled out as a factor that contributed to a developing sense of common identity in the face of "difference."[71] Opinion is currently divided as to whether this should be seen as part of a gradual or ongoing trend or as a comparatively abrupt realignment of concepts and values following a specific historical event: "the encounter with the barbarian."[72] Such confusion is not altogether surprising, however, given the complexity of the processes involved and the very nature of the evidence, which is both fragmentary and contested. As is usually the case, the answer lies somewhere in-between. While the experience of the Persian wars clearly had a profound effect upon the manner in which both contemporary and subsequent generations conceived (diverse) others and themselves, evidence for an intellectual engagement with non-Greek peoples *prior* to the fifth century has been hugely underrated. The idea that Greeks suddenly "noticed" foreign peoples during or shortly after their encounter with Persia appears untenable when aligned with material culture-based studies of the ancient Mediterranean stressing high levels of interconnectivity, mobility, and exchange.[73]

Whether contemporary scholarship is unduly preoccupied with matters of identity is a topic of some debate. Classics has shown itself to be no different from any other field of enquiry in that the interests of its practitioners often reflect the contemporary interests and concerns of a wider public.[74] This is far from surprising, however; bemoaning this fact simply implies a lack of understanding of how "history" is constructed and so develops over time.[75] Moreover, although undeniably the focus of a great deal of attention

---

[71] Malkin 2003a; Mitchell 2005; Kim 2009.

[72] For contrasting approaches, see E. Hall 1989; Kim 2009; Mitchell 2007 (discussed below); Malkin 2011.

[73] For which see contributions to van Dommelen and Knapp 2011a; Malkin 2011 (although with emphasis on Greek interest in fellow Greeks as opposed to "the terrestrial hinterland of their new foundations" [218]). For recent discussion of exchange in the eastern Mediterranean see Villing and Schlotzhauer 2006.

[74] See the (somewhat labored) introductory chapters of J. Hall 1997, 2002; but also Dougherty and Kurke 2003a—especially Joshua Ober's postscript which relates the preceding discussion of a variety of societal/subsocietal cultures in terms of "Sewellian thin coherence analysis," concluding: "the more squarely we face up to that multicultural Greek reality, the more clearly we can see why 'the political' could never be forgotten by the ancient Greeks" (Ober 2003, 243 cf. Sewell 1999). Culture and politics are thus mutually implicated. See also Walbank 1951.

[75] The intrusion of zeitgeist can in fact be an entirely positive phenomenon where it prompts new questions and approaches—provided it is self-aware (Malkin 2008b).

in recent years—a reaction to contemporary preoccupations with the politics of gender, ethnicity, or the status of minority groups within a multicultural society—a concern for identity has long been a salient feature of Classical scholarship. While the recent upsurge in scholarship documenting both the variety of identities by which an individual might choose to define him- or herself, and the means by which they did so, is a relatively new phenomenon, it would be naïve to suggest that identities were anything less of a concern to earlier generations of scholars—far less those dwelling in antiquity.[76] As far as past scholarship is concerned, the existence of such categories as "Greek," "Roman," and "barbarian" was largely taken for granted and as a result rarely questioned.[77] This does not mean that they were not—in themselves—considered hugely important, as we shall see when we set Jacoby's historical reconstructions in the context of the prevailing *mentalité* of their day.

That said, Classicists and historians have often been reluctant to engage directly with matters of identity. Over the twenty or more years that have elapsed since the publication of Edith Hall's seminal *Inventing the Barbarian* little, if anything, has changed when it comes to the manner in which Greek identity is conceptualized. Most have been content to follow the now-established orthodoxy of a switch from an ethnic identity (loosely defined or "aggregative") to an oppositional one based upon cultural criteria. This ultimately results in the now-familiar platitudes highlighting the importance of "self" and "other" in defining Greek—or more usually Athenian—identity.[78] Responses to this structuralist approach and the patter of identity-speak thus generated have ranged from tacit acceptance to blistering critique. James Davidson's (now somewhat notorious) *TLS* review of Hartog's *Memories of Odysseus* is undoubtedly the most extreme example of a concerted backlash against "other" scholarship, but by far the most common reaction has been to simply bypass such topics altogether.[79] A (spectacular) exception to this otherwise general rule can be found in Erich

---

[76] Sorabji 2006 is explicitly opposed to the idea that an interest in "self" was largely absent from early Greek philosophy. See also Morgan 2009, 30: "Ethnic groups, for better or for worse, have been an important aspect of the analysis of Greek and Roman political structures for well over a century, and throughout have been entwined with modern political preconceptions."

[77] Vlassopoulos 2007b.

[78] The defensive tone adopted by Cohen when introducing *Not the Classical Ideal* is somewhat telling in this respect (Cohen 2000b).

[79] Davidson 2002. For a more measured tone, see Gruen 2011a. Cf. Cohen 2000b (on iconography) and the overwhelming majority of work devoted to the study of "Greek colonization" in which the "Greekness" of the would-be colonist has—until relatively recently—invariably been assumed.

Gruen's recently published *Rethinking the Other in Antiquity*, which aims to bring about a sea change in the way in which ancient attitudes toward foreigners are conceptualized.[80] Conceived as a counterpoint to scholarly emphasis on negative stereotyping, this elegant rebuttal of the model of the Other highlights the prevalence of an alternative strand in ancient thought that was both affirmative and inclusive while acknowledging the fact that Jews, Greeks, and Romans occasionally accentuated the differences between themselves and foreigners. The extent to which this will have an impact on future scholarship remains to be seen, but an attempt at a more even-handed approach to ancient identity construction was long overdue and should be heartily applauded regardless of whether one finds Gruen's portrait of intergroup relations more "rose-tinted" than "warts and all."[81]

In the rare instances where genuinely innovative attempts have been made to apply theoretical frameworks imported from outside the discipline, these have proved remarkably illuminating, providing fresh paradigms and perspectives from which to consider old problems.[82] This is particularly notable in the case of archaeological studies of the western Mediterranean, notably Southern Italy and Sicily. However, their impact has been fairly marginal—or else has yet to be determined—when it comes to the way in which ancient identities are studied and conceptualized throughout Classics as a whole (with the study of ancient ethnography being perhaps the most obvious case in point).[83] There remains, in particular, a considerable gap separating the far more heterogeneous world of Classical archaeology (arrived at via problem-based fieldwork, distribution maps, inscriptions, and regional surveys) and mainstream studies predicated upon abstract/essentialized concepts of "Greek" culture and identity, self and other.

Bridging the gap between the empirical study of the material record and the more ephemeral world of the abstract *imaginaire* is far from straightforward—not least because it requires an element of speculative

---

[80] "To stress the stigmatization of 'the Other' as a strategy of self-assertion and superiority dwells unduly on the negative, a reductive and misleading analysis" (Gruen 2011a, 356).

[81] Cf. Harrison 2002a for discussion of the need for a frank approach to Greek society and culture. Although fundamentally different in many respects, Irad Malkin's *A Small Greek World* likewise advocates a shift away from simple binaries between Greek and barbarian during the Archaic period in favor of greater stress upon commonalities brought about by colonization: "there has been too much emphasis on 'boundaries' as defining ethnicity, with less attention paid to positive, deliberative, self-conscious practices aimed precisely at defining an overarching identity among Greeks." (Malkin 2011, 99).

[82] E.g., van Dommelen 2002; Antonaccio 2003; Malkin 2003b, 2011; Willi 2008.

[83] Siapkas 2003—an extreme example (see further below). Cf. Brock and Hodkinson 2000; Dougherty and Kurke 2003b; Lomas 2004a; and now Gruen 2011a.

reconstruction.[84] While essentially problematic, insofar as it runs directly counter to traditions of entrenched positivism endemic to Classics as a whole, an attempt to integrate the two remains, nonetheless, both important and worthwhile.[85] Attempting to find a satisfactory means of both framing and conceptualizing such problems is far preferable to struggling with frames of reference that bear little relation to the everyday complexity of the archaeological record. Analyses privileging demonstrable propositions and neatly defined categories (Greeks/natives) rapidly founder when confronted with material assemblages whose heterogeneity is often their *only* defining feature.[86] It remains true to say, however, that the manner in which we interpret such material as survives from antiquity relating to the description of peoples and poleis, their distinctive attributes and customs, is still largely dependent upon an *a priori* notion of Greek identity.

This would not, in itself, be a problem were it not for the fact that identities have become so inherently complicated. Theoretical studies of identity from outside the discipline have shed ever-increasing light on both the manifest complexities of social identities and the processes by which they are variously constructed and find expression.[87] Cultural theorists, historians, and anthropologists have meanwhile been engaged in exploring notions of connectivity, creolization, cultural hybridity, and individual agency, with recent work on culture theory providing a particularly rich vein of scholarship to which students of antiquity are increasingly turning in search of inspiration.[88] So, for example, cultural critics such as Stuart Hall have encouraged us to think of identity as a *production* as opposed to an already accomplished fact. Identity, Hall argues, is never complete: it is "always in

---

[84] The concept of the *imaginaire* referred to above derives primarily from that introduced by the philosopher and psychoanalyst Cornelius Castoriadis in *The Imaginary Institution of Society* (= *L'institution imaginaire de la société*) (Castoriadis 1998). Instead of becoming embroiled in a lengthy discussion of the Lacanian subtexts that might otherwise be seen lurking behind the use of such a term I would like to stress its (essentially) open and polysemous character. Rather than a self-enclosed system of interrelating terms specific to "Greek society" we have a free-flowing body of thought and practice, images and ideas, that cannot be mapped with any degree of exactitude since it is not a logically structured whole.

[85] While the widespread reluctance to address such issues in any detail reflects a general distrust of theoretical approaches to the historical past, endemic to Classics as a whole, the extent to which empirical approaches to the evidence are themselves predicated on their own assumptions makes them equally vulnerable to error—the more so in cases where the use of reflexive theoretical approaches is eschewed. Cf. Siapkas 2003.

[86] Van Dommelen and Knapp 2011a, 1 and passim.

[87] For examples see: Clifford and Marcus 1986; Stevenson 1989; Greenblatt 1991; Anderson 1991; Smith 1991; Young 1995, 2001 on hybridity; Gikandi 1996. For diasporas/diasporic experience, see S. Hall 1990; Gilroy 1993; Clifford 1994; Brah 1996; Gruen 2002; Kalra et al. 2005.

[88] Bhabha 1994; S. Hall 1990, 1996, 1997a, 1997b, 2003. Cf. Mitchell 2007; Antonaccio 2003, 2004; van Dommelen 2002; van Dommelen and Knapp 2011a; Jiménez 2011.

process, and always constituted within, not outside, representation."[89] Based upon almost a generation of work on culture, diasporic experience, and hybridity, this view problematizes "the very authority and authenticity to which the term, "cultural identity," lays claim."[90] Such arguments are highly significant for the way in which we study ancient identities, shifting the emphasis from preconceived notions of unitary cultures to identity as a "work in progress"—always changing in focus and subject to an ongoing play of culture, power, and knowledge.[91] They also have a significant bearing on how we study ancient ethnography, as we shall see.

One aspect of identity that has attracted increasing comment in recent years is that of the processes underpinning the formation and maintenance of ethnic groups and boundaries. The manner in which we conceptualize questions of ethnicity has, however, been challenged in a vanguard study by Johannes Siapkas.[92] Using theoretical frameworks developed by de Certeau and Bourdieu, Siapkas has argued that the drive for analytical precision when discussing matters of identity reduces ethnic identities to essentialized abstractions (exactly, in other words, what Barth's idea of ethnicity as a social construct was intended to circumvent).[93] Another fact that is frequently overlooked is that, quite apart from the conceptual overlap that can often occur between other common (yet potentially problematic) frames of reference such as "nation" or "race," terms such as "Greek" and "Italic" meant different things at different times to different people, making it difficult—perhaps even inadvisable—to align evidence drawn from periods of history that are chronologically remote without some consideration of the manner in which they relate to one another.[94] We are ultimately faced with a conundrum: How best to balance a (self-evident) need for analytical precision with terms of reference and models of understanding capable of highlighting the nuanced complexity lurking behind terms such as "Hellene."

---

[89] S. Hall 1990, 222.

[90] Ibid.

[91] Ibid., 225.

[92] Siapkas 2003.

[93] Ibid. Cf. Barth 1969; Cohen 1978; De Certeau 1988; Bourdieu 1990. For ethnic identity in general, see Phinney 2004. See also Morgan 2009, 24–25: "Part of the problem of trying to find clearly defined cases of ethnic expression lies with the desire for clarity and exclusivity . . . labelling is not an end in itself. . . ."

[94] Catherine Morgan, personal communication with author. Studies of both literary and material evidence often neglect such matters entirely, marshalling evidence from periods ranging from the early archaic to the imperial in support of arguments as to how identities were constructed. Hall's use of Strabo has been singled out for particular criticism on these grounds, an example of how, quite apart from anything else, discussions of how a coherent "Greek identity" came into being have a distinctly teleological flavor. Cf. (on J. Hall) Mitchell 2005, 2007.

While surveying the grand sweep of history there has long been a tendency to overlook the fact that "Greekness" constituted a myriad of identities, socially constructed and historically contingent. Modern notions of ancient "Greekness" have shown little care or attention for questions of context or chronology. Instead, such matters have all too often been swept aside in the scramble to interpret the evidence (providing ample testimony to the extent to which preconceived notions of identity have become entrenched). Matters look set to change, however. The last decade has in fact seen a rash of studies emphasizing the inherent complexity of ancient identities. Greek identity is now described as: "an extremely complex and fluid construction, or rather a system of constructions, and included multivocalities and ambiguities,"[95] while Greek ethnicity or Hellenicity are regarded as "multi-layered, constantly changing, and culturally constructed, concepts."[96] The fact that these studies have, by and large, focused on the western Mediterranean led many to assume that "identities" were far more complicated here than in central Greece and the east. In fact, this was simply a reflection of an upsurge in problem-based research making it to publication, since recently published material from across both the eastern Mediterranean and Black Sea regions is now equally suggestive of a hitherto unlooked-for complexity.[97] Classicists and historians can no longer be excused, in other words, for conceptualizing identities as essentialized or bounded entities. Laying such concepts to one side makes early ethnographic activity—notions of difference and the manipulation of foreign forms, images, and ideas—all the more significant in determining how identities were framed and constructed: part of an ongoing process as opposed to a *fait accompli*.

The monolithic entity of a homogenous "Greek" identity has nonetheless shown remarkable tenacity in the face of efforts to qualify, nuance, and ultimately deconstruct it. The vague and potentially misleading nature of the label "Greek," when employed in an archaic context, is matched only by its apparent usefulness in rendering coherent a broad range of traditions and

---

[95] Sourvinou-Inwood 2003, 140.

[96] Lomas 2004b, 2. Cf. Malkin 2001b and now Fearn 2011b, 3, stressing the diversity of fifth-century culture together with Hornblower's brilliant discussion of Archaic and Classical Greek identity (Hornblower 2008).

[97] E.g., Petersen 2010; Tsetskhladze 1998, 2001. Katherine Lomas has been noticeably forthright in highlighting the fuzziness surrounding concepts of citizenship/identity amongst the poleis of southern Italy; see Lomas 2000a, 2000b; 2004b; but not without Hornblower 2008, 53ff. Cf. J. Hall 2004; Burgers 2004; and Blok 2005 on Athens. For Greek identity in the west, see Barron 2004; Braccesi 2004; along with studies by Dominguez and Kerschner (both 2004) on Phocaea. For Herodotus's treatment of barbarians in the west, see Nenci 1990; Munson 2006. For diversity at Naucratis see Villing and Schlotzhauer 2006b.

practices whose differences often seem to outweigh their similarities.[98] Like Cavafy's barbarians, "Greekness" often emerges as something of a solution, when in reality defining when, where, and how Greek identity came into being is far from straightforward. For all the innovative and insightful comment from scholars such as Christiane Sourvinou-Inwood and Irad Malkin, there is little to indicate that the literary-historical mainstream has responded to such concerns in any significant way: buzzwords such as "ethnicity," "hybridity," and "Hellenization" come and go, but the institutional framework remains very much the same.[99]

While the subject of occasional discussion or critique, the model tabled in Jonathan Hall's *Hellenicity* can still be said to represent the *communis opinio* regarding both the manner and means by which Greek identity came into being.[100] Hall argued that Hellenic ethnic identity appeared quite late in the day (around the mid-sixth century B.C.) in the form of fictive claims to kinship,[101] until war with the barbarian engendered an abrupt switch from ethnic to cultural identity, defined in terms of polar oppositions.[102] The formation of a Hellenic self-consciousness has also been located somewhat further back in time in the early Archaic period: a direct result of increased population mobility, trade, and settlement overseas. At present, the precise mechanisms by which this came about have received scarce attention beyond vague allusions to "definition through difference"—with the notable exception of Irad Malkin's recent discussion of network theory (to which we shall return shortly).

---

[98] When discussing "Greekness" in the Early Iron Age, Catherine Morgan cites as widespread the "recognition that the construct of Greekness, which owes as much to nineteenth-century Europe as to the Greeks themselves, is an anachronism in this early period" (Morgan 2003, 3) See now Malkin 2011 for illuminating discussion.

[99] For wider discussion of disciplinary frameworks, see Humphreys 1978, 2004.

[100] For mixed reactions see: Siapkas 2003; Dench 2005; Mitchell 2005, 2007; Morgan 2009.

[101] In sum, the "putative subscription to a myth of common descent and kinship, an association with a specific territory and a sense of shared history" (J. Hall 2002, 9). This is in contrast to both previous broad-based definitions of ethnicity and arguments that saw the initial flowering of Hellenic identity as having occurred either in opposition to the threat posed by Achaemenid Persia in the fifth century B.C., or as a result of the experience of colonization from the eighth century B.C. onward. While Hall's thesis hinges upon Hellenic genealogy, supposedly reflecting charter myths of the archaic period, he is inclined to reject factors such as physical traits, language, religion, or cultural practices as largely ephemeral in comparison to a kin-based definition of ethnicity (J. Hall 2002, 12). Hall's theory of putative kinship does not in itself rule out the possibility of oppositional ethnicities as catalogues listing the sons of Hellene cannot help but exclude those unrelated to the *stammvater*. For further discussion of Hall's position as laid out in *Ethnic Identity*, see Sourvinou-Inwood 2005, 38–63.

[102] This is essentially the same model as that postulated by Edith Hall (albeit in an argument that places far less emphasis on archaeological materials and anthropological theory) some twenty years earlier.

The problems which arise from this, supposedly straightforward, switch from "ethnicity" to an identity defined according to cultural criteria come to light most readily in contexts such as Southern Italy and Sicily where a comparatively large quantity of problem-based research has now made it to publication. The results have been significant, casting doubt, in many cases, on the veracity of foundation myths promulgated by the cities throughout the region. Although of intrinsic historical value in themselves as "representations" reflecting fifth-century mindsets and preoccupations, colonial myths are often (at best) gross simplifications of historical processes that saw settlers of diverse origins band together to form communities in environments where their mutual similarities were highlighted against the backdrop of the comparatively alien cultures among which they had settled.[103] Even this merits some qualification, however, as the levels of difference encountered would have varied considerably depending on the region in question. The processes associated with encountering and mediating "differences within the same" must therefore have been equally significant.[104] This is not to say that definition through difference did not indeed occur, nor, for that matter, that Hall's thesis concerning theoretical elaborations of Hellenic identity occurring in the sixth century is any less important, merely that there is far more to be said on such matters and the discourses they engendered.

How do we explain the gap separating the initial intensification of contact with foreign peoples (the result of steadily increasing levels of mobility from the eighth century onward) and what are deemed the first overt manifestations of a Hellenic identity located in the mid-sixth century B.C.: the institutionalization of the circuit of—eventually—Panhellenic festivals, the founding of the Hellenion at Naucratis, and the construction of Hellenic genealogies?[105] The precise means by which the self-conscious

---

[103] Irad Malkin argues "overseas colonization informed and strengthened the nascent idea of Greekness primarily because of the newly perceived differences from various "Others" and because of the similarities of the initial colonial experiences. . . . What we call "colonization" . . . was a significant, formative historical power with currents running along the different lines of a Greek Wide Web, shaping archaic Greek society at large and making it more Greek into the bargain" (Malkin 2003b, 59, 72) However, see now Malkin 2011 (see above no. 73) reiterating the case for a network approach to collective identity but with emphasis on self-scrutiny among Greeks as opposed to contact with barbarians.

[104] Malkin 2003, 2011. For related discussion see Hornblower 2008. Hall is not alone in emphasizing that there may not—in many cases—have been a great deal *separating* settler and indigene in regions such as Southern Italy: J. Hall 2004, 2005; cf. Burgers 2004.

[105] See Malkin 2003b, 2011 for discussion. On Panhellenic games see Hornblower and Morgan 2007. On the Hellenion: Malkin 2011; Höckmann and Möller 2006; Sourvinou-Inwood 2005, 52–56; Hall 2002, 130; Möller 2000. On the Hesiodic catalogue see West 1985; Fowler 1998; Hunter 2005. Cf. Thomas 2001; Bertelli 2001.

assertion of Hellenic identities came about requires something more by way of explanation than the (vague and somewhat unsatisfactory) conclusion offered up in a recent study of Panhellenism to the effect that: "the process of finding and articulating difference through the early contacts must have been slow and tentative."[106] The latter is predicated on the idea that Hellenic identity was both expressed and defined in terms of a nexus of themes, ideas, and representations whose purpose was "to bridge and obscure the gap between the cultural and the political unities and disunities of the Greek world."[107] However, while Hellenic fragmentation has long been noted as problematic, frustrating any move toward greater unity of purpose, it might equally be argued that cultural and political disunities formed an intrinsic part of Hellenism and that the processes of negotiating these boundaries were themselves *constitutive* of identity.[108] It is here, I would argue, that "ethnographic" interests and representations have an important role to play.

Although posited on the notion that "ethnographic" interests and representations are fundamental to any understanding of Greek culture and identity, this study does not attempt to argue that ethnography or any wider discourse entailed the simple juxtaposition of Greek with non-Greek "other." Instead, it sees boundary negotiation and contestation as universal, generative processes intrinsic to cultural identities of any kind. The relationship between ethnographic representations and culture (Greek or otherwise) must therefore be redefined to fit this paradigm. If culture is best understood, in the words of Homi K. Bhabha, as an intrinsically "hybrid"

---

[106] Mitchell 2005, 415. A couple of likely mechanisms that may have contributed to this process are suggested with traveling poets/rhapsodes and sanctuaries, whose standing and reputation transcended their immediate local significance, being singled out—along with the Olympics and other festivals of broader regional significance (see Mitchell 2005).

[107] Mitchell 2007, xix. Ambitious and wide-ranging, Mitchell's study incorporates a variety of historic and material evidence from a period stretching from the time of Mycenaean collapse to the reign of Hadrian—with particular emphasis being placed on the sixth through fifth centuries B.C. As such, it is a valuable and welcome response to the current status quo even if it raises as many questions as it answers.

[108] Mitchell views contestation as a source of crisis, creating inherent problems for the integrity of the wider community of "Hellenes": "However . . . the plurality of foci for Panhellenic stories and representations of identity points to some of the deepest problems for the integrity of the symbolic community. That there was no single location for the generation of identity meant that local stories proliferated. As a result, there was an entrenched competition between local stories to assert their claim to being the principal source of Hellenic identity itself. So while on the one hand plurality created richness and diversity within the collective identity, it was also the root of its crisis" (Mitchell 2007, 8). See now M. Scott 2010, 260ff. emphasizing the disunities and fragmentation lurking behind the term "Panhellenism." For related discussion, see Hornblower 2008; Malkin 2011.

entity,[109] then the discursive interplay of ideas of identity and difference emerges as a thoroughly mundane activity: a reflexive positioning that could find expression in any area of cultural production as opposed to one that was restricted solely to prose.

Hellenic self-definition is commonly attributed to one of two strategies: "aggregation" on the one hand and "definition through difference" on the other. Setting the two strategies in opposition to one another is perhaps less useful, however, than highlighting the manner in which they can variously be said to overlap and interplay: "aggregation" can also serve to create "out groups" that by definition do not belong to the same mythic stemma.[110] The problem can in fact be approached in a variety of ways. Intercultural contact—whether between culturally similar groups or individuals whom we would today consider "Greek," or those of more varied beliefs and practices—would have generated information: knowledge derived from either firsthand experience or stories relating to similar encounters (whether real or imaginary). Once received it could be relayed orally or "represented" via iconography or text, only to be received, interpreted, and relayed again to ever-widening audiences.[111] However diverse or complex, the process thus engendered would have seen a whole range of groups and individuals actively participating in ethnographic activity—whether directly or indirectly. The overall importance of such "thinking about culture discursively" should not be underestimated, however, since it arguably played an important role in deciding what it meant to be "Greek" in the first place.

In order to fully appreciate the implications of this argument we must now retrace our steps to examine late-nineteenth- and early-twentieth-century conceptualizations of ethnography and identity in greater detail. This is important if we are to explain the apotheosis of the ancient ethnographer: a

---

[109] Bhabha 1994, 56: "For a willingness to descend into that alien territory—where I have lead you—may reveal that the theoretical recognition of the split-space of enunciation may open the way to conceptualizing an *international* culture, based not on the exoticism of multiculturalism or the *diversity* of cultures, but on the inscription and articulation of culture's *hybridity*." The notion that hybridity implies "relatively fixed forms of identity that met and mixed" (Gosden 2004, 69; Wallace-Hadrill 2008, 12) is therefore misconceived. While its purportedly biological connotations are viewed in some quarters as troubling and distasteful (e.g., Malkin 2004, 358) we should be careful to distinguish between lazy/ill-informed usage of the term as a shorthand for "mixed" and the elegant formulations of cultural critics such as Homi K. Bhabha and Stuart Hall. For exemplary treatment of the complexities involved in the context of Late Iron Age Iberia, see Jiménez 2011 together with van Dommelen 2002.

[110] For "aggregation": J. Hall 2002. On "Definition through difference": E. Hall 1989; Mitchell 2005, 409ff.; Gruen 2011a.

[111] For the extent to which the social status of the interlocutor governed the manner in which such information was subsequently "received," see Raaflaub 2004.

new breed of thinker and practitioner for whom the monumental clash with Persia was a necessary precursor.[112] The "invention" of Greek ethnography created a questionable distinction between what was purported to be the initial flowering of rational, objective, and scientific prose and the sort of popular or mythic traditions alluded to above and described in greater details below. It is also inextricably bound up in current thinking relating to the evolution and origins of "Great Historiography." This, in turn, bears ample testimony to the enduring legacy of the scholar whose dogged brilliance and steadfast determination produced volumes I to III of *The Fragmentary Greek Historians*.[113] Since Felix Jacoby was arguably responsible for deciding what constituted ethnographic inquiry in the first place, we must now explore how and why Jacoby might have sought to identify ethnography as a discrete body of enquiry, albeit one that was loosely defined, taking into account a range of factors—not least an intellectual milieu in which ethnographic concerns were very much to the fore. This in turn will have important implications for the manner in which we define the relationship between history, ethnography, and any overarching sense of collective "Greek" identity (topics to which we shall return in the final chapter).

1.5 Structuring Discourse, Inventing Genre: Felix Jacoby and Greek Ethnography

It would be hard to overemphasize the impact that Felix Jacoby's work had on subsequent scholarship. Not only was the monumental task of organizing and classifying the fragmentary Greek authors achieved in the face of great adversity but the various categories and genres thus created—largely as a matter of convenience—also proved extraordinarily resilient thereafter. What Oswyn Murray has elsewhere described as the "undifferentiated sphere of early Greek prose" was progressively ordered and compartmentalized into discrete bodies of enquiry: the various subspecies of historiography, namely, genealogy/mythography, ethnography, chronography, horography, and contemporary history, referred to collectively as *historiê*.[114] The attempt to identify

---

[112] E.g., Edith Hall's celebrated bid to demonstrate how ethnographic imaginings permeated the world of Attic drama (E. Hall 1989).

[113] International scholarship resolutely seeks to complete the project set in train by Jacoby: efforts are underway to produce Brill's new edition along with textual commentaries treating individual genres, see Fowler 2000 on mythography (vol. 1) and Harding's recent treatment of the Attidographers (Harding 2008). For Jacoby's life and career, see Chambers 2006.

[114] Summarized succinctly by Murray: "The origins of Greek history lie in the undifferentiated sphere of early Greek prose writing which was as much about myth, about the geography of the world and the customs of other peoples, as about the unfolding of events" (Murray 2000, 330).

discrete bodies of enquiry represented a significant departure from the chronological method employed by Jacoby's predecessors, the brothers Carl and Theodore Müller, whose *Fragmenta Historicorum Graecorum* had emerged at intervals between the years 1841 and 1870. This work possessed numerous shortcomings, however, which the precocious young Jacoby set out to rectify, at least in part, by implementing a new schema based on the evolution of literary and stylistic forms—the series of predefined genres outlined above. While the essential similarities between the various genres were explicitly acknowledged,[115] the idea that one could legitimately classify a body of literature as being variously "ethnographic," "chronographic," or "genealogical" was very much in line with a contemporary drive to organize and classify a vast body of materials and knowledge according to taxonomy.[116]

Closer examination of the structure and ordering of Jacoby's magnum opus reveals a puzzling discrepancy, however. While the original program published in 1909 envisaged a sequence beginning with testimonia to Hecataeus's *Genealogies* and *Description of the World* (vol. I), followed by:

Genealogy/Mythography (vol. II)
Ethnography (vol. III)
Contemporary History (*Zeitgeschichte des Griechischen Volkes*) (vol. IV)
Chronography (vol. V)

and *Local History* (vol. VI),[117] that laid out in the preface to the first volume of the *Fragmente* (published in 1923) diverges from this schema by placing ethnography in volume IV after *Contemporary History* together with horography. A further change occurred at some point prior to the publication of the third volume in 1950 when the structure of volume IV, formerly billed as *Geschichte von Völkern und Städten* (*Ethnographie und Horographie*),[118] was

---

[115] Jacoby himself noted—on more than one occasion—that the relationship between genres such as history and ethnography was "not clearly distinguished in ancient terminology" (Jacoby 1949, 289n110; 305n22). The latter ultimately proved incapable of supplying technical vocabulary to match many of the categories identified. Discussion of the various problems arising from this approach has since gathered momentum: see (among others) Zambrini 2006; Clarke 1999, 2008; Bowersock 1997; Schepens 2010, 2006b, 1997; Fowler 1996; Brunt 1980; Bravo 1971. The speed with which they subsequently became institutionalized owes a great deal to the simple fact that they exist in separate bound copies of *Die Fragmente der Griechischen Historiker*.

[116] A concern for classification was equally manifest among practitioners working within emerging subject areas such as geography and ethnography as they tackled basic (yet fundamental) questions of self-definition ranging from the scope of intellectual enquiry to the categories to be employed by library collections. For discussion of the classificatory systems to be employed in the ordering of geographical knowledge, see Mill 1898, 145–151.

[117] Jacoby 1909, 123. Further projected volumes included Biography (vol. 7) and Geography (vol. 8).

[118] Jacoby 1923, v.

reversed in favor of local history, thereby relegating ethnography to the sidelines of historiographical enquiry.[119] This requires some explanation.

Jacoby's initial conception of ethnography was initially unambiguous both with regards to its subject matter (the description of lands, their peoples, and their customs)[120] and mode of discourse—that is, descriptive in contrast to *narrative* (Greek) history (griechische Zeitgeschichte/Ἑλληνικά).[121] The idea of a gradual transition from ethnographic description to historical narrative was therefore of fundamental importance when it came to explaining the origins of Great Historiography. According to Jacoby, this entailed a "natural" evolution from the ethnographic excursuses embedded in Hecataeus's *Periodos Ges*, incorporating a description of the region, its regnal history, local wonders, and costume, to stand-alone treatises devoted to a single land or people (*Aigyptiaka, Lydiaka, Persika*). While it was envisioned that this new genre would have contained historical material, its subject matter—foreign lands and peoples—meant that it remained "ethnographic" in nature. A reflection of Jacoby's unwillingness to countenance the existence of a "Herodotus before Herodotus," this distinction has long been seen as both arbitrary and problematic.[122] The issue is at its most acute when it comes to one author in particular, Dionysius of Miletus, who by rights (and Jacoby's own reasoning) should have been attributed with the founding role in the emergence of Great Historiography.

---

[119] See Schepens 2010; Zambrini 2006, 200: "Dopo quasi cinquant'anni di elaborazione, l'impalcatura teorica a sostegno della raccolta deo *Frammenti* vede disgregarsi uno dei suoi pilastri principali: nel 1909 l'etnografia doveva costituire la III parte dei *Frammenti* . . . nel 1957 si ritrova in fondo insieme alla storia locale" (After almost fifty years of development, the theoretical framework underpinning *The Fragmentary Greek Historians* saw one of its principal pillars implode: in 1909 ethnography was destined for volume three . . . in 1957 it found itself at the end together with local history).

[120] "Die Beschreibung des Landes und der νόμοι der Bewohner bleibt immer Grundlage und Ausganspunkt für den Ethnographen" (The description of [foreign] lands and the customs of their inhabitants remains the basis and starting point for the ethnographer) (Jacoby 1909, 92).

[121] "Eine echte Ethnographie umfasst stets alles, was über das betreffende Land zu sagen ist. Wenn es daher mehrere Ethnographien über ein Volk gibt—und das ist bei allen bedeutenderen der Fall—so ist die spätere nicht die Fortsetzung, sondern die erweitere (um nur dies zu betonen) Neubearbeitung der früheren. Darin liegt einer wesentlichsten Unterschiede gegenuber den sich gegenseitig fortsetzen 'Ἑλληνικά.' Er erklärt sich daraus, dass die Gattung ihrem Ursprunge nach nicht erzählend ist, wie die griechische Zeitgeschichte, sondern deskriptiv" (A genuine ethnography is all-inclusive. If, therefore, there are several ethnographies concerning a people—and this is always the case where the more significant peoples are concerned—the later ones are not a continuation but an extended revision (and only this) of that which passed before. Therein lies an essential difference which distinguishes it [i.e. ethnography] from narrative Greek history. This explains why ethnography is not narrative by nature, as with contemporary Greek history, but descriptive) (Jacoby 1909, 92). See Zambrini 2006, 191.

[122] See Zambrini 2006, 192ff.

Jacoby's stance toward Dionysius was both ambivalent and contradictory from the outset. While he was content to link Dionysius's *Persika* to the invasion of Ionia "not only chronologically but also causally" ("nicht nur zeitlich, sondern zweifellos auch ursächlich") on the basis that the Ionian Greeks would have been in dire need of ethnographic information regarding their new overlords ("Man hatte das Bedürfnis, möglichst viel von dem herrschenden Volke zu erfahren; und dieses Bedürfnis hat die erste Ethnographie erzeugt" [They felt the need to learn as much as possible regarding the ruling nation and this need generated the first ethnography]), he was nonetheless unwilling to identify Dionysius as a predecessor of Herodotus since this would inevitably compromise the latter's originality.[123] What emerges from this all-too-brief excursus into Jacoby's arguments and methodology is that, while undoubtedly a masterpiece, the theoretical model that provided the bases for the *FGrHist* contained certain flaws that ultimately rendered it unworkable.[124]

During the course of time, the inherent inconsistency of this approach became increasingly apparent, forcing Jacoby to consider alternative ways by which ethnographic genre might be defined in order to preserve Herodotus's position as progenitor of historiographical enquiry. Analysis of Jacoby's personal correspondence with figures such as Eduard Meyer has revealed that, in addition to the drawn out (and highly personal) process of internal wrangling that marked the search for a definition of ethnography capable of sustaining his overarching schema for the emergence of historiographical enquiry, Jacoby continued to flirt with alternative formats for ordering the *FGrHist* long after the official announcement

---

[123] Although willing to acknowledge that Herodotus might have used Dionysius's *Persika* as a source ("Wenn er wirklich älter war als H., so ist es allerdings recht glaublich, dass dieser ihn benutzt hat" [If he really was Herodotus' senior it is certainly credible that he used it]; Jacoby 1913, col. 405), Jacoby remained vague and elusive when it came to matters of chronology, e.g., *Atthis* (100): "It may remain an open question how far the Περσικά before Herodotus gave also any detailed narrative concerning those peoples whom the Persians had subjected. . . . Modern writers seem for some time to have formed too grand a conception of this literature. . . .: they set forth hypotheses that made the authors of Περσικά little Herodotoi (especially Dionysius of Miletos, a figure difficult to grasp). . . ." The historical nature of the work is, however, hinted at in the article on Charon of Lampsacus where it is suggested (on chronological grounds) that the Περσικά encompassed the reign of Xerxes.

[124] The fragility of Jacoby's position is best summed up by Zambrini: "In ultima analisi l'anello di congiunzione tra Ecateo ed Erodoto si risolve più che nella presenza di un genere letterario nuovo, consistente e constatabile, nel galleggiamento di una singola opera e del nome di un personaggio oscuro in uno spazio cronologico, la cui definizione può essere discutibile" (In the final analysis the link between Hecataeus and Herodotus is resolved via the presence of a new literary genre that is both consistent and verifiable, in the viability of a single work and the name of a figure of uncertain chronology, whose definition is open to question) (Zambrini 2006, 195). See also Schepens 2010.

ETHNOGRAPHY BEFORE ETHNOGRAPHY | 33

of the project in 1909.[125] Unwilling to concede pole position to Dionysius, Jacoby opted for a different strategy entirely. In the years that followed, ethnography was radically downgraded in status—no longer the conduit between Hecataean thought and Herodotean inquiry, its historical content could safely be acknowledged. The full extent of this shift is apparent in Jacoby's *Atthis*:

> The name (not differing from Attika as to its sense) expresses the fact, and it is the nature of local history and of ethnography (which is related to it) to give history: Persika tell the history of Persia, and Λαμψακηνῶν Ὧροι the story of Lampsakos.[126]

The effective abandonment of "the evolutionary principle" expounded in 1909 (das Entwicklungsgeschichtliche prinzip) whereby ethnography constituted the link between Hecataeus and Herodotus, who began as an ethnographer but then "evolved" into a historian, has attracted comparatively little comment until relatively recently.[127] In fact, it appears to have gone largely unnoticed in scholarship on ancient historiography—it being generally assumed that Jacoby's views on ancient ethnography remained static throughout his career. Given the fact that Jacoby made no attempt to draw attention to the volte-face[128] this is not altogether surprising, but the end result was that the theory of a "genetic" relationship between ethnography and history went unqualified in spite of the fact that the finalized structure of the *Fragmente* that Jacoby would eventually bequeath to posterity rendered it essentially redundant.

1.6 Ethnography and Identity

Although Jacoby's conception of ethnography fluctuated over the years it should be emphasized both that this state of aporia was primarily linked to problems of historical reconstruction (as opposed to any wider sense of uncertainty as to how to define ethnography per se) and that much—if not

---

[125] See Schepens 2006a. A similar picture emerges from correspondence between Jacoby and Herbert Bloch. A series of letters relating to Jacoby's project has recently been published by Guido Schepens together with excerpts from Jacoby's notes and an annotated copy of the original plan (Schepens 2010).

[126] Jacoby 1949, 100. For discussion of the development and nature of local historiography and a cogent challenge to Jacoby's thesis that horography followed in the wake of Great Historiography, see K. Clarke 2008. Instead, K. Clarke highlights the (largely performative) contexts in which the past was presented to the polis, namely epic and lyric poetry, and epigraphy. Cf. Kowalzig 2007.

[127] Andrea Zambrini's paper, published in 2006, was entirely ground-breaking in this respect.

[128] E.g., Fowler 1996.

all—of these deliberations were undertaken in private.[129] Much of Jacoby's agonizing appears to have centered around the extent to which ethnographic accounts might be considered "historical" based on their content and subject matter. The categories of (foreign) "ethnography" and (Greek) "history" are never called into question in themselves—as will be seen below.

Like all those working in the late nineteenth and early twentieth centuries, Jacoby had little cause to be preoccupied with how to define Greek identity per se. Whereas the Humboltian Project had formerly emphasized the essential unity of humanity, advocating the study of its component parts as a means of understanding the greater whole, it rapidly gave way to a prevailing *mentalité* that fused language, culture, society, and state in a mystical and unassailable unity and conceived humanity's evolution and history in terms of developmental sequences of racially differentiated categories.[130] In accordance with attitudes prevailing at the time, Hellenic culture was conceived as a *national* culture: a static and/or homogenous entity whose existence was deemed largely self-evident (even in cases as ambiguous as Epirus or Macedon that could be explained away on evolutionary or empirical grounds).[131] The result was an idea of Greek identity and history that was both separate and distinct, a convenient starting point for Eurocentric narratives charting the rise of Western civilization.[132] Such attitudes are readily apparent, for example, in the published works of Jacoby's mentor and influential patron Ulrich von Wilamowitz Moellendorff to whom Jacoby dedicated the paper that won him his first lectureship at the University of Breslau in 1904/1905 (later reedited to become *FGrHist* 239).[133] Although the extent to which Wilamowitz's ideas regarding race and culture evolved during the course of his career remains highly controversial,[134] one can safely argue

---

[129] The end result is essentially the same insofar as contact with Persia remains the catalyst for the emergence of both ethnographic and historical genres, whether as a result of the invasion of Ionia or the conflicts that followed.

[130] See Wolf 1982, 13–19 stressing the role of anthropology in demarcating culture groups as bounded systems.

[131] The widespread enthusiasm for all things Greek in nineteenth-century Germany is well attested. See Marchand 1996 for discussion and references.

[132] For discussion see Vlassopoulos's provocative new study of the Greek polis (Vlassopoulos 2007b).

[133] Attempts to depict Wilamowitz as a racist antisemite invariably fall foul of the fact that the latter was instrumental in ensuring Jacoby's Jewish origins did *not* prove an insurmountable barrier to a successful academic career in the years prior to Hitler's rise to power—something Wilamowitz himself never lived to see. For an even-handed discussion highlighting the depth and complexity of this most brilliant of scholars, see Norton 2008. For intellectual output see countless works edited by William M. Calder.

[134] Criticism of Flaig (2003) and, to a lesser extent, Canfora (1985) has at times been scathing, e.g., LLoyd-Jones 1986, 295–296; 2004.

that Wilamowitz viewed the Greeks as possessing characteristics that rendered them unique among their (non-Greek) neighbors.[135] Had Wilamowitz and Jacoby held radically different views on something as fundamental as the nature of Greek identity it is unlikely that Wilamowitz would have gone to such lengths to secure a position for his talented protégé or that Jacoby would have been quite so keen to identify himself as Wilamowitz's pupil. Instead, it seems safe to assume that Jacoby saw himself as working in the same tradition as his illustrious patron (namely, *Altertumswissenschaft*),[136] together with others such as his doctoral supervisor—the celebrated philologist Hermann Diels.

The meaning and function of ethnography would have appeared similarly straightforward during the late nineteenth and early twentieth centuries,[137] making it possible to distinguish between the genres of horography and ethnography on the basis of subject matter alone: one pertained to Greeks and the other did not.[138] Ethnography itself was a burgeoning field. As the Great Powers extended their dominion to encompass vast swaths of territory, the ensuing need to administer these newly acquired territories effectively meant that local cultures rapidly became the objects of intense interest and scrutiny.[139] Foreign peoples became increasingly accessible and "safe"—a point highlighted by Talal Asad[140]—and the number of learned societies devoted to

---

[135] It should be noted that such arguments do not mean that Wilamowitz saw the Greeks as racially pure: "Der Fanatismus der reinen Rasse kann sich mit einigem Scheine auf die Griechen berufen, deren Sprache und Kultur auf ihrer Höhe eine unvergleichliche Einheit und Reinheit zeigt. Aber das ist das letzte Ergebnis einer langen Entwicklung, und zugrunde liegt gerade hier eine unübersehbare Mischung der Völker und der Kulturen, und selbst das arische Blut ist keineswegs rein" (The fanaticism of the pure breed may with some plausibility be imputed to the Greeks whose language and culture shows at its height unrivalled unity and purity. But this was the end result of a long period of development and rests on an incalculable mix of peoples and cultures, not consistently pure Aryan blood in itself) (Wilamowitz 1923, 26). See Flaig 2003, 122–127 in which Wilamowitz's views are assimilated (somewhat controversially) to that of the *völkisch* movement. Flaig refrains, however, from linking discussion of Wilamowitz's views on racial inequality to the extent to which such views prevailed throughout German scholarship as a whole.
[136] See Norton 2008, 87–89 for illuminating discussion of the relationship between *Wissenschaft* and intuition. For correspondence between Jacoby and Wilamowitz see now Schepens 2010, appendix B.
[137] On definitions see Fowler 2001, 97n3; Marincola 1999.
[138] Cf. G. E. R. Lloyd 2002, 17. See below for the politics of defining disciplinary boundaries. The extent to which Jacoby's conception of "Greekness" played a significant role in structuring his analyses can be seen in passages discussing the origins of Athens' local history: "One of the matters relating to the domain of culture is religious faith, which shows itself in Philochoros primarily as a history of the gods in Attica. . . . Matters are different in Ethnography and in Herodotus, who has distinct theological interests, even if they lie mostly in the direction of history: nobody can write the history of a people without describing its faith, and in the treatment of the νόμοι (which taken collectively represent the culture of the people) the τόπος περὶ θεῶν usually takes the first place" (Jacoby 1949, 139).
[139] Amselle 1998 provides an authoritative account of the extent to which the politics of anthropological enquiry have been allied to the activities and interests of the colonizing West.
[140] Asad 1973. Cf. Harris 1898 ("The Berbers of Morocco"); Read and Dalton 1898 ("Works of Art from Benin City"); Godden 1898 ("Nágá and Other Frontier Tribes of North-East India").

their study underwent a dramatic increase as a result.[141] Much of the ground-work was undertaken by individuals whose grounding in the Classics would, in many cases, have either equaled or outstripped any knowledge they might have possessed regarding the territories and/or societies that they had set out to alternately "discover" or "civilize."

The situation was much the same when it came to national organizations such as the Berliner Gesellschaft für Anthropologie, Ethnologie, und Urge-schichte (Berlin Society for Anthropology, Ethnology and Prehistory, BGAEU), founded in 1869 by Rudolf Virchow.[142] Although the BGAEU rapidly estab-lished a reputation for itself as the leading authority on ethnographic research, its members remained geographers, classicists, and philologists by training until such time as German universities became willing to incorporate subject areas such as prehistory and anthropology into university curricula. Leading classicists and historians also played an active role in this wider flowering of ethnographic and geographical knowledge, however. The earliest issues of *The Geographical Journal* are peppered with contributions by individuals such as J. L. Myres, attempting to reconstruct the maps employed by Herodotus; or, alternately, the formidable Colonel Holdich (R.E., C.B., C.I.E.), whose dis-cussion of "the origins of the Kafir of the Hindu Kush" is as much indebted to Arrian's account of the campaigns of Alexander as observations made "in the field."[143]

Although a nation-state of relative immaturity with comparatively minor territorial possessions, the Wilhelmian Germany of Jacoby's formative years displayed a notable enthusiasm for all things foreign.[144] This enthusiasm has

---

[141] In Britain notable examples include: the Royal Geographical Society (1830), the Anthropolog-ical Society of London (1863), followed by the Anthropological Institute of Great Britain and Ireland in 1870 (formed following merger of the Ethnological and Anthropological Societies of London). The first readership in Anthropology was created in Oxford in 1884, to be converted to a chair two years later. See Burrow 1966, 75–81.

[142] Marchand 1996, 175. An offshoot of the Versammlungen der deutschen Naturforscher und Ärzte (Conferences of German Natural Scientists and Doctors), a learned society founded in 1822, the activities of the BGAEU initially reflected the interests of its founding members, i.e., biological anthropology and pathology. See Zantop 1997 for the back history of the German co-lonialist imagination during the eighteenth and nineteenth centuries, highlighting the impor-tance of the novel as "a space for identification and projection" (103).

[143] Myres 1896 (see fig. 3); Holdich 1896, 43: "In the case of the Kamdesh Kafir . . . the tradition of Greek or Pelasgic origin seems likely to be verified . . . scientific enquiry has been converging on him from several directions, and it seems possible that the ethnological riddle connected with his existence will be solved ere long." Cf. also Markham 1893 on "Pytheas, the discoverer of Britain" (vol. 1); Maj.-Gen. Sir Frederic Goldsmid's discussion of the acropolis at Susa (1893); and Munro and Anthony on the exploration of Mysia, funded in part by grants from the Hellenic Society (1897). For discussion of J. L. Myres and other "geographical historians," see Clarke 1999, 45–65.

[144] For wider discussion, see Kundrus 2003 together with Friedrichsmeyer et al. 1998; Ames et al. 2005.

lately been the focus of considerable attention among scholars seeking to rehabilitate German anthropology of the prewar years: languishing in relative obscurity and tarred with infamy ever since its perverted doctrines of race were subsequently taken up and exploited by National Socialism.[145] In fact, German museums possessed ethnological collections that far outstripped those of Britain, while traveling shows or exhibitions (Völkerschauen) allowed paying members of the public to gaze upon the exotic garments and customs of far-off peoples, their coloring and physique.[146] Although state-run museums and colonial adventures both had an important role to play in forging a sense of collective *national* identity,[147] one of the most notable outcomes of such initiatives was the popularization of ethnographic interests and concerns.[148] These were by no means the preserve of Germany alone, however; instead, discourses of wonder proliferated across Europe as a whole, as exotic cultures increasingly became objects of popular consumption.[149]

---

[145] Such work has focused on the activities of prominent ethnologists such as Adolf Bastian (director of Berlin's ethnographic museum ca. 1873–1905) and Rudolph Virchow. In contrast to colleagues not only in Germany but also Britain, France, and the United States, they subscribed to a belief in the common dignity shared by all cultures, the basis for a comparative approach whose broadly humanistic goal was the greater understanding of human nature and society and, as such, an explicit reaction against contemporary tendencies to characterize non-Europeans as "savages" (Penny 2002; Penny and Bunzl 2003). While there is some danger of a whitewash here (the presence of nationalist attitudes and social Darwinism are certainly underplayed), studies of this nature highlight (intentionally or otherwise) the extent to which having an ethnographic museum/attendant exotica became an object of competition between municipalities and the possible attitudes/assumptions that such scientific curiosity entailed—effectively the "commodification" or consumption of ethnography.

[146] For the extent to which colonialism shaped social attitudes in Germany, see W. D. Smith 2005. Smith's discussion of cultural contexts is instructive and is worth quoting in full: "Cultural contexts and their elements are similar to *mentalités*, excepts that they are usually the products of conscious construction and are consciously recognizable by the people who incorporate them into their daily lives. They are not in most cases overtly political or ideological, but they can have political implications. They are not normally programmatic, but they constitute a storehouse of imagined meaningful relations that give significance to the terms in which the programs are stated. They often have the peculiar quality of being recognized not only by historians but by the people in whose heads they largely reside as well—though not usually recognized as the comprehensive frameworks that they actually are" (W. D. Smith 2005, 5). For analysis of the effects that the widespread popularity (and commercial success) of traveling shows, exhibitions and public lectures displaying foreign peoples had on the early history of Anthropology in Nineteenth-Century Britain see Qureshi 2011.

[147] See Marchand 1996, 175: "Virchow himself hoped that his organic scientific method would help to consolidate political unification by becoming the basis for a liberal and nondenominational cultural community." For discussion of the effects that decolonization had on the collective consciousness of the Weimar Republic emphasizing the role of binaries (notably that of *Kulturträger* [bearers of civilization] and *Völker* as they appear in *Mein Kampf*), see Klotz 2005, passim but esp. 143.

[148] For detailed discussion of the appetites and interests of working-class readers during the late nineteenth and early twentieth centuries, see Short 2003.

[149] A vast bibliography on this but see: Greenblatt 1991; Lidchi 1997; Driver 2001; Qureshi 2011. For discussion of popular ethnography in a postwar context, see Gates 1998, 235–236.

As anthropology developed into a full-fledged discipline serviced by a multitude of scholarly journals and periodicals, there was an exponential increase in the number of ethnographies produced. These were not, moreover, the work of enthusiastic amateurs alone—military personnel, colonial administrators, merchants, and adventurers—but also a growing number of professional academics. Claims to autopsy proliferated as ethnographic authority became increasingly contested; university-trained researchers were keen to distance themselves from their (nonprofessional) predecessors and/or contemporary rivals (irrespective of the levels of training received), challenging their knowledge or objectivity. According to the new discourse of professionalism, the authority to interpret human culture derived from one's ability to collate data according to preordained standards, generating results that would stand up to independent, scientific scrutiny. It followed, therefore, that anyone seeking to undertake research in the field required rigorous schooling in the latest analytical techniques. At the same time, those engaged in ethnographic research were increasingly keen to distinguish their work from other forms of representation in which aspects of human culture might be invoked or described: the travelogue, guidebook, or novel.

The manner in which the new discipline's remit was subsequently demarcated is in itself revealing. The cultural superiority of the (supposedly) enlightened European observer went hand-in-hand with that of his enlightened Greek predecessor.[150] As such it went largely unchallenged in the face of a veritable avalanche of knowledge and ideas relating to foreign peoples and so-called primitive cultures. There remained, accordingly, in both Classics and anthropology, as with society as a whole, a hierarchical distinction between Graeco-Roman studies, unambiguously associated with a "European," civilized past, and anthropological and ethnographic studies encompassing "everyone else"—including, notably, pre-Classical Greece and Rome. This distinction is nowhere more apparent than in comments made by R. R. Marett, writing in his preface to a collection of essays titled *Anthropology and the Classics* in 1908:

> The types of human culture are, in fact, reducible to two, a simpler and a more complex, or, as we are wont to say (valuing our achievements, I doubt not, rightly), a lower and a higher. By established convention Anthropology occupies itself solely with culture of the lower or simpler kind. The

---

[150] While reductive and unnecessarily condemnatory, the aggressive polemic of Bernal's *Black Athena* does reflect some degree of reality—albeit one that was ultimately far more nuanced and complex (Bernal 1987).

Humanities, on the other hand—those humanizing studies that, for us at all events, have their parent source in the literatures of Greece and Rome—concentrate on whatever is most constitutive and characteristic of the higher life of society.[151]

The enthusiasm for ethnographic material demonstrated by members of the Cambridge Ritual School was particularly notable but, like the Oxford Committee for Anthropology, committed to "inducing classical scholars to study the lower culture as it bears upon the higher,"[152] it was predicated upon a hierarchical ranking of cultures and societies—much like Frazer's epic, if misguided, undertaking, *The Golden Bough.*[153]

In order to understand this phenomenon we must turn our attention to the various ways in which culture was perceived within (early) anthropological studies. In this we are greatly aided by Jean-Loup Amselle's wide-ranging critique of "ethnological reason,"[154] a body of thought and practice arising from eighteenth- and nineteenth-century traditions of comparative nationalism and evolutionism but ultimately rooted in Classical Greek thought.[155] In a provocative reassessment of the intellectual foundations of cultural anthropology Amselle highlights the extent to which the work of pioneering anthropologists such as E. B. Tylor and Franz Boas drew on a notion of culture very much at variance with that formulated by Kant. While Kant's conception of *Kultur* was couched in terms of its intrinsic universality, the work of Tylor and Boas bears all the hallmarks of Herder's (rather more restricted) usage of a term reflecting "the sense of cultural inferiority felt by the Germans and the Russians vis-à-vis the more advanced nations" during the late nineteenth century.[156] This same "ethnic" usage of *Kultur* is linked in turn to

---

[151] Marett 1908, 3. Cf. Myres 1908, 121. Such views reflect the influence of one of the founding fathers of modern anthropology, E. B. Tylor, whose work on the evolutionary comparative method inspired a number of Classicists to embark upon *parallel* careers of anthropological enquiry, in an effort to rationalize the various social institutions of Graeco-Roman antiquity—notably James Frazer and Andrew Lang (Tylor 1891, 1; Burrow 1966, 236). For "Greek anthropology," see Sikes 1914.

[152] Marett 1908, 5.

[153] Burrow 1966. J. Harrison 1912 is a notable (and much celebrated) case in point. On Frazer's interest in the sequential relationship between magic, science, and religion and the influence on Durkheim see Skorupski 1976; cf. Durkheim 1912. For the balancing act attempted by the "Cambridge Ritualists," see Leonard 2005, 48; Beard 1992, 1999, 2002; Versnel 1990.

[154] "[T]he continuity-breaking procedure that extracts, refines, and classifies with the intention of isolating types, whether they be in the realm of politics (state society versus stateless society), economics (self-sufficient versus market economy), religion (paganism versus Islam), ethnicity or culture" (Amselle 1998, 1).

[155] Amselle 1998, 10. With reservations.

[156] Ibid., 26.

the term *Volk*, which, although synonymous with the German people when used in the singular, was invariably used "to designate cultures in general and primitive cultures in particular"[157] when applied in the plural—consider, by way of an example, Jacoby's *Geschichte von Städten und Völkern* (*Horographie und Ethnographie*).

The product of an academic tradition that was in many ways diametrically opposed to modernist-inspired groupings such as the Cambridge Ritualists, Jacoby's treatment of Herodotus and other fragmentary Greek authors must nonetheless be seen as arising from the same prevailing *mentalité*. Both reflect the creeping professionalization of Classics and anthropology, respectively, coupled with a more general tendency to distinguish between the aforementioned "uniqueness" of the Greeks and an equally homogenous mass: the exotic, uncivilized, nonwestern, non-Christian "other."[158] The fact that the German philological tradition prevailed in what was, for a time, a struggle for hegemony within the Anglo-American academy meant that anthropological approaches to Classical pasts were all but abandoned until their eventual reemergence in the work of individuals such as Sally Humphreys and Geoffrey Lloyd.[159] It is, as a result, only comparatively recently that the essential "foreignness" of the Greeks, long emphasized by those working under the aegis of the Recherches comparées sur les sociétés anciennes (Centre Louis Gernet), has been widely acknowledged by non-Francophone scholarship—fitting subjects in themselves for anthropological study.[160]

While it would be overly simplistic to suggest that the elevation of ethnography to the status of a science provides an effective rationale for the ease with which Greek ethnography came to be recognized as a discrete realm of

---

[157] Ibid.

[158] The relationship between anthropology and Classical studies has been anything but straightforward, characterized at different times by both close collaboration and deep (mutual) suspicion. Lang denied that it was possible to detect the "beastly devices of the heathen" in Homer although archaic survivals from a more primitive age are, however, deemed to have provided ready material for less scrupulous playwrights of the fifth century, who seemingly reveled in the "distressing vestiges of savagery and barbarism" (Lang 1908, 44; repeated by Murray 1908, 66). Cf. Sally Humphreys' authoritative and inspiring *Anthropology and the Greeks*.

[159] Leonard 2005, 49. The trail can be traced back to E. R. Dodds (1951), whose intellectual successors include G. E. R. Lloyd (1966); Geoffrey Kirk (1970, 1974); and Sally Humphreys (1978). For discussion and references, see Miriam Leonard's groundbreaking *Athens in Paris* (2005, 48–49): "Classics' flirtation with anthropology in the English academy at the beginning of this century was fully implicated in the wider debates of disciplinary formation in the move towards academic professionalisation. The exclusion of 'anthropology' from the canon of classical disciplines was . . . an important episode in early twentieth-century academic politics" (48). Cf. Leonard 2000; Stray 1998.

[160] Gernet 1976; R. Osborne 2006, 5. Cf. Detienne 2007. For more detailed discussion of the intellectual backdrop to the "Paris school," see Leonard 2005.

enquiry, it undoubtedly played an important role in shaping contemporary outlooks and approaches: a salutary reminder of the consequences and (potential) pitfalls of erecting epistemological barriers that subsequently become institutionalized, and the extent to which the initial demarcation and subsequent policing of these disciplinary boundaries is both politically charged and historically situated.[161] Opinion as to what constitutes "valid" ethnographic activity is inevitably shaped and constrained by the (perhaps questionable) assumption that ethnography, or indeed any other field of study, exists as some kind of static or stable entity.[162] It is only when disciplinary boundaries are subverted or broken down, allowing for extensive cross-fertilization of ideas between individuals working in a variety of fields, that we are reminded that the neat categories and definitions with which we work are both historically contingent and subjectively defined. Taken overall they demonstrate the extent to which the traditional view of ethnography as a subsection of Great Historiography ignores the fact that both ethnography and ethnographic activity constitute open-ended processes.

Around the very time that ethnography became established as a scientific discipline, efforts were simultaneously underway to problematize the various boundaries and categories upon which it depended for coherence. At a time when Jacoby was busily engaged in publishing parts I–II of *FGrHist*, containing the works (among others) of Herodotus's predecessors and contemporaries, Paris provided a haven for a dissident avant-garde keen to exploit ethnographic approaches in pursuit of its radical agenda. Inspired by a suggestion by Georges Henri Rivière, deputy director of the Musée d'Ethnographie du Trocadéro, the short-lived journal *Documents*, edited by the Surrealist Georges Bataille, went to press with "Doctrines," "Archéologie," "Beaux-Arts," and "Ethnographie" emblazoned on its cover.[163] *Documents* followed a number of set themes such as ritual, religion, and the sacred, collapsing the boundaries between notions idealized in Western culture and an unromanticized primitivism—moral and aesthetic hierarchies that the Surrealist project had set out to explode.[164] This was achieved via an eclectic collage of photographic studies and essays, intended to pose

---

[161] Cf. Humphreys 2004, 23: "[T]his imposition of disciplinary categories on ancient texts accompanied and encouraged linear narratives of evolution and progress, linked to the modern perception of the ancients as forerunners of the Enlightenment."

[162] Cf. Clifford 1988, 118.

[163] This engagement was far from superficial: Bataille founded the Collège de Sociologie in the late thirties, while *Documents* itself contained ethnographic texts by leading practitioners on subjects ranging from "Abyssinian Totemism" (Marcel Griaule, 1929) to "Cuban Music" (Alejo Carpentier, 1929). The Surrealist journal *Minotaure* (1936) also cited *ethnologie* in its rubric.

[164] Tythacott 2003, 219–220.

questions of relative value and classification. So, for instance, pictures from the interior of La Villette's slaughterhouse in Paris[165] or the Capuchin mortuary chapel of Santa Maria della Concezione in Rome[166] were subject to the same levels of scrutiny as masks from Cameroon[167] or human sacrifice in Central America.[168] This comprehensive overhaul of the objects and aims of ethnographical enquiry should alert us to the fact that not only the methods but also the ends to which cultural difference was analyzed and explored in antiquity may have differed from those with which we are familiar.

While the fruits of such collaboration between leading ethnologists, archaeologists, curators, writers, and poets have been amply documented elsewhere,[169] they provide ample proof of the fact that strategies of representation are both inherently political and historically situated.[170] Just as individuals such as J. L. Myres operated in an environment in which the boundaries separating institutions remained forever permeable and shifting, the Parisian avant-garde produced a very different way of thinking about culture and identity due to the prevailing conditions of the day. Unusual for the degree of self-conscious reflexivity it displayed,[171] its range and subject matter compares favorably with both Herodotean enquiry and current issues of journals such as *Ethnography* (although the latter is the more conservative of the two when it comes to layout and formatting).

Rethinking Greek ethnography will likewise entail broadening our definition of ethnography to encompass the varied means by which groups and individuals came to "think about identity from the point of view of an outsider." Altering the criteria as to what constitutes ethnographic activity and why has significant implications for understanding how the ethnographic genre emerged in the first place. Instead of a fifth-century epiphany preceded by hazy imaginings, it becomes part of a broader continuum of thought and practice in which cultural difference was variously represented

---

[165] Photo by Eli Lotar for Bataille's "Abattoir," (Bataille 1929, 328).

[166] Bataille, 1930.

[167] von Sydow, 1930.

[168] Hervé, 1930.

[169] Clifford 1988; Tythacott 2003.

[170] "The boundaries of art and science . . . are ideological and shifting, and intellectual history is itself enmeshed in these shifts. Its genres do not remain firmly anchored. Changing definitions of art or science must provoke new retrospective unities, new ideal types for historical description" (Clifford 1988, 118–119).

[171] Although the term "ethnographic surrealism" has since been coined in an effort to encapsulate the aims and ideals of Bataille and his associates, its inventor was at the same time keen to emphasize the extent to which this conceptual pigeonholing was something to be resisted (Clifford 1988, 117–119): "[M]y aim is to cut across retrospectively established definitions and to recapture . . . a situation in which ethnography is again something unfamiliar and surrealism not yet a bounded province of modern art and literature" (Clifford 1988, 117).

or "imagined" as groups and individuals sought variously to situate themselves in relation to fields of difference. Under such circumstances it would clearly be problematic to posit a steady process of evolution toward rational observation of cultural difference when the very opposite would, at times, appear to be the case. Pindar the poet carried equal authority, along with Homer, to contemporary logographers—at least as far as Herodotus was concerned.[172] The following chapters will emphasize the *range* of knowledge and ideas in circulation and the varied means by which they circulated before returning to the wider question of how the emergence of set-piece ethnographies, namely works subsequently referred to as *Persika* or *Lydiaka*, should be viewed in relation to both contact with "the barbarian" and the invention of Greek prose. The picture that emerges overall is one of dynamic exchanges of information and ideas arising from varying levels of contact and interaction between groups of different outlook and culture—all of them constitutive of identity. Each of the regions encountered in chapter 4 display marked differences in geographic location, topography, modes of subsistence, and levels of "connectedness"—whether viewed in terms of overland or maritime trade, participation in Panhellenic festivals and competitions, or links with both Greek and non-Greek-speaking populations scattered throughout the ancient Mediterranean. It follows, therefore, that they produced different meanings even if the majority of the materials employed to do so were essentially the same: mythic paradigms, figured pottery, coinage and knowledge and ideas relating to a variety of foreign peoples. Greek identities were, from the outset, hybrid, relational, and inventive, meaning different things at different times to different people, and ethnographic activity—the mechanisms and processes by which discourses of identity and difference were variously constructed and found expression—played an active role in deciding what it meant to be *Greek* in the first place.

1.7 Polarities Deconstructed

The modern tendency to conceptualize relationships between Greek and barbarian in terms of polarities is itself worthy of scrutiny. To this end, it is surely worth reminding ourselves that the concept of alterity was itself imported from anthropological theory. The setting was, once again, Paris—this time

---

[172] Material preserved within the Homeric corpus plays an important role in structuring the *Histories* from discussion surrounding conflicting accounts of Helen's elopement (implied in the case of Hdt. I 3–5 but cf. II 112–120), to questions of geography—the existence of a River Ocean (II 23)—and climate. For discussion of III 38 see chap. 2. For discussion of IV 29. Cf. IV 32 on Hyperboreans in Homeric *Epigoni*.

during the intellectual ferment of the 1960s. Although structural anthropology was as yet in its infancy, key individuals such as the noted Hellenist Louis Gernet provided a vital bridging mechanism by adopting a position at the intersection between disciplines as varied as Classical philology, history, and sociology.[173] Under the influence of leading thinkers such as Claude Lévi-Strauss, Gernet, followed by his intellectual successor Jean-Pierre Vernant, pioneered a variety of "anthropologie historique" not hitherto seen, in which anthropological models and paradigms were applied to Greek culture and society.[174] The starting point for this process was arguably Lévi-Strauss's critical engagement with the Oedipus myth: in all likelihood a reaction to Freudian psychoanalysis drawing heavily on the structural linguistics of Saussure. The result was an analysis framed in terms of a polarity of opposites soon to be a familiar feature of structural analysis and, in turn, Classics as a whole.[175]

Often forgotten or overlooked entirely, this intellectual pedigree is important if we are to understand how the Greek–barbarian paradigm achieved its position of unrivaled preeminence within Classical studies. The degree of salience that it was afforded reflects not only the wealth of material that could be explained in terms of a discourse of opposites—Greek–barbarian, self–other—but also the authority arising from its "scientific" origins within the social sciences, not least anthropological studies. While (poststructuralist) literary criticism also had an important role to play, it was equally predicated upon a juxtaposition of opposites, "Orient" and "Occident," and an "Orientalizing tradition" that took Aeschylus's *Persae* as its starting point.[176] However, if we accept Jean-Loup Amselle's epistemological critique of the models and paradigms underpinning anthropological thought as valid, the entire

---

[173] Leonard 2005, 47–49, see 44–45 for the relationship between Vernant's methodological approach and Lévi-Straussian structuralism. The complexities surrounding Lévi-Strauss's encounter with Classics is also highlighted: "It is this paradox of both a fundamental denial of philological methodology and the simultaneous reassertion of the importance of language which is one of the most interesting aspects of Lévi-Strauss' essay . . . the particular attention to the linguistic in his reading of mythology has meant that his structuralist account of ancient culture has paradoxically lent itself to the analysis of the literary expressions of its ideologies" (Leonard 2005, 58).

[174] In the years that followed, structural analysis was enthusiastically applied to a wide variety of textual and iconographic evidence before finally making its way into the Anglo-American academy. The impetus for this transfer derived from the publication of two books in particular: François Hartog's *Mirror of Herodotus* (originally published in 1980 and translated into English in 1988) and Edith Hall's *Inventing the Barbarian* (1989). See, for example: Gernet [1976] 1981; Vidal-Naquet [1981] 1998, [1970] 1996; Bérad [1984] 1989; Lissarrague [1987] 1990b. The trend is both noted and critiqued by Blok (Blok 1995, 118–126).

[175] For recent discussion, stressing the interpretative shortcomings of such an approach, see now Root 2011.

[176] Said 1978, 3, 21; Hall 1989, 99–100.

discourse on alterity begins to look very circular indeed since ethnographic studies, or, to use Amselle's phrasing, ethnology, is ultimately founded upon a cornerstone of (ancient) Greek political thought: the distinction between *ethnê* and poleis.[177]

Amselle's thesis is equally pertinent when it comes to wider questions of power relations variously referred to above in contexts ranging from the relationship between scientific argument, ethnocentric attitudes, and power relations to a perceived willingness to incorporate non-Greeks into a shared mythic past.[178] The extent to which the various elements of "ethnographic discourse" (loosely defined in the Foucauldian sense) can be analyzed in terms of wider questions of power and ideology deserves careful consideration, however. Amselle's analysis of the classificatory schemas employed in anthropological studies might be rooted in the past, but the alternative proposed (the *Mestizo Logics*) reflects modern interests and concerns, namely, a desire to arrive at a way of conceptualizing culture that does not automatically privilege the colonizing West. Applying such arguments to early ethnographic thought is unlikely to enhance our understanding of the intellectual and social milieus from which it emerged. The complex origins of ethnography do not lend themselves to reductive or totalizing statements regarding the power interests that a particular body of thought might have served. The dataset is too diverse and the topics too varied in scope. General pronouncements regarding the way in which a particular foreign people were perceived and represented are only helpful if our aim is to investigate the ideological bases of discursive strategies that would ultimately give rise to modern imperialisms—a different topic entirely that has already received comprehensive treatment by scholars working in a variety of disciplines.

While such analyses are necessarily dependent upon an essentialized notion of Greek identity (the Greek view of Egyptians, say), this study highlights the wide variety of contexts in which notions of Greek and Egyptian came into play and how that knowledge of Egypt existed as a complex patchwork of observed detail, speculation, and imaginings to which groups or individuals could selectively refer as and when the need arose. Although the relationship between the ethnographic subject and the ethnographer bears

---

[177] See Amselle 1997, 6: "For the Greeks, the notion of *ethnos* was a political category. It constituted one pole in the hierarchization that evolved between the two principle forms of societies: *polis* and *ethnos*. If the *polis* . . . was a precisely defined and valorized category, one in which the Greeks found their plentitude of being, the category of *ethnos*, in contrast, was vague and deprecatory." For recent discussion of the poleis–*ethnê* opposition, see Morgan 2009; Vlassopoulos 2007a; 2007b.

[178] For recent discussion, see Gruen 2011a.

some similarity to that discussed by Amselle, that is, one is invariably objectified, aestheticized, and described by the other, the degree of asymmetry involved varied hugely. Rather than a monolithic opposition between the West and Africa, we have a complex process of engagement that varied according to time or region concerned (the Northern Pontic shore, Southern Calabria, or Delphi/Olympia) and could apply to Greeks and non-Greeks alike. The institutional apparatus that played a central role in denying subject peoples their agency is itself noticeably absent and the modes of representation employed encompassed a wide variety of media and genre. While discourses of identity and difference might have played out in stereotypically "colonial" scenarios, they were equally prevalent in circumstances in which Greeks were very much the junior party—take Egypt again as an example.

Far from denying that ethnographic representation served the interests of particular groups and individuals I would merely like to highlight the importance of viewing such material in its local and regional context.[179] This is important from a methodological point of view as the study of ethnographies takes place against the backdrop of a world defined by mobility and exchange: an intricate web that connected (however indirectly) bustling ports of trade with isolated rural settlements located high in the Aspromonte, major metropoleis such as Corinth or Athens with Arcadia or the wilds of Scythia. It is a world of boundless complexity of which we retain only the barest fragments and whose appreciation and analysis is only going to be partial and subject to modern-day assumptions and preconceptions. Trade winds carried ships laden with passengers and cargo, images and ideas, from port to port on coasting voyages, or connecting island archipelagos. The tracks and byways that linked farmstead and village, *ethnê* and poleis were thronged with travelers and traders, armies and theoric embassies—a flow of goods and people but also of information.[180]

Whether this flow of information can be rendered in any way quantifiable or, indeed, accessible through anything other than a wild leap of the imagination is a question of fundamental importance. Gaps and silences in the evidence are inevitable as we are largely constrained by both the material available and the manner in which it can be interpreted: the discursive nature of Classics as a discipline means we invariably replicate ancient discourses and power relationships through our choice of themes and objects of study.[181]

---

[179] How it was deployed, when and to what ends, are important questions in their own right even if we have insufficient evidence to arrive at definitive answers regarding the "end product" or, for that matter, to identify its respective "winners" and "losers."

[180] *Od.* IX 125–30. On the network of ancient roads in the Peloponnese: Tausend 2006; cf. Pikoulas 1999. For the role of Greek elites as carriers of information, see Raaflaub 2004.

[181] Cf. Siapkas 2003; Humphreys 2004; Vlassopoulos 2007b.

While far from infallible, a synthetic approach that integrates material, iconographic, and literary evidence, remaining sensitive to questions of regional or local variation, individual agency, and—importantly—chronology is a viable basis for considering the manner in which Greek ethnographies and identities interrelated.

How such material should be organized conceptually is a matter of great importance. Decisions of this nature are both highly significant and complex—not least because they have a very direct bearing on the sorts of answers generated by any given study. While a variety of methods and paradigms are available, the network approach stands out as a heuristic device capable of accommodating varying levels of complexity at a scale ranging from the regional or local to "global" networks of trade and association.[182] Recent work has shown that the study of networks has much to offer the student of antiquity.[183] Following in the wake of Fernand Braudel's stately *The Mediterranean,* which saw the entire region characterized as an "exchange," criss-crossed by *réseaux,* scholars have increasingly sought to emphasize the high levels of "connectivity" linking cities, microregions, rural settlements, and ports of trade.[184] While the Mediterranean paradigm has been variously explored and qualified, analysis of its network-structure is now a field of study in its own right.[185] This field of study makes extensive use of social network theory and a variety of approaches imported from the sciences to examine the dynamic relationships between individual "nodes" (variously understood as points in space, objects, or individual agents) and the networks to which they were connected.

While the importance of networks linking founding city and *apoikia,* Panhellenic sanctuaries and far-flung populations, was, in many cases, either already well known or tacitly acknowledged, the manifest utility of a theoretical tool that permits researchers to model patterns of social and economic behavior makes it an important addition to the historian's arsenal. Tacit acknowledgment of a phenomenon is not the same as actively thinking through a factor or characteristic, shedding fresh light on old problems, or discovering entirely new ones in the process. Irad Malkin, the leading exponent of

---

[182] See Malkin 2003b, 2011; Malkin et al. 2007. For discussion of network approaches—and social network theory in particular—see Watts and Strogatz 1998; Watts 1999; Strogatz 2001; Barabási 2002.

[183] E.g., Malkin 2003; 2011; Malkin et al. 2007; Constantakopoulou 2007.

[184] Braudel 1966; Horden and Purcell 2000; Purcell 2003; Malkin 2003b, 2011; Morris 2003.

[185] See Purcell 2003 for discussion and references. Mediterranean paradigms have become increasingly politicized in the wake of initiatives aimed at formalizing Euro-Mediterranean partnerships (formerly referred to as the Barcelona Process). Cf. Xenakis and Chryssochou 2001; Adler et al. 2006.

the network approach, has linked the emergence and consolidation of networks—real or imagined—to "a new kind of 'Greek' convergence" throughout the Mediterranean world during the archaic period.[186] This study takes Malkin's recent work as a starting point for exploring the extent to which high levels of interconnectivity, mobility, and exchange might have contributed not only to the transmission of knowledge and ideas but also to the very processes through which identities were constructed.

1.8 Setting Sail: Homeric Paradigms and the Economies of Knowledge

Ethnographic interests, as we have seen, were not confined to any one particular genre. Evidence for an interest in foreign identities, manners, and customs is embedded within a broad range of literary and archaeological materials. Occasions on which this fascination with the foreign becomes apparent range from Pindar's observation that the nomadic Scythians despise anyone who does not possess a house borne on a wagon to images adorning Attic vases.[187] Both the apparent ubiquity and sheer variety of such material indicates that knowledge relating to foreign peoples was endemic to communities scattered across the length and breadth of the Mediterranean world. Viewed collectively, it constitutes a form of discourse that may legitimately be termed *ethnographic*—even if the material in which it is embedded is not ethnography per se. In a rejoinder to the assertion that ethnographic interests were not evident on any significant scale prior to the fifth century,[188] the ensuing chapters will employ a broad-based definition of "ethnography" to reconstruct something of the "thought world" into which early prose accounts emerged.[189] Although we cannot hope to recapture an objective historical reality, we can pose questions as to how individuals would have engaged with specific ideas or objects, as well as how, when, and why these might have affected their sense of identity, exploring the possibilities opened up by the multiplicity of constructions and receptions as groups and individuals "thought" selectively about culture, identity, and difference.

---

[186] Malkin 2003b, 59; 2011.
[187] Pind. Fr. 105ab.
[188] E. Hall 1989, 40–41.
[189] It has become something of a rallying call among more progressive elements within classical scholarship for historical productions to be grounded in actual, lived experience (Vlassopoulos 2007b, 236). The practice of placing one particular type of evidence on a pedestal has provoked controversy in the past: Cf. J. Hall 1997; 2002; Prag 2006; C. Muller 2007, 150n40 inveighing against Hannestad 2006.

In order to lay the foundations for what follows we must first turn to a body of knowledge and ideas that has become something of a battleground for rival approaches to early ethnographic thought. Precisely how Homeric epic should be interpreted in terms of its wider context, a world that was to a large extent defined by interconnectivity, mobility, and exchange, has presented a significant challenge to scholars seeking to explain the origins and nature of Greek identity, barbarian stereotypes, and early ethnographic interest. Debate has focused on two strands of enquiry. The first concerns Greek identity itself: When did it first arise, how was it expressed and disseminated, and to what extent was it a product of contact with peoples who could be defined as non-Greek? The second focuses on Greek representations of foreign peoples, together with the knowledge and interest of which they are indicative: When do they first become apparent, what form do they take, and what impact do they have on any common sense of Greek identity?[190] Scholars have reacted to these challenges in various ways, with recent treatments of the topic providing examples of not only the pervasive influence of unitary notions of culture and identity but also a number of exciting and highly innovative responses upon which the present study is variously reliant whether from a theoretical or methodological point of view. There are compelling reasons, therefore, why our discussion of early ethnographic enquiry must begin with Homer.

Another foundational document with a direct bearing on this discussion is Edith Hall's brilliant—if now controversial—*Inventing the Barbarian*.[191] Hall's approach to Homer was rendered particularly problematic by a need to reconcile the now famous diktat that Aeschylus's *Persians* was "the first file in the archive of Orientalism" with a desire to portray Homeric epic as being already infused with colonialist discourse. The epic poems are therefore viewed as constituting a profoundly ethnocentric discourse in which Asia was "tamed and subordinated" to the Western imagination—but only at a "non-literal level."[192] Hall's claim that epic poetry shows little interest in distinguishing between Greek and non-Greek is essentially true in many respects. However, this has far less to do with any concern for identity that may or may not be evident in the *Iliad* than the fact that searching for Greek–barbarian polarities in such a context is both misguided and profoundly anachronistic—quite apart from wider methodological concerns alluded to

---

[190] For diverse approaches: E. Hall 1989; J. Hall 1997, 2002; Murray 1988–1989; Ross 2005; Mackie 1996; Mitchell 2005, 2007; Gruen 2011a.
[191] E. Hall 1989.
[192] Just how Greek epic can be profoundly ethnocentric on one level and not on another is, however, far from clear.

above. It is surely unfair to expect Homer's *Iliad* to provide "a usable paradigm of the Greek/barbarian geopolitical boundary."[193] That said, Hall's thesis regarding the extent to which an interest in ethnic identity and foreign cultures was in evidence prior to the Persian Wars remains an established orthodoxy.[194]

By contrast, François Hartog's recent discussion of Homeric themes and paradigms as vehicles for a "poetic anthropology" provides a nuanced and almost poetic account of the way in which early Greeks set out both to explore and to map out the boundaries of human experience. In Hartog's eyes, the narrative space opened up by Odysseus's thwarted attempts to return to Ithaca provides an effective medium by which the principal categories by which society was ordered might be articulated.[195] The *Odyssey* is therefore an "anthropological text"—whether Greek or Homeric—and, as such, an adventure story whose purpose is as much "to see and explain the world as to explore it and represent it, 'inhabit' in and make it a world that was 'human,' that is to say Greek."[196] Although it is admitted, somewhat ruefully, that Odysseus is "not even particularly curious about the world," expressing only occasional interest in seeing Polyphemus and hearing the Siren's song, it is nonetheless asserted that "in Greece it all began with epic."[197]

Although rightly acclaimed for making the other "sing" in its efforts to emphasize the fluidity with which bipolar oppositions between Greek/barbarian, male/female, free/slave were constructed,[198] Hartog's work is ultimately predicated upon a reified and highly abstract notion of Greek identity rooted in a structuralist view of "self" versus "Other."[199] It remains questionable, therefore, as to how such an elegant and sophisticated thesis might have played out in reality.[200] One is left with the sense that the finesse that

---

[193] E. Hall 1989, 49.

[194] Cf. Finley 1979; Cartledge 1993; J. Hall 1997, 2002; Miller 1997, 2005. Although see Mitchell 2007; Gruen 2010.

[195] Hartog 2001, 17.

[196] Ibid., 25–26.

[197] Hom. *Od.* IX 229; XII 192; X 472; Hartog 2001, 9, 15–16.

[198] Davidson 2002.

[199] Albeit less so than in previous works (cf. Hartog 1988). Hartog's poetic anthropology is arguably predicated upon a notion of identity as both static and homogenous: Odysseus functions as a mobile marker whose travels test and in so doing delineate what it means to be Greek (Hartog 2001, 4–5).

[200] The use of such readings have rightly been criticized on the basis that they: "run the risk of focussing on basic synchronic categories, both mythic and social, to the exclusion of the specific historical circumstances at any one time and place" (Dougherty 2001, 7). This reflects a more general trend in which theoretical approaches to Greek identity have grown increasingly sophisticated, emphasizing both the importance and complexity of a far wider range of social identities.

Hartog displays for exploring collective *imaginaires* has yet to be brought to bear upon particulars relating to everyday experience. As far as models and paradigms go, however, there is no better starting point in our bid to reconstruct the way in which early ethnographic imaginings were structured and the means by which they circulated. Hartog's thesis encourages us to think beyond the "text" (which would, in any case, have been encountered aurally in the vast majority of cases) to the myriad of circumstances in which Homeric paradigms might have been called to mind by individual agents and the manner in which this related to their own sense of personal or group identity. While the full implications of this can only be the subject of speculation, we are left with a very clear sense of the richness and diversity of ideas and paradigms upon which an individual might realistically draw when seeking to conceptualize or explain "difference."[201] Scattered remnants such as the Aristonothos krater (discussed below) provide some indication of the extent to which epic models and paradigms were inextricably bound up in the cultural matrices of societies located the length and breadth of the ancient Mediterranean. But this is surely only the tip of the iceberg.

The extent to which epic paradigms played a role in early ethnographic thought has also been a matter of some concern for an author whose focus on the ethnographic imagination adopts a self-styled "historicizing approach."[202] According to Carol Dougherty's analysis, the *Odyssey* itself constitutes *an ethnographic text* and should be read accordingly. It follows, therefore, that while Hartog's "poetic anthropology" relates to the (Greek) human condition in general, Dougherty's is more introspective insofar as it:

> . . . interrogate[s] change and innovation at home (Greece) as much as it is to addresses the anomalies of new worlds abroad . . .
> . . . the product of a culture . . . that was trying to construct a reading of the worlds and peoples of its own mythic past in order to make sense of a tumultuous and volatile present. . . .[203]

For Dougherty as for Hartog, however, both Odysseus's journey home and ethnography as a *genre* entail a return to the—implicitly Greek—"self."[204] Odysseus emerges, yet again, as the embodiment of a culture's ethnographic

---

[201] These are explored, to a limited extent, in the following chapter in discussions relating to Cyclopes, Phoenicians, and Phaeacians.

[202] A term very much in vogue but whose definition seems to be entirely subjective; cf. Malkin 1998a.

[203] Dougherty 2001, 77, 9. Dougherty's ethnographic imagination functions primarily on an abstract, quasi-theoretical level.

[204] Ibid., 10.

imagination.[205] Are Homeric paradigms therefore indicative of "a hunger for expressing a cultural system," as Dougherty has claimed,[206] and what role did they play in determining the overall coherence of this system to start with? Is it perhaps possible to extend this argument to encompass a plurality of systems and a more general awareness of difference per se? If so, the role of imagined ethnographies in this process should not be underestimated; the great utility of Homeric paradigms arguably arose from the fact that they were primarily located in "mythic space" as opposed to any specific locale,[207] familiar to some and baffling to others. The reason, then, why Homer's *Odyssey* proved so popular was that it encapsulated a world in which identities were continually being explored, negotiated, and mapped out: the epics themselves function as the mobile, discursive operator to which Hartog alluded.[208] Viewed in its most basic terms the poems are systems in which a large variety of peoples are plotted and named in a manner not dissimilar to either the *Homeric Hymn to Apollo* or early periegetic accounts. The extent to which this reflects an abstract concept of geographical space has been discussed elsewhere and should not detain us here.[209] Instead, I would argue that works such as the *Iliad* are indicative of a broader interest in ethnography: questions of difference, places, and people. The epic is populated with an eclectic range of tribes, peoples, and races, usually led by some hero or similarly impressive "big man"; as such, it represents a self-conscious attempt to order individuals and societies within both the epic narrative and the world at large.

Previous scholarship has focused primarily upon the disappointingly small number of references to foreign peoples and a (similarly paltry) number of occasions on which some form of Greek–barbarian polarity might

---

[205] Both these and the arguments of Irad Malkin (discussed below) stand in marked contrast to the approach followed by Edith Hall in attempting to minimize both the impact and importance of ethnography prior to the fifth century B.C. Whether they can in turn be extended in a manner that links broader notions of an ethnographic discourse with the ongoing power play through which ideas of culture, history, and identity were routinely contested remains to be seen.

[206] Dougherty 2001, 10.

[207] Attempts to pin the epic narrative to various geographic locations have formed a core element of Homeric reception ever since the earliest performances: e.g., Hdt. IV 177, 183; Strab. XVII 8, 17 (lotus-eaters). A huge bibliography on this but see: Knight 1995, 125–127.

[208] There is of course nothing novel in the suggestion that foreign or mythical paradigms formed an important element of social discourse in antiquity. Increasing emphasis is placed on the unsettled nature of archaic society, including turbulent social-economic conditions, along with the resulting disruption of systems of representation, widely thought to have provoked marked changes in social practices ranging from burials to vase painting (Morris 1998; Shanks 1999; Dougherty 2001, 5).

[209] For the Homeric *Catalogue of Ships*, see below, chapter 3. See also Jacob 1991; Romm 1992; Malkin 1998a; Hartog 2001.

be evident. Attention has invariably centered, for example, upon the adjectival use of *barbaraphonous* in reference to the Carian host as an indication of some nascent concept of the barbarian.[210] The status of archery has also been examined, in particular whether there exists any evidence of a negative stereotype relating to "Oriental" archers. Although opinion on this subject is noticeably divided,[211] an interest in identity per se is apparent throughout the epic. Far from showing signs of disinterest in questions of difference, the manner in which identities are compared and contrasted is of pivotal importance to the narrative structure of the poem. Rather than sifting through epic and lyric poetry in search of the seeds of a later ethnological science—cases in which the habits and customs of non-Greek peoples are subject to obvious scrutiny—we need to explore how individuals might have engaged with the epic, the contexts in which they did so, and the results this might have had upon their own sense of identity and the way in which they viewed the world.

That Homeric heroes spoke a common language has become a touchstone for anyone arguing that archaic Greek identity remained loosely defined until the advent of the barbarian in the fifth century B.C.[212] Homeric heroes were, by this logic, largely the same. This orthodoxy has been challenged, however, in a study by Hilary Mackie that describes the *Iliad* as presenting two opposing speech-cultures, reflecting differences in preferred genre and style, civic function, and linguistic orientation.[213] The language used by the Homeric Achaeans is described as public and political, showing a marked preference for aggressive blaming as opposed to the more private, poetic, introspective, and praise-orientated approach favored by the Trojans. These differences reflect a contrast between two opposing models of social organization or cultural systems, leading the author to claim at one point that the epic presents "an ethnography of speech" for either side.[214]

That the implications of this argument have had little noticeable effect on Classical scholarship to date is due, in part, to the pronounced reticence of the author in interpreting the marked differentiation between the two sides.[215] Mackie dismisses the question as to whether one or the other is given preferential treatment as both misguided and anachronistic. While

---

[210] *Il.* II 867 (the earliest use otherwise being Heraclitus Fr. 107 on "barbarian souls"). The bibliography on this is extensive but see Hall 1989; Mackie 1996; Ross 2005 for discussion. Cf. Vannicelli 1989; Hall 2002 on Homeric usage of "Hellenes."

[211] Cf. Hall 1989; Mackie 1996; Mitchell 2007.

[212] Hall 1989.

[213] Mackie 1996, 161.

[214] Ibid., 5.

[215] "Differences drawn up between Greeks and Trojans are numerous, variable, and subtle, and they are not obviously reducible to any one evaluative scheme" (Mackie 1996, 9).

admitting that "In some respects the *Iliad* 'feminizes' the Trojans," she also asserts that "[t]he ethnic, cultural and linguistic differences the poet imagines appear to be descriptive and aesthetic, not prescriptive and evaluative."[216] While it is easy to see why the author might be keen to avoid the (now) tired clichés of other scholarship, ever keen to plot yet another "Other" against which the Greek self might be juxtaposed, the claim that linguistic and cultural difference can be represented in a manner that is value-free—essentially nonpolitical—is itself problematic. By Mackie's own reckoning both "Homer" and, by implication, his audiences were "thinking about culture" in a meaningful fashion and this, in itself, is significant.[217]

Although Homer's *Odyssey* is deemed by many to provide far more promising evidence of early ethnographic speculation than the *Iliad*, this is by no means universally accepted. While allowing for the fact that the *Odyssey* provides a more accurate reflection of the colonial zeitgeist, Hall's verdict that Odysseus's adventures "have little to do with . . . ethnography" is open to debate—as we shall see.[218] In fact, themes of cultural contact, conflict, and colonization all figure prominently within the narrative structure of the *Odyssey*. Take, for example, the account of the uninhabited island, rendered inaccessible to the landlubber Cyclopes by virtue of its location offshore, which dwells appreciatively upon its extensive natural resources and resulting potential for settlement.[219] Descriptions of people and place figure elsewhere also, however. Odysseus's account of Ithaca is similarly notable for the manner in which land and peoples are succinctly described with topography, flora, and local temperament all being enumerated in a manner that is at least suggestive of an overarching interest in place, people, and the manner in which they interrelate.[220] The connection drawn between the rugged nature of the landscape and local character is, at the same time, very much in keeping with later ethnographic pronouncements upon such subjects in Herodotus or the Hippocratic corpus.

The portrayal of other peoples is similarly indicative of ideologies linking the environment, lifestyle, and identity. The (aptly named) lotus-eaters are a good example. In their case, food is readily available and grows naturally of

---

[216] Mackie 1996, 80, 161
[217] Similar arguments relating to disinterested, nonpolitical discourses also feature in Rosalind Thomas's discussion of ethnographic material embedded within the various Hippocratic and philosophical treatises that emerged from fifth-century Ionia (Thomas 2000). Just what one would accrue by way of cultural capital by such displays of knowledge in a wider (Greek) context is a question to which we shall return below.
[218] Hall 1989, 49.
[219] *Od.* IX 131–139.
[220] *Od.* IX 21–27.

its own accord—a common characteristic of lands situated upon the very margins of human existence and a hallmark of Golden Age primitivism (more on this below).[221] The seductive nature of this existence would have been readily apparent to those accustomed to eking out a relatively harsh existence from the proverbially vigorous climate of central and mainland Greece. Odysseus's companions succumb immediately. Content to pass the rest of their days grazing on lotus flowers, they forget their homes, their loved ones, and, effectively, their identities as people who do not eat lotus flowers. On one level this story is clearly representative of any number of factors that might frustrate a *nostos* but it might also reflect more widespread concerns regarding the effects of foreign travel, intercultural contact, and acculturation: a degree of cultural propriety or conservatism, a sort of "each to his own" ethos, evident in Herodotus and elsewhere.

The economies of knowledge—systems of knowing and understanding, images and ideas—were based on networks and pathways that extended wherever goods or people traveled: Olympia, Olbia, or the cities of Magna Graecia. Alternately overlapping or intersecting, they connected people and place, past and present. Where ruptures and discontinuities occurred, they served merely to demonstrate the diverse complexity and manifest pliability of the larger whole, creating fluctuations in emphasis and multiple points of focus as opposed to bringing the flow of information and ideas to a standstill. While one could attempt to regulate the levels of contact between groups and individuals in a manner similar to that attributed to Libyan and Carthaginian traders by Herodotus,[222] complete isolationism was all but impossible and a trait associated with either nonhuman or dysfunctional polities such as pre-Lycurgan Sparta.[223]

Selectively mined by individual agents whose ability to do so varied according to a combination of historical circumstance, geographical location, and wider access to knowledge and resources drawn from outside their immediate community, this flow of information and ideas created individuals who

---

[221] *Od.* IX 82–104. For discussion see Steier 1927; Lamer 1927; Page 1973, 3–21; Herzhoff 1984, 1999. For attempts to localize see Hdt. IV 176 but Heubeck 1989, 17–18 (overly dogmatic?): "the λωτός plant, with its magical properties of suppressing the desire to return home, is symbolic of the insecurity of human existence poised precariously between the spheres of empirical reality and mythical unreality. It is, therefore, pointless to attempt, as so many scholars, both ancient and modern, have done, to identify either the λωτός plant itself or the country where it grows. In identifying the country as the Little Syrtis (iv 176ff.) Hdt., and scholars after him, showed no understanding of the function and nature of poetry." See Heubeck for further references, including M. Rosseaux, 1971, "Ulysse et les mangeurs de coquelicots," *Bull. Ass. Budé*, lxxi, 333–351 (not seen).

[222] Hdt. IV 196.

[223] Hdt. I 65. For further discussion, see Harrison 2007, 59–60.

were both knowledge-rich and those who, for a variety of reasons, were comparatively restricted in either their ability or willingness to engage in such activity. In this respect our sources are perhaps skewed in favor of the sorts of information accessible to elites—Pindaric odes being a notable case in point.[224] However, we must also envisage situations in which low-status individuals traveled, whether voluntarily as sailors, mercenaries, or craftsmen, or as a result of slavery. Although displaying knowledge of other places and peoples may well have formed part of elite self-fashioning for individuals ranging from the warrior-captains buried outside Eretria to Herodotus and his contemporaries. we should certainly not think of "ethnographic interest" as being limited to a particular "class."[225] Intercultural contact and interaction could take place on a variety of levels, and the majority of the concepts and media discussed above would have been accessible to some extent—however indirectly.

We are therefore obliged to speculate when it comes to the way in which everyday encounters between individuals of different outlook and culture might have played out—whether on the open steppe or among the jumble of workshops and storehouses at sites such as Pithekoussai or Piraeus. Traders and craftsmen would have swapped or relayed tales, negotiating language barriers, prejudices, and stereotypes by various means.[226] Vases might equally be glimpsed and "read" in contexts other than the symposium, and stories from epic, myth, or recent events might have been recounted over chickpeas and a cup of wine around even the meanest brazier.[227] In short, there is a great deal of this overarching discourse that we cannot hope to recover: the unwritten ethnographies that people carried "in their heads," as opposed to what was written down or depicted on krater or skythos. This has inevitable implications for our ability to gauge both the manner in which works such as Herodotus's *Histories* were received and the extent to which they reflect broader levels of interest and inquiry into questions of identity and difference. This is, in short, a picture somewhat at odds with the—widely subscribed-to—view that ethnic and cultural difference aroused little interest in the years prior to the Persian Wars.

The tendency to order fragmentary literary sources and material artefacts by genre and typology may have the advantage of being methodologically

---

[224] On Pindaric language: Silk 2007. For the influence of mobile, high-status individuals, see Raaflaub 2004.
[225] Malkin 1998a, 88ff. Fowler 1996.
[226] For Pithekoussai, see chapter 2. For Piraeus, see Vlassopoulos 2007b where such points form part of a wider discussion of the way in which historical narrative is generated.
[227] Cf. Xenophanes Fr. 18.

straightforward, but the end result is a narrative that appears convincing purely because it conforms to our own preconceptions. The general survey of knowledge relating to a variety of foreign peoples that follows in chapter 2 will consequently be organized according to loosely defined categories that span media and genre, emphasizing the varied, fluid, and malleable nature of ethnographic constructions permeating festival songs, stories told by the fireside, daily conversation in the agora, or images "read" (and discussed) amid the heady confines of the symposium. Although (inevitably) partial and incomplete due to both the vagaries of the evidence and the limits of space, this approach will highlight not only the potential range of information "in play" at any one time but also its manifest ubiquity. Chapter 3 will build on this discussion, exploring the various means by which information relating to foreign lands and peoples was organized, structured, and disseminated. Here the emphasis will be on highlighting and exploring the various interpretative frameworks to which an individual might have recourse in antiquity: How were they employed and why? The extent to which Greek identities resided, or were rather a product *of* a dialectical interplay of representational strategies, will then be analyzed in chapter 4 via a series of case studies focusing on Greater Olbia, Southern Calabria, and the imagined centers of Delphi and Olympia. Once it has been demonstrated that the discursive elements of Greek ethnography were—whether singly or collectively—*constitutive* of identity, chapter 5 will consider the implications such arguments pose for understanding the intellectual and social milieu that formed the backdrop to Herodotean discourse, the manner in which Great Historiography came into being, and the nature of Greek identity.

CHAPTER 2 | Populating the *Imaginaire*

THIS CHAPTER LEAPS BACKWARD and forward through imagined space, like the mind of the archetypal well-traveled man in Homer's *Iliad*[1] or, perhaps more famously, the mind of Odysseus, who "saw the cities of many men and knew their minds."[2] Its purpose in doing so is simply to populate the ethnographic *imaginaire*, highlighting the breadth and diversity of knowledge relating to a variety of foreign peoples in the years prior to the Persian Wars. Taking Homeric imaginings as a starting point (Cyclopes/Phaeacians), we swoop in from the northernmost margins of the *oikoumenê*, traversing in turn the imagined territories of the Hyperboreans, one-eyed Arimaspians, Scythians, and Amazons, before encountering the many tribes of Thrace. From here we turn to western Asia Minor and the Levant (Phoenicians/Lydians) before relocating once more to the sun-scorched realm of the Ethiopians. We then move on to Egypt, followed by brief excurses on past and present populations variously associated with lands less foreign: the (seemingly ubiquitous) descendants of Pelasgos and the inhabitants of Arcadia. By compiling what is effectively a gazetteer of some of the major categories of foreign peoples of whom knowledge is attested, this chapter paves the way for discussion of the interlocking systems of knowledge and understanding that provided both the material and the means by which groups and individuals were able to selectively "position" either themselves or others.[3]

---

[1] "ὡς δ' ὅτ' ἄν ἀίξῃ νόος ἀνέρος, ὅς τ' ἐπὶ πολλὴν γαῖαν ἐληλουθὼς φρεσὶ πευκαλίμῃσι νοήσῃ ἔνθ' εἴην ἤ ἔνθα, μενοινήῃσί τε πολλά . . ." (And as when the mind of a man darts, who having traversed far lands with sage mind wishes, "Oh to be here, or there," and desires for many things) (*Il.* XV 80–82). For a survey of the various categories of well-traveled men (mercenary commanders, specialists, traders and travelers, colonizers, marauders, and adventurers), see Raaflaub 2004.

[2] *Od.* I. 3. Dougherty 2001, 4; Hartog 2001. See further chapter 3.

[3] In order to cast the net as far as possible (and avoid undue repetition in later chapters) certain categories of foreign people have been omitted, e.g., Persians. For these, see below (chapter 5). See also Burkert 2004 (a concise overview of contact with, and knowledge of, the Ancient Near East, including Babylon and Persia).

2.1 Phaeacians and Cyclopes

While obviously paradigmatic—part of what François Hartog has referred to as the *Odyssey*'s "repertoire of otherness"—Homer's Cyclopes are described in a manner that can only be called ethnographic: a reflexive account of an alternative social world, albeit a perverted one.[4] The Cyclopes neither plant nor plough. Instead, they put their trust in providence, living on such cereals and grapes as can be found growing wild. They subsist predominantly on milk and cheese: staple foodstuffs of the pastoralist and a regime alien to audiences that identified (consciously or otherwise) with the self-styled "eaters of bread".[5] They are also described as lacking laws, assemblies, and the ability to build or sail in boats. Taking little account of their neighbors, they live an autonomous existence in isolated family groups in caves situated upon high mountaintops.[6] Small wonder, therefore, that the Cyclopean realm provides the setting for acts of transgression and violence. Polyphemus himself cares nothing for the gods, scorning even Zeus himself, protector of strangers and suppliants.[7] Accordingly, conventions of hospitality are inverted: the Cyclops feeds on his guests instead of offering sustenance and gifts before slaking his thirst with milk—a reminder of his pastoralist existence—and finally settles down to sleep, leaving his "guests" imprisoned and distraught.[8]

The tale of Polyphemus is widely acknowledged to represent a skillful reworking or synthesis of older folktales told throughout the ancient world.[9] Scholarly attention, however, has focused predominantly on identifying its various components and citing parallels, leaving it essentially unclear whether the barbaric *mores* of the Cyclopes is a narrative gloss unique to Homer or a more widespread phenomenon. While the dynamic by which primitive cultural practices and transgressive social norms are linked provides an effective rationale for Polyphemus's behavior, it may be something of an oversimplification to state that this opposition provides a clear archetype of the Greek–barbarian polarity.[10] Although the manners and customs of the Cyclopes clearly reflect the inverted criteria for a civilized society, invariably linked to the emergence of the polis and thus a quintessentially "Greek" *mentalité*, such values were by no

---

[4] Hartog 2001, 21–36.

[5] *Od.* IX 108, 219–249; X 101. For discussion of this "quasi-ethnographical description" of a pastoral lifestyle, see Vidal-Naquet 1996, 41ff.

[6] *Od.* IX 105–115, 125–130. For discussion see Dougherty 2001, 122–142; Hartog 2001, 24–36.

[7] *Od.* IX 275–276

[8] *Od.* IX 259–290, 298–306.

[9] For discussion and references see Heubeck 1989, 19–21; and (more generally) Hansen 1997.

[10] That Greek identity was defined in opposition to an inversion of itself during the archaic period is in fact widely opposed (e.g., E. Hall 1989; J. Hall 1997, 2002; Malkin 1998a). For an alternate view, see Winter 1995, 257: "What is more, the pairing of Trojans and Phoenicians helps to establish

means exclusive to "Greeks" during an Early Iron Age in which social and economic changes leading to increased social complexity and the development of towns represented pan-Mediterranean phenomena.[11] Where Cyclopes are invoked, they are clearly indicative of poets, vase painters,[12] and, by extension, their audiences, thinking about culture: the categories and norms that are considered universal and their various permutations—the extent to which the gigantic, murderous, and cannibalistic Laestrygonians, who likewise led a pastoral existence, could also be likened to Odysseus and his men by virtue of their being city-dwellers who held assemblies and were ruled by a *basileus*.[13]

In contrast, the Homeric Phaeacians provide a utopian vision of a society favored by the gods that enjoys wealth and *techne* in equal measure. Dwellers in the liminal island realm of Scheria, they again serve a paradigmatic function: although prone to somewhat unconventional familial arrangements (Alcinoos is married to his sister Arete)[14] and endowed with a bounty reminiscent of an earlier Golden Age, they live a pious, settled existence under the rule of a king, tilling the soil, excelling in crafts, and traveling extensively in their swift ships—but not engaging in trade.[15] This is significant insofar as it sets them at odds with the Homeric Phoenicians, proverbial traders and at times wily tricksters. Carol Dougherty has discussed this dynamic at some length, setting it in the context of a Greek Iron Age and the preoccupations of a society newly exposed to the combined stresses of long-distance trade, exploration, and settlement overseas.[16] The Phaeacians are pivotal to this "mapping out" of conflicting interests and ideologies: the mercantile entrepreneur versus the aristocratic buccaneer, who might inadvertently profit from gift exchange or the sale of plundered booty but who viewed commercial enterprise with disdain. As such, the Phaeacians provide the fulcrum for the two sets of oppositions around which the *Odyssey*'s ethnographic imaginings were structured.[17]

---

the opposition of both to Odysseus and the Greeks. In this respect, it is part of a well-attested pattern in later Greek literature, with respect not only to Phoenicians, but to Egyptians, Persians, Phrygians, and others as well: one of the ways in which 'otherness' is established is through distinctions of barbarian and civilized."

[11] For discussion of urbanization as a pan-Mediterranean phenomenon, see Osborne and Cunliffe 2005. Cf. Vlassopoulos 2007b; Morgan 2003; S. Morris 1997b on the hegemony of the polis-narrative in studies of the ancient world.

[12] Discussed in more detail in chapter 2. For a range of depictions spanning the early seventh through early fifth centuries on Protoattic, black- and red-figure and Chalkidian-Etruscan vases see *LIMC* s.v. "Kyklops".

[13] *Od.* X 103–124.

[14] *Od.* VII 61–73 (although the unambiguously favorable manner in which she is portrayed must surely have been sufficient to temper any negative reaction to the above).

[15] *Od.* VII 108–110, 114–132.

[16] Dougherty 2001, 122–142 esp. 145.

[17] Ibid., 103. Cf. Segal 1994, 30–33.

Modern "readings" of the Phaeacians vary widely. Some see their portrayal as unambiguously idyllic.[18] Charming and hospitable, their reception of Odysseus on his arrival is regarded an idealization of the colonial encounter: a generous welcome, marriage into the local elites, and subsequent acculturation. Others choose to emphasize a less rosy picture: dark undertones laced with menace, or at best an ambivalent portrayal that sees Alcinoos and his people as unambiguously "other."[19] Such ambivalence is hardly problematic as it would be surprising if ancient audiences were not equally varied in their readings. What is important, however, is the wider significance of this apparent problematizing and questioning of social models and paradigms—which must have been repeated or, alternately "imagined" each time the poem was recited (whether entirely or in part).[20] So, for example, the simile that likens the piercing of Polyphemus's eyeball to the action of a smith, who plunges a white-hot axe head or adze into cold water (τὸ γὰρ αὖτε σιδήρου γε κράτος ἐστίν), may well allude to or alternately have been "read" in the light of Hesiod's construction of the Cyclopes as skilled metalworkers (as opposed to ignorant savages).[21] The Cyclopes formed part of a mythical backdrop frequently alluded to not only by poets such as Hesiod but also later by enquirers such as the early logographers. The "Cyclopean walls" of Mycenae featured in Pherecydes's account of local aetiologies, an association echoed by a fragment of Pindar that also sees Cyclopes as builders.[22] As such, they suggest that for all their mythical or paradigmatic status—or perhaps because of it—Cyclopes provided an important cultural template as archetypal misanthropes, deviants, and craftsmen.

2.2 Hyperboreans

Another group that purportedly dwelt on the margins, at one remove from human civilization and entirely inaccessible to ordinary mortals, were the Hyperboreans. Although iconographic evidence for them is patchy, passing references in poetry and song would seem to indicate that they were well

---

[18] Ferguson 1975, 14: "[T]he first surviving utopia in European literature."

[19] Vidal-Naquet 1996, 50: "Peeping through the motif of the Phaeacians' hospitality is the image of a Phaeacia comparable to the land of the Cyclopes." Cf. Mitchell 2007, 51.

[20] For discussion of singing—episodic or otherwise—and its consequences see Malkin 1998a, 51–54 (in connection with *nostoi*); Shapiro 1993; Nagy 1992, 39–40.

[21] Hom. *Od.* IX 393; Hes. *Theog.* 139–146, 501–506. On the association between metalworking and the Homeric Phaeacians, see Dougherty 2001, chap. 5 and 123n2. For discussion of Homeric reworking of the Cyclopes, see Mondi 1983; Ahl and Roisman 1996, 115–118.

[22] *FGrHist* 3 F 12; Pind. Fr. 169. Schol. Eur. *Or.* 965. Echoes of which can perhaps be seen at *Od.* IX 185–186. See Ahl and Roisman 1996, 116–117. Cf. Bacchyl. II 67. On genealogy see: Hes. *Theog.* 139–146 and Hellanicus (*FGrHist* 4 F 88).

established within the popular imagination from a comparatively early stage.[23] There they are referred to as dear to the gods living in a blessed state: a people not dissimilar to the Ethiopians with whom the immortals often seek respite.[24] Their association with Apollo means they often figure in poetry and song whenever the god is invoked, whether in passing or in more detail.[25] They are first mentioned in a fragment of Hesiod where he portrays them as steppe nomads, inhabiting a region of lush pasture adjacent to the deep-flowing Eridanus and referred to as "well-horsed."[26] Although the section referring to the Eridanus is noticeably lacunose, a reference to amber follows shortly afterward—a product for which the river was famed in antiquity.[27] This is at variance with (vaguer) descriptions offered by later poets such as Pindar emphasizing luxuriant feasting, music, and lives free of sickness and old age.[28] As such, it suggests that poets such as Hesiod and others might have had recourse to a considerable range of ideas relating to Hyperboreans.

Although marginal by virtue of their location, the Hyperboreans played a significant role in both Delian and Delphic propaganda—a point to which we shall return in chapter 4.[29] While Pausanias reports the testimony of the semilegendary poetess Boio attributing the earliest prophecies at Delphi to a Hyperborean named Olēn—in which he is credited with not only establishing the oracle itself but also the invention of hexameter poetry—he ultimately follows Herodotus in upholding the Delian claim to having Olēn as founder.[30] What is noticeable is the extent to which both shrines were eager to capitalize

---

[23] See Bridgman 2004, 27–29 for discussion of their nonappearance in Homer. Hyperboreans figure prominently in modern debates ranging from the manner in which mythic geography was conceptualized to the relative importance of ideas of "hard" and "soft" primitivism in ancient thought. See variously: Campbell 2006, 88–93; Romm 1992, 60–67; 1989. Cf. Ramin 1979, 55–71; Ferguson 1975, 16–22; Bolton 1962. For ancient traditions linking the Hyperboreans with the Celts, see Bridgman 2004. Lasova 1996 sets them in the context of Graeco-Thracian interaction and a Palaeo-Balkan cult tradition, a popular theme for Bulgarian scholarship for which references are supplied.
[24] Campbell 2006, 84; Bridgman 2004, chap. 1; E. Hall 1989, 149; Lovejoy and Boas 1935. Cf. Rohde 1900, 178–242 on the history of utopian imaginings in Graeco-Roman literature, from Homer to Antonius Diogenes.
[25] Pind. *Ol.* 3. 16, *Isthm.* 6. 22–23, *Pae.* 8. 63; *Hom. Hymn. Bacch.* 28–29; Aesch. *Cho.* 373: "hyperborean good-fortune." Cf. *IG* II².1636.8.
[26] Hes. Fr. 98 20–24.
[27] Cf. Hes. *Theog.* 338. Herodotus disputed its existence entirely (III 115) while Pherekydes identified it with the Po (*FGrHist* 3 F 74).
[28] Pind. *Pyth.* 10. 29–43.
[29] As explored by Kowalzig 2007, 118–123. Cf. Delcourt 1955; Defradas 1972 (among others).
[30] Boio *ap.* Paus. 10.5.7–8. Cf. *Hymn. Hom. Ap.* 393–396 where Cretans from Knossos are installed as founders. However, Herodotus maintains instead that Olēn hailed from Lycia and composed "all the other traditional hymns which are sung on Delos," while the practice of singing praises to Opis and Arge had spread "to the rest of the Aegean islands and to Ionia" (IV 35). See Fontenrose 1978, 215–216; Chankowski 2008, 106–108. Cf. Kurke 2003, 2011 on the contested nature of Delphic authority.

upon association with pious Hyperboreans when competing for wider recognition. Herodotus himself questions their very existence on the basis that information relating to them was scant even amongst the Scythians and Issedones from whom they were supposedly not far removed.[31] As well as mentioning their appearance in Hesiod he refers to both the *Epigoni* attributed to Homer and a (supposedly well-known) story concerning a Hyperborean named Abaris, who circuited the world while carrying an arrow without pausing to eat anything.[32] Together with stories relating to the Scythian sage Anacharsis, this account has provoked considerable debate, with some scholars arguing that the Greeks themselves adopted shamanistic practices as a result of contact with steppe tribes north of the Black Sea. The debate has centered around one author in particular and another category of foreign people situated on the northern margins to whom we shall now turn.

2.3 Arimaspians

The "Arimaspians" are another category of foreign people that were apparently "good to think with." Knowledge regarding this one-eyed race can be traced back to an eponymous account attributed to one Aristeas of Proconnesus—a shadowy figure about whom we have very little secure information.[33] The *Arimaspea* itself is highly fragmentary but was purportedly a poetic account in which the author claimed to have visited the Issedones while in a trancelike state, acquiring in the process knowledge of the lands and peoples that lay beyond their borders as far as the River Ocean. The region is portrayed by Aristeas as one locked in turmoil. Everyone bar those inhabiting its farthest reaches (the Hyperboreans) is engaged in conflict with their neighbors—a

---

[31] Hdt. IV 32. He also extrapolated that they were matched by a people beyond the south wind: Hypernotians (Hdt. IV 36). See Campbell 2006, 89. For skepticism of another kind see modern scholarship on myth and ritual: Farnell 1907, 101–105 citing Ahrens (*De Graec. Ling. Dialect.* 1:341). Farnell vigorously upheld Ahrens' claim that Delian "Hyperboreans" "were not a people at all, but real ministers of the god who performed certain sacred functions for north Hellas" (Farnell 1907, 102). The evidence for the "fictitious ethnic significance" of the name is philological in nature and need not detain us here since the author freely admits both that "we cannot say when the false etymology first arose" (ibid., 103—although see *b* singling out Pind. *Ol.* 3. 31 as "the first" such case) and that instead of carrying a (foreign?) ethnic significance, the term "Hyperborean" was for a long time synonymous with "Northern Greeks" (itself indicative of a sense of difference—"ethnic" or otherwise). For related discussion, see Chankowski 2008, 107n121.

[32] Hdt. IV 36. Mentioned by Pindar as having visited Greece in the time of Croesus (Fr. 283). See Lasova 1996, 49–51; Bolton 1962, 158. The story was later sufficiently well known for it to feature in a speech by the orator Lycurgus mentioning both Abaris's divinatory powers and his peripatetic wanderings bearing Apollo's token (the arrow) (*FGrHist* 401c F 2).

[33] Birch 1950; Bolton 1962; Burkert 1963; Mayor and Heaney 1993.

species of gold-guarding griffins in the case of the Arimaspians.[34] The various (human) conflicts described are attributed to a series of westward migrations: the Arimaspians displaced the Issedones who in turn expelled the Scythians who then impinged on the Cimmerians.[35] Details concerning the Arimaspians are also said by Herodotus to have come via the Scythians but are dismissed as being derivative in nature: Aristeas, acting as a mouthpiece for his Issedonian interlocutors, is the only reliable source of information.[36]

The fragmentary state of the *Arimaspea* means that questions surrounding its likely origin/inspiration have provoked considerable debate. Imaginative reconstructions postulate various nomadic groups but it is the physical abnormality that invariably attracts the most attention.[37] Although indicative of the perceived antiquity of the tradition, Strabo's theory that the Arimaspians provided a template for Homer's one-eyed Cyclopes seems highly implausible.[38] This is something about which we know very little, however, and more thought should perhaps be given to factors governing the way in which ethnographies were variously "received" in antiquity.[39] Prior knowledge of a whole raft of popular and literary traditions, ideas, and imagery must have lent itself to any number of variant readings that we are now ill-equipped to recover.

There is little consensus as to how to categorize the fragmentary remnants of the *Arimaspea*. Described as vivid, quirky, and unconventional by Bowra, it demonstrates a certain playfulness in subverting whatever lingering preconceptions an audience might have cherished regarding either the manner or appearance of the one-eyed Arimaspeans.[40] Instead of being portrayed as

---

[34] Schol. on *P. V.* 830 claims, "Hesiod was the first to portray the monstrous griffins." See Bolton 1962, 73. Mayor and Heaney (1993) link them to fossil exposures in the gold-rich zones between the Altai and Tien Shan.

[35] Hdt. IV 11–13. The Cimmerian invasion of Asia described by Herodotus that occurred as a result is thus explained: these peoples are purported to have attacked Lydia during the rule of Ardys, son of Gyges, capturing all of Sardis bar the acropolis (I.15), settling in the area of Sinope (I.12), with raiding parties reaching as far as Ionia (I.6). See Dowden 1980; Braund 1999.

[36] This is challenged by S. West who points out that Herodotus was in all likelihood imposing his own interests and ideals upon the author whose original composition may have had a more theological focus (West 2004). Aristeas's influence is variously traced in the works of Hecataeus (*FGrHist* 1 F 193), Hellanicus (*FGrHist* 4 F 187), and Damastes (*FGrHist* 5 F 1)—not to mention Herodotus's testimonia (IV 14) and the ensuing description of the Issedonians (attributed by Bolton to Aristeas).

[37] Herodotus claimed that their name derived from the Scythian for "one" and "eye" (4.27). For discussion see: Bolton 1962; Mayor and Heaney 1993; Braund 1999; West 2004.

[38] Strab. I 12. The template is attested to in Hes. *Theog.* 144–145 but Hesiod also refers to the three sons of Gaia and Uranus as Κύκλωπες (139–146). For discussion of the relationship between the two see Heubeck 1989, 20–21.

[39] The influence that Herodotus exerted over the fourth-century ethnographers following in the wake of Alexander has been noted in a classic article by Murray, while Greenblatt has highlighted the markedly Herodotean flavor of accounts written by Columbus describing the Americas to the Spanish court (Murray 1972; Greenblatt 1991).

[40] Bowra 1956.

brutish savages, these powerful (στιβαρώτατοι), shaggy-haired (λάσιοι), one-eyed monstrosities appear as wealthy equestrians, indistinguishable from the Greek nobility (ἐν δ᾽ ἄνδρες ναίουσι πολύρρηνες πολυβοῦται), and are charming (χαρίεν), moreover, in appearance.[41] As such, they are more reminiscent of Homer's Pylian Lords: ἀφνειοὺς ἵπποισι, πολύρρηνας, πολυβούτας.[42] This playful inversion of the Homeric Cyclopes suggests a time of composition after—albeit not necessarily long after—the epics achieved widespread circulation. However, the work has also been linked to Ionian scientific enquiry of the mid-sixth to early fifth centuries B.C. This is not the time or the place to pursue these arguments since either date puts the Arimaspea well within our allotted timeframe. Instead, we should focus on both the manner and the means in which the Arimaspians were selectively "imagined". Can the Arimaspea shed any light upon the way in which the lands north of the Black Sea were regarded at the time of its composition, whether early on in the seventh century B.C. or, as Ivantchik would have it, amid the intellectual ferment of Ionia?[43]

The apparent playfulness of the poem may or may not have been apparent to contemporaries, it being equally possible that this is instead an example of foreign/alien paradigms being consciously reworked or formulated—part of a wider attempt to chart the boundaries of human existence. Modern discussions of such "imagining" have highlighted the extent to which it also functions as an act of *appropriation*, provoking similar questions concerning Aristeas's account; describing semimythical beings in far-off lands was evidently a popular activity. There are also suggestions, however, that the author of the Arimaspea was employing his subjects to think about culture in a very different way. In order to explore this further we need to turn to what is the longest extant fragment of Aristeas's work: a fragment of Longinus's On the Sublime discussed by Bowra in an influential article of 1952:

This also we note with great wonder:
Men dwell in the water, far from land on the open sea.
They are unfortunate wretches, for they suffer grievous toils,
with their eyes raised to the stars but their life amidst the waves.

---

[41] Hom. Il. 9. 154; 296 cf. Il. 16. 798; Bowra 1956, 9. Opinions differ as to whether these amount to fictional creations that consciously reference Homeric Cyclopes—however obliquely—or if they are genuine products of Central Asia folklore. Such questions are thankfully beyond the remit of the present study. But see Alföldi 1933; Bowra 1956; Bolton 1962; Phillips 1955—a mixture of both and Mayor and Heaney (1993) citing the almases of Central Asia.

[42] Aristeas Fr. 5.3.

[43] Ivantchik 1993. Hennig 1935 links Herodotus's account to trade with the inhabitants of what is now modern Siberia.

In truth, many are the prayers which they make,
lifting up their hands to the gods, with innards grievously upturned.

θαῦμ'ἡμῖν καὶ τοῦτο μέγα φρεσὶν ἡμετέρῃσιν.
ἄνδρες ὕδωρ ναίουσιν ἀπὸ χθονὸς ἐν πελάγεσσι·
δύστηνοί τινές εἰσιν, ἔχουσι γὰρ ἔργα πονηρά·
ὄμματτ'ἐν ἄστροισι, ψυχὴν δ' ἐνὶ πόντωι ἔχουσιν.
ἦ που πολλά θεοῖσι φίλας ἀνὰ χεῖρας ἔχοντες
εὔχονται σπλάγχνοισι κακῶς ἀναβαλλομένοισι.[44]

Bowra's analysis followed the earlier suggestions of Rhys Roberts by interpreting the fragment as a poetic conceit in which a description of the Greek practice of seafaring and navigation was placed in the mouths of a landlocked race utterly unacquainted with the sea. Bowra developed this argument considerably to reveal the paradoxical and horrific nature of this maritime existence as perceived by these unknown agents: Aristeas's men live wretchedly in the sea with their eyes fixed upon the stars. The attitude of prayer—hands raised to the gods—is accompanied by an oblique reference to what may reasonably be interpreted as a state of incontinence with some form of seasickness being implied.[45] The manner in which this fragment may reflect upon the *Arimaspea* as a whole is of course entirely open to speculation given our manifest ignorance as to its broader content. The suggestion that it is intended to function as a corollary to the colorful tales of the Issedones concerning their neighbors is not without merit (although one has the feeling that we are clutching at straws here!). If this *is* the case then juxtaposing what are portrayed as the strange and bizarre practices of the Greeks with the exploits of those constantly battling with griffins is somewhat reminiscent of the attitudes of cultural reflexivity variously hinted at in Presocratic philosophy, Pindar and Herodotus—all of them variously thinking about culture from the point of view of an outsider.[46]

Recently described as a form of "ethnological satire," this fragment has been set in the context of broader theories of social evolution—albeit with mixed results. James Romm has maintained that ". . . [t]he virtuous life of primitives is here contrasted with that of the so-called advanced peoples who greedily

---

[44] [Longinus], *Subl.* 10.4 = Fr. 7. The authorship of the passage was a matter of some uncertainty for both Longinus and Dionysius of Halicarnassus; the latter associated it instead with Cadmus of Miletus in *de Thuc.* 23. Bolton is likewise overtly skeptical as to the credibility of this fragment (Bolton 1962, 9). Bowra interprets it as reported speech attributed to Aristeas's interlocutors the Issedones (Bowra 1956, 4–5).
[45] Bowra 1956, 7–8.
[46] Ibid., 8n1 following the suggestion of Prof. A. Andrewes.

chase profit on the seas," linking this to the wider *topos* of seafaring, ". . . long associated in Greek literature with trade and commerce, social evolution, and consequent moral decline. . . ."[47] Quips associated with the Scythian sage Anacharsis provide a similar parallel for an (at best) ambivalent commentary on seafaring, delivered from the perspective of an outsider. While such criticism is interpreted by Romm as referring to "Hellenic" cultural achievements in particular,[48] it is also possible to see this in terms of a more general problematizing of the type lately attributed to Homeric epic (i.e., ostensibly pre-Hellenic). Given the uncertainty surrounding the date of composition it is hard to draw any firm conclusions from this, although it is worth highlighting that reflexive parodying of this kind also occurs in Herodotus.[49] We should nevertheless exercise a degree of caution when it comes to interpreting such comments in terms of an innate cultural reflexivity characteristic of the Ionian enlightenment. The play of ideas thus revealed is exceptional only insofar as it is retrievable and is unlikely to represent anything more than the tip of the iceberg given the sheer volume of "ethnographies" in circulation at any one time.

2.4 Scythians

"Scythians" are yet another category of foreign people of whom a certain degree of knowledge and interest appears to have been widespread long before the Persians arrived on the scene. Reference to both lordly Mare-milking milk drinkers (ἱππημολγῶν γαλακτοφάγων) and the Abii, "the most righteous of men," in the opening lines of book thirteen of the *Iliad* are widely accepted to reflect knowledge of nomadic populations north of the Black Sea.[50] Knowledge of "Scythians" proper becomes apparent in the Hesiodic fragments, where an eponymous Scythes is credited with devising a technique to produce bronze, while Phineus was reportedly pursued to "the land of the Milk-Eaters who use wagons as houses," subsequently identified as "Scythian."[51] From these rather hazy beginnings (we have already heard how Hyperboreans were

---

[47] Romm 1992, 74. Compared with *Od.* XI 121–137. For discussion of the literary and cultural view of sailing, see Dougherty 2001, chap. 3.
[48] "[I]t is the pursuits that stand out as the highest achievements of Hellenic culture—seafaring, athletic contest, symposia, and the use of the marketplace as a center of trade which come under strongest attack . . ." (Romm 1992, 76).
[49] Cases in which Greek customs are viewed from a Persian perspective are particularly notable in this respect: "lying" in the marketplace (Hdt. I 153), fighting techniques (VII 9), the rule of law (VII 101–104), and athletic competition for nonpecuniary gain (VIII 26) are all singled out for comment/critique.
[50] Hom. *Il.* XIII 5–6.
[51] Hes. Fr. 217b (Scythes); Fr. 97–98 (Milk-Eaters living in wagons).

also cast as horse-riding), "Scythians" went on to acquire the status of the archetypal steppe nomad whose defining characteristics included horseman-ship, drinking mares' milk, and houses mounted on wagons. The manner in which they were perceived in antiquity remains a matter of some debate. Attempts to link "mare-milking" with pacifism and vegetarianism are hard to rationalize as this might more plausibly be interpreted as a salient character-istic considered sufficiently bizarre to merit an epithet of sorts, an indication, in short, that mare-milkers were the subject of "ethnographic interest."[52] Like Polyphemus, another milk drinker not noted for his vegetarianism, the Scyth-ians of the popular imagination were associated with the immoderate drinking of unmixed wine, as demonstrated by the numerous references to "drinking in Scythian fashion" that can be found in lyric poetry. So, for example, drinking "Scythian style" was a rowdy and uncouth affair by Anacreon:

> Come now, this time let's drink
> not in this Scythian style
> with din and uproar, but sip
> to the sound of decent songs.

> ἄγε δηὖτε μηκέτ᾽οὕτω
> πατάγωι τε κἀλαλητῶι
> Σκυθικὴν πόσιν παρ᾽ οἴνωι
> μελετῶμεν, ἀλλὰ καλοῖς
> ὑποπίνοντες ἐν ὕμνοις.[53]

Evidence for knowledge of and/or interest in Scythia being prevalent in Sparta during the seventh through sixth centuries B.C. can perhaps be adduced from passing reference to "a Colaxaean horse" in Alcman's fragmentary

---

[52] Cf. Romm 1992 45n1. Milk-drinking has dubious connotations as either a symptom of pastoral primitivism or the outright savagery exhibited by Polyphemus. Cf. Pseudo-Scymnus 825–855; Lovejoy and Boas 1935, 324. Parodied by Aristophanes (Athen. *Deipn.* 226d)—this spares them harsh wet-nurses. The manifest inconsistencies surrounding sensationalist ethnographies of Scythians were criticized by Ephorus (Strab. VII.3.9.= *FGrHist* 70 F 42). Equally contentious is Romm's later assertion that *Il.* XIII 5–6 sees the Abii as blessed in the eyes of the gods as a result of their being "undemanding drinkers of milk rather than sumptuous feasters" (Romm 1992, 53): these are adjectives and not causal attributes. For constructions of pastoral nomadism/the Scythian "mirage," see Lévy 1981; Shaw 1982.

[53] Anac. Fr. 356b, trans. West. Immoderate drinking is thought characteristic of both Lydians (Critias Fr. 6) and Scythians (Anac. Fr. 356b). "What care I . . . for the bent-bowed Cimmerians, or the Scythians?" (Anac. *el.* 3, *P. Oxy.* 3722 Fr. 17 ii 7). Cf. Hdt. VI 84. See Hobden forthcoming for discussion. Archaeological evidence for a flourishing wine trade with the hinterland can be found at sites such as Cetățenii din Vali in the lower Danube basin, where the switch from amphorae to wineskins was made prior to transportation inland (Taylor 1994, 400).

Partheneion.[54] Opinion is divided as to whether this should be interpreted either as an allusion to a specific breed of horse, famed for its speed and thus recognized as being of superior quality to those available either in Greece or among the Veneti/Lydians/Ionians,[55] or as an indication that Colaxais (a figure from Scythian mythology) was known to both Alcman and his audiences.[56] A shared familiarity with Scythian material does not seem improbable in the light of additional references to tribes such as the Issedones;[57] however, the suggestion recently tabled by Zaikov that we can extrapolate, on this basis alone, an association with funerary ritual and hero cult is perhaps overly optimistic.[58] However, the important point is that the reference to Colaxaean horses must have been comprehensible, making Zaikov's assertion that Scythia was "immeasurably distant" from "such storehouses of mythological lore as . . . the *Odes* of Pindar" puzzling in the extreme.[59]

While a great deal of attention has been paid to the social function and ideological status of ideas and imagery relating to Scythians in contexts ranging from the iconography of the symposium to the writings of Herodotus and Hippocrates, numerous questions remain regarding the precise means by which constructions of "Scythianness" came into being. How did those living in antiquity know what they thought they knew about Scythians and Scythian attire—and why was it important? How were such details transmitted and what did they signify? We are now well accustomed to analyses in which Scythians are discussed in terms of what they can tell us about ethnocentric attitudes in antiquity, but the full implications of Scythians being "out and about"—not merely the butt of jokes in the plays of Aristophanes, or paradigms of alterity in the context of the symposium, but a mobile, fluid agglomeration of ideas and imagery that formed part of the everyday—have yet to be explored in any depth.[60] Pindar, certainly, expected his audience to be conversant with not only the domestic arrangements of Scythian nomads

---

[54] Alcm. Fr. 1. 59.
[55] Zaikov 2004, 77–80; Devereux 1965, 176; West 1965, 196; Puelma 1977, 29, 32; Schol. *P. Oxy.* 2389 Fr. 6 i.
[56] Zaikov 2004.
[57] Steph. Byz. s.v. *Issedones* = Alcman Fr. 156.
[58] Zaikov's argument must be considered unsatisfactory on a number of counts: first, the chronological framework upon which it is predicated is firmly rooted in the culture-history approach; secondly, much of the evidence is circumstantial/based upon comparative material.
[59] Zaikov 2004, 81.
[60] Cf. Romm 1992, 46ff. A case in point would be passing quips such as "you will end up among the Scythians," interpreted as a possible euphemism for being scalped. Whether this is merely a reflection of the geographical remoteness of Scythia having attained a proverbial quality or that some of the more colorful habits outlined in Herodotus book IV are sufficiently well known to be alluded to is impossible to say. For recent discussion of humorous depictions of foreigners in Greek art, see Cohen 2011.

but also the manner in which these governed an individual's social status: an effective inversion of contemporary social norms.

> . . . for among the nomadic Skythians the man is excluded
> from the folk
> who does not possess a house borne on a wagon,
> and he goes without glory. . . .

> . . . νομάδεσσι γὰρ ἐν Σκύθαις ἀλᾶται στρατῶν,
> ὅς ἀμαξοφόρητον οἶκον οὐ πέπαται,
> ἀκλεὴς <δ'> ἔβα. . . .[61]

How should this "odd tidbit" be evaluated? Bowra attributes it to the sort of travelers' tales one might encounter at Aegina, Corinth, or the Sicilian poleis— a ready source of exotica with which to fire the poetic imagination. While knowledge of Hesiod might be enough to explain the reference to horses drawn on wagons, Aristeas's *Arimaspea* has also been mooted as a possible source on Scythian customs. This may or may not be the case and is essentially unverifiable, but Bowra's comment that "Pindar's lively curiosity . . . also works in the common world, where it finds sustenance largely in legends but also in the talk of his own society"[62] should surely give us food for thought, as it is only via fragments such as these that we gain any insight into the sheer range of subjects this "talk" might have included. The level of detail on offer certainly suggests that Pindar was well informed: other authors mention the wagons of the Scyths but Pindar is the only one to mention the social exclusion of anyone *not* possessing a wagon.[63] West's conclusion that "For Pindar's Sicilian audience the essentials of the steppe lifestyle were evidently a commonplace" begs the immediate question of at what point and precisely how this came about.[64] Did such individuals rely primarily upon a

---

[61] Pind. Fr. 105ab.

[62] Bowra 1964, 370. For an attempt to reconstruct an intellectual and social milieu common to both Pindar and Thucydides, see Hornblower 2004.

[63] Cf. Aesch. *P.V.* 709–710; Hippoc. *AWP* 18. Even more intriguing is the somewhat macabre passage quoted by Zenobios as the basis for a proverb. The use of *skolios* (crooked) is surely value-laden: ". . . In truth, some men pretend in their speech to hate the dead horse lying in the open, but secretly with crooked jaws strip the skin from hooves and head . . ." (Fr. 203) (cf. Ogden 1997). Knowledge of the actual behavior of the Scythians is an essential precursor to understanding this reference, namely, ". . . the high regard in which the Scythians held horses . . ." and their declared aversion toward their meat (Bowra 1964, 371). We have to rely on the ancient authors for the fact that this anecdote relates to Scythians at all as they are not mentioned specifically in the surviving fragment.

[64] West 2002, 446.

combination of idle tittle-tattle and the poets for their information, or were they also avid consumers of works variously labeled as *Scythica* with which a number of fragmentary Greek authors are accredited?

Considerable attention has also been paid to the more general role that Scythians played in the Greek cosmos. This is important inasmuch as it lends weight to the argument that imagined Scythians were a feature of what might loosely be termed the "popular *imaginaire*." However, studies of this kind often project an overly static or essentialized notion of "Scythianness," largely at odds with the way in which such ideas were utilized and/or received.[65] To be sure Scythians might at times evoke ideas of primitivism and outright savagery, justice and naïve simplicity, but the tendency to focus solely upon ancient utopianism without addressing questions of broader social context is potentially misleading. From our point of view it is not enough merely to describe how an ethnocentric view of the cosmos placed nomad Scythians on the outer fringes of a series of concentric circles of historical and social evolution that had the Mediterranean world as its center. Instead, one must also attempt to reconstruct how such concepts were actively used/exploited on a day-to-day basis. Recent work by Lissarrague on the Greek symposium, along with points emphasized by Margaret Miller and Ivanchik,[66] would all seem to indicate that ethnographies of Scythia—here interpreted as any reference to the nexus of ideas and imagery connected with "Scythians"—were an important conceptual tool, long before the invention of the fifth-century barbarian.

The earliest iconographic depiction of figures generally referred to as "Scythian" occurs on the François Vase, a volute krater dated to circa 570 B.C.[67] Thereafter, they appear with increasing regularity in first black- and then red-figure vase painting, provoking widespread speculation as to their ethnic identity and social status. When defined in pictorial terms, "Scythianness" is generally understood to be signaled by one or more of the following: a distinctive pointed cap with long cheek flaps and occasionally a neck flap, a long-sleeved jerkin and trousers, and a compound bow and accompanying bow case-quiver (*gorytus*).[68] The extent to which such attributes were exclusive to ethnic Scythians or representative of a more generic nomadic lifestyle has long exercised scholars, particularly since Amazon and latterly Persian warriors

---

[65] E.g., Campbell 2006, 93–105. Efforts on behalf of later individuals such as Ephorus to both rationalize and revise the wide variety of traditions regarding Scythian barbarity surely demonstrates just how flexible or varied such constructions might be.

[66] None of whom, it should be stressed, would necessarily agree with this conclusion.

[67] Florence, Museo Archeologico Nazionale 4209, *ABV* 76.1. See Barringer 2004, 15ff. for detailed discussion.

[68] A celebrated example being a plate signed by Epiketos dating to ca. 520–500 B.C.: London, BM E135, Vulci, *ARV* 78.93. See Barringer 2004, 15; Pinney 1983, 129; Vos 1963, 40–51.

are represented in all but identical guise (with the result that unpicking this nexus of images and associations is a necessarily complex task).

Although wider discussion of the extent to which art and iconography provided a vehicle for a variety of ethnographic imaginings will be reserved for chapter 3, the exceptional prominence afforded to Scythians in modern discussions relating to the representation of foreigners makes it appropriate to cover such matters in some detail. Pioneering studies undertaken by Vos, Raeck, and Lissarrague have provided the initial bases for discussion by cataloguing instances in which barbarians feature in Attic vase-painting, rendering a large corpus of (otherwise widely dispersed) material accessible in the process. Vos interpreted Scythian archers as historical evidence for contact between Greeks and non-Greeks; the images in question not only were thought to represent "genuine" barbarians but also were linked to a corps of archers purported to have been stationed in Athens during the sixth century B.C. Linked to a more general flowering of ethnographic interest, later reflected in the work of Herodotus, their detailed rendering of equipment, costume, and physiognomy could therefore be used to reconstruct the customs and armaments of populations native to Scythia.[69] Such ideas have not gone unchallenged, however. While Welwei and later authors argued that they alluded instead to the mythical followers of Achilles and were therefore merely symbolic in nature, Lissarrague's *L'autre guerrier* focused on the manner in which archers, peltasts, and cavalrymen were variously depicted as an element of Athenian self-fashioning.[70]

Like many of those working under the auspices of the Centre Louis Gernet, Lissarrague's approach is grounded in the contextual analysis of ancient Greek culture and society, following in a tradition initiated in the 1960s by scholars such as Jean-Pierre Vernant and Pierre Vidal Naquet. As such it borrows heavily from anthropology in stressing polar relationships by which the marginal and liminal status of the Scythian archer was variously defined—often appearing in an ancillary role or as a passive spectator in departure or extispicy scenes.[71] The overall prominence of "Scythians" or Scythianized figures within the

---

[69] Vos 1963, no. 7, 6–39. The argument was subsequently taken up by Raeck as part of a wider initiative to document iconographic representations of barbarians during the sixth through fifth centuries B.C., encompassing Thracians, Scythians, and Persians (Raeck 1981). See also Frolov 1998; Ivanchik 2005.

[70] Welwei 1974, 9–32; Pinney 1983, 1984; Lissarrague 1990a; cf. idem. 2002.

[71] E.g., (in an ancillary role) on a belly amphora (Type A) by the Dikaios Painter: Hoplite flanked by archer, dog, and old man (London, British Museum E.255, from Vulci, *ARV* 31.2), or of a departure scene with extispicy on belly amphora by the Kleophrades Painter (Würzburg, Martin von Wagner Museum 507, from Vulci, *ARV* 181.1). For comment on Lissarrague's approach and the perceived "marginality" of archers, see Barringer 2004, 14–15, 17–18.

iconographic record was thought to reflect both their wider popularity and symbolic importance within the citizen *imaginaire* making them ideal subjects for semiotic analysis. When viewed in opposition to the paradigmatic representation of civic identity and the Greek city-state that was the hoplite hero, the alterity of the Scythian archer was deemed entirely self-evident with the result that alternative "readings"/attributes were effectively excluded. This view has only recently been challenged, encouraging us to look beyond the (somewhat atypical) confines of Athenian democratic society and consider afresh how such discourses functioned in such far-flung locations as Sicily, Cyrene, Olbia, and Emporias.[72]

The bases for many of these positivistic identifications relating to Scythians—in whatever guise—have since been questioned.[73] Alternative readings have stressed either that archer accoutrements served merely to denote status when heroic figures were depicted alongside members of their entourage, reflecting a complete disinterest in ethnography/realism, or that they reflect an element of elite self-fashioning, emulating the perceived wealth and opulence of an Oriental court.[74] Both views require further discussion and/or qualification. In the case of Miller's analysis, the tendency to subsume various categories of foreigner into the catchall term "Oriental" is both potentially unhelpful and notable for the extent to which it assumes a uniformly "occidentalist" outlook on behalf of its audience.[75] While challenges to the blanket assumption that "Scythian" attire should necessarily equate to Scythian ethnicity are not unwelcome, doing so via recourse to the monolithic construct of the "Oriental" merely raises further problems of interpretation.

There is in fact little difference between Miller's reading of the iconographic evidence and the "other" scholarship that she sets out to critique.

---

[72] Marconi 2004, 33; Vlassopoulos 2007b. See, however, Osborne 2004b, 52 for the opposing view: "[T]he chronological distribution of Skythians makes it highly unlikely that they are simply some random decorative element in a generic scene, and demands that we place the Sykthian with regard to a viewer with very specific interests. But if we are to place that viewer and those interests in any city at all, it is in Athens, and only in Athens . . ."

[73] Ivanchik 2005; Miller 1991, 1997.

[74] Cf. Ivanchik 2005, 121; Milller 1997, 1991. Miller argues: "In view of the evidence that some Athenians affected luxurious Oriental toreutics in their symposia, we should reconsider the *kidaris*—wearing symposiasts" (Miller 1991, 70–71). A particularly enigmatic example of the latter can be found on a cup by the Pithos Painter—a highly abstract depiction of a youth at a symposium, ca. 500 B.C. (Rhodes, Archaeological Museum 13386, Camirus, *ARV* 3.139.23). See Lissarrague 2002, 112, fig. 6.

[75] Miller's (somewhat reductive) analysis of the iconography of sympotic wares makes the leap from *kidaris* to the Achaemenid court explicit from the outset with potentially Scythian and Achaemenid attributes being effectively subsumed under the wider umbrella of "Oriental": *Kidaris* is ". . . adopted here because to the modern reader it connotes "Oriental hat" without any further geographic or ethnic restriction" that the more commonly employed "Scythian cap" might imply (Miller 1991, no. 2, 72).

Emulation of the sort postulated by Miller may equally be interpreted as an act of appropriation—thus allowing for a more pejorative undertone to the frivolous tastes of Athenian dandies.[76] The decision to focus solely upon depictions of Scythian attire in a sympotic context is similarly problematic. The same can also be said of Ivanchik's study devoted to archer imagery alone: skewing the analysis in favor of associating archer status with subsidiary roles of only secondary importance in comparison to heroic hoplite figures. Ivanchik's study takes an uncompromising look at the question of Scythian ethnicity—namely, whether this can be inferred from the imagery employed by those producing Attic vases. The argument that archer attributes are indicative of archer status and nothing more fails notably to address the question of how such an archetype came to be established in the first place. The distinctive details of dress and equipment must have originated from somewhere, and while it is perfectly reasonable to assert that "these are not ethnic Scythians," their identity on the vases themselves is to some extent a secondary consideration—at least from the point of view of the present study. In discussing the manner in which Scythian costume and archer status appear to correlate, Ivanchik comments:

> This fact alone raises doubts regarding the suggestion that costume of a "Scythian" type indicates the ethnic origin of a figure: otherwise, we should have to assume that Attic painters were literally obsessed by Scythian themes and ready to depict Scythians in any scene in which archers were deemed to have been participating.[77]

The extent to which Attic vase-painters were "obsessed" by Scythian themes can certainly be overstated, and we should undoubtedly be wary of our ability to assemble and to analyze materials that were previously widely dispersed in terms of both geographical prominence and chronology. They are, nonetheless, a recurrent feature in a variety of designs and images in what Ivanchik himself acknowledges to be "an imaginative pastiche of motifs" that shows little regard for reality.[78]

Considered in their broadest context, images of archers or those in Scythian attire clearly function on any number of levels—some of which at least relate to ethnic stereotypes linked with Scythians (real or imagined). Although an effective rebuff to (seemingly interminable) discussions as to whether archers represented on Attic vases are to be considered of Scythian, Persian,

---

[76] For a case in point: the Scythianized youths depicted in a deer hunt on a cup by the Bonn Painter (Basel, Antikenmuseum BS 438, Vulci, *ARV* 351.8).
[77] Ivanchik 2005, 101, 113.
[78] Ibid.

or Amazon ethnicity, the approaches adopted by Miller and Ivanchik are no less problematic in their attempts to shoehorn a medley of attributes and associations into monolithic categories without allowing for the sort of subtleties and nuances that would, for example, allow sculptors and vase painters to employ an Amazonomachy as an effective analogue for Greeks battling Persians.[79] Since the fact that Persian, Amazon, and Scythian could, on one level, be synonymous can be demonstrated beyond all reasonable doubt, imposing one particular schema upon such imagery would seem both ill-advised and unhelpful. Such analyses invariably fail to account for the knowledge concerning the actual origin of the Scythian costume—whether employed as a symbol for insobriety and intoxication, military *lachesse*, or marginal status. Questions of wider sociohistorical context are ultimately crucial for determining how individual images were read and interpreted.

From Scythians viewed and critiqued in the (private) context of the symposium, we now move to the public and monumental: ethnography, one might say, in the round. Two examples stand out: the *Persian Rider*, the remnants of an equestrian sculpture dated to the late sixth or early fifth century that was recovered from the Athenian Acropolis,[80] and a statue of a kneeling archer from Aegina, thought to depict Paris. This formed part of a sculptural group of painted marble that adorned the west pediment of the temple of Aphaia.[81] Carved from Parian marble and dated to c.490–480 BC, the group is a celebration of Aeginetan heroes linked to the second Trojan War (the east pediment commemorates the first Trojan war and depicts a similarly posed Herakles in archer guise but with armor and apparel that are resoundingly "Greek"). The group recently formed the basis of an exhibition of painted sculpture following the decision of Munich's Stiftung Archäologie and the Staatliche Antikensammlungen und Glyptothek to subject a portion of their collections to ultraviolet analysis (see fig. 2.1).[82] Although horrifying to anyone habituated to viewing Classical sculpture as white, polished marble, it offers compelling evidence that ethnographic interest relating to Scythian-archer types extended far beyond the minutiae of detail adorning sympotic wares.[83]

---

[79] Examples include the scene adorning a cup by the Painter of the Paris Gigantomachy (Vulci, *ARV* 417.4), the celebrated cup by the Triptolemos Painter (Edinburgh Royal Scottish Museum 1887.213, Italy, *ARV* 364.46), or the Nolan Amphora by the Oinokles Painter (Berlin, Staatliche Museum 2331, *ARV* 646.7).

[80] Acropolis no. 606. For discussion and references, see Eaverly 1995, 100–106, pls. 15–16; Fuchs and Floren 1987, 279, no.16, pl. 22.5.

[81] Furtwängler 1906. For recent discussion, see Watson 2011 together with further contributions to Fearn 2011b.

[82] Brinkmann et al. 2007. For an early attempt at reconstruction in color, see Furtwängler 1906, pl. 104.

[83] Marconi 2004, 33.

FIGURE 2.1 Sculpture of a kneeling archer, thought to represent
Paris, Temple of Aphaia, west pediment, ca. 490–480 B.C. ©
Stiftung Archäologie, Munich. Reproduced with kind permission of
Prof. Dr. Vinzenz Brinkmann.

While the various ideological implications of a "Scythianized" Paris have
been discussed elsewhere,[84] the attention to ethnographic detail (real or
imagined) has not hitherto been commented upon at any length as the
detailed patterning of the trousers and tunic remained undetected. In contrast, the partially preserved *Persian Rider* has prompted considerable debate
as to its identity ever since its discovery at a location west of the Erechtheion
in 1886 as the traces of paint are clearly visible to the naked eye. Although the
upper portion of the rider is now lost, the short chiton, leggings, and shoes
can still be seen with additional detail—including a belt—in the form of
bronze attachments. A fragment of arm indicates that the rider wore a long-
sleeved garment decorated with elongated lozenges that can also be seen on
the leggings. The rider's chiton sported teardrop-shaped elements in blue,
green, reddish brown, and red arranged in vertical rows, bordered with a
broad raised band bearing a skewed meander pattern.[85] His (red) shoes bore

[84] Hall 1989; Burnett 2005, 35.
[85] For full description, see Eaverly 1995, 100–106.

three bronze pegs, thought to represent fastenings. A section of the rider's quiver can also be seen featuring the same elongated diamond pattern.[86]

Variously identified as an honorific statue depicting Miltiades in Thracian costume, a captive Persian, a young Athenian in Scythian clothing, a Scythian officer in Athenian service, a mounted companion, or a "Scythian" adventurer, the statue is interpreted by Eaverly as a Persian on the basis of its footwear, which matches that associated with Persians in Achaemenid relief sculpture.[87] Rather than pursue questions of identity (Scythian, Greek, or Persian) or chronology, I would like to focus on how those visiting the sanctuary "received" such images. To what extent were they equipped to decode them and where did they obtain such information? Was the design alien and/or unfamiliar, or was it commonplace and thus entirely to be expected? How would it have chimed with images depicted on Attic pottery, which it closely resembles, or were such details gleaned instead from some merchant or trader? We have few answers, only questions, but the questions themselves open up new ways of thinking about the way in which images and ideas were read and interpreted. While their knowledge of foreign peoples might have been scanty at best, hazy or incorrect, it might equally be argued that at least someone must have been able to view Paris's "floppy Oriental hat" or the toggles fastening the shoes on the equestrian statue and decode the various ethnic/geographic associations with which they were imbued. Otherwise, why else would such motifs have been employed with such consistency? The fact that the stock characteristics of the nomadic, trousered horse archer were routinely reconfigured to represent a variety of groups and individuals, to the bewilderment of modern (and perhaps ancient) observers, does not detract from their ethnographic quality. By depicting an individual wearing a long-sleeved jerkin and trousers, the artist would have conjured up notions of a life spent on horseback in far cooler climes, perhaps even a notion of the landscape, ecology, and mode of subsistence characteristic of steppe nomads. Depiction of the gorytus or bow case would have been indicative of a specific way of fighting and a different set of cultural values. Whether or not these ethnographic references were correctly interpreted—or even recognized—by any given audience is largely immaterial. What is important is the recognition that these ideas were somehow "out there" or "in play" as part of a wider ethnographic *imaginaire*.

---

[86] Ibid.

[87] Eaverly 1995, 105–106. E.g., Studniczka 1891, 239 (captive Persian); Winter 1893 (young Athenian); Rouse 1902, 141 ("Scythian" adventurer); Wade-Gerry 1951, 212–221 (Thracian Miltiades); Vos 1963, 69 (Scythian officer); Stucky 1982 (mounted companion). See also von Roques de Maumont 1958, 11, for the suggestion that the figure in question represents the son-in-law of Peisistratos. Speculation as to its date is equally varied, ranging from 532 B.C. (celebrating Kimon's return from exile) to the first half of the fifth century B.C.—the point at which Persians first appear in Attic vase-painting.

2.5 Amazons

Another category of foreign people often (but by no means exclusively) depicted as archers were the Amazons. As a paradigmatic inversion of social norms, a society in which women lived independently scorning the company of men, their origins are hazy at best but they appear to have been a feature of the popular imagination by circa 700 B.C. onward. Doughty allies of the Trojans, they also feature in legendary combats with Bellerophon, Herakles, and Theseus, while Achilles' love for the Amazon queen Penthesileia was apparently well known.[88] References to them in Homer are therefore coupled with numerous iconographic depictions—most notably in vase painting—along with fragments of lyric poetry, early drama, and works by prose authors such as Pherekydes and, latterly, Herodotus.[89]

Their purported location may originally have been Thrace as indicated by what is perhaps the earliest depiction of a duel between Achilles and the Amazon queen on an inscribed terracotta relief (now on display in New York).[90] Rather than being named "Penthesileia," the vanquished female warrior to the left of Achilles is identified as "Ainia," the town in Thrace from which Penthesileia originated. The manner in which the Amazon homeland appears to shift progressively eastward is widely seen as an indication of the Greeks' expanding horizons.[91] The source of their original inspiration is a topic that has received much discussion.

The role these doughty warriors played vis-à-vis mainstream society as a basis for self-fashioning has received considerable attention to date.[92] They are referred to in verse and song by such stock epithets as "fearless in fight" or "the equal of men" (Ἀμαζόνας ἀντιανείρας)—this being arguably their

---

[88] Hom. *Il.* III 189–190, VI 186. The latter makes an appearance in both a scholion to *Iliad* XXIV 804 (Hesiod, Loeb ed. 509) and Procl., *Chrest.* Hesiod, Loeb ed. 507. Ahlberg-Cornell 1992, 69; Hardwick 1990.

[89] *Il.* III 188–189, VI 186; Pherekydes *FGrHist* 3 F 64; Pindar *Ol.* 8. 46–47; *Nem.* 3. 38; Aesch. *Supp.* 287–289; Hdt. IX 27.

[90] Metr. Mus. 42.11.33. Alhberg-Cornell 1992, 69.

[91] Such tales evidently survived down to Pindar's time even though the "official" Amazon home-land had by then shifted to lands adjoining the Ister (*Ol.* 8. 46–47). Cf. Bellerophon's exploits against the Amazons and Solymoi in Lycia (*Ol.* 13. 89–90; Hdt. I. 173. 2) Hellas and the nearby lands were themselves populated by an intricate patchwork of myths and legends including what are arguably archaic remnants, indicative of their former status as terra incognita. A similar process may perhaps be envisaged in the case of the Hyperboreans (contra Farnell 1907, 102ff.). (See above no. 31)

[92] On ancient perspectives on the Amazons: Erskine 2005; Gehrke 2005; Blok 1995; Henderson 1994; Hardwick 1990; Shapiro 1983. On their role as an element of propaganda/self-fashioning: Castriota 2005; Andres 2001; Cohen 2000; Stewart 1995; Hall 1989; Tyrell 1984; 1980; du Bois 1979; Pembroke 1967.

overarching and most transgressive quality.[93] Whether the Amazon template is in some way a reflection of the ways and customs of a tribe of steppe nomads in which women fought alongside men, which subsequently formed the basis for an entirely mythical society from which men were excluded altogether, is open to question.[94] Analysis of some of the iconographic evidence has suggested receptions of a different kind, however, as it has long been noted that some of the earliest depictions of Amazons include details reminiscent of Assyrian dress. A case in point would be a series of shield bands from Olympia that depict combats between armed warriors, one of whom was subsequently labeled ". . . Nthesila," dated to circa 575–550 b.c. Although there is little room for dogmatism in such matters, these would appear to form part of a more general trend in which non-Greeks and female monsters were depicted wearing half-length slit chitons similar to those portrayed in Assyrian glyptic art.[95]

Opinion is therefore divided as to how some of the earlier depictions should be interpreted. The absence of some of the most familiar encounters between heroes and Amazons from the epic traditions has led some to argue that rather than being linked to any one hero in particular, the mythical Amazons existed as a more general category of foreign-warrior-hero against which any hero might be expected to test his mettle. Discussion has focused on a sub-Geometric votive shield recovered from a *bothros* in the sanctuary of Hera at Tiryns.[96] Dating from circa 700–680 b.c., the outer face depicts a bearded and helmeted warrior brandishing a sword in his right hand, while his left grasps the helmet of his considerably smaller and unbearded female opponent.[97] The gender of this figure is confirmed by the fact that both she and a second subsidiary figure depicted to the right of the central tableau, beneath some species of waterfowl, wear highly decorated half-length slit chitons of the sort described above. The secondary figure is only partially preserved but the breasts of her stricken colleague can be faintly made out. She is shown grasping a spear that she aims at her attacker while grabbing his outstretched arm in her right hand. Two other male warriors are depicted:

---

[93] E.g. *Il.* III 171ff.

[94] Archaeological and literary evidence combined would certainly appear to suggest some tribal cultures did allocate women a fighting role. Cf. Hdt. IV 110–117 on the Sauromatae.

[95] Olympia Mus. B237 (band XXIVw). Kunze 1950, 149, 212, 50. See: Langdon 2008, 68; Ahlberg-Cornell 1992, 69; Lorimer 1947, 134–135.

[96] Nafplion Museum 4509, Diam. 40cm. First described as a plate in Schliemann and Dörpfeld 1885, 104–105, pl. XXIII.

[97] The initial identification of the scene as an Amazonomachy involving Penthesilea is attributed to Hampe 1936, 81; but see also Lorimer 1947; 1950, 170–171, pl. 9; von Bothmer 1957, 1–2, pl. I, 1a–b; Blok 1995, 356–373, pls. 4a–b; Langdon 2008, 56–57, 69–70, figs. 2.1, 2.5.

one subsidiary figure on the left who is shown facing the central tableau while fragments of the legs, lower torso, and head of a dead or dying warrior are picked out below in the same brownish red slip with added white details. Susan Langdon's recent study exploring the social function of Geometric figural style has taken the unusual step of extending discussion to incorporate the image adorning the shield's interior—a centaur, three does (one nursing a fawn), and a young stag—interpreting the whole as an allusion to rituals that marked a youth's coming of age.[98] That an Amazonomachy should appear in a ritual context is linked in this case to their sexual ambiguity as opposed to any specific knowledge of their customs or society—entirely absent, as Langdon points out, from the Homeric epic.[99] Whether or not one agrees with this (highly intriguing) attempt to link the shield and the images it portrays to a maturation ritual, the exterior clearly depicts fighting women wearing distinctive apparel, suggesting that contemporary audiences may well have been conversant with stories regarding the habits and customs of this strange race of warrior women.

It is important to note that it is only toward the end of the sixth century that Amazons begin to acquire elements of "Scythian" or rider accoutrements—the trappings of the horse nomad when depicted in iconography, equipped with bow, quiver, and the long sleeves/trousers that protect a rider's extremities from the elements. The same is true of the literary references in which references to horses and archery are only apparent in the fifth-century material. Prior to this their presence is nonetheless relatively easy to detect as they are invariably depicted clothed, often in patterned tunics, as opposed to heroically nude,[100] while any area of exposed flesh is often marked out with a white slip—the conventional manner of signaling femininity in a number of regional styles (of which Attic is the most notable).[101] Aside from this, however, they remain largely identical with their male opponents when it comes to arms and armor—there being little by way of deviation from the standard hoplite panoply.

---

[98] Langdon 2008, 66–70, 76 for detailed discussion and references relating to the archaeological context and associated interpretative problems.

[99] "Their ambiguity, which combines male and female natures to create a third, anomalous category, a woman as powerful and active as a man also renders them sacred 'active figures' of mediation . . ." (Langdon 2008, 76). For the discussion of the ages of Priam/Bellerophon see: Blok 1995, 146–147, 303–309; Goldberg 1998, 92–93. The mediatory role of Amazons has also been highlighted by Andrew Erskine and Hans-Joachim Gehrke in the context of relations between Greeks and non-Greeks, see Erskine 2005; Gehrke 2005.

[100] Cf. an inscribed Corinthian alabastron, ca. end of seventh century B.C., Samothrace, formerly at Imbros and a Laconian kylix, Rome, Coll. Stefani, by the Arcesilas painter, ca. 565–560 B.C., tondo depicts a naked Herakles confronting holding a sword in with arm extended holding the waist of one of two helmeted figures, both clothed and whose bodies are turned r. as if in flight.

[101] Cf. Chalcidian Hydria from Orvieto, Mus. Civ. 192. ca. 530 B.C.

From around the mid-sixth century onward, however, there is a marked change as aspects of (what has variously been interpreted as) Orientalia or Scythian attire are gradually imported with the result that individual warriors will variously sport a *kidaris* or compound bow/*gorytus* or, eventually, the full jerkin and trouser-suit characteristic of the Scythian archer.[102] Although such items were often liberally combined with elements of the hoplite panoply, *chiton* or *peplos*, the closing decades of the sixth century onward saw archer attire become the predominant mode of representation—in vase painting at least.[103] This can clearly be seen in a fifth-century example from the University of Liverpool's Garstang Museum of Archaeology: part of a red-figure cup on which a seated Amazon is visible (see fig. 2.2).

Whether or not one accepts the argument that these mythical *viragos* represent folk tales/memories of tribes such as the Sauromatae—reported by Herodotus to allow their wives to fight in battle—this did not find any obvious reflection in the manner in which they were depicted in iconography until the mid- to late sixth century B.C. This would seem to suggest that whatever their origin, imagined Amazons were conflated with what were in all likelihood ethnographic material/observations arising from contacts with populations situated north of the Euxine after an initial dalliance with Near Eastern forms and motifs. Alongside Hyperboreans, Scythians, and Arimaspians they were an aspect of the everyday and a means of problematizing—in this case—notions of male sovereignty and due propriety. That they were not "real"—insofar as one was unlikely to encounter one in real life—would have been in many senses immaterial. Their overall prominence in contexts ranging from praise poetry, popular myth, and the iconography of the symposium is indicative of deep-rooted social concerns—effectively externalized to either the distant mythical past or a territory lurking somewhere that was forever close to or beyond the boundaries of human knowledge. Whatever their origins or inspiration, they indicate that, from an early stage, a wide variety of groups and individuals were telling stories and alternately depicting or "reading" images of Ἀμαζόνας ἀντιανείρας: thinking through various problems and concerns via the medium of culture.

---

[102] E.g., Attic red-figure kylix, Berlin, Staatl. Mus. 2263, attributed to Oltos, *ARV*² 62, 85, ca. 530 B.C. Alternately, a plate by Paseas depicting a mounted archer facing left, bow in left hand, *gorytus* slung across left hip (Oxford, Ashmolean Mus. 310, from Chiusi, *ARV* 163.8).

[103] Exceptions abound, however. Cf. a volute krater by Euphronius depicting Herakles and Amazons in which the latter appear in the guise of both archer and hoplite (Arezzo, Museo Civico 1465, *ARV* 15.6). For Amazons depicted exclusively as hoplites see a spouted cup by the Nikosthenes Painter. Berlin, Staaliche Museen 2324, from Vulci, *ARV* 126.26.

FIGURE 2.2 Photo: Seated Amazon. Fragment of an Attic red-figure cup, height 5.75 cm, fifth century B.C. Liverpool, Garstang Museum C671. Reproduced with kind permission of the Garstang Museum of Archaeology, University of Liverpool. Photograph: J. R. Peterson.

2.6 Thracians

Allusions to Thrace as a land of "top-knotted" horsemen, famed for its metalworking, suggest a lively interest in Thrace and Thracians from at least the time of Homer.[104] While the geographical location of Thrace meant it was initially perceived as a somewhat liminal realm, home to the north wind,[105] it gradually acquired a reputation as a land rich in timber, grain, metals, fine horses,[106] and slaves,[107] through which the Hebrus River ran.[108] Aside from their "top-knottedness," an attribute they shared with the Trojans,[109] the inhabitants

---

[104] Hom. *Il.* XIII 4, 576; XXIII 808 cf. Hipponax Fr. 39. Hall 1989, 41 plays down their significance.

[105] Thracian Boreas: *Il.* IX 5, 23. 230; Tyrtaeus Fr. 12.3–6

[106] Hipponax Fr. 72.

[107] Hdt. V 23, VII 122; Thuc. 4. 108.

[108] Alcm. Fr. 45. Cf. ". . . land of plentiful vines and bountiful fruits" (Pindar, *Pae.* 2. Fr. 52b).

[109] Cf. Hipponax Fr. 115.

were variously conceived as brutal, warlike, and illiterate savages who were nonetheless capable of great feats of artistic expression, producing legendary musicians such as Orpheus, Musaeus, and Thamyras.[110]

Opinions vary, however, both as to how early signs of ethnographic interest in Thrace should be interpreted and the circumstances under which such information was initially obtained. Athenian activity in the region from the mid-sixth century onward is regularly cited as a potential source of knowledge relating to the land and its peoples: Miltiades's colonization of Chersonesus circa 540 B.C. is an obvious case in point, along with Pisistratus's reported involvement in silver mining in/around Pangaeum.[111] Pisistratus is also said to have employed Thracian mercenaries to bolster his power base on returning to Athens, ensuring, in doing so, that large numbers of Athenians enjoyed firsthand encounters with "Thrace." Developments such as these have been widely linked to the subsequent epiphany of "Thracians" in Attic vase-painting—often in the context of battle scenes.[112] We do, however, possess evidence for an active engagement with Thrace at a much earlier date: the result of (ongoing) investigations into circumstances surrounding the foundation of Thasos and the activities of Greek settlers on the adjacent mainland during the early archaic period.

Literary-led approaches to the study of Graeco-Thracian relations have provided the sole basis for conceptualizing interactions between tribes local to the region and settlers from islands such as Paros. Archaeological studies of Iron Age Thrace, however, have painted a very different picture of a relationship in which trade in prestige items had long had an equal (if not more important) role to play. Instead of a monolithic opposition between Greek and barbarian that was overwhelmingly antagonistic in nature, based largely on the poetry of Archilochus, all the evidence would appear to suggest not only that Thracian elites were already active participants in a pan-Mediterranean *koiné* prior to Parian settlement in the mid-seventh century B.C. but that when Greek-speaking settlers did arrive, they joined preexisting (native) communities adopting some of the ritual sites, customs, and perhaps practices of those they encountered.[113] There is certainly evidence for intensive interaction

---

[110] Referred to as sword-bearing (*machairophoroi*) by Thuc. 2. 96. 2. Thamyras: *Il.* II 594–600 see Tsiafakis 2000, 377 no. 54 for later references. When depicted in Attic vase-painting Thracian musicians are occasionally shown playing a musical instrument referred to—among other things—as the "Thracian cithara." Such associations make it unsurprising that Thrace was referred to as the home of music by Strabo's day (Strab. I 3. 17).

[111] For references and comment see: Shapiro 1983, 2000; Isaac 1986; Asheri 1990.

[112] Best 1969, 5–16; Raeck 1981, 67; Lissarrague 1990a.

[113] So, for example, stratified deposits from the pre-Greek settlement phases of the Artemision and Herakleion show evidence of ritual activity and structural features. For references and discussion, see Owen 2003, 12, nos. 54–55 together with Kostoglou 2011, 180–185.

between Greek-speaking and Thracian communities of a not-always-violent nature and that Parian symposiasts were, in general, comparatively well informed when it came to the manners and customs of the various tribes of Thrace.[114] So, for example, Archilochus mentions a particular tribe—the Saii—as the likely recipients of his recently abandoned shield, while an iambic fragment by the same author likens the practice of fellatio to the use of drinking straws by "beer-sucking Thracians" (and Phrygians).[115] Scattered references to the, at times, violent confrontations between Thracian tribes and colonists from Thasos in Archilochus[116] must be considered alongside the (fleeting) mention of what appears to be some form of embassy, marked by a gift of some kind. The allusion to diplomatic activity between Greek-speaking colonists and Thracians is rarely afforded as much attention, however, as a purported reference to "Thracian dogs," routinely cited as evidence of derogatory attitudes and pejorative stereotyping.[117]

The physical characteristics of Thracians were an established trope by the sixth century B.C. Xenophanes refers in passing to blue eyes and red hair as being stereotypical attributes when discussing whether the physiognomic traits of both Ethiopians and Thracians would apply to their gods.[118] An early example of the use of a red slip to denote foreignness in vase painting can be found in a Chalcidian amphora roughly contemporary with Xenophanes' fragment (ca. 550–540 B.C.), in which the Thracian king Rhesus is depicted with red hair and beard.[119] Other observed characteristics include the presence of tattoos on women—a custom that may have some bearing upon the fact that tattoos were also seen as indicative of servile status—and a number

---

[114] Owen 2003, 11.

[115] Archil. Fr. 42. See also Anacreon's "Lesbian love" (Fr. 13, cf. West 358) discussed by Gentili 1988, 95–96, no. 111. For the practice being a Lesbian invention: Theopompus Com. Fr. 35 Kock. Cf. Aristoph. *Eccl.* 920; Pherecrates Fr. 149 Kock. Hutchinson draws no such conclusions when discussing the same passage (Hutchinson 2001, 274–278). Other double entendres include the "Sindian fissure" (Hipponax Fr. 2a)—a reference to the Scythian Sindi? Cf. reference to "Thracian fillies" as a euphemism (Anacreon Fr. 417—West).

[116] Archilochus Fr. 92 cf. Pindar *Pae.* 2. 59–70 for campaigns against the Paeonians.

[117] Archil. Fr. 93a, b. That said, the translation of "Thracian dogs" depends on what now appears to be a (highly dubious) textual reconstruction that owes more to contemporary cultural attitudes toward non-Europeans during the early twentieth century than anything else. See Owen 2003, 7–10 for overview and comment. The hinge point would appear to be Hiller von Gaertringen's publication of 1934 in which "φ[ω]σὶ Θρέϊξιν δῶρ' ἔχων ἀκήρατον χρυσόν" (bearing gifts of purest gold for Thracian men) was replaced with "κυσί Θρέϊξιν" (Thracian dogs) (cf. *IG* XII (5) 445).

[118] Xenophanes Fr. A15, 16.

[119] Hom. *Il.* X; Hipponax Fr. 72. Malibu, J. Paul Getty Museum 96. AE. 1; True 1995, 415–429. It has been observed overall that representations of Thrace and Thracians peak during the fifth century B.C.—followed by a marked decline in the fourth. Although primarily associated with Thracians, red hair does, however, appear to have functioned as a generic signal of foreign identity (Tsiafakis 2000, 372n38).

of "ethnic" accoutrements: the distinctive crescent-shaped *pelte*; javelins and daggers; fawn-skin boots with tops turned down (*embades*); a thick woolen mantle (*zeira*); and animal-skin cap with tail hanging down behind (*alopekis*).[120]

Many of these attributes figure prominently in Attic vase-painting and are subject to the same caveats as Scythian attire. Regardless of whether or not they are being appropriated to form the basis for a semiotic dialogue through which hoplite/citizen identities were defined, they provide a clear indication that ethnographic ideas pertaining to Thrace were routinely exploited and manipulated. The fact that both Xanthus and Herodotus report how the industry, and in Herodotus's case the beauty, of a Thracian woman instills wonder in that archetypal observer, the Near Eastern monarch, may reflect a leitmotif running throughout the historical sources.[121]

2.7 Phoenicians

The absence of a conventional ethnographic treatment of Phoenicia is a notable feature of early ethnography (however defined). While this makes it difficult to maintain on the basis of literary evidence alone that knowledge of Phoenicians and their customs was particularly detailed or widespread, the material evidence paints a very different picture of sustained contact between "Greek" and Levantine populations from the Late Bronze Age onward in locations as far-flung as Thasos and Egypt, Cyprus and Sicily.[122] Largely associated with areas rich in mineral resources such as western Crete, Iberia, and Sardinia, the Phoenician expansion created a network of coastal settlements and trading stations between which mixed cargoes of ores, luxury goods, trinkets, and high-value prestige items were conveyed by "men in boats."

Precisely when, where, and how this occurred remain highly controversial questions. However, while we cannot be certain that the presence of imported ivories, bronze protomes, silver bowls, faience, perfume vessels, and seals alone constitutes unambiguous proof of contact with either Phoenicians or a resident population linked (however indirectly) to the Levant, stratigraphic

---

[120] Cf. Hdt. VII 75.

[121] Both are linked to etymological explanations: cf. *FGrHist* 765 F 8b, Hdt. V 12–14. In Xanthus's account it is Alyattes of Lydia who spies an immigrant woman from Mysia outside Sardis, while Herodotus relates the machinations of two would-be rulers of Paeonia (Pigres and Mastyes), whose attempt to attract the attention of Darius backfires so disastrously. See Harrison 2007; Pearson 1939, 128–129.

[122] Morris 1992, 125: "Understood as a revival, or survival, of Late Bronze Age Canaanite maritime trade, the Phoenicians do not 'appear' or 'arrive' in the West as much as they remain there." For discussion of the Phoenician trading empire, see Niemeyer 1990; Negbi 1992; Aubet 1993; Lipiński 2004; Sommer 2007.

sequences dating back to the late tenth and early ninth centuries from sites such as the Greek Sanctuary at Kommos in south-central Crete provide a (rather more secure) basis for arguing that both goods and people were present during the Early Iron Age since they contain both an abundance of transport amphorae *and* traces of cult activity.[123] Mixed populations including Canaanite and Aegean elements are also attested from an early date both at Al Mina and on Cyprus and Ischia respectively, with Greek and Levantine imports occurring alongside inscriptions in both Greek and Aramaic.[124] Opinion remains divided regarding the wider cultural impact of Phoenician settlement throughout the Aegean and wider Mediterranean worlds, but the characteristic opposition between "Greeks" and "Phoenicians," *apoikia* and *chora* versus *emporion*, now looks far less stable in the face of growing evidence for the systematic exploitation of territories throughout the western Mediterranean.[125]

This interpenetration of cultures manifested itself in various ways, including myths relating to legendary craftsmen such as the Telchines—largely associated with prominent centers of craft production including Rhodes, Cyprus, and Crete[126]—and Daidalos, the wanderings of Cadmus, legendary founder of Boeotian Thebes, and the adoption of the alphabet: all of them variously linked to the Levant.[127] These traditions are interpreted either as an indication of the extent to which ethnic and cultural distinctions tended to blur in a world where mobility and exchange formed the only constants or as the efforts of Athenian mythographers bent on stigmatizing those guilty of Medizing by drawing attention to the fact that they had barbarian skeletons lurking in the closet.[128] Archaic Sicily and the island of Thasos have both been singled out as regions where contact between Greek and Phoenician colonists resulted in cultural exchanges that were particularly intense.[129] Figures

---

[123] Shaw 2000.

[124] Morris 1992. For Phoenicians on Cyprus, see Lipiński 2004, 37–87; Karageorghis 2003; Coldstream 1969.

[125] Cf. Sommer 2007, 98; Boardman 1999; S. Morris 1992; Coldstream 1982. On Punic exploitation of Mediterranean landscapes see, most recently, van Dommelen and Bellard 2008.

[126] On the origins of the Telchines, see Strab. XIV 2.7 (Rhodes), Paus. IX 19.1 (Cyprus), Steph. Byz. s.v. Τελχίς (Crete, Sicyon).

[127] For Daidalos, see Morris 1992. For the alphabet, see Hdt. V 58; *FGrHist* 1 F 20 (also citing Danaus). On the Phoenician origins of Cadmus, see Hdt. II 49, IV 147, V 57–61. For discussion, see Gomme 1913; Vermeule 1971; Edwards 1979; Tourraix and Geny 2000; Miller 2005; Kim 2009, 40ff.; Gruen 2011a, 223–236.

[128] E.g., *FGrHist* 3 F 21 cf. Pl. *Menex.* 245c–d; Isoc. 10.68; 12.80. See Morris 1992, chap. 13; Miller 2005.

[129] See Malkin 2005 for the extent to which "cultic and mythic filters formed a middle ground for native populations and Greek and Phoenician colonists and functioned as charters, based on appropriated identities, for conquest and settlement." For the role that Phoenicians played in transmitting intellectual, ideological, and political influences between Greece and the high cultures of the Near East, see Raaflaub 2004.

such as Herakles-Melqart played an important role in mediating relationships between a variety of factions and interest groups: part of a colonial "middle ground" predicated—to a large degree—on knowledge of the habits and beliefs of one's immediate neighbors (however vague or inaccurate).[130] Skepticism as to whether the Homeric Phoenicians bore any relation to historical reality now appears ill-founded in the face of archaeological evidence. Although self-evidently fictionalized, both Odysseus's "lying tale" concerning his encounter with a Phoenician captain on Crete and Eumaios's story of abduction from the island of Syriê by traders whose stay lasted an entire year must have appeared entirely plausible to their audiences.[131]

Evidence from Homeric epic relating to Phoenicians can also be interpreted in a variety of ways. Phoenicians are portrayed both as cunning tricksters, merchants, and duplicitous slavers capable of acts of abduction and as lordly or noble types who, when the opportunity arises, refrain from depriving a vulnerable traveler of his booty.[132] Both the *Iliad* and the *Odyssey* refer to goods for which Phoenicians are famous: wrought metalwork and dyed purple and richly embroidered robes from well-peopled Sidon—a city, we are told, that is ruled by a king ($\Sigma\iota\delta o\nu\acute{\iota}\omega\nu\ \beta\alpha\sigma\iota\lambda\epsilon\acute{\upsilon}\varsigma$).[133] Although the picture that emerges from the *Odyssey* appears comparatively nuanced in comparison with the stray references to Sidonian craftsmanship embedded in the *Iliad*, it seems unlikely that either provide an entirely accurate or fair reflection of the knowledge current at the time—if not ubiquitously then at least in regions where contact took place on a regular basis.[134]

When assessed for its ethnographic accuracy, the manner in which Homeric Phoenicians are portrayed has been found sufficiently wanting as to be described as "flattened and one-dimensional" by Irene Winter, who sees in

---

[130] For Phoenicians on Sicily, see Thuc. VI 2.6. For Herakles/Melqart on Thasos, see Malkin 2005, 2011, 119ff. especially 128-129, 132-133; Bergquist 1973; van Berchen 1967. For the importance of mutual knowledge and (mis)understanding in constructing a colonial middle ground, see White 1991. For similar arguments regarding the mediatory role of Greek myth, see Erskine 2005; Gehrke 2005.

[131] Hom. *Od.* XIV 300; XV 388–484. Malkin 2005.

[132] For the Phoenician/Phaeacian opposition, see Dougherty 2001, 102–121. For detailed discussion of Homeric Phoenicians, see Winter 1995; Patzek 1996.

[133] *Od.* XV 117–118. And therefore an equal of Menelaus (*Od.* IV 614–619) Cf. II Chron. 2:14 (handicrafts); Ezekiel 27:23 (exotic textiles).

[134] *Od.* IV 612–619, XIII 272, XV 115–119, 415–416 cf. *Il.* VI 288–292, XXIII 740–745. On "noble Phoenicians" ($\Phi o\acute{\iota}\nu\iota\kappa\alpha\varsigma\ \mathring{\alpha}\gamma\alpha\nu o\mathring{\upsilon}\varsigma$) (*Od.* XIII 272) see Hoekstra 1989, 180: "Their activity in western Greek waters in Mycenaean times . . . cannot be proved or disproved, but as they only appear in the *Odyssey* and at *Il.* XXIII 744, it would not be surprising if . . . they are an anachronism introduced by an eighth-century Greek poet." Cf. Albright 1950; Dunbabin 1957; Muhly 1970; Wathelet 1974. Such views have now been discredited. See Winter 1995; Sommer 2007.

them a nexus of associations characteristic of the Asiatic barbarian.[135] This idea of the Phoenicians as literary trope finds echoes elsewhere (although with varying levels of emphasis being placed upon the practice of Oriental stereotyping). Given the paucity of the evidence the matter is unlikely to be resolved anytime soon, so while the proximity or familiarity of Phoenicians provides an (at least partial) explanation for their apparent absence from the ethnographic tradition—an argument that places them on a par with the inhabitants of Central and Southern Italy and Sicily as peoples considered not quite "other"—we can only point to a handful of cases in which references to their manners and customs made it into the sources. Referred to collectively as either *Phoinikes* or *Sidones* (the two are used almost synonymously in Homer's epics), their proverbial reputation as traders is well attested, but it is only when they come into direct competition with Greeks that they enjoy any degree of prominence in the historical record.[136]

2.8 Lydians

Both the knowledge and mimicry of Lydian ways and customs is explicitly referred to in a fragmentary poem attributed to Xenophanes of Colophon:

> And learning useless luxury from Lydia,
> while they were free from hateful tyranny,
> they'd go to the piazza in full purple robes,
> a thousand of them at the very least,
> proud in the splendour of their finely coiffured hair
> and sleek with unguents of the choicest scent.

> ἁβροσύνας δὲ μαθόντες ἀνωφελέας παρὰ Λυδῶν,
> ὄφρα τυραννίης ἦσαν ἄνευ στυγερῆς,
> ἤιεσαν εἰς ἀγορὴν παναλουργέ ἀφάρε᾿ ἔχοντες,
> οὐ μείους ὥσπερ χείλιοι ὡς ἐπίπαν,
> αὐχαλέοι, χαίτηισιν ἀγαλλόμεν εὐπρεπέεσσιν,
> ἀσκητοῖς ὀδμὴν χρίμασι δευόμενοι.[137]

---

[135] Winter 1995, 255, 257; Wathelet 1983, 242–243. For discussion of the extent to which Homeric Phoenicians match up to historical reality, see Winter 1995, 249–255; Patzek 1996; Raaflaub 2004. For Phoenicians in Herodotus, see Bondì 1990; Raaflaub 2004.

[136] Morris 1992, chap. 13 identifies the Persian Wars as the hinge point at which Phoenicians became unambiguously "other," citing Persia's almost total reliance on Phoenician sea power in the wars against the Greeks as the most likely cause.

[137] DK Fr. 3, trans. West. On this see Crielaard 2009, 61–63; Duplouy 2006; Morris 2000, 184–185; Kurke 1992; Lesher 1992, 61–65; Schäfer 1996, 97ff.; Defradas 1962a; Bowra 1941;

The manner in which this fragment should be interpreted has been the subject of much debate. It has been widely maintained that the willingness to indulge in the "useless luxury of the Lydians" that Xenophanes' fellow-citizens displayed provided an effective rationale for their downfall and the eventual subjugation of the city to "hateful tyranny" (τυραννίης ... στυγερῆς). It has also been suggested that the reference to "useless luxury" (ἀβροσύνας ... ἀνωφελέας) is indicative of an embryonic stereotype relating to decadent Orientals. Notwithstanding recent attempts to argue that there is insufficient evidence for the existence of the idea that luxury (tryphê) begat hubris prior to the Hellenistic period,[138] there seems little doubt that this carries moralistic undertones insofar as being haughty/boastful (αὐχαλέος) was clearly a means of setting oneself up for a fall.[139] Lydian customs are, in any case, clearly a subject of interest to both Xenophanes and his audience and—by extension—those of the ill-fated Colophonians also.

We should perhaps exercise a degree of caution, however, when it comes to associating this image of wealth and luxury with an explicitly *Oriental* archetype. Alcman's affirmation of his identity as a citizen of Sparta "rich in tripods" (Σπάρτας εἰμὶ πολυτρίποδος) may emphasize the fact that, had he been brought up in "the ancient dwelling place of his fathers," Sardis, he would have ended up an acolyte of Cybele bearing an offering dish, or a eunuch-priest decked out in gold, striking a noisy tambourine. But this is not necessarily evidence for a fully fledged denigratory stereotype relating to Lydia or "orientals" per se, rather a prelude to the (somewhat immodest claim) to have been elevated to a status greater than that of Candaules or Gyges through his acquaintance with the Muses.[140] Cities such as Samos and Sybaris were likewise proverbially wealthy and luxurious[141] and the

---

Fränkel 1925. A more general example of the mimicry of Lydian custom by the Greek cities is of course the adoption of coinage. Hipponax's use of μαυλιστήριον (Fr. 160) has traditionally been interpreted as referring to a type of (Lydian) coin—perhaps as pay for a prostitute?

[138] Gorman and Gorman 2007.

[139] In addition to this, there appears to be some link between cultural borrowing and historical causation. The emphasis upon *tryphê* alone may be overly simplistic and to some extent missing the point: the subject of cultural borrowing is of great interest to Herodotus being variously attributed to powers such as Persia and Athens with the implication that it is in some way linked to a restless imperial ambition (Harrison 2007). Knowledge of a (widespread?) interest in foreign customs and the ease with which certain practices might be adopted/appropriated seems to have provoked speculation as to whether or not this provided some deeper indication of the appetites/inclinations of a people that would find reflections in their actions and ultimately govern their fate.

[140] Alcman test. 2 (=Plut. *de exil.* 599e). See, however, Anacreon Fr. 136/481 *PMG*: "Λυδοπαθεῖς"—a byword for luxury cited in Aeschylus's *Persae* (41). See Kurke 1999, 168; 1992, 93–94.

[141] Lampsacus seems to function as a paradigm of lavish expenditure (tuna and savory sauce every day!) in a story relating the deeds of (at least one) prodigal son (Hipponax Fr. 26). See Crielaard 2009; Morris 2000, 178ff.

"usefulness" of Lydian customs was in any case something of a moot point. References to the use of baccaris, a Lydian unguent made from hazelwort, can be found in Semonides,[142] while a fragmentary poem by Hipponax appears to link the (unfortunately garbled) transliteration of a Lydian phrase, interpreted as a spell or incantation, with the description of an equally obscure cure for impotence.[143] Sappho was famously enthusiastic about Lydian fashions and styles,[144] and Hipponax was wont to line his nostrils with perfume "as used by Croesus".[145] Lydian banquets reportedly inspired Terpandros of Lesbos to invent a musical instrument called the *barbitos*:

> . . . which [*barbitos*] once Terpandros of Lesbos was first to invent, as he heard, during banquets of the Lydians, the voice-answering plucking of the high-pitched *pēktis* . . .[146]

We can be certain, therefore, that Lydia was familiar to many: passing allusions to foreign lands and peoples only make sense if the audience possesses a degree of background knowledge relevant to the subject. This is particularly true of proverbs, and those relating to Lydia seem to have been fairly common: "Gyges and all his gold don't interest me"[147] can be likened to Sappho's "I'd rather see her . . . than all the horse and arms of Lydia," where wealth, power, and military might all seem to be associated.[148]

Reference to a specific mountain in Lydia is notable in that it suggests a knowledge of "foreign" topography in archaic Megara: "I'll never place my neck beneath the galling yoke of my enemies, not even if Tmolus is upon my head" (Οὔποτε τοῖσ᾽ ἐχθροῖσιν ὑπὸ ζυγὸν αὐχένα θήσω δύσλοφον, οὐδ᾽ εἴ μοι Τμῶλος ἔπεστι κάρηι).[149] Knowledge of a more detailed sort is also in evidence when the road to Smyrna from the interior is described by Hipponax:

---

[142] Semonides: Fr. 16.

[143] Hipponax Fr. 92. Morris 2000, 185 sees this as invective targeting "the delicacy, eroticism, and orientalism" that formed the basis for the *habrosynē* ideology.

[144] Sappho Fr. 39; 98a 10–11. Cf. Lydian headbands splendid upon girls: Alcman Fr. 1. 67–68; Pindar's reference to a Lydian fillet at *Nem.* 8. 15.

[145] Hipponax Fr. 104. 22. Which suggests that Ian Morris's portrayal of Hipponax as championing "the middling tradition" is perhaps overly stark (Morris 2000, 185).

[146] Pind. Fr. 125. Cf. similar references to Lydian pipes (*Ol.* 5. 19) and a Lydian mode (*Ol.* 14.17; *Nem.* 4. 45).

[147] Archil. Fr. 19.

[148] Sappho Fr. 16. 19 cf. Fr. 132: "for all of Lydia."

[149] Theognis 1023–1024.—Assuming the identification is correct. Hdt. I. 93 notes the gold dust washed down from Mt. Tmolus as one of the few *thōmata* in Lydia worth speaking of while the tomb of Alyattes (Croesus's father) mentioned below is the only man-made wonder of any note.

... to Smyrna, through Lydia past the tomb of Attalus and the gravestone of Gyges and the column of [Seso]str[is] ... and the memorial of Tos, sultan of Mytalis, turning your belly towards the setting sun. . . .[150]

This provokes the question as to how widespread this practice of providing directions within a poem actually was? What was the purpose?

Linguistic appropriations will be discussed at greater length in a following chapter. However, the use of loan words such as the Lydian term for "priest"[151] and for "king" must suggest a degree of familiarity. The latter loan word occurs in the context of what is evidently some form of lampoon referring to the "sultan of Cyllene" (Κυλλήνης πάλμυν),[152] while elsewhere we have a (similarly irreverent) reference to a historical figure when it is alleged that κυνάγχα ("dog-throttler"), a stock epithet of Hermes as "ἀρχὸς φηλητέων," translates as "Candaules" in Lydian.[153] The presence of servile stereotypes can perhaps also be inferred in prayers uttered to Malis (a Lydian goddess identified with Athena) by a slave praying master won't beat him.[154] This association between Lydians and slaves is supported by evidence from Athens attesting to a female woolworker, a potter and a noted painter from the mid- to late sixth century B.C. (both men signed themselves as "Lydos").[155] Names such as these may not offer conclusive proof as to the identities of their owners but they do demonstrate that ideas about "Lydians" were in play at the time (even if, like East Greek and Lydian fine wares, it was sometimes difficult to tell individual "Lydians" and "Greeks" apart).[156] The status of Lydia is somewhat problematic as a result. References also encompass proverbial or heroic figures such as Croesus and Pelops.[157] It follows therefore that while stereotypes and pejorative attitudes can undoubtedly be detected we should perhaps be wary of assuming that prejudice against "the decadent Asiatic" can be equated with a discourse of "Orientalism" of the sort identified by

---

[150] Hipponax Fr. 42.
[151] Hipponax Fr. 4.
[152] Hipponax Fr. 3 also Fr. 38, 42, 72.
[153] Hipponax Fr. 3a. Cf. Hom. Hymn. Merc. 292.
[154] Hipponax Fr. 40.
[155] For discussion of "Lydos," see Canciani and Neumann 1978. Epigraphic and literary evidence offer conflicting indications regarding the Lydian presence in Athens: while only five funerary stelae commemorating Lydians were catalogued by Bäbler, Xenophon's Poroi has them marked out as typical of Athens' community of metics (2.3) (de Vries 2000, 356–358; Bäbler 1998, 87–91, 223–226).
[156] De Vries 2000, 356.
[157] Pind. Pyth. 1. 94 (Croesus); Ol. 9. 9 (Pelops). When depicted in Athenian vase-painting Croesus is invariably depicted as "Greek" up to and until the Achaemenid template was brought to bear upon any figure who might be considered remotely barbarian.

Edward Said.[158] While both Said's Orientalism and the "Occidental" view-point it implies are often ascribed an almost timeless quality, they are in fact the product of a particular set of structures and institutions and thus histor-ically situated phenomena, with at best a limited bearing on archaic and early classical Greece.

In vase painting meanwhile, the appearance of reclining symposiasts and turbaned komasts on painted wares from Chios and Miletus has recently been highlighted as evidence of cultural interchange between Lydia and the East Greeks.[159] How these were, in turn, received when traded further afield is a question requiring careful consideration. This needs to be borne in mind when we consider a late-sixth-century jug (*oinochoe*), signed by Xenokles the potter and Kleisophos, which purportedly depicts a Lydian symposium—a rather crude affair in which overweight drunkards cavort, collapse, and—in one case—defecate openly, in a graphic demonstration of the effects of exces-sive drinking.[160] Analysis of this scene by de Vries led to the conclusion that the use of various ethnic indicators signaling "Lydianess" makes it likely that it is Lydians who are being depicted. Attention focuses upon the wearing of turbans and boots (*kothornoi*), the use of both a dipping ladle to serve wine and a *phiale* as a drinking vessel (all deemed "Anatolian" in origin but ambig-uous in interpretation since they were variously adopted "among Greeks": early lyric poetry is rife with references to the use of ladles to serve wine), but ultimately it is the fact that the *oinochoos* (wine-pourer) is depicted wearing a loincloth that is deemed "[s]trikingly non-Greek."[161] Whether or not this is the case, a desire to depict East Greeks or Lydianess is arguably apparent.[162] It might also be argued that the fact that many of these practices/items of apparel were adopted by "Greeks" merely underlines the extent to which

---

[158] Said 1978. Cf. Spawforth 2001; Winter 1995; Hall 1989. For an alternative view, see Kim 2009, 127: "the overall impression of Sardis and the Lydians that we receive from the observation of Archaic Greek sources is overwhelmingly positive." Kim's view is that the material culture, intellectual traditions, and religious beliefs common to both Lydians and Greeks meant the latter ". . . could not rationally establish their ethnic superiority over the *barbaroi* . . ." (134).

[159] Lemos 2000. For examples see Lemos 2000, 389n87; Walter-Karydi 1973, 6, pl. 13, 109. On the practice of reclining at symposia see Boardman 1999, 122–131.

[160] Attic black-figure oinochoe signed by Kleisophos the painter and Xenokles as potter, ca. 520 B.C., Athens, National Archaeological Museum 1045; Pfuhl 1923, fig. 254; de Vries 2000, fig. 13.10 (drawing of Pfuhl fig. 254).

[161] De Vries 2000, 362. The latter hinges entirely upon the assumption that depictions of clothed wine waiters that were almost universal until the middle decades of the sixth century should have ceased so abruptly by ca. 530–520 B.C. that they would have been considered unambigu-ously alien/"other." Based as it is upon an isolated example and given the rapidity with which such changes came into place some caution is evidently required in this matter!

[162] In support of the latter it is (rightly) pointed out that the turban (*mitra*) was unambiguously associated with the peoples of Lydia in Achaemenid iconography (de Vries 2000, 359–360).

ethnographic observations could provide a basis for subsequent borrowing or self-fashioning. Lydian turbans, of various shapes and sizes, are also visible on a Klazomenian sarcophagus from Akanthos in Chalkidice in which men and women are depicted reclining at a banquet. In this case only some of the men depicted are wearing headdress; however, the women sport a variety of hats—variously embroidered (?) and tapering to a point that in some cases encroaches on the decorative field above.[163] Their identity is ambiguous since, by conventional standards and with the obvious exception of *hetairai* and slaves, women did not attend symposia—such practices being commonly associated with the kingdoms of the Near East.[164] Even if we are not entirely clear who is being depicted, it is evidently the intention of the artist to evoke a particular sociocultural milieu using a varied palette of symbols and motifs with which the viewing audience was conversant.

Lydian customs evidently posed something of a conundrum for Herodotus. While admitting that apart from the practice of prostituting their female children, Lydian *nomoi* differed little from those of the Greeks, the Halicarnassian felt it necessary to rationalize the means by which a kingdom that for a time exercised power over the Greek cities of Asia Minor should in his day possess a reputation for cowardliness and effeminacy.[165] The plausibility of his anecdote concerning Croesus's plea to Cyrus following an aborted uprising against their Persian conquerors is immediately suspect. In order to forestall the brutal punitive measures with which rebellious subjects were habitually punished, Croesus suggests that Cyrus adopt an alternative strategy, ensuring the long-term subservience of the population by depriving Lydian men of the right to bear arms while at the same time compelling them to wear soft shoes and chitons under their *himatia*. Such measures were accompanied by a new system of education in which boys were schooled in music, dance, and commerce—occupations that would leave them utterly effeminized and incapable of insurrection.[166]

---

[163] Crielaard 2009, 62, fig. 5; Kaltsas 1996–1997, 35–50, pls. 15, 21–22 (*non vidi*).

[164] Hdt. V. 18. See, however, chapter 4. Ambiguities of costume are by no means a novelty when it comes to the figurative art adorning the headpieces and wide fields of Klazomenian sarcophagi, however. Taken as a whole they provide an unusually rich array of "ethnographic" imagery, notably in battle scenes in which riders variously interpreted as Persians, Thracians, and Greeks engage each other in combat (e.g., G 11 = Izmir 3493 together with examples discussed by Schoppa 1933, 25). In some cases this has led to a degree of confusion as to which side should be considered Hellenes—it being assumed that "it is extremely unlikely that a battle between two sets of barbarians would be depicted on a Greek sarcophagus made for a Greek" (Cook 1981, 116). The result often hinges upon the presence or absence of facial hair or analogies with the imagery adorning Attic figured pottery—which is itself open to question, as we shall see.

[165] Hdt. I. 94. Lombardo 1990.

[166] Hdt. I 155–156.

While the fragment of Xenophanes already referred to makes it likely that Lydians possessed a reputation for luxury and softness prior to their conquest circa 540s B.C.,[167] Lydia seems to have featured significantly within the imagination of individuals ranging from Sappho and Alcman down until Pindar, signaling a wealth and sophistication to which many of her neighbors could only aspire. Elsewhere, a moralizing streak is perhaps apparent in a tale in which the ill-fated glutton King Cambles killed and ate his own wife, waking the next morning to find her hand protruding from his mouth.[168] However, if the manner in which Lydia and its affairs were portrayed seems at times contradictory, this reflects nothing more (or less) than the wide variety of traditions in circulation at any one time following successive changes in historical circumstance. Lydians were certainly useful analogues for commentators "thinking about culture": Xanthus's audiences were made aware of the fact that, just as Dorians and Ionians joshed over common terms and usages, the same was equally true of the Lydians and the Torrebians.[169]

2.9 Ethiopians

Early appearances in Homer and Hesiod would seem to indicate that Ethiopians were already well established within the popular imagination by the time the poems came into being. Part of a wider ethnographic discourse that transcended media and genre, they appear to have enjoyed a quasi-mythical status with considerable speculation regarding their precise location.[170] Homer's Ethiopians were geographically remote, with separate populations assigned to both eastern and western reaches of the world (although far greater emphasis appears to be placed on those residing in the east than their shadowy western counterparts). The itinerary attributed to Menelaus in the *Odyssey* is notably vague, representing something of a geographical hotchpotch (unless one is willing to allow for the fact that Σιδονίους is a generic reference to the Phoenician settlements in North Africa):

> Over Phoenician Cyprus and Cyrene I wandered, and Egypt, and I came to the Ethiopians, the Sidonians, and the Erembi, and Libya, where lambs are horned from birth.[171]

---

[167] In any case, a similar rationale seems to be at work in the minds of both authors?

[168] *FGrHist* 765 F 12.

[169] *FGrHist* 765 F 1, 13–16.

[170] For discussion see: Campbell 2006; Romm 1992; Snowden 1997, 1970; Schwabl 1962; Lesky 1959; Hadas 1935.

[171] Hom. *Od.* IV 84: "Κύπρον Φοινίκην τε καὶ Αἰγυπτίους ἐπαληθείς, Αἰθίοπάς θ᾽ ἱκόμην καὶ Σιδονίους καὶ Ἐρεμβοὺς καὶ Λιβύην, ἵνα τ᾽ ἄρνες ἄφαρ κεραοὶ τελέθουσι." The latter is a

Although some debate surrounds the issue as to whether Homeric Ethiopians were considered specifically African or black-skinned, the etymology of *Aithiopes* ("dark" or "burnt-faces") would appear to imply negritude and that physiognomic observations were a salient feature of "Ethiopianess" from the very outset.[172] So, for example, Odysseus's companion Eurybates is described as black-skinned and woolly-haired while Xenophanes invokes Ethiopian characteristics when outlining his relativist stance on anthropomorphic conceptions of the divine.[173] Examples such as these amount to some of the earliest evidence for an interest in a distinctively "African" physiognomy (dark skin and woolly or curly hair were invariably attributed to the increased proximity to the sun—hence the association with both east and south),[174] making it not unreasonable (where no evidence exists to the contrary) to conflate iconographic representations of black Africans with literary traditions regarding Ethiopians.[175]

This vague conflation of generic negritude and a specific geographical population inhabiting territories lying to the south of Egypt must to some degree reflect both the activities of traders operating out of Naucratis and the involvement of mercenaries from the cities of Asia Minor—Colophon among others—in campaigns undertaken by Psammetichus II against the Ethiopians and the Meroïtic kingdom of Kush (ca. 594–588 B.C.).[176] However, the travelers' tales that such expeditions must have generated can in all likelihood be linked—at least indirectly—to an apparent vogue for

---

peculiar detail upon which both Herodotus and Aristotle saw fit to comment (Hdt. IV 29; Arist. *H.A.* viii 28); its significance with regards to any wider "ethnographic turn" will be developed further below. While von Soden argued that this amounts to a claim that Menelaus circumnavigated Africa, recent commentators are more skeptical (cf. Soden 1959; S. West, S. 1988, 198). Strabo discusses Homeric geography at some length, including the manner in which "Sidonians" should be interpreted (Strab. I 2. 31).

[172] Contra Morris 1997. The precise meaning of Aeschylus's μελανθὲς ἡλιόκτυπον ("sun-burned race") has been the source of controversy (Aesch. *Suppl.* 154–155). Whatever one believes regarding ancient attitudes towards color prejudice, it remains plausible to argue that negritude and Ethiopianess go together.

[173] Hom. *Od.* IXX 246–247; Xenophanes Fr. 16.

[174] See Schäfer 1996, 151ff.; Lesher 1992, 90–93.

[175] The Hesiodic *Catalogue* also links Ethiopians to Africa as progenitor of the Libyans, Pygmies, and "Melanes"—again suggestive of negritude (Fr. 150, 17–19). Cf. Hes. *Theogn.* 984–985 and Mimnermus's Fr. 12—which places them in the east.

[176] The historical nature of these encounters is attested by both the material record and literary evidence ranging from the accounts of Herodotus to graffiti inscribed upon the colossus at Abu Simbel. See: Snowden 1983; Desanges 1982; Sauneron and Yoyotte 1952. For Pabis of Colophon and other "artists" who made their mark at Abu Simbel see Tod 1964, nos. 4, 6–7; Bernard and Masson 1957. For the evidence from Naucratis see contributions to Villing and Schlotzhauer 2006. For discussion of the extent to which mercenaries acted as a conduit of ideas about foreign lands and peoples, see Raaflaub 2004.

depicting Ethiopians in vase painting of the sixth century.[177] Black-skinned individuals are relatively common in art dating from the Bronze Age and references to Aithiopes may even be detectable in Mycenaean Greek.[178] Like the Hyperboreans, Ethiopians enjoy a reputation for piety but are associated in this case with Poseidon, while pseudo-Hesiod groups them with Libyans and Scythians as men "whose mind is superior to their tongue," alongside "black-skinned men," "subterranean men," and "the strengthless pygmies."[179]

Whatever their origins or inspiration, ideas and imagery relating to "Ethiopia" achieved widespread circulation. Archaeological assemblages from sites as far-flung as Sicily, Athens, and Byzantion have yielded objects that depict "Ethiopians"—or figures displaying an African physiognomy.[180] Whether we are in any way equipped to decode such representations is a moot point.[181] However, while their interpretation must in many cases remain open to speculation, they should clearly be conceived as objects of consumption: for example, perfume flasks shaped in the form of a human head in which elements of a stereotypically African physiognomy are picked out in meticulous detail.[182] Objects such as these appear in the material record from circa sixth century onward and were widely traded. While we can only speculate when it comes to any possible association between these and god-like Ethiopians—"the most beautiful of men"[183]—the same cannot be said of a series of Attic black-figure vases thought to depict the Homeric

---

[177] Linking such depictions directly to the Ethiopians' military repute may, however, be excessive (Snowden 1991, 27)—other factors were arguably in play.

[178] S. Morris 1997, 615.

[179] Hom. *Od.* I 22–26; Hes. Fr. 97 14–15. On pygmies see: Harari 2004; Lissarrague 2002. For Libyans see: Marshall 2001; Laronde 1990.

[180] The island of Cyprus would appear to have acted as an important conduit for such ideas/imagery due to its proximity to Egypt/the kingdoms of the Ancient Near East, e.g., a Chlorite pendant (ninth–eighth century B.C.) from Amathus depicting the head of an African (Met. no. 74.51.4393) and an early sixth-century faience vase in the form of two juxtaposed heads, one African and the other Syrian (Staatliche Museen, no. VI.3250); see Karageorghis 1988, 17, nos. 8, 30, 20. A motif derived from New Kingdom Egypt, the juxtaposed heads alluded to Pharaonic victories over Egypt's enemies to the North and South, see Webb 1978, 130n874, pl. XX. Cf. a fragment of a North Ionian black-figure amphora from Naucratis depicting the head and torso of an African: GR 1886.4-1. 1282 (Vase B 102.33).

[181] On racism in antiquity see Isaac 2006; 2004 but not without comments by Tuplin 2007b; 1999. See also Gruen 2011a, 197–220; Cohen 2011, 477–482; Lissarrague 2002; Vasunia 2001; Berad 2000; Miller 2000; Snowden 1997, 1991, 1970; Vercoutter et al. 1991; Bernal 1987; Said 1978. For earlier approaches, see Beardsley 1929.

[182] E.g., an aryballos in the shape of an African head, Attic, early fifth century, from the Lucifero necropolis: Lattanzi 2003, 36. Cf. Teracotta oinochoe in the shape of an African head, Attic, ca. 480 B.C., Metr. Mus. 00.11.1; and an Athenian red-figure Pelike by the Argos painter depicting an African youth and a camel now in St. Petersburg, Hermitage Museum 614, *ARV* 288, 11.

[183] Scylax, *Periplus* 112.

hero Memnon.[184] The fact that Memnon is invariably depicted as Caucasian while his retinue are black-skinned in appearance has provoked lively discussion as to whether hero status was in fact compatible with negritude in the first place.[185] Memnon appears as the leader of the Ethiopian contingent in the *Iliad*. As son of Eos, he is both explicitly tied to the east and the subject of a lost epic called the *Aithiopis*, a sequel to the *Iliad* in which Achilles avenges the former's killing of Antilochus, son of Nestor.[186]

A reputation for divine favor and piety has also been linked to the appearance of Negro heads both upon a large number of coins minted at Athens and Delphi during the sixth and (predominantly) fifth centuries B.C.[187] and as a decorative motif on *phialai*.[188] Alternative explanations for these appearances include their representing contingents in the Persian army, *sileni*, followers of Aphrodite or, alternately, an allusion to the fact that the name of Delphos's mother could be rendered as "black woman."[189] Representations such as the African face that features on one side of an Attic red-figure head-kantharos[190] (the reverse of which depicts the face of a Caucasian woman) are frequently cited as evidence of a derogatory juxtaposition of idealized Greek and ugly barbarian. Signs of a rigid Greek–barbarian polarity are also perceived in the case of groups such as the Negro alabastra—widely thought to reflect an upsurge in ethnographic interest in the wake of the Persian Wars.[191] Iconographic evidence of this kind does, however, predate the fifth century, as we have seen; we do, therefore, have reasonable evidence for a nexus of ideas in which Homeric Ethiopians and black Africans were variously conflated. Unlike the gods in Homer there is no veil separating individuals in antiquity from the trade in goods and images alluding to Ethiopian identities, manners,

---

[184] Hom. *Od.* XI 522. For references to Memnon and "spear bearing" Ethiopians in Pindar see: *Pyth.* 6. 31; *Nem.* 3. 61–63; 6. 49; *Isthm.* 5. 40–41; 8. 54. For the Ethiopian panoply, see Fraser 1935.

[185] Berad 2000; Miller 2000. The presence of Ethiopians in the Trojan host possessed great resonance in the light of the events of the fifth century. Cf. Kahil 1972, 282. See below for discussion of the implications of one of the attendants being labeled "Amasis."

[186] Hom. *Od.* IV 187–188.

[187] Triobol Athens, AR, ca. 510–500 B.C., Obv. Head of Athena; Rev. head of a Negro. East Berlin, Münzkabinett, Prokesch-Osten Coll. (acquired 1875); Seltman 1924 97, 200 pl. xxii; Simon 1970, 15–18. Cf. trihemiobol, Delphi AR, early fifth century, Obv. Negro head; Rev. Head of a goat. Brett 1955, 132 nos. 974–975 pl. 52 and similarly with ram's head reverse Head *HN²* 340–341.

[188] Phiale, AE, Plovdiv, National Archaeological Museum 3204. The exterior decoration includes a row of acorns and three concentric rows of Negro heads facing outward, which increase progressively in size. Cf. Terracotta *phiale*. Locri Epizephyrii, Muzio Archeologico Nazionale 6416, date uncertain. The interior is decorated with rows of palmettes, acorns, and Negro heads.

[189] Snowden 1970, 151.

[190] Attic red-figure head-kantharos, ca. 470 B.C., San Simeon, Hearst Castle no.529-9-688.

[191] Cf. Alabastron, white ground, early fifth century B.C. depicting a Negro in dotted tunic and trousers, holding a quiver in l. hand (reverse side depicts an armed Amazon). West Berlin, 3382. ARV² 269. *LIMC* s.v. "Aithiopes" 7. Elements of costume have undoubtedly been fused here.

and customs: anyone who knew their Homer would look upon such objects and, where appropriate, read them accordingly.[192] Rather than being the preserve of poets or Ionian thinkers, such items and images were part of the everyday figuring in stories and myths and lively images adorning plates, pots, and coins.

2.10 Egyptians

The vast power and wealth of Egypt rendered it a land of superlatives and an object of intense fascination.[193] Far from existing in isolation, however, the prose accounts penned by authors such as Hecataeus and Herodotus reflect a long back-history of engagement with the land and the people of Egypt. From around the eighth century B.C. onward, Egyptian trinkets were traded the length and breadth of the Mediterranean via Cyprus and Phoenicia in the Near East. Small, portable objects such as a bronze jug from Lefkandi in Euboea—perhaps dating to the ninth century—scarabs, beads, amulets, faience seals, ivories, vases and figurines were all circulating widely by the mid-seventh century.[194] Meanwhile, from the early seventh century onward, workshops on Rhodes began producing objects in faience and the islands of Samos and Crete became notable repositories of "Egyptianizing" artefacts.[195]

Although the circulation of such objects and imagery is rarely deemed to indicate anything more than a vague awareness of Egypt itself, due to its being relayed via intermediaries, figurines depicting ibis birds or the gods Bes and Horus must have been interpreted somehow, whether as exotica or through assimilation, while the subsequent reproduction and imitation of Egyptian forms denotes a certain level of interest on behalf of both artisan and audience.[196] In discussing the significance of Egyptian amulets recovered from the Greek sanctuary at Kommos, Shaw comments that while it may

---

[192] For the secluded nature of the Ethiopian realm—refuge for the gods: *Il.* I 423–424; XXIII 192–211; *Od.* I 22–23.

[193] For discussion of Greek conceptualizations of Egypt, see Froidefond 1971; A. B. Lloyd 1975, 1990; Smelik and Hemelrijk 1984, 1869–1876; Morris 1997; Vasunia 2001; Hartog 2002; Harrison 2003.

[194] Skon-Jedele 1994, passim; Boardman 1999, 113–114, fig. 131; Webb 1978; Austin 1970; *CAH* 3².1. chap.13; 3².2, chap. 35, 36a Braun; Pendlebury 1930. For traders operating between Samos and Egypt cf. Hdt. IV 152.

[195] E.g., the bronze jugs recovered from the Idaean Cave, Knossos, and Amnisos but also Lefkandi and Perachora: Skon-Jedele 1994, 1743–5; Burkert 1992; Boardman 1999, 113, fig. 129. See also the distinctive Bes figurines *LIMC* s.v. "Bes" 27b–g, 30; Boardman 1999, 147. For wider discussion of "Egyptianizing"/"Orientalizing," see Gunter 2009 and below. For detailed analysis of Archaic Greek faience-objects circulating from the mid-seventh to late sixth centuries B.C., see Webb 1978.

[196] See Boardman 1999, 112–114. Cf. *LIMC* s.v. "Sphinx" for the enthusiastic adoption of a motif.

have been the exotic nature of such talismans that made them preferable to products manufactured locally, "[i]t must also be said . . . that the choice of Egyptian deities reflects a degree of knowledge about the meanings they held for the Egyptians themselves."[197] Although Shaw is keen to emphasize the fact that the knowledge derived from the enthusiastic "sales pitch" of traders was in all likelihood vague and lacking in any depth, widespread ignorance and vague imaginings are every bit as significant as detailed insights—and no less political, insofar as the imagining and appropriation of foreign ideas and imagery possesses a significance that extends far beyond simple "borrowing."[198] Ann Gunter makes the case more strongly, arguing that the modern tendency to dismiss Egyptian and Egyptianizing objects recovered from tombs and sanctuaries as simple "curios," mementos, or trinkets and nothing more is in all likelihood mistaken in underestimating the importance of "distant origins."[199] Drawing on Mary Helms' work on cultural concepts relating to geographical space and distance,[200] Gunter highlights the extent to which goods such as these were signifiers of wealth and status that in some way "encapsulated" the lands from which they originated.[201]

Egyptian Thebes was evidently known to Homer as a place "where men's houses possess the greatest store of wealth" ("ὅθι πλεῖστα δόμοις ἐν κτήματα κεῖται"), a city with a hundred gates from which two hundred warriors with horses and chariots could sally forth.[202] While the emphasis on wealth may well reflect the activities of Greek marauders of the type alluded to in Odysseus's lying tales, it seems unlikely that textual parallels between Egyptian accounts of action to stem incursions by raiders at the end of the Bronze Age are anything other than circumstantial.[203] We might reasonably follow Sarah Morris both in her suggestion that the "houses" (δόμοι) in question refer to

---

[197] Shaw 2000, 170.

[198] Cf. Appadurai 1986; Miller 1997 on Athenian "receptivity" to foreign forms and images.

[199] Gunter 2009, 141–142: "[T]he sanctuary contexts in which Egyptian and Egyptianizing faience objects have been found offer further indications of their amuletic function. . . . To their ancient owners, these possessions were charged with the powers of particular foreign deities and afforded potent protection." Cf. Raaflaub 2004, 212 where the importance of objects is downplayed.

[200] Mary Helms' "ethnographic peregrination" explores the way in which elites exploit knowledge/experience of far-off lands in order to enhance their position: ". . . the symbolic significance accorded to geographical space and distance can acquire more dynamic dimensions as the characteristics or attributes of geographical distance are given overt expression in the affairs or activities of various political-religious practitioners" (Helms 1988, 64).

[201] Gunter 2009, 137–138.

[202] Il. IX 379–386 cf. Od. IV 125–132. Reference to "Polybus, who dwelt in Thebes" (Od. IV 125–127) has been interpreted as a garbled reference to a 19th Dynasty queen named Tausret, whose brief reign as pharaoh coincides roughly with that attributed to the Trojan War. For discussion and references, see Callender 2012.

[203] Od. XIV 246–258.

the mortuary temples and palace treasuries and in her caution when it comes to gauging when such observations were made (as this is certainly not a secure basis for down-dating the *Iliad*).[204] What is more significant, however, is that such information is embedded in the epic at all, along with another reference celebrating Egypt's fame as a country steeped in medical knowledge:

> Such cunning drugs had the daughter of Zeus, drugs of healing (φάρμακα μητιόεντα), which the Egyptian Polydamna, wife of Thon, had given her, for there the earth, the giver of grain, bears greatest store of drugs (ζείδωρος ἄρουρα φάρμακα), many that are healing when mixed, and many that are harmful; there every man is a physician (ἰητρὸς), wise above humankind; for they are of Paeëon's race.[205]

While there is some debate as to whether the river referred to as the "waters of Aegyptus" is indeed the Nile—first referred to by name in Hesiod's *Theogony* as offspring of Tethys and Ocean—Homeric audiences evidently had some idea of a country in which river and landscape were somehow conflated.[206] It is hard to gauge how this poetic "imagining" should be interpreted; the Nile was certainly a topic of abiding fascination for observers habituated to eking out a comparably precarious existence according to a capricious Mediterranean climate. We should perhaps be wary therefore of dismissing both this and subsequent speculation by authors such as Thales or Anaxagoras regarding such natural phenomena as nothing more than speculation of a quasi-geographical/scientific nature.[207] The act of imagining, assessing, and quantifying Egypt was not, during any period, a value-free exercise.

However hazy its origins, knowledge of Egypt undoubtedly spiraled from the reign of Psammetichus I (664–610 B.C.) following his decision to enlist the help of foreign mercenaries in a bid to assert his authority as ruler of Lower Egypt and throw off the Assyrian yoke. Those who served the Egyptian king were rewarded with grants of land close to the sea, on the Pelusian mouth of the Nile, with Carians settled on one bank and Ionians on the other.[208] Trade with Greece was also actively encouraged. Greeks and Carians continued to serve under Necho (610–595), who dedicated the armor he wore

---

[204] S. Morris 1997, 614–615. Cf. A. B. Lloyd 1975, 121; Burkert 1976.
[205] *Od.* IV 227–232.
[206] Hom. *Od.* IV 581; Hes. *Theog.* 338. Cf. Hdt. II 14; VII 102 together with Harrison 2000, 59–60.
[207] Cf. Shrimpton 1997, 175: "There is no reason to believe that his [Anaxagoras's] interest in Egypt went beyond accounting for certain of its physical characteristics" with postcolonial studies of geography and exploration emphasizing the politics of such enterprises (e.g., Driver 2001). Cf. Harrison 2007.
[208] Hdt. II 152–154. See Austin 1970, 14–15; Boardman 1999, 111–153.

while fighting in Syria in the sanctuary to Apollo at Branchidae, and successive pharaohs down to Amasis (570–526) who formalized the status of Naucratis, a trading settlement on the east bank of the Canopic branch of the Nile with a monopoly on all trade with the wider Mediterranean world.[209] During this time we have evidence for a great number of Greek-speaking soldiers and traders variously "making their mark" in Egypt—often quite literally as in the case of the irreverent scrawlings on the colossus at Abu Simbel, dating to the time of Psammetichus II's Nubian expedition.[210] A rather deeper engagement is apparent in the case of a votive inscription to Ammon as "Zeus of Thebes," dating to the mid-sixth century,[211] and a bronze apis inscribed with "PANEPI" dedicated by Socydes.[212] Equally suggestive is a tomb relief from Siwa commemorating the last resting place of Si-Amun (Man of Amun), in which a seated male is depicted as bearded and accompanied by a youth dressed in a *chlamys*.[213] The extent to which these are indicative of a specific knowledge or interest in Egyptian habits and customs is, of course, uncertain. We must allow for a wide variety of attitudes and experiences and, by extension, the possibility that some of this knowledge would have been carried back along the sea lanes as merchants, travelers and war-weary veterans variously returned from Egypt or sought opportunities elsewhere.

Receptions of Egypt can also be perceived in various areas of artistic endeavor along with patterns of thought and belief relating to the divine. Since there is neither the time nor the space to pursue such topics individually and at length, we shall resort instead to a brisk summary before moving on to address other categories of foreign people: the far-flung descendants of Pelasgos and a wild and woolly Arcadia. A great deal of attention has already been paid to the extent to which temple architecture and statuary followed Egyptian precedents during its early stages.[214] Meanwhile, scholars such as Walter Burkert have argued that Egyptian influence can be discerned in the manner in which a number of (supposedly Greek) gods were conceived. Perhaps the most prominent of these are Dionysius and Orphism in general—linked to Osiris and the promise of a blissful afterlife.[215] This is not altogether out of kilter with the image of Egypt cultivated by Herodotus as a country of

---

[209] See Hdt. II 159 (Necho's dedication); 178 (Naucratis). There exists a huge bibliography on the latter but see Boardman 1999; Möller 2000; Malkin 2003c, 2011, 81–93; Villing and Schlotzhauer 2006a.

[210] See Boardman 1999, 115–117, figs. 134–135. Cf. Hdt. II 161.

[211] *SEG* XXVII 1106.

[212] *SEG* XXVII 1116.

[213] Boardman 1999, 159, fig. 200.

[214] Boardman 1999; Kyrieleis 1996; Bietak 2001; Burkert 2004, 13–14, 72.

[215] Burkert 2004, 72ff.

great antiquity and wisdom that taught the Greeks the names of the gods (although with a number of subtle caveats and qualifications).[216] The dedication of a vase at Karnak depicting the sacred ship of Dionysius borne aloft by devotees has long been cited as indicating knowledge of practices common at Karnak/Luxor and Siwa, whereby gods traveled in boats on festival days—a practice that appears to have been translated to Athens, among other places.[217]

Further iconographic evidence for "receptions of difference" can be found in the style and subject matter adopted by vase painters from around the mid-seventh century onward. While John Boardman is adamant that "[t]hese isolated . . . scenes of course reflect no deeper awareness or influence of Egyptian practices or beliefs," the act of creating them must have entailed a significant level of contact and interaction as he also maintains that such parallels could not, in many cases, occur without the artists in question actually traveling to Egypt and viewing nonportable artworks (notably painted frescoes) in context.[218] So, for instance, depictions of Herakles using a sling to bring down the Stymphalian birds on a black-figure vase from Vulci are a reworking of traditional hunting scenes that formed a set piece in Egyptian art while images on the Vienna hydria from circa 510 B.C. offer a clear parody of Pharaonic iconography.[219] The choice of theme is, in the case of the Vienna hydria, a pertinent one: the myth of Bousiris, a mythical Egyptian king and eponym of a town in the Delta region. The image in question depicts a larger-than-life Herakles that is clearly modeled upon the "smiting Pharaoh" motif. Surrounded by Egyptians, he is shown in the act of trampling his enemies underfoot. Holding one priest by the ankle and dangling another by the throat, he bears down implacably on the altar on which the terrified Bousiris is shown crouched with arms outstretched in a gesture of supplication. The slaying of Bousiris was a popular theme whose earliest literary rendering comes in the form of fragmentary poems by Panyassis, a version subsequently refuted by Herodotus and Pherekydes.[220] The manner in which it is represented is significant for two reasons: not only are the king's retinue often depicted as black Africans with, in one later and somewhat notorious

---

[216] See T. Harrison 2000a; 2003b for discussion.

[217] Ionian amphora, Oxford, Ashmolean Museum 1924.264. Burkert 2004, 73; Boardman 1999, 137.

[218] Boardman 1999, 151, 153.

[219] Caeretan black-figure hydria, ca. 510 B.C., Vienna, Kunsthistorisches Museum AS IV 3576. Miller 2000, 418–419 discusses the likelihood that Egyptianizing Phoenician art provided the template: "The significance of this parody lies in the presumption of knowledge about and interest in Egyptian imperial iconographic traditions . . . on the part of the Greek viewer" (419). For Phoenician bowls depicting smiting Pharaohs, see Markoe 1985, 45–47. Cf. a relief of Seti I (1318–1301 B.C.) from Karnak on the northern exterior of the great hall (*Epigraphic Survey*, 1986, pls. 27, 29; Miller 2000, 418 no. 20).

[220] Pan. Fr. 26. k; Hdt. II 45; *FGrHist* 3 F 17.

example, tunics hitched up to reveal circumcised genitalia, but Bousiris himself is also on occasion depicted as black-skinned.[221] It has been suggested that Bousiris's differentiation reflects the fact that his transgressive act of sacrificing any foreigner who made landfall in Egypt placed him beyond "aristocratic 'internationalism'"; this represents a somewhat uncomfortable anomaly, however, for those wishing to keep the barbarian "other" waiting in the wings.[222]

While there may well be plausible grounds upon which to identify the fragmentary remnants of an Attic cup attributed to the Heidelberg Painter (see fig. 2.3) as the earliest known depiction of Bousiris's encounter with Herakles, we must remain open to the fact that the significance of the telltale *uraeus*—symbolic of the goddess Wadjet and pharaonic rule over Lower Egypt—was all but lost on an audience far better equipped to decipher the image depicted on the only other fragment of the vessel known to have survived from antiquity, the head of Herakles.[223] At the same time, it is equally possible that this distant echo of pharaonic iconography, a scale-lined skull cap from which a rearing asp can be seen protruding, evoked a wide array memories and associations relating to Egyptian manners and customs—real or imagined.

While opinions vary regarding the ethnic origin of the painter who signed himself as "Amasis," there is evidence to suggest that ideas about Egypt were nonetheless being bandied about relatively freely among his contemporaries in the Athenian Potters' Quarter.[224] Thought to have been working by the mid-sixth century, "Amasis" may or may not have been Egyptian in origin—or a slave (such questions are unlikely to be resolved). What is arguably more important is the fact that the Egyptian associations that his name conjured up are reflected in turn in the general badinage aimed in his direction. John Boardman is surely right in maintaining that two depictions of black Africans attending the Ethiopian king Memnon by his contemporary and rival Exekias (variously labeled Amasis and Amasos) are an attempt to poke fun at his

---

[221] E.g., the Vienna hydria (see above). For depiction of circumcised priests see an Attic red-figure pelike, attributed to the Pan Painter, ca. 470 B.C., Athens, National Archaeological Museum 9683, *ARV*² 554, 82. Responses vary from charges of overt racism to the suggestion that it is a strictly cultural opposition that is being constructed (cf. Bérard 2000, 393–394; M. C. Miller 2000, 429–430, fig. 16.7). For discussion of the tradition in antiquity, see Vasunia 2001, 185–193.

[222] M. C. Miller 2000, 420; Hall 1989.

[223] *LIMC* s.v. "Bousiris" no. 29; Brijder 1991, 374 pl. 127a; el Kalza 1970. See M. C. Miller 2000, 421–422, for discussion and references. Cf. a Milesian neck-amphora, mid-sixth century, Oxford, Ashmolean Museum G121.5. (See also fig. 2.3.)

[224] The potential foreignness of Greek potters and painters has long exercised scholars and art historians from the nineteenth century onward. While many have been willing to infer an Egyptian identity or time spent in either Ionia or Naucratis, the idea has been resisted by those unable or willing to allow for foreign ideas or influences upon Attic vase-painting—a quintessentially Greek art form. For East Greek pottery at Naucratis see Villing and Schlotzhauer 2006b.

FIGURE 2.3 Head of Bousiris. Attic black-figure sherd, Siana cup, ca. 565 B.C., attributed to the Heidelberg Painter. Palermo, Museo Archaeologico Regionale 1986. Redrawn from *LIMC* III pl. 131, Bousiris no. 29. Drawing by the author.

contemporary.[225] Whether or not Amasis was dark-skinned in appearance is, from the point of view of this study, largely immaterial. In contrast, the suggestion that one depiction of Amasis as Ethiopian or Egyptian included a phonetic rendering of a barbarized *epoisen* inscription (*aoiesn*), incorporating an Ionic eta (unusual in Athens at this date), is of considerable significance since it demonstrates an active concern for representing "difference"—in this case an outlandish accent.[226] Whether based in fact or fiction, this would seem to indicate that ideas, and even parodies, of Egyptians were common currency at the time.[227]

Representations of Egypt—or at least of a deity with whom Egypt was closely associated—can also be found on coins minted by the polis of Cyrene. Given the considerable distance separating the polis from Ammon's oracle at

---

[225] Boardman 1987, 148–149.

[226] Ibid., 149, fig. 8b.

[227] Outwith Athens we have fragments of a vase of East Greek type carrying a cartouche from Egypt and a painted wooden plaque recovered from the tomb of Hetepka, Sakkara as additional evidence of Egyptian influences/cross currents. Vase: Boardman 1987, 147, figs. 4a, b; Boardman 1999, 114, 139, fig. 164. Some understanding of Egyptian ritual can be inferred from a vase depicting a Dionysiac procession dedicated at Karnak, see Boardman 1999, 137–138, figs. 162–163. See also Bailey 2006 for discussion of a fragmentary East Greek amphora bearing the name of Apries.

Siwah, it is perhaps somewhat surprising that the figure of Zeus Ammon, horned and enclosed within a circular incuse, should figure so prominently on coins minted by the polis. The extent to which Libya and Egypt could be conflated can be seen, however, in references to "the fertile domain of Kronos' son on the Nile" (Νείλοιο πρὸς πῖον τέμενος Κρονίδα) in Pindar's *Pythian* 4.[228] Product of a union between the nymph Cyrene and Apollo, Zeus Ammon was hardly a local deity and it is hard to interpret his appearance as anything other than the opportunistic appropriation of an exotic cult figure for the purposes of self-aggrandizement. Moving on from Cyrene we have a variety of fragments all attesting to knowledge of or interest in Egypt. These range from the relatively mundane, in the case of Bacchylides' allusion to corn imports, with which his audiences were presumably familiar,[229] to Pindar's fanciful reference to:

> . . . Egyptian Mendes, by the bank of the sea,
> the end of the Nile's branch, where goat-mounting
> he-goats mate with women . . .[230]

Herodotus mentions a similar tale while recounting the reason why goats were not sacrificed in Egypt—albeit as a one-off occurrence.[231]

2.11 *Pelasgians*

The Pelasgians enjoyed a rather ambiguous status as both Greeks of the heroic age and a prehistoric non-Greek population that subsequently adopted Hellenic *nomoi*.[232] Their appearance in Homer (notably epithets) provided the

---

[228] Pind. *Pyth.* 4.55–57. Commentators are keen to defend Pindar of ignorance or uncertainty on this count, citing the Scholia's somewhat revealing suggestion that he may have been under the impression that the whole of Libya was consecrated to the god (Farnell 1961, 151). On charter myths, see Malkin 1987; 1994; 1998a, 20–21; 2005 (on Sicily in particular). See also J. Hall 1997, 2002; Kowalzig 2007, 33. The figure is sometimes identified as Apollo Delphinios (Irad Malkin, personal communication with author). See Marshall 2004, 134, 136 (with further references) for the suggestion that Ammon's presence reflects the influence of Libyan cultural traditions brought about by intermarriage with local populations together with Kane's analysis of the sculpture from the sanctuary of Demeter and Kore/Persephone (Kane 1998). For related discussion of cultural difference at Cyrene, see B. Mitchell 2000.

[229] Bacchyl. Fr. 20B 14–16.

[230] Pind. Fr. 201.

[231] It is reported not only that Egyptians refer to both he-goats and the god Pan by the same name (Μένδης) but that one he-goat in particular is singled out for veneration—creating considerable potential for confusion (Hdt. II 46). The Egypt of Herodotus's day was seemingly thronged with "tourists," creating any number of opportunities for information (accurate or otherwise) to be relayed further afield. See Assmann 2005 for the implications of this prolonged exposure to "enlightened" and inquisitive Greeks in what is portrayed as an asymmetrical relationship. On the attitudes of tourists see Redfield 1985.

[232] Cf. Hdt. I 57; II 51. For Greek constructions of prehistory, see Finkelberg 2005.

bases for a wide variety of stories and associations that showed little regard for consistency or genre—arguably just another case in which material preserved within the Homeric corpus provided any number of templates that could be adapted to suit the requirements of the day.[233] Mythic or poetic traditions could constantly be invoked or cited, feeding back into discussions concerning various peoples (foreign or otherwise) in order to explain points of similarity or difference. Pelasgians feature prominently in early prose accounts, appearing in any number of contexts: in Greece prior to their expulsion in Hellanicus, Hecataeus and Hieronymus of Cardia,[234] and in Ionia—again in Hellanicus.[235] Hecataeus reports that Thessaly was named after a king Pelasgos.[236] Hellanicus, meanwhile, places Pelasgians in Tyrrhenia—thus linking them with Etruscans and other Italic peoples—and Cyzicus.[237] This led to great confusion, even in antiquity (Herodotus famously tried—and failed—to make sense of it all).

The "problem" of the Pelasgians is arguably misconceived, however. Seen from the perspective of those propagating such myths, the Pelasgians were arguably a solution to any number of historical lacunae that required explanation. As a construct that illustrates the complexity of discourse relating to identity the Pelasgians are, unsurprisingly, extremely difficult to pin down. Problems only arise, however, if one expects the traditions surrounding them to be in any way consistent. Rather than thinking of Pelasgians as a historical population or idea that can be plotted and located, it might perhaps be more revealing to view them as an enigmatic construct that was variously appropriated and manipulated over time—solving some questions but raising others, contested in meaning but accumulating associations as they were successively incorporated into discourses of identity.[238] It is also worth noting, as Christiane Sourvinou-Inwood pointed out, that Pelasgians are often associated, both by virtue of (vague) chronology and geographical location, with early uses of the term "Hellas."[239] This may provide some clues as to the function and status of

[233] Pelasgian Argos *Il.* II 681; Dodonean Zeus as "Pelasgian" *Il.* XVI 233; in Crete *Od.* IXX 175–177. On Homeric Pelasgians see: Loptson 1981; and, more generally, Myres 1907; Lochner-Hüttenbach 1960; Briquel 1984.
[234] Hellanicus *FGrHist* 4 F 4; Hecataeus *FGrHist* 1 F 119; Hieronymus of Cardia *FGrHist* 154 F 17 Cf. Acusilaus (*FGrHist* 2 F 25a).
[235] Hellanicus *FGrHist* 4 F 92.
[236] Hecataeus *FGrHist* 1 F 14. See also Deiochus of Prokonnesos (*FGrHist* 471 F 7a, 8a).
[237] Hellanikos *FGrHist* 4 F 4.
[238] For recent discussion stressing inclusivity, see Gruen 2011a, 239–243.
[239] Sourvinou-Inwood 2003, 120–121n88. For Pelasgos son of Niobe/Zeus in Argos, see Acusilaus (*FGrHist* 2 F 25a); son of Argive Phoroneus (Hellanicus *FGrHist* 4 F 36). For links to Thessaly (*FGrHist* 4 F 91). Cf. on culture heroes/Deucalion (Deiochus *FGrHist* 471 F 7a, 8a).

the construct as an "other" against which self-proclaimed "Hellenes" might contrast themselves.[240]

2.12 Arcadia

From the Pelasgians we shall now move to consider another group who traced their ancestry back to the eponymous Pelasgos.[241] Arcadia was regarded as a somewhat liminal realm, marked out by its wild and mountainous terrain, and was routinely afforded the same treatment as supposedly "barbarian" peoples as a result (i.e., one that was "ethnographic" in nature).[242] This is invariably put down to prevailing stereotypes arising from entrenched notions of environmental determinism and a tendency to view a pastoral existence as "primitive." Is it merely the case, however, that the deterministic relationship between landscape and sacred/liminal status meant that such associations were to some extent automatic? Ascribing such views to "Greco-Roman society" in general and leaving it at that might be seen as a somewhat simplistic approach: the manipulation of imaginary cultural boundaries was an ongoing process that served explicitly political ends, as Catherine Morgan has highlighted.[243]

Why would these traditions have been circulating in the first place other than because they formed an important part of the way in which identities were mapped out or constructed? We have little by way of evidence for the way in which Arcadia and its inhabitants were both represented and perceived (aside, of course, from Homer) until the flurry of ethnographic treatments

---

[240] The incorporation of foreign and Homeric Pelasgians into genealogical poetry might equally be construed as an act of appropriation on behalf of those constructing genealogies.

[241] For Arcadian Pelasgians, see Hdt. I 146.

[242] For early interest in Arcadia, see Hom. *Il*. II. 603–614; *FGrHist* 1 F 6, 9, 29a–b; *FGrHist* 3 F 85, 86–87, 116–117; *FGrHist* 4 F 37, 162. See Ferguson 1975, 18–19, 21 (on Polyb. IV 20–21); Nielsen 1996, 1999, 2000; Campbell 2006, 78–84. See Scheer 2011, 12 for the argument that Homeric traditions played an important role in shaping ancient perceptions of Arcadia.

[243] Morgan 1999b. The relationship between landscapes and identities has received considerable attention in recent years (for a variety of scholarly perspectives see: McInerney 1999; Foxhall 2003; R. Osborne 2007a). In discussing whether we can identify landscapes in which social and economic practices are linked with the cultural identities of specific groups, Lin Foxhall has for instance argued that the evidence for land division in early Greece—typically characterized by small units of land that can be ploughed in a day—reflects specifically "agrarian" perspectives and ideologies that stand out from later modes of land use. It follows that ideals of private property/land use in all likelihood predated the monumentalization of urban centers as a manifestation of collective ethos/values (Foxhall 2003). It is from this—rather more embedded—perspective that we should arguably be considering ideas of primitive/egalitarian, golden age societies that do not engage in cultivation, etc. Rather than referring to "the Greek ethnographic view" as though it were some reified abstraction, we should pay more attention to reconstructing the sociocultural milieu in which such traditions might variously have circulated, the better to understand their wider function and purpose.

around the fifth century B.C. Questions remain as to how the literary material should be interpreted: as reflecting a bookish or antiquarian interest on behalf of observers based in Athens or Ionia or as signs that such questions were very much a current topic of interest, playing a vital role in an emerging sense of Arcadianness? Excluded from the "Hellenic club" and famously referred to as "eaters of acorns" (βαλανηφάγοι ἄνδρες) in an oracle reported by Herodotus, there is a very clear sense of Arcadian "difference."[244]

This chapter has demonstrated that, far from consisting of a paltry collection of hazily imagined "foreigners," the ethnographic *imaginaire* was in fact very crowded indeed long before Greece's celebrated encounter with "the barbarian." While we have surveyed a wide range of ideas relating to a variety of foreign or mythical peoples, transcending media and genre, we have by no means exhausted the list of foreigners with whom ancient audiences can be shown to have been familiar. In fact, such a list could continue almost indefinitely to encompass Libyans, Babylonians, and Issedones, not to mention Spartans, Aitolians, Macedonians, and Cretans. Having assembled this information, the next chapter examines the systems of knowledge and understanding that governed the way in which ideas relating to foreign peoples and places achieved widespread dissemination throughout the cultural *koiné* we now call "Greek." It will be argued that, far from being mere epiphenomena, "structures" such as these provided the mechanisms by which individual and community identities were defined, playing an active role in deciding what it meant to be Greek in the first place.

---

[244] Hdt. I 66. Georges 1994, 164 points out, however, that the techniques required to render acorns edible are actually quite sophisticated. For cogent discussion of the usefulness of an Arcadian identity, see Scheer 2011.

CHAPTER 3 | Mapping Ethnography

HAVING DEMONSTRATED THE RELATIVELY high levels of interest in and engagement with a wide variety of foreign or mythical peoples in the years prior to the Persian Wars, we shall now examine the interlocking systems of knowledge and understanding through which they found order and expression. Mapping out this "ethnography before ethnography" will entail consideration of individual categories such as epic poetry and list songs, epithets and stereotyping.[1] However, it will also stress their essential connectivity within an overarching *imaginaire*, unhampered by epistemic distinctions that privilege rational and objective prose—"fact" over fiction.

3.1 Naming and Describing

The history of humanity's engagement with questions of social and cultural difference is as old as society itself. There is neither time nor space here to explore the nature or origins of cognitive skills intrinsically bound up in evolutionary processes that accompanied the emergence of early human societies—what evolutionary anthropologists refer to as the "social brain."[2] It should also be emphasized that knowledge of foreign peoples—or, indeed, anything or anyone considered strange or different—does not have to be particularly detailed or even accurate for it to be important. Knowledge of foreign people can ultimately be pared down to two inherently basic and interrelated

---

[1] Cf. Robert 1980.

[2] The starting point for this study is contingent upon the survival of sources and materials relating to ancient Greece. Such myopic Hellenocentricity can perhaps be offset by recent/ongoing research into the perception of foreigners in ancient Egypt, China, and the Ancient Near East; see chapter 1, fn. 48 for references. For classificatory schemas in general, see Lloyd 1966, 2002; Goody 1977.

questions, namely: who or what lies beyond one's immediate community, the imaginative boundaries of which are subjectively defined, and by what criteria can they/it be effectively ordered and classified? This forms the essential basis for any intellectual engagement with "difference," however perceived, whether "vague"—as is often argued in the case of ideas relating to foreign peoples during the archaic period—or forensic in detail.[3] The processes of describing and classifying must always begin somewhere, however, and that somewhere is generally a name.[4]

3.1.1 Epithets

Names represent an intrinsic component of any wider ethnographic interest in that they identify the subject. They rarely exist in isolation, however. Instead, collective names are usually supplemented by additional information upon which identification can be "pegged." Such elements or attributes ascribed to an individual or group might refer to abstract qualities/geographical locations, but they may equally refer to patterns of behavior or common characteristics that then become cognate with the name itself, often taking the form of an epithet. Epithets, it will be argued, are significant both for the wider body of practice of which they are representative (the naming and describing of foreign peoples) and for the manner in which they function, once coined, as descriptive labels that may be incorporated into oral discourse or narrative—whether hexameters or prose.[5] Although transmitted to us as text via the medium of epic poetry, they would originally have functioned as building blocks/units of an (almost exclusively) oral discourse. This is important since the orality of early ethnography was a significant factor in determining the ease with which knowledge relating to foreign peoples and places was exchanged and disseminated.

Discussion of the role and significance of epithets as a means of representing people and place has largely centered upon the Homeric *Catalogue*

---

[3] "[N]aming and recognition are necessarily interrelated in their parallel structures of delineation and authority. For like recognition, naming also involves an act of classification. . . . One never names, one classes" (Goldhill 1991, 26–27, see 24–34 for discussion).

[4] The power of names and naming would have been deemed largely self-evident in antiquity. The ability to identify a specific group or individual brought with it certain powers associated with the ability to name a subject—witness Odysseus's reluctance to reveal his name to Polyphemus/the ensuing curse (*Od.* IX 528–535) or the concern expressed in curse tablets to offset the schemes of "unnamed" ill-wishers. For general discussion of the (perceived) risks of being named, see Eidinow 2007. For the power that comes with knowledge of the geographically distant, see Helms 1988. See Goldhill 1991, 27n50 for further references on cultural taboos relating to naming and its significance in Attic drama, oratory, and invective.

[5] Epithets of one sort or another are recognized as being typical of most narrative styles—up to and including prose. On the combination of personal/collective name and epithet/adjectival phrase, see Hainsworth 1968.

of Ships.[6] The wider significance of catalogue poetry in mapping people and place will be discussed below. For now, it is the function of the epithets themselves that needs to be addressed—in short, whether they can be thought of as being in any way "ethnographic." Around 180 places are named in the catalogue, divided between the 29 contingents that made up the Achaean host. Of these around 62 possess descriptive epithets—around 70 if looser geographical phrases are included—some of which are occasionally employed for more than one place. Scholarship has for some time been divided over how the catalogue should be interpreted. One view, championed notably by Page but widely subscribed to both before and since the publication of his *History and the Homeric Iliad*, was that it was based upon a detailed source dating from or not long after the historical expedition against Troy (i.e., circa mid- to late thirteenth century B.C.) and therefore that it amounted to a historical description of Mycenaean Greece. Those opposing such arguments pointed out (in some cases quite rightly) that the "special knowledge" that Page and others had argued for—supposedly the reflection of an earlier source that was explicitly concerned with the accurate description of places and their inhabitants—was in fact nothing of the sort, reflecting instead the formulaic use of stock phrases that owed more to metrical considerations that any historical reality.

The position adopted by Kirk, on the other hand, is largely representative of the more skeptical or conservative stance that many other scholars have adopted. Having classified and tabulated the epithets in question, Kirk concludes that they are in no way divergent from the Homeric formula style and, furthermore, that:

> the truth is that all the epithets (and other descriptive phrases) save about eight can be divided into one or other of four general categories of meaning. That a town is "well-built" or "walled," or "rocky" or "steep" in some sense, or "fertile" or "grassy" or "with many flocks" on the other hand, does not presuppose any

---

[6] A significant milestone in the study of oral hexameter style, Page's study of Homeric epithets highlighted the sheer range of name/noun-epithet formulas that were available to the poet as an aid to composition. The ensuing disagreement as to the specific role allotted to Homeric formulae in oral composition saw a clash of opinion between those who viewed the process as being essentially functional/mechanistic—in which the poet is merely abiding by the established rules of oral poetry—and those who, while acknowledging the importance of metrical considerations, stressed the richness and diversity of Homeric style. Cf. Page 1959, 222 (on oral epic): "[I]ts units are *formulas*, phrases ready-made, extending in length from a word or two to several complete lines, already adapted to the metre, and either already adapted or instantly adaptable to the limited range of ideas which the subject-matter of the Greek epic may require him to express"; and Austin 1975, 6: "Homer's style is paratactic . . . [but] his combination and repetition of formulas goes beyond parataxis to create for us a world rich in resonance and diversity." Cf. Allen 1910, 1921; Allison 1968; Clark 2004.

meticulous classification of particular places, since most ancient towns in ancient Greece fitted easily under one or more of these headings.[7]

An effective riposte to the claims forwarded by Page, this assessment militates against our attaching any explicitly *ethnographic* reading to such material. It is now widely agreed that the catalogue encompasses material that ranges from what could even be a period prior to the historical expedition against Troy down until the later stages of composition, with occasional archaisms and the format of the list itself being the only indicators of earlier influence from any supposed Mycenaean catalogue tradition. Both the overall format and layout are held to be overwhelmingly consistent with the established rules of Homeric formula style. Although it is widely accepted that the description of the Boeotian contingent contains an unusual level of detail and is in many ways an exception to the general rule, the manner in which epithets are deployed is largely determined by "the limited and conventionalised structure of the many verses whose primary purpose is to contain place-names."[8] The more general use of epithets has been interpreted in a variety of ways, with Parry insisting that they provide nothing but a heroic gloss to the narrative and others, such as Austin and Vivante, maintaining that a sense of meaning was retained throughout.[9] It should be noted, however, that both positions focus predominantly upon the epic verse as *text*—something that can be analyzed and dissected. Matters become more complicated, however, when we turn to the (far more nebulous) realm of the *imaginaire*: what happens, in short, once texts are heard, received, and understood.

The rigorous analysis of the various place names and epithets, tabulated in rows, is perhaps ill-suited to gauging the extent to which these formed part of wider discourses of identity and difference. Regardless of their accuracy or metrical value, the very authority of their source effectively guarantees that locations described as having "fine dance halls" or "swift horses" will henceforth be conceived or remembered as such. As a result, they are suggestive of a wider process in which identities were selectively imagined and constructed using Homeric materials.[10] While an appreciation of the rules governing the use of

---

[7] Kirk 1985, 175.

[8] Ibid., 176–177. Analysis of the Boeotian catalogue has highlighted how the use of epithets is driven by both functional imperatives and the need to enliven its recital with a dramatic climax to each verse—with occasional exceptions where a change of emphasis is required. As a result, the use of epithets in the catalogue overall is perceived as being both general in meaning and to a large extent arbitrary: mere "metrical fillers" that betray little interest in people/place (Kirk 1985, esp. 177–178). For discussion of the use of ethnics in Homer and elsewhere, see Fraser 2009, 1–4.

[9] Parry 1971; Austin 1975; Vivante 1982.

[10] Ridgway 1996; Malkin 1998a; Graziosi 2002; Hall 2005. For Pelasgians, see chapter 2.

specific formulae is important if we are to understand the manner in which epic poetry was both composed and recited, it does little to illuminate matters of reception—in particular, the way in which poetic material might subsequently be reworked and reimagined in everyday contexts. What does it mean if bent-bowed Paeonians (Παίονας ἀγκυλοτόξους) are elsewhere described as "spear-bearing" (ἄνδρας ἄγων δολιχεγχέας)?[11] Are such inconsistencies within a text important, or are we instead overly accustomed to dealing with narrative prose that can be read and rechecked by the lone individual, and in which extensive cross-referencing is effectively the norm? Is it safe to assume this (altogether more sophisticated) level of engagement with epic prior to the emergence of a prose tradition? Instead of seeing epithets as ethnographic fragments that must necessarily coalesce into a portrait that is both coherent and accurate, should we not see them as "mobile, discursive operators" that can be continually reworked as an element of discourse: snatches of ideas as opposed to lengthy excursuses (but no less important for all that).

3.1.2 Stereotyping

An epithet reflecting a belief relating to a group of people, to which another group or individual subscribes, can also be understood as a stereotype. To refer to Thracians as top-knotted (Θρήϊκες ἀκρόκομοι) is to imply that most— if not all—Thracians are top-knotted and that top-knottedness is thus a characteristic by which all Thracians are recognizable.[12] If, as has been argued, such practices are already endemic to Homeric epic, how should they be interpreted? Are they indeed indicative of knowledge of, or an interest in, foreign peoples and customs? Should they necessarily be the subject of censure, however implicit, as is perhaps implied by Edith Hall: the seeds of a process that would eventually produce "the Barbarian," a negative stereotype par excellence?[13] From a social-psychological perspective, stereotypes and stereotyping are an important means of making sense of the world and therefore possess a certain moral ambivalence.[14] While charges of Orientalism may not be entirely misdirected or out of place, far more attention needs to be paid to questions of social and historical context. Rather than simply focusing upon the extent to which they form the basis for erroneous or pejorative beliefs concerning particular groups, with the implied moral censure that comes

---

[11] Hom. Il. 2. 848; 21.155.

[12] Il. IV 533.

[13] "In a small number of epithets attached to certain ethnic groups, then, it looks as though the seed of later systematic ethnological science was germinating" (Hall 1989, 41). This "minimalist" interpretation is neither entirely convincing nor satisfactory, however. See further, chapter 5.

[14] McGarty et al. 2002, 186.

with it, we must also make some attempt to normalize stereotypes, placing them in their wider context as a cognitive function designed to help individuals deal effectively with social complexity on a day-to-day basis.

Some of the most insightful work on stereotyping has arisen in the context of postcolonial studies. Although some care is required in applying such theories to ancient societies, it provides a useful starting point for discussion of the manner in which knowledge relating to a variety of foreign peoples was both deployed and manipulated by active subjects.[15] Stereotypes are viewed as the "major discursive strategy" of colonial discourse:

> . . . a form of knowledge and identification that vacillates between what is always "in place," already known, and something that must be anxiously repeated . . . for it is the force of ambivalence that gives the colonial stereotype its currency.[16]

While the use of stereotypes is thus firmly situated in the "discursive and political practices of racial and cultural hierarchization,"[17] the extent to which such pronouncements are themselves historically situated should make us doubly cautious when it comes to inferring (modern) concepts of race and cultural hierarchization in an ancient context. The structures and power relationships underpinning the analyses of postcolonial theorists such as Bhabha differ profoundly from those which held sway in antiquity.[18] A recent (and highly sensitive) critique of Bhabha's views on stereotyping by Peter van Dommelen has nonetheless demonstrated that anachronistic notions of race or a "civilizing mission" can in fact be pared away from Bhabha's model with relative ease and that ambiguity and stereotypes specific to the period and locale are likely to have been every bit as prevalent in (ancient) colonial contexts as a result.[19]

---

[15] While long subject to question, the historicity of the Greek colonial paradigm has been disputed with much ferocity in recent years. Cf. Bérard 1960; de Angelis 1998; Osborne 1998b; Hurst and Owen 2005; Malkin 2008a. It would equally be too simplistic to interpret the evidence purely in terms of mutual antagonism between Orient and Occident (Cf. Hall 1989; Miller 1997; Thomas 2000; T. Harrison 2002a). For discussion of "conceptualisation," see Smelik and Hemelrijk 1984, 1856–1858.

[16] Bhabha 1994, 66.

[17] Ibid., 67.

[18] Although hierarchies of one sort or another undoubtedly existed in antiquity these rarely consisted (solely) of a unitary notion of Greek culture versus "the rest." Sumptuary laws attributed to Zaleucus of Locri Epizephyrii cite the citizens of Smyrna as the epitome of wanton luxury. See: Arist. Pol. 1274a; Diod. Sic. 12. 19–21; Dem. 24. 139–140; Polyb. 12. 16. For recent discussion of the extent to which racist attitudes were prevalent in antiquity see Cohen 2011, 477–482. See also Isaac 2004, 2006 together with Tuplin 2007b; 1999.

[19] Van Dommelen 2002, 128–129. See also van Dommelen 2002, 129: "Given the inherent complexity and confusion of colonial situations, I would argue that stereotypes . . . should be regarded as a common and recurrent feature of colonial encounters, although the *content* of the stereotypes is necessarily of a historically specific nature."

Recent work by social psychologists can provide us with useful comparanda and alternative routes of inquiry. It has been noted, for instance, that dependence amounts to a major cause of stereotyping when it comes to intergroup relations.[20] Observations of this nature add another dimension to the (decidedly ambivalent) manner in which Phoenicians are represented in Homeric epic:

Thither came Phoenicians, men famed for their ships,
greedy knaves, bringing countless trinkets in their black ship.

ἔνθα δὲ Φοίνικες ναυσικλυτοὶ ἤλυθον ἄνδρες,
τρῶκται, μυρί᾿ ἄγοντες ἀθύρματα νηῒ μελαίνῃ.[21]

The suggestion that Homeric epic might in some way reflect the day-to-day realities of contemporary society is of course not unprecedented. There is clearly a lot to be gained, however, by focusing on the link between social relationships and the practice of stereotyping (one of the major building blocks of ethnographic discourse), thus allowing a far clearer sense of the circumstances under which such traditions came into being.

Opinion as to the significance of stereotyping as practice is divided, as we have already seen. Edith Hall has played down the use of epithets, arguing that they reflect only a vague or patchy interest in, or knowledge of, foreign peoples, lacking the coherence and vigor of ethnological science.[22] However, this implies that the distinction between ethnological science and the use of epithets and stereotyping is entirely clear and straightforward—when in fact the reverse appears to be the case. It is in fact hard to think of any body of ethnographic material from antiquity that is *not* predicated upon stereotypes. Whether or not the application of stereotypes needs to be in any way systematic for it to be indicative of ethnographic interest is very much debatable. No simple conclusion is possible, but it is certainly somewhat anachronistic to expect anything resembling ethnological science to be manifest at this time—as we have seen when discussing how ethnographic enquiry has been both conceived and constructed by Classical scholarship.

The extent to which ethnographic tropes become effectively static or systematized is likewise open to question. While a number of stereotypes

---

[20] Corneille and Yzerbyt 2002.
[21] *Od.* XV 415–416. Cf. *Od.* XIV 287–289ff. Somewhat qualified by reference elsewhere to the Φοίνικας ἀγαυοὺς (XIII 272). See, in particular, Winter 1995 and chapter 2 for further discussion.
[22] Hall 1989, 41.

might exist regarding a particular group or polity, which one is used and when it is used will (in all likelihood) vary according to the context. Their formation should ultimately be conceived as occurring on an ad hoc basis: a process in which groups or individuals selectively affirm, deny, or gloss over a variety of known qualities and stock attributes associated with a specific category of foreigner.[23] Certain elements did achieve a degree of fixity in the case of written prose, but it should nevertheless be remembered that prose accounts form only one component of wider discourses of identity and difference. Stereotypes existed as a pool of knowledge into which one could dip as and when required. Just as a recent study of the Greek polis has posed the question as to how prejudices and stereotypes played out in multiethnic communities such as that at Piraeus, where archaeological and epigraphic evidence attest to individuals of different outlook and culture living side by side,[24] we need to factor stereotypes into our model of the overarching discourses of identity and difference that played out on quayside and harbor wall, dimly lit warehouses and sun-drenched streets, choked with traffic and filth.

Evidence for pejorative stereotypes regarding stupid or boring neighbors or rivals can be found in bountiful supply far beyond the confines of epic. They are, moreover, virtually indistinguishable from those relating to generic barbarians.[25] Epithets referring to generic characteristics of a particular place and people are evoked: "Sheep-rearing Asia"[26] or, in an echo, one assumes, of Homer, a reference to "top-knotted Thracians" at Salmydessus.[27] Elsewhere, the habitual use of Phrygian names when referring to pipers or slaves is interpreted as suggesting a well-established ethnic stereotype.[28] Generic references to Phrygian "foreigners" that occur in conjunction with remarks concerning slaves have, in at least one instance, been translated using the denigratory term "Wogs."[29] Reference

---

[23] Spears 2002, 127.

[24] Vlassopoulos 2007b.

[25] Demodocus Fr. 2: "The Chians are base, not just one and another not, but all except Procles— and Procles is a Chian" (Χῖοι κακοί, οὐχ ὁ μέν, ὅς δ᾽ οὔ, πάντες, πλὴν Προκλέους· καὶ Προκλέης δὲ Χίος). Cf. ibid. Fr. 1 on Milesians. A joke may perhaps be construed in referring to Heracleia as being in the land of the Cylicranians (Hermippus Fr. 4). For further discussion and references relating to Greek stereotypes, see Nielsen 2007, 7–8.

[26] Archilochus Fr. 227.

[27] Hipponax Fr. 115 (cursing an errant friend). The peculiarity of Thracian haircuts has been cited as a possible cause for comments made by Anacreon regarding the Thracian boy Smerdies (Anac. Fr. 347). Hutchinson 2001, 264–265. Cf. Theocritus 14.46; Il. IV 533. Allusions to a woman in Anacreon Fr. 347 are thought to refer to the personification of Thrace itself! (Hutchinson 2001, 270 Cf. Aesch. Pers. 181).

[28] E.g., Hipponax Fr. 118e.

[29] Hipponax Fr. 27 (trans. West).

to those of "Solecian speech" is equally linked to the use of the term "barbarian."[30] Such inferences are not altogether unproblematic, however, as we also see instances where supposed barbarians are represented as the pinnacle of refinement and taste; Alcman draws on popular conceptions contrasting a laughable country bumpkin (from Thessaly) with an urban sophisticate from Sardis:

He was no yokel,
No fool even among experts;
Not of Thessalian stock,
No shepherd from Nether Wallop
But from the centre of Sardis.

οὐκ ἦς ἀνὴρ ἀγρεῖος οὐ
δὲ σκαιὸς οὐδὲ παρὰ σοφοῖ
σιν οὐδὲ Θεσσαλὸς γένος,
Ἐρυσιχαῖος οὐδὲ ποιμήν,
ἀλλὰ Σαρδίων ἀπ᾽ ἀκρᾶν.[31]

Evidence for decidedly ethnocentric attitudes toward foreign customs and cultures can at times be found; Phocylides declares that "a small orderly city on a height is superior to foolish Nineveh,"[32] while *Isthmian* 6 states: "there is no city so alien or of such backward speech."[33] There is some ambiguity, however, as to whether such passages should automatically be understood to reflect a clear distinction between Greeks and non-Greeks. Nineveh was proverbially big—taking even the hardiest Old Testament prophets three days to cross (presumably fairly robust characters)—so it may be overly simplistic to cite such sentiments as being indicative of an all-encompassing contempt for "Asian cultures."[34] Granted, it is unlikely that the term βάρβαρος would be applied to a Greek community without carrying overwhelmingly negative connotations; but,

---

[30] For Soloeci see: Hipponax Fr. 27 cf. Anacreon Fr. 423 + S 313. Cf. Strab. XIV 2.28 on origins and Herodotus's use of σολοικίζειν ("to solecize") (IV 117) to describe the manner in which the Sauromatae garble their Scythian. For other servile stereotypes: prayers to Malis (Lydian goddess identified with Athena) uttered by a slave praying his master won't beat him (Hipponax Fr. 40).

[31] Alcm. Fr. 16 (trans. West).

[32] Phocylides Fr. 8 West.

[33] Pind. *Isthm.* 6. 24. The allusion to a linguistic community, in this case, is striking, there being a clear distinction made between the known/familiar and that which is other.

[34] See recently: Mitchell 2007, 20–21. The emphasis on "smallness" and orderly layout has inevitably attracted comment from those working on the history of the early polis/Hippodamian planning. See Shipley 2005.

on the other hand, numerous supposedly "Greek" populations—Epirotes, Aetolians, and Macedonians—were notorious for their uncouth dialect.[35] That Pindar can hark back to a time when Boeotians were referred to as "pigs" is similarly indicative of the extent to which lyric poetry is effectively riddled with material testifying to a clear perception of "difference" *within* the bounds of Hellas.[36]

One matter that might usefully be clarified is whether stereotypes should ever be considered as "just" literary *topoi*. The question was raised by Bohak in a rare (and recent) study of ancient stereotyping. Bohak's emphasis upon stereotypes as historically situated social facts, affecting the relationships between different social groups, is both useful and incisive.[37] It is doubtful, however, whether such arguments can be made to stand without acknowledging the politics underlying such representations. While it is of course entirely correct that some stereotypes became staple fare for ancient writers and audiences, this does not necessarily imply that they were in any way defused ideologically.[38] The ubiquity of epithets and stereotypes in the ancient sources points to both underlying knowledge regarding the habits and customs of "foreign" peoples—variously defined depending on the context—and the use of such knowledge as a means of constructing group identities. Being part of a group meant constructing an identity based upon knowledge of "others." An Athenian citizen would know that if you drank like a Scythian you would regret it the following morning;[39] that Laconian girls show their thighs;[40] that "Carian" and "mercenary" were virtually synonymous;[41] that Arcadians ate acorns; that Libyans rode camels; and that Amazons bore bows, ate raw flesh, and deferred to no man.[42] Passing references to such "facts" demonstrates that they were something understood. In cases where there were a number of stereotypes concerning one particular group, the resulting montage might be termed an "ethnic portrait."[43] It is open to question, however, as to whether there is any real difference between this phenomenon and the systematic science that Edith Hall associates with the fifth century B.C.[44]

---

[35] Malkin 2001a; Hall 2001; Sourvinou-Inwood 2002.

[36] Pind. Fr. 83.

[37] Bohak 2005, 209; cf. Dench 1995.

[38] Said 1978; 1993.

[39] See chapter 2.

[40] Ibyc. Fr. 339 cf. Anac. Fr. 399.

[41] For stereotypes linking Carians with mercenary service, see Archil. Fr. 216: "and what's more I shall be called an auxiliary like a Carian" (καὶ δὴ 'πίκουρος ὥστε Κὰρ κεκλήσομαι). Reference is also made to a Carian-made shield grip (Anac. Fr. 401). For mercenary service in Babylon and Ascalon, see Alc. Fr. 48, 350. For invaluable discussion andreferences, see Raaflaub 2004, 206–210. For Carians at Naucratis see Williams and Villing 2006b.

[42] Aesch. *Supp.* 287–289; Hdt. I 66.

[43] Bohak 2005.

[44] Hall 1989, 40–41.

Emma Dench has adopted a different line of argument altogether, casting doubt on whether ethnographical discourse can be explained solely in terms of "internal" factors:

> While, at times, under certain conditions, Greek and Roman images of Italian peoples tend towards non-specific generalizations, on the whole this discourse is characterised by considerable attention to detail. Certainly, detail is selected out and framed according to persisting patterns of "ways of seeing," but these images by and large do not give the impression of being purely the products of Greek and Roman imaginations.[45]

Emphasizing the inherent complexities associated with the processes of stereotyping, Dench advocates studying the material record in order to illuminate what Greeks and Romans failed to see and therefore the processes of perception that governed or dictated what they in turn wanted to see.[46]

The use of epithets and stereotyping was ultimately constitutive, then, of identities. A form of social knowledge, they are best conceived as mobile, discursive systems of understanding that people carried in their heads. Stereotypes could find voice in a variety of contexts: the agora, theater, or symposium. That they affected individual perception and were an important factor in defining both individual and group identities is important; that we might find their ubiquity unsettling or distasteful is not.

3.2 Listing and Imagining

One of the most obvious ways in which this plethora of information might be both organized and communicated is via the construction and recital of lists.[47] List songs and catalogues formed an important part of early hexameter poetry—a predominantly oral tradition whose survival has in many cases been dependent upon its being incorporated into epic verse.[48] Those

---

[45] Dench 1995, 22.

[46] Ibid., 23.

[47] Goody 1977 discusses the impact of a shift "from utterance to text" (75) on systems of thought and classificatory schemas, disputing the argument that lists are ever "natural" (108ff.) (contra Minchin 1996 et al. on oral societies). On the practical benefits of listing, Goody states that it "increases the visibility and definition of classes, makes it easier for the individual to engage in chunking, and more particularly in the hierarchical ordering of information which is critical to recall" (111).

[48] The *Iliad* contains a variety of material that might plausibly represent preexisting catalogue poetry—sometimes referred to as the Little Catalogues of the *Iliad*. These include the list of the Greek army in the battle with Hector (*Il.* XIII 685ff.), the seven towns offered by Agamemnon to Achilles (*Il.* IX 150ff., 292ff.), as well as a number of tales to which hints are made that might have included catalogues: the Seven against Thebes (*Il.* IV 376ff.), those who assembled to hunt the Calydonian Boar (*Il.* IX 527ff. esp. 544–545), and *Iliad* III. 161ff. concerning Helen's suitors. Cf. Cingano 2005 on Hes. frr. 196–204.

found in Homeric epic characteristically enumerate aspects of regional geography—usually in the form of epithets, demographic groupings, and the genealogies of local heroes—systematically arranged according to geographical location, albeit often as an aid to memory.[49] It would be all too easy to underestimate the importance of this genre in the history of early ethnographic thought: surviving only in fragments, amended in places, and at times the victim of modern conceptions of lists as "boring" or unimaginative. In contrast, when performed before an assembled audience they played a significant role in wider discourses of identity and difference, not least because they brought pleasure to their listeners, inspiring wonder and delight; they were objects, in other words, of consumption.[50] Lists also function as important mechanisms of signification—representations—whose ability to segment, order, condense, and transform places, events, groups, or individuals carries a potency far beyond that of simple utterance.[51]

Works such as the *Catalogue of Ships* in book two of the *Iliad* achieve a new dimension when recited aloud from memory.[52] (It might even be argued that they were didactic in nature.) The audience would be an active participant in this process, following the poet in their mind's eye as he recited the list of warriors and war bands. For some these would be words learned by heart with the result that any major slip-up or omission on behalf of the bard would immediately be noted. For others it would be new or at least unfamiliar: a catalogue of far-off or familiar places, collected together as an ordered whole. The fact that individual contingents could presumably have been included or omitted (either intentionally or due to a slip of memory) would have created the potential for alternative or competing versions whose veracity might be disputed or gainsaid in a manner similar to that found in Presocratic debate.[53] To what extent, however, was the very *act* of describing the various participants according to their points of origin

---

[49] For discussion see: Minchin 1996, 11–13.

[50] For the pleasure of listening: *Il.* VII 127–128 cf. Ap. Rhod. *Argon.* 2. 762–772.

[51] Goody 1977, 110 and passim. I do not, however, agree with the overarching thesis that writing, and with it literacy alone, would have prompted speculation of a sort that made it almost inevitable that classificatory systems would grow ever more complex. The latter is too closely linked with attempts to rationalize the emergence of early philosophical enquiry: G. E. R. Lloyd's *Polarity and Analogy* (1966) is cited by Goody at 102.

[52] For the catalogue in general, see Mommsen 1850; Allen 1910, 1912; Austin 1965; Giovannini 1969; Hope Simpson, and Lazenby 1970; Nachtergael 1975; Visser 1997. For discussion of historical traditions relating to the Heroic Age and early Archaic Greece, see Finkelberg 2005.

[53] Graziosi 2002. Catherine Osborne (1987; 2006) has challenged the notion that Presocratic philosophers were engaged in a model philosophical dialogue of argument/counterargument of the sort championed by Parmenides, arguing instead that philosophical inquiry could take a variety of forms: "To suggest that our favourite philosophers offer revisionary systems, not counter argument, is not, after all, to say that they merely talk past each other in a wilderness

actually constitutive of a shared sense of group identity, a form of "performance ethnography"?[54]

Listing or citing far-flung places could serve any number of purposes. Charting the geographic boundaries of the known world by reciting a list of places conceived of as being "at the furthest reaches" can serve to emphasize the fame of the individual concerned.[55] Such boundaries are conceived to be coterminous with the limits of human achievement:

> . . . truly has Theron now reached the furthest point
>   with his achievements and
>   from his home grasps the pillars
>   of Herakles. What lies beyond neither wise men
>   nor fools can tread. . . .[56]

As well as the functional attributes of such "geographic metaphors"—glorifying the achievements of, in this case, Theron of Acragas—these operate as a structuring device, framing the mythic narrative.[57] Through such poems we gain a clear picture of a world consisting of three continents: Europe, "broad Asia," and Africa, surrounded by Oceanus.[58] The lands adjoining these boundaries are populated by a mixture of mythic and semimythical beings, providing the setting for tales such as Taygeta's pursuit.[59] These communities range from—at the farthest extremes—the utopian communities of the Hyperboreans, sacred to Apollo, and semidivine Ethiopians, also associated with the Homeric Memnon, to the paradigmatic inversion of Greek norms and values that was the Amazon polity.[60] Such regions are predominantly visited by gods and heroes—Apollo and Herakles being just two examples—with mythic and "real" geographies being in many cases conflated.[61] The limits of

---

where no one listens and no one hears. It is to say that they listen and they respond; but . . . in a style that recent analytic philosophers have found it hard to hear or understand" (C. Osborne 2006, 245). For the role of nineteenth- and early-twentieth-century conceptions of scientific enquiry, see chapter 1.

[54] Cf. other instances of catalogue poetry: *The Hunters of the Boar* (Stes. Fr. 222)

[55] Direct reference to more far-flung locations seem also on occasion to resemble proverbs: with reference to Karthaia on Keos, "I will (not) trade it for Babylon of plains" (*Pae.* 4. Fr. 52d). How much knowledge this implies concerning Babylon or even Karthaia (notably devoid of plains) is uncertain.

[56] Pind. *Ol.* 3. 43–45. Cf. *Pyth.* 10. 27–30; *Nem.* 4. 69; *Isthm.* 4. 14; 41–42; 6. 23 and *Isthm.* 2. 41–42 on bounds of generosity.

[57] Kurke 1991, 53.

[58] Pind. *Ol.* 7. 18; *Pyth.* 9. 6–9.

[59] Pind. *Ol.* 3. 25–32.

[60] Memnon: *Pyth.* 6. 31; *Nem.* 3. 61–63; 6. 49; *Isthm.* 5. 40–41; 8. 54. For Amazons, see: *Ol.* 8. 47; 13. 87; *Nem.* 3.38; Fr. 172.

[61] Pind. *Ol.* 8. 46–48; 3. 14ff. The upper Danube region or Istrian land, referred to elsewhere as the "shady springs of Ister," is also the land of the Hyperboreans (*Ol.* 3. 14; 26; *Pyth.* 10. 30–34).

the known world are effectively delineated in an ode honoring Aristokleidas of Aigina recounting the epic journey of the Argonauts across the Inhospitable Sea[62] to "the dark-faced Kolchians" at the mouth of the Phasis, traversing Oceanus and the Red Sea, overland to Libya, the Mediterranean shore, and then home to Iolkos.[63]

The mapping and cataloguing of foreign places and peoples by means of recited lists has much in common therefore with the so-called periegetic accounts that formed some of the earliest prose-writing. The listing of itineraries had an obvious practical function but the politics and poetics of such exercises need also to be borne in mind. The *Homeric Hymn to Apollo* appears to be arranged in order to chart the places where the god received a cult, in much the same way as odes composed by authors such as Pindar on the Aiakidai.[64] The wider implications of such poetic "voyages" remains open to question; should they be interpreted as over arching charter myths or claims to cultural preeminence?[65] Some would, no doubt, have possessed a particular resonance in the immediate aftermath of the Persian Wars in commemorating the heroes who fought at Troy. It follows therefore that while it may be difficult to gauge the full import of the allusions made, we can be more than certain that, in Kurke's words: "the poet's imagery was culturally grounded and meaningful to his audience. . . systematically deployed in service of the poetic program."[66] Lists functioned as systems of understanding and while they might bear little resemblance to later prose traditions, from a functional point of view there is very little to choose between them. Although on occasions restrained, Herodotus's unabashed appetite for listing and itineraries is abundantly clear.

The practice of reciting list songs and catalogues replete with epithets is closely linked to the construction of genealogies. An effective means of organizing notions of people and place, these often provided the basis for some of the earliest catalogue poetry. There is considerable evidence that genealogy functioned as an important heuristic tool for conceptualizing identities throughout the ancient Mediterranean (and beyond).[67] Hellenic genealogy—including

---

[62] Pind. *Nem.* 4. 203.

[63] Pind. *Nem.* 4. 13. Cf. Fr. 172.

[64] Cf. *Nem.* 10. 4–18 on Argive heroes with the six strophes that make up the core of the *Nemean* 4 amounting to a catalogue of the Aiakidai and the lands in which they receive hero's honors (Kurke 1991, 51; Willcock 1995). Other catalogues focus notably on the Aiakidai: *Ol.* 8, *Pyth.* 8, *Nem.* 3–8, *Isthm.* 5, 6, 8. For the relationship between catalogue poetry and epinicia, see d'Alessio 2005.

[65] For "inventions" cf. *Ol.* 13. 17–23; 65: dithyramb and bridle/bit.

[66] Kurke 1991, 11.

[67] The role played by genealogy in the Old Testament is particularly notable. See: Gen. 5; 9.18; 10 (The Table of Nations). For related discussion, see Gruen 2011a; J. Scott 2010; Romm 2010, 228ff.

the Hesiodic *Catalogue of Women*—has recently been singled out as the basis for defining Greek ethnicity with fictive kinship taking preference over physical traits, religion, language, or cultural orientation.[68] To what extent is this view valid, however, and can anything further be said regarding the role of genealogy in the ancient Mediterranean? While the various problems arising from Jonathan Hall's—perhaps overly schematic—treatment of archaic Greek identity have already been recounted, it might also be suggested that genealogies were equally effective as a means of conceptualizing *difference*[69] and could just as easily be invoked when relating conflict between "kin."[70]

It is not merely Hellenic genealogy alone that has attracted scholarly attention in recent years, however. The manifest utility of genealogy as a means of defining identities made it an obvious choice, it is argued, when describing indigenous populations. Following a line of argument first laid down by Elias Bickerman in a classic article of 1952, Irad Malkin has demonstrated that mythic figures such as Odysseus and other "returning heroes" (*Nostoi*) were employed to mediate encounters with non-Greek others and conceptualize identity/ethnicity in the Archaic and Classical periods.[71] A notable characteristic of "Nostos genealogical ethnography" as identified by Malkin is that it was normally applied to peoples living at one remove from those with whom Greek traders and colonists habitually came into contact. Odysseus figures prominently in such narratives as the archetypal "returning hero," particularly linked with the wild and unknown and therefore typical of the "Greek ethnographic model for regarding and defining Others: heroic genealogy," linked in this case to the Euboian colonies of Pithekoussai and Kyme.[72]

These mythic articulations functioned as a means of collective representation, adopted in some cases by the native populations themselves. However,

---

[68] J. Hall 1997, 2002. For the social/political dynamics of the catalogue, see Irwin 2005a.

[69] The oppositional nature of these practices becomes clear when one examines the contexts in which genealogies are recited in Homeric epic—often when two heroes meet, they exchange greetings and recite their lineage to their opponent as either a prelude to conflict or reconciliation.

[70] Cf. Aeolian Smyrna (Mimnermus Fr. 9). Although to some extent obvious, the latter reflects an uncomfortable truth for anyone attempting to narrate the means by which a coherent sense of Greek identity emerged: kinship and genealogies are not necessarily a force for unity and are just as capable of acting as a means of defining difference.

[71] Malkin 1998a.

[72] *Theogony* 1011–18; Malkin 1998a, 160. Odysseus is identified as progenitor of those ruling the Tyrsenoi (Etruscans) siring two sons: Latinos and Agrios, an association further supported by the fact that the Etruscan Utuse is in fact a transliteration from Euboian dialect. Such eponyms are supposedly characteristic "of a maritime perspective (sea to shore)" (Malkin 1998a, 178). Cf. Erskine 2005; Dench 1995, 36. The *Nostoi* were also suitable for explaining migrations—unlike what is termed migration ethnography and distinct from "other kinds of Grecocentric ethnographies" that either sought to retrospectively assimilate foreigners to migratory Arcadians or the like, or the practice entertained by later Greek cities of creating their own *nostos* associations (Malkin 1998a, 179).

the *Nostoi*—and by extension the writings tracing them—were not merely cultural representations but representations with a tangible impact upon Greek/non-Greek relations: the myths played an "active role . . . in filtering, shaping and mediating cultural and ethnic encounters."[73] It is here that Bickerman and Malkin differ hugely as, aside from pushing the adoption of Greek myths of origin far back into the archaic period and replacing "scientific authority"[74] with "Homeric epic and its heroes,"[75] Malkin's brand of "New Historicism" opens up avenues of enquiry entirely alien to Bickerman's generation. Questions of agency, however, remain: the scenario is still one in which somewhat dull and unimaginative natives are progressively seduced by the glamour of a (Greek) heroic past. Should we envisage this as a form of "cultural seepage" of the sort associated with Etruria: a one-way process in which Greeks remained impervious to the cultural influence of others?[76]

Andrew Erskine adopts a different (and rather more nuanced approach) to explaining why, in his words, "the transmission of tradition would appear to be in one direction—from Greek to non-Greek."[77] Although critical of the view that Greeks considered themselves at all times and in all places superior to "natives," Erskine identifies the practice of using (Greek) mythology to incorporate "others" into a shared Hellenic past of myths and heroes as being intrinsically Greek:

> Far from excluding, they [the Greeks] used myth to include others. They were willing to share their own heritage and to bring cities like Lycian Xanthos within the community of Greeks. What they were not willing to do, however, was to embrace the past of other peoples, because that would run counter to the very idea of what it was to be Greek.[78]

While it would be inaccurate to say that Erskine fails to acknowledge the power dynamic underpinning decisions to adopt or exclude local mythic traditions from both historiographical accounts and everyday interactions between Greeks and non-Greeks, the impression of disinterested altruism that emerges from this conclusion reflects a highly idealized and altogether

---

[73] Malkin 1998a, 5.

[74] "Under the double impact of Greek power and Greek science, the barbarians, mostly ignorant of their own primitive history, as soon as they had become a bit hellenized, accepted the Greek schema of *archaiologia*" (Bickerman 1952, 73).

[75] Malkin 1998a. Noted explicitly at 176 cf. 29, 170. See also Erskine 2005, 129 and passim; Hall 2002, 104–111; Dench 1995, 35ff.

[76] Malkin 1998a, 170.

[77] Erskine 2005, 121.

[78] Ibid., 134. See now Gruen 2011a.

abstract notion of "Greek community," its interests and concerns.[79] This can, in part, be explained on methodological grounds. Although keen to distance himself from Bickerman and "look beyond historiography" to examine the manner in which Greeks and non-Greeks interacted, Erskine's carefully argued analysis remains primarily literary in focus, rarely encroaching on anything that might reasonably be considered representative of the day-to-day realities of cross-cultural interaction, namely, the material evidence.[80] Any attempt to understand the intricate web of myth and local tradition upon which Greek historians drew for inspiration must, however, include a thorough exploration of the specific local and regional contexts from which they emerged. If we compare Erskine's account to Christiane Sourvinou-Inwood's detailed reconstruction of the manner in which the Hylas myth served to integrate non-Greek elements into Chian polis-ritual, we see glaring differences in approach—although both authors concur that Greek settlers invariably sought to assimilate local indigenous traditions to Greek mythological and ritual schemata.[81] It is only by adopting a synthetic approach, incorporating both textual and archaeological materials, that we will achieve a fully rounded picture of the way in which discourses of identity and difference played out throughout Southern Calabria and further afield.[82]

Two factors should make us wary of the assumption that the transmission of tradition was in all cases a one-way phenomenon—however compelling the evidence may (at first) appear. First, consider the accumulating mass of scholarship demonstrating the degree of receptivity toward Near Eastern ideas and motifs in early epic during the Early Archaic period: How "Greek" were the Greeks, in actual fact, at this point in time?[83] While the diffuse

---

[79] Cf. Kim 2009, 43–44 stressing the Greeks' desire to acknowledge their "debts to the Near East and . . . to be acknowledged as part of that civilized world." For discussion of the extent to which attitudes toward non-Greeks shifted over time, see ibid. but also Dench 1995, 44ff. Similar worries arise in the case of Erich Gruen's recent study highlighting the affirmative and inclusive nature of ancient thought (Gruen 2011a).

[80] Where such discussion does occur it is couched in fairly general terms and from a somewhat Hellenocentric perspective that does little to remedy the marked imbalance between external (Greek) and internal views, e.g., interpreting the increase in the use of imported ceramics as grave goods in South Italy from the late sixth century onward *solely* in terms of an "increasing familiarity with Greek practices and commodities" (Erskine 2005, 123). Cf. Morgan 2009, 14; Antonaccio and Neils 1995 (with reference to Morgantina).

[81] Cf. Sourvinou-Inwood 2005, passim but especially 67–79, 329–345, 365–370. While the end product might be the same—an ostensibly "Greek" myth—the processes that gave rise to it are laid bare: a degree of misogyny combined with chauvinistic ethnocentrism on behalf of the Milesian colonists, who were nonetheless acquainted with (and therefore not completely impermeable to) local Anatolian custom.

[82] When examined in isolation, textual and archaeological materials provoke different sets of questions, different methods and approaches, and different answers.

[83] Cf. Erskine 2005, 150ff.

collection of poems and list songs relating the deeds of gods and heroes must surely have had an equally important role in mediating difference between Greeks, can we indeed separate the two processes in anything like a meaningful fashion, or should we instead view the Iron Age populations of regions such as Sicily and Southern Italy as subscribing to the same values and sharing common interests with their Greek contemporaries, playing a (to some degree) active role in the promulgation of stories relating to the *nostoi*? The mounting evidence for active engagement by Italic peoples in networks of trade and association during the same period should serve to underline the fact that these were not parochial tribesmen but communities who were in many cases at a similar level of social and political development to contemporary "Greeks" and whose elites appear to have been equally at home at the great, so-called Panhellenic sanctuaries such as Delphi and Olympia (see further below).[84] The pan-Mediterranean *koiné* of myths and heroes that emerged may, in the case of Homer, have been "Greek" in origin but to view it as cultural property of Greeks alone is something else entirely.

Other, perhaps less subtle, approaches to colonial genealogies see them as nothing more or less than mythical projections legitimating overseas expansion: acts of representation and appropriation that merely render Asia or the Other "known" to the Greeks.[85] The relationship between myth and colonization is arguably rather more complex, however—quite apart from the potential problems arising from trawling the sources for what is effectively a retrojection of fifth-century perspectives: "the supernatural agent of disorder."[86] Whatever our concerns regarding the wider currency of the *Nostoi* and other mythical figures, their overall importance as mobile discursive operators should not be underestimated.

3.3 Enquiring

Nostos identifications have much in common with the so-called analytical identifications of Hecataeus of Miletus and other mythographers active from the sixth century. In fact, it might reasonably be argued that the interests and enquiries of these individuals formed part of a wider continuum of thought linking Homeric genealogies, the *Nostoi,* and the prose study of the genealogical

---

[84] See below, chapter 4. On syncretism more generally: Malkin 2005; 2011 highlights the mediatory role played by Herakles/Melqart on Sicily. For a similar approach to Homeric heroes, and others, in relation to Lycia, see Gehrke 2005.

[85] "Known" in the Saidian sense of the word and therefore legitimating "the actions of colonisers and express[ing] the spirit of the age" (E. Hall 1989, 48; cf. Dougherty 1993).

[86] E. Hall 1989, 50.

and mythological traditions endemic to Archaic–early Classical Greece. What, however, do we mean by "myth" and what exactly does "mythography" entail? If we set aside wider questions regarding the usefulness (or, indeed, advisability) of subdividing broad-based historiographical enquiries by genre, we are left with huge problems regarding how to define ancient conceptions of myth.[87] This uncertainty, in turn, makes it difficult to point to a genre or mode of enquiry that was concerned exclusively with "myth," as opposed to more wide-ranging concerns that were variously (but by no means exclusively) ethnographic, geographical, or historical in nature.

Modern definitions of myth as "a story in which some of the characters are gods,"[88] or simply a "traditional tale" that carries relevance in the present,[89] often seem rather inadequate, or even banal, when confronted with a diverse (and often inherently contradictory) range of opinions both as to what constituted *mythos* and what the term itself implied.[90] While we should perhaps resign ourselves to the lack of a secure and universally applicable definition of myth, an interest in aetiology, etymology, and "origins" in general is readily apparent throughout the sources. An interest in establishing the origins or "First Finder" ($\pi\rho\hat{\omega}\tau\sigma\varsigma$ $\epsilon\hat{\upsilon}\rho\epsilon\tau\dot{\eta}\varsigma$) of various cults and institutions can be seen in Hecataeus's work and elsewhere, raising inevitable questions as to what, if anything, such interests imply. What does it mean, say, for Democles to pronounce on the Phoenician origins of a specific musical instrument/dirge?[91] The same might also be said of Charon of Lampsacus's note that Phobus was the first to throw himself into the sea from the Leucadian Rocks[92] or Acusilaus's assertion that rites in Samothrace were initiated in honor of the Cabeiri.[93] More general points such as the origins of various mythological races are also discussed, for example, Phaeacians and Giants in Acusilaus.[94] Who wants to know these things and why? The answer must surely go beyond some bookish interest in local history for its own sake.

---

[87] For discussion, see Kirk 1970, chap. 1; 1973; 1974, 13–29; Buxton 1994; Harrison 2000, 196–198, 206–207; Csapo 2005, 1–9.

[88] Northrop Frye cited by Kirk 1970, 10; Harrison 2000a, 197n58. See also Kirk 1974, 27.

[89] See: Bremmer 1987, 1; Burkert 1979a, 23; 1979b, 1–34. Kowalzig 2007 follows Burkert's conception of myth where aetiologies are concerned: "Aetiology creates a religious world that is tied to visible localities and lived local customs. It is always engrained in the physical world, linked with the tangible reality of cults and rituals, shrines and objects of cult. . . . [It] . . . has a share in everyday religious practice; and it creates social explanations of items in use by a community of myth-tellers" (25). For examples of the more traditional view of aetiology as a form of primitive scientific explanation, see works cited at Kowalzig 2007, 25n44.

[90] See T. Harrison 2000, chaps. 6 and 7 for discussion.

[91] *FGrHist* 2, F 20; cf. Xanthos on Torrhebus and Torrhebian melodies: *FGrHist* 765 F 1.

[92] *FGrHist* 262 F 7a.

[93] *FGrHist* 2 F 20. For discussion of "firsts" in Herodotus, see Harrison 2000a, chap. 7.

[94] *FGrHist* 2 F 4, 35.

Pearson's (brief) summation of Charon's work contains a number of comments and assumptions that provide much food for thought in this respect. The comments are, in part, a reaction to Müller's suggestion that Charon, like Hellanicus, wrote a *Ktiseis* dealing with the founding of cities. Well aware of the problems of attributing fragments to a particular work, Pearson declares the matter to be open-ended, adding:

> The interest of these legends is that they are of a particular romantic variety that appealed to Alexandrian taste, not in the Homeric nor precisely in the Hesiodic tradition. The occurrence of both of them in the work of Charon is also interesting as suggesting that he liked to present parallel legends and for that reason might be classed as an elementary student of folk-lore.[95]

The observation that such authors appear to draw upon traditions that are in many ways a departure from both Homeric and Hesiodic traditions is significant: a plethora of myths and aetiologies that were explicitly local in origin. Their "romantic nature" finds obvious parallels, moreover, in the charter myths of cities such as Cyrene and the poleis of Magna Graecia. It has already been mentioned that stories concerning the seduction or rape of hapless nymphs are widely interpreted as presenting a mythical analogue for power relationships between indigenous populations and Greek colonists (see above). Colonial or charter myths have been variously interpreted as forms of early ethnography, evoking a sense of place and people.[96] The study of these myths arguably demonstrates an interest in foundations, identity, and origins—but the two are rarely considered side by side. Instead, many have followed the traditional approach of viewing Charon and his contemporaries very much in terms of a developmental framework:

> His fragments, such as they are, suggest that his method resembled that of Herodotus . . . they exhibit . . . a love of digression . . . , a taste for the curious tale and aetiology, combined with a desire to write serious history.[97]

---

[95] Pearson 1939, 150.

[96] Dougherty 1993; Malkin 1998a. Cf. on colonial myth: Pherekydes of Athens on the population of Ionia prior to Ionian colonization under Androclus, founder of Ephesus (*FGrHist* 3 F 155). On Cyzicus: the expulsion of the Pelasgian Doliones (*FGrHist* 471 F 8a). On Lampsacus/Lampsace Charon (*FGrHist* 262 F 7a, b) and on its prior inhabitants the Bebryces (*FGrHist* 262 F 8). Foundation myths that invoke elements of topography and landscape: nymphs, river gods, etc. feature prominently in areas such as S. Italy and Sicily. Documenting these was common practice among praise poets seeking to eulogize a victor's hometown. How different are they from traditional explanations of origins—e.g., the Spartoi and Thebes? (See above, chapter 2.) There was clearly a widespread desire to describe and unify disparate place in accounts of heroes' wanderings—within the realms of the imagination (Herakles, Jason); cf. Deiochus *FGrHist* 471 F 2,4 on the Argonauts. For further discussion of the relationship between foundation myths and ethnicity, see Sourvinou-Inwood 2005.

[97] Pearson 1939, 150. For the origins of these views, see chapter 1.

Leaving both Herodotus and "serious history" aside, the love of curious tales and aetiologies—and particularly "digressions"—are surely reminiscent of "ethnography" as conventionally defined; it's just, as it were, that the subject matter is all wrong.

If one were looking for an author whose work reflected ethnographic concerns, Charon of Lampsacus would certainly be a good starting point. The traits that would (under other circumstances) have earned him the title of "mythographer," including parallel tales and so forth, suggests that Charon was indeed aware of variant traditions. The tale concerning Arcas and the hamadryad nymph provides an aetiological myth for the Arcadians (with the requisite oak trees in attendance) and could easily be read as an account explaining the origins of Arcadia and Arcadians rather than as a piece of romantic whimsy that served no other purpose than to delight both its audience and subsequent generations of Alexandrian scholars.[98] The role of such "invented traditions" in both providing a focus for and, simultaneously, constructing identities was perhaps sufficiently evident to merit the research of individuals such as Charon and Hellanicus.

An interest in origins per se may suggest that such tales figured prominently in everyday discourse and that they were reported for a reason. Explaining the link between people and place was obviously important. This might not constitute "ethnography" as we understand it but if it served a similar function to contemporaries then this is surely what mattered. Even if some of the material we possess is pure speculation on behalf of the authors as opposed to genuine local traditions, they are nonetheless the product of the same intellectual milieu, the same desire to investigate and explain difference. Nor are these purely abstract constructs. Such claims would have either arisen from or be supported by cults, statues, and so forth upon which such tales could be pinned.[99] How do these stories relate to identities, however? Where do they come from and in what contexts were they rehearsed? Given the fact that distinguishing between mythic and historical pasts was little more than a rhetorical strategy for early writers (who seem equally unclear as to how myth should be defined), attempting to separate rational or "scientific" ethnography from genres such as "mythography" is unlikely to produce anything other than a false dichotomy. Stuart Hall's description of identities as "the names we give to the different ways we are positioned by, and position ourselves within the narratives of the past"[100] might encourage

---

[98] *FGrHist* 262 F 12b.

[99] The manner in which tales told about the past—invented traditions—could form the basis of a shared sense of identity is now widely acknowledged. See Hobsbawm & Ranger 1983; Gehrke 2001; and Flower 2002 (Sparta).

[100] S. Hall 1990, 225. For the significance of names in particular, see Fraser 2009.

the suggestion that an interest in aetiologies, myths, and fables of the sort that Hecataeus and Pherekydes are studying would have acted as a mechanism for understanding both local identities—and could in other words be considered as signs of an ethnographic interest—and the past.[101]

3.4 Celebrating Place and People

3.4.1 Epinicia

Widely received and commissioned at great expense, epinician poetry was a genre whose chief purpose was to celebrate "place" and people: the *laudandus*, his *oikos*, and the polity from which they originated. While the composition of epinicia can be traced back as far as Ibycus of Rhegion in the sixth century B.C., the surviving remnants of this most ephemeral of art forms are likely to represent only the very tip of the iceberg when it comes to the number of epinicia in circulation at any one time—even in the case of celebrated individuals such as Pindar.[102] While it would be far too simplistic to describe these as ethnography per se, there were occasions on which these had recourse to "foreign" manners and customs. A notable example occurs in *Isthmian* 5 when Pindar describes Theban festivals and cult in the light of those performed at Argos, Sparta, and Aegina before an Aeginetan audience:

> ἐν μὲν Αἰτωλῶν θυσίαισι φαενναῖς
> Οἰνεΐδαι κρατεροί,
> ἐν δὲ Θήβαις ἱπποσόας Ἰόλαος
> γέρας ἔχει, Περσεὺς δ᾽ ἐν Ἄργει, Κάστορος δ᾽ αἰχ—
> μὰ Πολυδεύκεός τ᾽ ἐπ᾽ Εὐρώτα ῥεέθροις.
> ἀλλ᾽ ἐν Οἰνώνα μεγαλήτορες ὀργαί
> Αἰακοῦ παίδων τε. . . .

---

[101] Barbara Kowalzig has argued that enquiries into matters such as the origins of cults and rituals arguably played an important role in explaining difference: "Aetiology is the narrated form of diversity in Greek religion. In accounting for diversity, giving an identity to a place and a community of myth-tellers, lies aetiology's greatest potential for acting as a tale of social relevance" (Kowalzig 2007, 25). As such, it could arguably be viewed as reflecting ethnographic interests: a mechanism for understanding people, place, and any associated peculiarities or customs that either might possess. Cf. Hecataeus on "Mycenae" and "Oineus" (*FGrHist* 1 F 22, 15); Pherekydes on "Teos" (*FGrHist* 3 F 102); Ion of Chios on "Chios" (*FGrHist* 392 F 1). See Fowler 1996; Woodbury 1980; Risch 1947. Can one reasonably distinguish between etymology as a scientific method and popular etymology: Fowler 1996, 72n77; Immerwahr 1966; Kowalzig 2007, 26 take an alternative approach in arguing that aetiology abolishes history by denying change through time.

[102] Hornblower and Morgan 2007a, 1. For the circumstances surrounding performance/reperformance of Pindaric odes, see Currie 2005, 16–18; Carey 2007.

In the splendid sacrifices of the Aitolians
the mighty sons of Oineus have their honour
while in Thebes it is the horse-driving Iolaos;
it is Perseus in Argos, and the spearmen Kastor and
Polydeukes by the streams of the Eurotas;
but in Oinona it is the great-hearted spirits
of Aiakos and his sons. . . .[103]

Elsewhere, Theban cult, myths of origin (Σπαρτοί), and cult buildings are all variously alluded to, although the poet appears to refrain from direct comment on forms of government or constitution.[104] Stray references and allusions scattered throughout the rest of the corpus indicate that a wider knowledge of Amazons, the Euxine, and Ethiopians was in many cases assumed (see chapter 2 for discussion).

Moreover, it has recently been noted that the "implied opposition between *oikeion* and *allotrion*, what is one's own as opposed to what is foreign, [is] frequent and important in Pindar generally."[105] This is significant if we recall the fragmentary paean cited at the beginning of this study: Pindar's apparently relativist stance that implies knowledge of the variability of human custom. In sum, there appears to be very little separating ethnographer and poet; that Herodotus should draw upon an epinician authority suggests that the boundaries separating logographer and composer of praise poetry were entirely permeable and that the processes of mutual scrutiny and comparison were in fact endemic. Epinicia provided a vehicle for such comparisons, at times placing little-known local deities center stage, such as Theia of many names, Mother of the Sun,[106] at others evoking local landscapes and imagery—a theme to which we shall return below in our discussion of coinage.

Although it is easy in hindsight to adopt a totalizing perspective that views Greek culture as a homogenous entity, reflecting identity constructs that are essentially bipolar in nature,[107] it is worth considering whether poems such

---

[103] Pind. *Isthm.* 5, 30–35, trans. Race.

[104] *Ol.* 7, 13 (Thebes); *Pyth.* 9. 82; *Isthm.* 1. 30, 7. 10; Fr. 29 (Sparta); *Nem.* 4 (cult buildings). Hornblower and Morgan 2007a, 5, 39.

[105] Hornblower 2004, 117. Some care is indeed required with regards to the notion of shared cultural values if one reflects upon the conceptual permutations of the term ξένος, used throughout the odes to denote "foreigners." The ubiquity of the latter raises questions as to the role of the implied opposition between *oikeion* and *allotrion*. See: *Ol.* 8. 29; 9. 67; *Isthm.* 6. 70 passim. cf. Zeus Xenios: *Ol.* 8. 21; *Nem.* 11. 8 cf. *Ol.* 10. 14 for strictness at Locri. The spatial characteristics of epinician poetry and the manner in which it's structured around the oikos and an attendant theme of homecoming have been greatly elucidated by those such as Kurke 1991.

[106] Pind. *Isthm.* 5, 1. For epinkia as a window on individual/collective identities, see now Hornblower 2008.

[107] References to the curve-bowed Medes (Persia), Carthaginians, and Etruscans are fairly transparent allusions to contemporary politics: *Pyth.* 1. 72; 75–79; *Nem.* 9. 28; *Isthm.*5. 49 cf. *Paean* 2. 59–70 for campaigns against the Paionians in Thrace.

as Pindar's could not also function in more general terms as a means of storing and organizing information regarding the *nomoi* of different categories of others, some foreign—but many less so, encompassing communities both far removed and close at hand; their cults, myths of origin, and topographical setting—historically grounded and spatially located within a wider *oikoumenē*. The shifting frames of reference and heightened sensitivity to questions of identity and difference make epinicia a highly appropriate medium for self-conscious reflection: a mechanism for thinking about people and place. While the sense of a cacophony of competing voices is to some extent lost, both the esteem in which such works were held and the enthusiasm with which they were consumed remain readily apparent.

3.4.2 Greek Coinage and its Reception

If ethnographic discourse is to be understood as an exchange of ideas and information, then the production and use of coinage demands our attention. While the narrative potential of an image stamped upon a small disk of precious metal might seem paltry when compared to that of sculpture or vase painting, let alone texts, they were nonetheless commissioned and executed with a specific purpose in mind: to "speak" to the user and tell stories about people and place.[108] These stories ranged from allusions to a foundation myth, or some other "historical" event, to elements of local flora, fauna, and topography, an eclecticism of subject matter matched only by early Greek prose.[109] The "static image" on a coin can rarely, as a result, be entirely divorced from popular or narrative traditions, whether by providing some sort of aetiological explanation or a more prosaic reference to local cult. Representations of river gods and nymphs are not uncommon, together with devices symbolic of agricultural or mineral wealth—often in conjunction with a genitive ethnic identifying the people or polis on whose behalf it was struck.[110] As such, they provide an effective basis not only for shaping a collective perception of the (civic) self, but also the manner in which it might be

---

[108] See Skinner 2010; for discussion. For a survey of approaches to narrative in Greek art, see Stansbury O'Donnell 1999: "Structurally and mechanically it is possible for the visual arts to present stories. Understanding how an ancient viewer might have participated and understood a pictorial narrative, however, is a difficult task" (9).

[109] Cf. Murray 2000, 330.

[110] The possessive element of the genitive ethnic ("of the [. . .] people/polis") anticipates the possibility that people who needed some reminder of this fact might also view the coin. Butcher draws attention to the use of genitive ethnics as a means of marking out different communities as well as more technical differences such as the size and shape of flan, generating "a feeling of distinction among the users" (Butcher 2005, 145). For further discussion of coinage and identity, see Nielsen 2007, 67; Osborne 1998, 117. For ethnics on coins, see Fraser 2009, 69ff. and Appendix 2.

read or understood by *others*.[111] Exploring the manner in which coins were read, "received," and understood can therefore deepen our understanding of an important—yet frequently overlooked—mechanism for transmitting knowledge and ideas of an "ethnographic" nature beyond the confines of the communities of whom they were emblematic.[112]

While validation of a coin depends primarily upon its matching those already in circulation (that is, possessing a particular legend, motif, or weight), the imagery itself often alluded to common elements of experience that served as a basis for some wider form of "collective identity." Although the early electrum coinages of Ionia display a bewildering diversity of types, a fact that often renders it exceptionally difficult to ascertain their point of origin,[113] coins from cities such as Cyzicus consistently incorporated images of a tunny fish (Cyzicus) in their design.[114] The regularity with which these were employed seems to indicate that they functioned as a form of civic "badge," since they even appear on fractional issues.[115] In the case of Cyzicus, fractions of the electrum stater depict the distinctive tail of the tunny or, alternately, one or more fish heads,[116] with an entire fish featuring prominently on larger denominations. This can reasonably be interpreted as a reference to the annual migration of tuna shoals from the Black Sea into the Mediterranean—an important (and potentially highly lucrative) event for communities inhabiting the coastal littoral that presumably resulted both in a dramatic upsurge in fishing activity and a noticeable shift in dietary patterns as the widely sought-after fish became readily available.[117]

---

[111] For the relationship between aetiological myth, ritual, and the creation of imagined pasts and identities see Kowalzig 2000, 2007.

[112] While the extent to which coinage came to be embedded in social relations within the polis has received considerable attention, consideration of its external impact has been hampered by uncertainty regarding wider patterns of monetary circulation. For the argument that coins functioned unambiguously as symbols of identity, achieving widespread circulation—albeit according to regional patterns of trade and association—see Skinner 2010. It should also be noted that of the 1,035 poleis catalogued by Hansen et al., only 444 are currently known to have possessed mints—of which only a hundred or so are known to have been in operation by 480 B.C. (Hansen and Nielsen 2004, 148; Kim 2001, 10–11).

[113] A subject of long running concern for numismatists: Babelon 1897; Gardner 1907/1908, 111; Head *H.N.*; Jenkins 1990, 17.

[114] Cf. Cyzicus AR Hemiobol. 0.41g. Obv: forepart of a crested boar, behind tunny. Rev. K reversed. Garstang Museum of Archaeology 106. *SNG* Cop. 52.

[115] These *type parlants* or "canting types" are relatively commonplace: Rhodos minted coins bearing the image of a rose, Selinous's coins carried an image of the selinon, etc. For further discussion, see Skinner 2010; MacDonald 1922, 7–8, 20; Head *H.N.* lviii.

[116] Both regarded as delicacies by later authors, e.g., Ath. *Deip.* VII 303a, 303e (Aristotle Fr. 206).

[117] Pausanias's account of the sanctuary at Delphi includes a description of a bronze bull that the citizens of Corcyra dedicated to Apollo, together with a similar dedication at Olympia, following a bumper catch of tunny-fish (Paus. X 9. 3–4).

Evidence for what might loosely be termed "ethnographic receptions" of images struck on coins can perhaps be found in Pindar's *Pythian* 6.6 and 12.2–3 for two citizens of Acragas: Xenocrates, winner in the chariot race of 490 B,C, and the flautist Midas—also victorious in 490 B.C. Indeed, coins minted by the polis of Acragas have already been singled out as a body of source material that might plausibly have been accessible to the poet prior to his visit to the city circa 476 B.C.[118] Although one might be tempted to dismiss passages emphasizing aspects of Acragantine topography as little more than artistic hyperbole, details such as these were evidently intended to both interest and entertain, raising interesting parallels when it comes to the content and subject matter of equally early Greek prose.[119] Depicting or describing aspects of the local environment, flora, or fauna can often send out decidedly mixed messages, however, indicating a more complicated sense of identity. The coins issued by the polis of Cyrene are a notable case in point.

From the very outset (ca. 570 B.C.), Cyrene minted coins depicting the silphium plant or its attributes (see fig. 3.1).[120] A "salient feature" of the polis's identity, coins struck in Cyrene invariably depict either the ῥίζα (root or stem) of the silphium, with more detailed representations also including the root itself, or the heart-shaped fruit that it bore.[121] As a wild "cash crop," silphium fused aspects of natural landscape and environment with that of trade and merchandise. Its representation both on coins and, potentially, in song, amounts to both the effective "commodification" of a polis and the creation of what is effectively a recognized logo or "brand."[122] If we follow Rutter's example in scrutinizing *epinicia* for signs of intertextual references between the two media, this emerges as something more than a numismatic curiosity reflecting the quirky nature of Cyrenaican coinage.

---

[118] Rutter 2000, 75–76; Carey 1981, 104; cf. *Ol.* 2. 9. However, Rutter's analysis of Sicilian coin types stops short of considering the wider implications of the (potentially) widespread circulation of such symbols and imagery, encouraging the view that they enjoyed only "discreet patterns of circulation" and were therefore primarily "self-referential" in nature (Butcher 2005, 145, 147). Internal or outward-projecting discourses are commonly viewed as mutually exclusive categories: Butcher 2005, 151, 154. Cf. Dougherty 1993; Malkin 1998a.

[119] Cf. Hornblower 2004.

[120] *Ferula tingitana* cf. Theophr. *Hist. pl.* 9.1.7. Cf. Solon Fr. 39; Hdt. IV 169; Hermippus Fr. 63; Plin. *HN* 19 38–46 (Liddle and Scott s.v. σίλφιον). See Micheli et al. 2000, chap. 1 for discussion. For the close relationship between Cyrene and local indigenous populations, who played a crucial role in the harvesting of silphium, see Laronde 1990; Marshall 2001, 2004. For contact with the wider Greek world, see Gill 2004.

[121] The popular association between Battos's proverbial wealth and the silphium was strengthened by the fact that coin minted in Cyrene invariably carried this emblem and that the trade in silphium was itself incredibly lucrative. The consumption/use of silphium can be compared with that of frankincense: a luxury commodity whose consumption/use was taken for granted by those who could afford it. Cf. Hdt. IV 169 where detailed discussion of the silphium's properties, mode of production, and means of supply is evidently regarded as superfluous.

[122] See Klein 2000 and Anderson 1991, respectively, for the significance of logos in consumer society and national discourse.

FIGURE 3.1 Silver tetradrachm of Cyrene AR 15.46g ca. 525–480 B.C., recovered from Naucratis. Obv. Cyrene seated, facing left; left field, silphium bearing fruit; test cut, rev., type effaced (BM1886, 0802.12). Reproduced with kind permission of the Trustees of the British Museum.

That floral and vegetal imagery play a significant role in praise poetry, often in conjunction with evocations of landscape or environment, has long been acknowledged. Aside from a marked emphasis upon agricultural wealth, widely interpreted as allusions to the abundance of produce for which Cyrene was famed,[123] considerable attention has also been paid to the

---

[123] In this case, the uncultivated wilds of Cyrene's territory are held to be analogous with both populations native to the region and the eponymous nymph, whose capture/seduction and subsequent "taming" forms a necessary precursor to a prosperous and flourishing landscape (Castillo

manner in which vegetal or floral imagery was routinely employed both as a metaphor for the (transient) fame and fortune with which an athletes' labors come into fruition and an eroticizing element through which the "ripeness" and youthful fecundity of the eponymous nymph were emphasized.[124] While one must bear in mind that *Pythian* 4 is by far the longest ode in the collection—a fact that might skew the evidence in its favor—and the (undoubted) popularity of floral imagery as a means of illustrating aristocratic *arete*, questions remains as to whether the use of words with explicitly "vegetal" connotations in poems dedicated to Cyrene simply refer to its proverbial fertility or the trysts of an amorous Olympian.[125] In fact, the interpretation of a number of otherwise seemingly obscure references within *Pythian* 4, 5, and 9 may be subtly nuanced to reflect allusions to the silphium crop. The result, when combined with more generic references to cult, environment, and topography, is an unexpectedly detailed portrait of the polis or territory in question.

While there is little ground for dogmatism in such matters, it can plausibly be suggested that even if Pindar's choice of imagery does *not* amount to a conscious allusion to the silphium crop, his audience may well have drawn upon these or similar images in order to illustrate their imaginings. A case in point would be the eulogy offered to "the sweet garden of Aphrodite"[126] on the plain of Libya:

ὁ Βάττου δ᾿ ἕπεται παλαι—
ὸς ὄλβος ἔμπαν τὰ καὶ τὰ νέμων,
πύργος ἄστεος ὄμμα τε φαεννότατον
ξένοισι.

But the ancient prosperity of Battos continues,
nevertheless, as it bestows now this, now that,
bastion for the city and most splendid light for foreigners.[127]

1996, 166–167). Although it is generally accepted that such themes figured prominently in the iconographic programs deployed by so-called colonial foundations, little attention has been paid to whether the longstanding preference for silphium-related imagery in the polis's coinage found echoes elsewhere.

[124] Epithets such as wheat- or fruit-bearing Libya are commonplace (*Isthm.* 4. 53b; *Pyth.* 4. 7). The many references to healing in Pythian 4 have been attributed to both the medicinal qualities of silphium (by no means its only use for which it was employed) and the esteem in which Cyrene's doctors were held (Race 1997, 258). For further discussion see Castillo 1996, 165–169; Salvador 1996.

[125] Analysis of the frequency with which the figurative use of plant imagery occurs within Pindar's poetry reveals a marked concentration in poems eulogizing victors from Cyrene when compared to the rest of the corpus (contra McCracken 1934, 343). Of the 105 examples catalogued by McCracken in poems and fragments the use of ῥίζα (2/4): *Pyth.* 4 15; 9 8 and φυτεύω (5/11): *Pyth.* 4 15, 69, 144, 256 are particularly notable (McCracken 1934).

[126] *Pyth.* 5. 24; 52.

[127] *Pyth.* 5. 55–57. The plant was notoriously difficult to cultivate but flourished wild of its own accord—perhaps offering some explanation for τά καὶ τά νέμων (56). Farnell's reading of "in equal proportions awarding this and that = good and bad fortune" seems unnecessary (Farnell

There remains, perhaps unsurprisingly, considerable room for ambiguity. That the foundation prophecy includes, when taken with the verb φυτεύειν (to plant), what may or may not be understood as a punning reference to ἀστέων ῥίζαν (root of cities),[128] means that references to plants or stems and planting could all plausibly be associated with the silphium crop (although "planting a colony" is in itself a widely used phrase). As if to counter any uncertainty this is accompanied by a reference to the oracle of Zeus Ammon.[129] Any discrepancy arising from the fact that oracle and polis are geographically remote from one another within "spacious Libya"[130] is thus neatly elided: as two sides to the same coin they represent a conceptual whole.

Taken overall, these are rare and tantalizing glimpses of the ways in which coinage could potentially be exploited as a vehicle for both constructing and "reading" personal or group identities. Coinage did not just operate in isolation "as a boundary phenomenon, articulating the border between the citizen community and its others."[131] Instead, the widespread circulation of these symbols, stories, and traditions contributed to a widening sense of connectedness and common identity, arrived at through *confronting* difference through a variety of media.[132] That this occurred according to regional patterns of trade and association does not detract from the point overall: the exchange of knowledge, images, and ideas generated fresh bases for collective self-perception and definition. The widespread circulation of coined identities during the Archaic and early Classical periods resulted in a complex exchange of knowledge and ideas: histories, stories, peoples, and places all variously juxtaposed on a Braudelian scale—raising obvious questions of reception. While knowledge of certain non-Greek populations seems to have been fairly common currency throughout the Greek world, the levels of mutual knowledge connecting early poleis and, most importantly, the various means by which it was transmitted, remain remarkably ill-defined. With its

---

1961, 176). The reference to ὄμμα is in this case ambiguous, carrying the sense of "anything dear or precious" (Liddle and Scott s.v. ὄμμα), while Πύργος ἄστεος may itself refer to the stem of the plant as depicted on the coins with Πύργος taking the meaning of "tower." Φαεννός may likewise be metaphorical allusion to either the splendor of the silphium or a reference to the fact that the plant's stem bears a passing resemblance to an ancient lighthouse?

[128] "Ἐπάφοιο κόραν ἀστέων ῥίζαν φυτεύσεσθαι μελησιμβρότων Διὸς ἐν Ἄμμωνος θεμέθλοις" (Pyth. 4 14–16). On this see Braswell who disagrees with Farnell's identification of the ἀστέων ῥίζαν as Cyrene as opposed to Thera, arguing that φυτεύσεσθαι carries a passive sense (Braswell 1988, 83; Farnell 1961, 151).

[129] Pyth. 4 16, 57 cf. Hymns Fr. 36.

[130] Pyth. 4 42.

[131] Kurke 1999, 316.

[132] Cf. Howgego: "We may at least ponder whether the coins themselves, as a mass-produced and circulating medium, handled by everyone, may have had an active role in spreading and fixing notions of identity" (Howgego 2005, 17).

characteristic focus on locally recognized cult, modes of subsistence, ancestry, and origins, Greek coinage may ultimately have played an active (and hitherto largely overlooked) role in this process.

3.5 Visualizing

Ethnographic discourse had an important iconographic dimension with visual cues to foreign identities being all but ubiquitous in some cases. They can be found adorning pots traded in agoras and potters' quarters up and down the Mediterranean, on coins, wrought metalwork, and sculpture—points of intersection where "readings" are selectively construed according to a complex nexus of ideas and values, half-truths and imaginings.[133] The apparent ease with which images or motifs could migrate from gems to coins and vases suggests that the visual fields with which individuals sought to conceptualize and problematize questions of identity were not ordered by rigid typology. While questions of reception must remain very much open-ended, they cannot be ignored altogether as we extend our analysis beyond the (comparatively well demarcated) confines of the Attic-citizen *imaginaire*, to encompass a wider world of wild imaginings, hazy half-truths, curiosity, and ignorance.[134] Rather than viewing these as merely foreshadowing what was later to come, that is, an enlightened, rational, discourse conforming (albeit in the loosest terms) to modern standards of intellectual enquiry,[135] we should instead focus on questions of function and context—namely, in cases where it is possible to discern such things, how these ideas were employed, how they were *received*, and what this tells us about wider levels of knowledge, interest, and understanding in foreign cultures, identity, and difference.

Discussions tracing the history and evolution of ethnographic thought have traditionally paid little—if any—attention to the material or iconographic evidence. Where vase painting and sculptural representations are discussed it is generally in contexts specific to a particular social group/setting (Athenian symposiasts)[136] or represents an effort to gauge the levels of knowledge/overall accuracy with which a barbarian "type" was represented (Thracians or "Scythian" archers—of which we shall hear more below). It is

---

[133] For parallel discussion of the politics underpinning modern "imaginings"/visual representation, see Said 1978; S. Hall 1997; Lidchi 1997; Penny 2002. For an overview of how Greeks represented others, see Sparkes 1997.

[134] See above fn. 179. See also Greenblatt 1991; Romm 1989, 1992; Campbell 2006 for discussion of hazy/imagined knowledge of life on the margins. For receptions (variously interpreted) see E. Hall 1989; Miller 1997; Harrison 2002; Antonaccio 2003, 70 on Athens/Persia.

[135] Cf. E. Hall 1989; Thomas 2000; and Skinner 2002a.

[136] See further below but also Cohen 2000; Lissarrague 1990b, 2002; Miller 1991.

worth noting, however, that although our ability to relate visual representations of the foreign to literary traditions concerning the same is of considerable importance, it is far from paramount as this study is more concerned with the play of ideas rather than factual content or accuracy per se. From this point of view, the information contained in textual sources is only important insofar as it forms the basis for *our* interpretation of the images concerned. If we can detect instances in which there appears to be a conscious interplay between textual traditions and iconography, then this is obviously worthy of note, and ideas written down are self-evidently important in their own right; however, it would be dangerous to assume that the images we encounter on vases and elsewhere should necessarily correspond to literary traditions with which we are familiar.[137]

Although theoretical discussion of the underlying problems associated with "reading" Greek images has largely centered on the mythological, the characteristic blurring of categories and concepts relating to early representations of intercultural contact makes this a highly appropriate starting point since we cannot always be certain if foreign peoples are being depicted in the first place. The essential plurality of Greek myth coupled with the discursive role that images played in its formulation and dissemination[138] created an expressive world in which "foreignness" could be expressed in a wide variety of ways. The fact that visual cues alluding to a particular ethnic group—real or imagined—could convey vastly differing associations, ideas, and messages depending on the audience or context meant that ideas relating to "the foreign" were being continually rehearsed. Although there is much uncertainty surrounding the manner in which collective identities emerged during the early Archaic period, establishing a consensus as to what was or was not "familiar" must have played an important role in a process in which knowledge of the foreign or exotic was necessarily implicated.

Although confronted by a (seemingly) vast body of evidence, it is worth reminding ourselves both that this body of material is merely the fragmentary remnants of what must have existed in antiquity and that any discussion of the manner in which foreign peoples were represented in visual media is inevitably constrained by our ability to "read" the figurative styles employed

---

[137] On our ability to "read" Greek vases, see Goldhill and Osborne 1994; Carpenter 1991. Isaac (2004) argues that images allow us to step outside the (textual) sources and their various agendas to examine more general *mentalités*—a point open to debate. The decision to privilege one type of evidence to the exclusion of another is invariably problematic: questions of social context are arguably vital if we are to bypass modern interpretative schemas (Sourvinou-Inwood 1991).

[138] Goldhill and Osborne 1994, 5. It is clear that "representations of foreign peoples" cannot be considered without recourse to the more general theme of monsters/monstrous serving as a metaphor for particular ethnic groups (Dougherty 2003).

by individual artists. Although it is sometimes possible to read foreign imagery into designs and motifs that would remain otherwise enigmatic (for example, differences in armor schematically represented), this requires a level of detail beyond that of the (to our eyes) generic man, woman, or warrior types characteristic of Geometric pottery. The result of this initial ambiguity as to whom or what is being represented is that ethnographic interest and imaginings appear seemingly out of the blue once recognizably Scythian, Thracian, or Ethiopian types are discernable. We should be extremely cautious, however, in making such assumptions: absent (or inscrutable) evidence does not necessarily equate to evidence of absence when it comes to gauging the relative levels of engagement with questions of identity and difference.

One phenomenon that has been both widely observed and commented upon is the manner in which ideas of the foreign appear to have been inextricably bound up in discourses of power and sovereignty. This forms the central focus of Michael Shanks's discussion of the production of proto-Corinthian aryballoi as a technology of power.[139] Self-consciously deployed by an embattled social elite seeking to bolster its authority within the emergent city-state, this new visual field was entirely the result of the great social-political upheaval generated by an ongoing shift in power structures.[140] This gave rise to stories relating the experiences of travel and, by extension, a concern for alterity, expressed in terms of the feminine, animal, vegetable, or ultimately death and the divine—a potent means of defining the relationship between underclass and overlord. Discussion of "Art, design and the constitutive imagination in the early city state"[141] therefore reinterprets the Orientalizing style as an interest in the "aesthetics of sovereignty and power,"[142] as opposed to addressing how this knowledge was obtained and how it related to the wider world in general. Can we extend this view to encompass the myriad of contexts from which Corinthian wares have been recovered as a result of long-distance trade, placing such usages of "Oriental" imagery on a par, say, with the various representations or receptions of "difference" embedded in Homeric epic—as perceived by Hartog and Dougherty, Mackie, or Ross?[143] Does a taste for such Oriental imagery necessarily equate to clear knowledge of the lands and artistic styles upon which they drew for inspiration? Did they carry connotations of Egypt, Assyria, or Phoenicia, or were

---

[139] Shanks 1999.
[140] Ibid., 212. On early Corinth in general see: Salmon 1984; Morgan 1988, 1998, 2001. For critique of accounts of Orientalization focusing on various aspects of social stratification, see S. Morris 1997b.
[141] Shanks 1999, 210.
[142] Ibid., 213.
[143] See above: Introduction; cf. Hartog 2001; Mackie 1996; Ross 2005.

they merely deemed aesthetically pleasing—with no further thought being given to their selective "referencing" of decorative styles, ideas, or values, already in circulation?[144]

The extent to which ideas associated with Homeric Cyclopes provided a heuristic tool for conceptualizing foreign peoples in general and the potential dangers arising from intercultural contact and interaction in particular has already been highlighted in an earlier chapter. This would appear to be linked to the apparent vogue for depicting the blinding of Polyphemus in vase painting, from around the early seventh century B.C.—a period in which contact and interaction between Greek-speaking populations and their neighbors was widespread and sustained.[145] Events in *Odyssey* book IX are variously depicted on a proto-Attic amphora and vases from Argos (675–650 B.C.)[146] and Eleusis.[147] As well as demonstrating that the folk tale relating to Odysseus's encounter with the Cyclopes was already popular in this period, images such as these have been linked in many quarters—by dint of their widespread association with the Greek colonial experience—to early ethnographic thought.

Manufactured from local clays and of a "hybrid" type—equally reminiscent of Italo-Geometric traditions—one krater in particular has become a notable cause célèbre. Inscribed with the name of its maker, in all likelihood a Euboean name Aristonothos, the vessel in question was discovered at Caere's Cerveteri cemetery and dates from circa 700 to 650 B.C.. The exterior depicts two images juxtaposed: the blinding of Polyphemus by Odysseus and his companions (see fig. 3.2) and a naval engagement between two ships.[148] This is widely interpreted as a naval battle reflecting the at times fierce rivalry that existed between Etruscans and newcomers to the region (based largely on the fact that the two opposing vessels differ visibly in design).[149] On this occasion, the argument for an ethnographic reading or "turn" derives largely from its association with *Odyssey* book IX and the

---

[144] For ideas and motifs in circulation see: Burkert 1992; M. West 1997. See, however, Gunter 2009, chap. 3 for critique of the (modern) tendency to use visual style to interpret objects in terms of anachronistically conceived "national" identities.

[145] Dougherty 2003, 40; Snodgrass 1998.

[146] Argive crater Fr. Argos C149; H. 24.5.

[147] Attic MPA Eleusis amphora from Eleusis H. 1.42m c.670 BC. Coupled with gorgons pursuing Perseus—their decapitated sister behind them. For alternative interpretations see Langdon 2001. Cf. Laconian cup by the Rider Painter. Paris, Cals. Med. 190. W. 21.4; (484) Pseudo Chalcidian neck amphora from Vulci. Polyphemus group, London B154, H. 30. For further depictions spanning the sixth through early fifth centuries B.C. see: *LIMC* s.v. Kyklops.

[148] Dougherty 2003, 47. See also: Spivey 2007, 248–250; Izzet 2004; Snodgrass 1998; Malkin 1998a, 166–167; Schweitzer 1955.

[149] One might note, in support of this, various traditions relating to Tyrrhenian "pirates" a label whose subjectivity is self-evident (e.g., *Hymn Hom. Bacch.* 6–8ff.). Cf. the English usage of "privateers" in a later, Elizabethan, age (Rodger 2004).

FIGURE 3.2 The blinding of Polyphemus. Aristonothos Krater (side B), ca. 650 B.C., from Caere. Rome, Musei Capitolini 6. Drawn from photo. Drawing by the author.

accompanying Phaeacian/Cyclopes dynamic described by Kurke. This leads to the argument that the two images should likewise be read in conjunction with one another, with each scene reflecting different ways of thinking about the colonial encounter—one mythological, the other veristic.

Such arguments are far from straightforward, however. In fact, there is some degree of uncertainty as to whether an exclusively Hellenocentric reading of the imagery is entirely appropriate given the bicultural circumstances surrounding its manufacture and subsequent deposition.[150] The images could equally represent an Etruscan reading of the *Odyssey*, perhaps illustrating the dangers posed by Greek corsairs. Polyphemus's cannibalism might also be interpreted in multiple ways depending on the audience in question: while it may well have acted as a cipher for distant or alien peoples it may equally have referred to those located somewhat closer to home given the frequency with which relationships between communities that we now think of as "Greek" were marred by acts of transgressive violence and the inversion of social norms. Under such circumstances, it is perhaps advisable to emphasize the potential for a multiplicity of readings, the better to ponder the thoughts or associations that such a piece might have engendered in a society in which people of different outlook and culture lived "cheek by jowl." Whatever the particulars surrounding the Aristonothos krater, both its maker and its wider user-audience appear to be making ready use of hybrid forms, observed difference, and mythical paradigms to think about identities: What happens when they meet and why?[151] Although the krater might not conform

---

[150] Implicit in such arguments is the assumption that interpreting the vase in such a fashion would have been the sole preserve of a Greek. This is by no means the case as the Etruscan fascination with Utuse/Odysseus is well documented (see Malkin 1998a, 156–177). See above and Hemelrijk 1984, 81–83. On Etruscans/Greek myth more generally see Spivey 2007; Izzet 2005. For Euboean/Etruscan interaction, see Ridgway 1990, 1996, 2000, 2004.

[151] See Dougherty 2003 for full discussion. Depictions of Odysseus confronting the Sirens found upon a Corinthian aryballos may similarly be representative of the often ambivalent relationship between seafarer and landsman: (LC) Boston, MFA 1901.8100. H. 10.2. From Boeotia. Localization

to a stark Greek–barbarian polarity, a self-conscious awareness of cultural difference is readily apparent.

3.6 Consuming

Another means by which we can usefully frame and explore questions of identity is via the idea of consumption. While the period circa 750–500 B.C. is widely perceived as one of great social, political, and economic up-heaval—symptoms, in part, of wider trends toward increasing urbaniza-tion and the emergence of the polis societies[152]—material and poetic culture provided two distinct (yet inherently complementary) means by which archaic Greeks could render their world intelligible.[153] The same period saw a marked increase in a desire for things, especially foreign things, a desire contingent upon a diffusion of knowledge relating to spe-cific commodities employed as a basis for self-fashioning.[154] This "con-sumer culture" emerged at a time when both people and commodities were increasingly mobile. The diffusion of, and desire for, knowledge is arguably reflected in poems such as the *Odyssey* and elsewhere.[155] Stories and songs were themselves widely regarded as luxurious and highly desir-able commodities, compared, on occasion, to Phoenician cargoes, synony-mous with luxury goods.[156]

Just as processes of trade and interaction can be mapped with ever-increasing clarity—throwing the Finleyan model of a primitive economy into increasing disarray in the process—so our picture of the economies of knowledge has become increasingly sophisticated. Trade in material goods—both luxury items and so-called staples such as wine and oil—is a topic of ongoing research in which empirical evidence for the movement of goods is not hard to come by. The excavated remains of a series of shipwrecks discovered in the western Medi-terranean have made a notable contribution to our understanding of trade throughout the region (at least with regards to the nonperishable commodities

---

of the Siren myth to the S. Italian shoreline (Strab. I 22, 23; V 247; VI 258) may either be indicative of interaction with local tribes during the early trade for metals or the nature of the coastline itself from a mariner's perspective: lined with cliffs and treacherous in places (cf. Malkin's "ship-to-shore-perspective"—of which we shall hear more below—and Snodgrass 2000 on "A view from the sea." See Malkin 1998a, 189 for the various locations and associated traditions. For the early prominence of Sirens on worked metal objects see Muscarella 1962.

[152] Malkin 1998a, 9; Osborne and Cunliffe 2005; Shipley 2005.
[153] S. Morris 1997a, 539.
[154] Foxhall 1998, 298; 2005.
[155] Hom. *Od.* I 330–332.
[156] Pind. *Pyth.* 2. 67–68; *Nem.* 8. 21; Foxhall 1998, 303. See above for the inherent desirability of myths and Malkin 1998a, 6.

that variously made up their cargo).[157] There remains plenty of debate, however, surrounding the precise volume of goods that traveled, their relative value or importance, and just how their use should be interpreted once they reached their final destination.[158] It is also far from clear how much this movement of goods indicates a similar mobility when it comes to people. Who crewed these vessels and in what numbers?[159] Such questions may or may not find answers but they are unlikely to detract from our wider picture of a world defined by widespread mobility and exchange.[160] As such they provide a convenient starting point for tracing signs of ethnographic interest prior to the supposed invention of the genre in the fifth century B.C.[161]

It would clearly be difficult to argue that the widespread mobility of goods and people was not matched by an equally widespread pooling of knowledge and ideas. Indeed, an interest in knowledge and ideas was in all likelihood intimately bound up with the desire to consume, or to appropriate foreign luxury items in the first place. As such, knowledge was itself an object of consumption. Rather than being universally accessible one might envisage that access to products and knowledge from far-off places would at times convey a degree of status upon the individual agent (the extent to which this was the case would of course vary depending upon the context).[162] Access to information and luxury goods went hand in hand. Both *Odyssey* IX 196–215 and Hesiod's *Catalogue*[163] have been widely interpreted as reflecting the popularity of Thracian wines. Odysseus's tale referring to the protection of Maron is understood as an allusion to the town of Maroneia on the south coast of Thrace.[164] The gift

---

[157] Antonaccio 2001, 135.

[158] On the value of painted pottery: Gill 1991, 1994.

[159] Opinion is in many cases divided as to whether such vessels should be identified (in this case) as being of either Greek or Etruscan origin. For diverse views see Gori et al. 2006. The number of shipwrecks dating from the Archaic and early Classical periods is comparatively small, however.

[160] The mobility of groups and individuals is well attested: *Od.* I 182–184; IX 125–130 (οἷά τε πολλὰ . . . θάλασσαν), etc. See Raaflaub 2004 for discussion of the various categories this might involve.

[161] Although see G. E. R. Lloyd: "Trading relations do not necessarily imply a deep mutual understanding between, or even much mutual curiosity concerning, the societies in question" (G. E. R. Lloyd 1979, 237).

[162] On ideas of craft and "distance" associated with luxury commodities such as sandalwood, frankincense, and ebony, and wider analysis of the relationship between power, knowledge, and geographical distance, see Helms 1988, 111ff. For more general studies on consumption, see Glennie 1995; Mansvelt 2005. Davidson 1997 explores such themes using Athens as a case study. Duplouy's study of elite culture from the tenth through fifth centuries B.C. focuses on *modes de reconnaissance sociale* as crucial mechanisms through which elite status was contested and defined (Duplouy 2006).

[163] Hes. Fr. 238.

[164] See Isaac 1986; Graham 1978, 2001; Owen 2000, 2003 for interaction and settlement in Thrace. See also above, chapter 2.

of wine with which the hero was subsequently rewarded (among other things) is eulogized at some length, making the association all the more explicit at *Odyssey* IX 204-205: "wine . . . sweet and unmixed, a drink divine" (οἶνον . . . ἡδὺν ἀκηράσιον, θεῖον ποτόν). Although a priest of Apollo in the *Odyssey*, Hesiod's Maron can boast Dionysius as his great-grandfather—further reinforcing the associations with viticulture.[165] In each case, the assembled audience was presumably assumed to be fully capable of interpreting such allusions, reveling in a sense of shared knowledge and connoisseurship.

It is similarly hard to interpret material such as Pindar's Fragment 106, recounting the provenance of good things, as anything other than a very clear indication that these were ideas with which his assembled audience was assumed to be conversant: "knowing," for instance, that the best hunting dogs came from Laconia, that goats which milked well came from Skyros, and that both Argive arms and Theban chariots were without peer.[166] While it is at times hard to gauge how specific objects or images might have been perceived, evidence from authors such as Herodotus suggests this ability to link items of material culture with identities: Athenian pottery (banned from the sacred precincts of Aegina and Argos), the "Dorian" peplos and "Ionian" chiton, and the golden cicadas and linen undergarments that signaled an affinity with Ionia.[167] "Foreign" products might in other cases be so endemic as to become an indispensable element of cultural identities. The use of frankincense both in the symposium and ritual is a notable case in point: according to Xenophanes of Colophon, the burning of incense was an important element of any good dinner party along with good wine and conversation, while virtuous souls can look forward to "shady frankincense trees" (λιβάνων σκιαρᾶν) in Pindar's Hades.[168] Just as the use of drinking services or hoplite weaponry in protohistoric Italy should be interpreted as an active strategy for self-definition as opposed to evidence of creeping Hellenization, the use of Orientalizing or Achaemenid designs and imagery in proto-Corinthian and Attic vases suggests something more than a mere fascination for Orientalia or "Perserie."[169]

---

[165] Heubeck 1989, 25. It is worth noting in addition that early coinage from Thrace makes ready use of themes associated with viticulture: grapes, garlands, and Dionysius. See Kraay 1976; Carradice 1995. Cf. a Chian didrachm, AR, 7.2, *SNG* Vol. III 2858: early coins from Chios commonly depict grapes, amphorae, and a sphinx.

[166] cf. Pindar 107ab; the excellence of Naxian whetstones: *Isthm.* 6. 74 later endorsed by Pliny *NH* 36.54, 164; 37.109.

[167] Hdt. V 58; Thuc. I. 6. See: Antonaccio 2003, 62–65; Cohen 2001 (on items of dress).

[168] Xenophanes Fr. 2; Pindar Fr. 129. While the latter may be invoked to indicate the "otherness" of death it is entirely possible that the use of *libanos* and other such loan words relating to "oriental imports" had been totally assimilated (contra. Burkert 1992, 20, 36).

[169] Cf. Dench 1995; Miller 1997; Mitchell 2007.

While we can be confident that the archaeologically attestable processes of consumption and trade generated knowledge and information of a broadly "ethnographic" nature, questions remain as to how these transactions were perceived both in antiquity and the present day.[170] Lesky's assertion that it was the innate inquisitiveness of *Greek* traders—men "with their eyes open" whose interests strayed beyond the merely practical—falls rather wide of the mark. This is arguably a (rather simplistic) explanation for the perceived evolution from periegetic account to discussions of foreign manners and customs reflecting the (somewhat questionable) assumption that such individuals were sufficiently entrenched in their identities as "enlightened Greeks" as to be entirely immune to external influence and thus in a position merely to *observe*.[171] Trade, intercultural contact, and consumption were factors endemic to the Mediterranean world. Material artefacts and ideas—whether stories told of far-off lands, mythical fabulae, or obscure etymologies—were continually being employed discursively to construct identities (of whatever kind).

Having made some attempt to map out this "ethnography before ethnography"—the structures through which ideas relating a variety of foreign or mythical peoples were variously ordered and found expression—the next chapter strikes out beyond the well-traveled and much discussed worlds of those most reified of subjects, the civic *imaginaire* of democratic Athens and Ionian scientific enquiry, to take a closer look at the way in which ethnographic discourse might have played out in practice "on the ground." To do so is important since the study of early Greek prose has—until relatively recently—been largely devoid of attempts to relate the (apparently) bookish interests and pursuits of its authors to the "lived experience" and social worlds of their contemporaries as revealed by the material record.[172] Instead

---

[170] Herodotus's tale of the mute transactions undertaken by Carthaginian and Libyan merchants (IV 196) demonstrates an implicit awareness of the potential dangers arising from contact and/or interaction—notably the serial abductions of women that form the narrative starting point for the *Histories* as a whole. In what is self-evidently a paradigmatic account, Herodotus describes how, when such meetings occur, goods are left on the shore so that no one has to communicate directly. The other party can then inspect the merchandise before engaging in a form of mute bargaining. Although direct contact (with its attendant knowledge-transfer—and any subsequent repercussions) is thus seemingly averted, there is a sense that even exceptional and elaborate precautions such as these are unlikely to prove effective in the long run (Harrison 2007).

[171] Lesky 1966, 219.

[172] The invention of prose has been linked primarily to the emergence of the democratic city state (Goldhill 2002) but this can hardly account for prose traditions emanating from Ionia and should probably be revised to reflect the diverse origins of the authors preserved in Jacoby's *FGrHist*.

of treating these as two separate discourses running in parallel, a series of case studies will be employed to demonstrate that the interests and concerns of authors such as Herodotus and Hecataeus were firmly embedded in a socio-intellectual milieu in which discourses of identity and difference were forever being constructed or received in an ongoing play of culture, power, and knowledge.[173]

[173] See S. Hall 1990.

CHAPTER 4 | Mapping Identities

HAVING IDENTIFIED SOME OF the major building-blocks upon which "ethnographic discourse" might be founded—knowledge relating to a variety of foreign peoples, both Greek and non-Greek, and the mechanisms by which it was deployed—it is now time to extend our analysis to encompass unfamiliar settings and far-flung locations: the wilds of Scythia, Magna Graecia, and, at the "imagined center," the great Panhellenic sanctuaries at Delphi and Olympia. This broad canvas is necessary in order to demonstrate that discourses of identity indicative of a self-conscious engagement with questions of cultural difference were not only widespread well before their supposed epiphany during the fifth century B.C.—the point at which Greek identity is purported to have switched from "ethnic" to cultural criteria[1]—but also intrinsic to the processes by which identities (of any kind) were constructed. If "ethnographic discourse" was indeed manifest in a variety of contexts outwith traditional genre-writing—and therefore just as important in contexts in which we have little or no literary evidence for an interest in the manners and customs of one's neighbors or those further afield—then it should be possible to map its various features and contours, in a manner sensitive to local nuances and complexities: the networks of trade and association that connected settler and indigene, thriving metropolis and remote farming community. Time, space, and the availability of evidence mean that this will remain a partial and somewhat uneven treatment of the period in question; our survey will alternately zoom in and out, focusing upon particular questions or locales in some detail while merely alluding to others in passing. Although the result may be a somewhat

---

[1] E. Hall 1989; but especially J. Hall 1997, 2002.

bumpy and uneven ride around the Greek world, this is wholly to be expected when tracing the history of ideas in a world defined by mobility and exchange.

Before we proceed any further, however, it is worth pausing to reiterate one very important point. While the discourses of identity and difference encountered below provided both the material and the *means* by which group or individual identities might be selectively constructed,[2] they need not (and should not) be interpreted in terms of a homogenous group identity—whether "Greek," "native," or "barbarian." Instead, the emphasis upon an essential plurality of identities as socially constructed and historically contingent reflects a conviction that these were essentially *ongoing* processes that were never static or fixed, and in which the stark delineation of conceptually bounded ethnic groups has little if any role to play. Scholars are now remarkably cautious when discussing the extent to which those involved in the earliest phases of Greek settlement would have been conscious of any shared sense of Hellenic identity, defined in opposition to the "barbarian" peoples they encountered. The traditional criteria upon which such judgments would be based have variously been qualified in recent years: the idea of a common language—supposedly implicit in the term "barbarian"—is a gross oversimplification of a situation that saw a multitude of regional dialects sit side-by-side with, in some cases, widespread bilingualism or at least the (apparently widespread) ability to negotiate language barriers in circumstances where contact took place on a regular basis.[3] Allusions to shared descent from a common Hellenic stock are offset by the fact that intermarriage between groups of different outlook and culture was entirely commonplace, while the overall fluidity of the Olympian pantheon allowed for a generous measure of syncretism between local and imported deities.[4] This is *not* to say that the populations in question did not encounter cultural difference but rather that it is unlikely to have equated to a neat Greek–barbarian polarity.

---

[2] Although somewhat inexact and prone to misuse and generalization, the term "social knowledge" reflects the extent to which the information and ideas that circulated in antiquity were selectively deployed by individual agents in order to both situate and define themselves as variously belonging to one of any number of identity groups (male/female, settler/indigene, farmer/nomad, uplander/townsman, etc.).

[3] Morpurgo Davies 2002, 168: "'Greek' was and remained an abstract concept which subsumed all different varieties, much as a federal government subsumes the component states."

[4] On language: J. Hall 1995, 1997, 2002; Arena 1996; Munson 2005; but see Harrison 1998. For intermarriage/bilingualism, see J. Hall 2005, 280; 2002, 100–102, 113–117; Coldstream 1993; Hodos 1999; Marshall 2004. For bilingualism throughout antiquity in general, see Adams et al. 2002. For gods/syncreticism, see Dothan 2003; Greaves 2004; Malkin 2005; Kleibrink 2006.

4.1 Between Boundless Steppe and a Welcoming Sea: Olbia and its Environs

Our first port of call on this voyage of exploration is the Northern Pontic Region and the city of Olbia and its localities in particular, extending our discussion of ideas relating to Scythia and "Scythians" to encompass their supposed place of origin (see fig. 4.1).[5] It should be made clear from the outset that the archaeology and history of the region have long been bedeviled by controversy. While the rising tide of nationalism and regional autonomy that marked the end of the Cold War swept away the political barriers to scholarly collaboration between western academics and those working in the former Soviet bloc, the fundamental differences in attitude and approach that were their legacy have proved every bit as divisive.[6] As a result, a series of hugely impassioned—and often bitter—debates regarding the way in which material and literary evidence should be interpreted have yet to run their course. The negative effects of both this and a turbulent historical past have only partially been offset by the work of the Danish National Research Foundation's Centre for Black Sea Studies, which has played a pioneering role in fostering international collaboration and the rapid dissemination of high-quality research.[7] With such caveats in mind, it will nonetheless be useful to sketch a rough framework of events for the period in question, before proceeding to more detailed discussion of instances in which a self-conscious engagement with "foreign" identities, manners, and customs can reasonably be inferred.

4.1.1 Negotiated Heterogeneity: From Earliest Contacts to the Fifth Century B.C.

Located on the western shore of the Bug liman, the city of Olbia occupied a slightly elevated position overlooking a low stretch of shoreline upon which

---

[5] This study is greatly indebted to a recent upsurge in publication on the history/archaeology of the Northern Pontic Region in languages other than Russian and Ukrainian, allowing far wider access to materials and evidence previously inaccessible to anyone for whom Russian-language scholarship remains something of a closed book. Rather than providing an accurate reflection of work previously undertaken by successive generations of scholars, the references that follow provide merely a starting point for those wishing to pursue such matters further with the titles of certain key texts reproduced in English for ease of referral. For histories of Russian scholarship of the eighteenth and nineteenth centuries and Soviet era, see Tunkina 2003; Petersen 2010, 23–28.
[6] The apparent ease with which individuals such as E. H Minns positioned themselves between academic traditions, west and east, still stands out as being exceptional even before the Cold War, however (Minns 1913).
[7] E.g., Guldager Bilde, Højte and Stolba 2003; Guldager Bilde and Stolba 2006; Guldager Bilde and Petersen 2008; Lejpunskaja et al. 2010.

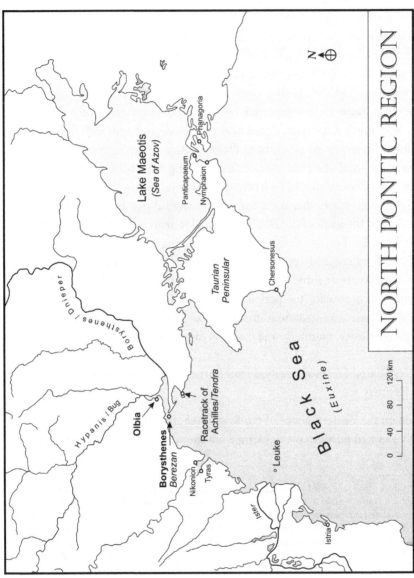

FIGURE 4.1 Regional map of the Northern Pontic Region. Redrawn from A. Bresson et al., eds., 2007, *Une koinè pontique: cités grecques, sociétés indigènes et empires mondiaux sur le littoral nord de la mer noire (VIIe s.a.C.–IIIe s. a.C.)*, 18, fig. 1. Map by the author.

ships might easily be beached. Now partially submerged under the waters of the Bug (Hypanis), the site is approximately triangular in shape. It is bordered to its west by a formidable ravine, while to the northwest a series of man-made barriers mark the successive ebb and flow of human habitation that occurred in conjunction with alternating levels of prosperity (see fig. 4.2). The acropolis incorporated two *temene* divided by a road running north–south and an agora, while from the fifth century B.C. there emerged an increasingly urbanized "lower town"/harbor area adjacent to the Bug—a major trade route and one of the principal waterways linking the coastal emporia with the settlements and trading stations of the interior.[8]

The settlement at Olbia was preceded by an earlier site at Berezan on a former peninsula some 40 kilometers to the southwest (now reduced to an island due to rising sea levels).[9] Although traditionally attributed a leading role in settling the region, it seems highly unlikely that Miletus was the only city from which the newcomers came. While a Milesian contingent may have been prominent, we must therefore envisage one or more communities defined primarily in terms of their heterogeneity.[10] It has now become commonplace to point out that the overwhelming majority of early settlers are likely to have consisted of adult males in boats. This fact alone would have rendered intermarriage with the local population an obvious desideratum if the settlement were to have any long term viability, leading to a degree of bilingualism, creolization, and cultural hybridity characteristic of colonial societies.[11]

Trade would also have created extensive opportunities for intercultural contact even if we remain essentially unclear as to its precise nature. Many of the commodities circulating during this (or indeed any other) period leave

---

[8] Vinogradov & Kryžicky 1995; Rusjaeva 2003. For detailed overview and critique of both the research history of Olbia and its findings, see Petersen 2010, 41–51.

[9] Tsetskhadze et al. 1999; Solovyov 1999, 2001.

[10] While widely subscribed to, the idea that Miletus played a leading role in opening up the Euxine may in part represent a historical mirage: a combination of later sources—Pliny's famous statement that the city founded 90 colonies (*N.H.* 5.122)—and a tendency for settlements subsequently to emphasize their Milesian pedigree (cf. Strab. XIV 1.6). See Avram et al. 2004, 924, for discussion of historiographical tradition. Even the "Milesianess" of Miletus at the time can itself be overstated: recent scholarship has been at pains to point out that (quite apart from the need to allow for the involvement of other groups/individuals from across Ionia) archaic Miletus was itself a highly cosmopolitan city whose inhabitants proved highly adaptable when confronted with interests and customs not their own (Greaves 2002, 2004).

[11] Braund 2007a, 40–41. These may well be reflected in (confused) references to Greeks who variously "went native" and other "half-Hellenes" mentioned in Herodotus and elsewhere (a topic to which we shall return below). See: Hdt. IV 17, 108; Rusyayeva 2007, 101–102. Cf. Sourvinou-Inwood 2005; Marshall 2004 citing onomastic evidence from Cyrene. The latter is discussed by Mason 1976, 377–387. Further references can be found at Marshall 2004, 128n2.

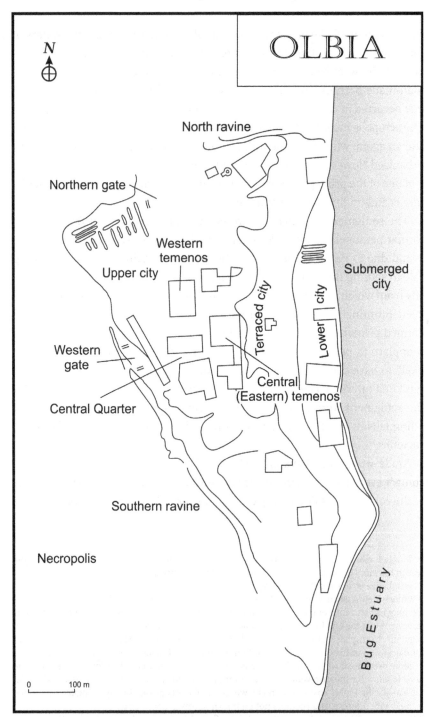

FIGURE 4.2 Map of Olbia. Redrawn from S. D. Kryzhitskiy, "Excavations at Olbia in the Past Three Decades," in D. Braund and S. D. Kryzhitskiy, eds., 2007, *Classical Olbia and the Scythian World: From the Sixth Century BC to the Second Century AD*, 8, fig. 2. Map by the author.

little by way of archaeological signature. In some cases this has led scholars to be extremely cautious when it comes to assessing the nature and overall intensity of trading activity across the Northern Pontic Region and beyond.[12] While other (less reticent) commentators have confidently asserted that first grain and then the slave trade[13] provided the basis for both local wealth and that of steppe Scythia as a whole, Berezan and Olbia were also ideally placed not only to take advantage of local resources—in particular the rich fish stocks of the river estuary that would later be eulogized by Herodotus—but also to act as a central hub for processing and stockpiling of objects and materials from further afield.[14] Whatever the relative importance of the various commodities involved, the movement of goods and people (whether enslaved or free) is likely to have contributed yet further to a community defined more by its heterogeneity than any single or homogenous cultural identity.

The material record is certainly suggestive of an influx of goods of diverse origins. In the case of Berezan, trade links with Egypt may be inferred—however indirectly—from a faience vessel in the form of a fish dating to the late sixth century and a late archaic paste pendant of Horus.[15] The recovery of pottery from Samos, Chios, Ephesus, and possibly Smyrna dating to the seventh century B.C. suggests participation in wider networks of trade and exchange incorporating the cities of Ionia.[16] While the practice of cabotage, coasting voyages by ships loaded with mixed cargoes sailing from port to port, makes it unnecessary to infer direct contact with the various centers mentioned, connections of this kind provided at least one mechanism by which knowledge and ideas might be transmitted between nodes.[17] Trade in precious metals is suggested by the mention of "Lydian plate" in a letter inscribed on lead tablets dating from the late sixth century, discovered in Olbia's agora.[18]

---

[12] E.g., Greaves 2007.

[13] Most recently the latter has been favorably compared with the trade in cereals as being a far more lucrative source of revenue (Gavriljuk 2003).

[14] Hdt. IV 53. For the wider importance of the salting and preservation of fish—including sturgeon and tunny—as part of the local/regional economy, see Bekker-Nielsen 2005; Demir 2007. For trade in metals, see Domanskij and Marčenko 2003, 35.

[15] Faience vessel: B.82.315 (Solovyov 1999, 87 fig. 77); Horus pendant: B.87.313 (ibid. 57 fig. 41); Webb 1978, no. 507. Other faience vases recovered from Olbia/Berezan that are catalogued by Webb include a seated figure with drum, an Achelous head, a hedgehog aryballos, and a locust/grasshopper; see Webb 1978, nos. 411, 855, 932, 953 for discussion and references.

[16] See Posamentir 2006, 161-166 (in which the evidence for which locally-produced finewares is also addressed) together with Lejpunskaja 2010, 126–131 (finewares); Lawall et al. 2010 (transport amphorae). See also Tsetskhladze 1998a.

[17] Similar conclusions can be drawn from Klazomenian amphoras recovered from Olbia, dated to ca. 530–500 B.C., that are marked with dipinti identified as the letter B from the Corinthian/Megarian alphabet (SEG L 703).

[18] SEG XLVIII 1011.

Copper splashes, ingots, and the remains of ovens were also recovered among the remains of two buildings in the Osnovnoj area on Berezan Island providing evidence for craft production and the possible importing of copper ore.[19] In short, we have every reason to believe that both settlements enjoyed regular and sustained contact with both the Northern Pontic Region and the wider (Mediterranean) world.

Opinions vary hugely as to the initial (and subsequent) status of the settlement at Berezan, not to mention the ethno-cultural makeup of its inhabitants. It is generally agreed, however, that the transfer of at least a proportion of the settlers to the mainland site of Olbia overlooking the estuary circa 600 B.C. would have opened up the surrounding landscape for agricultural exploitation (rendering contact with local populations all the more likely).[20] Whether the absence of evidence for indigenous populations should be interpreted as evidence of absence or as merely a reflection of the methodologies, paradigms, and sampling strategies employed in an attempt to detect them remains highly controversial, however.[21] Attempts to downplay the level of interaction between settlers and local populations—by denying that the latter even existed—remain highly questionable.[22] Such comments are a symptom of the ongoing and bitter dispute between those that interpret the early settlement data in terms of a predominantly non-Greek community, home to a scattering of Ionians prior to a subsequent influx of colonists, and those who see the community as "Greek" from the start. Evidence cited in support of the

---

[19] Dated to the end of the seventh/first half of the sixth century B.C. these structures are interpreted as workshops whose combined output is thought to have far exceeded the needs of the local population, leading to speculation that objects manufactured on site would have been traded back to the mother city—trade with the interior being seemingly discounted. Metallurgical analysis of the copper ore suggests a point of origin somewhere in the Carpathian-Danube basin (Domanskij and Marčenko 2003, 30–35).

[20] Some 107 rural sites are now attested for the late sixth century B.C.; see Petersen 2010, 53.

[21] These might, in many areas, profitably be expanded to encompass the analysis of faunal assemblages, human remains, paleobotanical evidence, geology, and geomorphology. The latter is best exemplified in the *chora* of Metapontion (with astounding results) but has yet to be implemented on any significant scale elsewhere. In the case of Metapontion, analysis of the skeletal remains of some 700 individuals recovered from the Pantanello necropolis and the urban necropolis at Crucina (300 apiece), together with the pre-Greek Iron Age necropolis, has revealed that those dwelling in the Metapontine *chora* were genetically closer, when it came to certain shared characteristics, to the nearby Italic populations than those dwelling in the city (Carter 1998, 2004, 2006). Cf. Rusyayeva 1999 passim; 2007, 101.

[22] Cf. Kryžickij 2006, 107: "We may now state two important points, which leave no room for doubt. First, there was no settled barbarian population in the Lower-Bug region by the time of the Greek colonisation. . . . Nor do we have any grounds for supposing that there were nomadic barbarians in this area either. . . ." Carter is more circumspect, pointing out that there remains a great deal of data that has yet to be explored in any detail: "In general . . . field archaeologists working in the Black Sea, as well as the Mediterranean, could be more sensitive to the importance of evidence that habitually ends up in the back dirt" (Carter 2006, 199).

argument for a lack of contact between Scythians and Greeks prior to the former's migration from the northern Caucasian Steppe includes the lack of destruction layers from sites throughout the Northern Pontic Region; the fact that none of the major settlements were, by and large, enclosed by walls until the fifth century B.C.; and the fact that only a comparatively low number of graves judged "ethnically Scythian" have been recorded for the archaic period throughout the region as a whole.[23] Such arguments are at best tenuous, as we shall see. The sheer impracticality of walling a settlement during its early stages, when manpower and materials were both lacking, is hard to over-look,[24] while changes in the manner in which local populations buried their elites cannot be discounted. We should be wary of the assumption that burial practices were both uniform throughout the region and equally traceable ar-chaeologically. The apparent absence of destruction layers from excavated sites during the period in question is certainly an interesting phenomenon but insufficient grounds on which to argue that conflict of any kind was en-tirely absent until the late sixth or early fifth centuries—since the archaeology of violence is notoriously ephemeral. There is, in short, no reason to suspect anything other than a relatively high level of contact between early settlers and traders and local populations from the very outset as evidenced by the extensive pottery finds at sites located deep within Scythian territory.[25]

The agricultural exploitation of an expanding *chora* must have created countless opportunities for contact between local populations (peaceful or oth-erwise), further contributing to the diffusion of knowledge and ideas relating to Scythia and Scythians. While the relative importance of the long-distance grain trade between the Northern Pontic Region and the cities of the Aegean during these early stages has to some extent been downplayed, trade of some sort was apparently underway by at least the mid-sixth century B.C. with cargoes of wine and oil making the return journey.[26] Agricultural production

---

[23] Some 39 in total: Tsetskhladze 2002, 83. For detailed discussion of the mortuary evidence for the region, see Petersen 2010.

[24] See, however, Højte 2008, 153–155.

[25] Some of the earliest deposits include a fragment of a Wild Goat oinochoe from Trachtemirov city-site, dated to circa 630–600 B.C., depicting the head of a griffin—a notable occurrence in a land in which tales of Arimaspians and gold-guarding griffins are supposed to have circulated (Hdt. IV 27). For discussion see Vachtina 2003 who argues for intensive contact and interaction, characterizing the region as "one vast contact zone" (Vachtina 2003, 23).

[26] It is entirely possible, moreover, that sections of the local population were in at least some cases already engaged in growing cereal crops if the variegated practices reported by Herodo-tus—not to mention shadowy archaeology—are anything to go by (Bresson 2007, 56). For an alternative view, see Noonan 1973; Tstetskhladze 1998a, 54–63. On the grain trade in general, see Noonan 1973 and De Angelis 2002 on Megara Hyblaea. For an early start to trade in luxury foodstuffs, see Foxhall 1998.

does appear to have flourished from comparatively early on, however. While we cannot expect a fully fledged grain trade to have sprung into existence almost as soon as settlers transferred to the mainland site at Olbia, the potential for raising crops must have been obvious to individuals far more attuned to agrarian production than we are today, making it all the more likely that measures would have been put in place to exploit this potential with alacrity.[27] Such links are important: once established, they would have provided a conduit for ideas and information regarding Scythia to be transmitted to centers such Miletus and Athens, with its Potters' Quarter relaying them in turn the length and breadth of the Mediterranean via the medium of figured pottery.

A high degree of cross-cultural interaction can reasonably be assumed throughout the region in spite of repeated claims that Greek-speaking colonists arrived in "virgin" territory in which neither nomadic nor sedentary populations had yet to gain a substantial foothold. The nature of the relationship between settlers and local indigenous groups is equally the subject of controversy, however. Attempts to explain the ever-increasing amounts of precious metals recovered from the tumuli of local elites purely in terms of protection money should perhaps be resisted: we are ultimately ill-equipped to gauge the complexities of dealings between settled and nomadic or semi-nomadic communities.[28] The tendency to interpret the accumulated wealth of the Scythian elites as money extorted from Greek settlers is not unrelated, however, to the (now largely discredited) theory of a "Scythian Protectorate" under which Olbia was supposedly allowed to flourish following the southerly migration of the nomadic tribes to territories adjoining those of poleis such as Olbia and Panticapaeum.[29] Given the positioning of the settlement of Berezan, and latterly Olbia itself, either astride or closely adjacent to the main artery of communication with the interior, it is highly likely that contact of some sort did occur—whether as a result of trade in hides, furs, slaves, or honey, or the fact that settled or nomadic populations (whose movements are notoriously difficult to detect archaeologically) either occupied the area

---

[27] For the importance of agricultural production for the economic prosperity of the city, see Petersen 2010, 53; Kryzhytskyy and Krapivina 2003, 515; Bujskich 2006, 115–121.

[28] E.g., Tsetskhladze 2002, 84; 1998b, 63–67. It follows that while protection money may on occasions have been paid in an attempt to guarantee the safety of settlers or those traveling inland to trade, such wealth could also be derived from tolls levied upon the movement of goods (and people?), revenues arising from the trade in slaves, pelts (which was doubtless extensive for all the fact that it is hard to trace archaeologically), and/or the leasing of lands/territories for agricultural exploitation.

[29] See Petersen 2010, 53–54 for critique of this model. The idea of a so-called Scythian Protectorate arises from Herodotus IV 78–80 (Kryzhitskiy 2005). Some scholars have even seen this as a sign of Achaemenid influence from the late sixth century onward (SEG XLVII 1164; Fedoseev 1997).

on a permanent basis or periodically moved through the region in search for pasture. The decision to settle on the Berezan peninsula at some time circa 625–600 B.C. may itself be indicative of an explicit awareness of local populations characteristic of early settlement and colonization in general: Irad Malkin's "ship to shore" perspective.[30] The ever-wary settlers may, in other words, have chosen a defensible location where contact could easily be regulated, thereby offering a degree of security should relations with the local population turn sour.[31]

Debate surrounding the extent to which the populations of "emporia," emerging urban centers, and *chora* included a "barbarian" component has, for a long time, been equally misguided.[32] Although the likelihood that early settlers intermarried with local women in both the initial and successive generations is readily acknowledged along with the presence of slaves and other dependents, the complexities arising from this cross-cultural mix have only now begun to be explored in any detail.[33] Instead, debate revolves around the twin polarities of "Greek" and "barbarian": terms of reference that under the circumstances appear both conceptually loaded and clumsy.[34] The principal criteria singled out as being indicative of Scythian ethnicity include dwelling type (dugout or semidugout); the presence of handmade pottery conforming to forms judged to be ethnically "Scythian"; mortuary practices (crouched burials and grave goods including "Scythian" weaponry, mirrors, stone dishes, and jewelery); and personal names.[35] The assumption that these practices can be seen as indicative of ethnic identity per se is, however, somewhat out of step with received notions regarding how material practices relate to notions of identity.[36] A number of factors need also to be taken into account

---

[30] Malkin 2001, 188; 2005, 239; 2011, 48ff.

[31] For trade between Olbia and the Scythian hinterland, see Leypunskaya 2007; Gavriljuk 2008.

[32] See, however, Petersen 2010.

[33] For a landmark publication of the mortuary evidence, see Petersen 2010 together with contributions to Guldager Bilde and Petersen 2008. Gavriljuk 2003 makes the (somewhat dubious) assertion that sixth- and fifth-century Olbians would have had little need for slaves, arguing instead that they were a major export to Chios with cargoes of wine making the return journey.

[34] Cf. Petersen 2010, 114: "We may stress the presence of a great variety of objects and burial features which have different cultural affiliations, but their reception in the burials of Archaic Olbia is much more blurred and complex than we may like to admit. . . ."

[35] See Petersen 2010, table 4 together with Tsetskhladze 1998a, 2001, 2004; Vanchugov 2001; Solovyov 2001; Kryžickij 2007b; Gavriljuk 2010.

[36] Jones 1997; Stark 1998; Hannestad 2007. Similarly tendentious are the assertions that the presence of stone dishes can be linked to the presence of "barbarian" women from the wooded steppe, thought to be responsible for introducing such practices, and that the recovery of handmade pottery from domestic contexts is indicative of either interaction with or the presence of indigenes. Cf. Rusyayeva 2007, 101. For more reasoned discussion, see Petersen 2010, 101–103, fig. 2.28 where the possibility of a cultic function is mooted based on the traces of soot, fat, and fire. The author does not attribute them to a specific ethnic group, however.

such as the location of production centers, the availability of materials, and the extent to which trading relationships between settled and nomadic groups might have contributed to their prevalence in specific contexts and locales.

In the case of Olbia, the appearance of mirrors decorated in what is commonly referred to as the "Scythian animal style" (Graves 87, 136, 170, 174, 245, 258), alongside those deemed more obviously "Greek" (e.g., Herakles stealing the tripod, Grave 62), is attributed to the presence of one or more workshops in Olbia itself.[37] The apparent diversity of decorative styles is interpreted as evidence of a stylistic repertoire that could be tailored to meet a variety of tastes.[38] The presence of either one or the other in a funerary context is unlikely to bear any direct relation to any sense of ethnic identity to which the interred may (or may not) have subscribed.[39] Questions of consumption and taste need to be explored further if we are to appreciate the significance of the finds deposited as grave goods at Olbia. They reflect patterns of consumption, the result of active choices that we are, in most cases, ill-equipped to decipher.[40]

Where dugouts and pit dwellings are concerned, there are immediate problems regarding terms of analysis and basic methodology. Just what exactly constitutes a dugout appears to vary hugely according to the excavator or site in question. Features interpreted as such are usually described in at best cursory detail and published as a planned view accompanied by a photo (depicting what is essentially a hole in the ground).[41] As far as settlement data in general is concerned, the problem can be approached in a number of ways. While dugouts might well have been characteristic of local populations, they are also a feature of early Milesian settlement throughout the Black Sea and

---

[37] For discussion and references, see Petersen 2010, 92.

[38] Petersen 2004.

[39] Elsewhere in the Mediterranean, the use of metalwork as an indicium of ethnic identity has been questioned as brooches previously considered unambiguously "Greek" are now recognized to reflect the influence of populations inhabiting south/central Italy (see also below).

[40] While pioneering studies such as that undertaken by Rostovtzeff have gone to great lengths to highlight the importance of Iranian influences in shaping the forms used in Scythian metalwork, the reception of such trends and the manner in which they related to identities—whether ethnic, religious, or social—remains essentially moot (Rostovtzeff 1922). Documenting such material (in often lavish style) and attempting to link particular assemblies to named individuals remains the primary objective for many of those working in the field, e.g., Alekseyev 2005; Rolle 1989; Jacobson 1995; but see also Koltukhov and Vdovichenko 2001 for the cultural biography of a single artefact.

[41] Stratigraphical relationships are rarely documented to such a degree as to allow the reader to assess the data independently, e.g., Solovyov 1999, 32–33, figs. 10–13. Kryžickij 2003 discusses the problems surrounding the reconstruction of Greek architecture in the Northern Black Sea region. My thanks to Zosia Archibald for timely advice on matters pertaining to Black Sea archaeology.

Ionia.[42] "Pit-dwellings" appear to have been prevalent in Anatolia, Lycia, Pamphylia, and Cilicia, at sites such as Göltepe, Karataş, and Gordion, over a period extending from the Bronze to Iron Ages.[43] This merely strengthens the suspicion that, rather than being indicative of the presence or influence of local peoples upon "Greek" colonists, the use of construction techniques of this type by settlers in the Northern Pontic Region could equally be a reflection of intercultural contact between settlements such as archaic Miletus and neighboring populations.[44] If we cast our eyes further afield, no sign of dugouts has been discovered at the fortified settlement at Porthion, an archaic site northeast of the modern city of Kerch perched high on a plateau overlooking the straits that link the Kuban region with the Crimea.[45] Instead, archaeologists have uncovered evidence of a small building (approximately 6.9 x 2.2 meters) constructed of mud brick on a stone foundation, dated by some proto-Thasian amphorae that were recovered in situ dating to the second half of the sixth or first third of the fifth century B.C.[46] Similar caution is necessary when it comes to employing projectiles and other forms of weaponry recovered during excavations as evidence: arrowheads of a type matching "Scythian" designs were widely used in both hunting and warfare—a point to which we shall return below when discussing the iconographic evidence for the representation of "Scythians" in and around Olbia.[47]

---

[42] Tsetshkladze 2004; Kryžickij 2007a.

[43] Tsetshkladze 2004, 267–268.

[44] Some care also needs to be exercised in distinguishing between the various uses to which dugouts were put (which included storage spaces and workshop areas as well as domestic space suited for groups or individuals). It should be noted that domestic architecture recorded in settlements in the region surrounding Olbia display a diversity that cannot be narrowed down to one technique in particular. See Tsetshkladze 2004, 247–248 for summary and further references.

[45] Vachtina 2003.

[46] Equally anomalous with regards to the late Archaic rural settlements of Olbia is a small rural temple situated some 13.5 kilometers north of the city, on a cliff overlooking the Bug liman (Golovacheva and Rogov 2001). The structure (commonly referred to as Kozyrka II) is some 12 x 8 meters in area, constructed according to a megaron-type plan: two adjacent rooms on a west-east alignment, whose unfired mud-brick walls are faced with limestone slabs (ibid., figs. 1.3; 2.1; 3). While the presence of an altar points to the structure being a cult building, no votives—or any other material connected with cult activities—has been found, aside from the bones of a child's hand found deposited in a pit south of the altar. Although recorded examples of above-ground stone buildings remain very much the exception to the rule throughout the period in question, the structure at Kozyrka demonstrates that blanket distinctions between different construction techniques are an unsuitable basis for tackling questions of identity and difference.

[47] Although the processes surrounding it are unclear, the adoption of technologies from local populations would appear to be proven beyond all reasonable doubt. Of the items of weaponry found in the large number of graves at Olbia, bronze arrowheads are by far the most common (although see Petersen 2010, 104–106 and below for interpretation), generally associated with a variety of other artefacts including tools and ceramics—occurring in numbers ranging from isolated finds to fifty or more (Petersen 2004). Swords, daggers, and knives also occur for which see Petersen 2010, 77–78, 87–89. Other distinctive features include the fact that the interred is on rare occasions positioned upright along with the use of seaweed as a means of lining the graves, the presence of red ochre, and faunal remains (ibid., 103 for discussion and references).

While there is considerable archaeological and epigraphic evidence for discourses of identity and difference in and around the city of Olbia, the city appears to have enjoyed a somewhat obscure reputation vis-à-vis the rest of the Greek-speaking world—as demonstrated by the oblique treatment it received from Herodotus.[48] Herodotus refers to a town as Borysthenes[49] in a variety of contexts as both a trading center and as a city on the Hypanis whose inhabitants refer to themselves as "Olbiapolites."[50] The term "Borysthenites" is reserved for Scythian agriculturalists living adjacent to the Dnieper (Borysthenes) to the west.[51] As far as the epigraphic record is concerned, two city ethnics are employed: Borysthenes, dated to circa 550–25 B.C.,[52] and Olbia itself—thus bearing out Herodotus's account. The apparent tendency of outside observers to conflate the Bug (Hypanis) with the larger, and surely far better known, Dnieper is suggestive of both a vague appreciation of local geography (not unsurprising in itself, given the sheer size of the estuary that the two rivers shared) and an apparent insouciance when it came to eliding local differences—that were no doubt keenly felt—in favor of a catchall term. Convenience, it seems, took precedence over any concern for geographical accuracy. In this we get some inkling of the gap separating local perspectives and the reports offered by external commentators whose descriptions of local Greek-speaking populations were at times highly ambivalent.[53]

Whether Herodotus actually journeyed to Olbia at all remains a matter of some debate.[54] The absence of any reference to clothing and dress in his account of the region could be interpreted in a variety of ways: it is equally possible that by the fifth century B.C., or even earlier, knowledge of Scythian costume was so widely disseminated as to be commonplace. If this is indeed the case then West's argument—that Scythia was so far beyond the ken of the Halicarnassian or of Greeks in general as to preclude the exercise in self-definition brilliantly elucidated by François Hartog—may itself need to be qualified. It seems unlikely, in any case, that the widespread ignorance of Scythia postulated by West would have proved an insurmountable barrier to ideas of Scythia and Scythians being employed as foils for the various

---

[48] West 2004.
[49] Hdt. IV 78.5.
[50] Hdt. IV 24.1, 17.1.
[51] Hdt. IV 18, 53.
[52] *SEG* XXXVI 693. Cf. *SEG* XLVIII 1024.1 (ca. 530–510 B.C.). See Braund 2007a, 1997.
[53] Herodotus writes of "the Greeks of the Black Sea and the Hellespont" or simply "the Greeks of the Black Sea/Euxine" but just what this meant to contemporaries is unclear. We cannot be certain whether the phrase would have conveyed a sense of regional or cultural difference, marking out those concerned as in some ways different from Miletus or Athens (Braund 2005, 4).
[54] Notable skeptics have included Armayor 1978.

polarities that Hartog saw to be in play.[55] Steppe culture was undoubtedly alien to those residing in Athens or Sicily, but we have to question its "incommensurability" in the light of the wealth of evidence to the contrary already encountered in chapter 1. Although levels of knowledge and interest must have varied hugely, variability alone was no bar to its forming the basis for abstract speculation—however vague or ill-informed.[56]

West's suspicion that Herodotus has something to hide stands in stark contrast to the arguments tabled by David Braund stressing the essential accuracy of the Halicarnassian's account of Olbia and its environs.[57] Questions of sources and veracity have a long history in Herodotean scholarship, however, and it should be pointed out that whatever the outcome of such discussions, a significant level of interest and engagement with the region is assumed by both parties.[58]

The extent to which Herodotean problematizing of Scythian ethnicity relates to preceding traditions regarding the region and its peoples remains to be determined as early knowledge of the region prior to Herodotus is extremely difficult to gauge. While Hecataeus appears to have included the names of native settlements in his description of the region, the manner in which this relates to the Herodotean account is largely open to question—although Herodotus is keen to correct the identification of the Melanchlaeni as "Scythian."[59] The suspicions, voiced by West among others, that we have lost the vast proportion of literary works relating to the region seem not unjustified when one considers the number of Ionian logographers whose works indicate an interest in Scythia.[60] Whatever we choose to make of these works and their relationship to wider questions surrounding the fragmentary Greek authors, the overall impression gained is one of significant interest and engagement with the lands and peoples north of the Black Sea.[61]

---

[55] Hartog 1988; West 2002, 448.

[56] Further (trenchant) critique of Hartog's thesis can be found in Dewald's review of 1990. Rather more convincing is West's argument that reference to the Cauldron of Ariantes—commonly understood as a claim to autopsy—may instead be rendered as "they indicated this much to me by way of illustration" (IV 81). The latter is more commonly translated as "they showed" or "offered to show" me (West 2002, 442).

[57] Braund 2005, 2008.

[58] For recent discussion of these "conversations," see Braund 2008. Cf. Woolf 2009; 2010 for cross-cultural dialogue in the Roman west.

[59] FGrHist 1 F 185; Hdt. IV 20.2. That Hecataeus might have described the Euxine as being shaped "like a Scythian bow"—a point picked up by later authors—seems at least plausible if the comments of Ammianus are anything to go by (Res Gestae XXII 8.10). See Hind 2001.

[60] West 2002, 2004.

[61] Authors following in the wake of the Halicarnassian are notably less inclined to distinguish between the respective groups, raising further questions of reception. For further discussion, see Braund 2008.

Although reports of Hellenic-Scyths, the Callippidae,[62] muddy the waters considerably, it remains questionable whether these local or regional perspectives regarding cultural difference were in the main transmitted back to centers such as Miletus or Athens. It is equally questionable how established cultural traditions relating to Mare-milking milk drinkers, derived from Homer or Hesiod, might have mediated contacts between settlers and the populations they encountered. It is to these questions that we now turn below.

4.1.2 Points of Contact and Receptions of Difference

We shall now turn to examine certain aspects of intercultural contact and interaction in more detail. In doing so we will bolster the overarching thesis that the intellectual engagement with questions of identity and difference ascribed to fifth-century logographers was in fact an entirely ubiquitous phenomenon throughout the period in question. We shall begin with the cult of Achilles from which some degree of cultural interchange can reasonably be inferred.[63] Adopted as a charter myth by Milesian colonists, the cult benefited from the high regard in which sailors habitually held Achilles. We have literary and epigraphic evidence to the effect that the cult was both present and highly popular on the north shores of the Black Sea, where it would appear to have played a key role in an emerging regional identity. Graffiti inscribed on clay disks has provided a valuable source of information in this respect, although we cannot be certain that they can be linked to cult activity in all cases. The disks begin to appear from around the second half of the sixth century B.C. onward and range from approximately 3 to 6 centimeters in diameter. As well as carrying an abbreviation of Achilles' name (A, AXI, AXIΛΛ, AXIΛΛΕ, AXIΛΛΕΙ), many of them also sport simple drawings that include daggers, swords, human figures, and snakes. Evidence for the cult is not confined to Olbia and its emporion, however, since a significant proportion of the disks (thirty-nine) come from the settlement of Beikush, some 40 kilometers to the west of Olbia at the junction of the Berzeran and Beikush inlets.[64] Additional evidence for the importance of the cult of

---

[62] Hdt. IV 17.1.

[63] See, most recently, Bujskikh 2007; Hupe 2007.

[64] *IOSPE* I 53; 130–144; IV 17/18, also I 145/6, 149, 155/6, 158, 685. Hedreen 1991; Rusyaeva 2007. The majority have been recovered from domestic contexts as opposed to shrines. Their interpretation remains somewhat uncertain but the association of Achilles with board games means they may very well have functioned as gaming pieces. Where Achilles' name appears in the dative they would appear to have been votives (Hedreen 1991). For graffiti from the lower city of Olbia, see Rusjaeva 2010.

Achilles can be found some kilometers to the southeast of Olbia at a site referred to in antiquity as the "Racetrack of Achilles" (modern Tendra).[65]

The link connecting Achilles with Scythia has already received considerable attention. Pinney has used both literary and iconographic evidence to postulate a link between Achilles and Scythia dating back to the epic tradition. Pinney would see Achilles as the leader of the Scythians during the Trojan War, a tradition ignored by Homer but that supposedly made its way into the *Aithiopis*. Although in many ways attractive, this is inferred from one fragment of Alcaeus and the blithe assumption that this fact could have subsequently escaped the notice of artists and commentators. Another (rather more convincing) approach has subsequently been proposed by one of Pinney's students, Guy Hedreen.[66] Hedreen's study of the cult of Achilles concluded instead that the key to understanding the relationship between Achilles and Scythia lay in the *Aithiopis* itself. According to Hedreen, the Milesian colonists, familiar with traditions such as those preserved in the *Aithiopis* that mentioned the "White island's" proximity to Scythia, founded the cult in response. The argument is predicated upon the Milesians' familiarity with early Ionic prose, the works of Hecataeus and earlier traditions now lost, as well as epics. According to such traditions, the Nile and Ister represented two extremes. Scythia, with the Ister, represented the ends of the earth: an antipode to the land of the Ethiopians. Ethiopia was also reputed to be the last resting place of a fallen hero, in this case Memnon, who was brought there by his mother Eos (also mentioned in the *Aithiopis*). Achilles and the "White" island are therefore arrayed in opposition to Memnon and Ethiopia in a manner characteristic of early Ionian science. Unable to abide each other's company as immortals, Memnon and Achilles were likewise kept apart in death (a similar logic underpins Herodotus's tale relating to the expulsion of Adrastus from Sicyon).[67]

While such explanations are perfectly plausible there may be other factors at play. If we compare some of the qualities for which Achilles was famed, it is tempting to speculate that the tendency to link the hero to this particular part of the world reflects an awareness of the (at times) savage and warlike nature of its peoples, their essential "otherworldliness" in comparison to contemporary

---

[65] Tunkina 2007. Another altar has been discovered at the mouth of the Borysthenes River and yet another on the island of Leuke, allegedly the place to which the hero's corpse was brought by his mother following his death (*Aithiopis*; cf. Proclus *Chrest.* 2). We have fifth-century graffiti (*SEG* XXX 869–872) as well as inscribed dedications from the fifth or fourth century B.C. See: *SEG* XL 610 for Thetis and Achilles worshipped alongside one another.
[66] Hedreen 1991.
[67] Hdt. V 67.

norms. Aside from reflecting the extent to which relations between settlers and indigenous populations were marked by violence, knowledge of Scythian habits and customs (however vague) might equally have given rise to associations with Achilles, the wild warrior whose behavior was at once splendid and transgressive.[68] It is not only Achilles, however, who provided a conceptual bridge between groups of different outlook and culture; in a region where archery figured so prominently the same might be said of Apollo as archer god par excellence. Although no doubt a reflection in part of the regard in which Apollo was held in what was purportedly the metropolis, it might reasonably be wondered whether it is merely happy coincidence that sees an archer god playing a prominent role in the religious life of a city whose non-Greek neighbors were famously skilled in archery. Whether or not this aspect of Apollo's persona was emphasised to any greater degree at Olbia in comparison to elsewhere, there is an obvious potential for a figure of this nature acting as a common point of reference in a community of diverse origins—including local elements arrived at through intermarriage with local elites.[69] Scholars have argued that the relationship between the two principal manifestations of Apollo—or rather their followers—was one of mutual antagonism, with Apollo Delphinios being supposedly imported from the Ionian homeland by refugees fleeing Persian encroachment.[70] These refugees remained largely marginalized in a society where the original colonists formed the backbone of the landowning elite. The fact that Apollo Ietros was eventually supplanted by Apollo Delphinios is seen as an indication that these Milesian émigrés had finally become established and thus gained the upper hand.[71]

The fact that an early form of coinage at Olbia took the form of bronze dolphins has led some scholars to interpret these in the light of the cult of Apollo Delphinios—a deity with whom dolphins were closely associated.[72] As such they are juxtaposed with what is commonly referred to as "arrowhead money." As the first coined money to achieve widespread circulation throughout the region, these were routinely dedicated to Apollo Ietros as votives in both Olbia and elsewhere.[73] Whether the appearance of arrowhead money

---

[68] See Bujskikh 2007 for discussion and references.

[69] Rusyayeva 2007, 101.

[70] E.g., Rusjaeva 2003.

[71] The potential circularity of such arguments should perhaps provide grounds for caution. It should, for instance, be recalled that we have evidence for Apollo Delphinios being present in the city from as early as the sixth century B.C. A less antagonistic relationship can perhaps be perceived in a graffito adorning a red-figure kylix dating from the early fifth century B.C., "shared (cup) of Delphinios and Healer," recovered from a tumulus far inland at Zhurovka (Rusyayeva 2007, 99, fig. 12).

[72] Nocita 2000, 217–230; Martinelli 2000, 231–247.

[73] For discussion, see Rusyayeva 2007, 98–99. For their appearance in burials being equivalent to that of single coins, see Petersen 2010, 104–106.

should be considered as just another example of the extensive variation in material practice characteristic of the wider Greek-speaking world or as an explicit reflection of interactions between local indigenous populations is open to question. As well as demonstrating the importance of trade as a driving factor in relationships between settlers and nomad groups, this might be interpreted as evidence that incoming settlers devised a system of monetary exchange that reflected the interests and tastes of the local population, implying not only prior interest and understanding but also a desire to create a basis for some sort of "meaningful exchange."[74]

Evidence of intercultural contact—or rather the problems of communication that inevitably arise when two language groups meet—can perhaps be found in a series of bone plaques inscribed with Orphic "texts."[75] Rather than interpreting these in terms of the celebrated gold leaves inscribed with directions intended to guide the soul on its journey through the underworld, recovered from funerary contexts in locations as far-flung as Magna Graecia, Thessaly, and Crete, it is the Pythagorean tables of opposites and a concern for duality underlying much of Presocratic philosophy that are cited as a likely source of inspiration.[76] These bone plaques, along with onomastic evidence derived from an inscribed bronze mirror of purportedly "Scythian" type dated to circa 500 B.C.,[77] have been convincingly linked to a desire to communicate religious beliefs and identities in circumstances where communication may have been less than straightforward:

> The cultural consequences of cultural encounter come precisely in material form. The knowledge of difference leads to its more explicit articulation, ideas under pressure get themselves down in writing.[78]

---

[74] See Rusyayeva 2007 for the argument setting this in the context of a wider initiative to promote the cult of Apollo among the local population.

[75] For recent discussion, see Onyshkevych 2002; Osborne 2008; Petersen 2010. References to Dionysius: Dubois 94a, b, c. Apollo: Dubois 93 (from Berezan). Particularly notable is a dedication to Apollo Didymaios from Bezeran ca. 550–525 B.C. The dedication is followed by a sequence of numbers (7-70-700-7000) and images (wolf, lion, bowman, dolphin) and a concluding promise of peace and blessing (SEG XXXVI 694). Cf. Penkova 2003, 605–617 for the highly tendentious argument that the text is linked to oral (religious) traditions of Thracian origin as defined by Al. Fol.

[76] Olbia, fifth century B.C.: SEG XXVIII 659–661; XXXII 796; XXXV 1822. Alternative interpretations include their use in cult ritual as the basis of a sermon with the wider enthusiasm for an Orphic-Dionysius being linked to aristocratic support for a tyranny.

[77] Relating to the name Lenaios. See Petersen 2010, 93n69 citing Guldager Bilde 2003, 31 (non vidi). Cf. Heraclitus DK12 B14a. See R. Osborne 2008 for discussion of later examples. Presocratic philosophy and cult practice emerge as being far more closely related to one another than is widely thought—a point rendered all the more interesting if we remember that some of the earliest references noting "ethnic" traits and characteristics can likewise be found in Heraclitus.

[78] R. Osborne 2008, 337.

According to Osborne, it is the manner in which (Greek) cult practices are articulated in material form that marks Olbia out. If this is the case, it provides compelling evidence for intercultural exchange and the transmission of ideas and values in a community in which ideas and objects relating to distinctive peoples and customs were apparently commonplace.[79]

The free exchange of ideas cannot be taken for granted, however, if Herodotus's tale of the series of unfortunate events that befell individuals such as Scyles and Anacharsis is in any way representative of religious interaction between Greeks and Scythians.[80] Dabbling in foreign cults and importing new modes of worship are portrayed as perilous tasks in a land noted for its cultural conservatism and a particular aversion to Greek habits and customs.[81] Take, for example, Scyles' secret initiation into the rites of Dionysius, which so scandalized his subjects that he was allegedly put to death as soon as he returned to them from the city of Olbia;[82] or the hostile response to Anacharsis's enthusiasm for Cybele that caused him to slip into the woods at Hylaea to perform rites in her honor: summary execution by means of bow and arrow shot by King Saulius himself.[83] The extent to which these stories reflect historical attitudes has been commented upon at some length with opinions differing as to how much weight should be attributed to what appear to be—to all intents and purposes—cautionary tales. It is notable, however, that in each case the narrative structure presupposes knowledge of foreign lands and customs.[84]

Although a degree of caution is required, other types of "meaningful exchange" can perhaps be inferred. Tales relayed by Herodotus, which purportedly represent variations upon a Scythian genealogical myth, provide a more obvious reflection of empirical knowledge of both the local topography and ethnic groups native to the region.[85] Three versions are

---

[79] Moving from the mystical to the mundane: a graffito on a chalice from Berezan ca. 500 B.C. has been interpreted as alluding to a Macedonian cap of a similarly conical shape: [.] ΟΚΟΛΗΚΑΥΣΙΑΙΚΑ ΥΣΙ [.] *SEG* XLIII 496; Saatsoglou-Paliadeli 1993, 141–142.

[80] See Braund 2008 for discussion of these and similar episodes pointing to a wider engagement between Greek and Scythian interlocutors.

[81] Hdt. IV 76.

[82] Hdt. IV 78–80.

[83] Hdt. IV 76. Scholarly excitement surrounding the discovery of an engraved ring as well as coins minted by Histria (amongst other places) marked ΣΚ, ΣΚΥ, ΣΚΥΛ. It is assumed, largely on this basis, that the Scythians controlled the coast between the Bug and the Dneister (see Sekerskaya 2001). The so-called Priest's letter also mentions damage to an altar to "the Mother of the gods" at Hylaea: see Braund 2007a, 49–50; Rusyayeva 2007, 94–102.

[84] In this instance the Scythians both know about and heartily disapprove of the ecstatic rites that were a feature of the cult (Hdt. IV 79).

[85] Hdt. IV 5; 8–10.

recounted.[86] The first (attributed to the Scythians) describes how Targi-taos, the first man, was the product of a union between Zeus and the daughter of the river Borysthenes. The second relates to Herakles and is attributed to "the Greeks living beside the Euxine." Having driven Gery-on's cattle as far as the (then uninhabited) land of Scythia, Herakles lay down to rest, only to discover when he awoke that his horses had been stolen. After much searching he discovers the culprit, a woman dwelling in a cave at a place called Hylaea, described as half-woman and half-ser-pent.[87] In response to Herakles' demand that she return his property she replied that she would only consent to do so if the hero had sex with her. The fruit of this union were the eponymous offspring destined to act as progenitors for the tribes that would in the future inhabit the region: Agathyrsus, Gelonus, and Scythes. Scythes was the only one of the three to fulfill the tasks stipulated by Herakles in order to determine who would stay and rule the land on reaching adulthood.[88] The third version explains the westward migration of the Scythians as a result of pressure from the Massagetae, a move that displaced the original inhabitants (the Cimmerians) and precipitated the invasion of Asia Minor.

Given the extent to which anguipede creatures feature in myths concerning early populations throughout mainland Greece, not to mention the veritable flood of images and ideas emanating from the Ancient Near East, it would perhaps be overly optimistic to claim that Scythia acted as an important con-duit for such ideas—particularly if the soundest evidence we have for such ar-guments is the creative output of workshops reflecting a form of Graeco-Scythian

---

[86] The degree of confusion that surrounds the origins of the Scythians for whom three separate myths are cited, without any indication of preference on behalf of the author, is seen by West as indicative of a lack of firsthand knowledge (West 2002). (This seems excessively severe, how-ever.) For discussion of possible cosmological associations, see Hinge 2008, 375–378.

[87] Snake-limbed maidens enjoy some prominence in the iconographic record; in her study of the way in which human, vegetal, and serpentine elements are variously combined in divine im-agery, Ustinova has traced the prevalence of at times androgynous tendril-limbed creatures throughout the Ancient Near East as well as the Graeco-Roman Mediterranean, arguing as a result that Argimpasa-Aphrodite and the anguipede nymph should logically be conflated. Usti-nova's arguments are largely predicated upon iconographic evidence, mostly dated to the fourth century B.C.—at least where Scythia is concerned—upon which basis it is argued that Scythia played a vital role in the diffusion of anguipedes throughout Mediterranean and beyond: [Which] "may well have started from Scythia and the Northern Balkans" (Ustinova 2005, 76). This seems unlikely, as while its presence in Scythian mythology must presumably be acknowledged (it should be noted that the snake-like being is only mentioned explicitly in the version attributed to "the Greeks living beside the Euxine"), it might just as easily have originated in myths told by the colonists.

[88] See Rusyayeva 2007, 95–96, who sees this as symptomatic of the Greek–barbarian opposition interpreted as both an archetype for mixed marriages between Greek and Scythian and a tem-plate for closer interaction between their respective deities.

hybridity that makes it largely impossible to determine their sources of inspiration.[89] Herakles' tryst with the snake-limbed maiden is sufficiently reminiscent of other colonial myths in which amorous Olympians or heroes consort with nymphs and so on to make us suspect that this says as much about those who relayed the tale to Herodotus, their interests and agendas, than those it purported to represent. This does not mean that an exchange in images and ideas did not occur, merely that it may have been a two-way process as nomads and settlers attempted to establish some form of "middle ground."[90] The recent discovery of a fragment of Fikellura pottery inscribed with a graffito referring to an altar to Herakles at Hylaea suggests that elements of this myth may actually have been commemorated through cult activity—a means of naturalizing Scythia and Scythians, incorporating them into wider models of understanding by which the origins of different tribes and peoples might be explained.[91]

Discourses of identity also played out in relief sculpture and iconography.[92] One of the most famous fifth-century representations of a "Scythian" from outside Athens, an inscribed stele dedicated to Leoxos, son of Molpagoras, was recovered from the necropolis at Olbia in 1895 (see figs. 4.2 and 4.3).[93] Although only partially preserved, each side of the stele depicts the torso and upper thigh of a figure, one a young nude—presumably the deceased—adopting the standard pose of a youth leaning on a spear with arm outstretched, the other resting casually on his hip (Side A). The opposing side is more unusual, however, since it features a figure clad in rider costume (trousers and a long-sleeved jerkin), facing left (Side B). The individual in question carries a bow/gorytus slung at his hip in the usual fashion and is holding an arrow point down, as if examining it for flaws (the angle is quite acute, a result, one assumes, of restrictions of space). An accompanying epigram relates that Leoxos died far from home, presumably while on campaign (it is invariably assumed that this campaign was against the Scythians). The stele has been variously interpreted but scholarly opinion has tended to see the young nude as Leoxos and the figure in rider costume as either a Scythian or an Amazon warrior (arguments for the identification of

---

[89] In contrast, the so-called Scythian animal style certainly appears to be a distinctive attribute of Scythian art but figurative elements are far harder to pin down.

[90] See Braund 2008. Cf. Rusyayeva 2007, 95–96 where this is seen as a very one-sided process.

[91] SEG XLII 710. Cf. Hesiod, Fr. 150. While the sherd itself is dated to ca. 550–30 B.C., the dating of the letter remains controversial. See Braund 2007a, 46n31; Hinge 2008, 378 for discussion and references.

[92] Although identified by Vladimir Nazarčuk as depicting a satyr's head facing left, the image on a body fragment on a black-figure lekythos (ca. 510–490 B.C.) might reasonably be interpreted as an individual wearing a "Scythian" cap with lappets. See Nazarčuk 2010, 150, pl. 76 B-31 for discussion and references.

[93] See Vos 1963, pl. XV; Petersen 2010, fig. 2.11.

FIGURE 4.3 *Stele of Leoxos*. Drawn from photo: M. F. Vos, 1963, *Scythian Archers in Archaic Attic Vase-Painting*, pl. XV. Drawing by the author.

the figure as an Amazon hinge on the fact that the figure in question is depicted wearing bracelets),[94] it being assumed that this is a paradigmatic rendering of polar opposites: idealized Greek versus barbarian.

The images in question might be read in a variety of ways, however. While some have chosen to depict the stele as depicting the deceased and his attendant or squire,[95] another theory might equally be suggested: although the epigram informs us that Leoxos "died far from the city" (ὅτι τῆλε πολέ[ως πρὸ]), it offers no clues as to how he arrived there. Granted, the easiest means of traveling long distances along the coast was by sea, but given that we are offered no indication as to where it was that Leoxos died, we must at least be willing to entertain the possibility that he may have traveled overland and died fighting somewhere in the hinterland. Were this indeed the case, it seems likely that he would have chosen to travel on horseback (a family that could afford to commission a funerary stele was presumably well placed both economically and geographically to avail itself of mounts, harnesses, etc.), raising obvious questions as to his choice of attire. What would Leoxos have worn while traveling

---

[94] See Jajlenko (*SEG* LIV 696) for the argument that it is a man that is being depicted. The so-called bracelets could easily be interpreted as an attempt to depict the cuffs of a long-sleeved "jump-suit" characteristic of stylized renderings of rider costume.

[95] Himmelmann 1956. Those objecting to this have highlighted the fact that the two figures are of equal size, a point with which Pinney concurs (Hiller 1975, *Grabreliefs*, 44n119, 36–40, 151–152, pl. 4; Pinney 1983, 139–140 and n. 103). Pinney went one or two steps further, however, in not only interpreting it as a pairing of hero and archer reminiscent of Attic vase-painting (while acknowledging that this is the only known case of such a pairing from outside Attica) but also insisting that the youthful nude is in fact Achilles and that his "Scythian" counterpart should instead be seen as Apollo in the semblance of Paris (Pinney 1983, 139–140). Although the latter ties in with her broader thesis concerning the hero's death and the manner in which he came to be associated with Scythia, supported by a barrage of iconographic material in which Achilles, Apollo, and Paris are variously depicted, the overall complexity of this model makes it difficult to accept that it is in fact correct. Pinney's conclusion that: "As Achilles confronts the god, about to die but still untouched, he is shown briefly as *daimoni isos*" (Pinney 1983, 141) is thus needlessly elaborate and essentially unconvincing.

abroad: Would he have dressed as any proper Greek should, in tunic and chlamys, or would he have donned clothing more suited to the environment and terrain? When fighting, would he have retained the lance or javelin of the hippeis or the weapon most commonly associated with the region's native inhabitants—the bow and quiver? While to some extent banal, such questions are important if we are to determine how individuals/agents might have chosen to portray themselves, provoking very real concerns as to whether we are in any way justified in "reading" such images in terms of an unambiguous depiction of a Greek–barbarian polarity.

If Leoxos died sometime in the early fifth century B.C., as is commonly suggested, then there is every chance that his family may have lived in the region for several generations, perhaps intermarrying with local populations on more than one occasion. In fact, the manner in which the two figures are depicted makes it difficult to rule out the possibility that both in fact represent Leoxos, one in the guise of the young nude and the other as warrior.[96] There may therefore be little need to see this as the juxtaposition of a doomed hero and vengeful deity, brandishing the dart that will eventually bring about the death of Achilles.[97]

The possibility that Leoxos might at times have donned Scythian attire ties back into debates surrounding both the interpretation of "Scythians" depicted on Attic vases and the identity of the equestrian statue from the Athenian acropolis—the so-called *Persian Rider*. The argument that these represented Athenians "dressed up" might be thought to appear somewhat more credible when viewed in the light of such material.[98] It is questionable, however, whether this is necessarily the case: Just because such practices may have been common on the Black Sea littoral, there is no need for them to have extended as far as Athens—a more complex range of associations are likely to have been in play. Although far later than the period in question, echoes of Leoxos's behavior can perhaps be found in

---

[96] Pia Guldager Bilde has observed that the stele may very well reflect the cultural complexity of the region as opposed to a polarity of opposites and that idealized concepts of warrior and citizen identities had simply been adapted to suit the mode of warfare most suited to that environment (Petersen 2004; 2010, 73–74, citing Bilde 2003, 130). Cf. Vinogradov 1997, 230–241.

[97] It should also be noted that the act of examining an arrow for flaws has many Near Eastern precedents and would later (?) find expression in imagery depicting various divine or heroic archers. The examples cited by Pinney of Apollo brandishing an arrow pointing in the direction of his enemy, including the red-figure hydria by the Eucharides Painter, are at least one remove from cases in which the gesture is depicted. The precise origins of the motif itself are impossible to pinpoint with any degree of certainty; it can be found in vase painting and gems in the Greek world during the Archaic and Classical periods as well as liberally dispersed throughout the iconographic programs deployed by various Near Eastern monarchies.

[98] Miller 1991, 1997.

Dio Chrysostom's (somewhat fanciful) pen-portrait of Olbia, epitomised in a handsome young lad called Callistratus, whom he encounters on horseback, dressed in Scythian garb:

> Suspended from his girdle he had a great cavalry sabre, and he was wearing trousers and all the rest of the Scythian costume, and from his shoulders there hung a small black cape of thin material, as is usual with the people of Borysthenes.[99]

Dio's Olbians speak a debased Greek, grow shaggy beards "like the ancient Greeks described by Homer," and are so fond of the *Iliad* that they know it by heart.[100] A literary construction drawing upon centuries of ethnographic tradition, Dio's Olbia encourages us to ponder the manner in which earlier generations of Olbians would have appeared to contemporaries from outside the region.

It seems reasonable to conclude, based upon the evidence outlined above, that discourses of identity played out in a variety of ways during the period in question. While it is commonly argued that ethnographic interests and concerns did not come to the fore until after the clash with Persia, the history and archaeology of Greek settlement in the Northern Pontic Region tells a markedly different story of an active engagement with foreign manners and customs.

4.2 Reconstructing Identities in Southern Calabria: An Archaeology of discourse[101]

From windswept Olbia and the wilds of Scythia we shall now proceed to the southernmost tip of the Italian peninsula—what was referred to variously

---

[99] *Or.* 36.7.

[100] For discussion and further references see Bäbler 2007. The popularity of Homeric themes can, in later times, be inferred from the "scenes from the life of Achilles" that adorn four identical *gorytus* covers dating from the fourth century B.C. Rendered in beaten gold, the covers include scenes of the young Achilles being taught archery. Apparently mass-produced, they were recovered from tombs in Chertomlyk, Dnepropetrovsk district as well as Melitopol, Ilintsy, and Kostov-on-Don (Heinen 2001, 10–15, figs. 6–7). Based on the latter, David Braund has argued that: "[T]he Scythian taste for Achilles, particularly in the military paraphernalia of its elite, . . . suggests that Achilles could offer a constructive point of contact between Greek and Scythian culture" (Braund 2007a, 52). See, however, Rusyayeva 2007, 97–98 who sees this as an exclusively elite phenomenon associated with the Bosphorus.

[101] "Archaeologies of discourse" have been much in vogue among scholars studying the humanities following their popularization by Michael Foucault (Howarth 2002; Foucault 1972). Some qualification is required, however, as while Foucault's objective was a "pure description of discursive events" (Foucault, 1972, 27), it must be acknowledged that description can never be

in antiquity as Oinotria, Italia, and Brettia (the land of the Bruttii).[102] While the distances involved are considerable, this is all but identical to the imaginative leap that Herodotus performs when casting around for geographic parallels that might elucidate his description of the Taurian peninsula, citing first Cape Sunium on the Attic coast before settling on the territory of the Iapygians on the "heel" of Italy.[103] Broadly equivalent with the administrative boundaries of the modern *regione* of Reggio Calabria, the area in question is not the territory of the Iapygians (located further to the north) but that which extends south of the isthmus created by the gulfs of Southern Eufemia and Squillace—ancient Napetinos and Skylletikos—to the Straits of Messina. Comparatively understudied (at least in comparison to other parts of the Mediterranean) and for a long time poorly understood, Southern Calabria might be regarded as a challenging environment in which to posit discourses of any kind—let alone those that might be reasonably be termed "ethnographic." Discourses of identity and difference, however, were just as prevalent here as on the fringes of the Asian steppe. Before we proceed to map out the various ways in which ideas relating to "foreign" lands and peoples might have circulated throughout this (ostensibly obscure) backwater of the western Mediterranean, we will begin with a number of caveats and preliminary observations concerning the nature and limitations of the evidence available for study, its wider landscape setting, and the extent to which research into the archaeology and history of the region has been shaped by external interests and concerns—both ancient and modern.

"pure" and that the process of identifying statements that make up a historically specific discourse is itself inherently subjective. As far as both this chapter and the study as a whole are concerned, "archaeologies of discourse" take on a more literal meaning: something akin to the use of trial trenching on an archaeological site in order to trace the plan of underlying structures. Rather than extrapolating connecting walls and other features, this study is engaged in the search for ideas. It is therefore an act of reconstruction and by definition *speculative*.

[102] "Brettia" is commonly understood to extend from Lucania (Laus/Crathis Rivers), south to the Straits of Messina, incorporating the Leucopetra peninsula. Brettia: Polyb. IX 7. 10; Strab. VI 1.5. n *Brettiane Chora* is found also in Polyb. I 56. 3. Although often used, "Bruttium" is a modern appellation with no ancient authority as both the name of the people and that of the region were cognate: in *Bruttiis, Bruttii provincia*, etc. For Italia, see Antiochus of Syracuse (*FGrHist* 555 F 3; Arist. *Pol.* 1274a 24; 1329b 7, 11) (see further below) and n *Rheginon Cherronesos*: Plut. *Crass.* 10. 7.

[103] Hdt. IV 99. 13–15. While perhaps attributable to the author's purported links to Southern Italy, this is a far cry from the status of modern Calabria, a neglected backwater now languishing in relative obscurity. Comparative study of the archaeology of the Northern Pontic Region and Southern Italy is now not uncommon, however; e.g., Petersen 2010; Attema 2008.

4.2.1 Framing the Argument: Contact, Interaction, and Systems of Exchange

First, much of what follows will focus primarily on the material record since we have little by way of historic or ethnographic material relating to Calabria for the period in question. In order to make this study "work" effectively it will be necessary to draw upon material recovered both from the more northerly regions of Campania, Puglia and Basilicata, and the island of Sicily across the Straits.[104] Digressions of this nature are hardly inappropriate, however, in the light of archaeological evidence for trade in ores and worked metal (jewelery, weaponry, etc.) encompassing Sicily, South/Central Italy and Sardinia, and a string of ports extending all the way to the Levant.[105] While demonstrating Calabria's historic role within both the "pan-Italian exchange system"—elements of which can be traced back to at least the Late Bronze Age[106]—and long-distance trade, this also provides some indication as to the likely interests and aspirations that prompted Greek-speaking settlers from Euboea (and elsewhere) to begin venturing westward from the eighth century B.C. onward.[107]

---

[104] Hodos 1999. The decision to draw upon data from outside the study area reflects the assumption that practices of a similar nature are likely to have encompassed Calabria itself. Where such inferences are made they must remain sensitive to the constraints imposed by local patterns of trade and association and a varied/rugged topography—there being some risk that this might otherwise constitute an overly generalized and/or essentially self-validating approach. For the wider importance of Calabria's role in connecting Sicily and central Italy, leading to extensive levels of contact and the emergence of a distinct cultural zone encompassing the southern reaches of the Tyrrhenian Sea, see Bietti Sestieri 1980–1981; Procelli 1996.

[105] See J. Hall 2005; Burgers 2004 for discussion of contacts linking Illyria, Crete, and Puglia. For exchange networks connecting Calabria with centers to the north: a series of iron swords dated to the early eighth century B.C.: Albanese Procelli 1995, 42; Ridgway 1995, 84–85. On exchange networks encompassing Sicily: bronze spears/axes dating to the early eighth century from Tre Canali, Giarratana, San Cataldo, and Mendolito (Procelli 1993, 233); pendants from Modica and Segesta (de la Genière 1968, 62n90; Kilian 1970, pl. 277, no. 5.7); figurines from Tre Canali, Taormina, and Centuripe (la Rosa 1968, 75, 125)—interpreted by Hodos (1999, 72) as evidence for a metalworking *koiné*.

[106] So, for example, Iron Age populations on both sides of the Straits are traditionally referred to as "Sicels" in the light of literary evidence recounting the migratory activities of various prehistoric populations (e.g., *FGrHist* 555 F 1) and perceived similarities in material culture. For discussion of Sikel identity, see Cordano 2002; Antonaccio 2004. For discussion of approaches to the literary and material evidence in Italian prehistory, see Loney 2002.

[107] Evidence for the latter can be found in mortuary evidence from Sala Consilina in the Vallo di Diano (Campania), which can be compared with material from Calabria and western Lucania—primarily fibulae and ceramics—while the analysis of imported fine-wares found at Rhegion and neighboring Zancle provide ample testimony to the importance of long-distance trade (Vallet 1958; de la Genière 1968; Mercuri 2004). The field is largely dominated by Francophone scholarship including the landmark studies of J. de la Genière on Greek/native interaction during the South Italian Iron Age (de la Genière 1968) and Georges Vallet's bid to situate the poleis overlooking the Straits of Messina in their wider context of pan-Mediterranean networks of maritime trade and exchange (Vallet 1958). Practical matters pertaining to seafaring are discussed in Snodgrass 2000. For recent discussion of cultural identity and interaction in Sicily, see Willi 2008.

Trade was not the only factor connecting Southern Calabria to the wider world during the period in question, however. Instead, a complex patchwork of shifting political allegiances and competing spheres of influence created an at times volatile admixture resulting in acts of territorial aggrandizement, piracy, and open warfare. While we will return to such matters in due course it can reasonably be argued that we have more than enough evidence to assume levels of contact and interaction conducive to the transmission of knowledge and ideas relating to foreign lands and peoples—however patchy or uneven.[108] Since the manner in which goods and ideas circulate is very much reliant upon modes of subsistence and networks of communication, the following section will describe some of the more important characteristics by which Southern Calabria and its various microregions were variously defined before offering a brief assessment of the current state of research into the region's archaeology.

4.2.2 Landscape and Identity in Southern Calabria

The topography of Southern Calabria has undoubtedly played a vital role in shaping the history of the region. The mountainous hinterland of the Aspromonte forms a jagged backbone that runs the length of the peninsula before terminating abruptly at the Straits of Messina (reputedly the lair of Scylla in Homer's *Odyssey* and the scene of much seismic activity) (see fig. 4.4).[109] Both the climate and hydrology of the region make it an attractive region for settlement. Lofty mountain peaks (some well in excess of 1,000 meters) ensure consistently high levels of precipitation in autumn and winter months, with snow cover extending into late spring. These combine to feed numerous streams and rivers, whose descent to the coast has, over millennia, contributed to alluvial plains ripe for cultivation. These plains are for the most part narrow, disappearing almost completely in places, with the result that the adjoining waters of the Tyrrhenian and Ionian seas would have provided the most straightforward mode of communication between coastal settlements as well as a ready source of sustenance. Conditions are, however, ideal for sustaining fruit trees, figs, almonds, chestnuts, and arable crops. Olives thrive throughout the region up to an altitude of circa 600 to 650

---

[108] Herodotean tales of a coastal reconnaissance undertaken by Persian spies are too closely associated with the—no doubt apocryphal—account of Darius's motivation for invading Europe to be taken seriously (III 135–138). For illuminating discussion of this together with the broader topic of geographical exploration, see Harrison 2007.
[109] See Strabo for the perils faced by ancient mariners (VI), portrayed more as a botherance by Dunbabin (Dunbabin 1948, 195–196) and, for more recent discussion Snodgrass 2000.

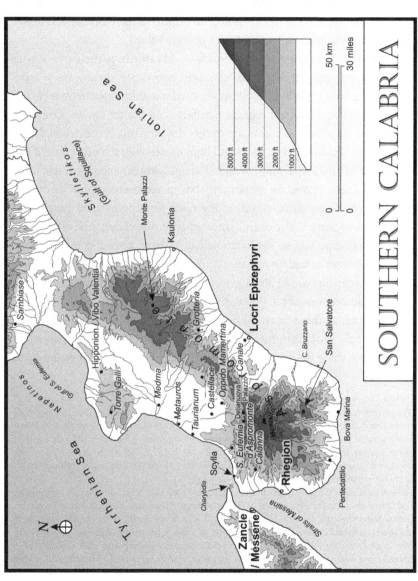

FIGURE 4.4   Southern Calabria. Regional map showing major sites and topography. Map by the author.

meters,[110] while vines are found considerably higher where soils and levels of exposure are favorable.[111] Rich in natural resources, the region was heavily wooded in antiquity, providing a valuable source of timber and pitch (produced from the processing of pine resin), as well as game for hunting.[112] The prevalence of high pasture for livestock also constituted a valuable resource, linked in some quarters to the etymological origins of the name by which the region came to be known: Ἰταλία (more on this below).

Given the likely importance of livestock—and cattle in particular—as part of the local and regional economy, we might also expect droveways to have played an important role in facilitating seasonal transhumance between areas of high pasture and lowland regions unaffected by winter snows. Overland routes connecting the two coasts are to this day very much constrained by a topography of winding river valleys and high passes with the exception of the principal "land bridges" through which trade/movement appear to have been channeled. These played an important role in connecting settlements on either side of the isthmus, negating the need for lengthy (and potentially risky) coastal voyages.[113] The overall impression is one of dynamic interaction within a landscape whose exploitation would have provided the primary source of subsistence and/or wealth[114] while trade, craft production, and other "economic" activities would also have contributed to the movement of goods and people among centers of population, whether by land or sea.

Factors such as these must all be borne in mind when considering how and why people, materials, and ideas might have circulated throughout the region. Again, there is a marked contrast with the chora of Olbia or the open

---

[110] Foxhall 2007b, 112.

[111] The extent to which this mountainous hinterland remained untamed and/or exploited remains very much a moot point. We should certainly be wary of assuming a direct correlation between sudden breaks in elevation/topography and sociocultural boundaries (Purcell 2003; R. Osborne 2007a). Such points will be dealt with at greater length below when we focus in on one hilltop site in particular that although located deep in the interior was very much connected with wider networks of practice, belief, trade, and exchange.

[112] Strab. VI 1.9. Later taxed by Rome but no doubt exploited, to at least some degree, during the period in question. On the exploitation of Calabrian pine (*Pinus nigra* Arn. ssp. *laricio* Poiret var. *Calabrica* Delamare) see: Dionys. XX. Fr. Mai, 5, 6. The lower slopes of the Aspromonte carry larch, beech, oak, and chestnut trees—the region as a whole being one of the major sources of timber in modern Italy. Finds of a variety of arrowheads at Locri along with *arule* depicting deer have both been interpreted as testifying to the popularity of hunting in the hinterland (Lattanzi 1989, 17n68, tav. IV, 1 (see further below). On topography/communications in general see: Dunbabin 1948, 200–210.

[113] The overall significance of trans-isthmian trade/communications has been emphasized by Vallet 1958; Will 1973; Guzzo 1981. A combination of naval power and the fortification of Scyllaeum by Anaxilas may have afforded some degree of control over shipping passing the Straits (Strab. VI 1.5). Cf. Vallet 1958. See also the *Homeric Hymn* for the dangers posed by Tyrrhenian "pirates" (cf. chap. 3 on Aristonothos krater).

[114] Foxhall 2003a.

landscapes of Scythia, where major waterways provide ready access to the interior. In the case of Southern Calabria, while the bustling sea-lanes would have contributed to thriving ports where knowledge and ideas might be freely exchanged, the pattern of rural life—seasonal transhumance in search of mountain pasture, the sowing and reaping of crops, and the exploitation of "wild" landscapes for seasonal foods, game, and fuel—would have been equally important in dictating the circumstances under which individuals would have been able to tap into knowledge of places and people beyond their immediate environs.[115] Occasions on which this might have been possible may have included visits to local sanctuaries timed to coincide with a particular agricultural festival, the occasional trip to the nearest urban center to sell produce or buy what could not be supplied locally, or a gathering of friends during which tales might be swapped regarding the various images depicted on imported figured pottery.

4.2.3 Materials in Circulation, Ideas in Play

Having explored some of the factors that might have contributed to the ebb and flow of knowledge and ideas throughout the region, we can now turn to the historic and archaeological materials. Historians and archaeologists have traditionally focused their attentions on the polis sites of Rhegion and Locri Epizephyrii, together with their various subcolonies and dependencies (see fig. 4.4). All of these have been located and investigated to some extent.[116] Locri's rapid expansion during the seventh century resulted in settlements being founded at Medma[117], Metauros,[118] and Hipponion[119] in stark contrast to Rhegion's sole reported foundation at Pyxous dating from the fifth century B.C.[120] Archaeological exploration of the intervening territories has been comparatively limited in all but recent years: a reflection, arguably, of both the widespread shortage of financial resources capable of sustaining anything other than developer-led interventions and the (still) widely held assumption that there was little, if any, settlement activity beyond the coastal littoral

---

[115] Foxhall 2006b, 273. See Braun 2004 for knowledge circulating throughout the western Mediterranean and beyond.

[116] Both Rhegion and Locri were the subject of pioneering excavations by the redoubtable Paolo Orsi during the nineteenth through early twentieth centuries, with periodic investigations of a more limited nature taking place in later years, constrained, in the case of Rhegion, by the fact that the ancient city lies directly beneath modern Reggio. See Mercuri 2004 for discussion and references.

[117] Thuc. V.5.3; Ps. Skymnos 308; Strab. VI 1.5.

[118] Steph. Byz. 437.3. Originally founded as a Chalkidian settlement by Zancle? (Solin. 2.11).

[119] See (variously): De Franciscis 1960; Settis 1965, 116–117; Musti 1976, 88–89. For general discussion of Locrian expansion see Dunbabin 1948, 163–170.

[120] Diod. 11.59.4.

during the archaic-classical periods.[121] Such views are increasingly being challenged, however, in the light of ongoing investigation of the rural landscapes of the interior (of which we shall hear more below).[122] Our ability to gauge levels of interaction between groups of different outlook and culture is somewhat hampered by the fact that, with a few notable exceptions, little evidence has been found—and thus little attention paid overall—to the indigenous/prehistoric populations themselves, the study of which has traditionally suffered from a far more widespread interest in the civilizations of Greece and Rome.[123]

Settlement data relating to the prehistoric populations of Southern Calabria is, for the most part, either sparse or poorly published with the (predominantly fourth-century) hilltop site of Oppido Mamertina being the exception that proves the rule.[124] Surface scatters of sherds and other materials provide indications of activity at locations such as Palmi,[125] Sant'Eufemia D'Aspromonte,[126] and Pentedattilo (see fig. 4.4).[127] Mortuary evidence is relatively abundant in comparison—in particular the necropoleis at Canale-Janchina,[128] Castellace,[129] Calanna,[130] and Gioia Tauro[131] (ancient Metauros)—but has long lacked anything by way of systematic analysis. Where the latter has occurred, the results have provoked as many questions as they answered. At the necropolis at Gioia Tauro for instance, the earliest phases of burials have been interpreted as

---

[121] E.g., S. Morris 2007, 388; J. Hall 2007, 117. A notable exception can be found in the excavations at Southern Eufemia in Aspromonte—of which we shall hear more below. See also the remains of a mid-sixth-century sanctuary identified by an Archaic-period inscription discovered out of context. Strabo VI 1.2 does in fact make the claim that " [οἳ] (τοὺς Ἕλληνας) πρότερον μέν γε καὶ τῆς μεσογαίας πολλὴν ἀφῄρηντο, ἀπὸ τῶν Τρωικῶν χρόνων ἀρξάμενοι. . . ." (Beginning from the time of the Trojan War, the Greeks seized much of the interior from its inhabitants.)

[122] Recent work relating primarily (but not exclusively) to the chora of Rhegion has provided an invaluable window upon the wealth of material contained within the archives of the regional Soprintendenza—much of which has received only summary publication. See: Givigliano 1978; Costabile 1980; Sabbione 1981; Costamagna 1986, 1997, 2000; Cordiano 1988, 1995, 2000. Cf. Osanna 1992 for an overview of the chorai situated along the Ionian coast (Locri-Taranto). More generally, the journal Kokalos and the Taranto proceedings provide a useful digest of ongoing research—albeit in somewhat cursory detail.

[123] Broad treatment of historical questions can be found in Carratelli 1976.

[124] See Costamagna and Visonà 1999; Mercuri 2004, 262.

[125] Loc. San Leo: Pacciarelli 1989–1990, 23–24.

[126] Cordiano 1997, 1–16.

[127] Mercuri 2004, 264.

[128] Orsi 1912; Mercuri 2004.

[129] De la Genière 1964; Givigliano 1987; Costamagna in Costamagna and Visonà 1999, 251–252; Pacciarelli 1999, 73–74.

[130] De Francisis 1956, 1962; de la Genière 1964, 1968.

[131] De Francisis 1960, 21–67; Sabbione 1977, 1981, 1986. See Mercuri 2004, 260–262 for useful summary and bibliography.

indicating a mixed population, a reflection of both the heterogeneity of some of the early assemblages of grave goods (coarse-ware vases and sub-Geometric pottery) and the fact that "natives" and "Greeks" were apparently buried side by side.[132] Although some caution is required in this respect as such judgments are invariably based upon the nature of the grave goods alone (e.g., biconical urns and pitchers marking "native" burials while Attic black-figure vases are associated with "Greeks"), we cannot of course rule out the possibility that they were selected for deposition precisely because they signaled some notion of identity or difference given the (impressive) range of imported goods deposited in the graves.[133] These include Corinthian fine wares (up until ca. mid-sixth century)[134] and the full range of Chalkidian wares, alongside—to a lesser degree—Ionian bucchero,[135] Cretan and Rhodian aryballoi, Chian and Phoenician amphorae, Samian lekythoi, and the fragments of one or more Etruscan kantharoi. While we should be wary of inferring ethnic affiliations on the basis of material evidence alone, the sheer diversity of imported materials deposited is suggestive of precisely the sorts of (comparatively high) levels of interregional connectivity that would both encourage and facilitate the exchange of knowledge and ideas regarding different types of "foreigner"—whether defined in terms of the various categories encountered in chapter 2 or those located somewhat closer to home in an adjoining settlement or the mountainous hinterland.[136]

The lack of any (systematic) treatment of mortuary evidence at a local or regional level has recently been offset in a landmark study addressing questions of intercultural contact and early settlement throughout the region during the Early Archaic period.[137] The conclusions arising from Laurence

---

[132] Although yet to receive full publication, the Gioia Tauro cemeteries contain some 3,500 tombs dating from the seventh through fifth centuries B.C., providing a valuable insight into both the consumptive practices (?) and (likely) cultural preferences associated with death and burial. Changes in funerary ritual are also readily apparent: switching progressively from inhumation burials to cremation and back to inhumation again—this time in tile-covered graves.

[133] The accessibility of such goods altered over time: Mercuri contrasts the range of materials recovered from the tombs at Torre Galli with the later cemetery at Canale-Janchina—the former is seen to be indicative of limited/periodic contacts with the wider Mediterranean world, with little attempt being made to imitate imported goods locally. At Canale-Janchina, meanwhile, a far greater range of imported goods are present and indigenous pottery styles are seen as mimicking those of the newly arrived (Euboean) settlers (Mercuri 2004, 198–199, 201–202).

[134] Typical examples include two proto-Corinthian aryballoi, nos. 34188–34189 (tomb 105) and 34190 (tomb 195), mid-seventh century B.C., Agostino 2005, 189n40, cf. Lo Porto 1964.

[135] E.g., Bucchero alabastron, East Greek, no. 34213 (tomb 197), first half of sixth century B.C., Agostino 2005, 188n36; cf. Jacopi 1931, 47, fig. 13.

[136] While the extent to which this constituted an open conduit for ideas and information can of course be exaggerated, Pindar's likening of songs to Phoenician cargo suggests that both poet and audience were equally aware of the manner in which long-distance trade and exchange contributed to the transmission of knowledge and ideas (Pyth. 2.67).

[137] Mercuri 2004.

Mercuri's analysis of the grave goods from the Canale-Janchina cemetery pose a significant challenge to the widely held belief that the region constituted something of a cultural backwater in which Euboean settlers had only a passing interest.[138] Instead, local populations appear to have been actively engaged in wider networks of trade and exchange, contributing to the wider circulation of material goods, ideas, and information.[139] The selective deposition of ceramics and fibulae at the Canale-Janchina cemetery would appear to be indicative of both an interest in identities and cultural difference and the active appropriation of "different ways of doing things."[140] Engaging in such processes appears to have formed an important part of both constructing local identities and a means of defining elite status via consumption (see above).

The discourses of identity that Mercuri brings to light should not be thought of as acting solely in isolation, however. The recital of epic, genealogical, and lyric poetry, whether formally or in the form of stray quips and maxims, would each have contributed to the shared pool of knowledge and ideas, evoking specific notions of people/place. Although hailing from well outside the study area, the incised inscription adorning "Nestor's cup" from Pithekoussai is a celebrated (and controversial) example of the manner in which epic poetry might be self-consciously cited and/or exploited in hot spots of diversity.[141] Did the owner of "Nestor's cup," a migrant, perhaps, from Euboea, also possess some knowledge of Homer's top-knotted Thracians or the Mare-milking milk drinkers—not to mention the blameless Ethiopians or Hyperboreans—and to what extent did they shape his view of the world?

Mortuary data of the sort recovered from Gioia Tauro is open to a variety of interpretations, however. On this occasion, the marked shift in cultural profile that had occurred by the mid-sixth century B.C. is traditionally seen as clear indication of the rapid acculturation of an indigenous population succumbing to the allure of Hellenic mores.[142] Similar patterns of behavior have

---

[138] Ibid.

[139] Mercuri's discussion of intercultural contact in the early Archaic period raises a number of questions regarding whether we are right to treat the categories of Euboean/native as coherently defined and conceptually distinct entities (cf. Papadopoulos on Achaeaness) (see below).

[140] See Duplouy 2006.

[141] Debate surrounding the various ethnicities present at Pithekoussai has been at times intense. For the debate surrounding Nestor's cup see: Ridgway 1996; Malkin 1998a. On diasporic hotspots, see Sommer 2007.

[142] E.g., Mercuri 2004, 261: "L'élément grec pénètre cependant rapidement la culture indigene et devient predominant, soumettant à une acculturation totale la population locale. . . ." (However, Greek influences quickly penetrated indigenous culture and soon came to dominate resulting in the complete acculturation of the local population.) Cf. Greco 2003.

been attributed to the shadowy populations that purportedly inhabited the site upon which Epizephyrian Locri was later founded,[143] although much of the evidence for this has unfortunately been lost as a result of excavation.[144] One might reasonably question the reliability of interpretative schemas in which Hellenization is portrayed as a logical outcome, however, since Hellenic identity was far from static and homogenous.[145] Instead, the perceived homogenization of material practices must be viewed in its local and regional context: the result of processes in which all parties were actively engaged.[146]

Narratives of a very different kind must also be taken into account when considering historical attitudes regarding the land and peoples of Southern Calabria: a tangled web of assumptions and biases (ancient and modern) that have been slow to dissipate. Modern views of the region's geography have often been projected onto the past.[147] However, the logic of such assumptions must necessarily be challenged, as in spite of being portrayed in modern historical documents as barren and poverty-stricken, Southern Calabria would have appeared spectacularly rich and fertile to anyone accustomed to the rural landscapes of mainland Greece.[148] Far from being impoverished,

---

[143] According to Polybius, the initial phases of settlement saw colonists co-habiting with indigenes (Polyb. 12.5.10).

[144] As a result, the only concrete evidence of intercultural contact and/or interaction relating to this period that survives is the mortuary evidence preserved in the Canale-Janchina cemetery. For what remains see: Orsi 1912; Foti 1976, 358; Sabbione 1982, 277–298—based, in part, upon ceramic evidence; *RE* xiii.2 1310.

[145] In fact, while the tendency to interpret the archaeological record in terms of the progressive acculturation of native populations succumbing to the allures of Hellenic civilization reflects a profoundly Hellenocentric bias, other/additional problems include erratic and infrequent publication of archaeological materials and the sheer quantity of data thrown up by development, presenting huge challenges for an already overstretched archaeological service.

[146] Cf. recent work on the Sibaritide in Northern Calabria, which has instead adopted a self-styled landscape archaeological approach, widening the sphere of analysis to encompass the emergence of urban identities and the resulting contrasts that may have arisen with the rural lifeways of those inhabiting the upland Pollino massif (e.g., Attema 2003).

[147] "The two great mountain groups of the Sila and the Aspromonte, have formed in all times wild and rugged tracts, covered in dense forests almost impenetrable to civilization . . . modern travellers speak with great admiration of the beauty and fertility of the coasts of Calabria. But these advantages are limited to a small portion of the country; and it is probable that even when the Greek settlements on the coast were the most flourishing, neither culture nor civilization had made much progress in the interior" (*Dictionary of Greek and Roman Geography* [1854], ed. William Smith). Dunbabin 1948, 201 observes: "The inhabitants have from the days of the Bruttians to this a reputation for backwardness and incivility." Cf. Gissing 1901.

[148] Take areas such as the Southern Argolid, for example, approximately 50 percent of which is deemed uncultivable due to its predominantly thin soils and an annual rainfall that frequently falls below the level considered necessary to sustain arable farming (Forbes 1993, 214). Mean annual rainfall in Calabria currently ranges from 6 centimeters at sea level to 20 centimeters in the mountains (Le Pera and Sorriso-Valvo 2000). For ancient accounts of luxuriant flora/fauna, see Strab. VI 1.5.

the agricultural wealth of the cities of Magna Graecia was in many cases so famous as to be proverbial (e.g., Sybaris, Metapontum)[149] while the colonialist assumptions that have at times underpinned narratives of Hellenization have been countered by recent research stressing both the agency of local indigenous populations and the extent to which trends in urbanization were already in evidence, long before Greek settlers became firmly established in the region.[150]

One of the most immediate problems that faces the historian seeking to map identity discourse in Southern Calabria and, to some extent, Magna Graecia as a whole is the relative paucity of historic/literary evidence for the period in question. Aside from some scattered references preserved in later authors such as Strabo or Dionysius of Halicarnassus and stray remarks from Herodotus and Thucydides, information regarding the way in which local identities were framed and constructed is remarkably hard to come by. What little material as survives regarding the various pre-Greek/native populations is largely restricted to narrative accounts of a sequence of prehistoric migrations to Italy from Greece and the circumstances surrounding the founding of the (various) colonies. Where material does survive, moreover, it requires careful handling as the fifth-century context from which it emerged may well have influenced its overall content and scope. Proximity to Sicily and events such as the revolt of Ducetius would have left questions of ethnic origin highly politicized. The picture, insofar as a clear one exists at all, is largely one of confusion as to how and by what criteria the various groups should be defined—there being little agreement on such matters even in antiquity.[151]

Some headway may, however, be achieved if we examine the reports of fifth-century authors such as Antiochus of Syracuse and Pherekydes of Athens. Both felt inclined to write on the early history of the region in question, one from a more general, historical point of view and the other in his study of the diverse genealogical traditions by which people and place were variously connected. The indigenous inhabitants are referred to as "Oinotrians"

---

[149] Wealth as opposed to decadence: see a recent challenge to the idea that Sybarite luxury provided an effective rationale for the polis's eventual downfall—the earliest recorded instance in which excessive wealth ($\pi\lambda o\hat{v}\tau o s$) begets (in turn) luxury ($\tau\rho v\phi\acute{\eta}$), surfeit ($\kappa\acute{o}\rho o s$), hubris, and ultimate destruction (Gorman and Gorman 2007 on *Deip.* 12.520c; cf. Bernhardt 2003; Ampolo 1993). The authors are perhaps unduly skeptical on this point as, while Athenaeus's treatment of the Hellenistic historians is undoubtedly problematic (see Pelling 2000), the transgressive nature of Sybarite luxury may well have been highlighted by those favorable to Croton (albeit by way of apologia). For Metapontum's dedication of a golden harvest at Delphi see *FGrHist* 555 F 13.
[150] Burgers 1998, 2004; Osborne and Cunliffe 2005; Attema 2003.
[151] See the markedly guarded comments of Dionysius of Halicarnassus (Dion. Hal. I. 12–13).

and the region as a whole as "Oinotria"—an appellation linked, it is thought, to early wine production and subsequent trade,[152] or the wider importance of communal banqueting in mediating relationships between settlers and local populations. While Antiochus refrains from comment concerning the ethnic origins of the Oinotrians, the eponymous Oinotros is listed by Pherekydes as one of the fifty offspring of Pelasgos and Deianeira (along with Peucetios, eponym of the Picenes).[153] This in all likelihood reflects the belief that both Oinotros and the people who took his name were actually migrants from Arcadia or, alternately, that those inhabiting the region only assumed the name once the migrant Oinotros rose to power. King Italos, another eponymous hero who later emerged as something of a culture hero, is credited by Aristotle with converting the nomadic Oinotrians to a settled, law-abiding existence of which communal dining was a component part.[154]

Hellanicus, another noted genealogist, offers an alternative etymology for Italia/Italoi. Although colorful in the extreme, this provides tantalizing glimpses of early contacts between Greek-speaking settlers and local populations. Hellanicus's lively etymology describes an episode in which one of Geryon's cattle escaped from its herd and wandered the length and breadth of the peninsula before fording the Straits and crossing to Sicily. Herakles' attempts to communicate with the local inhabitants while searching for the stray calf were repeatedly met with the word *witoulos*—the term they used for "calf"—and as a result, the lands over which the calf had roamed were subsequently named "Witoulia."[155] Just as "Oinotria" is suggestive of early interactions being governed by commensal dining or viticulture, an etymology focusing on intercultural contact arising from the procurement of cattle is too much of a coincidence to be ignored. What is striking, however, is the non-Greek origin of the term, which, along with a supposed link to Pelasgians—a group whose origins (real or imagined) were sufficiently nebulous to confound later authors such as Herodotus—suggests active theorizing on behalf of one or more parties and an attempt to integrate local populations into the wider genealogical framework.[156]

---

[152] A possible derivative of *oinótron* "vine prop" (J. Hall 2005, 270).

[153] *FGrHist* 3 F 156. Cf. Soph. *Tript.* Fr. 541; Dion. Hal. I. 12–13.

[154] His arrival would subsequently give rise to another shift in identity from Oinotrians to Italoi (Ath. *Pol.* 7.9.3 cf. *FGrHist* 555). See Scheer 2011 for wider discussion of Arcadian foundation myths.

[155] Hellanicus's claim that the term derives from the Latin for "calf" (*vitulus*) is, to some extent, supported by Timaios insofar as the explanations refer to cattle (*FGrHist* 4 F 111 = Dion. Hal. I 35; *FGrHist* 42 F 556). However, Timaios stresses the Greek origins of Italia, linking the name to the ancient term for "bull" (*italos*)—a reflection, it is argued, of the fact that the area was particularly rich in livestock.

[156] Malkin 1998a; Hall 2002. See also Dench 1995, 44 where Hellanicus's cross-cultural interests are contrasted with the more "Bickermanesque" Timaios.

The absence of a narrative account by which historians might seek to order the past—ignoring issues and concerns aroused by the dissonances between the varied bodies of evidence—can, however, have its benefits. Classical historians have, at times, been overly preoccupied with making the data "fit" what literary evidence we possess. Where Italian prehistory is concerned, this has often taken the form of employing tribal names inherited from ancient Greek authors to denote specific cultural groups, taking it for granted all the while that the information transmitted by their various interlocutors was at all times accurate and reliable.[157] Some caution is required, however, when it comes to the way in which these literary attestations of identity are integrated with broader archaeological enquiry. (We have already had cause to consider the implications of culture-historical paradigms in our discussions of Scythia.)[158]

Although foundation myths and legends do suggest some ways in which local populations were conceptualized, both their provenance and dating are in many cases uncertain as they are almost entirely reliant upon later sources. Stories surrounding the foundation of Rhegion involving a violent incident in which local populations had to be driven away by force from a site overlooking the Straits provides one such example.[159] The apparent interest with which stories surrounding the various cities were evidently regarded is arguably indicative of their overall importance as narratives that might be selectively deployed to situate groups and individuals. Viewed in this light, historicity is very much a secondary consideration. We must instead take individuals such as Antiochus at their word and assume that they at least provide an accurate reflection of the sorts of stories circulating in the fifth

---

[157] The extent to which these accounts have influenced archaeological interpretation is hard to gauge but there are strong grounds for arguing that literary-led perspectives have resulted in arguments that are essentially circular and self-validating in nature, with artefacts and assemblages being equated with specific "cultures" or ethnic groups and vice versa. Although very much an emerging field of scholarship, the latter has seen a marked shift in focus from literary-led studies employing a culture-history approach, to problem-based scholarship stressing the dynamic and often tumultuous nature of Iron Age societies in which interregional trade, competition for resources, urbanization, and social mobility were already prevalent to varying degrees (see further below plus Herring and Lomas 2000; Ridgway et al. 2000; Burgers 2004; Osborne and Cunliffe 2005).

[158] Italian prehistory has for a long time remained closely wedded to theories and methodologies rooted in intellectual debates dating back to the country's unification and the pervasive influence of Croce (Loney 2002). This typically results in the mapping of tribal identities in terms of discrete, bounded entities that were somehow static and impermeable.

[159] According to Antiochus of Syracuse, Rhegion was a Chalcidian colony: the inhabitants of Zancle (known as Messina from ca. 490 onward) sent for colonists from Chalcis and appointed one Antimnestos as *oikistes* (*FGrHist* 555 F 10). Other sources attesting to Chalcidian origins include Thuc. 6.44.3; Ps.-Skymnos 311–312; Diod. 14.40.1). A variant tradition preserved by Dionysius of Halicarnassus has Artimedes of Chalcis as founder (Dion. Hal. *Ant. Rom.* 19.2), while the involvement of Peloponnesian Messenians is also attested. For discussion of an oracular response and foundation traditions concerning Rhegion, see Manni 1980; Malkin 1987, 31ff.; Londey 1990.

century B.C. In contrast, archaeological evidence for the external use of collective ethnics for both Rhegion and Locri, dating from the late sixth century onward, provides what is perhaps the soundest indicator that both communities were perceived as coherent identity groups both internally and externally.[160]

4.2.4 The Play of Identities, Knowledge, and Difference

Having completed this (albeit partial) sketch of some of the overarching characteristics of Southern Calabria—encompassing general issues relating to archaeological and historic interpretation—we shall now embark upon more focused discussion of specific sites and assemblages in which the "play" of identities can readily be perceived. We shall begin with the *Nostoi*—an intricate patchwork of tales and associations that proved so important in mediating contacts between groups of different outlook and culture. Aside from providing a ready means of conceptualizing relationships between foreign peoples, the *Nostoi* have also featured in discussions surrounding both the role of extramural cults/sanctuaries in defining territory and the extent to which they reflect prior contact and interaction with indigenous groups dating back (in some cases) to the Mycenaean period.[161]

That this network of stories and myths encompassed Southern Italy, and Calabria in particular, is already well established.[162] One figure that stands out in particular is Philoctetes, the owner of the bow and arrows of Herakles whose festering wound so disturbed his companions that they abandoned him on Lemnos, only to return when a captured seer prophesized that Troy would otherwise remain impregnable. Philoctetes is reported to have founded various settlements associated with local indigenous peoples either inhabiting or adjoining the territory of Croton on his way back from Troy—notably the Chones. It seems likely therefore that stories concerning the hero

---

[160] Evidence of this and a similar nature is important in demonstrating that ideas of a Locrian or Rhegian identity were not only subscribed to by "insiders" and but also noted by outsiders in contexts ranging from their immediate locality to major Panhellenic sanctuaries. See: Rhegion: *SEG* XI 1205 (ca. 500 B.C.), *SEG* XXIV 303–305 (sixth–fifth centuries B.C.), *ML* 63.12. Earlier evidence of its external individual use can be found in *SEG* XLVIII 1252 (ca. 550–500 BC). Locri: *SEG* XI 1211 (ca. 525–500 BC), *SEG* XXIV 304–305 (sixth–fifth centuries B.C.). The internal use of a city ethnic occurs on coins minted by Rhegion from the late sixth century onward (evidence from Locri being far later due to an initial reluctance to mint coin).

[161] E.g., de Polignac 1995, 95.

[162] For Italy see Phillips 1953; Bérard 1957, 323–383; Malkin 1998a, 1998b; J. Hall 2005; Kowalzig 2007, esp. 288ff. Strabo mentions a heroon dedicated to Draco near Laos (in modern Basilicata) and an associated oracle stating that "Many of Laos will one day perish about Laoian Draco" (VI 1.1). Such dire predictions are likely to reflect the damage wrought by Oscan-speaking peoples during the fifth century B.C. A heroon to Polites is reported near Temesa (VI 1.5)

were common currency between early settlers and non-Greek-speaking groups native to the region.[163]

Another figure associated with (again) the northern reaches of Calabria is Epeios, celebrated architect of the Trojan horse. On returning from Troy, Epeios is reputed to have dedicated his tools at Lagaria in a sanctuary dedicated to Athena.[164] Although reportedly famous throughout the region, the sanctuary soon sank into such obscurity that by the Roman period its location was considered something of a mystery. Its rediscovery centuries later on the Timpone della Motta, a low hilltop overlooking the Sibaritide some 12 kilometers from the ancient site of Sybaris near the modern village of Francavilla Marittima, has been an important milestone in the history of the region.[165] While securely identified as a sanctuary dedicated to Athena, the wider interpretation of the site has become a matter of controversy following the suggestion that the location of the Athenaion was in some way dictated by cult activities previously undertaken by non-Greek populations.[166] Such arguments have been hotly contested—most notably by François de Polignac in an important study of the role of extra-urban cults in the demarcation and control of territory.[167] In fact, de Polignac goes so far as to explicitly single out Francavilla Marittima, arguing: "There is no evidence for ascribing to the autochthonous peoples who visited these places any specifically religious purpose, until after

---

[163] See Malkin 1998b for discussion. For the mainstream tradition that saw the hero return to Thessaly see: *Il.* II 717; *Od.* III 190 cf. Soph. *Phil.* 1421–1430. Strabo (VI 1.3) reports that Petelia, the metropolis of the Chones, was founded by Philoctetes after he left Meliboea. Crimissa, near Croton, is also mentioned in a passage citing Apollodorus's *On Ships*. See Musti 1991; Giangiulio 1991 for discussion of the role Philoctetes played in relations between Croton and Sybaris. Links are attested with Sybaris and at Macalla near Croton (Lycoph. *Alex.* 919–929, cf. [Aristotle] *Mir. Ausc.* 107. For these and further discussion, see *OCD*³ s.v. 'Philoctetes'. N.b. that this reference is absent from the hardback edition of this volume). After colonizing the promontory the hero is reported to have moved into the interior to found Chone—an indigenous center. (Although whether such traditions date back to the period in question is entirely moot.) For Philoctetes in Sicily see Nenci 1991; and Lacroix 1965, 5–21 for Southern Italy as a whole. Other "Achaeans" are mentioned by Strabo VI 1, 12.

[164] Strabo VI 1.4. De La Genière 1991.

[165] De La Genière 1989; Russo 1996; Kleibrink 2006.

[166] Maaskant-Kleibrink 2000.

[167] Polignac's withering critique of the notion that the Greeks of Southern Italy were in any way influenced by indigenous cult practice formed part of a broader reaction against the idea that these cults were either native in origin or a reflection of precolonial/Mycenaean contacts that were subsequently revived. Explicitly opposed to the notion that the existence of important extra-urban cults was a phenomenon unique to the colonial foundations of the western Mediterranean, in which cult practices dating to the pre-Greek Iron Age were intentionally preserved in order to facilitate the control and/or assimilation of indigenous populations, Polignac asserted that: "It is fair to say that not a single sanctuary has produced material proof of any continuity with a previous cult . . . these establishments left no vestiges of religious activity, which suggests that the relevant societies never attained a level of development in which religion constituted an autonomous and public domain clearly indicated by special arrangements made to accommodate it" (Polignac 1995, 96). The contrast with the (more advanced) Greeks could not be clearer and the question of continuity was rendered essentially "meaningless" as a result. Cf. Guzzo 1990.

the arrival of the Greeks."[168] The recent publication of some of earliest phases of the site means this is no longer a tenable position, however. Building Vb, one of a number of timber longhouses situated on the Timpone della Motta, has been interpreted by its excavators as an apsidal structure referred to as a "sacred house," in which members of the local elite were busily engaged in ritual activities from at least the eighth century B.C. These rituals involved "extraordinary weaving" on a monumental loom equipped with badly fired but well-burnished impasto weights, of considerable workmanship and over twice the size of those normally used in weaving. The discovery of an unusually high quantity of ash and animal bones in which a variety of bronze jewelery was also found also suggests the presence of a ritual hearth.[169]

Although pottery evidence is suggestive of at least some level of contact with Greek-speaking traders or merchandise from the nearby settlement that would later emerge as the polis of Sybaris, the extent to which this might have acted as a conduit for information concerning local cult practice is impossible to determine. In the absence of any literary evidence it is difficult to gauge the extent to which the site was well known in antiquity or whether Greek-speaking settlers were attracted to the locality by its reputation—as well as by more material or strategic considerations. There is therefore a marked difference in opinion regarding the manner in which both the site and its inhabitants are likely to have fared at the hands of Achaean settlers.[170] The apparent destruction of the site might in fact be attributed to a variety of factors ranging from hostile attack and deliberate demolition to accidental causes. It was replaced by three temples constructed of timber and, in a subsequent building phase, mud brick with stone foundations (seventh through sixth centuries B.C.). More importantly, at least one of the new structures appears to have functioned as an Athenaion that remained in use until at least the fifth century.[171] The decision to dedicate the sanctuary to Athena is arguably significant in the light of the goddess's widespread association with *techne*—and weaving in particular—perhaps implying a degree of continuity in cult activity.[172]

---

[168] De Polignac 1995, 96n16.

[169] Kleibrink 2006.

[170] Depending on whether one perceives interaction predominantly in terms of peaceful coexistence or mutual antagonism this may be interpreted as demolition, accidental burning, or destruction by fire (Attema 2008).

[171] De La Genière 1989, 494–495.

[172] The excavators have speculated that sacred weaving may have continued to take place on site, citing the activities depicted upon the Verucchio throne as possible grounds for comparison. In addition to this, the recovery of large numbers of loom weights from later contexts suggests that weaving (of whatever kind) remained an important activity at Lagaria well into the sixth century

Let us assume, for the time being at least, that continuity of some kind or other did in fact occur (whether through a cult offered to Athena or the on-going practice of sacred weaving). It seems highly unlikely that the Achaean settlers merely hit upon the right cult through sheer serendipity; instead, it seems reasonable to argue that there must have been some appreciation of or interest in the ritual activities undertaken at the site prior to their arrival—knowledge that might reasonably be described as "ethnographic"—and that this formed the basis for subsequent decisions as to how future generations lived and worshipped there. Some degree of syncretism would seem to be apparent on this basis but this should not be perceived as evidence for the "indigenization" of "Greeks."[173] Instead, the archaeological sequences on the Timpone della Motta are indicative of some form of "knowledge transfer" between the resident population and newcomers to the region. These new-comers arguably demonstrated an active engagement with ideas and values that were perhaps not dissimilar to their own. The gap separating Greek settler and Italic indigene was perhaps not quite as wide as de Polignac assumed.

Knowledge of tribes native to Northern Calabria can in fact be demon-strated, or at least inferred, at a location far removed from Magna Graecia. While no doubt familiar with Sybaris, a city with treasuries at both Olympia and Delphi reported to contain rich dedications[174] and by that time a byword for opulence and luxury, a sharp-eyed visitor to the sanctuary at Olympia might have wondered at the likely identity of the Serdaioi. The Serdaioi are mentioned on a bronze plaque commemorating a treaty with Sybaris and her allies dated to circa 550–525 B.C.[175] How would such questions have been answered and where did the information come from? Would the resident priests or officials have been able to supply the necessary information if asked, and to what extent would they have found it necessary to define their subject in relation to the other neighboring tribes, perhaps leading to a gen-eral discussion of the defining characteristics of the various Italic peoples native to the region? Such flights of fancy may at one level appear frivolous but the network of knowledge and ideas to which they refer can now only be

---

(De La Genière 1991, 64–66, figs. 7–12). The types in question are of the pyramidal type com-monly associated with "Greek" cultural practices. Whether this represents anything out of the ordinary is rather more difficult to establish given the overall importance of weaving as a day-to-day "economic" activity. For a different view on continuity see de Polignac 1995, 96.

[173] De Polignac 1995, 96.

[174] Delphi: Strab. IX 3.8; Partida 2000, 261–263. Olympia: Paus. VI 19.9; Mertens-Horn and Viola 1990, 240–246. On dedications see: Ath. 605A–B; Papadopoulos 2002.

[175] Kunze 1961; Jeffery 1961, 456, pl. 77, no. 1b; Greco 1990. For discussion of comparatively high levels of elite mobility in the (non-Greek) west, see Antonaccio 2007.

restored by imaginative leaps of this nature. The extent to which contemporaries carried such facts and figures as might easily be recalled "in their heads" has an important bearing upon the manner in which discourses of identity and difference played out over time and space.

4.2.5 Notions of Place

Nostos ethnography and a lively interest in local cult aside, there is far more to be said concerning the "play" of knowledge and ideas relating to foreign lands and peoples. The consumption of material objects and images was equally important.[176] We have already seen in an earlier chapter how Etruscan metalwork from the sixth through fifth centuries B.C. included depictions of Scythians or Amazons—those from Capua being notable examples. In the absence of supporting evidence we cannot necessarily assume that objects such as these circulated *within* our study area itself but the same cannot be said of the black-figure pottery carrying depictions of "Scythians" that certainly did, with some of the earliest examples dating back to at least the mid- to late sixth century B.C.[177] These, along with the prominence afforded to Scythian habits and customs in epinicia honoring victors from Syracuse, suggest that ideas regarding Scythia and Scythians were already circulating freely throughout the region well before the fifth century B.C.

While many of the most celebrated depictions of Egyptians or Ethiopians discussed in an earlier chapter were discovered in Etruscan cemeteries located further to the north, there seems little doubt as to whether such ideas and images extended as far as Southern Calabria. This is borne out by the Attic black-glaze aryballos in the shape of an Ethiopian's head from the Contrada Lucifero necropolis at Locri, now on display in the Museo Nazionale in Reggio-Calabria.[178] The aryballos offers a detailed depiction of an Ethiopian physiognomy and was presumably intended to act as a container for some exotic product—scented or refined oils and so forth. The precise means by which it reached its final resting place after its original starting point in the Athenian Potters' Quarter can only be guessed at: such items were effectively mass-produced and easily transportable. It is unlikely, therefore, that the specimen from Lucifero traveled alone to locations where such images and

---

[176] The presence of objects of Etruscan origin both at "Greek" sites and among the grave goods at the Canale-Janchina necropolis suggests trading links of some sort or another were already well established by at least the eighth century B.C.

[177] Cf. a white-ground lekythos published by Orsi (Tomb 1614, Contrada Lucifero necropolis, Locri) depicting an Amazon armed with bow and axe standing before a palm tree (Orsi 1917, 137–138, fig. 45).

[178] (Tomb 448.) See Orsi 1912, 16, fig. 20; Lattanzi 2003, 36.

forms were entirely unfamiliar. Were it possible to map the routes such objects took as they traveled the length and breadth of the Mediterranean world, the result would be an intricate web of pathways connecting manufacturing centers, storage depots, and distribution centers (whether quayside stalls or booths lining the agora)—from which individual pieces might then depart on solo journeys in the possession of their one or more owners, before finally being lost, disposed of, or deposited in funerary contexts whose distance from their initial point of manufacture might range from a few minutes' walk to thousands of kilometers.[179]

This is significant insofar as just what *did* travel with Greek pots along their various networks of distribution is uncertain.[180] The distribution of fine-ware pottery presupposes cultural *koiné* of some sort but we cannot assume that the images with which various pots were variously adorned were universally intelligible, conveying the same information and ideas to all observers. While we may be able to trace the circulation of pots both spatially and chronologically, the interpretation of such imagery would have been dependent upon a whole host of factors no longer accessible to us, rendering questions of reception far from straightforward. In the case of the Lucifero aryballos, the lack of accompanying inscriptions or graffiti mean the image could have been interpreted in any number of ways, calling to mind tales of Homeric Memnon, Apollo's blameless companions, or the scorching effect of less moderate climes (see above, chapter 2).

Where transmission of some sort has evidently occurred we can at least demonstrate that the image in question actually matters, even if its transferral to another medium is motivated by nothing more than a whimsical desire to depict "pointy-headed people on horseback." The manner in which such objects and imagery were both viewed and interpreted outwith an Athenian context is rarely, if ever, discussed in any detail—a peculiar oversight that holds true for both Greek and non-Greek contexts: the poleis of Locri, Rhegion, or Messina or the city-states of Etruria.[181] Take, for example, the fragmentary depiction of a Chian komast from Rhegion dating from the seventh through sixth centuries B.C. Although described as a running satyr, the individual depicted appears to be wearing a turban, raising interesting questions as to how such imagery would have been understood: Would it have been assimilated with the Scythian cap (*kidaris*), as Miller has maintained, or is such blurring of categories more a reflection of modern ideas

---

[179] See Appadurai 1986; Gosden and Marshall 1999.
[180] See R. Osborne 2007b for related discussion.
[181] Cf. Boardman 1999, who is essentially dismissive of the ability of non-Greeks to appreciate "Greek art"; and Arafat and Morgan 1994 stressing interest and engagement.

and agendas relating to Orientalism?[182] Since East Greek ceramics are relatively common in the region's archaeology during the early Archaic period, the reception of such objects and imagery is clearly a matter of some importance.

Another—not unrelated—problem that needs to be addressed is the extent to which a taste for the foreign equated to knowledge and interest in foreign places and people. Given the fact that fine wares from Corinth form a significant proportion of the material assemblage for sites located throughout the study area,[183] is it therefore possible that proto-Corinthian or Corinthian pottery carried with it a resonance of "wealthy Corinth": a specific sense of place of which the ancient consumer would have been explicitly aware? Aryballoi of similar form and design are also thought to have been produced locally during the sixth century B.C., a reflection of the way in which local networks of trade and exchange were progressively adapting in response to foreign forms and ideas.[184] These were reworked or appropriated by craftsmen local to the region whose creative engagement with cultural difference represented an active process entirely at odds with narratives of passive acculturation/Hellenization.

Objects/things are not defined solely by their materiality. We have already heard how particular products and commodities may have become synonymous with their point of origin. Approached from this perspective, an assemblage of pottery represents a host of overlapping ideas about people and place—however ephemeral or transitory—effectively frozen in time and space: the point at which they were lost, broken, or deposited in a grave. Until that final act or event removed them from circulation they retained the potential to act as vehicles for specific notions of place that were effectively encoded in their form and decorative style. Corinthian, East Greek, Etruscan, Chian, Attic, Chalkidian, and, at times, Laconian imports circulated relatively freely alongside locally manufactured fine wares such as the Chalkidian-style black-figure vases that were produced in Rhegion during the sixth through fifth centuries B.C. If such objects were at times recognized or (at the very least) *classified* according to their place of origin, then mapping their

---

[182] See: Miller 1991, 1997. It is difficult to estimate the extent to which elements of cultural difference would have been discernible to the ancient viewer in Rhegion or Locri, firmly situated in their own sociocultural milieu with tastes and preferences that were (potentially) far removed from our perhaps overly schematized view of the "imagined world" of the Athenian citizen. Cf. Lemos 2000 tracing the interplay between artistic traditions emanating from Anatolia and East Greek pottery and vase painting.

[183] Evidence for a taste for imported fine wares is apparent from the eighth century onward at the Canale-Janchina necropolis (Orsi 1912; Mercuri 2004).

[184] Cf. Boardman 2004; Jones and Buxeda i Garrigós 2004 (for an archaeometric perspective).

distribution is in some ways analogous to charting the interplay of specific ideas and values associated with Ionia, the Aegean, Sparta, or Etruria.

In the case of pottery, differences in form and style are not only representative of "different ways of doing things" (by different people) but also evocative—to varying degrees—of a specific sense of place. Take, for example, Panathenaic amphorae: as prizes in the Panathenaic games they were distinctive in both form and design. Each amphora had the capacity to carry approximately ten gallons of oil from a grove sacred to Athena. Labeled "one of the prizes from Athens," one side depicted Athena Promachos while the other showed the event for which the prize was awarded.[185] These prized commodities were already in circulation by circa 530 B.C.—perhaps as a result of reforms instituted by the Pisistratids—and, as prestige goods, appear to have been equally sought after by non-Greek elites.[186]

Coins represent another category of "speaking" object that achieved widespread circulation throughout the study area during the period in question. Although Locri did not mint its own coinage until quite late, Rhegion issued drachms on the Euboic standard from circa 510 B.C. inscribed with a Chalkidian script.[187] These were produced using the distinctive incuse technique characteristic of the cities of Southern Italy, interpreted in some quarters as signaling an Achaean identity (in spite of the fact that it was periodically employed not only by Rhegion but also Taras—a city whose Achaean ties are less than obvious).[188] In fact, while the incuse technique may in some

---

[185] An example from the British Museum is a case in point; although effectively unprovenanced, it is said to have originated in Southern Italy/Sicily: Black-figured Panathenaic amphora, Euphiletos Painter, ca. 530–520 B.C. GR 1836.2–24.177 (Cat. Vases B 137). See Kluiver 1995, 83 for "foreign interest" in Athens and links between Tyrrhenian amphorae and the earliest Panathenaic vases.

[186] See Hornblower and Morgan 2007, 5; Lippolis 2004, 46–50; Lo Porto 1967.

[187] C. Boehringer 1984–5, 111–112; Rutter *HN*³ 2468.

[188] While a recent study by John K. Papadopoulos represents an important bid to bring the study of coinage into the mainstream of archaeological enquiry, making a number of important suggestions concerning the significance attributed to the minting of identities in a colonial context and the role that the southern Italian city states played in the spread of coinage, the claim that notions of "Achaeaness" were communicated via images referencing "prehistoric notions of value" is highly questionable: "the images and emblems chosen are taken not from the contemporary cultural landscape of the historic Akhaians, but actively recall the world of the heroic Akhaians of the Bronze Age" (Papadopoulos 2002, 123). That the imagery depicted on coins amounts to an important contribution to discourses of identity and difference is now widely accepted, however, singling out images of cattle (to take just one example) and using them to trace an unbroken continuum back to the Bronze Age Vapheio Cup A, Mycenaean frescoes from Knossos, and, in other cases, Linear B, seems needlessly far-fetched (e.g., Papadopoulos 2002, 29). Put simply, it seems unnecessary to historicize or mythologize the monetary value of a bull in a society in which agriculture formed the primary means of subsistence, prestige, and wealth and any similarities that do occur may simply arise from the fact that depictions of bulls will (necessarily) share common attributes. For recent discussion, see Kowalzig 2007 on

contexts have become representative of a local or regional sense of Achaean-ess connecting poleis such as Sybaris, Croton, Caulonia, and Metapontum, it seems far more likely that its appearance was closely related to the activities of specialist die-cutters who plied their trade throughout the region as a whole.[189]

The earliest types minted by Rhegion convey a great deal of information to the interested observer. Those issued prior to the tyrant Anaxilas's rise to power depict a man-faced bull, widely interpreted as a riverine deity repre-senting the Apsias, with a locust above. These were followed by a series of staters and drachms on the Euboic standard with a lion mask facing on the obverse, reflecting the arrival of Samian refugees in Messina early in the fifth century.[190] From circa 485 B.C., Rhegion's mint switched to the Attic standard, depicting thereafter the mule biga (obv.) and running hare (rev.) on both tetradrachms and fractions.[191] Such images may reasonably be linked to a form of self-promotion—whether on behalf of a tyranny or the polis as a whole. Coins struck by Rhegion were by no means the only issues in circula-tion, however. While Rhegian coins boast of lush pasture (cattle), the pres-ence of a tripod on Crotoniate coins may be understood as both a reference to the founding of the colony and the mines at Temesa. Meanwhile, Meta-pontion's ear of corn is invariably interpreted as an allusion to the city's agrarian wealth. There remains, however, considerable ambiguity sur-rounding the precise quantity of coined money that was in circulation at any one time since hoard evidence from Calabria is strongly regional in flavor—with the notable exception of the Taranto hoard, which, although situated well outside Calabria itself, demonstrates the extent to which coined money could travel.[192] Since such matters have already been discussed in an earlier

---

Bacchylides' *Ode* 11 and the cult of Artemis at Metapontum, stressing the mutability of Achaean (or, indeed any other) identity in a fifth-century context: "the song goes to the heart of the deli-cate issue of competing ethnic identities in southern Italy" (298).

[189] The technique may equally owe something to the repoussé technique characteristic of indige-nous metalworking traditions. Once established such practices may well have become institu-tionalized (for a variety of reasons) but the extent to which they communicated a sense of shared (Achaean) ethnicity remains difficult to ascertain; stamped incuses served the very practical function of demonstrating that coins had not been plated.

[190] The device had been a standard feature of Samian issues since at least the late sixth century: e.g., AR drachm, Samos, OBV: winged boar. REV: lion's head facing, ca. 530–500 B.C., *SNG* Vol: VII 1237. Cf. Caltabiano 1993, 17–18, 25–26; Rutter *HN*³ 2469; *SNG Cop. Italy* 1924–1927.

[191] Caltabiano 1993, 17–18, 53–56; Rutter *HN*³ 2472ff.; *SNG Cop. Italy* 1924–7.

[192] At one extreme we have the Taranto hoard (*IGCH* 1874), around 600 silver coins deposited in a vase sometime around 510 B.C. As well as coins from Sicily (Selinus, Himera, Naxos) it included issues from Calabria (Sybaris, Croton), Campania (Poseidonia), central Greece (Athens, Corinth), Cyrene, Ionia (Phocaea), and the Aegean (Chios, Mende, Thasos). Other hoards recov-ered from across Calabria are either less extensive and/or varied. These include the Sambiase

chapter there is no need to pursue such matters further other than to emphasize the extent to which the "play" of identities thus revealed was very much
part of the everyday existence of the region's inhabitants.

Notions of place also had an important role to play in the emergence of
polis centers such as Rhegion and Locri. At some point during their early
history the communities that came to occupy the sites of Rhegion and Locri
would have found it necessary to establish a common set of *nomima*.[193] This
can be seen as a process of negotiating and mediating difference both within
nascent citizen communities and with surrounding and outlying populations (whether "Greek" or non-Greek).[194] Precisely how this came about in
the case of Rhegion and Locri is far from clear, but it was clearly a topic of
some importance if the observations made by later commentators such as
Thucydides are anything to go by.[195] Self-conscious reflection on the relative
merits of "different ways of doing things" saw individuals and communities
tap into a wider pool of knowledge and ideas, participating in a wider discourse in which "ethnographic interest" had an important role to play.

One (highly visible) means by which material identities might plausibly
have been formulated or expressed is through the use of architectural orders
in monumental construction. The monumentalization of the urban centers

---

hoard (just east of modern Lamezia Terme) (*IGCH* 1872), consisting of 45 silver coins originating from Sybaris and Corinth (a mere two) dated to around 520 B.C. A burial from Gerace
near Locri dated to around 490 B.C. contained a silver drachma minted by Croton/Temesa
(*IGCH* 1880), while *IGCH* 1881, a pot hoard from Curinga (some 30 km SW of Catanzaro) contained some 300 incuse coins including staters from Caulonia, Metapontion, and Taras. A further 600 silver coins are attested at Cittanuova, some 45 km NE of Rhegion, deposited in a
burial dating to around 470–460 B.C. Although only a fraction of the hoard has been recorded,
the latter contained coins from Laus, Poseidonia, Caulonia, Sybaris, and Croton. Other hoards
recorded for Calabria include *IGCH* 1873, 1882, 1883, 1885–1887, 1891, spanning the period ca.
510 B.C. down until the mid-fifth century with at least another 3 attributed to "Southern Italy"
(*IGCH* 1877–1879).
[193] The significance of the latter as a means of defining identities within the Greek world has
recently been highlighted, with particular emphasis being placed upon the importance of the
colonial experience in developing a sense of "Greek" identity. It was this sense of growing connectedness that was arguably at the root of any wider sense of "Greek" identity. Malkin sees
nomima as: "reflecting or even defining the collective identity of a political community," their
deployment constituting "a very Greek experience of identity and connectedness" (Malkin
2003a, 67–69).
[194] See Malkin 2003a. Coinage constitutes just one element of the nomima of a polis, as we have
seen, and although references to coinage in particular are comparatively sparse within ancient
literature, there is considerable evidence that the wider topic, including other fundamentals
such as religious calendar, weights, and measures, was considered important by contemporaries (Thuc. VI 4. 4).
[195] E.g., Thuc. VI 5. 1 discussing the poleis of Sicily. Cf. the interests and concerns of early Greek
logographers mentioned above. Euboic influence can be traced in elements of the Rhegian
calendar (Trümpy, *Monat.* 43–44) and local scripts (Jeffery 1961). Some caution is required in the
use of such material as foundation narratives invariably reflect a variety of agendas.

of Rhegion and Locri, which appears to have taken place during the sixth century B.C., would presumably have necessitated some degree of consensus regarding the architectural orders, units of measure, and ratios to be employed. Consensus on such issues must have preceded, or at least developed in tandem with, the introduction of an orthogonal plan sometime around the mid-sixth century B.C. In the case of Locri, this was accompanied by the structure commonly referred to as the U-shaped Stoa, the Marasà Sud/Sanctuary of Aphrodite, Marasà and the "Casa Marafioti," a Doric temple with foundation trenches dating to circa 540–530 B.C., which were variously constructed or monumentalized at around this time.[196]

4.2.6 The Case for Difference: The Western Locrians

In an effort to explore the manner in which regional and local identities variously found expression we shall now sharpen our focus to one polis in particular: Locri Epizephyrii. Founded during the opening decades of the seventh century,[197] Locri's early history was reportedly plagued by civil unrest prior to the appointment of Zaleucus as *nomothetes*. The move resulted in what was purportedly the oldest set of written laws in the Greek world; reportedly attributed to Athena herself after she appeared to Zaleucus in a dream.[198] Locri subsequently acquired the reputation for being well ordered, a quality that remained, in many people's eyes, its defining characteristic. Vague references to this effect in authors such as Pindar suggest that the city

---

[196] Orsi 1911, 27–67. Barra Bagnasco 1996; Parra 1998, 314. Dieter Mertens has argued that the fusion of Doric and Ionic elements was a means of actively signaling local/regional identities in the case of the Achaean colonies (Mertens 1990), raising questions as to whether similar processes can be identified elsewhere across the region. The argument, which has much to recommend it, was subsequently taken up by Jonathan Hall (J. Hall 1997, 137; cf. Barletta 1990) as part of a wider initiative to highlight other forms of material culture through which identity might be signaled. Comparisons with the various mother-cities thought likely to have influenced the choices made will in all likelihood remain inconclusive, however, due to a distinct paucity of evidence from poleis such as Helike (now totally submerged) (Papadopoulos 2002, 28). Although it remains entirely plausible that the monumentalizing trend exhibited by poleis such as Locri and Rhegion went hand in hand with attempts to construct a civic identity that distinguished them from their peers, whether it is indeed viable to think of Dorian and Ionian identities as representing two mutually exclusive ethnicities during the period in question is similarly moot (J. Hall 1997). Cf. Snodgrass 1986 on peer–polity interaction in Sicily. For discussion of the Achaean poleis of Southern Italy, see Morgan and Hall 1996.

[197] Archaeological survey dates the foundation to early seventh century (Sabbione 1982, 277–293) but accounts vary: Strab. VI 1.7. (after the founding of Croton in 710 and Syracuse 733); Polyb. 12.6b.9 circa the first Messenian War (ca. 735–717 BC); Eusebius: sometime between Olympiads 25.1 or 26.4 (679/8 or 673/2).

[198] The sources for this are late: Arist. *Pol.* 1274ª 22 and Fr. 555; Iambl. *VP* 130, 17. See Gagarin 1986, 58–59, 129–130, no. 27. Although seemingly dating from the fourth century, the Locrian Tables may preserve traces of the latter, attesting to a local calendar of twelve months with an additional intercalary month (Niutta 1977, 266) along with various sumptuary laws.

may have been regarded as something of a cultural backwater—largely introvert and somewhat provincial in outlook.

The question as to which Locrians founded Locri was debated even in antiquity.[199] A number of parties were in all likelihood involved although there is little scope for certainty in such matters. Tarentines may have participated but it is equally possible that Locri's foundation narrative was subsequently remodeled to reflect that of Taras.[200] Traditions relating to Taras may well have arisen from a desire to forge an alliance with the city in the face of an overbearing Italiote League, headed by Croton, during the mid-sixth century B.C.[201] In order to legitimate these ties both Taras and Locri would (presumably) have had to remodel their respective pasts or identities in order to accommodate the other—all the while aware of the threat posed by an "Achaean" confederacy whose common ethnic identity had apparently become its defining ideology.[202] Locri appears to have implemented a process of cultural realignment at the same time that she entered into an accord with Taras—whose ties to the Doric ethnos were well established. This must have been predicated on relatively detailed knowledge of Tarantine myths and customs in order for the city to effectively"become Dorian."[203] Material expressions of the city's—newfound—Dorian affinities can perhaps be seen in the pediment sculpture from the Marasà sanctuary dated to the latter half of the fifth century in which Sparta's decision to send the Dioscuri to the aid of the stricken polis (which had earlier appealed for aid) was commemorated.[204]

Another (rather more unusual way) in which distinctive attributes of Locrian society found expression can be found in the Locrian *pinakes*. Recovered in large numbers from not only the city and its environs but also its various "colonial" offshoots located on the Tyrrenhian seaboard, these clay tablets carry reliefs linked to a cult that enjoyed widespread popularity throughout the Greek world during the period in question—that of Kore/

---

[199] Although how early this speculation began is uncertain: Ephor. Fr. 138 apud Strab. VI 1.7; Ps.-Skymnos 312–316. See Dunbabin 1948, 35–37.

[200] Elsewhere it is maintained that Locri was both a colony of Sparta and that citizens from Locri had aided that city in the (first) Messenian War (Paus. III 3.1).

[201] Sourvinou-Inwood 1974, 189. See also: Van Compernolle 1992, 762–763; Bérard 1957, 199–209; Niutta 1977, 260–261.

[202] This was a (presumably) opportunistic move as the non-Achaean Taras had initially been a part of the same league prior to seceding.

[203] Paus. III 19. 11–13; Strab. VI 1. 10; Diod. VIII 32; Justin xx 2–3.

[204] The decision ensured that Locri and her allies carried the day, winning a decisive victory at the battle of the Sagra. See: Bicknell 1966; Redfield 2003, 205; Malkin 2003, 62ff.; Currie 2005, 264.

Persephone.[205] They are unique to Locri and, as such, provide us with an interesting case study of Greek difference. James Redfield has explored the significance of the images displayed on the *pinakes* in great detail, only to conclude that the social organization of Locri Epizephyrii set it apart from other leading Greek city-states during the archaic period. Redfield credits the Locrians with inventing a "third way" in which community solidarity reflected or relied upon the mediation of sexual difference and the closed exchange of women of elite status through marriage.[206] In view of the apparent singularity of this social model, the question as to whether contemporaries (whether in neighboring poleis or further afield) were in any way sensitive to these differences acquires considerable importance.[207] Aspects of this "third way" are perhaps encapsulated in the manner in which the worship of Persephone at Locri was seemingly conflated with that of Aphrodite, as demonstrated by the imagery depicted on the *pinakes*.[208] Redfield's innovative claim that the fusion of nuptial and funerary imagery is indicative of Orphic concepts of marriage and death (both symbolic rites of passage that would ultimately lead to a blessed state)[209] merely highlights the point that we should, wherever possible, take local difference into account in the study of Greek deities rather than assuming a Panhellenic, community-oriented approach to cult.[210] "Differences within the same" were many and varied.[211]

This brings us to another topic over which the women of Locri have aroused a storm of controversy—namely, the presence or absence of sacred prostitution within the city. Debate centers around the interpretation of one structure in particular: a central colonnaded building overlooking a rectangular space (approximately 55 x 66 meters), located in the area of the Centocamere and facing toward the sea. Constructed at some point during the sixth century B.C., this was positioned adjacent to the port quarter and south of the circuit wall (which deviates abruptly from its course in order to avoid the earlier structure).

---

[205] According to later sources the sanctuary at Locri was renowned throughout Italy (Diod. Sic. 27.4.2; Livy, IXXX18.3).

[206] Redfield 2003.

[207] The extent to which commentators such as Herodotus appear to have had an eye for cases in which traditional social/gender norms were subverted makes it not unreasonable to expect that, if Redfield's theories relating to the Locrian women were to be correct, evidence for their reception should be preserved in the sources. Cf. Hdt. I 181, 199; II 35, 60; IV 168, 186, 193.

[208] The images described have been variously interpreted but are widely regarded as "wedding ex-votos" (MacLachlan 1995, 210), in which aspects of the two deities are amalgamated, provoking considerable controversy as to their significance and/or meaning. For discussion see Skinner 2005; Graf 2000; MacLachlan 1995, 218; Sourvinou-Inwood 1991; 1978, 109, 120.

[209] Redfield 2003, 367–369, 384–385. For wider discussion of interpretative problems surrounding mortuary practice at Locri, see Petersen 2010, 269; Redfield 2003, 220.

[210] Sourvinou-Inwood 1978, 101–103.

[211] A phrase coined by Irad Malkin (Malkin 2003b).

Although open on the seaward side, its remaining sides were lined with porticoes behind which a series of small rooms were situated—six on either side, to which a further five were added during a later phase of construction. Around 371 *bothroi* were discovered in the central space containing the remains of sacred meals and votive terracottas of male figures such as Dionysius; however, the recovery of two vases carrying dedications to Aphrodite (dating to the fourth century) has encouraged speculation that the sanctuary was in fact the location for ritualized prostitution and that the small rooms that lined the porticoes were booths in which *hetairai* could carry out their sacred duties.[212]

Such arguments are far from straightforward, however, since the entire concept of sacred prostitution has recently been denounced as a "historiographic myth."[213] In the case of Locri, the literary evidence is overwhelmingly late and merits a fair degree of skepticism: Justin's epitome of the first-century B.C. author Pompeius Trogus dates to 477/476 B.C. a vow undertaken by the citizens of Locri in which they promised to prostitute their virgin daughters at the festival of Aphrodite should they manage to overcome their assailant, Leophron, tyrant of Rhegion. Leophron was, at the time, either in the process of besieging the city or threatening to do so.[214] Sacred prostitution need not be the only interpretation, however; Redfield's hypothesis that the booths in question were intended as communal dining facilities at which both sexes were present seems equally—if not more—likely, finding parallels with Etruscan practices and a more general tendency to associate ideas of a blissful afterlife with banqueting and symposia.[215] Tomb paintings aside, this found expression in forms such as the plaques and reliefs in which men and women are depicted reclining on couches.[216] The need to interpret such scenes in terms of courtesan/reveler as opposed to a loving couple is, however, questioned; instead, Redfield links these to the wider emphasis on the importance of happiness and mutual fulfillment for *both* sexes, perceiving the *pinakes* as a celebration of the duality of the wife in which sensual and matronly qualities enjoyed equal status. This was, insofar as we can tell, profoundly *different* from

---

[212] Similar rooms have been interpreted as facilities for communal dining elsewhere—the thesis remains a source of biding controversy.

[213] Pirenne-Delforge 2009. For discussion see: Pirenne-Delforge 2009, 2007, 1994; Budin 2008. Cf. Dillon 2002, 199–202.

[214] Just. *Epit.* 21.3. Another author, Clearchus of Soli (ap. Ath. 12.516a), also claimed that rituals of this nature were commonplace at Locri, although Pompeius's report may be the starting point for this statement (which is implied to be more of a one-off). For discussion see Redfield 2003, 411–416; Skinner 2005.

[215] Communal dining in sanctuaries is also attested at Kalapodi in East Locris and Isthmia: Morgan 1994, 113; 2003, 117–118.

[216] Redfield 2003, 383–384 on type 10/11 P 50.

more traditional attitudes regarding the role of women in ancient society—as expounded by (predominantly) male authors.

Although just what was going on at Locri is likely to remain unclear, it remains entirely possible that whatever distinguished Locri from neighboring poleis and those further afield was in some way reflected in the *pinakes* and the rituals with which they were associated. The manner in which they should be interpreted has certainly been debated at some length[217] but whatever the answers to such questions turn out to be, it seems not unreasonable to take the various traditions and stories relating to maidens, cult practice, and prostitution as evidence of a degree of interest (and perhaps bewilderment) as to goings-on within the city. Take, for example, the outrageous behavior attributed to Dionysius II of Syracuse sometime around the mid-fourth century B.C. According to the (unswervingly hostile) sources, after being deposed in a coup d'état Dionysius sought sanctuary at Locri, exploiting his maternal link to the city. Clearchus and Strabo present different accounts of events that ensued thereafter: Clearchus has Dionysius ravishing young maidens of noble birth and generally acting in a deplorable fashion while Strabo describes a string of outrages in which the ex-tyrant not only exercises his droit de seigneur but also compels maidens to dance around naked and chase doves while wearing oddly matched shoes.[218]

Aside from being a hallmark of typically tyrannical behavior this is arguably a reflection of the special position that girls of a marriageable age enjoyed within Locrian society. It has in fact been suggested that the bizarre antics that the hapless maidens were compelled to undertake in Strabo's account may be seen as a confused refraction of some form of initiatory rite performed in honor of Aphrodite—with whom doves were closely associated.[219] Whatever the truth of the matter, both tales imply a certain level of

---

[217] Arguing at one extreme, Prückner has suggested a reading of the *pinakes* that sees them as recreating snapshots of a ritual undertaken at the festival of Aphrodite in which young girls were prostituted (Prückner 1968). This is likely to be wholly excessive (and is, in any case, impossible to substantiate) but there are certainly distinctive elements regarding the imagery portrayed (the manner in which the respective deities/animals with which they were associated are represented and the overall prominence of women in performing sacrifices, etc.), which may have been noticeable to outsiders. The poems of Nossis, composed during the fourth century, are undoubtedly important, containing numerous references to hetairai making dedications, thereby suggesting that prostitutes may have played a prominent role in cult activity, enjoying wealth and, perhaps, status not far removed from that of women/girls from other sectors of society (Skinner 2005).
[218] ap. Ath. 12.541d; Strab. VI 1.8.
[219] Redfield 2003, 288–289; Skinner 2005.

observation/interest/understanding (or otherwise) of the habits and customs attributed to Locrian maidens. Whether they are accurate or not is largely immaterial. The fact that they survive at all raises questions as to how many other stories of a similar nature were in circulation at any one time that might reveal an interest in people and place.[220]

Having ranged fairly freely across Southern Calabria and some of its adjoining territories, we shall now pause to consider a particular point in space and time—a sort of case study within a case study that focuses upon issues of identity at their most basic and fundamental. Located in what amounts to a void separating the poleis of Rhegion and Locri, literally "on the margins" amid what was quite possibly disputed territory, it is precisely the sort of place where one would expect identities/ethnicities to be at their most strident.[221] What we have instead is a paradox: deafening silence—at least where the literary evidence is concerned—and an enigmatic material assemblage, the implications of which will be discussed below.

4.2.7 Conflict, Connectivity, and Exchange: The View from the Margins

At an elevation of 1,260 meters, some 20 kilometers inland and around 50 kilometers from the poleis of Rhegion and Locri Epizephyrii, respectively, the hilltop site at San Salvatore is somewhat at odds with established views on the nature of Greek settlement in Magna Graecia.[222] Far from hugging the coastal lowlands and fertile agricultural plains, the site demonstrates that populations that we would now consider to be culturally "Greek" were busily exploiting the rich pasture and timber resources of the mountainous hinterland as early as the sixth century B.C.[223] Located in a strategic position overlooking access routes both to and from the rich agricultural land of a high plateau, known locally as the Campi di Bova, the site assumed its present form during the late sixth through early fifth centuries B.C. At or around this time, the summit of the hill was leveled and enclosed by a perimeter wall of approximately 34 meters (N-S) by 29 meters (E-W), roughly square, with what appears to be a range of buildings or series of "rooms" projecting into

---

[220] Another interpretation applied to stories concerning the votum is that they reflect the practice of the Opuntian Locrians in sending two maidens to Troy as an act of atonement for the outrages perpetrated by Ajax (Sourvinou-Inwood 1974, 1978, 1991). If correct, this would provide further evidence of a wider interest in (Greek) nomoi and of the latter being progressively received and reworked according to local interests and agendas.

[221] Cf. Morgan 2001b, 83.

[222] Foxhall 2007a, 52; cf. S. Morris 2007, 388; J. Hall 2007, 117.

[223] Foxhall 2006, 2007a. However, see now Visonà 2009; 2010 (Monte Palazzi); Brizzi and Costamagna 2010, 593 (Palazzo).

the interior. A substantial tower some 7 square meters was located on its southern side, with at least one building located a little way to the south, outside the main enclosure. According to the results of a magnetometry survey conducted in 2006, a defensive earthwork of some sort may also have extended across the ridge, presumably with a view to controlling access to the site on its southern side—from which it is most accessible.[224] These concerns for security appear to have been well founded since the site's history came to an abrupt close a century or so after it was initially constructed following an armed assault and ensuing conflagration.[225]

The comparative remoteness and apparent inaccessibility of the (modern) site is somewhat at odds with the range of materials recovered during excavations.[226] These indicate that its inhabitants were actively engaged in wide-ranging networks of knowledge, trade, and exchange. The presence of imported products—black-glazed fine wares, wine and oil (products most commonly associated with the numerous fragments of transport amphorae recovered from across the site), and jewelery (in the form of a faience bead), along with evidence of indigenous craft traditions—gives some indication of both the likely subsistence level and cultural predilections of its occupants. They apparently not only possessed the means to obtain such goods but also subscribed to a set of cultural values or practices that involved the consumption of luxury items such as refined oils and the use of drinking services.[227] Did they also tap into knowledge and ideas relating to a variety of foreign lands and peoples?

---

[224] Foxhall 2007a. On the wider significance of fortifications both within Calabria and throughout Greece as a whole, see Adamesteanu 1982; Snodgrass 1982; Guzzo 1982.

[225] Evidence for the former can be found in the numerous sling bullets and projectile points recovered during excavations, located, in almost all cases, in a destruction layer that showed clear evidence of sustained burning. Since the identities of both attackers and attacked remains something of an enigma, questions regarding their cultural affiliations and political loyalties must necessarily be explored via the material record (Foxhall 2007a; Skinner 2007).

[226] Although further work is undoubtedly required before any firm conclusions can be drawn regarding its local and regional context, the settlement at San Salvatore does not appear to have existed in isolation. Field survey on the northern edge of the Campi di Bova undertaken in 2006 revealed the existence of the (decidedly smaller) site at Monte Grosso on a terraced hilltop, some 1,307 meters above sea level (Yoon 2006). It bears some resemblance to the site at San Salvatore from the point of view of its material assemblage and topographical position overlooking the valleys of the interior. Fortifications dating to the sixth century B.C. are also reported to have been identified on a hilltop overlooking the Petrace River Basin (contrada Palazzo)—later the site of the Italic stronghold commonly referred to as Oppido Mamertina (Visonà 2009, 10; Brizzi 2008; Agostino and Sica 2009).

[227] The presence of luxury commodities can be inferred from the discovery during the 2006 field season of items such as a globular aryballos thought to date from the fifth century B.C. or earlier (Foxhall 2007a). See above for the relationship that existed between consumption and self-fashioning.

Although the sociopolitical and economic significance of the site in relation to the surrounding area remains essentially unclear, both the hybrid nature of this assemblage and its inland location make it likely that San Salvatore formed a point of contact for peoples of different outlook and culture—indeed, one of the most intriguing and important aspects of the site is its potential to illuminate the precise terms on which such contact occurred.[228] Although interest in the chora of Rhegion has flourished since the pioneering work of Vallet, Will, and Guzzo, with the major emphasis being on the control of movement and resources, discussion of the history and archaeology of the region has focused predominantly upon political geography and the at-times fraught relations that existed with Locri. Much energy (and ink) has been expended upon the question of where the frontiers between the two adjoining territories could be said to lie and the relevance of fragmentary snippets of Stesichorus in determining the same, leaving largely unanswered numerous questions concerning the way in which the adjoining lands were settled and exploited and the manner in which their inhabitants perceived themselves relative to one another.[229]

This is far from straightforward, however, as there is (as yet) no direct evidence to suggest that those inhabiting the settlement at San Salvatore were directly dependent upon either of its neighboring poleis. Just as recent studies of the site of L'Amastruola in southern Puglia have questioned whether the settlement was in any way linked to the nearby polis of Taras, it remains entirely ambiguous as to how the inhabitants of San Salvatore would have viewed themselves in relation to sites such as the coastal settlement at Mazza, isolated rural farmsteads, or the evolving poleis of Rhegion and Locri—and vice versa.[230] We are therefore faced with a barrage of unanswered questions as to not only how local populations, poleis, and rural "Greek" settlements interacted on a political and economic level but also how Greek they were in the first place.

While we have both literary and epigraphic evidence attesting to conflict between the poleis during the Archaic–early Classical period,[231] whether such material forms a viable starting point for archaeological interpretation is open to debate. Recent discussion of territorial expansion and conflict in

---

[228] Foxhall 2007a.

[229] Cordiano 1995, 2006. See Berlinzani 2002 for the way in which a myth concerning the musical contest between Eunomos and Ariston was employed to frame the conflict.

[230] Foxhall 2007a. See Attema 2003 for discussion of similar questions arising from research in the Sibaritide.

[231] A number of inscribed dedications from Olympia celebrating one or more victories by Rhegion over Locri and a fragment of Stesichorus (see fn. 14, above) being among the most notable (Cordiano 1995; Berlinziani 2002; Visonà 2009).

Southern Calabria during the sixth through fifth centuries B.C. is valuable as a case in point in this respect.[232] Accounts offered by Cordiano and Visonà regarding the role that border forts and garrisons played in securing territory during a period of mounting tensions between the poleis of Southern Italy are both erudite and persuasive; however, their authors are noticeably reticent when it comes to the role that local indigenous populations played in such processes. The only factors that the civic elites of Locri and Rhegion were required to take into account—according to such analyses— were the expansionist ambitions of their rivals in neighboring poleis, it being assumed from the outset that their chorai were effectively contiguous and that local populations were either entirely absent or remained nothing more than bystanders as territories to which they had formerly laid claim were progressively subdivided between the neighboring Greek colonies.

Applying such arguments represents something of a challenge for archaeologists and historians. We have abundant evidence that identities were expressed quite forcibly—up to and including armed conflict, but the means by which these were articulated are largely lost. Problems also surround the manner in which we conceptualize the various groups involved in that, however careful one is in emphasizing the generalizing nature of terms such as "Greek" and "native," the assumption that the two categories were easily distinguished is at times difficult to demonstrate. One of the most nuanced and balanced discussions of the manner in which native identities were constructed and expressed during the period in question starts from the position that the broad distinction between the Italic and Greek (or Italiote) people of Southern Italy was a significant one.[233] An important contribution to the debate surrounding the politics of identity in Southern Italy during the Archaic–early Classical period, the study in question sees the construction and reformulation of native identities as having occurred as a result of

---

[232] Cordiano 1995, 2006; Visonà 2009, 2010. From a methodological point of view, Cordiano adopts an entirely traditional approach to the problem of how best to align material, epigraphic, and literary evidence. The latter provides a framework for interpreting a range of archaeological materials—by far the most notable of which is the sixty-century walled site of Serro di Tavola (described as a phrourion). Both the morphology of the latter and its location astride important routes of communication find a number of parallels at San Salvatore (Costamagna 1986, 495–502; Cordiano 2006; 1995, 83–88, 104–107). The site's location on the northern margins of the Piani d'Aspromonte is particularly striking, inviting the conclusion that it was constructed with a view to controlling access to the fertile agricultural land of the high plateau (Cordiano 1995, 84).

[233] Herring 2000, 45n2. This position is largely predicated upon the Greek–barbarian dichotomy present in authors of the fifth century or later and is thus very much aligned with the approach to identity pioneered by Jonathan Hall in which literary evidence is held to be the preeminent indicium of ethnic identity.

external influence—namely, contact with *Greeks.*[234] This thesis is supported by ethnographic examples of cases in which contact with Europeans encouraged exclusive ethnic identities, rightly emphasizing the historical significance of modern, European expectations—reflecting well-defined notions of the nation state—in determining the strategies pursued by the colonized.[235]

This argument has considerable implications for any attempt to stress the exclusivity of Greek identity and the manner in which this might have affected native identities.[236] While drawing attention to the fact that native identities are less likely to have been exclusive, it has been suggested that "[i]ncreased contact with the Greek coastal cities is likely to have increased the native sense of a distinct and exclusive identity" and that this resulted in the material expression of native cultural identities via regional styles of matt-painted pottery.[237]

Problems of a similar nature are neatly encapsulated in an assemblage of weaponry recovered from the site at San Salvatore, which, although modest in size, carries significant implications for understanding its eventual fate while at the same time providing the start point for a discussion as to the manner in which social or political identities were framed and constructed through the discursive use of material culture. As such, it represents a valuable opportunity to study questions of intercultural contact and/or conflict in a region in which our understanding of interactions between shadowy local populations and early Greek-speaking settlers remains hazy at best. Far from revealing a rigid ethno-cultural boundary separating different identity groups, it suggests that relationships between early city-states and local populations, whether settler or indigene, were often far from clear-cut.[238]

The interpretation of the assemblage in question is anything but straightforward given that its most notable characteristic is perhaps its heterogeneity. In the case of the weaponry, the items include thirteen bronze-cast, socketed arrowheads; a javelin point; a spearhead; and several fragments of bronze-scale armor. It might similarly be characterized as heterogeneous from a culture-historical point of view also, with matériel considered both typically "Greek" and "native" recovered—quite literally—side by side. Although all the

---

[234] Albeit while attempting to play down the gap separating settlers and the indigenous populations during the eighth through seventh centuries B.C. and that intercultural contact might have encouraged an awareness of contrasting identities on both sides (cf. Malkin 1998a).

[235] Herring 2000, 63–64. The assumption that Greek identity was relatively well defined at the time and thus an effective analogue for that of modern Europeans in a colonial context is to some extent tendentious, however.

[236] "The Greek settlers, with their emerging concept of exclusive citizenship, which we might liken to ideas of nationality, would have been far more aware of their cultural identity than their native neighbours" (Herring 2000, 62).

[237] Herring 2000, 62n41.

[238] See Petersen 2010, 298; Lomas 2004b, 8.

arrowheads recovered are of types regarded as characteristically "Greek"—albeit with a pedigree stretching back to Scythia—they are unlikely to function as a reliable indicium of ethnic identity. Any simplistic correlation between material culture and identity seems inherently unlikely given the manifest complexities of interactions between settlers, traders, and indigenes throughout the region that date back to at least the eighth century B.C.[239]

Another object recovered from one of the earliest phases of the site presents us with a range of possibilities as to its origins and interpretation. An alabastron in the shape of a kore figurine, dating from the mid-sixth century B.C., was recovered underneath a floor of a structure located to the southwest of the main enclosure (see fig. 4.5).[240] Widely thought to be East Greek in origin and a reflection of Egyptian/"Oriental" influences, Kore figurines of this kind are widely associated with the cult of Persephone. While examples have also been found at Rhegion and at Locrian foundations such as Metauros, the nearest cult center is the Mannella sanctuary at Locri.[241] Outside Magna Graecia, close parallels exist with the votives dedicated at the extramural sanctuary of Demeter and Persephone at Cyrene.[242] It is, however, unclear whether the maiden in question represents the work of craftsmen serving the sanctuaries at Locri and would have been recognized as such by contemporaries or whether this is a generic model whose origins would have gone unremarked.[243]

Although elusive and enigmatic, the site of San Salvatore encourages us to think in terms of a landscape populated by mixed groups who selectively employed different aspects of material culture in order to negotiate questions of power and identity.[244] Instead of trying to identify elements of the site assemblage that might be considered either distinctly "Italic" or "Greek,"

---

[239] See above for parallel discussion concerning the Leoxos stele: individuals born and reared in Southern Calabria might justifiably be expected to make equally pragmatic decisions regarding their chosen dress/materiel.

[240] The kore was deposited face down and the charcoal deposit with which it was associated, along with three small jugs while a fourth jug with a pierced base was set in the floor itself, as a means of pouring libations into the earth below (Foxhall 2007a). For the cult of Demeter/Kore in the Greek countryside, see Cole 2000.

[241] Cf. Costamagna and Sabbione 1990, 99n112.

[242] White 1984.

[243] Other material recovered from the fifth-century destruction layer included a tile stamp marked with a qoppa—an archaic script that formed the initial letter of both Croton and Corinth—and an inscription on a locally made Ionic cup of the late sixth century B.C. The graffito—presumably the name of its owner—includes the use of a 3-bar sigma, a practice associated on occasion with Rhegion but more commonly with sites further to the north such as Siris and, again, Croton (Jeffery 1961; Foxhall 2007a). If we return to the idea of nomima being a defining element of local identity then it is essentially unclear as to how such evidence should be interpreted.

[244] See Petersen 2010, 298: "The local and, perhaps, strategies of social mobility, competition and power struggles may provide the best basis from which to understand identity formations rather than polarized perceptions of 'Greeks and Others.'"

FIGURE 4.5 Photo: Kore alabastron from San Salvatore, mid-sixth century B.C. Reproduced with kind permission of Prof. Lin Foxhall, Bova Marina Archaeological Project. Photograph: Lin Foxhall.

one might argue that it is the essential heterogeneity of the material assemblage that in fact holds the key to how questions of identity should be framed and conceptualized. Rather than visualizing Southern Calabria as being neatly divided between the chorai of the local poleis, with any areas in which "Greek" finds are not present being the preserve of Italic groups, we should perhaps envisage a more fluid situation in which questions of power and identity were being continually renegotiated and mapped out anew. Far from representing a smooth and linear process that saw native cultures subsumed and acculturated by a rising tide of Hellenism, the manner in which identities were negotiated and contested formed part of an ongoing process, largely tied to the control of the economic resources capable of sustaining an elite lifestyle. "Hellenic" or "Italic" identities could be assumed or discarded as and when required. The rigid distinction between "Greek" and "native" underpinning de Polignac's interpretation of cult activity on the Timpone della Motta or the analysis of matt-painted pottery styles is unlikely to be helpful when it comes to conceptualizing the ongoing processes by which knowledge and ideas were exchanged between groups and individuals of different outlook and culture. The discursive construction of identities played out across time and space as groups and individuals selectively positioned themselves in relation to both the narratives of the past and other people.[245] Knowledge of "others" was freely exchanged, exploited, and/or manipulated on a day-to-day basis; material objects, images, and "texts" were all variously capable of evoking cultural difference—to be read and "understood" by active agents, immersed in a sea of ethnographic imaginings gleaned from epic and lyric, everyday parlance, sculpture, and vase painting.

4.3 The Imagined Centre: Identity and Difference at Delphi and Olympia

From the shores of Magna Graecia we shall now return to the center (both literally and metaphorically): the sanctuary at Delphi, location of the *omphalos*— Gaia's navel and thus the center of the world—and the sanctuary of Zeus at Olympia (see fig. 4.6).[246] As constituent parts of the "imagined center" these sanctuaries formed key points of reference for an ever-widening circle of individuals and communities from approximately the eighth century B.C. onward.[247] Between them they contributed toward the spread of ideas and values constitutive of a common sense of Greek identity, whether via participation in Panhellenic games, or reference to an oracle that purportedly played a key role in guaranteeing the long-term success of a whole range of civic and communal enterprises—not least the foundation of settlements

---

[245] S. Hall 1990. For discussion of the link between mortuary practice and proximity to urban centers such as Taras, see Petersen 2010, 299.

[246] Cf. Pind. Pyth. 4.74; Bacchyl. 4.4; Aesch. *Eum.* 40, 166. On the significance of Delphi's claim to mark the center of the world see Defradas 1954, 108–110; Gernet 1981, 323; Burkert 1983, 126–127; Cole 2004, 74ff.

[247] A huge bibliography on this but see variously: Snodgrass 1980, 2005; Malkin 1987, chap. 1; Morgan 1990, 1993; Osborne 1996, 232. For "imagined centers": Malkin 2003b.

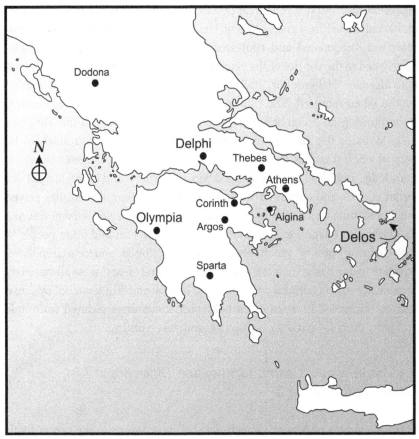

FIGURE 4.6 The imagined center: Delphi and Olympia. Map by the author.

overseas.[248] The manner in which this came about have been variously elucidated via a number of theoretical frameworks—studies in peer-polity interaction and the wider processes of state-formation and network theory—but
there are many aspects of their history and archaeology that remain
enigmatic.[249]

One factor that has been consistently remarked upon is the extent to
which these sanctuaries provided a backdrop for the staging of regional or
local identities, rival claims and (often) animosities, before a wider Panhellenic audience.[250] The controlled environment that they provided for acts of

---

[248] Such views were notably opposed by Defradas (1954), who disputed the historicity of Delphi's
involvement in colonization, to be qualified variously by Amandry 1956; Parke and Wormell
1956; Forrest 1957; Malkin 1987.
[249] Renfrew and Cherry 1986 (peer-polity interaction); Morgan 1990 (state-formation); Malkin
2003b; 2011 (Networks).
[250] E.g., Morgan 1990.

self-aggrandizement and expression on behalf of individuals and communities created veritable crucibles of Greek difference—whether in outlook, origin, or opinion. The resulting cacophony of competing voices and identities found material form in treasuries and inscribed votives, freestanding monuments, and epinicia—not least the songs of praise poets such as Pindar and Bacchylides, evoking local settings, identities, and difference before a diverse audience.[251] The great Panhellenic sanctuaries functioned on a quasi-international level as centers of cross-cultural contact and interaction between Greek-speaking populations and neighboring polities, states, and empires (west and east). Historical evidence for this is amply supported by a material record attesting to the diffusion of objects and ideas from the Ancient Near East, Egypt, and elsewhere. Part of a wider phenomenon commonly referred to as "Orientalizing," this process of cultural diffusion resulted in the circulation of craft objects (carved ivories, decorated metalwork, faience amulets, and so forth), knowledge, and people between social elites via complicated networks of trade, intermarriage, and gift-exchange. As such, it is now widely perceived to have played a key role in the unfolding story of "Greek" culture and society although with differing emphases, as we shall see.[252] While Hellenists might once have explained the genesis of Greek art and culture in terms of an exclusively "Greek miracle," evidence for contact between Iron Age Greece, Crete, and the Levant dating back to the ninth and tenth centuries B.C. means scholars are now more likely to stress an essential openness to the influence of "the high cultures of the Semitic Near East." This is very much the case if we turn to Ann Gunter's recent (and arguably groundbreaking) reappraisal of relations between the Aegean and the kingdoms of the Near East in terms of "a much broader set of interactions centred on the Neo-Assyrian Empire and its frontiers both east and west."[253] What was the wider significance of these various shifts and changes,

---

[251] Some of the more recent treatments of such topics include: Hornblower and Morgan 2007b; Currie 2005; Pedley 2005; Neer 2003; van Straten 2000; Alcock and Osborne 1994; Morgan 1993, 1990.

[252] Cf. Gunter 2009; Burkert 1992; S. Morris 1997b; 1992; Markoe 1996; Boardman 1996; M. West 1997; Osborne 1998a.

[253] Gunter 2009, 5. While an important (and long overdue) critique of a general tendency to either downplay or simply ignore the same, Gunter's study perpetuates the pendulum-like effect that appears to be the defining characteristic of debate on interaction between the Iron Age Aegean and the Near East—albeit against an expanded historical/geographical backdrop (see Gunter 2009 passim and works cited in fn. 65). The results are impressive but not entirely unproblematic: although the comprehensive rebuttal of the modern predilection for essentialized concepts of "Greece"/the "Orient" (1–16) and a related tendency to equate visual styles with national cultures (ibid., chap. 3) is well-founded, the suggestion that Greeks were sufficiently familiar with foreign imports as to render reference to "exotica" or "novelties" to which Greeks could respond/borrow from as redundant may be an overstatement (3). More importantly, Gunter's denial that Greeks would have perceived "the Orient" as an undifferentiated entity is

however, in a world in which membership of social elites was, to some extent at least, "defined and communicated by means of a symbolic currency in non-Greek objects"?[254]

This chapter will explore the extent to which knowledge relating to the lands and peoples from which such goods originated was, to some degree, constitutive of "Greekness" itself. Rather than seeking to simply explain or qualify a "Greek miracle," through close analysis of art forms and craft traditions, it will broaden its perspective to encompass the way in which ideas relating to cultural identity and difference were variously articulated and understood. In doing so it will demonstrate that a significant back history of interest and engagement with questions of cultural difference can be traced through the study of artefacts, iconography, and historical materials, further undermining the (now commonplace) assumption that ethnographic interests only emerged as a result of contact with Persia.

4.3.1 (Re)constructing Difference at Delphi and Olympia

It is already widely acknowledged that the great Panhellenic sanctuaries played a key role in determining what it meant to be Greek in the first place. Sometime around the mid-seventh century B.C., Thessalian machinations associated with the seizure of Delphi resulted in the Amphiktyonic genealogy being reconfigured to accommodate the sons of a newly inserted King Hellen, the bases by which "Hellenes" were subsequently be defined. The ability to claim a Hellenic pedigree, however remote, is purported to have formed the essential criteria for determining one's eligibility to compete in the Olympic games—as Jonathan Hall has argued. This emphasis on genealogy as the preeminent basis for conceptualizing the community of the Hellenes has been variously praised and qualified.[255] There are many other ways, however, in which Delphi and Olympia may have contributed to a developing sense of what it meant to be "Greek" in the first place.[256] In order to pursue

---

somewhat at odds with the argument that the Neo-Assyrian empire actively constructed a shared sense of "Assyrian identity" among the social elites of the various vassal states that lined its periphery via mechanisms such as the ritual exchange of prestige goods, etc. If, as Gunter argues, the Assyrians were successful in this respect, then a degree of perceived homogeneity would be entirely expected from the point of view of "outsiders," for all the fact that particular states/elite individuals operated at the margins of these transcultural networks.

[254] J. Hall 2007, 346; Duplouy 2006; Raaflaub 2004.

[255] See: Siapkas 2003; Dench 2005; Mitchell 2005.

[256] There were, of course, other sanctuaries that functioned on both an interstate and interregional level, not least those on the Isthmus at Corinth and at Nemea, Samos, and Dodona. The decision to focus on Delphi and Olympia reflects both the (entirely mundane) constraints of time/space and their centrality to narratives tracing the emergence of an overarching sense of Greek identity. Olympia, with its purported exclusivity, is traditionally contrasted with sites such

these further we need to lay aside any preconceived notions of "Greekness" to consider the practical implications of ever-increasing levels of contact and interaction between groups of different outlook and culture in settings marked out for that purpose.

While the heterogeneous world of the Homeric heroes has been variously interpreted as providing a mechanism (or mechanisms) for negotiating questions of cultural difference, the same is only partly true of sanctuaries such as Delphi and Olympia. A long-term interest in gauging the historical significance of institutions such as the Pytho or the Olympic games in relation to a number of broad-based narratives—the criteria by which "Greek" identities were selectively defined or the need to obtain divine sanction for various collective enterprises including the foundation of colonies/settlement overseas—has seen a great deal of scholarly attention focused on matters outwith everyday activity at the sanctuaries themselves. Aside from the basic recognition that they played an active role in disseminating ideas, values, and knowledge constitutive of a wider sense of Greek identity, whether by providing arenas in which an international elite could meet, engage in agonistic and cult activities, or consult an oracle whose power and prestige was progressively enhanced in the process, questions regarding the manner in which cultural difference was perceived are rarely considered in any detail.[257] Instead, there is an implicit assumption that membership of the "Hellenic club" was, to all intents and purposes, unambiguously defined and that non-Greeks themselves were de facto excluded from such settings. Discussion of the material record appears meager in comparison, a result, in part, of uneven levels of publication,[258] with the majority of attention focused on establishing the precise nature or mechanics of oracular divination, the logistics associated with organizing the respective games, or the economics of dedication (whether material or ideological).

More emphasis might usefully be placed on the manner in which questions of identity and difference played out in these arenas and whether these can in turn be tied to interests and discourses rarely associated with

---

as the Heraion at Samos, where non-Greek involvement is readily attested (see further below). For the early history of the Panhellenic sanctuaries and further references, see Davies 2007; Pedley 2005, 119–164; de Polignac 1995 [1984]; Morgan 1994; 1993; 1990.

[257] Nielsen 2007 being the exception that proves the rule.

[258] Extensive in some cases and negligible in others: cf. volumes of Olympische Forschungen; Fouilles de Delphes, Isthmia and Nemea—in which architectural analysis, art, and epigraphy often take precedence over finds recording and stratigraphy. For an all-too-rare example of the systematic publication of site data, see Felsch 2007; 1996. For new approaches, see Alcock and Osborne 1994; Hägg and Marinatos 1993; Morgan 1990; M. Scott 2010.

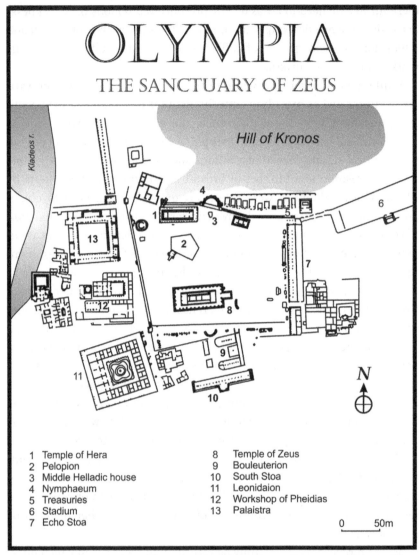

OLYMPIA
THE SANCTUARY OF ZEUS

Kladeos r.

Hill of Kronos

1	Temple of Hera	8	Temple of Zeus
2	Pelopion	9	Bouleuterion
3	Middle Helladic house	10	South Stoa
4	Nymphaeum	11	Leonidaion
5	Treasuries	12	Workshop of Pheidias
6	Stadium	13	Palaistra
7	Echo Stoa		

N

0   50m

FIGURE 4.7 The Sanctuary of Zeus at Olympia. Redrawn from A. Mallwitz, 1988, "Cult and Competition Locations at Olympia," in W. J. Raschke, ed., *The Archaeology of the Olympics: The Olympics and Other Festivals in Antiquity*, 82, fig. 6.2. Map by the author.

"goings-on" at "the imagined center." While it is somewhat unusual to characterize such spaces as areas of intercultural contact per se given the inherent "Greekness" of the setting, it will be argued that Greek difference was no more on show or being acted out than in an arena where states and individuals staked their claim to the cultural capital, kudos and everlasting

fame arising from agonistic competition (see fig. 4.7).[259] While we have traditionally looked to the margins for occasions on which identities (ethnic or
otherwise) developed in opposition to one another, the discursive interplay of
ideas and images—identified in earlier chapters—is equally in evidence at
the center of all things "Greek." Differences of various kinds were openly
displayed and, in turn, scrutinized by various groups and individuals: foreign objects, past events, and peoples were selectively viewed, remembered,
or "imagined" by diverse audiences who then employed them to construct
their own sense of identity.

4.3.2 "Reading" Objects, Viewing People: Everyday Activities at the Center of all things "Greek"

Our knowledge of the earliest phases of activity at the sites is largely depen-
dant upon the material record, often patchy and open to a variety of interpretations. Although the object of extensive—if uneven—study, as alluded to
above, it is only comparatively recently that the earliest phases of Iron Age
activity have received detailed discussion in Catherine Morgan's study of the
origins and development of cult practice at Delphi and Olympia.[260] Placing
the archaeology center stage, Morgan traces the manner in which material
evidence reflects shifting patterns of activity relating to the economics of
dedication, craft production, and technological innovation with a view to examining the sanctuaries in terms of both their local and regional contexts
and any wider role they might have played in the emergence of early state
societies. We should, however, be wary of subsuming such processes into the
all-encompassing narrative tracing the origins and history of the polis—as
Morgan has herself pointed out.[261] Other, no less important, factors were also
at work as knowledge and ideas relating to people and places were variously
absorbed, assimilated, and subsequently relayed. It seems highly likely, for
example, that in the years prior to Sparta's invasion of Messenia, gatherings
such as these were a source of key intelligence regarding the relative strengths
and weaknesses of neighboring states.[262] Although highly tentative in nature,

---

[259] Nielsen 2007, 98: "[T]he Olympic Games . . . provided one of the socio-political arenas in
which the great multitude of Hellenic *poleis* competed with each other through their dedications
and their athletes and in this way ideologically constructed and sharpened their own peculiar
local identity and existence." Cf. Antonaccio 2003, 72; Sewell 1999, 56.

[260] Morgan 1990.

[261] For the overweening influence of the polis, see Vlassopoulos 2007a; 2007b Morgan 2003;
2001b; S. Morris 1997b, 64ff.

[262] One of the most archaeologically visible states in the years preceding its conquest, Messenia
fades away abruptly thereafter (Morgan 1990, 192–193). Cf. Kaplan 2006, 145 for discussion of
Persian attempts to use Greek sanctuaries for intelligence-gathering. See also Russell 1999.

suggestions such as these should encourage us to pay far closer attention to the varying outlooks and agendas of those visiting major Panhellenic sanctuaries: How did they regard what they found there and how was the information that they gained subsequently employed?[263]

Exactly who visited these spaces can in some cases be gauged by the various rules and regulations regarding participation. In the case of Olympia, a panel of judges was convened to decide who had the right to compete and who was barred from proceedings: the *Hellanodikai* ("Judges of the Hellenes"). Although the origins of this magistracy are far from clear, it would appear to have replaced an earlier board of *diaitetes* at some point between 525–500 and 476 B.C.,[264] there being some ambiguity as to whether athletic competitions were open to non-Greeks prior to the fifth century B.C.[265] Inscribed lists recounting victors' names and cities of origin are another obvious point of reference, however, they represent only those who distinguished themselves by winning in the various agones, as opposed to providing an accurate reflection of the range of individuals present at any one time either as competitors or spectators.[266] Far less certainty surrounds the state of affairs that prevailed at the other major competitions where such records do not exist making it difficult, if not impossible, to rule out the presence of others whose status as Hellenes might also have been open to question.[267] However, it might reasonably be wondered how often such adjudication was required and the frequency with which individuals whose Hellenic credentials were either disputed or suspect were ejected from proceedings or alternatively allowed to participate.[268] This process of adjudication would have affected groups normally considered unambiguously "Greek"—as noted by Jonathan Hall. The game of genealogical one-upmanship that occurred when Alexander I asserted his right to compete at Olympia may not, in other words, have been at all

---

[263] For wider discussion of the relationship between geographic/ethnographic knowledge and imperial mindsets, see Harrison 2007.

[264] Nielsen 2007, 20–21.

[265] Cf. Nielsen 2007, 19–20: "While there is no reason to doubt that the Olympic Games were *de facto* a Hellenic phenomenon in the Archaic period it should nevertheless be noted that we have no information about any Barbarian who *wanted* to compete in the Olympics prior to Alexander whose ethnic identity could both be acknowledged and denied to be Hellenic" (author's italics).

[266] See Nielsen 2007, 18–21. For discussion of the problems arising from the list of Olympic victors attributed to Hippias of Elis, see J. Hall 2001, 160–161, appendix B.

[267] Lynette Mitchell's suggestion that the other three major sanctuaries may have exercised the same degree of ethnic exclusivity where athletic competitions are concerned cannot, unfortunately, be verified due to a lack of evidence (Mitchell 2005). Cf. S. Morris 1997b, 65: "Once we turn to a Greek sanctuary, the population we must imagine is likely to include foreigners, women, slaves, and other noncitizens." For Ionian exclusivity, see Hdt. I 143.

[268] See Nielsen 2007, 22–28; Crowther 2004, 135–140 for detailed discussion of the extent to which athletic nudity constituted a "boundary marker" separating Greeks/barbarians and the date at which this distinction, widely attested during the classical period but entirely absent in Homeric epic, came into play.

unusual.[269] It is worth pointing out, moreover, that the decision of the judges only related to the royal house of Macedon with the remainder of the population enjoying an at-best ambivalent status. One might reasonably ask how this worked out in real terms as, even if we restrict ourselves solely to the retinue that accompanied Alexander I to Olympia, we must surely envisage a sizeable cohort befitting an individual of rank, speaking (at best) woolly Greek and with manners or dress peculiar to many.[270] Mingling among other parties variously encamped on land adjacent to the sanctuary, would they have swapped tales regarding the foreign tribes and peoples that they had encountered, whether via firsthand experience or hearsay?.

There were other reasons for visiting the emerging Panhellenic sanctuaries, however. In the case of Delphi (see fig. 4.8), aside from a more general enthusiasm for *theoria* there was also the desire to consult the oracle, whose existence from the early eighth century B.C. would have provided an additional focus of interest and activity beyond that of agonistic competition. One day was set aside for nine months of the year for consulting the Pythia, with favored states and polities being granted the right of *promanteia*.[271] Prophecy by the Pythia was apparently supplemented by cleromancy—perhaps a more regular occurrence if divination took place on auspicious days.[272] The increasing prestige that resulted from involvement in initiatives such as city foundations and settlement overseas created an ever-increasing circle of devotees and admirers. Even if we have to make due allowance for the dubious historicity of some aspects of the story, Herodotus's account of the lengths to which the Lydian king Croesus went to secure favorable oracles from Delphi is significant.[273] Far from experiencing any difficulty in gaining access to the Pythia, Croesus's emissaries seem to have been more than welcome at the sanctuary.[274] The sumptuous dedications made in order to propitiate the god and the persistent questioning may

---

[269] Herodotus recounts the aplomb with which Alexander I of Macedon established his right to participate; the king's Argive descent was duly demonstrated and the monarch went on to a joint victory in the foot race (Hdt. V 22). See J. Hall 2001, 154–158 (and above for further discussion of genealogy). Thomas Heine Nielsen has recently argued that ethnic exclusivity may in fact be a fifth-century phenomenon: a reflection of the heightened sense of self-awareness resulting from the confrontation with Persia, her vassals and allies—notably Macedon (Nielsen 2007, 20).

[270] For perception of Macedon, see J. Hall 2001; Sourvinou-Inwood 2002. Cf. Saatsoglou-Paliadeli 1993.

[271] Morgan 1990. Cf. R. Osborne 1996, 192ff.; Malkin 1987; Roux 1976, 75–79; Amandry 1950. For pilgrimage to Delphi, see Arnush 2005.

[272] See Malkin 1987, 29–31 for discussion of sources relating to oracular lots at Delphi, qualifying—but not dismissing—Amandry's arguments relating to the same (Amandry 1950).

[273] Hdt. I 46–55. For alternative interpretations of Croesus's motives and their portrayal, see Parke 1984; Kurke 1999, 130ff.; Kaplan 2006.

[274] Cf. Kaplan 2006, 136 commenting on the length to which Mardonius was forced to go to obtain oracles from the shrines of Central Greece (Hdt. VIII 133–135): "Even at this stage direct access to local Greek shrines was difficult for a foreigner." For further dedications by Persians toward Greek deities, see Hdt. VI 97, 118; VII 191; VIII 133–135.

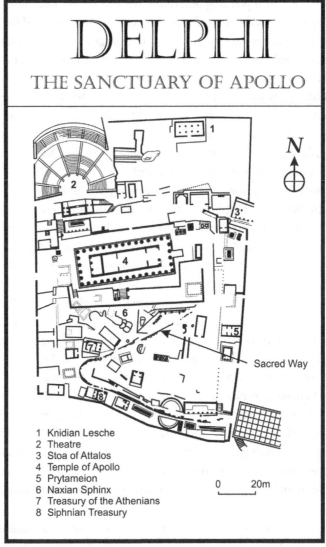

DELPHI

THE SANCTUARY OF APOLLO

N

1 Knidian Lesche
2 Theatre
3 Stoa of Attalos
4 Temple of Apollo
5 Prytameion
6 Naxian Sphinx
7 Treasury of the Athenians
8 Siphnian Treasury

Sacred Way

0   20m

FIGURE 4.8 Delphi, The Sanctuary of Apollo. Redrawn from
C. Morgan, 1990, *Athletes and Oracles*, 128, fig. 19. Map by the author.

have been ill-fated, but the implication is that those representing foreign monarchs may well have rubbed shoulders on a regular basis with the great and the good from various Greek-speaking communities.[275] Even if Croesus's motives—together with those of fellow royal dedicants of Lydian, Egyptian, or Persian

---

[275] The comparison with modern-day state funerals as an opportunity for informal politicking is well made (Morgan 1990, 177). For Saïte dedications in Greek sanctuaries, see Hdt. II 159, 182; Kaplan 2006, 134.

origin—were either misconstrued or misrepresented by the Greeks, as Philip Kaplan has recently argued,[276] the end result cannot be denied, namely a "foreign" presence in a quintessentially Greek setting.[277]

4.3.3 Delphi and Colonization

The gathering of envoys from communities seeking the oracle's sanction provided an ideal opportunity for exchanges of information and ideas. Opinion is, however, divided as to the extent to which the oracle itself would have acted as a repository of knowledge capable of independent action. The advantages arising from a level of connectedness unmatched by any other state or divinatory institution have been variously emphasized or downplayed as a result. Morgan's trenchant critique of the—widely subscribed-to notion—that Delphi acted as what was essentially "a clearing house for the dissemination of geographical and political information" should make us highly cautious when it comes to assuming the significance of Delphi during the late eighth through seventh centuries B.C.[278]

Our understanding of the earliest forms of consultation is bedeviled by uncertainty regarding the basic historicity of reported oracles[279]—whether due to distortion resulting from later colonial interaction or creative embellishment arising from their centrality to foundation traditions reflecting a

---

[276] I am especially grateful to Kostas Vlassopoulos for bringing this, together with several other works cited elsewhere, to my attention.

[277] Although it is highly likely both that many aspects of these "intercultural transactions . . . were interpreted in different ways by the various parties involved" (Kaplan 2006, 151) and that individual dedicants were motivated by a variety of factors—the need for strategic intelligence, friends and allies, or the desire to establish some degree of regional hegemony—other aspects of Kaplan's thesis are less convincing. To argue that Xerxes' sacrifice at Troy (Hdt. VII 42) "was not motivated by specific, detailed knowledge of the deity and the Greek myth associated with the site" (Kaplan 2006, 136) seems unduly pessimistic since the Persians clearly made it their business to understand local cults relating to "foreign deities"—see, for example, the Cyrus Cylinder (BM90920) (Brosius 2000, 10–12). For Homer/Troy cf. Haubold 2007; Gruen 2011b, 79. See also Parke 1984 for Croesus's motivations (the need to counter Sibylline predictions that the dynasty was doomed to fall), together with S. Morris 1997b, 65–66, building upon arguments tabled by Oscar Muscarella (1989; 1992, 40–43): "Near Eastern rulers negotiat[ed] their credentials with Greek gods, in the absence of permanent and powerful rulers who would remember and honor them on future visits and in future generations" (65).

[278] Morgan 1990, 172. See also R. Osborne 1996, 194: "Settling abroad did indeed demand information, but that information will have come rather from the dense network of exchange which there is good reason to believe already existed in the late eighth century BC . . . Delphi's role was above all a political one." For alternative views, see Dunbabin 1948, 38–39 citing Corinthian and Chalkidian traders as informants; Snodgrass 1980, 120; 1986, 53–54. See also Kaplan 2006, 144n57 and Malkin's discussion of Dorieus's enquiry to the Pythia during the early sixth century B.C. (Hdt. V 42.2), where the potential for preexisting oracular literature relating to regions such as Libya is tacitly acknowledged (Malkin 1987, 78–81).

[279] Fontenrose 1978; Londey 1990.

variety of interests and agendas. There is clearly a distinction to be made here between the wider effect of individuals converging on Delphi—many of whom were already busily engaged in trade and exploration throughout the western Mediterranean—and the Pythia's ability to *systematically* exploit such knowledge as it retained to its own advantage. Morgan is primarily preoccupied with questioning the notion that Delphi itself would have acquired the power and authority based on its exclusive access to information of political significance during its earliest stages. It follows, however, that one can quite readily allow for a more gradual accumulation of knowledge characteristic of diviners and oracular institutions, as documented in modern ethnographic studies,[280] while simultaneously acting as an "information exchange."[281]

Whether Delphi merely sanctioned or actively prescribed is, to some extent, immaterial from the point of view of an ongoing trend of intellectual engagement with ideas relating to foreign lands and peoples. The precise number of states consulting during the earliest phases is likewise of limited relevance when it comes to the significance (or otherwise) of any wider systems of understanding current at the time; assessing Delphi's role in terms of what it would *eventually* turn out to be does little to advance our understanding of its historical significance during earlier periods. While concern regarding the true extent of the Pythia's involvement in alternately directing or sanctioning early colonisztion is altogether well founded, whether Delphi's use of geographical knowledge could, at any time, have been characterized as *systematic* is open to question. Thinking about foreign lands and peoples in a haphazard or ad hoc fashion is no less significant—a point much labored by postcolonial critics and historians[282]—while manifest ignorance was rarely (if ever!) a barrier to active theorizing in the ancient world.

4.3.4 Eclectic Spaces? Material Identities, Intercultural Contact, and Receptions of "Difference"

Herodotus's reference to the dedications as evidence for what would emerge as a tragic case of misunderstanding, Croesus's fateful decision to attack Persia, is itself suggestive of the extent to which sanctuaries acted as repositories of knowledge, where artefacts and ideas of another sort might

---

[280] As acknowledged by Morgan (1990, 177) citing ethnographic parallels for examples of the practice of subsidiary questioning as a means of gauging the most appropriate response.
[281] Morgan 1990, 176–177.
[282] Greenblatt 1991; cf. Romm 1992.

be selectively archived or preserved.[283] While reported cases in which the origins of some of the dedications were disputed suggest that these may not have been questions upon which all parties necessarily would have seen eye to eye, tales of a nature similar to those recounted by Herodotus would in all likelihood have circulated freely (regardless of whether they were genuine or not). The "histories" of individual artefacts, namely, their purported origins and the circumstances surrounding their deposition, would undoubtedly have evolved over time given their heavy reliance on popular tradition.[284] Those seeking to know the histories of the various objects on show would have presumably directed their enquiries to a resident priest or official—or alternately drawn their own conclusions based on prior knowledge or hearsay and whatever was visible by way of inscription. Although remarkably detailed when it came to locations in which specific items were stored, the fragmentary remnants of the annual inventories undertaken by the treasurers of Athena describing the contents of the Parthenon (434–295 B.C.) indicate that, where written records were available, there remained considerable room for doubt or uncertainty regarding matters of provenance.[285] We might reasonably assume a system whereby votive objects would have remained on display for a considerable period of time before being removed to another location within the sanctuary for either storage or burial as part of periodic attempts to reduce clutter.[286]

There is far more that could be said, however, regarding the manner in which major Panhellenic sanctuaries acted as points of intercultural contact and interaction. We have already heard mention of an inscribed dedication at Olympia recording a treaty between the Serdaoi and Sybaris: another indication that as well as acting as regional and "Panhellenic" centers, sanctuaries

---

[283] Croesus is also credited with dedicating the property of a political rival Pantaleon whom he had previously tortured and put to death (Hdt. I 92). For interpreting oracles and assessing risk, see Barker 2006; Eidinow 2007.

[284] E.g., Hdt. I 51. For Delphic traditions about Croesus and the availability of written records, see Kaplan 2006, 138–139; Flower 1991; Thomas 1989; Parke 1984.

[285] Harris 1995. These inscribed marble fragments list a wide variety of objects ranging from items of furniture and musical instruments to boxes of nails of unknown origin, offering valuable insights into the internal arrangements of a classical temple building in which shelves and cupboards lined the cella walls and the floors were piled high with individually labelled storage boxes. Examples include: 10 Milesian couches (*IG* I³, 343 (434/3); an ivory lyre and plectrum (*IG* II², 1388 add. p. 798 lines 79–80 (398/7); and bronze nails gilded in silver and gold (*IG* II², 1419, 1408, 1424a) (Harris 1995, 57, 91–92, 150–151).

[286] Objects dedicated to a deity could neither be removed from the sanctuary in question nor reused for other purposes. For general discussion of practical problems relating to dedicatory behavior in a Classical context, including the problem of cluttering, see van Straten 2000, esp. 213–215. Broader discussion of the spatial dynamics of the major Panhellenic sanctuaries can be found in M. Scott 2010.

evidently enjoyed a reputation that transcended political and cultural boundaries. Dedications of weaponry linked to Etruscans or various Italic tribes have variously been interpreted as either "the weapons of the vanquished," dedicated by victorious Greeks, or of active participation by non-Greeks in cult activity.[287] The deposition of votives originating from the western Mediterranean merits further consideration, however, in the light of ongoing discussions concerning the manner in which such materials should be interpreted.[288]

In discussing the bone and amber fibulae recovered from Greek sanctuaries such as Olympia and Perachora, Shepherd dismisses the possibility that these could be in any way indicative of the presence of non-Greeks from the very outset.[289] Matters are far from straightforward, however, as while it is clearly inappropriate to simply adduce ethnicity from the origin and/or decorative style of the artefact dedicated, the assumption that native Italians and Sicilians would not a priori have been present at such sanctuaries might reasonably be questioned.[290] While one should of course be cautious when it comes to interpreting such data, the bald distinction between "Greek" and "native" that Shepherd implies might usefully be nuanced to reflect the cultural hybridity arising from the mixed marriages that she openly acknowledges may have been the norm "back in the Greek colonies."[291]

It remains, in contrast, entirely possible that not only objects originating from the Italian peninsula but also *people* may have experienced relatively high levels of mobility. A fragmentary inscription on a Laconian stemless cup of circa the mid- to late sixth century B.C., recovered from the sanctuary of Aphaia on Aegina, provides at least some indication that this may in fact have been the case. It has the distinction of being the first Etruscan inscription identified in Greece and is interpreted as a dedication of the "talking inscription" type.[292]

---

[287] For discussion see Antonaccio 2007, 278ff. Cf. Rausch 2004.

[288] In some circumstances it could be argued that whether a particular item was dedicated by a Greek or not is to some extent immaterial. Objects that fell into recognizable categories due to a distinctive form or décor would possess a cultural biography all of their own, evoking notions of Etruria, say, or Sidon, regardless of who dedicated them or their reasons for doing so. Cf. the ban on Attic cups mentioned above (Hdt. V 88).

[289] "It is hard to see what interest of native Italians and Sicilians in Greek sanctuaries could have been in the 8th and 7th centuries so we can probably rule them out as the dedicators" (Shepherd 1999, 288). The largest concentration of fibulae of this type recovered to date can be found at Perachora. For their distribution throughout the wider Greek world see: Blinkenberg 1926, 197ff.; 1931, 86, nos. 103–105; Payne 1940, 170.

[290] Cf. Shepherd 1999, 289.

[291] Cf. Antonaccio 2007, 270–271. For intermarriage, see above.

[292] mipl [. . .] xinur. See, variously Cristofani 1994; Naso 2000, 202–204.

Alessandro Naso used this as a basis for questioning whether the range of Italic materials recovered across the Aegean, including, by implication, sanctuaries such as that at Olympia, might usefully be reevaluated.[293] This has potentially far-reaching consequences as votives originating from Italy/Sicily account for what is undoubtedly the lion's share of non-Greek dedications from Olympia.[294] In the case of Delphi, the same author has recently suggested that the bronze fittings of a folding stool (a type widely associated with magistrates) can in fact be attributed to a workshop local to Felsina in Etruria.[295]

That Etruscans and various Italic peoples should have been present at sanctuaries such as Olympia is not altogether surprising in spite of the games' purported exclusivity.[296] Carla Antonaccio has recently gone so far as to suggest that precolonial dedications by non-Greek elites at Olympia effectively prefigure the dedicatory practices of the western Greek colonies.[297] The historic evidence for treasuries belonging to Caere and Spina at Delphi is well known, and Colonna has gone so far as to argue that the structure referred to as Treasury 10 may be Etruscan in style.[298] The inscription adorning the Cippo dei Tirreni has been variously interpreted as referring to either a dedication of the spoils of war made on behalf of the Etruscans or a reference to "Apollo Tyrrhenos,"[299] while we have it on Pausanias's authority that the first barbarian to make a dedication to Zeus at Olympia was an Etruscan ruler named Arimnestos.[300]

---

[293] Naso 2000, 204. Although some caution must be observed in this respect it being difficult to generalize where archaic sanctuaries are concerned—as Kilian-Dirlmeier so aptly demonstrated! Cf. Serra Ridgway 1990.

[294] Kilian-Dirlmeier 1985. See also Antonaccio 2007, 227; Philipp 1992, 1994. See Hall 2002, 159 and Snodgrass 2005, 432–433 for discussion of Kilian-Dirlmeier's findings—notably the problem of categorization by geographical land mass; more than 70 artefacts are listed—approximately 9 percent of the total recovered during excavations.

[295] Naso argues that this is in all likelihood the remains of a dedication made in the treasury of Spina in the sanctuary of Apollo by an Etruscan magistrate hailing from either Spina or Felsina (Naso 2000, 202).

[296] For discussion see J. Hall 2002, 154. Irene Winter follows Gunther Kopcke in arguing that the Phoenician imports that occur in votive deposits at sanctuaries such as Samos, Ephesus, and Olympia may in part represent dedications made by sea captains seeking safe passage: Winter 1995, 253; Kopcke 1992.

[297] Antonaccio 2007, 277. The especially close relationship between Olympia and the west is noted by Morgan (Morgan 1990, 34n18).

[298] Torelli 1993, 63–64; Colonna 2000.

[299] Colonna 1993, 61–67. See further Amandry 1987, 124–126. Antonaccio (2007, 278–283) discusses the interpretation of weaponry recovered from Panhellenic sanctuaries. Those broadly in favor of interpreting the latter as booty include: Philipp 1992; Shepherd 1999; Hermann 1983, but this cannot be extended to encompass Late Hittite shields and Cypriot helmets as Antonaccio has highlighted (280).

[300] Paus. V 12.5. The latter was purported to have dedicated a bronze throne, perhaps similar to those recovered from sites such as Verucchio and Chiusi, which was reportedly still visible in Pausanias's day. See: Antonaccio 2007, 278; Colonna 1993, 53–55.

Whatever the historicity of this claim, material evidence from the sanctuaries themselves indicates that a range of objects would have been on display to the interested viewer. Long before Hieron dedicated a number of inscribed helmets at Olympia in commemoration of his victory over the Etruscans at the Battle of Cumae in 474 B.C., Etruscan artefacts featured prominently as votives in many of the major sanctuaries.[301] To some extent this is of course indicative of networks of trade and exchange linking the Etruscan- and Greek-speaking inhabitants of Southern Italy with communities further afield. In cases where objects are not inscribed, however, we must also allow for the fact that a certain number of these items may have been dedicated by those with far closer links to their point of origin. There are, moreover, grounds for supposing that dedications of Etruscan objects in Greece may not simply be contingent upon the colonization of Southern Italy and the resulting interaction this engendered— whether through conflict or trade—as argued by Kunze.[302] Although subject to disruption at some point during the tenth through ninth centuries B.C., trade and interaction seem to have picked up at some point during the ninth century B.C., making it equally plausible that sanctuaries such as Delphi and Olympia provided a focus of activity for non-Greek elites also.[303]

While items such as fibulae are prominent in numerical terms at Olympia, their overall visibility is far from clear. The same cannot be said, however, for the various items of weaponry, including a large number of shields dated to the eighth century B.C. (estimates range between sixteen and twenty-one), which were apparently cut and/or pierced in order to allow them to be suspended from nails—presumably as part of some sort of display.[304] The same is also true of a number of fragments of greaves, including one specimen that was fastened with laces—which appear to have been treated in a similar fashion—as well as assorted basins and belts, horse bits, and bridle fittings.[305]

---

[301] Paus. VI 19.7. On the ideological significance of these dedications as booty, see Morgan 2001, 24–27—qualified by Antonaccio 2007, 279. For dedications in Etruscan sanctuaries, see Glinister 2003.

[302] Kunze 1951.

[303] That said, evidence from other sanctuaries such as the Heraion on Samos reflect a different order of magnitude: just over 15 percent of the votives recovered have been classified as "Greek" with the remainder composed of major contributions from Mesopotamia, Cyprus, Egypt, Phoenicia, North Syria, and Phrygia—including ivories from Andalusia (Kilian-Dirlmeier 1985, 243). At Perachora, meanwhile, the proportion of Greek to non-Greek artefacts dedicated is less than 22 to 78 percent.

[304] Naso 2000, 198 revises Hermann's estimate down from around 20 to 16. There is no evidence regarding the storage and display of the 138 or so shields that Diane Harris estimated to be present in the Parthenon (excluding those present in the Chalkotheke, Erechtheion, and Opisthodomos) (Harris 1995, 109).

[305] While dedications of ceramics are overall poorly represented, this is likely to be more a reflection of the predilections of collectors and excavators, whose primary concern has long remained the recovery of bronzes and statuary. Excavations at Miletus and Samos have documented dedications of bucchero pottery dating to mid- to late seventh century B.C. (Naso 2000, 197).

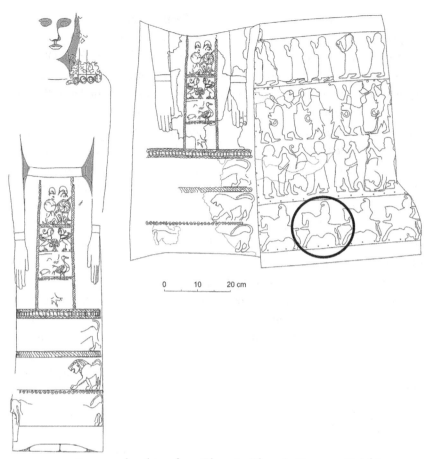

FIGURE 4.9 Bronze sphyrelaton from Olympia. Olympia Museum: Height ca. 1.2m. Redrawn from B. Borell and D. Rittig, 1998, *Ol-Forsch* 26, pls. 57, 54. Drawing by the author.

Perhaps equally (if not more) prominent items include a series of bronze plaques testifying to the skill of craftsmen operating, in part, out of Sidon and elsewhere (see fig. 4.9). While precisely who dedicated them and the manner in which they did so remain something of a mystery, we are equally unclear as to how such images were subsequently "read" and interpreted. Much attention has been paid to the ways in which objects and imagery might have contributed to the Orientalizing trend evident in artistic styles from circa ninth century B.C. onward, there being some disagreement among scholars as to whether the Greeks were little more than passive receptors to these influences or whether they actively engaged with them, progressively reworking Near Eastern forms and motifs to suit a specifically "Greek" idiom—as mentioned above. Discussion of the extent to which Near Eastern epic influenced the Greek canon has therefore taken center stage as opposed to wider issues of reception (a reflection—at least in part—of the fragmentary state of the evidence and the entirely speculative nature of any subsequent attempt at reconstruction). The bronze sphyrelata from Olympia provide a striking case in point. Hammered out from sheets of bronze that were then riveted together, the sphyrelata are traditionally cited as reflecting an important stage in the evolution of Greek figurative sculpture.[306] They are all less than life-size and consist of depictions of women picked out in relief. Figure 4.9 depicts one of three recovered, probably Cretan in origin from the late seventh century or thereabouts. Scholars generally distinguish between the "Greek" figured decoration on the front panels and those depicted on the reverse,[307] thought to reflect the work of an Oriental workshop—a reflection of the perceived differences in style, subject matter, and the overall depth of relief. One detail in particular that might usefully be singled out is the troop of armed riders depicted in the lowest panel, proceeding right to left, carrying spears or lances and wearing pointed caps.[308]

Although cursory and to some extent schematic, this survey of objects and imagery recovered from Delphi and Olympia encourages the view both that circumstances at the sanctuaries would have been conducive to the gradual accumulation of knowledge concerning a variety of foreign places and peoples and that this in turn may have been relayed to visitors by individuals working within the temple hierarchy. The assembled wealth dedicated by present and past generations would have attested to the antiquity and prestige of the sanctuary; "foreign" dedications from far-flung locations may, therefore, have received equal (if not more) attention as objects more familiar. Levels of interest and understanding among those visiting the sanctuaries would have varied hugely of course, but we can safely presuppose knowledge of Homer and Hesiod and perhaps some level of familiarity with catalogue poetry. The extent to which these modes of understanding either coalesced or became progressively systematized should not be overstated. Immersed in this free-flowing current of ideas Herodotus and his contemporaries showed little inhibition, however, in drawing selectively upon disparate bodies of knowledge and materials in support of their "enquiries."[309]

---

[306] Boardman 2006; Mattusch 1988, 42ff.

[307] E.g., Boardman 2006.

[308] Equally exotic are the numerous bronze griffin-head attachments from cauldrons (regularly cited as a source for inspiration for tales of Arimaspians [e.g., Olympia Mus. B 945]) (Boardman 1996, fig. 34) or, alternately, a North Syrian bronze plaque with figured decoration depicted in relief, Olympia; seventh century B.C. (Olympia Mus. B 1950; H. 15.7 cm) (Boardman 1999, fig. 53).

[309] Modern preoccupations with marking the point at which archaic imaginings gave way to systematic science can often fall prey to anachronism (cf. E. Hall 1989; Thomas 2000).

Another notable feature of these imagined centers is the extent to which certain categories of foreign people rose to prominence in popular traditions by which the origins of such sites were explained. The role that Hyperboreans played in Delian propaganda has already been touched upon in an earlier chapter,[310] and we have Herodotus's word to the effect that the majority of the stories about them originated from Delos.[311] Herodotus recounts how the sacred objects are now conveyed to Delos after the initial embassy undertaken by the two women, Hyperoche and Laodice, and the five Perphereis failed to return. Unwilling to risk further losses, the Hyperboreans resorted to passing the sacred objects to their neighbors, with instructions that they should in turn be passed on, journeying via Dodona and across Euboea, before arriving at Tenos. From there they were taken by sea to the sanctuary on Delos.[312] Another tale, again attributed to the Delians, relates to an earlier visit by two maidens, Arge and Opis, to make offerings to Eileithyia in return for an easy labor at childbirth. The two maidens arrived with a divine retinue and are described as being worshipped throughout the Aegean islands and Ionia (as well as on the island of Delos itself) by women seeking their favor. It would seem, therefore, that by the time Herodotus was undertaking his enquiries, Hyperboreans were exceptionally prominent in traditions concerning Delos. The extent to which such tales can be projected back into the past is essentially unclear: are they, by and large, a fifth-century phenomenon or did Hyperboreans feature in Delian propaganda from the outset?

The Hyperboreans also appear to have featured in an aetiological myth concerning the origins of the olive wreaths awarded to victors at Olympia. Evidence for this can be found in Pindar's third *Olympian*, composed for Theron of Acragas circa 476 B.C. Pindar narrates how Herakles persuaded the Hyperboreans to allow him to take some olives to plant at Olympia, having encountered them on an earlier journey to the region in the hunt for Artemis's doe:

---

[310] For Hyperboreans on Delos, see Kowalzig 2007, 118–123. For the interpretative problems raised by the myths as relayed by Herodotus, see Sale 1961; Chankowski 2008, 106–108 (focusing on the Hyperborean offerings). Cf. Delcourt 1955; Defradas 1972. A tradition reported by Pausanias relates that Olēn "was the first to give prophecy there, and the first to chant in hexameters," which is widely interpreted as preserving an earlier account in which mythical foreign peoples were consciously invoked in order to bolster the fame and standing of the oracular shrine at Delphi (Paus. V 7. 8). See above, chapter 2.
[311] Hdt. IV 33.1. Although their "ethnic" significance has been disputed on philological grounds. See section 2.2 (above) and Farnell 1907, 101–105 for discussion and references.
[312] Hdt. IV 33. The death of Hyperoche and Laodice is also linked to a hair-cutting ritual practiced by the girls and boys of the island, focusing upon the tomb in which they were reportedly buried (Hdt. IV 34). See Chankowski 2008, 106–107 for further discussion and references.

> ... and Pisa too
> bids me lift up my voice, for from there
> come divinely allotted songs to men
> whenever for one of them, in fulfillment of Herakles'
> ancient mandates, the strict Aitolian judge
> places above his brows
> about his hair
> the gray-coloured adornment of olive, which once
> Amphitryon's son brought
> from the shady springs of Ister
> to be the fairest memorial of the contests at Olympia,
> after he persuaded the Hyperborean people,
> Apollo's servants, with his speech. . . .[313]

The pious Hyperboreans, servants of Apollo, would appear to have been just as important in establishing the origins of games sacred to Olympian Zeus as they were in myths concerning Apollo's birthplace on Delos.[314] In the case of Delphi, some form of apologia may be detected in a tale relayed by Bacchylides that sees Croesus "who of all mortals had sent the most gifts to holy Pytho" and his daughters being rescued from the pyre and spirited away to live among the Hyperboreans.[315] Piety is an attribute widely associated with the Hyperboreans, as we have seen while a reputation for divine favor and piety may likewise be linked to the appearance of Ethiopians on coins minted both at Athens and Delphi during both the sixth and (predominantly) fifth centuries B.C.[316] In the case of Delphi, these were interpreted by Babelon as depicting the legendary Delphos, founder of the sanctuary, thereby providing an aetiology for the site, or as offerings to Apollo.[317]

---

[313] Pind. *Ol.* 3. 9–16, trans. Race.

[314] Reference to the Ἑλλανοδίκας . . . Αἰτωλὸς (12) highlights the ambivalent status of Aetolia as a whole—birthplace, on the one hand, of those empowered to dictate who was a Hellene while on the other a region whose inhabitants were effectively barbarized by Thucydides in a notorious passage citing reports that the Eurytanians spoke nearly incomprehensible Greek and ate their flesh raw (ἀγνωστότατοι δὲ γλῶσσαν καὶ ὠμοφάγοι . . .) (Thuc. III 94.5). Eleans claimed pre-Dorian descent. See Farnell 1961, 25–26 who censures Pindar's placing of the olive in the far north.

[315] The graphic description of the fall of Sardis and the unhappy fate suffered by Delphi's most generous patrons was obviously a cause of some embarrassment. Bacchylides *Ol.* 3 21–62.

[316] Triobol Athens, AR, ca. 510–500 B.C., Obv. Head of Athena; Rev. head of a Negro. East Berlin, Münzkabinett, Prokesch-Osten Coll. (acquired 1875); Seltman (1924) 97, 200 pl. xxii; Simon 1970, 15–18. Cf. trihemiobol, Delphi AR, early fifth century, Obv. Negro head; Rev. Head of a goat. Brett 1955, 132, nos. 974–975, pl. 52 and similarly with ram's head reverse Head *HN²* 340–341. The suggestion that this might also refer to the fact that the name of Delphos's mother could be rendered as "black woman" has already been mentioned.

[317] See Kowalzig 2007, 56ff.; Lacroix 1974 for discussion. Others interpret them as depicting Ethiopians in Xerxes' army (Graindor 1955, 108) or Sileni (Simon 1970).

We must break with such discussions however and return to the topic in hand—leaving Delphi and Olympia awash with foreign objects and peoples, a rowdy hubbub of competing voices speaking with different dialects and inflections, where knowledge and ideas were freely exchanged. Although far more could be said regarding the manner in which discourses of identity and difference played out during the period in question, we have sufficient material here to support the conclusion that evidence for elements constitutive of an "ethnographic discourse" can be found in the most unlikely or challenging of settings—far beyond the cozy confines of Ionia or the civic *imaginaire* of a democratic Athens. The historical engagement with questions of culture and difference traced both in this and preceding chapters sheds a very different light not only on the way in which Greek identity itself has been constructed and conceptualized but also the genesis of what would later be termed Great Historiography. While the decision to focus on *imaginaires* has at times left us grasping at shadows, we have now reached the point at which we can examine how this early interest in ethnography relates to the sudden upsurge of ethnographic prose that occurred during the fifth century B.C. and how this in turn should inform our understanding of Herodotus's intellectual and cultural milieu. A number of tentative observations will also be made concerning the nature of both Great Historiography and Greek identity, respectively. Each of these, it should be emphasized, are weighty topics in their own right, meriting not one but several monographs apiece. They are, however, interconnected to such a degree as to require synthetic treatment—however partial. While it may not be possible to think through the various connections in a systematic manner, we have come far enough to begin the process of drawing the various narrative threads together to form a series of preliminary conclusions.

CHAPTER 5 | The Invention of Greek Ethnography

HAVING EXPLORED HOW DISCOURSES of identity and difference might have played out in localities ranging from the wilds of Scythia to the rugged landscapes of Calabria, zooming in and out alternately before a final excursus on the imagined centers of Delphi and Olympia, it is now time to return to discussion of the circumstances surrounding the emergence and subsequent circulation of stand-alone treatises devoted to a single land or people.[1] While we have abundant evidence demonstrating that the *practice* of ethnography was widespread long before it became common to describe "foreigners" (of whatever kind) in prose, the emergence of these accounts still amounts to a significant development in the history of a wider ethnographic discourse that shifted effortlessly between hexameter poetry, vase painting, painted sculpture, and praise poetry. Although it is wholly unlikely that we will ever have sufficient evidence to fix the invention of Greek ethnography to a particular point in time and space, we do need to think more broadly about both the nature of this invention and its consequences. How much significance should be attributed to the textualization of ethnographic discourse and under what circumstances did it occur? What triggered this development and what impact did it have on the way in which groups and individuals thought about questions of culture and identity? How inclusive or exclusive was this new form of discourse and how did it relate to other media? Although some, if not all, of these topics have already featured in the preceding chapters, they each have some bearing on the overarching question as to whether scholars were ultimately correct in singling out the invention of

---

[1] It has already been mentioned both that these could relate to Greeks and non-Greeks alike and that modern attempts to impose disciplinary boundaries upon this "undifferentiated sphere of early Greek prose" may owe more to contemporary mindsets than any ancient reality (O. Murray 2000, 330). See chap. 1, no. 115.

Greek ethnography as the event that laid the foundations for the emergence not only of Great Historiography but also of Greek identity itself.

The invention of ethnographic prose is widely associated with a sudden shift from hazy and loosely organized ideas about what it meant to be Greek to an oppositional identity based on cultural criteria.[2] Greeks are suddenly seen as being self-consciously aware of cultural differences that marked them out from Egyptians, Scythians, and Thracians—differences that allowed them to both conceive and, for the very first time, articulate what it meant to be Greek in the first place. Classicists and historians have invariably (and perhaps justifiably) associated the emergence of Greek ethnographic interests with the appearance of prose accounts describing the habits and customs of foreign peoples. The fact that both of these were ultimately (and again, perhaps not unreasonably) explained in terms of contact with Achaemenid Persia and the polyglot horde of the Great King renders this an explicitly fifth-century phenomenon—although several commentators have recently (re)stated the case for a late sixth-century date on the basis that this was the point at which Ionian Greeks first encountered "the barbarian."[3] Earlier signs of interest in foreign manners and customs have been downplayed as unsystematic and lacking in focus as a result.

As we have seen, however, the idea that unprecedented levels of barbarian contact provided the catalyst for early ethnographic prose must now be revised to accommodate two important factors. First, there is the material evidence for contact between peoples of different outlook and culture: a degree of interconnectedness not hitherto appreciated or largely ignored due to insufficient data and/or a tendency to consider Greek identity and culture as existing in relative isolation.[4] Secondly, there is the complicated back history of attempts to assert intellectual control over that which lay beyond the known or familiar via a complex array of discursive and political practices. These would appear to have continued unabated as the first prose accounts began to be disseminated in oral and written form—the presumption being that the vast majority of their audience would have encountered them orally—raising questions as to what, if anything, changed when prose came

---

[2] E. Hall 1989; J. Hall 1997; 2002.

[3] See L. Mitchell 2007; H. J. Kim 2009. For Jacoby's views on the origins of ethnographic enquiry, see chap. 1. See H. J. Kim forthcoming for judicious argument concerning the origins of this term.

[4] For a radically different approach stressing the interconnectedness of the ancient Mediterranean, see van Dommelen and Knapp 2011a. For discussion of the sorts of frameworks and methodologies that might replace such thinking, see Vlassopoulos 2007b *passim* but especially 8–9 citing the thought-provoking comments of Eric Wolf (Wolf 1982, 4–5).

to the fore. Alternatively, is the privileging of prose anachronistic from the point of view of contemporary audiences for whom "thinking about culture" was a day-to-day reality? Is it possible that a combination of cultural attitudes and lack of evidence has caused modern scholarship to identify ethnographic genre as the preeminent mode of intellectual engagement with questions of identity and difference when in fact this was not the case?[5] While there is obviously a danger of overstressing such arguments we must remain sensitive to the fact that the primacy of ethnographic genre may not have been self-evident to those wandering the streets of Piraeus or Syracuse—not least because this was something from which they may have felt excluded.

This brings us back to wider questions of self-fashioning, power, and knowledge. In recognizing the primacy of ethnographic discourse as a textual genre we are effectively recognizing the claims to authority, power, and knowledge of a relatively small number of individuals originating from a comparatively restricted sector of the population: individual adult males from a handful of city-states who possessed sufficient wealth and standing to pursue their research at least semi-independently—even if they did end up having to supplement their income via private/public commissions.[6] The environment in which they operated was highly competitive so trumping one's rivals was a desideratum, whether as a means of securing gainful employment or of establishing oneself as the preeminent authority on a given topic, and the rules governing source-citation were more honored in the breach.[7] Factors such as these need to be borne in mind when considering the way in which prose accounts of foreign lands and peoples should ultimately be interpreted—other interests and agendas were certainly in play. In short, the disinterested study of cultural difference by naturally inquisitive and enlightened Greeks represents, at best, an idealized view of ethnographic enquiry, and the origins and function of ethnographic enquiry are anything but straightforward.

The idea that the self-conscious prose study of a foreign land and its inhabitants is a practice peculiar to Greeks has already been alluded to. However, this singularity may, on one level, be something of a red herring. While it is undoubtedly true that prose accounts of the habits and customs of foreign peoples *are* a phenomenon that is almost entirely unique in the Greek world, the same could equally be said of a wide variety of different forms of

---

[5] For examples regarding Pindar and Homer see above chap. 1 and passim.
[6] For wider discussion see R. Thomas 2000.
[7] Ibid., together with a vast bibliography including Fehling 1989; S. West 1991; Rhodes 1994; Fowler 1996; Clarke 1999.

knowledge that made the transfer into prose.[8] It is therefore, perhaps, the invention of Greek prose that should be both stressed and explained as opposed to ethnography per se with its rich back history incorporating everything from lyric poetry to the images stamped on coins. This revolution in thought and practice undoubtedly had a colossal effect on the way in which knowledge was selectively ordered and scrutinized. It might even be argued that some of the more distinctive attributes of Greek ethnography can in part be attributed to the experience of writing in or otherwise engaging with prose, as Simon Goldhill has suggested—an important point to which we shall now turn.[9]

The invention of Greek prose *was* arguably a revolutionary development from the point of view of ethnographic enquiry: a new form of technology that facilitated critical self-reflection on behalf of both author and audience via the juxtaposition of various categories of the known and familiar with that which was deemed alien or different. While the previous chapters have been dedicated to demonstrating the extent to which discourses of identity and difference can be seen to have played out via the selective manipulation of a wide variety of subliterary materials, iconography, and material culture, the formulaic manner in which this knowledge came to be presented in written form and at length constitutes a very different mode of delivery and thus an abrupt shift in register in this wider ethnographic discourse. All of a sudden, the well-traveled man who had seen the cities of many men and knew their minds had to display his knowledge in a very different fashion in order to receive acclaim.[10] Since knowledge of foreign peoples was not in itself a novelty per se, it is worth exploring the extent to which this was linked to new claims to authority and new ways of thinking. The impetus for such displays—which were by no means limited to ethnography alone—arguably arose as much from circumstances within the Greek world as from those without.

The most convincing explanation for this development offered to date is that such changes are in some way linked to the emergence of the democratic city-state, namely Athens, and the democratic subject—the Athenian citizen.[11] Emphasis on factors such as active participation in collective decision-making, a self-critical awareness of language and its uses, and a culture in

---

[8] See above together with comparative work by H. J. Kim 2009 (China) and contributions to Raaflaub and Talbert 2010.

[9] See Goldhill 2002 for discussion and references.

[10] *Il.* XV 80–82; *Od.* I 3.

[11] See Goldhill 2002, 116: "I find it hard to see any direct, causal connections . . . [b]ut I also find it hard to think of the invention of prose and the invention of democracy as unrelated developments. . . . Indeed, it is not easy to imagine how a citizen would conceive of himself as a citizen without the performance of the law court and Assembly, without his sense of his city's history of war, without his awareness of Athens as a capital of culture."

which the competitive display of knowledge supplanted divine inspiration as the basis of authority are all eminently persuasive. However, such arguments may well attribute excessive weight to Athenian influences at the expense of the Ionian cities of Asia Minor.[12] One is left wondering whether a narrative stressing the centrality of Athens might ultimately be the product of a body of evidence that is irrevocably skewed in its favor. A triumphalist, Athenocentric narrative of progress and enlightenment appears highly seductive, but this may in part be a result of the explanatory schema to which we have become accustomed. The tattered remnants of works that constituted Herodotus's intellectual milieu makes it difficult to assess the extent to which his predecessors and contemporaries were already grappling with similar problems and concerns.[13]

The question as to whether this interest in "what lies beyond" constituted a response to a specific set of stimuli (threat of invasion, encounter with invading forces) is fairly straightforward. The effects of textualization and the vigorous competition between individuals whose standing was in some way dependent on displaying such knowledge are somewhat harder to gauge, however. Further work is undoubtedly required before this problem can be unraveled in full. The aim of this book has been merely to problematize the entire process of imposing disciplinary categories on the ancient sources and marshalling them in such a way as to support a linear narrative of evolution and progress.[14] Viewed in its appropriate context, the invention of ethnographic prose is every bit as interesting and important as the old model of a fifth-century epiphany in reaction to unprecedented levels of contact with non-Greeks. In order to demonstrate this more fully we shall now turn to what is, if not the earliest, then certainly the largest piece of ethnographic prose to survive in its entirety: the *Histories* of Herodotus of Halicarnassus. In doing so we return to broader, overarching questions introduced in chapter 1 regarding the origins and nature of Greek ethnography, from Homer to Herodotus, the sense of collective identity upon which it was predicated, and the implications these pose for the study of Great Historiography.

5.1 Ethnography and Identity, from Homer to Herodotus

First, some caveats are necessary since a chapter heading titled "from Homer to Herodotus" could easily be misconstrued. Rather than signaling an analysis founded on evolutionary perspectives and profoundly unimaginative

---

[12] Although the contribution of Ionia is explicitly acknowledged; e.g., Goldhill 2002, 10.
[13] See above; and Fowler 1996.
[14] Humphreys 2004, 23.

periodization, it highlights a number of very important points. Situated in an established tradition of narrative spanning East and West, Homer's composition bears all the hallmarks of contact and interaction between peoples of different outlooks and culture. "Homer" stands for any number of rhapsodes and poets who showed an evident interest in exploring questions of identity and difference, drawing selectively upon preexisting information and ideas regarding foreign peoples, wherever it suited their artistic program. Reference to Homer highlights both the many nuances and complexities of the Homeric corpus and the fact that Homer continued to be sung, read, explored, and critiqued throughout the period in question.[15] "Homer" should not simply be understood in terms of the text that has made its way down to us via the offices of Alexandrian bibliophiles but in terms of the multiple versions, audiences, and receptions of tales that structured the outlook and consciousness of the populations under discussion—providing them with paradigms with which to think *through* everyday encounters, problems, and dilemmas. These poems were performed before "knowing audiences" actively engaged in the construction of meaning: thinking about culture—whether their own or that of "others"—and imagining far-off lands and places: Egypt and Arcadia, Scythia and Sparta.

"Herodotus," as it turns out, is no less complex. Although grounded rather more securely in historical events, the author of the *Histories* remains largely divorced from his intellectual context—a prose tradition of which we possess only fragments by authors of whom we know (comparatively) little. While the *Histories* themselves undoubtedly represent a narrative that is all but complete, with only the odd loose end here or there, we must also take into consideration a back history of multiple versions; the drawn-out process of composition and publication; and the influence exerted by epic tradition, multiple audiences, and receptions.[16] "From Homer to Herodotus" reflects the continuity of interests and concerns extending far beyond the desire to preserve *kleos*. Viewed in context they fulfill similar functions via the juxtaposition of various categories, paradigms, and concepts. Both provide a medium for "thinking about culture": vehicles for reflection that both actively theorize and, at the same time, constitute identities since each in their way reveals background knowledge of a variety of foreign peoples, however "vague" or diffuse. There is not, on one level, a great deal separating the tales of Polyphemus or the "ethnographies of

---

[15] Cf. Graziosi 2002.
[16] See variously: Lattimore 1958; Fornara 1971a, 1971b; Dewald 1998; Boedecker 2002; Marincola 2006; Stadter 2006.

speech" embedded in the *Iliad*[17] from Herodotean problematizing of Greek and non-Greek categories that are blurred from the very outset. Pelasgians can be found lurking in (what seems like) each and every closet, and idealized notions of Hellenic virtue and solidarity are repeatedly offset by acts of savage retribution and abject servility.[18]

With this in mind we shall now examine the intellectual world of Herodotus of Halicarnassus: What implications does this significant back history of ethnographic activity pose for our understanding of not only the intellectual and social milieu from which he emerged but also the *Histories* as a whole? Discussion of the factors that shaped Herodotus's overall outlook and approach have placed particular emphasis on first Athens and then Ionia as intellectual hothouses that played a crucial role in shaping his development. Many followed Jacoby in stressing the importance of the historian's encounter with Periclean Athens, but others have been equally keen to highlight the importance of Ionia—most recently as part of the concerted backlash against Edith Hall's *Inventing the Barbarian*, contrasting Ionia's uniquely cosmopolitan outlook with the starkly antibarbarian rhetoric emanating from a less enlightened and pluralistic Athens.[19] Matters are far from straightforward, however, as this opposition between a (somewhat idealized) point of contact between East and West—the proverbial "cultural melting pot"—and the ethnocentric attitudes and negative stereotyping is itself open to question.[20] We should, moreover, be extremely wary of the modern (and ancient) impulse to variously try to "explain" the achievement of Herodotus since the narratives thus generated are often partial in focus and both self-validating and teleological in equal measure.

The modern preoccupation with "explaining" Herodotus has given rise to a variety of analytical approaches. The influence of epic and storytelling traditions has received widespread attention, notably the shared concern for preserving the glory of men and the prominence of folk tales within the narrative.[21] However, this occurs primarily in the context of discussion surrounding the

---

[17] Mackie 1996.

[18] Cf. Hdt. I 1–5, 56–58; II 50–52; III 142–143; IV 17, 136–142; IX 120. On the general muddying that occurs from the outset in book one and *passim* see: Harrison 2007, on Pelasgians see above in chapter 2. For the ambiguity surrounding identities in "Greater Olbia" see Braund 2007a; Petersen 2010; and chapter 4.

[19] E.g., M. C. Miller 1997; R. Thomas 2000. For a recent critique of Hall's analysis of the role of the barbarian in Attic drama, see Papadodima 2010.

[20] The argument has effectively come full circle as a recent study by Lynette Mitchell highlighting Ionia's long-term engagement with "Asia" has suggested that the mid-sixth-century invasions of Ionian territory may have generated barbarian stereotypes that foreshadowed (what would later become) the mainstay of Athenian propaganda (L. Mitchell 2007, 15).

[21] A vast bibliography but see now Kurke 2011, 362ff.

extent to which Herodotus's *Histories* can be said to be rational and historical as opposed to any serious attempt to reassess the role of ethnography within the narrative. Considerable emphasis has also been placed on the enduring influence of the Ionian Enlightenment—or the work of "the Milesians"— based on both direct references to Thales, Protagoras, and Hecataeus and modes of argument reminiscent of Xenophanes, likewise a critic of Homer and noted relativist to whom comments relating to anthropomorphism and the unknowability of the gods are attributed.[22]

In a classic study stressing the overarching importance of the Presocratics and Ionian rationalism in shaping Herodotus's approach, A. B. Lloyd has sought to emphasize the extent to which Herodotus shared interests with Hecataeus of Miletus "and, doubtless, many other enquirers" of his day.[23] Lloyd's Herodotus is writing within an established tradition and follows previous authors and/or contemporary trends by including lengthy excurses on Scythia and (most notably) Egypt.[24] While Hecataeus is singled out as his immediate predecessor and the point at which Greek lore and epic *evolved* into the prose genre,[25] reference is also made to both the early *periplus* accounts and the systematizing tendencies of authors such as Hesiod— variously preoccupied with imposing conceptual order upon human society, nature, and the divine.[26] Broad similarities in approach and chosen subject matter among early prose authors writing on Egypt can meanwhile be linked, albeit tentatively, to the pedagogic role of Homeric epic, described as a notable repository of "ethnographic lore."[27]

---

[22] Hdt. II 3. The latter led to the assertion that the *Histories* were best viewed as: "part of the thought-world that had been created already in the sixth century BC by the philosophical and scientific thinkers who worked in Miletus . . . and in other Ionian cities" (Gould 1989, 7). On Herodotus's conception of the divine see Harrison 2000a.

[23] A. B. Lloyd 1975, 167. While the advent of rational prose is portrayed as both a momentous and radical break in approach, matters of "context" and the back history of ethnographic interests and activity are also addressed (ibid., 156–170). Cf. Goldhill 2002; D. Müller, D. 1981; Nestle 1908; Immerwahr 1966 152–153; 1956, 280.

[24] A choice of subject paralleled in the Hippocratic corpus's *Airs, Waters, Places* (cf. the opening lines of chapter 13): Scythians/Egyptians being the archetypal barbarians of Europe and Asia respectively whose peculiarities had long since attained the status of *thaumata* (A. B. Lloyd 1975, 167). Cf. Immerwahr 1966, 319: a position predicated on the preexistence of an ethnographic tradition with established *topoi*, thought to have developed in tandem with the ever-increasing expansion of eastern empires.

[25] Hecataeus is explicitly referred to as drawing on "a rich store of ethnographic lore" (A. B. Lloyd 1975, 134).

[26] A. B. Lloyd 1975, 125. However, both the ethnographers themselves and the discipline they practice (nascent or otherwise) remain unambiguously "Greek"—there being little cause to question such matters during the mid-seventies. Material expressions of "ethnographic interest" are omitted entirely but this is hardly surprising given the context—preface notes for a commentary on Herodotus's book two.

[27] A. B. Lloyd 1975, 123, 140

Whilst Herodotus's debt to sophists such as Protagoras has received considerable attention,[28] equal—if not more—weight has been placed on the widespread use of analogy and inference linked to early medical and scientific writers.[29] This idea has been developed by Rosalind Thomas in a recent study that places Herodotus squarely in the context of a late fifth-century Ionia and makes him less a product of "the Milesians" than of contemporary discourses on natural philosophy and the ethnography of health. While the emphasis on stylistic parallels with technical treatises, as well as a wider discursive milieu in which scientific and philosophical debates were articulated using the language of persuasion, is a veritable tour de force, success here has to some extent displaced earlier attempts at a more wide-ranging appreciation of Herodotus's intellectual affinities and the back history of engagement in questions of identity and difference alluded to by A. B. Lloyd.[30] The tendency to view such patterns of thought and behavior purely in evolutionary terms affects the way in which we approach early signs of ethnographic activity: "thinking about culture from the point of view of an outsider." Rather than regarding them as developmental stages, we should perhaps pay more attention to how these might variously have been employed by contemporaries. How significant was it, for example, that the process of imagining and mapping was already well underway in Hesiod's day? How did this poetic "casting about" in search of boundaries relate to the use of genealogy and myth as a means of progressively ordering people and place—not to mention the peregetic accounts whose circuits would eventually come to include "digressions" in which a particular theme, aetiology, or people might be elaborated upon? In what contexts, for example, was such knowledge displayed and was such information to some extent required or expected by contemporary audiences?

Instead of viewing Homeric epic or Hecataeus' discussion of local myth and geography as something to be tolerated prior to the Halicarnassian's taking center stage, should we not instead turn our attention to tracing the continuities between them, or alternately follow Strabo in his assertion that Homer was the first geographer? Can the concern for geography that runs

---

[28] "At least as far as the historical parts in the work are concerned, the most that can be said—but it is decisive—is that Herodotus learned from the σοφοί how to apply reason and ἱστορίη to the study of man and society" (Shimron 1989, 117). Cf. Dewald and Marincola 1987; Dihle 1962a, 1962b; Nestle 1908.

[29] G. E. R. Lloyd 1966, 1979; and, most notably, Lateiner 1986, 1989.

[30] In addition, this talk of Ionian context risks overlooking the fact that Herodotus left Ionia—at least as far as we know—fairly early in his career. Also referred to as Herodotus of Thurii, he was clearly influenced by his travels elsewhere and regardless of whether the mass migration of Ionian intellectuals is overstated or not intellectual activity thrived outside Ionia itself.

throughout the *Histories* shed any light on the manner in which earlier works might have been received by contemporaries? The recent assertion that, at the time of Hecataeus' researches, myth constituted "the currency of cultural debate" provides much food for thought.[31] If we look beyond historiography to examine local contexts it soon becomes clear that this debate included both Greek and non-Greek material. Take, for example, the continuity in cult activity on the Timpone della Motta near Sybaris, or the process of engagement that gave rise to the Hylas ritual, interpreted by Christiane Sourvinou-Inwood as evidence for religious interaction between the Milesian settlers who founded Chios and local Anatolians.[32] In the light of such encounters it would have been more surprising if the researches of Hecataeus had not turned up material that left him open to charges of "philo-barbarism" much akin to those leveled at Herodotus.[33] One thing is certain: Our determination to see Herodotus in context should arguably be matched by a willingness to afford the same treatment to earlier authors and contemporaries.[34] In doing so we change the way in which we think about the *Histories* and their broader relationship to an established engagement with questions of identity and difference.

We shall now pause briefly to recap before proceeding to discuss the implications thus posed for the relationship between ethnography and history. It has been argued both that there was a significant quantity of ethnographic activity prior to the Persian Wars and that the information thus generated was actively employed in discourses of identity and difference. In addition to

---

[31] Fowler 2001, 97. Cf. Malkin 1998a, 2005.
[32] See Sourvinou-Inwood 2005, 366, emphasizing the extent to which local Mysian nexuses of Innana/Ishtar + Dumuzi/Tammuz were Hellenized by the newcomers: "[T]he Milesians who founded Kios . . . encountered a local mythicoritual nucleus that . . . included 'lamenting for, and calling out the name of, a dead youth-especially on a mountain.' . . . The Anatolian ritual may simply have inspired the selection to generate a ritual . . . that is, the observed similarity of a local ritual with Greek ones may have simply triggered off the deployment of the Greek ritual schemata of search or lament. Or, perhaps, the influence of the local nexus had been stronger, perhaps some non Greek mythicoritual had gone into the making of the Hylas nexus."
[33] Bertelli 2001, 89. Cf. F 20: Danaus and the introduction of writing; F 119: Greece previously inhabited by barbarians. For criticism of Herodotus, see Plut. *De Malign.* For Greek attitudes toward the mythic traditions of non-Greeks, see Erskine 2005; Dench 1995; and above, chapter 3.
[34] Hecataeus of Miletus is an obvious case in point. The latter's treatment by modern scholarship is often quite revealing: on the one hand both his achievements and contribution to the field of historiography have been wildly exaggerated, based largely on the (often uncritical) acceptance of the corpus of fragments collected by Felix Jacoby. On the other there is scathing disdain for an author perceived as banal and unimaginative. Cf. Thomas's somewhat dismissive: "Neither the Homeric epics nor Hecataeus' dry works on geography and genealogy at the turn of the sixth and fifth centuries are quite enough to "explain" the achievement of the *Histories*" (Thomas 2000, 1). Such judgments tell us very little, however, as to why Hecataeus thought it necessary to write such works to begin with.

this, evidence for an interest in culture and identity can be either found or extrapolated in contexts outwith genre writing as part of the everyday, shifting in focus according to region or locale but constant nonetheless. This engagement was equally important in shaping the intellectual backdrop to both Homer *and* Herodotus, making it all but impossible to claim that enquiry into the manners and customs of foreign peoples only took off in earnest as a result of the Persian Wars. Once this is cast into doubt, a sudden switch to a cultural identity of the type argued for by Edith and Jonathan Hall seems equally improbable. Culture and identity had long been matters of concern and contestation. Questions also surround the evolutionary schema by which "ethnography" morphed into "history," forcing us to reformulate our theories concerning the emergence of Great Historiography. Instead of something resembling a "big bang" phenomenon, we are confronted instead with an ongoing continuum, shifting in tempo and focus, and subject to an ongoing "play" of culture, power, and knowledge.[35]

Ethnographic interest did not stop at the barbarian. In fact, as we have seen, "Greek ethnography" is a classificatory label not altogether suited to the wide-ranging eclecticism of early prose authors. Formulated in an era of entrenched Hellenism, imperial mindsets, and Eurocentric and empirical attitudes, it elides the many subtleties and nuances indicative of more reflexive interests and concerns. This was not only an exercise in self-fashioning undertaken from the fastness of a colonial episteme but part of a wider interest and engagement with questions of culture, identity, and difference. Herodotus's Spartans were subjected to much the same scrutiny as a variety of non-Greek peoples, while other prose authors such as Hellanicus wrote on topics ranging from Thessaly and Arcadia to Egypt and Scythia.[36]

This in turn has important implications for past, present, and future interpretations of Herodotus's *Histories*. Classificatory labels are hugely important insofar as they remain inextricably tied up in current thinking relating to both the emergence of Great Historiography and the anatomy of Herodotean discourse. We have already seen how Jacoby's formulation of ethnography was perhaps overly static; the knock-on effect of this is that parts of the *Histories* are routinely described as "ethnographic" and others as "historical"— it being implied that the two are at all times separate and distinct. Jacoby maintained that they represented two different stages in Herodotus's intellectual development, subsequently grafted together to form an overarching narrative but still showing signs of their former nature. While seeking to

---

[35] S. Hall 1990.
[36] E.g., *FGrHist* 4 F 37, 53–54, 64–65, 201.

qualify Jacoby's thesis on a number of counts, Charles Fornara was equally convinced of the fact that the ethnographic material within works such as the *Histories* amounted to effective digressions wherein the "rules" of conventional historiography were temporarily suspended.[37] Such arguments have continued to resonate down to the present day with recent commentators such as Rosalind Thomas still maintaining a distinction between the ethnographic and historical sections of the *Histories*.[38] This is, of course, wholly justified—at least in part—since the two modes of discourse differ markedly from one another: the description of cultures versus the sequential narrative of events in order of chronology. Cultural analysis and historical narrative are closely interrelated, however, as Lattimore so famously pointed out when discussing how best to define an Arabian *logos*.[39]

The extent to which ethnography and history are intertwined has long been acknowledged.[40] François Hartog employed structural analysis to argue that Herodotus the ethnographer and Herodotus the historian are indistinguishable and that the *Histories* needed to be read as an integrated whole.[41] More recently, Rosaria Munson has cast the Halicarnassian as part moralist and part political theorist, projecting intrinsically Greek concerns onto far-off lands and peoples so that ethnographic and historical *logoi* essentially mirror each other when it comes to the problematics they address.[42] Herodotus is still conceived as operating in two separate personas, however, as "relativistic ethnographer" and "absolutist historian," producing a narrative

---

[37] Fornara 1983, 15.

[38] "We seem in fact to find such methods and connections particularly prominent, not so much in the narrative sections about the past and the last books where the story of the Persian Wars gathers momentum, though even there frequent digressions are inserted, but in the sections treating the ethnography and geography of the known world" (R. Thomas 2000, 26).

[39] Lattimore 1958, 14: "This passage has been called the Arabian Logos; and if there is any such thing as an Arabian Logos, this must be it. But it is not an organised free-standing anthropology of Arabia or the Arabians, rather a sequence of notices which grows organically out of its place of occurrence in the Persian progress." See also Harrison 2007, 53–56; Payen 1997, 95ff.

[40] Notably by Immerwahr emphasizing "the importance of basic ethnographic concepts for the understanding of history" (Immerwahr 1966, 323). This forms a marked contrast with modern historiography: "In their historical works, many Greeks included barbarian history, ethnography and geography; it is something that we have deliberately omitted from our own accounts of Greek history, all for the worse" (Vlassopoulos 2007, 229).

[41] Hartog 1988. See Dewald's review article of 1990 for response to the argument that the ethnography of bk. 4 concerning "the imaginary Scythians" reflects the strategy pursued in books 7–9.

[42] Munson 2001, 13, on the opposition drawn between the "silent Assyrians" (Hdt. I 194) and the hydraulic feats of Near Eastern kings: "By setting the pragmatics of everyday life, exotic but legitimate, side by side with the behaviour of the powerful agents of history, his ethnographies represent a crucial part of a discourse at once 'democratic' (almost in the modern sense of the word) and anti-imperialistic."

in which ethnography and history run in tandem but remain separate and distinct.[43]

Rather than seeing ethnography and history as two distinct areas of practice, we might instead see "thinking about culture from the point of view of an outsider" as intrinsically bound up in explaining past events—and, by extension, the present. The major cause of hostilities between Greeks and non-Greeks, Persian *nomoi* are inextricably linked to the human events that Herodotus set out to commemorate. To explain the rise of Persia it is necessary to understand Persian manners and customs—of which the overarching *nomos* of expansion from which Xerxes was ultimately unable to escape is arguably the most important.[44] The restlessness of Persia is borne out in an appetite for the *nomoi* of others, creating an unsettling (if unspoken) parallel with Athens.[45] Contact with Persia also forms the "red thread" by which the *Histories* are unified: as successive lands and peoples fall under (or, in some cases, resist) the imperial yoke their *nomoi* are selectively examined and critiqued.[46]

Ethnographic enquiries can be detected at every level of Herodotean analysis, not just in the earlier books charting the Persians' rise to power, constructing an opposition between a fragmented Hellas and the wealth and might of Asia. Here Babylon provides a full third of the annual tribute necessary to sustain the Great King's court and army,[47] while his most recent acquisition, Egypt, possessed wonders and a history that dwarfed common

---

[43] Munson 2001, 18. "[O]ne diachronically recounts unique events of the past and relies on chronological and causal continuity; the other synchronically describes permanent conditions and customary actions in the present in a discontinuous catalogue form" (ibid., 2). Cases in which these intersect in Herodotean narrative—examples include Persian acquisitiveness (I 135), Lydian effeminacy (I 155), and constitutional reform instituted by Athens and Sparta (I 65–66, V 66) —make the latter eminently contestable.

[44] Hdt. VII 8. See (variously) Immerwahr 1966, 321–322; Evans 1961.

[45] Hdt. I 135. Cf. *Ath. Pol.* 2. 7–8. For discussion of Athens' incipient imperialism as portrayed in the *Histories* and elsewhere, see Harrison 2007, 57–59; 2002, 553; Clarke 1999, 223; Payen 1997, 348–349; Moles 1996; Stadter 1992; Redfield 1985, 114; Fornara 1971b. For parallels between Herodotus's narrative recounting the Persian invasion of Greece and the Sicilian expedition, see Harrison 2000b; Rood 1999.

[46] Immerwahr 1966. Cf. Payen's *Les îles nomades*, which argues that, in addition to the Greek–barbarian polarity outlined in the proem, Herodotus's *Histories* reflect a division between conquerors and their (would-be) victims: "Il semble que Hérodote propose un autre partage; preparé de longue main, entre les conquérants et ceux qui refusent l'assujettissement. Sans annuler le premier, il se superpose à lui car, dans l'*Enquête*, Grecs et Barbares sont à même d'occuper les deux positions" (Herodotus appears to propose another, long-established division between conquerors and those who resist subjection. Without dispensing with the former, he superimposes the second since Greeks and barbarians occupy both positions in the *Histories*) (Payen 1997, 161). For related discussion of historical emplotment and metanarratives, see Vlassopoulos 2007b, 229ff.

[47] Hdt. I 192.

reckoning. Ethnography and political ideology collide when it comes to ideas about how oracles should be read—not by one individual, as in the case of Croesus[48]—while Ionian servility and ineffectiveness are similarly rationalized, their nature and customs being ultimately determined by climate, demonstrating repeatedly that they did not want to be free.[49]

This is, on one level, by no means a novel argument; it was already expounded at some length by Immerwahr.[50] Immerwahr's views on Greek identity did, however, necessitate some (slightly awkward) posturing in relation to quasi-ethnographic treatment of "Greeks":

> [T]he Greek material . . . is throughout formally subordinated to the Eastern sequence by being attached to Eastern accounts in sections. In this respect, the Greek stories are treated in a manner resembling (in a general way) the ethnographic material.[51]

While Immerwahr and others remained essentially uncomfortable with the idea that ethnographic techniques might also be applied to Greeks,[52] a more wide-ranging ethnographic interest encompassing both Greeks and non-Greeks renders this less problematic.[53] It follows that instead of having to make allowances for "a gradual transition from true ethnography to historical *logoi*,"[54] we must instead recalibrate our notion of Great Historiography to allow for a pervasive interest in, and engagement with, cultural analysis and concepts of identity. Having done so, we must consider the implications thus posed for Herodotean audiences: What, if anything, changes if they are all—to a greater or lesser degree—engaged in ethnographic activity, and how

---

[48] See Barker 2008 for recent discussion. On oracles in general: Harrison 2000a.

[49] E.g., Hdt. III 143 (with a somewhat resigned air): *"οὐ γάρ δή, ὡς οἴκασι, ἐβούλοντο εἶναι ἐλεύθεροι."* Cf. IV 137–139.

[50] "It must be remembered that to Herodotus historiê means investigation, irrespective of subject matter. . . . Man is part of the world as a whole and cannot be understood without inquiry into the world as it affects him. This (rather than biographical accident) is the real reason for the inclusion of ethnography and geography in his work" (Immerwahr 1966, 315).

[51] Ibid., 34–35.

[52] On "Greek ethnographies": "[S]ince the Persians and other Eastern powers attacked all nations; among these peoples we must count the Greeks with their 'ethnographic' *logoi*" (Immerwahr 1966, 318).

[53] Cf. Payen 1997, 108: "Cette exigence impérieuse, par laquelle tous les peuples extraient de la diversité de leur coutumes un principe de resemblance, qui ne se confond en rien avec un repli sur soi . . . ou avec un universalisme dissolvant, ne recoupe pas le clivage entre Grecs et Barbares. «Roi» ou «maitre», le *nomos* est, au singuliér, l'affirmation d'une alterité vitale." (This imperative, whereby peoples of diverse customs retain a degree of semblance, which is not to be confused with a retreat into the self . . . or with a fluid universalism, does not coincide with a division between Greeks and barbarians. *Nomos* [custom] alone is "King" or "master" in affirming an essential otherness.)

[54] Immerwahr 1966, 323.

should this affect our reading of the *Histories* overall? Rather than being over-whelmed by the encyclopedic detail presented in the *Histories,* would an audience well-versed in the works of authors such as Hecataeus, Pindar, and Homer, and adept at "reading" Greek coins or the images painted on red- and black-figure vases, have taken such things entirely in their stride?

Viewed from this perspective, the *Histories* represent less a break from established tradition, the product of a Damascene moment or biographical accident, than part of an ongoing engagement in questions of identity and difference: a mode of travel and a way of understanding a diverse world as encountered at Panhellenic sanctuaries, the rural hinterland of Calabria, and the North Pontic region.[55] Just as Bataille and his contemporaries experimented with different ways of thinking about culture and identity, Herodotus's *Histories* cut across cultural boundaries to examine, critique, and compare; whereas the Massagetae become intoxicated on the smoke of a certain plant, the Greeks imbibe wine to excess—and so forth and so on.[56] By this reckoning Herodotus's *Histories* are no less monumental: a study of lands and peoples linked by the red thread of Persian imperial expansion and a mapping out of what it meant to be Greek, forever aware of the fact that the wheel of history was continuing to turn. Looking back into the past in an attempt to make sense of a tangled mass of stories and traditions, the historian incorporates multiple perspectives, conscious all the while that there is no master-narrative with which everyone will be equally satisfied. It is therefore anticipated that many might disagree with the assertion that Athens' contribution to the Persian Wars was a decisive factor in ensuring that the allies prevailed, and that those who sat idly by might bristle when tarred with the same brush as those who gave material aid to Xerxes.

Heterogeneous, pluralistic, and open-ended, the *Histories* do not need to be parceled up awkwardly into sections that deal with foreign peoples "ethnographically," but only afford similar attention to "Greeks" by virtue of some overarching narratological schema.[57] The fact that an interest in *nomos,* reflecting the sentiment "custom is king," appears to be entirely representative of a more general social and intellectual milieu should come as no great

---

[55] Clifford 1988, 10; cf. Hartog 2001.

[56] Hdt. I 202.

[57] This is precisely what Immerwahr (1966) and others have attempted: "the Greek material . . . is throughout formally sub-ordinated to the Eastern sequence by being attached to Eastern accounts in sections. In this respect, the Greek stories are treated in a manner resembling (in a general way) the ethnographic material" (34–35); and "since the Persians and other Eastern powers attacked 'all nations' among these peoples we must count the Greeks with their 'ethnographic' *logoi*" (318).

surprise in the light of evidence, outlined in earlier chapters, for an interest in culture and difference stretching back as far as our sources will allow encompassing epic and lyric poetry, "Orientalizing" styles, and luxury commodities. "Ethnography" was not the passive yokemate of history but part of a larger whole, whose richness and diversity reflected the complexities of the sociocultural milieu from which it emerged. Ill-suited to modern paradigms and analytical frameworks, it saw knowledge of foreign peoples and places as inextricably bound up with understanding the course of human events, the construction of identities, and the process of enshrining both within collective memory.

The extent to which the *Histories* can be analyzed in terms of wider questions of power and ideology is likewise a matter of debate. On the one hand the work is undoubtedly a celebration of the Greek victory over the barbarian even if this is via a "warts and all" portrayal that shows Greeks, whether singly or collectively, in a less than positive light. This, together with its detailed descriptions of foreign lands and peoples—significant insofar as the author makes a conscious link between geographical and ethnographic knowledge and imperial expansion—makes it entirely reasonable to view the *Histories* in the context of a wider "history of empires" as an "imperial" text. In applying the work of noted postcolonial theorist Simon Gikandi to the Herodotean project, Thomas Harrison has convincingly argued that "the very frame of [the] *Histories* reflects and reinforces the structure of attitudes that allows for the expansion of Greek power."[58] This view expresses the nuances and subtleties of Herodotus's position on the cusp of several empires, past, present, and future. While it would, as Harrison points out, be altogether crude to view Herodotus as an imperialist, his efforts can nonetheless be viewed in the context of the grand metahistorical narrative of European imperialism, providing—among other things—a useful template for Hellenistic authors seeking a framework in which to describe the conquered peoples of Asia in the wake of Alexander's conquests.[59] On the other hand, there is as much to be gained from examining the intellectual and social milieux that gave rise to the *Histories*—as I hope this study has demonstrated. Questions of power and discourse are equally prevalent, as we have already seen, but this complicated back history of identity discourse cannot easily be arranged into a single, overarching narrative of Orient versus Occident, Greek versus barbarian.

---

[58] Harrison 2007, 60.
[59] Ibid., 61; Clarke 1999, 68–69; O. Murray 1972.

5.2 Inventing the Greek

The processes of naming, describing, and narrating are, as Simon Goldhill and Robin Osborne have observed, "overlapping and mutually implicative processes."[60] Native to an Ionian city under Persian suzerainty that claimed Dorian origins, with ancestral ties to both Greek and Carian communities and firsthand experience of stasis and exile, Herodotus would have been perhaps more aware than most that identities constitute "the names we give to the different ways we are positioned by, and position ourselves within the narratives of the past."[61] It is to this process of positioning that we shall now turn.

Greek identities were a product of an ongoing process of "positioning" relative to the narratives of the past and other people. This positioning gave rise to "enunciations"—narratives, images, and ideas—"cuts" of identity that were selectively deployed in a process where meanings were continually unfolding: images were repeatedly viewed and "read," proverbs heard or recited.[62] The complexities of this cultural "play" cannot be summarized in terms of the simple binaries of "Greek–barbarian" since meaning is itself never fixed. Contexts change and individual interests and agendas vary, so that while polar categories can in one instant be arrayed in opposition to one another—take, for example, the Scythian–hoplite pairing so prominent in Athenian vase-painting—they are better conceived as different points along a sliding scale: the archer can be "read" in a multiplicity of ways as "youth," "nomad horse archer," "Paris" or "low-status auxiliary."[63] A degree of caution is therefore required in cases where "enunciations" of identity come to the fore. Perhaps one of the most celebrated examples of this comes when the Athenian ambassadors protests their city's loyalty to the Greek cause. Although problematized and questioned to some extent, τὸ Ἑλληνικόν (literally "the Greek thing") still stands, as far as modern scholarship is concerned, as a statement of Greek identity and the basis upon which (some) Greeks united against a common enemy.[64] In addition to this we have the programmatic statement laid out in the proem referring to "Greeks" and "barbarians" (τὰ μὲν Ἕλλησι, τὰ δὲ βαρβάροισι) while the structuring/symmetry, whether implicit or explicit, of both geographic and ethnographic accounts are all

---

[60] Goldhill and Osborne 1994, 6.
[61] S. Hall 1990, 225.
[62] Ibid., 1990, 230.
[63] Cf. E. Hall 1989; S. Hall 1990; J. Hall 2005. For discussion of the depiction of auxiliaries on Attic vases, see Lissarague 1990a.
[64] Hdt. VIII 144.2.

variously held to be indicative of a work in which the boundaries between "Greek" and "barbarian" were essentially clear-cut.

We have only to scratch the surface, however, in the case of the *Histories*, to discover occasions on which this (apparently) neat polarity is cast into doubt. From the very outset we have the blurring of boundaries that takes place as hapless maidens are transported the length and breadth of the Mediterranean in a sequence that links Argos and Phoenicia, Troy and Colchis, providing, in the process, aetiologies for both Europe and the Medes.[65] Prehistoric populations defy easy categorization, and societies are capable of evolving, adopting different forms of government, no longer carrying arms, or, in some cases, "going native."[66] Although some exchanges of *nomoi* are frowned upon, for example Scyles' wish to carry out the Bacchic rites, others occur without mishap.[67] Exceptions and inconsistencies abound: not all Ionians are Ionian, the status of Macedon is disputed, and Spartans call everyone from outside Sparta "foreigner."[68] The Athenian claims that "kinship" (ὅμαιμον), a "common language" (ὁμόγλωσσον), and shared cultural practices (ἤθεα ὁμότροπα) formed the basis for an unbreakable solidarity between Greeks are no less problematic.[69] Herodotean audiences would have been all too aware that such rhetoric was very much at odds with the internecine conflict in which they had become embroiled. Many of them would also have been aware of Athens' move both to restrict the right of citizenship to those who could prove descent on both sides and promote myths of autochthony over kinship ties linking the city to Ionia. Such claims can either be read as darkly ironic or as an impassioned appeal to Athens, and the Hellenic community in general, to lay aside their differences and promote a common peace. They are, in short, shot through with politics as opposed to universally acknowledged truths.

Attempts to pinpoint the precise point at which the community of Hellenes first came into being are fraught with difficulty. Although great emphasis has been placed upon either the unprecedented levels of intercultural contact that arose as a result of the Persian Wars, or subsequent Athenian attempts to bolster a faltering alliance with rhetoric and propaganda, can the same really be said for the vast majority of the "Greek" world? While

---

[65] Hdt. I 1–4, IV 45, VII 62.

[66] Cf. I 65, 155, IV 17.

[67] Cf. I 135, IV 76–80.

[68] I 43–44 (Ionia); V 22 (Macedon). Cf. II 158: "βαρβάρους δὲ πάντας οἱ Αἰγύπτιοι καλέουσι τοὺς μὴ σφίσι ὁμογλώσσους." (And the Egyptians refer to all those who do not speak the same language as them as barbarians.)

[69] Morpurgo-Davies 2002. See now Zacharia 2008.

Athenocentric attitudes often lead us to extrapolate attitudes and ideas on the basis of a dataset that is wholly unrepresentative of Greek-speaking communities scattered the length and breadth of the ancient Mediterranean, the most effective way of tackling this problem can instead be found in the "bottom-up" approach recently advocated by Catherine Morgan. Morgan argues, quite rightly, that we must first achieve a far clearer understanding of a wide range of factors underlying regional interconnectivity that affected the variety of associations and identities constructed by groups and individuals before proceeding to discuss the "identities" themselves.[70] This is important if we are to trace "the chronological development, and balance between, often highly localised ties of place and broader notions of people and/or geography."[71] Where such analyses have been undertaken, the results rarely appear to tally with the traditional model of a switch from "aggregative" to "cultural identity." Polarities do occur but their emphasis varies according to the context that prevailed at any one time, there being many cases in which reference to the non-Greek barbarian is patently irrelevant.[72] We need, in other words, to focus on *processes* of self-definition, in which ethnographic knowledge and interests had—as we have seen—an important role to play, as opposed to "outcomes," namely Greek (or any other) identity.[73]

Attempts to structure or manipulate a history of events in order to highlight convergences that would serve to underline wider notions of community are self-evidently important. Cases in which ancient authors sought to equate one barbarian war with another are a notable case in point, for example, Pindar's pairing of the battles of Salamis and Plataea with Cyme and Himera.[74] Modern historians are perhaps all too eager to follow suit in this respect, voicing their disappointment in at least one case that their particular encounter with the barbarian went unnoticed by major authors such as Herodotus. We therefore find Heinen claiming that the meeting of Greeks and Scythians in the north Pontic region was "one of the historical encounters of Europe and Asia,"[75] which occurred earlier and was therefore potentially more significant than the clash with Persia:

> One would expect . . . Herodotus to have seized the opportunity of treating contacts of Greeks and Scythians in harmony with his *leitmotiv*, that is as an

---

[70] C. Morgan 2009.
[71] Ibid., 25.
[72] See Farinetti 2003 on the polarity between Orchomenos and Thebes, Thessalians and Phocians.
[73] C. Morgan 2009.
[74] Pind. *Pyth.* 1 72–80.
[75] Heinen 2001, 5.

example of the encounter between Europe and Asia. But this is not the case. He has barely a word for the courageous Greek settlers of the northern coast of the Black Sea.[76]

Emphasis on the "inventive" fifth-century B.C. as the point at which Greek identity came into being has recently been qualified by Lynette Mitchell, as we have already seen, although she is keen to distinguish between the "cultural community" that formed its precursor and the political community of Hellenes.[77] This represents something of a challenge, as "culture" is rarely apolitical, but perhaps a greater difficulty surrounds the notion that we are looking for one community in particular.

In a world where collective identity is both heterogeneous and relational, it might be better to follow Benedict Anderson in arguing that "*Imagined Communities* are to be distinguished, not by their falsity/genuiness, but by the style in which they are imagined."[78] The preceding chapters have demonstrated the broad similarities regarding the manner in which diverse groups and individuals engaged in discourses of identity and difference. Rather than tailoring our analysis according to essentialized notions of identity, reflecting modern notions of the nation-state, we might adopt a different perspective, one that embraces diversity and heterogeneity of the sort that we find in the material record. Stuart Hall writes that diasporic experience is defined "not by essence or purity, but by the recognition of a necessary heterogeneity and diversity; by a conception of 'identity' which lives with and through, not despite, difference; by *hybridity*."[79] Hybrid identities were continually being reformulated—then as now—and ethnographic activity, or "positioning," formed an intrinsic part of this process. Rather than being a phenomenon restricted to the "colonial" margins, where local elites would later feel it necessary to celebrate athletic victories at great expense using obscure and inaccessible prose in order to distinguish themselves from their non-Greek neighbors,[80] this discourse was at the very center of all things "Greek"—it framed it and gave it meaning. Relative ignorance and lack of information

---

[76] Ibid. Such views are rationalized in a footnote (5–6n4) on the basis that an overarching narrative schema makes the author more interested in Darius' expedition from Asia to Europe, where the Scythians north of the Black Sea were to be found, than relations between Greeks and European Scythians who originated in Asia (IV.11, cf. I. 201, 215).

[77] "Although the development of a cultural community created the preconditions for the politicisation of the community, the existence of the cultural community did not itself fulfil the conditions for the existence of the political community" (Mitchell 2007, 3).

[78] Anderson 1991, 15; S. Hall 1990, 237.

[79] S. Hall 1990, 235.

[80] Cf. Hornblower on "the assertive language of hellenism" (Hornblower 2004, 372).

proved no barrier whatsoever to imagined acts of appropriation and enquiry, whether as part of a wider project casting out to the farthest reaches of the *oikoumene* or investigating contexts closer to home. Discourses of identity and difference did not suddenly appear as if out of the blue, the result of one event or individual. Instead, they were both endemic and meaningful, from antiquity up until the present day. Our ability (or willingness) to interpret them ultimately depends upon how we position ourselves in relation to both the narratives of the past and other people.

5.3 Ancient Ethnography: Future Directions, New Approaches

An all-inclusive history of ethnographic thought could easily encompass multiple volumes and a lifetime of painstaking research.[81] It should come as no surprise, therefore, if a book-length treatment of the topic contains glosses and ellipses relating to a wide range of topics. A study of this nature could obviously be extended to encompass additional or, alternately, more in-depth case studies, detailed discussion of the various bodies of evidence encountered above, or a more systematic analysis of the way in which the characteristics attributed to a particular category of "foreigner" were selectively described from the point of view of an outsider. As it is, these are all projects for the future. In what follows, I intend merely to highlight the importance of several key topics whose investigation should be considered a priority before bringing this study to its conclusion.

First, although this study is predicated upon a broad-based notion of ethnography that can encompass both Greeks and non-Greeks, comparatively little attention has been paid to the way in which Greek difference may have been scrutinized and critiqued, whether via prose accounts describing Thessaly, Boeotia, Crete, or the Argolid;[82] epic and lyric poetry; or the sanctuaries and festivals that provided Greeks with the opportunity to meet and mingle— whether at the supposed epicenters of Panhellenism, the great sanctuaries of Delphi and Olympia, or the less celebrated (but in many ways equally important) interregional sanctuaries at Kalapodi in East Locris and elsewhere.[83] Here as elsewhere, discourses of identity and difference were every bit as important as those involving non-Greeks when it came to deciding what it meant to be

---

[81] K. E. Müller 1972 is a formidable case in point.

[82] E.g., *FGrHist* 4.

[83] Felsch 1996, 2007. The problem has recently been outlined and theorized with great eloquence in Malkin 2011 but with an emphasis on networks and collective identity.

Greek in the first place. The extent to which cultural and political disunities formed an intrinsic part of Hellenism and were actually constitutive of Greek identity is far too weighty a topic to be dealt with in this present volume, however, and will be treated elsewhere.

Secondly, far more could be said regarding wider questions of power and agency. This is particularly true in the case of the initial textualization of ethnographic discourse—by which I mean the processes whereby a select portion of this knowledge was effectively canonized to form what would later be perceived as a literary genre. The impact of the effective institutionalization of this knowledge vis-à-vis the inhabitants of the many *ethnê* and poleis to whom it was (or was not) communicated needs to be assessed, not least because knowledge of foreign peoples and customs would have continued to circulate by diverse means throughout this period. As always, the level of accuracy and the modes of transmission would have varied hugely, but the fact that much of it would have derived from real-life encounters makes it highly likely that it would have either undercut or otherwise qualified the information enshrined within the putative ethnographic canon.[84] The lack of any disciplinary framework, together with the fact that that "canonical" texts were not (insofar as we can tell) subjected to periodic bouts of scrutiny and refinement that would ultimately lead to the accounts of once-celebrated authors being rendered obsolete as more information became available, is perhaps the strongest argument against perceiving ancient ethnography as a proto-scientific discipline: other interests and agendas were invariably in play.[85] What we can say is that ethnographic description permeated everything from medical treatises to Attic drama to be eagerly consumed by knowing audiences. The precise role that such information played in a wider intellectual environment shaped by intercultural contact, mobility, and exchange is a question that will preoccupy researchers for years to come. The (now commonplace) notion that overall levels of ethnographic activity[86] decreased markedly during the course of the fifth century B.C., only to experience a dramatic resurgence in the wake of Alexander's conquests, may likewise be called into question if one accepts the so-called long view of discourses of identity and difference as forming an unbroken continuum, incorporating periodic flurries of literary or iconographic activity that might then give way

---

[84] Albeit one that was loosely defined, incorporating authors such as Homer where appropriate.
[85] The explosion of literary activity that occurred did witness the publication of "rival" accounts of regions such as Scythia but since we possess little, if any, of these bar the (putative) title it is difficult to assess how they relate to one another.
[86] As measured by the number of set-piece ethnographies attested in our sources.

to other media and modes of enquiry.[87] Again, this is a topic that merits far more time and attention than is currently available.

This study has attempted to build upon successive generations of scholarship by casting a critical eye over the way in which concepts of identity, ethnography, and history (ancient and modern) have influenced the way in which we think and write about the past.[88] Its conclusions can be summarized as follows: the postmodern conception of ethnography as "thinking and writing about culture" reflexively is far broader than that to which classicists and historians habitually subscribe. Whereas Greek ethnography has traditionally been (and arguably continues to be) conceived as a prose genre predicated on the opposition between Greek "self" and the barbarian Other, evidence for an interest in the manners and customs of foreign peoples can be found across a wide range of subliterary, iconographic, and material evidence, encompassing both Greeks and non-Greeks alike. This "ethnography outwith ethnography" is in many ways remarkably compatible with the more reflexive and theoretically refined postcolonial, postmodern conception of ethnography as practice.

The fifth-century origins of ethnographic prose have also encouraged the assumption that ethnography itself was a fifth-century phenomenon.[89] However, even a limited survey of this wider discourse of identity and difference demonstrates that this was not in fact the case. Chapters 2 and 3 of this book demonstrate both that the so-called ethnographic *imaginaire* was awash with a wide variety of foreign or mythical peoples from at least the early Archaic period onward and that this information found order and expression via a complex array of structures incorporating everything from epithets and stereotypes to amulets and the images stamped on coins.

While the self-conscious reflection on the differences separating Greek and non-Greek had been seen as a significant step-change from the supposedly vague and unfocused ethnographic musings that had hitherto been the norm, a more detailed examination of the material, iconographic, and literary evidence reveals that the systematic juxtaposition of the known and unfamiliar had a rich and varied back history, and that such discourses were,

---

[87] Based on the evidence discussed above it is difficult to believe that identity-construction suddenly became less of a priority or that interest in foreign lands or peoples somehow went away or was replaced by something else entirely. (An interest in local history, for example, might legitimately be viewed as ethnographic.) For related discussion see above, together with Clarke 2008.

[88] For discussion of teleological approaches to the history of ideas, described as "the mythology of prolepsis," see Q. Skinner 2002a, 73 and passim.

[89] The catalyst for this ethnographic interest was invariably seen as the Persian Wars.

in all likelihood, one of the constitutive elements of Greek identity, if not the major one.

Whereas Greek ethnography had traditionally been tied to an overarching narrative about how and why a bounded sense of Greek cultural identity came into being, this study has argued that discourses of identity and difference were part of a wider process of "positioning" that was continually unfurling both across space and throughout time as groups and individuals scattered the length and breadth of the Mediterranean world sought to locate themselves in relation to the narratives of the past and other peoples. This in turn has implications for the modern tendency to view Greek ethnography as an important staging post in a linear narrative describing how Great Historiography (i.e., narrative history) emerged in the form of Herodotus's *Histories*. Devised in the early twentieth century by the great philologist and historian Felix Jacoby, this developmental schema has continued to resonate throughout historiographical scholarship and beyond—not least because the categories by which Jacoby selectively ordered the fragmentary Greek historians remain firmly entrenched to this day despite numerous challenges highlighting their dubious heuristic value and somewhat ad hoc application. The extent to which Jacoby struggled to reconcile an ingenious act of historical reconstruction—that saw Herodotus's *Histories* as both the apogee of ethnographic enquiry and the starting point for the (entirely new) genre of Great Historiography—with the dazzling complexities of the textual sources is only now becoming clear as a result of recent work by Zambrini and Schepens. The relationship between ethnography and history is important but it is rooted in this notion of reflexive positioning of a community or individual with a view to explaining past events—and by extension the present— as opposed to the sequential development of discrete realms of enquiry.

While entirely plausible in many respects, the idea that Greek ethnography (and identity) was effectively *invented* either following or during the Greek encounter with Persia reflects a specific set of historically situated preconceptions, attitudes, and ideas relating to the nature of Greek identity, the hegemonic position of Greek civilization within Western thought and culture, and the diametric opposition between foreigners/the barbarian and a (highly) reified notion of Greek cultural identity. A different set of presuppositions produce a very different narrative stressing the intrinsic hybridity of culture and identity and the extent to which discourses of identity and difference can be traced back long before the supposed apotheosis of the barbarian. The heterogeneity of the Greek world is repeatedly borne out in material, culture-based studies tracing the complicated networks of trade and exchange that connected the inhabitants of the ancient Mediterranean with communities scattered further afield—Greek and non-Greek alike. This represents a challenging environment for classicists and historians seeking to hone their ideas regarding the origins and nature of Greek identity and culture but it also throws up new questions, fresh insights, and problems from which new histories are even now emerging.

ABBREVIATIONS

Aesch. *Cho. Pers.*	Aeschylus, *Choephoroe, Persae*
Aesch. *Supp. P.V.*	Aeschylus, *Suppliants, Prometheus Bound*
AFLS	*Annali della Facoltà di Lettere e Filosofia dell'Università di Siena*
AJA	*American Journal of Archaeology*
Alcm.	Alcman
AM	*Mitteilungen des Deutschen Archäologischen Instituts, Athenische Abteilung*
Anac.	Anacreon
AnnArchStorAnt	*Annali del Seminario di studi del mondo classico: Sezione di archeologia e storia antica*
AnnPisa	*Annali della Scuola Normale Superiore di Pisa*
Annuario	*Annuario della Scuola Archeologia di Atene*
ARAB	*Ancient Records of Assyria and Babylonia*
Arch.	Archilochus
Aristoph. *Eccl.*	Aristophanes, *Ecclesiazusae*
Arist. *H.A.*	Aristotle, *Historia Animalium*
Aristotle *Mir. Ausc.*	Pseudo Aristotle, *de Mirabilibus Auscultationibus*
ARV²	J. D. Beazley, *Attic Red-Figure Vase Painters*, 2nd ed. (Oxford: Oxford University Press, 1963).
ASMG	*Atti del Sodalizio glottologico milanese*
Athen. *Deipn.*	Athenaeus, *Deipnosophistae*
Ath. *Mitt.*	*Mitteilungen des Deutschen Archäologischen Instituts, Athenische Abteilung*
AttiTaranto	*Atti del Convegno di studi sulla Magna Grecia, Taranto*
Bacchyl. *Ol.*	Bacchylides, *Olympian Odes*

BAR	*British Archaeological Reports*
BCH	*Bulletin de correspondance héllenique*
BTCGI	*Bibliografia topografica della colonizzazione greca in Italia e nelle isole tirreniche*, G. & G. Nenci, Vallet (Pisa/Rome, 1977–present).
Bull. Ass. Budê	*Bulletin de l'Association Guillaume Budê*
CAH²	*Cambridge Ancient History²*, 14 vols. (Cambridge: Cambridge University Press, 1970–2000).
CAJ	*Cambridge Archaeological Journal*
Diod.	Diodorus Siculus
Dion. Hal.	Dionysius of Halicarnassus
Dion. Hal. *De Thuc.*	Dionysius of Halicarnassus, *On Thucydides*
DNa	Darius inscription from Naqsh-i-Rustam (a)
DNb	Darius inscription from Naqsh-i-Rustam (b)
FGrHist	*Die Fragmente der Griechischen Historiker*
GB	*Grazer Beiträge: Zeitschrift für die klassische Altertumswissenschaft*
Hdt.	Herodotus
Hes. *Theog.*	Hesiod, *Theogony*
Hippoc. *AWP*	Hippocrates, *Airs, Waters, Places*
Hom. *Il*	Homer, *Iliad.*
Hom. *Od.*	Homer, *Odyssey*
Hom. *Hymn. Ap.*	*Homeric Hymn to Apollo*
Hom. *Hymn. Bacch.*	*Homeric Hymn to Dionysius*
Hom. *Hymn. Merc.*	*Homeric Hymn to Hermes*
HSCP	*Harvard Studies in Classical Philology*
IG	*Inscriptiones Graecae*
IGCH	*Inventory of Greek Coin Hoards*
JDAI	*Jahrbuch des deutschen archäologischen Instituts*
JHS	*Journal of Hellenic Studies*
Just. *Epit.*	Justin, *Epitome* (of Pompeius Trogus)
LIMC	*Lexicon Iconographicum Mythologiae Classicae*
[Longinus] *Subl.*	Pseudo Longinus, *On the Sublime*
Lycoph. *Alex.*	Lycophron, *Alexandra*
MJBK	*Münchner Jahrbücher der Bildenden Kunst*
ML	R. Meiggs and D. Lewis, *A Selection of Greek Historical Inscriptions to the End of the Fifth Century BC*, rev. ed., 1988
OCD³	S. Hornblower and A. Spawforth, eds., *The Oxford Classical Dictionary*, 3rd rev. ed. (Oxford : Oxford University Press, 2003)

Pan.	Panyassis of Halicarnassus
Paus.	Pausanius
Pind. *Isthm.*	Pindar, *Isthmian Odes*
Nem.	*Nemean Odes*
Ol.	*Olympic Odes*
Pyth.	*Pythian Odes*
Pae.	*Paeans*
Pl. *Menex.*	Plato, *Menexenus*
Plut. *Crass.*	Plutarch, *Life of Crassus*
de exil.	*On exile*
PMG	D. L. Page, *Poetae Melici Graeci*, 1962
Polyb.	Polybius
P. Oxy.	*Oxyrhynchus Papyri*
Procl. *Chrest.*	Proclus, *Chrestomathia*
RE	A. Pauly, G. Wissowa, and W. Kroll, *Real-Encyclopädie der Classischen Altertumswissenschaft* (Leiden: Brill, 1893–).
RFIC	*Rivista di filologia e di istruzione classica*
HN²	B. V. Head, *Historia Numorum: A Manual of Greek Numismatics*, 2nd ed. (New York: Durst, 2001).
Schol. Eur. *Or.*	Scholia to Euripides' *Orestes*
Schol. P. Oxy.	Scholia to the Oxyrhynchus Papyri
SEG	*Supplementum Epigraphicum Graecum*
Soph. *Tript.*	Sophocles, *Triptolemus*
SNG Cop.	*Sylloge Nummorum Graecorum: The Royal Collection of Coins and Medals, Danish National Museum*, 8 vols., reprint ed. (West Milford, N.J.: Sunrise Publications, 1982).
SRPS	*Società romana e produzione schiavistica*
Steph. Byz.	Stephanus of Byzantium
Strab.	Strabo
Theophr. *pl.*	Theophrastus, *Historia Plantarum*
Thuc.	Thucydides
TLS	*The Times Literary Supplement*
Trümpy, *Monat.*	C. Trümpy, *Untersuchungen zu den altgriechischen Monatsnamen und Monatsfolgen*, Bibliothek der klassischen Altertumswissenschaften, Reihe 2, N.F., vol. 98 (Heidelberg: Universitätsverlag C. Winter, 1997).
VDI	*Vestnik Drevnej Istorii*
ZPE	*Zeitschrift für Papyrologie und Epigraphik*

BIBLIOGRAPHY

Adamesteanu, D. 1982. "Quadro storico delle fortificazioni greche della Sicilia e della Magna Grecia." In *La fortification dans l'histoire du monde grec. Actes du colloque international. La fortification et sa place dans l'histoire politique, culturelle et sociale du monde grec, Valbonne, décembre 1982*, ed. P. Leriche and H. Tréziny. Paris: Éditions du centre national de la recherche scientifique, 105–111.

Adams, J. N., M. Janse, and S. Swain, eds. 2002. *Bilingualism in Ancient Society: Language Contact and the Written Word*. Oxford: Oxford University Press.

Adler, E., F. Bicchi, B. Crawford, and R. A. Del Sarto, eds. 2006. *The Convergence of Civilisations: Constructing a Mediterranean Region*. Toronto: University of Toronto Press.

Agar, M. H. 1980. *The Professional Stranger: An Informal Introduction to Ethnography*. London: Harcourt Brace Jovanovich.

Agostino, R. 2005. *Nel territorio dei Tauriani*. Palmi: Soveria Mannelli.

Agostino, R., and M. M. Sica, eds. 2009. *Sila Silva. ho drumós... hón Sílan kaloûsin. Conoscenza e recupero nel Parco Nazionale d'Aspromonte*, III. *Palazzo: una struttura fortificata in Aspromonte*. Soveria Mannelli: Rubettino.

Ahl, F., and H. Roisman. 1996. *The Odyssey Re-Formed*. Ithaca, N.Y.: Cornell University Press.

Ahlberg-Cornell, G. 1992. *Myth and Epos in Early Greek Art. Representation and Interpretation*. SIMA 100. Goteborg: Astrom.

Ahrens, H. L. 1839–43. *De graecae linguae dialectis*. Göttingen: Vandenhoeck and Ruprecht.

Albright, W. F. 1950. "Some Oriental Glosses on the Homeric Problem." *AJA* 54: 162–176.

Albanese Procelli, R.M. 1995. "Contacts and Exchanges in Protohistoric Sicily." *Acta Hyperborea* 6: 33–49.

Alcock, S., and R. Osborne, eds. 1994. *Placing the Gods: Sanctuaries and Sacred Space in Ancient Greece*. Oxford: Clarendon Press.

———. 2007. *Classical Archaeology*. Oxford: Basil Blackwell.

Alekseyev, A. Y. 2005. "Scythian Kings and 'Royal' Burial Mounds in the Fifth and Fourth Centuries BC." In *Scythians and Greeks: Cultural interactions in Scythia, Athens and the Early Roman Empire (Sixth Century BC—First Century AD)*, ed. D. Braund. Exeter: University of Exeter Press, 39–55.

Alföldi, A. 1933. "Review of M. Rostowzew: Skythien und der Bosporos, Band 1: Kritische Übersicht der schriftlichen und archäologischen Quellen. Berlin, H. Schoetz & Co., 1931." *Gnomon* 9: 561–572.

Allen, T. W. 1910. "The Homeric Catalogue." *JHS* 30: 292–322.

———. 1921. *The Homeric Catalogue of Ships.* Ed. with commentary. Oxford: Clarendon Press.

Allison, J. E. 1968. *Geographic and Ethnic Formulas in Homer and the Catalogue of Ships.* Chapel Hill: University of North Carolina Press.

Aloni, A. 2001. *Iambic Ideas: Essays on a Poetic Tradition from Archaic Greece to the Late Roman Empire.* Oxford: Rowman & Littlefield.

Alonso-Núñez, J.-M. 2003. "Herodotus' Conception of Historical Space and the Beginnings of Universal History." In *Herodotus and His World: Essays from a Conference in Memory of George Forrest*, ed. P. Derow and R. Parker. Oxford: Oxford University Press, 145–152.

Amandry, P. 1950. *La mantique apollinienne à Delphes. Essai sur le fonctionnement de l'oracle.* Paris: E. de Boccard.

———. 1956. "Les thèmes de la propagande delphique." *Revue de philologie* 30: 268–282.

———. 1987. "Trépieds de Delphes et du Péloponnèse." *BCH* 111, 79–131.

Ames, E., M. Klotz, and L. Wildenthal, eds. 2005. *Germany's Colonial Pasts.* Lincoln and London: University of Nebraska Press.

Ampolo, C. 1993. "La citta dell'eccesso: Per la Storia di Sibari fino al 510 a.C." In *Sibari e la Sibaritide. Atti del Trentaduesimo Convegno di Studi sulla Magna Grecia, Taranto-Sibari, 7–12 Ottobre 1992 (Taranto)*, ed. A. Stazio and S. Ceccoli. Taranto: Istituto per la Storia e l'archeologia della Magna Grecia, 13–54.

Ampolo, C. 1993. "La citta dell'eccesso: per la Storia di Sibari fino al 510 a.C." In *AttiTaranto* 32: 13–54.

Amselle, J.-L. 1998. *Mestizo Logics: Anthropology of Identity in Africa and Elsewhere.* Trans. Claudia Royal. Stanford: Stanford University Press.

Anderson, B. 1991. *Imagined Communities: Reflections on the Origins and Spread of Nationalism.* London: Verso.

Andres, S. 2001. *Le Amazzoni nell'immaginario occidentale: il mito e la storia attraverso la letteratura.* Pisa: Edizioni ETS.

Angrosino, M. 2007. *Doing Ethnographic and Observational Research.* London: Sage.

Antonaccio, C. 2000. "Review of Malkin, I. (1998) The Returns of Odysseus: Colonization and Ethnicity, University of California Press: Berkeley." *American Journal of Philology* 121, no. 4 (Winter 2000): 637–641.

———. 2001. "Ethnicity and Colonization." In *Ancient Perceptions of Greek Ethnicity*, ed. I. Malkin. Cambridge, Mass.: Harvard University Press, 113–157.

———. 2003. "Hybridity and the Cultures within Greek Culture." In *The Cultures within Greek Culture: Contact, Conflict, Collaboration*, ed. C. Dougherty and L. Kurke. Cambridge: Cambridge University Press, 57–74.

———. 2004. "Siculo-Geometric and the Sikels: Ceramics and Identity in Eastern Sicily." In *Greek Identity in the Western Mediterranean*. Mnemosyne, supp. 246, ed. K. Lomas. Leiden: Brill, 55–81.

———. 2007. "Elite Mobility in the West." In *Pindar's Poetry, Patrons, and Festivals: From Archaic Greece to the Roman Empire*, ed. S. Hornblower and C. Morgan. Oxford: Oxford University Press, 265–287.

Antonaccio, C., and J. Neils 1995. "A New Graffito from Archaic Morgantina." *ZPE* 101: 261–277.

Antonetti, C., ed. 1997. *Il dinamismo della colonizzazione greca. Atti della tavola rotunda Espansione e colonizzazione greca di età arcaica: metodolgie e problemi a confronto, Venezia, 10–11/11/1995.* Napoli: Loffredo.

Appadurai, A., ed. 1986. *The Social Life of Things: Commodities in Cultural Perspective.* Cambridge: Cambridge University Press.

Arafat, K., and C. Morgan. 1994. "Athens, Etruria and the Heueneburg: Mutual Misconceptions in the Study of Greek-Barbarian Relations." In *Classical Greece: Ancient Histories and Modern Archaeologies*, ed. I. Morris. Cambridge: Cambridge University Press, 108–134.

Arena, R. 1996. "The Greek Colonization of the West: Dialects." In *The Greek World: Art and Civilisation in Magna Graecia and Sicily*, ed. G. P. Carratelli. New York: Rizzoli, 189–200.

Armayor, O. K. 1978. "Did Herodotus Ever Go to the Black Sea?" *HSCP* 82: 45–62.

Arnush, M. 2005. "Pilgrimage to the Oracle of Apollo at Delphi: Patterns of Public and Private Consultation." In *Pilgrimage in Graeco-Roman and Early Christian Antiquity*, ed. I. Rutherford and J. Elsner. Oxford: Oxford University Press, 97–111.

Asad, T., ed. 1973. *Anthropology and the Colonial Encounter.* London: Ithaca Press.

Asheri, D. 1990. "Herodotus on Thracian Society and History." In *Hérodote et les peuples non grecs. Entretiens sur l'Antiquité classique: Vandoeuvres-Genève, 22–26 Août 1988*, ed. G. Nenci and O. Reverdin. Genève: Fondation Hardt 35, 131–164.

Assmann, J. 2005. "Periergia: Egyptian Reactions to Greek Curiosity." In *Cultural Borrowings and Ethnic Appropriations in Antiquity*, ed. E. S. Gruen. Stuttgart: F. Steiner, 37–59.

Atkinson, P., A. Coffey, S. Delamont, J. Lofland, and L. Lofland, eds. 2001. *Handbook of Ethnography.* London: Sage.

Attema, P. 2003. "From Ethnic to Urban Identities? Greek Colonists and Indigenous Society in the Sibaritide, South Italy: A Landscape Archaeological Approach." In *Constructions of Greek Past: Identity and Historical Consciousness from Antiquity to the Present*, ed. H. Hokwerda. Groningen: Egbert Forsten, 11–25.

———. 2008. "Conflict or Coexistence? Remarks on Indigenous Settlement and Greek Colonization in the Foothills and Hinterland of the Sibaritide Northern Calabria, Italy." In *Meeting of Cultures—Between Conflicts and Coexistence*, ed. P. Guldager Bilde and J. H. Petersen. Aarhus: Aarhus University Press, 67–100.

Aubet, M. E. 1993. *The Phoenicians and the West: Politics, Colonies, and Trade.* Cambridge: Cambridge University Press.

Austin, J. N. H. 1965. *Catalogues and the Catalogue of Ships in the Iliad.* Berkeley: University of California Press.

Austin, M. M. 1970. "Greece and Egypt in the Archaic Age." *Proceedings of the Cambridge Philological Association* 2: 22–34.

Austin, N. 1975. *Archery at the Dark of the Moon: Poetic Problems in Homer's Odyssey.* Berkeley: University of California Press.

Avram, A., J. Hind, and G. Tsetskhladze. 2004. "The Black Sea Area." In *An Inventory of Archaic and Classical Poleis*, ed. M. Hansen and T. H. Neilsen. Oxford: Oxford University Press, 924–973.

Babelon, E. 1897. *Les origines de la monnaie considérées au point de vue économique et historique.* Paris: Firmin-Didot.

Bäbler, B. 1998. *Fleissige Thrakerinnen und wehrhafte Skythen: Nichtgriechen im klassischen Athen und ihre archäologische Hinterlassenschaft.* Stuttgart and Leipzig: Teubner.

———. 2007. "Dio Chrysostom's Construction of Olbia." In *Classical Olbia and the Scythian World: From the Sixth Century BC to the Second Century AD,* ed. D. Braund and S. D. Kryzhitskiy. Proceedings of the British Academy 142. Oxford: Oxford University Press, 145–160.

Bailey, D. M. 2006. "The Apries Amphora—Another Cartouche." In *Naukratis: Greek Diversity in Egypt. Studies on East Greek Pottery and Exchange in the Eastern Mediterranean,* ed. A. Villing and U. Schlotzhauer. London: British Museum Press, 155–157.

Bakker, E., I. De Jong, and H. Van Wees, eds. 2002. *Brill's Companion to Herodotus.* Leiden: Brill.

Barabási, A. -L. 2002. *Linked: The New Science of Networks.* Cambridge, Mass.: Perseus.

Barker, E. 2006. "Paging the Oracle: Interpretation, Identity and Performance in Herodotus' History." *Greece & Rome* 53, no. 1: 1–29.

Barletta, B. A. 1990. "An 'Ionian Sea' Style in Archaic Doric Architecture." *AJA* 94, no. 1: 45–72.

Barnes, J. 1982. *The Presocratic Philosophers.* London: Routledge & Kegan Paul.

Barra Bagnasco, M. 1996. "Il culto extramuraneo di Afrodite." In *I Greci in Occidente. Santuari della Magna Grecia in Calabria,* ed. E. Lattanzi et al. Naples: Electa, 27–30.

Barringer, J. M. 2004. "Scythian Hunters on Attic Vases." In *Greek Vases: Images, Contexts and Controversies,* ed. C. Marconi. Leiden: Brill, 13–25.

Barron, J. 2004. "Go West, Go Native." In *Greek Identity in the Western Mediterranean.* Mnemosyne, supp. 246, ed. K. Lomas. Leiden: Brill, 259–266.

Barth, F. 1969. *Ethnic Groups and Boundaries: The Social Organization of Culture Difference.* Oslo: Universitets fortaget.

Bataille, G. 1929. "Abattoir." *Documents* 6: 328–329.

———. 1930. "L'espirit moderne et le jeu des transpositions." *Documents* 8: 489–493.

Beard, M. 1992. "Frazer, Leach and Virgil: The Popularity and Unpopularity of the Golden Bough." *Comparative Studies in Society and History* 34: 203–224.

———. 1999. "The Invention and Re-Invention of 'Group D': An Archaeology of the Classical Tripos." In *Classics in 19th and 20th Century Cambridge: Curriculum, Culture and Community,* ed. C. Stray. Cambridge Philological Society, supp. Vol. 24. Cambridge: Cambridge University Press, 95–134.

———. 2002. *The Invention of Jane Harrison.* Cambridge, Mass.: Harvard University Press.

Beardsley, G. H. 1929. *The Negro in Greek and Roman Civilization: A Study of the Ethiopian Type.* Baltimore: Johns Hopkins University Press.

Bekker-Nielsen, T., ed. 2005. *Ancient Fishing and Fish Processing in the Black Sea Region.* Aarhus: Aarhus University Press.

Bentley, J. H. 1993. *Old World Encounters: Cross-Cultural Contacts and Exchanges in Pre-Modern Times.* Oxford: Oxford University Press.

Benz, F. L. 1972. *Personal Names in the Phoenician and Punic Inscriptions. A Catalogue, Grammatical Study and Glossary of Elements.* Rome: Biblical Institute Press.

Bérad, C. 2000. "The Image of the Other and the Foreign Hero." In *Not the Classical Ideal: Athens and the Construction of the Other in Greek Art,* ed. B. Cohen. Leiden: Brill, 390–413.

Bérad, C., ed. 1989. *A City of Images: Iconography and Society in Ancient Greece.* Princeton, N.J.: Princeton University Press.

Bérard, J. 1957. *La colonisation grecque de l'Italie méridionale et de la Sicile dans l'antiquité.* Paris: Presses Universitaires.

———. 1960. *L'expansion et la colonisation grecques jusqu'aux Guerres médiques.* Paris: Aubier.

Bergquist, B. 1973. *Herakles on Thasos: The Archaeological, Literary and Epigraphic Evidence for his Sanctuary Reconsidered.* Uppsala Studies in Ancient and Near Eastern Civilisations 5. Uppsala: University of Uppsala.

———. 1990. "The Archaic Temenos in Western Greece: A Survey and Two Enquiries." In *Le sanctuaire grec. Entretiens sur l'Antiquité classique: Vandoeuvres-Genève, 20–25 Août 1992,* ed. A. Schachter. Genève: Entretiens Hardt 37, 109–152.

Berlinzani, F. 2002. "Leggende musicale e dinamiche territoriali: Reggio e Locri nel VI secolo." In *Identità e prassi storica nel Mediterraneo greco,* ed. L. Moscati Castelnuovo. Milano: Edizioni ET, 23–33.

Bernal, M. 1987. *Black Athena: The Afro-Asiatic Roots of Greek Civilisation.* New Brunswick, N.J.: Rutgers University Press.

Bernard, A., and O. Masson. 1957. "Les inscriptions grecques d'Abou Simbel." *Revue des études grecques* 70: 1–46.

Bernhardt, R. 2003. *Luxuskritik und Aufwandsbeschränkungen in der griechischen Welt.* Historia Einzelschriften 168. Stuttgart: Franz Steiner Verlag.

Bertelli, L. 2001. "Hecataeus: From Genealogy to Historiography." In *The Historian's Craft in the Age of Herodotus,* ed. N. Luraghi. Oxford: Oxford University Press, 67–95.

Best, J. G. P. 1969. *Thracian Peltasts and their Influence on Greek Warfare.* Groningen: Wolters-Noordhoff.

Bhabha, H. K. 1994. *The Location of Culture.* London and New York: Routledge.

Bichler, R. 2001. *Herodots Welt.* Berlin: Akademie Verlag.

Bichler, R. 2010. *Historiographie—Ethnographie—Utopie, Gesammelte Schriften, 3: Studien zur Wissenschafts-und Rezeptionsgeschichte.* Wiesbaden: Harrassowitz.

Bickerman, Elias J. 1952. "Origines Gentium." *Classical Philology* 472: 65–81.

Bicknell, P. 1966. "The Date of the Battle of the Sagra River." *Phoenix* 20, no. 4: 294–301.

Bietak, M. 2001. *Archaische griechische Tempel und Altägypten.* Wien: Verlag der Österreichischen Akademie der Wissenschaften.

Bietti Sestieri, A. M. 1980–81. "La Sicilia e le isole eolie e i loro rapporti con le regioni tirreniche dell'Italia continentale dal Neolitiico alla colonizzazione greca." *Kokalos,* nos. 26–27: 8–66.

Billerbeck, M. 2006. *Stephani Byzantii Ethnica.* Vol. 1, A-Γ. Berlin: de Gruyter.

Birch, C. M. 1950. "Lives and Works of Aristeas." *Classical Journal* 46, no. 2 (November): 79–83.

Blinkenberg, C. 1926. *Fibules grecques et orientales.* Lindiaka V. Copenhagen: F. Host & Son.

———. 1931. *Lindos I. Les petits objets.* Berlin: W. de Gruyter.

Bloch, R. S. 2002. *Der Judenexkurs des Tacitus im Rahmen der griechisch-römischen Ethnographie.* Historia Einzelschriften 160. Stuttgart: Franz Steiner Verlag.

Blok, J. H. 2005. "Becoming Citizens: Some Notes on the Semantics of 'Citizen' in Archaic Greece and Classical Athens." *Klio* 87, no. 1: 7–40.

Blok, J. L. 1995. *The Early Amazons: Modern and Ancient Perspectives on a Persistent Myth.* Leiden: Brill.

Boardman, J. 1987. "Amasis: The Implications of His Name." *Papers on the Amasis Painter and His World. Colloquium Sponsored by the Getty Centre for the History of Art and the Humanities and Symposium Sponsored by the J. Paul Getty Museum*. Malibu, Calif.: J. Paul Getty Museum, 141–153.

———. 1996. *Greek Art*. 4th ed. London: Thames & Hudson.

———. 1999. *The Greeks Overseas: Their Early Colonies and Trade*. 4th ed. London: Thames & Hudson.

———. 2001. *Greek Gems and Finger Rings: Early Bronze Age to Late Classical*. New expanded ed. London: Thames & Hudson.

———. 2004. "Copies of Pottery: By and for Whom?" In *Greek Identity in the Western Mediterranean*. Mnemosyne, supp. 246, ed. K. Lomas. Leiden: Brill, 149–162.

———. 2006. "Sources and Models." In *Greek Sculpture: Function, Materials and Techniques in the Archaic and Classical Periods*, ed. O. Palagia. Cambridge: Cambridge University Press, 1–31.

Boedecker, D. 2002. "Epic Heritage and Mythical Patterns in Herodotus." In *Brill's Companion to Herodotus*, ed. E. Bakker, I. De Jong, and H. Van Wees. Leiden: Brill, 97–117.

Boedecker, D., and K. A. Raaflaub. 1998. *Democracy, Empire and the Arts in Fifth-Century Athens*. Cambridge, Mass.: Harvard University Press.

Bohak, G. 2005. "Ethnic Portraits in Greco-Roman Literature." In *Cultural Borrowings and Ethnic Appropriations in Antiquity*, ed. E. S. Gruen. Stuttgart: F. Steiner, 207–238.

Bolton, J. D. P. 1962. *Aristeas of Proconnesus*. Oxford: Oxford University Press.

Bonacci, E. 2002. "La difesa di una polis: Metaponto e i Lucani tra V e IV secolo a.C." In *Identità e prassi storica nel Mediterraneo greco*, ed. Moscati Castelnuovo. Milano: Edizioni ET, 63–91.

Bondi, S. F. 1990. "I Fenici in Erodoto." In *Hérodote et les peuples non grecs. Entretiens sur l'Antiquité classique: Vandoeuvres-Genève 22–26 Août 1988*, ed. G. Nenci and O. Reverdin. Genève: Fondation Hardt 35, 255–287.

Bottini, A. 1996. "The Impact of the Greek Colonies on the Indigenous Peoples of Lucania." In *The Greek World: Art and Civilisation in Magna Graecia and Sicily*, ed. G. P. Carratelli. New York: Rizzoli, 541–548.

Bourdieu, P. 1977. *Outline of the Theory of Practice*. Trans. Richard Nice. Cambridge: Cambridge University Press.

———. 1990. *The Logic of Practice*. Trans. Richard Nice. Stanford: Stanford University Press.

Bouzek, J. 2001. "Cimmerians and Early Scythians: The Transition from Geometric to Orientalising Style in the Pontic Area." In *North Pontic Archaeology: Recent Discoveries and Studies*, ed. G. R. Tsetskhladze. Colloquia Pontica 6. Leiden: Brill, 33–45.

Bovon, A. 1963. "La représentation des guerriers perses et la notion de Barbare dans la première moitié du Ve siècle." *BCH* 87: 579–602.

Bowersock, G. W. 1997. "Jacoby's Fragments and Two Greek Historians of Pre-Islamic Arabia." In *Collecting Fragments = Fragmente Sammeln*, ed. G. W. Most. Göttingen: Vandenhoeck & Ruprecht, 173–186.

Bowie, E. 2010. "The Trojan War's Reception in Greek Lyric, Iambic and Elegiac Poetry." In *Intentionale Geschichte: Spinning Time in Ancient Greece*, ed. L. Foxhall, H.-J. Gehrke, and N. Luraghi. Stuttgart: Franz Steiner Verlag, 57–87.

Bowra, C. 1941. "Xenophanes, Fragment 3." *Classical Quarterly* 35: 119–126.

———. 1956. "A Fragment of the Arimaspea." *Classical Quarterly* 6: 1–11.

———. 1964. *Pindar.* Oxford: Oxford University Press.

Braccesi, L. 2004. "The Greeks on the Venetian Lagoon." In *Greek Identity in the Western Mediterranean.* Mnemosyne, supp. 246, ed. K. Lomas. Leiden: Brill, 349–362.

Brah, A. 1996. *Cartographies of Diaspora: Contesting Identities.* London: Routledge.

Brandt, H. 1992. "Panhellenismus, Particularismus und Xenophobie Fremde in griechischen Poleis der klassischen Zeit." *Eos* 80: 191–202.

Braswell, B. K. 1988. *A Commentary on the Fourth Pythian Ode of Pindar.* Berlin: Walter De Gruyter.

Braudel, F. 1966. *The Mediterranean and the Mediterranean World in the Age of Philip II.* Trans. Sian Reynolds. 2 vols. New York: Harper & Row.

———. 1995. *A History of Civilizations.* Harmondsworth, U.K.: Penguin.

Braun, T. 2004. "Hecataeus' Knowledge of the Western Mediterranean." In *Greek Identity in the Western Mediterranean.* Mnemosyne, supp. 246, ed. K. Lomas. Leiden: Brill, 287–347.

Braund, D. 1997. "Greeks and Barbarians: The Black Sea Region and Hellenism under the Early Empire." In *The Early Roman Empire in the East,* ed. S. E. Alcock. Oxford: Oxbow, 121–136.

———. 1999. "Greeks, Scythians and Hippake, or 'Reading Mare's-Cheese.'" In *Ancient Greeks West and East,* ed. G. R. Tsetskhladze. Leiden: Brill, 521–530.

———. 2003. "The Bosporan Kings and Classical Athens: Imagined Breaches in a Cordial Relationship (Aisch. 3.171–172; [Dem.] 34.36)." In *The Cauldron of Ariantas: Studies Presented to A. N. Ščeglov on the Occasion of his 70th Birthday,* ed. P. Guldager Bilde et al. Aarhus: Aarhus University Press, 197–209.

———. 2004. "Herodotus' Spartan Scythians." In *Pontus and the Outside World: Studies in Black Sea History, Historiography, and Archaeology,* ed. C. J. Tuplin. Leiden: Brill, 25–43.

———, ed. 2005. *Scythians and Greeks: Cultural Interactions in Scythia, Athens and the Early Roman Empire (Sixth Century BC—First Century AD).* Exeter: University of Exeter Press.

———. 2007a. "Greater Olbia: Ethnic, Religious, Economic, and Political Interactions in the Region of Olbia, c. 600–100 BC." In *Classical Olbia and the Scythian World: From the Sixth Century BC to the Second Century AD,* ed. D. Braund and S. D. Kryzhitskiy. Proceedings of the British Academy 142. Oxford: Oxford University Press, 37–77.

———. 2007b. "Parthenos and the Nymphs at Crimean Chersonesos: Colonial Appropriation and Native Integration." In *Une koinè pontique: cités grecques, sociétés indigènes et empires mondiaux sur le littoral nord de la mer Noire (VIIe s. a.C. –IIIe s. p.C.),* ed. A. Bresson et al. Bordeaux: Ausonius, 191–201.

———. 2008. "Scythian Laughter: Conversations in the Northern Black Sea Region in the 5th Century BC." In *Meeting of Cultures—Between Conflicts and Coexistence,* ed. P. Guldager Bildeand and J. H. Petersen. Aarhus: Aarhus University Press, 347–368.

Braund, D., and S. D. Kryzhitskiy, eds. 2007. *Classical Olbia and the Scythian World: from the Sixth Century BC to the Second Century AD.* Proceedings of the British Academy 142. Oxford: Oxford University Press.

Bravo, B. 1971. "Remarques sur l'érudition dans l'antiquité." *Acta Conventus XI "Eirene"*: 325–335.

Bremmer, J. 1987. "What Is a Greek Myth?" In *Interpretations of Greek Mythology*, ed. J. Bremmer. London: Croom Helm, 1–9.

Bresson, A. 2007. "La construction d'un espace d'approvisionnement: les cités égéennes." In *Une koinè pontique: cités grecques, sociétés indigènes et empires mondiaux sur le littoral nord de la mer Noire (VIIe s. a.C. –IIIe s. p.C.)*, ed. A. Bresson et al. Bordeaux: Ausonius, 49–69.

Bresson, A., A. Ivantchik, and J.-L. Ferrary, eds. 2007. *Une koinè pontique: cités grecques, sociétés indigènes et empires mondiaux sur le littoral nord de la mer Noire (VIIe s. a.C. –IIIe s. p.C.)*. Bordeaux: Ausonius.

Brett, A. B. 1955. *Catalogue of Greek Coins*. Boston: Museum of Fine Arts.

Briant, P. 1990. "Hérodote et la societé perse." In *Hérodote et les peuples non grecs. Entretiens sur l'Antiquité classique: Vandoeuvres-Genève, 22–26 Août 1988*, ed. G. Nenci and O. Reverdin. Genève: Fondation Hardt 35, 69–105.

———. 2002. *From Cyrus to Alexander: A History of the Persian Empire*. Trans. Peter T. Daniels. Winona Lake, Ind.: Eisenbrauns.

Bridgman, T. 2004. *Hyperboreans: Myth and History in Celtic-Hellenic Contacts*. New York: Routledge.

Brijder, H. A. G. 1991. *Siana Cups II: The Heidelberg Painter*. Amsterdam: Allard Pierson Museum.

Brinkmann, V., R. Wünsche, U. Koch-Brinkmann, S. Kellner, J. Köttl, O. Herzog, R. Batstone, S. Ebbinghaus, and A. Brauer. 2007. *Gods in Color: Painted Sculpture of Classical Antiquity. Exhibition at the Arthur M. Sackler Museum, Harvard University Art Museums, in Cooperation with Staatliche Antikensammlungen and Glyptothek, Munich [and] Stiftung Archäologie, Munich, September 22, 2007–January 20, 2008*. Munich: Stiftung Archäologie.

Brizzi, M. 2008. "La fortificazione di contrada Palazzo di Oppido Mamertina (RC)." In *La Calabria tirrenica nell'antichità: nuovi documenti e problematiche storiche. Atti del convegno (Rende 23–25 Novembre 2000)*, ed. G. De Sensi Sestito. Palmi: Soveria Mannelli, 465–474.

Brizzi, M., and L. Costamagna. 2010. "Il sito fortificato di Serro di Tavola Aspromonte." In *Grecs et indigènes de la Catalogne à la mer Noire. Actes des rencontres Ramses 2006–2008*, ed. H. Tréziny. Paris: Errance; Aix-En-Provence: Centre Camille Jullian, 581–594.

Briquel, D. 1984. *Les Pélasges en Italie: Recherches sur l'histoire de la légende*. Paris: de Boccard.

Brock, R., and S. Hodkinson, eds. 2000. *Alternatives to Athens: Varieties of Political Organization and Community in Ancient Greece*. Oxford: Oxford University Press.

Brosius, M. 2000. *The Persian Empire from Cyrus II to Artaxerxes I*. LACTOR 16. London: London Association of Classical Teachers.

———. 2011. "Keeping up with the Persians: Between Cultural Identity and Persianization in the Achaemenid Period." In *Cultural Identity in the Ancient Mediterranean*, ed. E. S. Gruen. Los Angeles: Getty Research Institute, 135–149.

Brown, T. S. 1973. *The Greek Historians*. Lexington, Mass.: DC Heath.

Brulé, P. 2003. *Women of Ancient Greece*. Edinburgh: Edinburgh University Press.

Brunt, P. A. 1980. "On Historical Fragments and Epitomes." *Classical Quarterly* 30: 477–494.

Budin, S. 2008. *The Myth of Sacred Prostitution in Antiquity.* New York: Cambridge University Press.

Bujskich, S. B. 2006. "Die Chora des pontischen Olbia: Die Hauptetappen der räumlich-strukturellen Entwicklung." In *Surveying the Greek Chora: Black Sea Region in a Comparative Perspective,* ed. P. Guldager Bilde and V. F. Stolba. Aarhus: Aarhus University Press, 115–139.

Bujskikh, S. B. 2007. "Der Achilleus-Kult und die griechische Kolonisation des unteren Bug-Gebiets." In *Une koinè pontique: cités grecques, sociétés indigènes et empires mondiaux sur le littoral nord de la mer Noire (VIIe s. a.C. –IIIe s. p.C.),* ed. A. Bresson et al. Bordeaux: Ausonius, 201–213.

Bunnens, G. 1983. "La distinction entre Phéniciens et Puniques chez les auteurs classiques." *Atti del i Congvegno internazionale di studi fenici e punici* 1: 233–238.

Burgers, G.-J. 1998. *Constructing Messapian Landscapes: Settlement Dynamics, Social Organization and Culture Contact in the Margins of Graeco-Roman Italy.* Amsterdam: J. C. Grieben.

———. 2004. "Western Greeks in their Regional Setting: Rethinking Early Greek-Indigenous Encounters in Southern Italy." *Ancient West and East* 3, no. 2: 252–282.

Burgess, J. S. 2004. *The Tradition of the Trojan War in Homer and the Epic Cycle.* Baltimore: Johns Hopkins University Press.

Burke, P. 2009. *Cultural Hybridity.* Cambridge: Polity Press.

Burkert, W. 1963. "Review of Bolton, J. D. P. 1962. Aristeas of Proconnesus." *Gnomon* 35: 235–240.

———. 1976. "Das hunderttorige Theben und die Datierung der Ilias." *Wiener Studien* 10: 6–21.

———. 1979a. *Structure and History in Greek Mythology and Ritual.* Berkeley: University of California Press.

———. 1979b. "Mythisches Denken. Versuch einer Definition an Hand des griechischen Befundes." In *Philosophie und Mythos. Ein Kolloquium,* ed. H. Poser. Berlin: W. de Gruyter, 16–39.

———. 1983. *Homo Necans: The Anthropology of Ancient Greek Sacrificial Ritual and Myth.* Trans. Peter Bing. Berkeley: University of California Press.

———. 1987. "The Making of Homer in the 6th Century: Rhapsodes versus Stesichorus." In *Papers on the Amasis Painter and His World. Colloquium Sponsored by the Getty Centre for the History of Art and the Humanities and Symposium Sponsored by the J. Paul Getty Museum.* Malibu, Calif.: J. Paul Getty Museum.

———. 1990. "Herodot als Historiker fremder Religionen." In *Hérodote et les peuples non grecs. Entretiens sur l'Antiquité classique: Vandoeuvres-Genève 22–26 Août 1988,* ed. G. Nenci and O. Reverdin. Genève: Fondation Hardt 35, 1–33.

———. 1992. *The Orientalizing Revolution: Near Eastern Influence on Greek Culture in the Early Archaic Age.* Trans. Margaret E. Pinder. Cambridge, Mass.: Harvard University Press.

———. 2004. *Babylon, Memphis, Persepolis. Eastern Contexts of Greek Culture.* Cambridge, Mass.: Harvard University Press.

Burn, A. R. 1962. *Persia and the Greeks.* London: Edward Arnold.

Burnet, J. 1892/1930. *Early Greek Philosophy*. London: A & C Black.

———. 1914. *Greek Philosophy: Thales to Plato*. London: Macmillan.

Burnett, A. 2005a. "The Roman West and the Roman East." In *Coinage and Identity in the Roman Provinces*, ed. C. Howgego, V. Heuchert, and A. Burnett. Oxford: Oxford University Press, 171–181.

———. 2005b. *Pindar's Songs for Young Athletes of Aegina*. Oxford: Oxford University Press.

Burnett, A. P. 1985. *The Art of Bacchylides*. Cambridge, Mass.: Harvard University Press.

Burrow, J. 1966. *Evolution and Society: A Study in Victorian Social Theory*. Cambridge: Cambridge University Press.

Buschor, E. 1919. "Das Krokodil des Sotades." *MJBK* 11: 1–43.

Butcher, K. 2005. "Information, Legitimation, or Self-Legitimation? Popular and Elite Designs on the Coin Types of Syria." In *Coinage and Identity* in the Roman Provinces, ed. C. Howgego, V. Heuchert, and A. Burnett. Oxford: Oxford University Press, 143–156.

Butler, J. 1990. "Performative Acts and Gender Constitution: An Essay in Phenomenology and Feminist Theory." In *Performing Feminisms: Feminist Critical Theory and Theatre*, ed. S. E. Case. Baltimore and London: Johns Hopkins University Press, 270–282.

———. 1997. *Excitable Speech: A Politics of the Performative*. London and New York: Routledge.

———. 2004. *Undoing Gender*. London and New York: Routledge.

Buxton, R. 1994. *Imaginary Greece: The Contexts of Mythology*. Cambridge: Cambridge University Press.

Calame, C. 1990. *Thésée et l'immaginaire athénien: legende et culte en Grèce antique*. Lausanne: Editions Payot.

Callender, G. 2012. "Female Horus: The Life and Reign of Tausret." In *Tausret: Queen and Pharaoh of Egypt*, ed. R. H. Wilkinson. Oxford: Oxford University Press.

Caltabiano, M. C. 1993–1995. "La monetazione di Rhegion nell'età della tirannide." *Klearchos* 35–37: 137–148, 103–124.

Campbell, G. 2006. *Strange Creatures: Anthropology in Antiquity*. London: Duckworth.

Canciani, F., and G. Neumann. 1978. "Lydos, der Sklave?" *Antike Kunst* 21: 17–22.

Canfora, L. 1985. "Wilamowitz: Politik in der Wissenschaft." In *Wilamowitz nach 50 Jahren*, ed. W. M. Calder III, H. Flashar, and T. Lindken. Darmstadt: Wissenschaftliche Buchgesellschaft.

Carey, C. 1981. *A Commentary on Five Odes of Pindar*. Salem, N.H.: Ayer.

———. 2007. "Pindar, Place, and Performance." In *Pindar's Poetry, Patrons, and Festivals: From Archaic Greece to the Roman Empire*, ed. S. Hornblower and C. Morgan. Oxford: Oxford University Press, 199–211.

Carpenter, T. H. 1991. *Art and Myth in Ancient Greece*. London: Thames & Hudson.

Carradice, I. 1987. "The 'Regal' Coinage of the Persian Empire." In *Coinage and Administration in the Athenian and Persian Empires: Proceedings of the Ninth Oxford Symposium on Coinage and Monetary History*, ed. I. Carradice. BAR International Series 343. Oxford: Oxbow.

———. 1995. *Greek Coins*. Austin: University of Texas Press.

Carradice, I., and M. Price. 1988. *Coinage in the Greek World*. London: Seaby.

Carratelli, G. P., ed. 1996. *The Greek World: Art and Civilisation in Magna Graecia and Sicily*. New York: Rizzoli.

Carter, J. C. 1998. *The Chora of Metaponto: The Necropoleis*. Austin: University of Texas Press.

———. 2004. "The Greek Identity at Metaponto." In *Greek Identity in the Western Mediterranean*. Mnemosyne, supp. 246, ed. K. Lomas. Leiden: Brill, 363–390.

———. 2006. "Towards a Comparative Study of Chorai West and East: Metapontion and Chersonesos." In *Surveying the Greek Chora: Black Sea Region in a Comparative Perspective*, ed. P. Guldager Bilde and V. F. Stolba. Aarhus: Aarhus University Press, 175–207.

Cartledge, P. 1993. *The Greeks: A Portrait of Self and Others*. Oxford: Oxford University Press.

Castells, M. 1997. *The Power of Identity*. Oxford: Blackwell.

Castillo, S. 1996. *Thalia: un estudio del léxico vegetal en Pindaro*. Zaragoza: Gorfi.

Castoriadis, C. 1998. *The Imaginary Institution of Society*. Cambridge, Mass.: MIT Press.

Castriota, D. 2005. "Feminizing the Barbarian and Barbarizing the Feminine: Amazons, Trojans, and Persians in the Stoa Poikile." In *Periklean Athens and its Legacy*, ed. J. M. Barringer and J. M. Hurwit. Austin: University of Texas, 89–102.

———. 2000. "Justice, Kingship, and Imperialism: Rhetoric and Reality in Fifth-Century BC Representations following the Persian Wars." In *Not the Classical Ideal: Athens and the Construction of the Other in Greek Art*, ed. B. Cohen. Leiden: Brill, 443–481.

Chagnon, N. A. 1997. *Yanomamö*. Fort Worth: Harcourt Brace.

Chambers, M. 2006. "La vita e la carriera di Felix Jacoby." In *Aspetti dell'opera di Felix Jacoby. Seminari Arnaldo Momigliano, Scuola Normale Superiore di Pisa 18–19 dicembre 2002, Pisa*, ed. C. Ampolo. Pisa: Ed. della Normale, 5–29.

Chankowski, V. 2008. *Athènes et Délos à l'époque classique: recherches sur l'administration du Sanctuaire d'Apollon délien*. Paris: de Boccard.

Cifarelli, M. 1998. "Gesture and Alterity in the Art of Ashurnasirpal II of Assyria." *Art Bulletin* 80, no. 2 (June 1998): 210–228.

Cingano, E. 2005. "A Catalogue within a Catalogue: Helen's Suitors in the Hesiodic Catalogue of Women Frr. 196–204." In *The Hesiodic Catalogue of Women: Constructions and Reconstructions*, ed. R. Hunter. Cambridge: Cambridge University Press, 118–153.

Clark, M. 2004. "Formulas, Metre and Type-Scenes." In *The Cambridge Companion to Homer*, ed. R. Fowler. Cambridge: Cambridge University Press, 117–138.

Clarke, K. 1999. *Between Geography and History: Hellenistic Constructions of the Roman World*. Oxford: Oxford University Press.

———. 2008. *Making Time for the Past: Local History and the Polis*. Oxford: Oxford University Press.

Clifford, J. 1988. *The Predicament of Culture: Twentieth-Century Ethnography, Literature, and Art*. Cambridge, Mass.: Harvard University Press.

———. 1989. "Notes on Travel and Theory." *Inscriptions* 5: 177–188.

———. 1994. "Diasporas." *Cultural Anthropology* 9, no. 3: 302–338.

Clifford, J., and G. Marcus, eds. 1986. *Writing Culture: The Poetics and Politics of Ethnography*. Berkeley: University of California Press.

Coffey, A. 1999. *The Ethnographic Self: Fieldwork and the Representation of Identity*. London: Sage.

Cohen, A. 2011. "The Self as Other: Performing Humour in Ancient Greek Art." In *Cultural Identity in the Ancient Mediterranean*, ed. E. S. Gruen. Los Angeles: Getty Research Institute, 465–490.

Cohen, B. 2000a. "Man-Killers and their Victims: Inversions of the Heroic Ideal in Classical Art." In *Not the Classical Ideal: Athens and the Construction of the Other in Greek Art*, ed. B. Cohen. Leiden: Brill, 98–132.

———, ed. 2000b. *Not the Classical Ideal: Athens and the Construction of the Other in Greek Art.* Leiden: Brill.

———. 2001. "Ethnic Identity in Democratic Athens and the Visual Vocabulary of Male Costume." In *Ancient Perceptions of Greek Ethnicity*, ed. I. Malkin. Cambridge, Mass.: Harvard University Press, 235–274.

Cohen, R. 1978. "Ethnicity: Problem and Focus in Anthropology." *Annual Review of Anthropology* 7: 379–403.

Cojocaru, V., ed. 2005. *Ethnic Contacts and Cultural Exchanges North and West of the Black Sea from the Greek Colonization to the Ottoman Conquest.* Iasi: Trinitas.

Coldstream, J. N. 1969. "The Phoenicians of Ialysos." *Bulletin of the Institute of Classical Studies* 16: 1–7.

———. 1982. "Greeks and Phoenicians in the Aegean." In *Phönizier im Westen*, ed. H. G. Niemeyer. Mainz: Philipp von Zabern, 261–275.

———. 1993. "Mixed Marriages at the Frontiers of the Early Greek World." *Oxford Journal of Archaeology* 121: 89–107.

Cole, S. G. 1994. "Demeter in the Ancient Greek City and its Countryside." In *Placing the Gods: Sanctuaries and Sacred Space in Ancient Greece*, ed. S. Alcock and R. Osborne. Oxford: Clarendon Press, 199–217.

———. 2000. "Demeter in the Ancient Greek City and its Countryside." In *Greek Religion*, ed. R. Buxton. Oxford: Oxford University Press, 133–155.

———. 2004. *Landscapes, Gender, and Ritual Space: The Ancient Greek Experience.* Berkeley: University of California Press.

Coleman, J. E., and C. A. Walz, eds. 1997. *Greeks and Barbarians: Essays on the Interactions between Greeks and Non-Greeks in Antiquity and the Consequences for Eurocentrism.* Bethesda, Md.: CDL Press.

Colonna, G. 1993. "Doni di Etruschi e di altri barbari occidentali nei santuari panellenici." In *I grandi Santuari della Grecia e l'Occidente*, ed. A. Mastrocinque. Trento: Università, 43–67.

———. 2000. "Elmo." In *Mache: La battaglia del Mare Sardonio: Studi e ricerche*, ed. P. Bernardini, P. G. Spanu, and R. Zucca. Cagliari-Oristano: La memoria storica-Mythos.

Comaroff, J., and J. Comaroff. 1992. *Ethnography and the Historical Imagination.* Boulder, Col.: Westview Press.

Constantakopoulou, C. 2007. *The Dance of the Islands: Insularity, Networks, the Athenian Empire and the Aegean World.* Oxford: Oxford University Press.

Cook, R. M. 1981. *Clazomenian Sarcophagi.* Mainz: von Zabern.

Corbato, C. 1952. *Studi Senofanei.* Trieste: Università di Trieste.

Corcella, A. 1984. *Erodoto e l'analogia.* Palermo: Sellerio.

Cordano, F. 2002. "Le identità dei Siculi in età arcaica sulla base delle testimonianze epigrafiche." In *Identità e prassi storica nel Mediterraneo greco*, ed. L. Moscati Castelnuovo. Milano: Edizioni ET, 115–137.

Cordiano, G. 1988. "I rapporti politici tra Locri Epizefiri e Reggio nel VI secolo a.C. alla luce di Arist. Rh. 1394b–1395a (=Stesichorus, Fr. 281b Page)." *Rendiconti dell'Istituto Lombardo* CXXII: 39–47.

———. 1995. "Espansione territoriale e politica colonizzatrice a Reggio (ed a Locri Epizefiri) fra VI e V Secolo a.C." *Kokalos* 41: 77–121.

———. 1997. "L'espansione territoriale di una polis in ambito coloniale: aspetti e problematiche generali alla luce del caso di Rhegion." *Annali della Facoltà di Lettere e Filosofia dell'università di Siena* 18: 1–16.

———. 2000. "Per una carta archeologica della zona confinaria tra Rhegion e Lokroi Epizephyrioi." *Annali della Facoltà di Lettere e Filosofia dell'Università di Siena* 21: 19–31.

———. 2006. "Avamposti militari Reggini e Locresi lungo l'antico fiume Halex: Qualche altre considerazione." In *Nuove richerche storico-topografiche sulle aree confinarie dell'antica chora di Rhegion*, ed. G. Cordiano, S. Accardo, C. Isola, and A. Broggi. Pisa: Edizioni ETS, 55–60.

Corneille, O., and V. Y. Yzerbyt. 2002. "Dependence and the Formation of Stereotyped Beliefs about Groups: From Interpersonal to Intergroup Perception." In *Stereotypes as Explanations: The Formation of Meaningful Beliefs about Social Groups*, ed. C. McGarty, V. Y. Yzerbyt, and R. Spears. London: Cambridge University Press, 111–127.

Cornford, F. M. 1912. *From Religion to Philosophy: A Study in the Origins of Western Speculation*. London: Edward Arnold.

Costabile, F. 1980. "Ricerche di topografia antica tra Motta S. Giovanni e Reggio Calabria 1969–1973." *Rivista Storica Calabrese* 11, no. 2: 11–27.

Costamagna, L. 1986. "Il territorio di Reggio: problemi di topografia." *AttiTaranto* XXVI: 475–512.

———. 2000. "Tra Rhegion e Lokroi Epizephyrioi: nuovi dati archeologici sul confine ionico." *Annali della Facoltà di Lettere e Filosofia dell'Università di Siena* 21: 1–17.

Costamagna, L., and C. Sabbione 1990. *Una città in Magna Grecia: Locri Epizefiri*. Reggio Calabria: Laruffa.

Costamagna, L., and P. Visonà, eds. 1999. *Oppido Mamertina, Calabria, Italia: Ricerche archeologiche nel territorio e in contrada Mella*. Roma: Gangemi.

Counillon, P. 2007. "L'ethnographie dans Le Périple du Ps.-Skylax entre Tanaïs et Colchide." In *Une koinè pontique: cités grecques, sociétés indigènes et empires mondiaux sur le littoral nord de la mer Noire (VIIe s.a.C. –IIIe s. p.C.)*, ed. A. Bresson et al. Bordeaux: Ausonius, 37–49.

Crielaard, J.-P. 2009. "The Ionians in the Archaic Period: Shifting Identities in a Changing World." In *Ethnic Constructs in Antiquity: The Role of Power and Tradition*, ed. T. Derks and N. Roymans. Amsterdam: Amsterdam University Press, 37–84.

Cristofani, M. 1994. "Un etrusco a Egina." *Studi Etruschi* 59: 159–162.

———. 1996. "Sostratos e dintorni." In *Etruschi e altre genti dell'Italia preromana: mobilità in età arcaica*, ed. M. Cristofani. Roma: Giorgio Bretschneider, 49–57.

Crowther, N. B. 2004. *Athletika: Studies on the Olympic Games and Greek Athletics*. Hildesheim: Wiedmann.

Csapo, E. 2005. *Theories of Mythology*. Oxford: Blackwell.

Currie, B. 2005. *Pindar and the Cult of Heroes*. Oxford: Oxford University Press.

Curtis, J., and S. Razmjou. 2005. "The Palace." In *Forgotten Empire: The World of Ancient Persia*, ed. J. Curtis and N. Tallis. London: British Museum Press, 50–103.

d'Agostino, B. 1996a. "The Colonial Experience in Greek Mythology." In *The Greek World: Art and Civilisation in Magna Graecia and Sicily*, ed. G. P. Carratelli. New York: Rizzoli, 209–214.

———. 1996b. "The Impact of the Greek Colonies on the Indigenous Peoples of Campania." In *The Greek World: Art and Civilisation in Magna Graecia and Sicily*, ed. G. P. Carratelli. New York: Rizzoli, 533–540.

D'Alessio, G. B. 2005. "Ordered from the Catalogue: Pindar, Bacchylides, and Hesiodic Genealogical Poetry." In *The Hesiodic Catalogue of Women: Constructions and Reconstructions*, ed. R. Hunter. Cambridge: Cambridge University Press, 217–239.

Dalley, S. 2005. "Semiramis in History and Legend." In *Cultural Borrowings and Ethnic Appropriations in Antiquity*, ed. E. S. Gruen. Stuttgart: Franz Steiner Verlag, 37–59.

Darbo-Peschanski, C. 2007. "The Origin of Greek Historiography." In *A Companion to Greek and Roman Historiography*, ed. J. Marincola. Oxford: Blackwell, 27–38.

Davidson, J. 1997. *Courtesans and Fishcakes: The Consuming Passions of Classical Athens*. London: Fontana Press.

———. 2002. "Too Much Other? François Hartog and the Memories of Odysseus." *TLS*, April 19.

Davies, J. K. 2007. "The Origins of the Festivals, Especially Delphi and the Pythia." In *Pindar's Poetry, Patrons, and Festivals: From Archaic Greece to the Roman Empire*, ed. S. Hornblower and C. Morgan. Oxford: Oxford University Press, 47–71.

De Angelis, F. 1998. "Ancient Past, Imperialist Present: The British Empire in T. J. Dunbabin's the Western Greeks." *Antiquity* 72: 539–549.

———. 2002. "Trade and Agriculture at Megara Hyblaia." *Oxford Journal of Archaeology* 3: 299–310.

De Certeau, M. 1988. *The Writing of History*. New York: Columbia University Press.

De Francisis, A. 1960. "Metauros." *Atti e memorie della Società Magna Grecia* 3: 21–67.

De Hoz, J. 2004. "The Greek Man in the Iberian Street: Non-Colonial Greek Identity in Spain and Southern France." In *Greek Identity in the Western Mediterranean*. Mnemosyne, supp. 246, ed. K. Lomas. Leiden: Brill, 411–428.

De La Genière, J. 1964. "Note sur la chronologie des nécropoles de Torre Galli et Canale Janchina." *Mélanges d'Archéologie et d'Histoire* 76: 7–23.

———. 1968. *Recherches sur l'âge du fer en Italie méridionale I: Sala Consilina*. Naples: Institute Français de Naples, Centre Jean Bérard Publications 1.

———. 1989. "Francavilla Marittima." *Bibliografia topografica della colonizzazione greca in Italia* 7: 492–497.

———. 1991. "L'identification de Lagaria et ses problèmes." In *Épéios et Philoctète en Italie: donées archéologiques et traditions légendaires. Actes du colloque, Lille, 1987*, ed. J. De La Genière. Naples: Cahiers du Centre Jean Bérard 16, 55–66.

De Libero, L. 1996. *Die archaische Tyrannis*. Stuttgart: Franz Steiner Verlag.

De Luna, M. 2003. *La comunicazione linguistica fra alloglotti nel mondo greco: da Omero a Senofonte*. Studi e testi di storia antica 13. Pisa: Edizioni ETS.

De Polignac, F. 1994. "Mediation, Competition, and Sovereignty: The Evolution of Rural Sanctuaries in Geometric Greece." In *Placing the Gods: Sanctuaries and Sacred Space in Ancient Greece*, ed. S. Alcock and R. Osborne. Oxford: Clarendon Press, 3–19.

———. 1995. *Cults, Territory, and the Origins of the Greek City-State*. Trans. Janet Lloyd. London: University of Chicago Press.

D'Ercole, M. C. 2011. "Sharing New Worlds: Mixed Identities around the Adriatic Sixth to Fourth Centuries B.C.E." In *Cultural Identity in the Ancient Mediterranean*, ed. E. S. Gruen. Los Angeles: Getty Research Institute, 465–490.

De Vries, K. 2000. "The Nearly Other: The Attic Vision of Phrygians and Lydians." In *Not the Classical Ideal: Athens and the Construction of the Other in Greek Art*, ed. B. Cohen. Leiden: Brill, 338–364.

Defradas, J. 1954. *Les thèmes de la propagande delphique*. Paris: Klincksieck.

———. 1962a. "Le Banquet de Xénophane." *Revue des études grecques* 75: 344–365.

———. 1962b. *Les élégiaques grecs*. Paris: Presses Universitaires.

———. 1972. *Les thèmes de la propagande delphique*. 2nd ed. Paris: Librairie C. Klincksieck.

Delcourt, M. 1955. *L'oracle de Delphes*. Paris: Payot.

Demir, M. 2007. "The Trade in Salt-Pickled Hamsi and Other Fish from the Black Sea to Athens during the Archaic and Classical Periods." In *The Black Sea: Past, Present and Future: Proceedings of the International, Interdisciplinary Conference, Istanbul, October 14–16, 2004*, ed. G. Erkut and S. Mitchell. Ankara: British Institute at Ankara.

Dench, E. 1995. *From Barbarians to New Men: Greek, Roman, and Modern Perceptions of Peoples of the Central Apennines*. Oxford: Clarendon Press.

———. 2005. "Review of J. Hall, Hellenicity: Between Ethnicity and Culture, Chicago, 2002." *Classical Review* 55 (1): 204–207.

———. 2007. "Ethnography and History." In *A Companion to Greek and Roman Historiography*, ed. J. Marincola. Oxford: Blackwell, 493–503.

Denti, M. 2002. "Linguaggio figurativo e identità culturale nelle più antiche communità greche della Siritide e del Metaponto." In *Identità e prassi storica nel Mediterraneo greco*, ed. L. Moscati Castelnuovo. Milano: Edizioni ET, 33–63.

Derks, T., and N. Roymans, eds. 2009. *Ethnic Constructs in Antiquity: The Role and Power of Tradition*. Amsterdam: Amsterdam University Press.

Derow, P., and R. Parker, eds. 2003. *Herodotus and His World: Essays from a Conference in Memory of George Forrest*. Oxford: Oxford University Press.

Desanges, J. 1982. *Recherches sur l'activité des Méditerranéens aux confins de l'Afrique: VIe siécle avant J.-C.-IVe siécle après J.-C.* Lille: Atelier Reproduction des thèses, Université Lille III.

Descoeudres, J.-P., ed. 1990. *Greek Colonists and Native Populations*. Oxford: Clarendon Press.

Detienne, M. 2007. *The Greeks and Us: A Comparative Anthropology of Ancient Greece*. Trans. Janet Lloyd. Cambridge: Polity Press.

Devereux, G. 1965. "The Kolaxaian Horse of Alcman's Partheneion." *Classical Quarterly* 15: 176–184.

Dewald, C. 1990. "Review of Hartog, F. 1988 the Mirror of Herodotus: The Representation of the Other in the Writing of History, University of California Press, Berkeley." *Classical Philology* 853: 217–224.

———. 1998. "Introduction." *Herodotus: The Histories*. Trans. Robin Waterfield. Oxford: Oxford University Press, Ix–Xli.

Dewald, C., and J. Marincola. 1987. "A Selective Introduction to Herodotean Studies." *Arethusa* 20: 9–40.

———, eds. 2006. *The Cambridge Companion to Herodotus*. Cambridge: Cambridge University Press.

Di Cosmo, N. 2010. "Ethnography of the Nomads and 'Barbarian' History in Han China." In *Intentionale Geschichte: Spinning Time in Ancient Greece*, ed. L. Foxhall, H.-J. Gehrke, and N. Luraghi. Stuttgart: Franz Steiner Verlag, 297–325.

Díaz-andreu, M., and S. Lucy, eds. 2005. *Archaeology of Identity: Approaches to Gender, Age, Status, Ethnicity and Religion*. London: Routledge.

Dihle, A. 1962a. "Aus Herodots Gedankenwelt." *Gymnasium* 69: 22–32.

———. 1962b. "Herodot und die Sophistik." *Philologus* 106: 207–220.

Diller, A. 1937. *Race Mixture among the Greeks before Alexander*. Urbana: University of Illinois Press.

Dillon, M. 2002. *Girls and Women in Classical Greek Religion*. London: Routledge.

Dodds, E. R. 1951. *The Greeks and the Irrational*. Berkeley: University of California Press.

Domanskij, J. V., and K. K. Marčenko. 2003. "Towards Determining the Chief Function of the Settlement of Borysthenes." In *The Cauldron of Ariantas: Studies Presented to A. N. Ščeglov on the Occasion of his 70th Birthday*, ed. P. Guldager Bilde et al. Aarhus: Aarhus University Press, 29–37.

Domínguez, A. J. 2004. "Greek Identity in the Phocaean Colonies." In *Greek Identity in the Western Mediterranean*. Mnemosyne, supp. 246, ed. K. Lomas. Leiden: Brill, 429–456.

Dörrie, H. 1972. "Die Wertung der Barbaren im Urteil der Griechen." In *Antike und Universalgeschichte*, ed. R. Stiehl and G.A. Lehmann. Münster: Aschendorff, 146–175.

Dothan, T. 2003. "Aegean and the Orient: Cultic Interactions." In *Symbiosis, Symbolism, and the Power of the Past: Canaan, Ancient Israel, and their Neighbors from the Late Bronze Age through Roman Palaestina: Proceedings of the Centennial Symposium, W. F. Albright Institute of Archaeological Research and American Schools of Oriental Research*, ed. W. G. Devereux and S. Gitin. Jerusalem, May 29–31, 2000. Winona Lake: Eisenbrauns, 189–214.

Dougherty, C. 1993a. *The Poetics of Colonization: From City to Text in Archaic Greece*. Oxford: Oxford University Press.

———, ed. 1993b. *Cultural Poetics in Archaic Greece: Cult, Performance, Politics*. Cambridge: Cambridge University Press.

———. 2001. *The Raft of Odysseus: The Ethnographic Imagination of Homer's Odyssey*. Oxford: Clarendon Press.

———. 2003. "The Aristonothos Krater: Competing Stories of Conflict and Collaboration." In *The Cultures within Greek Culture: Contact, Conflict, Collaboration*, ed. C. Dougherty and L. Kurke. Cambridge: Cambridge University Press, 35–56.

Dougherty, C., and L. Kurke, eds. 2003a. *The Cultures within Greek Culture: Contact, Conflict, Collaboration*. Cambridge: Cambridge University Press.

———, 2003b. "Introduction." In *The Cultures within Greek Culture: Contact, Conflict, Collaboration*, ed. C. Dougherty and L. Kurke. Cambridge: Cambridge University Press, 1–22.

Dowden, K. 1980. "Deux notes sur les Scythes et les Arimaspes." *Revue des études grecques* 93: 487–492.

Draycott, C. M. 2010a. "Convoy Commanders and Other Military Identities in Tomb Art of Western Anatolia around the Time of the Persian Wars." In *Proceedings of the 17th AIAC 2008, Bollettino di Archeologia Online*: http://151.12.58.75/archeologia/index.php?option=com_content&view=article&id=66&itemid=66

———. 2010b. "What Does Being 'Graeco-Persian' Mean? An Introduction to the Papers." In *Proceedings of the 17th AIAC 2008, Bollettino di Archeologia Online*:

http://151.12.58.75/archeologia/index.php?option=com_content&view=article&id=66&itemid=66

Drews, R. 1973. *The Greek Accounts of Eastern History*. Cambridge, Mass.: Harvard University Press.

Driver, F. 2001. *Geography Militant: Cultures of Exploration and Empire*. Oxford: Blackwell.

Du Bois, P. 1979. "On Horse/Men, Amazons, and Endogamy." *Arethusa* 12: 35–49.

Dubovsky, P. 2006. *Hezekiah and the Assyrian Spies: Reconstruction of the Neo-Assyrian Intelligence Services and Its Significance for 2 Kings 18–19*. Biblica et Orientalia 49. Rome: Pontificio Istituto Biblico.

Dueck, D. 2000. *Strabo of Amasia: A Greek Man of Letters in Augustan Rome*. London: Routledge.

Dunbabin, T. J. 1948. *The Western Greeks: The History of Sicily and South Italy from the Foundation of the Greek Colonies to 480 BC*. Oxford: Clarendon Press.

———. 1957. *The Greeks and their Eastern Neighbours*. London: Society for the Promotion of Hellenic Studies.

Duplouy, A. 2006. *Le prestige des élites: recherches sur les modes de reconnaissance sociale en Grèce entre les Xe et Ve siècles avant J.-C*. Paris: Les Belles Lettres.

Dupont, P. 2003. "Crucible or Damper?" In *The Cauldron of Ariantas. Studies Presented to A. N. Ščeglov on the Occasion of his 70th Birthday*, ed. P. Guldager Bilde et al. Aarhus: Aarhus University Press, 239–247.

———. 2007. "Le Pont-Euxin archaïque: lac milésien ou lac nord-ionien?" In *Une koinè pontique: cités grecques, sociétés indigènes et empires mondiaux sur le littoral nord de la mer Noire (VIIe s. a.C. –IIIe s. p.C.)*, ed. A. Bresson et al. Bordeaux: Ausonius, 29–37.

Durkheim, É. 1912. *Les formes elementaires de la vie religieuse: Le systeme totemique en Australie*. Paris: Alcan.

———. 1915. *The Elementary Forms of Religious Life*. Trans. Joseph Ward Swain. London: Allen & Unwin.

Dziobek, E., and M. A. Raziq. 1990. *Das Grab des Sobekhotep. Theben Nr. 63. Archäoligische Veröffentlichungen 71*. Mainz am Rhein: Philipp von Zabern.

Eaverly, M. A. 1995. *Archaic Greek Equestrian Sculpture*. Ann Arbor: University of Michigan Press.

Edwards, M. W. 1991. *The Iliad: A Commentary*. Vol. 5, Books 17–20. Cambridge: Cambridge University Press.

Edwards, R. B. 1979. *Kadmos the Phoenician: A Study in Greek Legends and the Mycenaean Age*. Amsterdam: Hakkert.

Eidinow, E. 2007. *Oracles, Curses, and Risk among the Ancient Greeks*. Oxford: Oxford University Press.

Einhorn, D. 1917. *Xenophanes. Ein Beitrag zur Kritik der Grundlagen der Bisherigen Philosophiegeschichte*. Wein und Leipzig: Wilhelm Braumüller.

El Kalza, S. 1970. *Ο Βούσιρις εν τη ελληνική γραμματεία και τέχνη*. Athens: Self-published by author.

Ellen, R. F., ed. 1984. *Ethnographic Research: A Guide to General Conduct*. London: Academic Press.

Erbse, H. 1969–83. *Scholia Graeca in Homeri Iliadem*. Berlin: W. de Gruyter.

Eriksen, T. 1993. *Ethnicity and Nationalism: Anthropological Perspectives*. London: Pluto.

Erskine, A. 2001. *Troy between Greece and Rome: Local Tradition and Imperial Power.* Oxford: Oxford University Press.

———. 2005. "Unity and Identity: Shaping the Past in the Greek Mediterranean." In *Cultural Borrowings and Ethnic Appropriations in Antiquity,* ed. E. S. Gruen. Stuttgart: F. Steiner Verlag, 121–137.

Evans, J. A. S. 1961. "The Dream of Xerxes and the 'Nomoi' of the Persians." *Classical Journal* 57: 109–111.

Evans, S. 2008. "The Recitation of Herodotus." In *The Children of Herodotus: Greek and Roman Historiography and Related Genres,* ed. J. Pigoń. Newcastle upon Tyne: Cambridge Scholars Publishing, 1–16.

Farinetti, E. 2003. "Boeotian Orchomenos: A Progressive Creation of a Polis Identity." In *Constructions of Greek Past: Identity and Historical Consciousness from Antiquity to the Present,* ed. H. Hokwerda. Groningen: Egbert Forsten, 1–11.

Farnell, L. R. 1907. *The Cults of the Greek States.* Vol. 4. Oxford: Clarendon Press.

———. 1961. *A Critical Commentary to the Works of Pindar.* Amsterdam: Adolf M. Hakkert.

Faubion, J. D. 2001. "Currents of Cultural Fieldwork." In *Handbook of Ethnography,* ed. P. Atkinson, A. Coffey, S. Delamont, and L. Lofland. London: Sage, 39–60.

Fearn, D., ed. 2011a. *Aegina: Contexts for Choral Lyric Poetry. Myth, History, and Identity in the Fifth Century BC.* Oxford: Oxford University Press.

———. 2011b. "Aegina in Contexts." In *Aegina: Contexts for Choral Lyric Poetry. Myth, History, and Identity in the Fifth Century BC,* ed. D. Fearn. Oxford: Oxford University Press, 1–28.

Fedoseev, N. F. 1997. "Zum achämenidischen Einfluß auf die historische Entwicklung der nordpontischen griechischen Staaten." *Archäologische Mitteilungen aus Iran und Turan* 29: 309–319.

Fehling, D. 1989. *Herodotus and his "Sources." Citation, Invention and Narrative Art.* Trans. J. G. Howie. Leeds: Cairns.

Felsch, R. C. S., ed. 1996. *Kalapodi: Ergebnisse der Ausgrabungen im Heiligtum der Artemis und des Apollon von Hyampolis in der antiken Phokis.* Mainz am Rhein: Philipp von Zabern.

———, ed. 2007. *Kalapodi II. Ergebnisse der Ausgrabungen im Heiligtum der Artemis und des Apollon von Hyampolis in der antiken Phokis.* Mainz am Rhein: Philipp von Zabern.

Ferguson, J. 1975. *Utopias of the Classical World.* London: Thames & Hudson.

Ferrari, F. 1992. "Dileggio e rispetto dei Nòmima nel Fr. 215M. di Pindaro." *Atti dell'Accademia Peloritana dei Pericolanti, Classe di Lettere, Filosofia e Belle Arti* 67: 71–82.

Finkelberg, M. 2005. *Greeks and Pre-Greeks: Aegean Prehistory and Greek Heroic Tradition.* Cambridge: Cambridge University Press.

Finley, M. 1979. *The World of Odysseus.* 2nd ed. London: Harmondsworth.

Flaig, E. 2003. "'Towards Rassenhygiene': Wilamowitz and the German New Right." In *Out of Arcadia: Classics and Politics in Germany in the Age of Burckhardt, Nietzsche and Wilamowitz,* ed. I. Gildenhard and M. Ruehl. London: Institute of Classical Studies. 105–127.

Floyd. D. 1990. "The Sources of Greek Ἵστωρ 'Judge, Witness.'" *Glotta* 68: 157–166.

Flower, H. I. 1991. "Herodotus and Delphic Traditions about Croesus." In *Georgica: Greek Studies in Honour of George Cawkwell,* ed. M. Flower and M. Toher. London: Institute of Classical Studies, 57–77.

Flower, M. 2000. "From Simonides to Isocrates: The Fifth Century Origins of Fourth Century Panhellenism." *Classical Antiquity* 19, no. 1 (April): 65–102.

———. 2002. "Invention of Tradition in Classical and Hellenistic Sparta." In *Sparta: Beyond the Mirage*, ed. A. Powell and S. Hodkinson. London: Classical Press of Wales and Duckworth, 191–218.

Foley, H. 1982. *Reflections of Women in Antiquity*. New York: Gordon and Breach.

Foley, J. 1997. "Oral Tradition and Its Implications." In *A New Comapanion to Homer*, ed. I. Morris and B. Powell. Leiden: Brill, 146–174.

Fontenrose, J. 1978. *The Delphic Oracle: Its Responses and Operations with a Catalogue of Responses*. Berkeley: University of California Press.

———. 1988. *Didyma: Apollo's Oracle, Cult, and Companions*. Berkeley: University of California Press.

Forbes, H. 1993. "Ethnoarchaeology and the Place of the Olive in the Economy of the Southern Argolid, Greece." In *La production du vin et de l'huile en Méditerranée*, ed. M.-C. Amouretti and J.-P. Brun. Paris: de Boccard, 213–226.

———. 2007. *Meaning and Identity in a Greek Landscape. An Archaeological Ethnography*. Cambridge: Cambridge University Press.

Fornara, C. W. 1971a. "Evidence for the Date of Herodotus' Publication." *JHS* 91: 25–34.

———. 1971b. *Herodotus. An Interpretive Essay*. Oxford: Oxford University Press.

———. 1983. *The Nature of History in Ancient Greece and Rome*. Berkeley: University of California Press.

Forrest, W. G. 1957. "Colonisation and the Rise of Delphi." *Historia* 6: 160–175.

Forsdyke, S. 2005. "Revelry and Riot in Archaic Megara: Democratic Disorder or Ritual Reversal?" *JHS* 125: 73–93.

Foti, G. 1976. "La topografia di Locri Epizefirii." *AttiTaranto* 16: 343–362.

Foucault, M. 1972. *The Archaeology of Knowledge*. Trans. A. Sheridan-Smith. London: Tavistock.

Fowler, R. L. 1996. "Herodotus and his Contemporaries." *JHS* 116: 62–87.

———. 1998. "Genealogical Thinking, Hesiod's Catalogue and the Creation of the Hellenes." *Proceedings of the Cambridge Philological Society* 44: 1–19.

———. 2000. *Early Greek Mythography*. Vol. 1, *Text and Introduction*. Oxford: Oxford University Press.

———. 2001. "Early Historiē and Literacy." In *The Historian's Craft in the Age of Herodotus*, ed. N. Luraghi. Oxford: Oxford University Press, 95–116.

———. 2003. "Herodotus and Athens." In *Herodotus and His World: Essays from a Conference in Memory of George Forrest*, ed. P. Derow and R. Parker. Oxford: Oxford University Press, 305–318.

———. ed. 2004. *The Cambridge Companion to Homer*. Cambridge: Cambridge University Press.

Foxhall, L. 1998. "Cargoes of the Heart's Desire: The Character of Trade in the Archaic Mediterranean World." In *Archaic Greece: New Approaches and New Evidence*, ed. N. Fisher and H. Van Wees. London: Classical Press of Wales and Duckworth, 295–311.

———. 2003. "Cultures, Landscapes, and Identities in the Mediterranean World." In *Mediterranean Paradigms and Classical Antiquity*, ed. I. Malkin. *Mediterranean Historical Review* 18 (December): 75–92.

———. 2005. "Village to City: Staples and Luxuries? Exchange Networks and Urbanization." In *Mediterranean Urbanization 800–600 BC*, ed. B. Cunliffe and R. Osborne. Oxford: Oxford University Press.

———. 2006a. "Excavations at San Salvatore." In *Bova Marina Archaeological Project. Preliminary Report, 2006 Season*, ed. J. Robb. Cambridge. Department of Archeology, 23–40.

———. 2006b. "Environments and Landscapes of Greek Culture." In *A Companion to the Classical Greek World*, ed. K. H. Kinzl. Oxford: Blackwell, 245–280.

———. 2007a. "Classical Greek Excavations at San Salvatore." In *Bova Marina Archaeological Project. Preliminary Report, 2007 Season*, ed. J. Robb. Cambridge, Department of Archeology, 51–75, 81–82.

———. 2007b. *Olive Cultivation in Ancient Greece: Seeking the Ancient Economy.* Oxford: Oxford University Press.

Foxhall, L., and J. Salmon, eds. 1998. *When Men Were Men: Masculinity, Power and Identity in Classical Antiquity.* London: Routledge.

Fränkel, H. 1925. "Xenophanesstudien." *Hermes* 60: 174–192.

Fraser, A.D. 1935. "The Panoply of the Ethiopian Warrior." *AJA* 39: 35–45.

Fraser, P. M. 2009. *Greek Ethnic Terminology.* Oxford: Oxford University Press.

Frazer, J. G., Sir 1932. *The Golden Bough: A Study of Magic and Religion.* 3rd ed. London: Macmillan.

Friedrichsmeyer, S., S. Lennox, and S. Zantop, eds. 1998. *The Imperialist Imagination: German Colonialism and its Legacy.* Ann Arbor: University of Michigan Press.

Froidefond, C. 1971. *Le mirage égyptien dans la littérature grecque d'Homère à Aristote.* Aix-en-Provence: Ophrys.

Frolov, E. D. 1998. "The Scythians in Athens." *VDI* 1: 135–142.

Fuchs, W., and J. Floren, 1987. *Die Griechische Plastik.* Vol. 1, *Die Geometrische und Archaische Plastik.* Munich: Beck.

Furtwängler, A. 1906. *Aegina. Das Heiligtum der Aphaia.* Munich: Verlag der K. B. Akademie der wissenschaften.

Gagarin, M. 1986. *Early Greek Law.* Berkeley: University of California Press.

Garbini, G. 1996. "The Phoenicians in the Western Mediterranean through to the Fifth Century B.C." In *The Greek World: Art and Civilisation in Magna Graecia and Sicily*, ed. G. P. Carratelli. New York: Rizzoli, 121–132.

Gardner, P. 1908. "The Gold Coinage of Asia before Alexander the Great." *Proceedings of the British Academy* 3: 107–139.

Garraffo, S. 1984. *Le riconiazioni in Magna Grecia e in Sicilia. Emissioni argentee dal VI al IV secolo a.C.* Palermo: Centro di Studi per l'Archeologia greca.

Gates, L. 1998. "Of Seeing and Otherness: Leni Riefenstahl's African Photographs." In *The Imperialist Imagination: German Colonialism and its Legacy*, ed. S. Friedrichsmeyer, S. Lennox, and S. Zantop. Ann Arbor: University of Michigan Press, 233–246.

Gavriljuk, N. A. 2003. "The Graeco-Scythian Slave Trade in the 6th and 5th Centuries BC." In *The Cauldron of Ariantas. Studies Presented to A. N. Ščeglov on the Occasion of his 70th Birthday*, ed. P. Guldager Bilde et al. Aarhus: Aarhus University Press, 75–87.

———. 2008. "Social and Economic Stratification of the Scythians from the Steppe Region Based on Black-Glazed Pottery from Burials." In *Meeting of Cultures—Between Conflicts and Coexistence*, ed. P. Guldager Bilde and J. H. Petersen. Aarhus: Aarhus University Press, 237–262.

―――. 2010. "Handmade Pottery." In *The Lower City of Olbia (Sector NGS) in the 6th Century BC to the 4th Century AD*. Vols. 1–2, ed. N. A. Lejpunskaja et al. Aarhus: Aarhus University Press, 335–354.

Geertz, C. 1973. *The Interpretation of Cultures*. New York: Basic Books.

Gehrke, H .J. 2001. "Myth, History, and Collective Identity: Uses of the Past in Ancient Greece and Beyond." In *The Historian's Craft in the Age of Herodotus*, ed. N. Luraghi. Oxford: Oxford University Press, 286–314.

―――. 2005. "Heroen als Grenzgänger zwischen Griechen und Barbaren." In *Cultural Borrowings and Ethnic Appropriations in Antiquity*, ed. E. S. Gruen. Stuttgart: F. Steiner Verlag, 50–67.

―――. 2010. "Representations of the Past in Greek Culture." In *Intentionale Geschichte: Spinning Time in Ancient Greece*, ed. L. Foxhall, H.-J. Gehrke, and N. Luraghi. Stuttgart: Steiner Verlag, 15–33.

Gentili, B. 1988. *Poetry and its Public in Ancient Greece: From Homer to the Fifth Century*. Baltimore: Johns Hopkins University Press.

Georges, P. 1994. *Barbarian Asia and the Greek Experience: From the Archaic Period to the Age of Xenophon*. Baltimore: Johns Hopkins University Press.

Gerber, D.E. 1999a. *Greek Elegiac from the Seventh to the Fifth Centuries BC*. Cambridge, Mass.: Harvard University Press.

―――. 1999b. *Greek Iambic Poetry from the Seventh to the Fifth Centuries BC*. Cambridge, Mass.: Harvard University Press.

Gernet, L. 1976. *Anthropologie de la Grèce antique*. Paris: Maspero.

―――. 1981. *The Anthropology of Ancient Greece*, Trans. John Hamilton and Blaise Nagy. Baltimore: Johns Hopkins University Press.

Giangiulio, M. 1991. "Filottete tra Sibari e Crotone: osservazioni sulla tradizione letteraria." In *Épéios et Philoctète en Italie: donées archéologiques et traditions légendaires. Actes du colloque, Lille, 1987*, ed. J. De La Genière. Naples: Cahiers du Centre Jean Bérard 16, 37–53.

―――. 2010. "Collective Identities, Imagined Past, and Delphi." In *Intentionale Geschichte: Spinning Time in Ancient Greece*, ed. L. Foxhall, H.-J. Gehrke, and N. Luraghi. Stuttgart: Steiner Verlag, 121–135.

Gikandi, S. 1996. *Maps of Englishness: Writing Identity in the Culture of Colonisation*. New York: Columbia University Press.

Gill, D. W. J. 1991. "Pots and Trade: Spacefillers or objets d'art?" *JHS* 111: 29–47.

―――. 1994. "Positivism, Pots and Long-Distance Trade." In *Classical Greece: Ancient Histories and Modern Archaeologies*, ed. I. Morris. Cambridge: Cambridge University Press, 99–107.

―――. 2004. "Euesperides: Cyrenaica and its Contacts with the Greek World." In *Greek Identity in the Western Mediterranean*. Mnemosyne, supp. 246, ed. K. Lomas. Leiden: Brill, 391–410.

Gilroy, P. 1993. *The Black Atlantic*. London: Verso.

Giovannini, A. 1969. *Étude historique sur les origines du Catalogue des Vaisseaux*. Berne: Éditions Francke Berne.

Gissing, G. 1901. *By the Ionian Sea: Notes of a Ramble in Southern Italy*. London: Chapman & Hall.

Givigliano, G. P. 1978. *Sistemi di comunicazione e topografia degli insediamenti di età greca nella Brettia*. Cosenza: Edizioni «Il Gruppo».

————. 1987. "Castellace." *Bibliografia topografica della colonizzazione greca in Italia* 5: 95–97.

Glennie, P. 1995. "Consumption within Historical Studies." In *Archaeology Consumption: A Review of New Studies*, ed. D. Miller. London: Routledge, 164–203.

Glinister, F. 2003. "Gifts for the Gods: Sanctuary and Society in Archaic Tyrrhenian Italy." In *Inhabiting Symbols: Symbol and Image in the Ancient Mediterranean*, ed. J. B. Wilkins and E. Herring. London: Accordia Research Institute, 137–147.

Godden, G. M. 1898. "Nágá and Other Frontier Tribes of North-East India." *Journal of the Anthropological Institute of Great Britain & Ireland* 28: 2–52.

Goldberg, M. Y. 1998. "The Amazon Myth and Gender Studies." In ΣΤΕΦΑΝΟΣ: *Studies in Honour of Brunilde Sismondo Ridgway*, ed. K. J. Hartswick and M. C. Sturgeon. Philadelphia: University Museum, University of Pennsylvania, 89–100.

Goldhill, S. 1991. *The Poet's Voice: Essays on Poetics and Greek Literature*. Cambridge: Cambridge University Press.

————. 2000. "Civic Ideology and the Problem of Difference: The Politics of Aeschylean Tragedy." *JHS* 120: 34–56.

————. 2002. *The Invention of Prose*. Oxford: Oxford University Press/The Classical Association.

Goldhill, S., and R. Osborne, eds. 1994. *Art and Text in Ancient Greek Culture*. Cambridge: Cambridge University Press.

————. eds. 2006. *Rethinking Revolutions through Ancient Greece*. Cambridge: Cambridge University Press.

Goldsmid, F. 1893. "The Acropolis of Susa." *Geographical Journal* 15: 437–444.

Golovacheva, N. V., and E. Y. Rogov. 2001. "Note on the Rural Temple on the Northern Edge of the Archaic Chora of Olbia." In *North Pontic Archaeology. Recent Discoveries and Studies*, Colloquia Pontica 6, ed. G. R. Tsetskhladze. Leiden: Brill, 143–149.

Gomme, A. W. 1913. "The Legend of Cadmus and the Logographi." *JHS* 33: 53–72, 233–245.

Goody, J. 1977. *The Domestication of the Savage Mind*. Cambridge: Cambridge University Press.

Gori, S., and M. C. Bettini. 2006. *Gli Etruschi da Genova ad Ampurias. Atti del XXIV Convegno di studi etruschi ed italici, Marseille-Lattes, 26 settembre–1 ottobre 2002*. 2 vols. Pisa: Istituti Editoriali e Poligrafici Internazionali.

Gorman, R. J., V. B. Gorman. 2007. "The Tryphê of the Sybarites: A Historiographical Problem in Athenaeus." *JHS* 127: 38–60.

Gosden, C. 2004. *Archaeology and Colonisation. Cultural Contact from 5000 BC to the Present*. Cambridge: Cambridge University Press.

Gosden, C., and Y. Marshall. 1999. "Cultural Biography of Objects." *World Archaeology* 31: 169–178.

Gould, J. 1989. *Herodotus*. London: Weidenfeld & Nicolson.

————. 1994. "Herodotus and Religion." In *Greek Historiography*, ed. S. Hornblower. Oxford: Clarendon Press, 91–107.

Graf, F. 2000. "The Locrian Maidens." In *Greek Religion*, ed. R. Buxton. Oxford: Oxford University Press, 250–271.

Graham, A. J. 1978. "The Foundation of Thasos." *BSA* 73: 61–98.

————. 1982. "The Colonial Expansion of Greece." *CAH²* III, no. 3: 83–162.

———. 2001. *Collected Papers on Greek Colonization*. Leiden: Brill.

Graindor, P. 1955. "Mélanges d'archéologie." *Bulletin of the Faculty of Arts, University of Egypt* 3 (II): 105–110.

Grammenos, D. V., and E. K. Petropoulos, eds. 2003. *Ancient Greek Colonies in the Black Sea* III. Thessaloniki: Archaeological Institute of Northern Greece.

Gras, M., M. H. Tréziny, and H. Broise. 2004. *Mégara Hyblaea*. Vol. 5, *La ville archaïque: l'espace urbain d'une cite grecque de Sicile*. Rome: École Française de Rome.

Graziosi, B. 2002. *Inventing Homer: The Early Reception of the Epic*. Cambridge: Cambridge University Press.

Greaves, A. 2002. *Miletos: A History*. London: Routledge.

———. 2004. "The Cult of Aphrodite in Miletos and Its Colonies." *Anatolian Studies* 54: 27–33.

———. 2007. "Milesians in the Black Sea." In *The Black Sea in Antiquity. Regional and Interregional Economic Exchanges*, ed. V. Gabrielsen and J. Lund. Aarhus: Aarhus University Press, 9–23.

Greco, E. 1990. "Serdaioi." *Annali dell'Istituto Universitario Orientale di Napoli, Dipartimento di Studi del mondo classico e del Mediterraneo antico, sezione di archeologia e storia antica* 12: 39–57.

———. 2003. "La colonizziazone greca in Italia meridionale: profilo storico-archaeologico." *Il fenomeno coloniale dall'antichità ad oggi (Roma, 19 e 20 marzo 2002). Atti dei convegni lincei, 189*: 17–35.

Greenblatt, S. 1991. *Marvellous Possessions: The Wonder of the New World*. Oxford: Clarendon Press.

Grote, G. 1862. *A History of Greece*. London: John Murray.

Gruen, E. S. 2002. *Diaspora: Jews amidst Greeks and Romans*. Cambridge, Mass.: Harvard University Press.

———. 2005a. "Persia through the Jewish Looking-Glass." In *Cultural Borrowings and Ethnic Appropriations in Antiquity*, ed. E. S. Gruen. Stuttgart: F. Steiner Verlag, 90–105.

———, ed. 2005b. *Cultural Borrowings and Ethnic Appropriations in Antiquity*. Stuttgart: F. Steiner Verlag.

———. 2011a. *Rethinking the Other in Antiquity*. Princeton: Princeton University Press.

———, ed. 2011b. *Cultural Identity in the Ancient Mediterranean*. Los Angeles: Getty Research Institute.

———. 2011c. "Herodotus and Persia." In *Cultural Identity in the Ancient Mediterranean*, ed. E. S. Gruen. Los Angeles: Getty Research Institute, 67–85.

Guettal Cole, S. 2010. "'I Know the Number of the Sand and the Measure of the Sea': Geography and Difference in the Early Greek World." In *Geography and Ethnography. Perceptions of the World in Pre-Modern Societies*, ed. K. A. Raaflaub and R. J. A. Talbert. Chichester: Wiley-Blackwell, 197–214.

Guldager Bilde, P. 2003. "Ved det Gæstmilde hav?" *Sfinx* 3: 128–133.

Guldager Bilde, P., J. M. Højte, and V. F. Stolba, eds. 2003. *The Cauldron of Ariantas. Studies Presented to A.N. Ščeglov on the Occasion of his 70th Birthday*. Aarhus: Aarhus University Press.

Guldager Bilde, P., and V. F. Stolba, eds. 2006. *Surveying the Greek Chora. The Black Sea Region in a Comparative Perspective*. Aarhus: Aarhus University Press.

Guldager Bilde, P., and J. H. Petersen, eds. 2008. *Meetings of Cultures—Between Conflicts and Coexistence*. Aarhus: Aarhus University Press.

Gunter, A. C. 2009. *Greek Art and the Orient*. Cambridge: Cambridge University Press.

Guzzo, G. P. 1981. "II territorio dei Brutti." *Società romana e produzione schiavistica* I: 115–135.

———. 1982. "Fortificazioni della Calabria settentrionale." In *La fortification dans l'histoire du monde grec. Actes du colloque international. La fortification et sa place dans l'histoire politique, culturelle et sociale du monde grec, Valbonne, décembre 1982*, ed. P. Leriche and H. Tréziny. Paris: Éditions du centre national de la recherche scientifique, 201–209.

———. 1990. "Myths and Archaeology in South Italy." In *Greek Colonists and Native Populations*, ed. J.-P. Descoeudres. Oxford: Clarendon Press, 131–142.

———. 1996. "The Encounter with the Bruttii." In *The Greek World: Art and Civilisation in Magna Graecia and Sicily*, ed. G. P. Carratelli. New York: Rizzoli, 559–562.

———. 2002. "L'identità contraddittoria." In *Identità e prassi storica nel Mediterraneo greco*, ed. L. Moscati Castelnuovo. Milano: Edizioni ET, 137–159.

Hadas, M. 1935. " Utopian Sources in Herodotus." *Classical Philology* 30: 113–121.

Hägg, R., and N. Marinatos, eds. 1993. *Greek Sanctuaries: New Approaches*. London: Routledge.

Hainsworth, B. 1993. *The Iliad: A Commentary*. Vol. 3, Books 9–12. Cambridge: Cambridge University Press.

Hainsworth, J. B. 1968. *The Flexibility of the Homeric Formula*. Oxford: Clarendon Press.

Hall, E. 1989. *Inventing the Barbarian: Greek Self-Definition through Tragedy*. Oxford: Clarendon Press.

———. 2002. "When Is a Myth not a Myth? Bernal's 'Ancient Model.'" In *Greeks and Barbarians*, ed. T. Harrison. Edinburgh: Edinburgh University Press, 133–152.

Hall, J. 1995. "The Role of Language in Greek Ethnicities." *Proceedings of the Cambridge Philological Society* 41: 83–100.

———. 1997. *Ethnic Identity in Greek Antiquity*. Cambridge: Cambridge University Press.

———. 2000. "The East within the Cultural Identity of the Cities of Magna Graecia." *AttiTaranto* 39: 389–401.

———. 2001. "Contested Ethnicities: Perceptions of Macedonia within Evolving Definitions of Greek Ethnicity." In *Ancient Perceptions of Greek Ethnicity*, ed. I. Malkin. Cambridge, Mass.: Harvard University Press, 159–186.

———. 2002. *Hellenicity: Between Ethnicity and Culture*. Chicago: University of Chicago Press.

———. 2003. "'Culture' Or 'Cultures'? Hellenism in the Late-Sixth Century." In *The Cultures within Greek Culture: Contact, Conflict, Collaboration*, ed. C. Dougherty and L. Kurke. Cambridge: Cambridge University Press, 23–34.

———. 2004. "How 'Greek' Were the Early Western Greeks?" In *Greek Identity in the Western Mediterranean*. Mnemosyne, supp. 246, ed. K. Lomas. Leiden: Brill, 35–54.

———. 2005. "Arcades His Oris: Greek Projections on the Italian Ethnoscape?" In *Cultural Borrowings and Ethnic Appropriations in Antiquity*, ed. E. S. Gruen. Stuttgart: F. Steiner, 259–285.

———. 2007. "The Creation and Expression of Identity: The Greek World." In *Blackwell Studies in Global Archaeology: Classical Archaeology*, ed. S. E. Alcock and R. Osborne. Oxford: Basil Blackwell, 337–355.

Hall, S. 1990. "Cultural Identity and Diaspora." In *Identity: Community, Culture Difference*, ed. J. Rutherford. London: Lawrence and Wishart, 222–237.

———. 1997a. "The Spectacle of the 'Other.'" In *Representation. Cultural Representations and Signifying Practices*, ed. S. Hall. London: Sage, 223–290.

———. 1997b. "The Work of Representation." In *Representation. Cultural Representations and Signifying Practices*, ed. S. Hall. London: Sage, 13–74.

———, ed. 1997c. *Representation. Cultural Representations and Signifying Practices*. London: Sage.

———. 2003 [1996]. "New Ethnicities." In *Identities. Race, Class, Gender and Nationality*, ed. L. M. Alcoff and E. Mendieta. Oxford: Blackwell, 90–96.

Hammersley, M., and P. Atkinson. 1983. *Ethnography: Principles in Practice*. London: Tavistock.

Hampe, R. 1936. *Frühe griechische Sagenbilder in Boiotien*. Athens: Deutsches Archäologisches Institut.

Hannestad, L. 2007. "Handmade or Wheel-Made: A Note on the Issue of a Northern Pontic Cultural Koinè." In *Une koinè pontique: cités grecques, sociétés indigènes et empires mondiaux sur le littoral nord de la mer Noire (VIIe s. a.C. –IIIe s. p.C.)*, ed. A. Bresson et al. Bordeaux: Ausonius, 141–149.

Hannestad, L., and V. Stolba. 2006. *Chronologies of the Black Sea Area in the Period, C. 400–100 BC*. Aarhus: Aarhus University Press.

Hansen, H. M., and T. H. Nielsen, eds. 2004. *An Inventory of the Archaic and Classical Polis*. Oxford: Oxford University Press.

Hansen, W. 1997. "Homer and the Folktale." In *A New Companion to Homer*, ed. I. Morris and B. Powell. Leiden: Brill, 442–462.

Harari, M. 2004. "A Short History of Pygmies in Greece and Italy." In *Greek Identity in the Western Mediterranean*. Mnemosyne, supp. 246, ed. K. Lomas. Leiden: Brill, 163–190.

Harding, P. 2008. *The Story of Athens: The Fragments of the Local Chronicles of Attika*. London: Routledge.

Hardwick, L. 1990. "Ancient Amazons—Heroes, Outsiders or Women?" *Greece & Rome* 37, no. 1: 14–36.

Harmatta, J. 1990. "Herodotus, Historian of the Cimmerians and the Scythians." In *Hérodote et les peuples non grecs. Entretiens sur l'Antiquité classique: Vandoeuvres-Genève, 22–26 Août 1988*, ed. G. Nenci and O. Reverdin. Genève: Fondation Hardt 35, 115–131.

Harman, R. 2009. "Viewing Spartans, Viewing Barbarians: Visuality in Xenophon's Lakedaimoniōn Politeia." In *Sparta: Comparative Approaches*, ed. S. Hodkinson. Swansea: Classical Press of Wales, 361–382.

Harris, D. 1995. *The Treasures of the Parthenon and Erechtheion*. Oxford: Clarendon Press.

Harris, W. B. 1898. "The Berbers of Morocco." *Journal of the Anthropological Institute of Great Britain & Ireland* 28: 61–75.

Harrison, J. E. 1912. *Themis: A Study of the Social Origins of Greek Religion*. Cambridge: Cambridge University Press.

Harrison, T. 1998. "Herodotus' Conception of Foreign Languages." *Histos* 2: Http://
Www.Dur.Ac.Uk/Classics/Histos/1998.

———. 2000a. *Divinity and History: The Religion of Herodotus*. Oxford: Clarendon
Press.

———. 2000b. *The Emptiness of Asia: Aeschylus' Persians and the History of the Fifth
Century*. London: Duckworth.

———. 2000c. "Sicily in the Athenian Imagination: Thucydides on the Persian
Wars." In *Ancient Sicily from Aeneas to Cicero*, ed. C. J. Smith and J. Serrati. Edinburgh: Edinburgh University Press, 84–96.

———, ed. 2002a. *Greeks and Barbarians*. Edinburgh: Edinburgh University Press.

———. 2002b. "The Persian Invasions." In *Brill's Companion to Herodotus*, ed.
E. Bakker, I. De Jong, and H. Van Wees. Leiden: Brill, 551–578.

———. 2003a. "'Prophecy in Reverse?' Herodotus and the Origins of History." In
Herodotus and His World: Essays from a Conference in Memory of George Forrest, ed.
P. Derow and R. Parker. Oxford: Oxford University Press, 237–255.

———. 2003b. "Upside Down and Back to Front: Herodotus and the Greek Encounter with Egypt." In *Ancient Perspectives on Egypt*, ed. R. Matthews and C. Roemer.
London: UCL Press, 145–156.

———. 2007. "The Place of Geography in Herodotus' Histories." In *Travel, Geography and Culture in Ancient Greece and the Near East*, ed. C. Adams and J. Roy.
Oxford: Oxbow, 44–66.

———. 2010. *Writing Ancient Persia*. London: Duckworth.

Hartog, F. 1988. *The Mirror of Herodotus: The Representation of the Other in the Writing
of History*. Trans. Janet Lloyd. Berkeley: University of California Press.

———. 1998. "Premières figures de l'historien en Grèce: historicité et histoire." In *Figures de l'intellectuel en Grèce ancienne*, ed. N. Loraux, C. Miralles. Paris: Belin, 123–141.

———. 2000. "The Invention of History: The Pre-History of the Concept. From
Homer to Herodotus." *History and Theory* 39: 384–395.

———. 2001. *Memories of Odysseus: Frontier Tales from Ancient Greece*, Trans. Janet
Lloyd. Edinburgh: Edinburgh University Press.

———. 2002. "The Greeks as Egyptologists." In *Greeks and Barbarians*, ed. T. Harrison. Edinburgh: Edinburgh University Press, 211–228.

Harvey, D. 1990. *The Condition of Postmodernity: An Enquiry into the Origins of Cultural
Change*. Oxford: Blackwell.

Haubold, J. 2007. "Xerxes' Homer." In *Cultural Responses to the Persian Wars: Antiquity to the Third Millennium*, ed. E. Bridges, E. Hall, and P. J. Rhodes. Oxford:
Oxford University Press, 47–63.

Haynes, S. 1965. *Etruscan Bronze Utensils*. London: Trustees of the British Museum.

Head, B. V. 1911. *Historia Numorum*. Oxford: Clarendon Press.

Hedreen, G. 1991. "The Cult of Achilles in the Euxine." *Hesperia* 60, no. 3: 313–330.

Heinen, H. 2001. "Greeks, Iranians and Romans on the Northern Shores of the Black
Sea." In *North Pontic Archaeology. Recent Discoveries and Studies*, ed. G. R. Tsetskhladze. Colloquia Pontica 6. Leiden: Brill, 1–23.

Heinimann, F. 1945. *Nomos und Physis: Herkunft und Bedeutung einer Antithese im
griechischen Denken des 5. Jahrhunderts*. Basel: F. Reinhardt.

Helms, M. W. 1988. *Ulysses' Sail: An Ethnographic Odyssey of Power, Knowledge, and
Geographical Distance*. Princeton: Princeton University Press.

Henderson, J. 1994. "Timaeo Danaos: Amazons in Early Greek Art and Pottery." In *Art into Text in Ancient Greek Culture*, ed. S. Goldhill and R. Osborne. Cambridge: Cambridge University Press, 85–138.

Henkelman, W., and M. Stolper. 2009. "Ethnic Identity and Ethnic Labelling at Persepolis: The Case of the Skudrians." In *Organisation des pouvoirs et contacts culturels dans les pays de l'empire achéménide. Actes du colloque organisé au Collège de France par la « Chaire d'histoire et civilisation du monde achéménide et de l'empire d'Alexandre » et le « Réseau international d'études et de recherches achéménides » GDR 2538 CNRS. 9–10 novembre 2007*, ed. P. Briant and M. Chauveau. Paris: de Boccard, 271–329.

Hennig, R. 1935. "Herodots Handelsweg zu den sibirischen Issedonen." *Klio* 28: 248–254.

Herring, E. 2000. "'To See Ourselves as Others See Us!' The Construction of Native Identities in Southern Italy." In *The Emergence of State Identities in Italy in the First Millennium BC*, ed. E. Herring and K. Lomas. London: Accordia Research Institute, 45–77.

Herring, E., and K. Lomas, eds. 2000. *The Emergence of State Identities in Italy in the First Millennium BC*. London: Accordia Research Institute.

Herring, E., R. D. Whitehouse, and J. B. Wilkins. 2000. "Wealth, Wine and War. Some Gravina Tombs of the 6th and 5th Centuries BC." In *Ancient Italy in Its Mediterranean Setting: Studies in Honour of Ellen Macnamara*, ed. D. Ridgway et al. London: Accordia Research Institute, 235–257.

Herrmann, H. V. 1983. "Altitalisches und Etruskisches in Olympia." *Annuario della Scuola Archeologica di Atene e delle Missioni Italiane in Oriente* 61: 271–294.

Hervé, R. 1930. "Sacrifices humains du Centre-Amérique." *Documents* 4: 205–214.

Herzhoff, B. 1984. "Botanische Beobachtungen zu einem homerischen Pflanzennamen." *Hermes* 112: 257–271.

———. 1999. "Lotos." *Neue Pauly* 7: 449.

Heubeck, A. 1989. "Books IX–XII." In *A Commentary on Homer's Odyssey*. Vol. II, Books IX–XVI, ed. A. Heubeck and A. Hoekstra. Oxford: Clarendon Press, 3–146.

Heubeck, A., and A. Hoekstra. 1989. *A Commentary on Homer's Odyssey*. Vol. II, Books IX–XVI. Oxford: Clarendon Press.

Heubeck, A., S. West, and J. B. Hainsworth. 1988. *A Commentary on Homer's Odyssey*. Vol. I, Introduction and Books I–VIII. Oxford: Clarendon Press.

Hiller, H. 1975. *Ionische Grabreliefs der ersten Hälfte des 5. Jahrhunderts v. Chr.* Tübingen: Wasmuth.

Hiller von Gaetringen, F. 1934, "Noch einmal das Archilochosdenkmal von Paros." *Nachrichten von der Gesellschaft der Wissenschaften zu Göttingen*. Philol.-Hist. KI.1 (1934–36): 41–56.

Himmelmann-Wildschuetz, N. 1956. *Studien zum Ilissos-Relief*. Munich: Prestel.

Hind, J. G. F. 2001. "A Sea 'Like a Scythian Bow' and Herodotus' 'Rugged Peninsula' Hist. 4.99." In *North Pontic Archaeology. Recent Discoveries and Studies*, Colloquia Pontica 6, ed. G. R. Tsetskhladze. Leiden: Brill, 25–33.

Hinge, G. 2003. "Scythian and Spartan Analogies in Herodotus' Representation: Rites of Initiation and Kinship Groups." In *The Cauldron of Ariantas. Studies Presented to A.N. Ščeglov on the Occasion of his 70th Birthday*, ed. P. Guldager Bilde et al. Aarhus: Aarhus University Press, 55–75.

———. 2008. "Dionysos and Herakles in Scythia—the Eschatological String of Herodotos' Book 4." In *Meeting of Cultures—Between Conflicts and Coexistence*, ed. P. Guldager Bilde and J. H. Petersen. Aarhus: Aarhus University Press, 369–398.

Hobden, F. 2013. *The Symposion in Ancient Greek Society and Thought.* Cambridge: Cambridge University Press.

Hobsbawm, E., and T. Ranger, ed. 1983. *The Invention of Tradition.* Cambridge: Cambridge University Press.

Höckmann, U., and A. Möller. 2006. "The Hellenion at Naukratis: Questions and Observations." In *Naukratis: Greek Diversity in Egypt. Studies on East Greek Pottery and Exchange in the Eastern Mediterranean,* ed. A. Villing and U. Schlotzhauer. London: British Museum Press, 11–22.

Hodkinson, S., ed. 2009a. *Sparta: Comparative Approaches.* Swansea: Classical Press of Wales.

———. 2009b. "Was Sparta an Exceptional Polis?." In *Sparta: Comparative Approaches,* ed. S. Hodkinson. Swansea: Classical Press of Wales, 417–472.

Hodos, T. 1999. "Intermarriage in the Western Greek Colonies." *Oxford Journal of Archaeology* 18: 61–78.

Holdich, T. H. 1898. "The Origins of the Kafir of the Hindu Kush." *Geographical Journal* 7: 42–48.

Hölscher, T. 1973. *Griechische Historienbilder des 5. und 4. Jahrhunderts v. Chr.* Würzburg: K. Triltsch.

———. 2011. "Myths, Images, and the Typology of Identities in Early Greek Art." In *Cultural Identity in the Ancient Mediterranean,* ed. E. S. Gruen. Los Angeles: Getty Research Institute, 47–65.

Hommel, H. 1937. "Toxotoi 2." *RE* VI A, 2: 1855–1858.

Hope Simpson, R., and J. F. Lazenby. 1970. *The Catalogue of Ships in Homer's Iliad.* Oxford: Clarendon Press.

Horden, P., Purcell, N. 2000. *The Corrupting Sea: A Study of Mediterranean History.* Oxford: Blackwell.

Hornblower, S. 1994. "Introduction: Summary of Papers; the Story of Greek Historiography; Intertextuality and the Greek Historians." In *Greek Historiography,* ed. S. Hornblower. Oxford: Clarendon Press.

———. 2004. *Thucydides and Pindar: Historical Narrative and the World of Epinikian Poetry.* Oxford: Oxford University Press.

———. 2008. "Greek Identity in the Archaic and Classical Periods." In *Hellenisms: Culture, Identity, and Ethnicity from Antiquity to Modernity,* ed. K. Zacharia. Aldershot: Ashgate, 37–58.

Hornblower, S., and C. Morgan. 2007a. "Introduction." In *Pindar's Poetry, Patrons, and Festivals: From Archaic Greece to the Roman Empire,* ed. S. Hornblower and C. Morgan. Oxford: Oxford University Press, 1–45.

———, ed. 2007b. *Pindar's Poetry, Patrons, and Festivals: From Archaic Greece to the Roman Empire.* Oxford: Oxford University Press.

Howarth, D. 2002. "An Archaeology of Political Discourse? Evaluating Michel Foucault's Explanation and Critique of Ideology." *Political Studies* 50, no. 1: 117–135.

Howgego, C. 2005. "Coinage and Identity in the Roman Provinces." In *Coinage and Identity in the Roman Provinces,* ed. C. Howgego, V. Heuchert, and A. Burnett. Oxford: Oxford University Press, 1–19.

Humphreys, S. C. 1978. *Anthropology and the Greeks*. London: Routledge.

———. 1987. "Law, Custom and Culture in Herodotus." *Arethusa* 20: 211–220.

———. 1997. "Fragments, Fetishes and Philosophies: Towards a History of Greek Historiography after Thucydides." In *Collecting Fragments/Fragmente Sammeln*, ed. G. W. Most. Göttingen: Vandenhoeck and Ruprecht, 207–224.

———. 2004. *The Strangeness of the Gods: Historical Perspectives on the Interpretation of Athenian Religion*. Oxford: Oxford University Press.

Hunter, R., ed. 2005. *The Hesiodic Catalogue of Women: Constructions and Reconstructions*. Cambridge: Cambridge University Press.

Hunter, R., and I. Rutherford, eds. 2009. *Wandering Poets in Ancient Greek Culture: Travel, Locality and Pan-Hellenism*. Cambridge: Cambridge University Press.

Hunter, V. J. 1994. *Policing Athens: Social Control in the Attic Lawsuits*. Princeton: Princeton University Press.

Hupe, J. Von 2007. "Aspekte des Achilleus Pontarches-Kultes in Olbia." In *Une koinè pontique: cités grecques, sociétés indigènes et empires mondiaux sur le littoral nord de la mer Noire (VIIe s. a.C. –IIIe s. p.C.)*, ed. A. Bresson et al. Bordeaux: Ausonius., 213–225.

Hurst, H., and S. Owen, eds. 2005. *Ancient Colonizations: Analogy, Similarity and Difference*. London: Duckworth.

Hurter, S. M. 2004. "Crickets/Grasshoppers/Locusts: A New View on Some Insect Symbols on Coins of Magna Graecia and Sicily." *Nomismatika Khronika* 23: 11–20.

Hussey, E. 1995. *The Presocratics*. London: Duckworth.

Hutchinson, G. O. 2001. *Greek Lyric Poetry: A Commentary on Selected Larger Pieces*. Oxford: Oxford University Press.

Højte, J. M. 2008. "The Cities That Never Were. Failed Attempts at Colonization in the Black Sea." In *Meeting of Cultures—Between Conflicts and Coexistence*, ed. P. Guldager Bilde and J. H. Petersen. Aarhus: Aarhus University Press, 149–162.

Iliakis, M. 2009. *The Bactrian "Mirage": Iranian and Greek Interactions in Western Central Asia*. Ph.D. dissertation, University of Liverpool.

Immerwahr, H. R. 1956. "Aspects of Historical Causation in Herodotus." *Transactions of the American Philological Association* 87: 241–280.

———. 1966. *Form and Thought in Herodotus*. Cleveland: Western Reserve University Press.

Ingold, T. 2008. "Anthropology is not Ethnography." *Proceedings of the British Academy* 154, 2007 Lectures: 69–92.

Irigoin, J. 1952. *Histoire du texte de Pindare*. Paris: Klincksieck.

Irwin, E. 2005a. "Gods among Men? The Social and Political Dynamics of the Hesiodic Catalogue of Women." In *The Hesiodic Catalogue of Women: Constructions and Reconstructions*, ed. R. Hunter. Cambridge: Cambridge University Press, 35–85.

———. 2005b. *Solon and Early Greek Poetry: The Politics of Exhortation*. Cambridge: Cambridge University Press.

Irwin, E., and E. Greenwood, eds. 2007. *Reading Herodotus: A Study of the Logoi in Book 5 of Herodotus' Histories*. Cambridge: Cambridge University Press.

Isaac, B. 1986. *The Greek Settlements in Thrace until the Macedonian Conquest.* Leiden: Brill.

———. 2004. *The Invention of Racism in Classical Antiquity.* Princeton: Princeton University Press.

———. 2006. "Proto-Racism in Graeco-Roman Antiquity." *World Archaeology* 38, no. 1: 32–48.

Ivanchik, A. I. 2005. "Who Were the 'Scythian' Archers on Archaic Attic Vases?" In *Scythians and Greeks. Cultural Interactions in Scythia, Athens and the Early Roman Empire Sixth-Century BC—First Century AD*, ed. D. Braund. Exeter: University of Exeter Press, 100–114.

Ivantchik, A. 1993. "La datation du poème l'Arimaspée d'Aristéas de Proconnèse" *L'Antiquité Classique* 62: 35–67.

———. 2007. "Une koinè nord-pontique: en guise d'introduction." In *Une koinè pontique: cités grecques, sociétés indigènes et empires mondiaux sur le littoral nord de la mer Noire (VIIe s. a.C. –IIIe s. p.C.)*, ed. A. Bresson et al. Bordeaux: Ausonius, 7–15.

Izzet, V. E. 2004. "Purloined Letters. The Aristonothos inscription and Krater." In *Greek Identity in the Western Mediterranean.* Mnemosyne, supp. 246, ed. K. Lomas. Leiden: Brill, 191–210.

———. 2005. "The Mirror of Theopompus: Etruscan Identity and Greek Myth." *Papers of the British School at Rome* 73: 1–22.

Jacob, C. 1991. *Géographie et ethnographie en Grèce ancienne.* Paris: Colin.

Jacobs, D. C., ed. 1999. *The Presocratics after Heidegger.* New York: Sunny Press.

Jacobson, E. 1995. *The Art of the Scythians: The Interpretation of Cultures at the Edge of the Hellenic World.* Leiden: Brill.

Jacoby, F. 1909. "Über die Entwicklung der griechischen Historiographie und den Plan einer neuen Sammlung der griechischen Historikerfragmente." *Klio* 9: 80–123.

———. 1913. "Herodotos." *RE*, supp. 2: 205–520.

———. 1923–1958. *Die Fragmente der griechischen Historiker.* Vols. 1–3. Berlin: Weidmann.

———. 1949. *Atthis: The Local Chronicles of Ancient Athens.* Oxford: Clarendon Press.

Jacopi, G. 1931. *Scavi nelle necropoli camiresi 1929–30. Clara Rhodos IV.* Bergamo: Instituto Italiano d'Arti Grafiche.

Janko, R. 1992. *The Iliad: A Commmentary.* Vol. 4, Books 13–16. Cambridge: Cambridge University Press.

Jantzen, U. 1972. *Ägyptische und orientalische Bronzen aus dem Heraion von Samos.* Bonn: Deutsches Archaologisches Institut.

Jeffery, L. H. 1961. *The Local Scripts of Archaic Greek: A Study of the Origin of the Greek Alphabet and Its Development from the Eighth to the Fifth Centuries B.C.* Oxford: Clarendon Press.

Jenkins, G. K. 1990. *Ancient Greek Coins.* London: Seaby.

Jiménez, A. 2011. "Pure Hybridism: Late Iron Age Sculpture in Southern Iberia." *World Archaeology* 43, no. 1: 102–123.

Jones, C. P. 1996. "The Panhellenion." *Chiron* 26: 29–56.

Jones, R., I. Buxeda, and J. Garrigós. 2004. "The Identity of Early Greek Pottery in Italy and Spain: An Archaeometric Perspective." In *Greek Identity in the Western Mediterranean.* Mnemosyne, supp. 246, ed. K. Lomas. Leiden: Brill, 83–114.

Jones, S. 1997. *The Archaeology of Ethnicity: Constructing Identities in the Past and Present.* London: Routledge.

Kahil, L. 1972. "Un nouveau vase plastique du potier Sotadès au Musée du Louvre." *Revue archéologique* 2: 271–284.

Kalra, V.S., R. Kaur, and J. Hutnyk. 2005. *Diaspora and Hybridity*. London: Sage.

Kaltsas, N. 1996–97. "Κλαξιομεvιακές Σαρκοφάγοι Από Το Νεκροταφείο Τησ Ακάνθου." *Αρχαιολογικόv Δελτίον* 51–52: 35–50.

Kane, S. 1998. "Cultic Implications of Sculpture in the Sanctuary of Demeter and Kore/Persephone at Cyrene, Libya." In *La Cirenaica in età antica. Atti del convegno internazionale di studi, Macerata, 18–20 maggio 1995*, ed. E. Catanni and S. Marengo. Pisa and Rome: Instituti Editoriali e Poligrafici Internazionali, 289–300.

Kamal, A. Forthcoming. *Foreigners in New Kingdom Egypt*. Ph.D. dissertation, University of Liverpool.

Kaplan, P. 2006. "Dedications to Greek Sanctuaries by Foreign Kings in the Eighth through Sixth Centuries BCE." *Historia* 55: 129–152.

Karageorghis, V. 1988. *Blacks in Ancient Cypriot Art*. Houston: Menil Foundation.

———. 2003. "Cult of Astarte in Cyprus." In *Symbiosis, Symbolism, and the Power of the Past: Canaan, Ancient Israel, and their Neighbors from the Late Bronze Age through Roman Palaestina: Proceedings of the Centennial Symposium, W.F. Albright Institute of Archaeological Research and American Schools of Oriental Research, Jerusalem, May 29–31, 2000*, ed. W. G. Devereux and S. Gitin. Winona Lake, Ind.: Eisenbrauns, 215–222.

Karageorghis, V., and I. Taifacos, eds. 2004. *The World of Herodotus: Proceedings of an International Conference held at the Foundation Anastasios G. Leventis, Nicosia, September 18–21, 2003*. Nicosia: A. G. Leventis Foundation.

Karttunen, K. 1992. "Distant Lands in Classical Ethnography." *GB* 18: 195–204.

———. 2008. "Phoebo Vicinus Padaeus: Reflections on the Impact of Herodotean Ethnography." In *The Children of Herodotus: Greek and Roman Historiography and Related Genres*, ed. J. Pigoń. Newcastle upon Tyne: Cambridge Scholars Publishing, 17–25.

Kerschner, M. 2004. "Phokäische Thalassokratie oder Phantom-Phokäer? Die frühgriechischen Keramikfunde im Süden der Iberischen Halbinsel, aus der ägäischen Perspective." In *Greek Identity in the Western Mediterranean*. Mnemosyne, supp. 246, ed. K. Lomas. Leiden: Brill, 115–148.

Kilian-Dirlmeier, I. 1985. "Fremde Weihungen in griechischen Heiligtümern vom 8. bis zum Beginn des 7. Jahrhunderts v. Chr. 32." *Jahrbuch Des Römisch-Germanischen Zentralmuseums*, 215–254.

Kilian, K. 1970. *Früheisenzeitliche Funde aus der Südostkropole von Sala Consilina (Provinz Salerno)*. Heidelberg: Kerle.

Kim, H. 2001. "Archaic Coinage as Evidence for the Use of Money." In *Money and Its Uses in the Ancient Greek World*, ed. A. Meadows and K. Shipton. Oxford: Oxford University Press, 7–23.

Kim, H. J. 2009. *Ethnicity and Foreigners in Ancient Greece and China*. London: Duckworth.

———. 2013: The Invention of the 'Barbarian' in Late 6th Century BC Ionia." In *Ancient Ethnography: New Approaches*, ed. E. Almagor and J. E. Skinner. London: Bloomsbury/Bristol Classical Press, 25–48.

Kirk, G. S. 1962. *The Songs of Homer*. Cambridge: Cambridge University Press.

————. 1970. *Myth: Its Meaning and Function in Ancient and Other Cultures.* Cambridge: Cambridge University Press.

————. 1973. "On Defining Myth." *Phronesis*, supp. 1: 61–69.

————. 1974. *The Nature of Greek Myths.* Harmondsworth: Penguin.

————. 1985. *The Iliad: A Commentary. Vol. I, Books 1–4.* Cambridge: Cambridge University Press.

————. 1990. *The Iliad: A Commentary. Vol. II, Books 5–8.* Cambridge: Cambridge University Press.

Kleibrink, M. 2006. *Oenotrians at Lagaria Near Sybaris. A Preliminary Report on the Excavation of Two Timber Buildings on the Timpone Della Motta Near Francavilla Marittima, Southern Italy.* London: Accordia Research Institute.

Klein, N. 2000. *No Logo: Taking Aim at the Brand Bullies.* London: Flamingo.

Kleine, O. F. 1828. *Stesichori Himerensis Fragmenta.* Berlin: Ge. Reimer.

Klotz, M. 2005. "The Weimar Republic. A Post-Colonial State in a Still-Colonial World." In *Germany's Colonial Pasts*, ed. E. Ames, M. Klotz, and L. Wildenthal. Lincoln and London: University of Nebraska Press, 135–147.

Kluckhohn, C. 1961. *Anthropology and the Classics.* Providence: Brown University Press.

Kluiver, J. 1995. "Early 'Tyrrhenian': Prometheus Painter, Timiades Painter, Goltyr Painter." *Bulletin Antieke Beschavung* 70: 55–103.

Knight, V. H. 1995. *The Renewal of Epic: Responses to Homer in the Argonautica of Apollonius.* Leiden: Brill.

Koch, H. 1912. *Dachterrakotten aus Campanien mit Ausschluss von Pompei.* Berlin: G. Reimer.

Kocybala, A. X. 1978. *Greek Colonization on the North Shore of the Black Sea in the Archaic Period.* Philadelphia: University of Pennsylvania.

Koltukhov, S.G., and I. I. Vdovichenko. 2001. "A Work of Scythian Archaic Art from the Collection of the Bakhchisarai Museum Crimea." In *North Pontic Archaeology. Recent Discoveries and Studies*, ed. G. R. Tsetskhladze. Colloquia Pontica 6. Leiden: Brill, 231–235.

König, J., and T. Whitmarsh. 2007. "Ordering Knowledge." In *Ordering Knowledge in the Roman Empire*, ed. J. König and T. Whitmarsh. Cambridge: Cambridge University Press, 3–39.

Konstan, D. 1987. "Persians, Greeks and Empire." *Arethusa* 20: 59–74.

————. 2001. "To Hellenikon Ethnos: Ethnicity and the Construction of Ancient Greek Identity." In *Ancient Perceptions of Greek Ethnicity*, ed. I. Malkin. Cambridge, Mass.: Harvard University Press, 29–50.

Kopcke, G. 1992. "What Role for Phoenicians?" In *Greece between East and West: Tenth-Eighth Centuries B.C.*, ed. G. Kopcke and I. Tokumaru. Mainz: Philipp von Zabern, 103–113.

Kostoglou, M. 2011. "Iron, Connectivity and Local Identities in Iron Age Thrace." In *Material Connections in the Ancient Mediterranean. Mobility, Materiality and Identity*, ed. P. Van Dommelen and A. B. Knapp. London and New York: Routledge, 170–189.

Kowalzig, B. 2000. "Singing For the Gods: Aetiological Myth, Ritual and Locality in Greek Choral Poetry of the Late Archaic Period." DPhil, Oxford.

————. 2007. *Singing for the Gods: Performances of Myth and Ritual in Archaic and Classical Greece.* Oxford: Oxford University Press.

Kraay, C. 1976. *Archaic and Classical Greek Coins*. London: Methuen.

Krapivina, V. V. 2003. "Bronze Weights from Olbia." In *The Cauldron of Ariantas: Studies Presented to A. N. Ščeglov on the Occasion of his 70th Birthday*, ed. P. Guldager Bilde et al. Aarhus: Aarhus University Press, 117–131.

Kravitz, K. F. 2003. "A Last-Minute Revision to Sargon's Letter to the God." *Journal of Near Eastern Studies* 62, no. 2 (April): 81–95.

Kryzhytskyy, S. D., and V.V. Krapivina. 2003. "Olbian Chora." In *Ancient Greek Colonies in the Black Sea* III, ed. D.V. Grammenos and E. K. Petropoulos. Thessaloniki: Archaeological Institute of Northern Greece, 507–561.

Kryžickij, S. D. 2003. "On the Problem of the Reliability of Reconstructions of Greek Architecture in the Northern Black Sea Region." In *The Cauldron of Ariantas. Studies Presented to A. N. Ščeglov on the Occasion of his 70th Birthday*, ed. P. Guldager Bilde et al. Aarhus: Aarhus University Press, 227–239.

———. 2006. "The Rural Environs of Olbia: Some Problems of Current Importance." In *Surveying the Greek Chora: Black Sea Region in a Comparative Perspective*, ed. P. Guldager Bilde and V. F. Stolba. Aarhus: Aarhus University Press, 99–115.

———. 2007a. "Origines et développements d'une koinè architecturale dans les cités grecques et les étalissements hellénisés indigènes de la région nord-pontique VIe S.—Ier s. a.C." In *Une koinè pontique: cités grecques, sociétés indigènes et empires mondiaux sur le littoral nord de la mer Noire (VIIe s. a.C. –IIIe s. p.C.)*, ed. A. Bresson et al. Bordeaux: Ausonius, 127–133.

———. 2007b. "Criteria for the Presence of Barbarians in the Population of Early Olbia." In *Classical Olbia and the Scythian World: from the Sixth Century* BC *to the Second Century* AD, ed. D. Braund and S. D. Kryzhitskiy. Proceedings of the British Academy 142. Oxford: Oxford University Press, 17–22.

Kryžickij, S.D., V.V. Krapivina, N.A. Lejpunskaja, and V.V. Nazarov 2003. "Olbia—Berezan." In *Ancient Greek Colonies in the Black Sea* III, ed. D.V. Grammenos and E. K. Petropoulos. Thessaloniki: Archaeological Institute of Northern Greece, 389–505.

Kuhrt, A. 2002. *"Greeks" and "Greece" in Mesopotamian and Persian Perspectives.* J. L. Myres Memorial Lecture 21. Oxford: Leopard's Head Press.

Kundrus, B. 2003. *Moderne Imperialisten. Das Kaiserreich im Spiegel seiner Kolonien.* Köln: Böhlau Verlag.

Kunze, E. 1950. *Archaische Schildbänder*, Olympische Forschungen II. Berlin: W. de Gruyter.

———. 1961. *Olympia Bericht* 7. Berlin: W. de Gruyter.

Kurke, L. 1991. *The Traffic of Praise: Pindar and the Poetics of Social Economy*. Ithaca, N.Y.: Cornell University Press.

———. 1992. "The Politics of Ἀβροσύνη in Archaic Greece." *Classical Antiquity* 11, no. 1 (April): 91–120.

———. 1999. *Coins, Bodies, Games, and Gold: The Politics of Meaning in Archaic Greece*. Princeton: Princeton University Press.

———. 2003. "Aesop and the Contestation of Delphic Authority." In *The Cultures within Greek Culture. Contact, Conflict, Collaboration*, ed. C. Dougherty and L. Kurke. Cambridge: Cambridge University Press, 77–100.

———. 2011. *Aesopic Conversations: Popular Tradition, Cultural Dialogue, and the Invention of Greek Prose*. Martin Classical Lectures. Princeton: Princeton University Press.

Kyrieleis, H. 1996. *Der grosse Kuros von Samos*. Samos 10. Berlin: Deutsches Archaologisches Institut.

La Rosa, V. 1968. "Bronzetti indigeni della Sicilia." *Cronache di Archeologia* 7: 7–136.

———. 1996. "The Impact of the Greek Colonists on the Non-Hellenic inhabitants of Sicily." In *The Greek World: Art and Civilisation in Magna Graecia and Sicily*, ed. G. P. Carratelli. New York: Rizzoli, 523–532.

Lacroix, L. 1965. "La légende de Philoctète en Italie méridionale." *Revue belge de philologie et d'histoire* 43: 5–21.

———. 1974. *Etudes d'archéologie numismatique*. Paris: de Boccard.

Lamer, H. 1927. "Lotophagen." *Revue ses études grecques* 13: 1507–1514.

Lang, A. 1908. "Homer and Anthropology." In *Anthropology and the Classics: Six Lectures Delivered before the University of Oxford*, ed. R. R. Marett. Oxford: Clarendon Press, 44–66.

Lansky, J. 1991. "Fünf Briefe Felix Jacobys an Eduard Meyer." In *Eduard Meyer (1855–1930). Zu Werk und Zeit. Wissenschaftliche Zeitschrift der Humboldt-Universität zu Berlin, Reihe Geistes und Sozialwissenschaften* 40.9: 61–69.

Langdon, S. 2001. "Beyond the Grave: Biographies from Early Greece." *AJA* 105, no. 4: 579–606.

———. 2008. *Art and Identity in Dark Age Greece, 1100–700 B.C.E.* Cambridge: Cambridge University Press.

Laronde, A. 1990. "Greeks and Libyans in Cyrenaica." In *Greek Colonists and Native Populations*, ed. J.-P. Descoeudres. Oxford: Clarendon Press, 157–168.

Lasova, T. 1996. *The Hyperboreans: A Study in the Paleo-Balkan Tradition*. Sofia: St. Kliment Ohridski University Press.

Lateiner, D. 1986. "The Empirical Element in the Methods of Early Greek Medical Writers and Herodotus: A Shared Epistemological Response." *Antichthon* 20: 1–20.

———. 1989. *The Historical Method of Herodotus*. Toronto: University of Toronto Press.

Lattanzi, E., ed. 1989. *Locri Epizefiri. III. Cultura materiale e vita quotidiana*. Firenze: Le Lettere.

———. ed. 2003. *Il Museo Nazionali di Reggio Calabria*. Rome: Gangemi Editore.

Lattimore, R. 1958. "The Composition of the Histories of Herodotus." *Classical Philology* 53: 9–21.

Lavelle, B. M. 1992. "Herodotus, Skythian Archers, and the Doryphoroi of the Peisistratids." *Klio* 74: 78–97.

Lawall, M. L., N. A. Lejpunskaja, P. D. Diatroptov, and T. Samojlova. 2010. "Transport Amphoras." In *The Lower City of Olbia (Sector NGS) in the 6th Century BC to the 4th Century AD*, ed. N.A. Lejpunskaja et al. Vols. 1–2. Aarhus: Aarhus University Press, 355–405.

Lee, R. B. 1979. *The Kung San: Men, Women and Work in a Foraging Society*. Cambridge: Cambridge University Press.

Lehmann, P. 1946. *Statues on Coins of Southern Italy and Sicily in the Classical Period*. New York: H. Bittner.

Lejpunskaja, N. A. 2010. "Late Archaic Painted Tableware." In *The Lower City of Olbia (Sector NGS) in the 6th Century BC to the 4th Century AD*, ed. N.A. Lejpunskaja et al. Vols. 1–2. Aarhus: Aarhus University Press, 121–142.

Lejpunskaja, N. A., P. Guldager Bilde, J. M. Højte, V. V. Krapivina, and S. D. Kryžickij, eds. 2010. *The Lower City of Olbia (Sector NGS) in the 6th Century* BC *to the 4th Century* AD. Vols. 1–2. Aarhus: Aarhus University Press.

Lemos, A. 2000. "Aspects of East Greek Pottery and Vase Painting." In *Die Ägäis und das westliche Mittelmeer. Beziehungen und Wechselwirkungen 8. bis 5. Jh. v. Chr.*, ed. F. Krinzinger, G. Wlach, M. Kerschner. Wien: Verlag der Österreichischen Akademie der Wissenschaften, 359–373.

Lenfant, D. 2007. "Greek Historians of Persia." In *A Companion to Greek and Roman Historiography*, ed. J. Marincola. Oxford: Blackwell, 200–209.

Leonard, M. 2000. "The Politiques de l'amitié: Derrida's Greeks and a National Politics of Classical Scholarship." *Proceedings of the Cambridge Philological Society* 46: 45–78.

———. 2005. *Athens in Paris. Ancient Greece and the Political in Post-War French Thought.* Oxford: Oxford University Press.

Le Pera, E., and M. Sorriso-Valvo. 2000. "Weathering and Morphogenesis in a Mediterranean Climate, Calabria, Italy." *Geomorphology* 34: 251–270.

Lerat, L. 1952. *Les Locriens de l'Ouest.* Paris: de Boccard.

Lesher, J. H. 1992. *Xenophanes of Colophon.* Toronto: University of Toronto Press.

Lesky, A. 1959. "Aithiopica." *Hermes* 87: 26–38.

———. 1966. *A History of Greek Literature.* Trans. James Willis and Cornelis de Heer. London: Methuen.

Lévy, E. 1981. "Les origines de mirage scythe." *Ktema* 6: 57–68.

Lévy-Bruhl, L 1910. *Les fonctions mentales dans les sociétés inférieures.* Paris: Presses universitaires de France.

Lewis, S. 2000. "The Tyrant's Myth." In *Sicily from Aeneas to Augustus*, ed. C. Smith and J. Serrati. Edinburgh: Edinburgh University Press, 97–106.

———. 2002. "Representation and Reception: Athenian Pottery in its Italian Context." In *Inhabiting Symbols: Symbol and Image in the Ancient Mediterranean*, ed. J. B. Wilkins and E. Herring. London: Accordia Research Institute, 175–192.

———, ed. 2006. *Tyrants and Autocrats in the Classical World.* Edinburgh: Edinburgh University Press.

Leypunskaya, N. A. 2007. "Olbian-Scythian Trade: Exchange Issues in the Sixth to Fourth Centuries BC." In *Classical Olbia and the Scythian World: From the Sixth Century* BC *to the Second Century* AD ed. D. Braund and S. D. Kryzhitskiy. Proceedings of the British Academy 142, Oxford: Oxford University Press, 121–134.

Lidchi, H. 1997. "The Poetics and Politics of Representing Other Cultures." In *Representation. Cultural Representations and Signifying Practices*, ed. S. Hall. London: Sage, 151–222.

Lipiński, E. 2003. "Phoenician Cult Expressions in the Persian Period." In *Symbiosis, Symbolism, and the Power of the Past: Canaan, Ancient Israel, and their Neighbors from the Late Bronze Age through Roman Palaestina: Proceedings of the Centennial Symposium, W. F. Albright Institute of Archaeological Research and American Schools of Oriental Research, Jerusalem, May 29–31, 2000*, ed. W. G. Devereux and S. Gitin. Winona Lake, Ind.: Eisenbrauns, 297–308.

———. 2004. *Itineraria Phoenicia.* Leuven: Peeters.

Lippolis, E. 2004. "The Cultural Framework of the Polis and Sport in the Greek West." In *Magna Graecia: Athletics and the Olympic Spirit on the Periphery of the*

Hellenic World, ed. N. Stampolidis and Y. Tassoulas. Athens: Museum of Cycladic Art, 39–53.

Lissarrague, F. 1990a. *L'autre guerrier: archers, peltastes, cavaliers dans l'imagerie attique*. Paris and Rome: Éd. de la Découverte; de Boccard.

———. 1990b. *The Aesthetics of the Greek Banquet: Images of Wine and Ritual*. Trans. A. Szegedy-Maszak. Princeton: Princeton University Press.

———. 2002. "The Athenian Image of the Foreigner." In *Greeks and Barbarians*, ed. T. Harrison. Edinburgh: Edinburgh University Press, 101–124.

Littauer, M. A. 1968. "A Nineteenth and Twentieth Dynasty Heroic Motif on Attic Black-Figured Vases." *AJA* 72: 150–152.

Lloyd, A. B. 1975. *Herodotus Book Two*. Leiden: Brill.

———. 1990. "Herodotus on Egyptians and Libyans." In *Hérodote et les peuples non grecs. Entretiens sur l'Antiquité classique: Vandoeuvres-Genève, 22–26 Août 1988*, ed. G. Nenci and O. Reverdin. Genève: Fondation Hardt 35, 215–245.

Lloyd, G. E. R. 1966. *Polarity and Analogy. Two Types of Argument in Early Greek Thought*. Cambridge: Cambridge University Press.

———. 1979. *Magic, Reason and Experience in the Origin and Development of Greek Science*. Cambridge: Cambridge University Press.

———Lloyd, G. E. R.. 2002. *The Ambitions of Curiosity: Understanding the World in Ancient Greece and China*. Cambridge: Cambridge University Press.

Lloyd-Jones, H. 1986. "Wilamowitz." *Classical Review, New Series* 36, no. 2: 295–300.

———. 2004. "Review of I. Gildenhard and M. Ruehl, eds., *Out of Arcadia: Classics and Politics in Germany in the Age of Burckhardt, Nietzsche and Wilamowitz*. BICS, supp. 79. London: Institute of Classical Studies, School of Advanced Study, University of London, 2003." BMCR 2004.02.43, available at http://bmcr.brynmawr.edu/2004/2004-02-43.html

Lochner-Hüttenbach, F. 1960. *Die Pelasger*. Wien: Gerold.

Lomas, K. 1996. "Greeks, Romans and Others: Problems of Colonialism and Ethnicity in Southern Italy." In *Roman Imperialism: Post-Colonial Perspectives* 3, ed. J. Webster and N. Cooper. Leicester: Leicester Archaeological Monographs, 135–144.

———. 2000a. "Cities, States and Ethnic Identity in South-East Italy." In *The Emergence of State Identities in Italy in the First Millennium BC*, ed. E. Herring and K. Lomas. London: Accordia Research Institute, 79–90.

———. 2000b. "The Polis in Italy: Ethnicity and Citizenship in the Western Mediterranean." In *Alternatives to Athens: Varieties of Political Experience and Community in Ancient Greece*, ed. S. Hodkinson and R. Brock. Oxford: Oxford University Press, 167–185.

Lomas, K., ed. 2004a. *Greek Identity in the Western Mediterranean*. Mnemosyne, supp. 246. Leiden: Brill.

———. 2004b. "Introduction." In *Greek Identity in the Western Mediterranean*. Mnemosyne, supp. 246, ed. Lomas. Leiden: Brill, 1–14.

Lombardo, M. 1990. "Erodoto storico dei Lidî." In *Hérodote et les peuples non grecs. Entretiens sur l'Antiquité classique: Vandoeuvres-Genève 22–26 Août 1988*, ed. G. Nenci and O. Reverdin. Genève: Fondation Hardt 35, 171–204.

Londey, P. 1990. "Greek Colonists and Delphi." In *Greek Colonists and Native Populations*, ed. J.-P. Descoeudres. Oxford: Clarendon Press, 117–127.

Loney, H. L. 2002. "Themes and Models in the Development of Italian Prehistory." *Journal of Mediterranean Archaeology* 15 (2): 199–215.

Long, A. 1999. *The Cambridge Companion to Early Greek Philosophy*. Cambridge: Cambridge University Press.

Lo Porto, F. G. 1964. "Satyrion (Taranto): Scavi e richerche nel luogo più antico insediamento laconico in Puglia." *Notizie degli scavi di Antichità*: 177–279.

———. 1967. "Tombe di atleti tarentini." *Atti e memorie della Società Magna Grecia* 8: 31–98.

Loptson, P. 1981. "Pelasgikon Argos in the Catalogue of Ships 681." *Mnemosyme* 34: 136–138.

Lorimer, H. L. 1947. "The Hoplite Phalanx with Special Reference to the Poems of Archilochus and Tyrtaeus." *Annual of the British School at Athens* 42: 76–138.

———. 1950. *Homer and the Monuments*. London: Macmillan.

Lovejoy, A., and G. Boas. 1935. *Primitivism and Related Ideas in Antiquity*. Baltimore: Johns Hopkins University Press.

Lubtchansky, N. 2005. *Le cavalier tyrrhénien: répresentations équestres dans l'Italie archaïque*. Rome: École Française de Rome.

Luckenbill, D. D. 1926. *Ancient Records of Assyria and Babylonia*. Chicago: University of Chicago Press.

Lund, A. A. 2005. "Hellenentum und Hellenizität: Zur Ethnogenese und zur Ethnizität der antiken Hellenen." *Historia* 54: 1–17.

Luraghi, N. 1994. *Tirannidi arcaiche in Sicilia e Magna Grecia: Da Panezio di Leontini alla caduta dei Dinomenidi*. Firenze: Olschki.

———. 2001a. "Introduction." In *The Historian's Craft in the Age of Herodotus*, ed. N. Luraghi. Oxford: Oxford University Press, 1–15.

———. 2001b. "Local Knowledge in Herodotus' Histories." In *The Historian's Craft in the Age of Herodotus*, ed. N. Luraghi. Oxford: Oxford University Press, 138–161.

———. ed. 2001c. *The Historian's Craft in the Age of Herodotus*. Oxford: Oxford University Press.

———. 2002. "Becoming Messenian." *JHS* 122: 45–69.

Ma, J. 2008. "Mysians on the Çan Sarcophagus? Ethnicity and Domination in Achaemenid Military Art." *Historia* 57: 243–254.

Maaskant-Kleibrink, M. 2000. "Early Cults at the Athenaion at Francavilla Marittima as Evidence for a Pre-Colonial Circulation of Nostoi Stories." In *Die Ägäis und das westliche Mittelmeer. Beziehungen -Wechselwirkungen, 8. bis 5. Jh. v. Chr.*, ed. F. Krinzinger. Wien: Verlag der Österreichischen Akademie der Wissenschaften, 165–185.

Macdonald, J. M. 1922. *The Uses of Symbolism in Greek Art*. Ph.D. dissertation, Bryn Mawr College.

Mackay, E. 2002. "The Evocation of Emotional Response in Early Greek Poetry and Painting." In *Epea & Grammata: Oral and Written Communication in Ancient Greece*, ed. I. Worthington and J. Foley. Leiden: Brill, 55–71.

Mackie, H. 1996. *Talking Trojan: Speech and Community in the Iliad*. London: Rowman & Littlefield.

MacLachlan, B. C. 1995. "Love, War and the Goddess in Fifth-Century Locri." *Ancient World* 26, no. 2: 205–223.

Malkin, I. 1987. *Religion and Colonization in Ancient Greece*. Leiden: Brill.

———. 1994. *Myth and Territory in the Spartan Mediterranean*. Cambridge: Cambridge University Press.

———. 1997. "Categories of Early Greek Colonization." In *Il dinamismo della colonizzazione greca*, ed. C. Antonetti. Napoli: Loffredo, 25–38.

———. 1998a. *The Returns of Odysseus: Colonization and Ethnicity*. Berkeley: University of California Press.

———. 1998b. "The Middle Ground: Philoktetes in Italy." *Kernos* 11: 131–141.

———. 1999. "Ulysse Protocolonisateur." *Mediterraneo Antico* 2, no. 1: 243–261.

———. 2001a. "Greek Ambiguities: Between 'Ancient Hellas' and 'Barbarian Epirus.'" In *Ancient Perceptions of Greek Ethnicity*, ed. I. Malkin. Washington, D.C.: Center for Hellenic Studies and Harvard University Press, 187–212.

———. 2001b. "'Introduction.'" In *Ancient Perceptions of Greek Ethnicity*, ed. I. Malkin. Washington, D.C.: Center for Hellenic Studies and Harvard University Press, 1–28.

———, ed. 2001c. *Ancient Perceptions of Greek Ethnicity*. Washington, D.C.: Center for Hellenic Studies and Harvard University Press.

———. 2002a. "A Colonial Middle Ground: Greek, Etruscan, and Local Elites in the Bay of Naples." In *The Archaeology of Colonialism*, ed. C. L. Lyons and J. K. Papadopoulos. Los Angeles: Getty Research Institute, 151–181.

———. 2002b. "Exploring the Validity of the Concept of 'Foundation': A Visit to Megara Hyblaia." In *Oikistes: Studies in Constitutions, Colonies, and Military Power in the Ancient World. Offered in Honor of A. J. Graham*, ed. V. B. Gorman and E. W. Robinson. Leiden: Brill, 195–224.

———. 2003a. "'Introduction.'" Ed. I. Malkin. *Mediterranean Paradigms and Classical Antiquity, Mediterranean Historical Review* 18, no. 2 (December): 1–8.

———. 2003b. "Networks and the Emergence of Greek Identity." Ed. I. Malkin. *Mediterranean Paradigms and Classical Antiquity, Mediterranean Historical Review* 18, no. 2 (December): 56–75.

———. 2003c. "'Tradition' in Herodotus: The Foundation of Cyrene." In *Herodotus and His World: Essays from a Conference in Memory of George Forrest*, ed. P. Derow and R. Parker. Oxford: Oxford University Press, 153–170.

———, ed. 2003d. *Mediterranean Paradigms and Classical Antiquity. Mediterranean Historical Review* 18 (December): Routledge.

———. 2004. "Postcolonial Concepts and Ancient Greek Colonization." *Modern Language Quarterly* 65, no. 3 (September): 341–364.

———. 2005. "Herakles and Melqart: Greeks and Phoenicians in the Middle Ground." In *Cultural Borrowings and Ethnic Appropriations in Antiquity*, ed. E. S. Gruen. Stuttgart: Franz Steiner Verlag, 238–257.

———. 2008a. "Review Of: Henry Hurst, Sara Owen, eds., *Ancient Colonizations. Analogy, Similarity & Difference*. London: Duckworth, 2005." BMCR 2008.11.08, available at http://bmcr.brynmawr.edu/2008/2008-11-08.html.

———. 2008b. "You Can't Go Home Again: 'Apoikiai' and 'Metropoleis' in the Ancient Mediterranean." Paper presented at Triennial Meeting of the Greek and Roman Societies, Oxford, July 31.

———. 2011. *A Small Greek World: Networks and the Ancient Mediterranean*. New York: Oxford University Press.

Malkin, I., C. Constantakopoulou, and K. Panagopoulou. 2007. "Preface: Networks in the Ancient Mediterranean." *Mediterranean Historical Review* 22, no. 1: 1–9.

Malkin, I., and M. Jameson. 1998. "The Gravestone of Latinos of Rhegion." *Athenaeum*: 477–486.

Manni, E. 1980. "L'oracolo delfico e la fondazione di Regio." *Perennitas. Studi in onore di Angelo Brelich*. Rome: Edizioni dell'Ateneo, 311–320.

Mansvelt, J. 2005. *Geographies of Consumption*. London: Sage.

Marchand, S. 1996. *Down from Olympus: Archaeology and Philhellenism in Germany, 1750–1970*. Princeton: Princeton University Press.

Marconi, C. 2004. "Images for a Warrior. On a Group of Athenian Vases and their Public." In *Greek Vases: Images, Contexts and Controversies*, ed. C. Marconi. Leiden: Brill, 27–40.

Marcus, J. 2001. *"Orientalism."* In *Handbook of Ethnography*, ed. P. Atkinson, A. Coffey, S. Delamont, and L. Lofland. London: Sage, 109–118.

Marett, R. R., ed. 1908. *Anthropology and the Classics: Six Lectures Delivered before the University of Oxford*. Oxford: Clarendon Press.

Marincola, J. 1997. *Authority and Tradition in Ancient Historiography*. Cambridge: Cambridge University Press.

———. 1999. "Genre, Convention and innovation in Graeco-Roman Historiography." In *The Limits of Narrative: Genre and Narrative in Graeco-Roman Antiquity*, ed. C. Krauss. Leiden: Brill, 281–342.

———. 2001. *Greek Historians*. Oxford: Oxford University Press.

———. 2006. "Herodotus and the Poetry of the Past." In *The Cambridge Companion to Herodotus*, ed. C. Dewald and J. Marincola. Cambridge: Cambridge University Press, 13–29.

Markham, C. R. 1893. "Pytheas, the Discoverer of Britain." *Geographical Journal* 16: 504–523.

Markoe, G. 1985. *Phoenician Bronze and Silver Bowls from Cyprus and the Mediterranean*. Berkeley: University of California Press.

———. 1996. "The Emergence of Orientalizing in Greek Art: Some Observations on the Interchange between Greeks and Phoenicians in the Eighth and Seventh Centuries B.C." *Bulletin of the American Schools of Oriental Research* 301: 47–67.

Marshall, E. 2001. *Images of Ancient Libyans*. DPhil, Exeter.

———. 2004. "Women and the Transmission of Libyan Culture." In *Women's influence on Classical Civilization*, ed. F. Mchardy and E. Marshall. London: Routledge, 127–137.

Martin, R. P. 2003. "The Pipes Are Brawling: Conceptualizing Musical Performance in Archaic Athens." In *The Cultures within Greek Culture: Contact, Conflict, Collaboration*, ed. C. Dougherty and L. Kurke. Cambridge: Cambridge University Press, 153–180.

Martinelli, C. 2000. "I <<delfini>> di Apollo: note sulla prima monetazione di alcune colonie milesie del Ponto Eusino fra VI e IV secolo a.C." *Annali dell'Istituto Italiano di Numismatica* 47: 231–247.

Masson, O. 1976 "Grecs et Libyens en Cyrénaïque d'après les Témoinages de l'epigraphie." In *Assimilation et résistance à la culture gréco-romaine dans le monde ancien*, ed. M. Pippidi. Paris: Les Belles Lettres, 377–387.

Matthews, L. S 1898. "Bullroarers Used by Australian Aborigines." *Journal of the Anthropological Institute of Great Britain & Ireland* 28: 52–61.

Mattusch, C. 1988. *Greek Bronze Statuary: From the Beginnings through the Fifth Century B.C.* Ithaca, N.Y.: Cornell University Press.

Mayor, A., and M. Heaney. 1993. "Griffins and Arimaspians." *Folklore* 104, nos. 1/2: 40–66.

McCracken, G. 1934. "Pindar's Figurative Use of Plants." *American Journal of Philology* 55: 340–346.

McDowell, L., ed. 1997. *Undoing Place? A Geographical Reader*. London: Arnold.

McGarty, C., V. Y. Yzerbyt, and R. Spears, eds. 2002. *Stereotypes as Explanations: The Formation of Meaningful Beliefs about Social Groups*. London: Cambridge University Press.

McGlew, J. F. 1993. *Tyranny and Political Culture in Ancient Greece*. Ithaca, N.Y.: Cornell University Press.

McInerney, J. 1999. *The Folds of Parnassos: Land and Ethnicity in Ancient Phokis*. Austin: University of Texas Press.

——. 2001. "Ethnos and Ethnicity in Early Greece." In *Ancient Perceptions of Greek Ethnicity*, ed. I. Malkin. Cambridge, Mass.: Harvard University Press, 51–73.

McKirahan, R. 1994. *Philosophy before Socrates*. Indianapolis: Hackett.

McNiven, T. J. 2000. "Behaving Like an Other: Telltale Gestures in Athenian Vase Painting." In *Not the Classical Ideal: Athens and the Construction of the Other in Greek Art*, ed. B. Cohen. Leiden: Brill, 71–98.

Megaw, J. V. S., and R. M. Megaw. 1990. "Italians and Greeks Bearing Gifts: The Basse-Yutz Find Reconsidered." In *Greek Colonists and Native Populations*, ed. J.-P. Descoeudres. Oxford: Clarendon Press, 579–606.

Mercuri, L. 2004. *Eubéens en Calabre à l'époque archaïque: formes de contacts et d'implantation*. Rome: École Française de Rome.

Merkelbach, R., and M. L. West. 1967. *Fragmenta Hesiodea*. Oxford: Clarendon Press.

Mertens-Horn, M., and L. Viola. 1990. "Archaische Tondächer west griechischer Typologie in Delphi und Olympia," *Hesperia* 59: 235–250.

Mertens, D. 1990. "Some Principal Features of West Greek Colonial Architecture." In *Greek Colonists and Native Populations*, ed. J.-P. Descoeudres. Oxford: Clarendon Press, 373–384.

Meuli, K. 1935. "Scythica." *Hermes* 70: 122–176.

Michalowski, P. 2010. "The Universe in Early Mesopotamian Writings." In *Geography and Ethnography: Perceptions of the World in Pre-Modern Societies*, ed. K. A. Raaflaub and R. J. A. Talbert. Chichester: Wiley-Blackwell, 147–168.

Micheli, M.E. Santucci, A., Bacchielli, L. 2000. *Il santuario delle Nymphai Chthoniai a Cirene: il sito e le terrecotte*. Rome: L'Erma di Bretschneider.

Mill, H. R. 1898. "The Classification of Geography." *Geographical Journal* 11, no. 2: 145–152.

Millar, F. 1993. *The Roman Near East, 31 BC–AD 337*. Cambridge Mass. and London: Harvard University Press.

Millender, E. 2002. "Herodotus and Spartan Despotism." In *Sparta: Beyond the Mirage*, ed. A. Powell and S. Hodkinson. London: Classical Press of Wales and Duckworth, 1–62.

——. 2009. "The Spartan Dyarchy: A Comparative Perspective." In *Sparta: Comparative Approaches*, ed. S. Hodkinson. Swansea: Classical Press of Wales, 1–67.

Miller, D., ed. 1995. *Acknowledging Consumption: A Review of New Studies*. London: Routledge.

Miller, M. C. 1991. "Foreigners at the Greek Symposium?" In *Dining in a Classical Context*, ed. W. J. Slater. Ann Arbor: University of Michigan Press, 59–83.

——. 1997. *Athens and Persia in the Fifth Century BC: A Study in Cultural Receptivity*. Cambridge: Cambridge University Press.

——. 2000. "The Myth of Bousiris: Ethnicity and Art." In *Not the Classical Ideal: Athens and the Construction of the Other in Greek Art*, ed. B. Cohen. Leiden: Brill, 413–442.

———. 2002. "Review of Irad Malkin ed. 2001 *Ancient Perceptions of Greek Ethnicity*. Center for Hellenic Studies Colloquia, 5. Cambridge, MA: Harvard University Press, 2001." *Bryn Mawr Classical Review* (August 12): n.p.

———. 2005. "Barbarian Lineage in Classical Greek Mythlogy and Art: Pelops, Danaos and Kadmos." In *Cultural Borrowings and Ethnic Appropriations in Antiquity*, ed. E. S. Gruen. Stuttgart: F. Steiner, 68–90.

———. 2011. "'Manners Makyth Man': Diacritical Drinking in Achaemenid Anatolia." In *Cultural Identity in the Ancient Mediterranean*, ed. E. S. Gruen. Los Angeles: Getty Research Institute, 97–134.

Minchin, E. 1996. "The Performance of Lists and Catalogues in the Homeric Epics." In *Voices into Text: Orality and Literacy in Ancient Greece*, ed. I. Worthington. Leiden: Brill, 3–21.

———. 2001. *Homer and the Resources of Memory: Some Applications of Cognitive Theory to the Iliad and the Odyssey*. Oxford: Oxford University Press.

Minns, E. H. 1913. *Scythians and Greeks*. Cambridge: Cambridge University Press.

Miracle, P., and N. Milner, eds. 2002. *Consuming Passions and Patterns of Consumption*. Cambridge: Mcdonald Institute for Archaeological Research.

Mitchell, B. J. 2000. "Cyrene: Typical or Atypical." In *Alternatives to Athens*, ed. R. Brock and S. Hodkinson. Oxford: Oxford University Press, 82–102.

Mitchell, L. 2005. "Ethnic Identity and the Community of the Hellenes: A Review." *Ancient West and East* 4, no. 2: 409–421.

———. 2006. "Greeks, Barbarians and Aeschylus' Suppliants." *Greece & Rome* 53, no. 1: 205–224.

———. 2007. *Panhellenism and the Barbarian in Archaic and Classical Greece*. Cardiff: Classical Press of Wales.

Moers, G. 2010. "The World and the Geography of Otherness in Pharaonic Egypt." In *Geography and Ethnography: Perceptions of the World in Pre-Modern Societies*, ed. K. A. Raaflaub and R. J. A. Talbert. Chichester: Wiley-Blackwell, 169–181.

Moles, J. 1996. "Herodotus Warns the Athenians." *Papers of the Leeds International Latin Seminar* 9: 259–284.

Möller, A. 2000. *Naukratis: Trade in Archaic Greece*. Oxford: Oxford University Press.

Momigliano, A. 1975. *Alien Wisdom: The Limits of Hellenisation*. Cambridge: Cambridge University Press.

———. 1990. *The Classical Foundations of Modern Historiography*. Sather Classical Lectures 54. Berkeley, Los Angeles, and London: University of California Press.

Mommsen, A. 1850. "Der Homerische Schiffskatalog in ser Ilias." *Philologus* 5: 522–527.

Monachov, S. J. 2003. "Amphora from Unidentified Centres in the North Aegean." In *The Cauldron of Ariantas. Studies Presented to A. N. Ščeglov on the Occasion of his 70th Birthday*, ed. P. Guldager Bilde et al. Aarhus: Aarhus University Press, 247–261.

Mondi, R. 1983. "The Homeric Cyclopes: Folktale, Tradition and Theme." *TAPA* 113, 17–38.

Morel, J.-P. 1997. "Problématiques de la colonisation grecque en Méditerranée Occidentale: L'exemple des Réseaux." In *Il dinamismo della colonizzazione greca. Atti della tavolla rotunda espansione e colonizzazione greca di età arcaica: Metodolgie e problemi a confronto, Venezia, 10–11/11/1995*, ed. C. Antonetti. Napoli: Loffredo, 59–70.

Morgan, C. 1988. "Corinth, the Corinthian Gulf and Western Greece during the 8th Century BC." *Annual of the British School at Athens* 83: 313–338.

———. 1990. *Athletes and Oracles: The Transformation of Olympia and Delphi in the 8th Century BC*. Cambridge: Cambridge University Press.

———. 1991. "Ethnicity and Early Greek States: Historical and Material Perspectives." *PCPS*: 131–163.

———. 1993. "The Origins of Pan-Hellenism." In *Greek Sanctuaries: New Approaches*, ed. R. Hägg and N. Marinatos. London: Routledge, 18–44.

———. 1994. "The Evolution of a Sacral 'Landscape': Isthmia, Perachora, and the Early Corinthian State." In *Placing the Gods: Sanctuaries and Sacred Space in Ancient Greece*, ed. S. Alcock and R. Osborne. Oxford: Clarendon Press, 105–143.

———. 1998. "Ritual and Society in the Early Iron Age Corinthia." In *Ancient Greek Cult Practice from the Archaeological Evidence*, ed. R. Hägg. Stockholm: Åström, 73–90.

———. 1999a. "The Archaeology of Ethnicity in the Colonial World of the Eighth to Sixth Centuries BC: Approaches and Prospects." *Frontieri e confini. Atti Taranto* 37: 85–145.

———. 1999b. "Cultural Subzones in Early Iron Age and Archaic Arcadia?" In *Defining Ancient Arcadia: Symposium, April 1–4, 1998*, ed. T. H. Nielsen and J. Roy. Acts of the Copenhagen Polis Centre 6. Kæbenhavn: Kongelige danske Videnskabernes Selskab, 382–457.

———. 1999c. "The Human Figure in Eighth-Century Corinthian Vase Painting." In *Céramique et peinture grecques. Modes d'emploi*, ed. M.-C. Villaneuva Puig, F. Lissarague, P. Rouillard, and A. Rouveret. Paris: La Documentation Française, 279–287.

———. 2000. "Politics without the Polis: Cities and the Formation of the Achaian Ethnos, Ca. 800–500 BC." In *Alternatives to Athens: Varieties of Political Organization and Community in Ancient Greece*, ed. R. Brock and S. Hodkinson. Oxford: Oxford University Press, 189–211.

———. 2001a. "The Corinthian Aristocracy and Corinthian Cult during the Eighth Century BC." In *Peloponnesian Sanctuaries and Cults*, ed. R. Hägg. Stockholm: Aström, 45–51.

———. 2001b. "Ethne, Ethnicity, and Early Greek States, Ca. 1200–480 B.C.: An Archaeological Perspective." In *Ancient Perceptions of Greek Ethnicity*, ed. I. Malkin. Cambridge, Mass.: Harvard University Press, 75–112.

———. 2001c. "Symbolic and Pragmatic Aspects of Warfare in the Greek World of the 8th-6th Centuries BC." In *War as a Cultural and Social Force*, ed. L. Hannestad and T.B. Nielsen. Aarhus: Aarhus University Press, 20–44.

———. 2002. "Ethnicity: The Example of Achaia." In *Gli Achei a l'identità etnica degli Achei d'Occidente*, ed. E. Greco. Paestum: Pandemos, 95–116.

———. 2003. *Early Greek States beyond the Polis*. London : Routledge.

———. 2004. *Attic Fine Pottery of the Archaic to Hellenistic Periods in Phanagoria*. Phanagoria Studies. Vol. 1. Leiden: Brill.

———. 2009. "Ethnic Expression on the Early Iron Age and Early Archaic Greek Mainland. Where Should we be Looking?" In *Ethnic Constructs in Antiquity. The Role of Power and Tradition*, ed. T. Derks and N. Roymans. Amsterdam: Amsterdam University Press, 11–36.

Morgan, C., and K. Arafat. 2001. "Imported Fine Pottery of the Archaic-Early Hellenistic Periods in the Collection of the Temryuk Museum Taman Peninsula." In *North Pontic Archaeology: Recent Discoveries and Studies*, ed. G. R. Tsetskhladze. Colloquia Pontic 6. Leiden: Brill, 365–399.

Morgan, C., and J. Hall. 1996. "Achaian Poleis and Achaian Colonisation." In *Introduction to an Inventory of Poleis*, ed. H. M. Hansen. Copenhagen: Acts of the Copenhagen Polis Centre, 164–233.

Morgan, C., and S. Hornblower, eds. 2007. *Pindar's Poetry, Patrons and Festivals: From Archaic Greece to the Roman Empire*. Oxford: Oxford University Press.

Morpurgo-Davies, A. 2002. "The Greek Notion of Dialect." In *Greeks and Barbarians*, ed. T. Harrison. Edinburgh: Edinburgh University Press, 153–171.

Morris, I. 1996. "Negotiated Peripherality in Iron Age Greece." *Journal of World Systems Research* 2: 1–8.

———. 1998. "Archaeology and Archaic Greek History." In *Archaic Greece: New Approaches and New Evidence*, ed. N. Fisher and H. Van Wees. London: Duckworth/ Classical Press of Wales, 1–92.

———. 2000. *Archaeology as Cultural History: Words and Things in Iron Age Greece*. Oxford: Blackwell.

———. 2003. "Mediterraneanization." In *Mediterranean Paradigms and Classical Antiquity*, ed. I. Malkin. New York: Routledge, 30–55.

Morris, I., and B. Powell, eds. 1997. *A New Companion to Homer*. Leiden: Brill.

Morris, S. 1992. *Daidalos and the Origins of Greek Art*. Princeton: Princeton University Press.

———. 1997a. "Homer and the Near East." In *A New Companion to Homer*, ed. I. Morris and B. Powell. Leiden: Brill, 599–623.

———. 1997b. "Greek and Near Eastern Art in the Age of Homer." In *New Light on a Dark Age. Exploring the Culture of Geometric Greece*, ed. S. Langdon. Columbia: University of Missouri Press, 56–71.

———. 2003. "Islands in the Sea: Aegean Polities as Levantine Neighbors." In *Symbiosis, Symbolism, and the Power of the Past: Canaan, Ancient Israel, and their Neighbors from the Late Bronze Age through Roman Palaestina: Proceedings of the Centennial Symposium, W.F. Albright Institute of Archaeological Research and American Schools of Oriental Research, Jerusalem, May 29–31, 2000*, ed. W. G. Devereux and S. Gitin. Winona Lake, Ind.: Eisenbrauns, 3–16.

———. 2007. "Linking with a Wider World: Greeks and 'Barbarians.'" In *Classical Archaeology*, ed. S. E. Alcock and R. Osborne. Oxford: Blackwell, 383–400.

Moscati Castelnuovo, L. 2002a. "Introduzione: Quale identità?" In *Identità e prassi storica nel Mediterraneo Greco*, ed. L. Moscati Castelnuovo. Milano: Edizioni ET, 15–23.

———, ed. 2002b. *Identità e prassi storica nel Mediterraneo Greco*. Milano: Edizioni ET.

Muhly, J. D. 1970. "Homer and the Phoenicians." *Berytus* Xlx: 19–64.

Muller, C. 2007. "Insaissables Scythes: discours, territoire et ethnicité dans le Pont Nord." In *Identités ethniques dans le monde grec antique*, ed. J.-M. Luce and R. Christian. Toulouse: Presses Universitaires du Mirail, 141–158.

Müller, C., and T. Müller. 1841–1870. *Fragmenta Historicorum Graecorum*. Paris: Didot.

Müller, D. 1981. "Herodot—Vater des Empirismus? Mensch und Erkenntnis im Denken Herodots." In *Gnomosyne: Menschliches Denken und Handeln in der frühgriechischen Literatur: Festschrift für Walter Marg zum 70. Geburtstag*, ed. G. Kurz, D. Müller, and W. Nicolai. Munich: Beck, 299–318.

Müller, K. E. 1972, 1980. *Geschichte der Antiken Ethnographie und Ethnographischen Theoriebildung.* Wiesbaden: Franz Steiner.

Munn, M. H. 1993. *The Defense of Attica. The Dema Wall and the Boiotian War of 378–375 b.c.* Berkeley: University of California Press.

Munro, J. A. R., and H. M. Anthony. 1897. "Explorations in Mysia." *Geographical Journal* 9, no. 2: 150–168.

Munson, R. V. 2001. *Telling Wonders: Ethnographic and Political Discourse in the Work of Herodotus.* Ann Arbor: University of Michigan Press.

———. 2005. *Black Doves Speak: Herodotus and the Languages of Barbarians.* Washington, D.C.: Center for Hellenic Studies.

———. 2006. "An Alternate World: Herodotus and Italy." In *The Cambridge Companion to Herodotus*, ed. C. Dewald and J. Marincola. Cambridge: Cambridge University Press, 257–273.

Murray, G. G. A. 1908. "The Early Greek Epic." In *Anthropology and the Classics: Six Lectures Delivered before the University of Oxford*, ed. R. R. Marett. Oxford: Clarendon Press, 66–93.

Murray, O. 1972. "Herodotus and Hellenistic Culture." *Classical Quarterly* 22: 200–213.

———. 1987. "Herodotus and Oral History." In *Achaemenid History II, The Greek Sources*, ed. H. Sancisi-Weerdenburg and A. Kuhrt. Leiden: Brill, 93–115.

———. 1988–1989. "Omero e l'etnografia." *Kokalos* 34–35: 1–13.

———. 2000 [1996]. "History." In *Greek Thought: A Guide to Classical Knowledge*, ed. J. Brunschwig and G. E. R. Lloyd. London: Belknap Press, 328–338.

———. 2001. "Herodotus and Oral History Reconsidered." In *The Historian's Craft in the Age of Herodotus*, ed. N. Luraghi. Oxford: Oxford University Press, 314–325.

Muscarella, O. W. 1962. "The Oriental Origin of Siren Cauldron Attachments." *Hesperia* 31: 317–329.

———. 1989. "King Midas of Phrygia and the Greeks." In *Anatolia and the Ancient Near East: Studies in Honor of Tahsin Özgüç*, ed. K. Emre et al. Ankara: Türk Tarih Kurumu Basimevi, 333–344.

———. 1992. "Greek and Oriental Cauldron Attachments: A Review." In *Greece Between East and West: Tenth–Eighth Centuries b.c.*, ed. G. Kopcke and I. Tokumaru. Mainz: Philipp von Zabern, 16–45.

Musti, D. 1976. "Problemi della storia di Locri Epizefirii." *Atti Taranto* 27: 23–146.

———. 1991. "Lo sviluppe del Mmito di Filottete da Crotone a Sibari: tradizioni achee e troiane in Magna Grecia." In *Épéios et Philoctète en Italie: donées archéologiques et traditions légendaires. Actes du colloque, Lille, 1987*, ed. J. sde la Genière. Naples: Cahiers du Centre Jean Bérard 16, 21–35.

Myres, J. L. 1896. "An Attempt to Reconstruct the Maps Used by Herodotus." *Geographical Journal* 8: 605–631.

———. 1907. "A History of the Pelasgian Theory." *JHS* 27: 170–225.

———. 1908. "Herodotus and Anthropology." In *Anthropology and the Classics: Six Lectures Delivered before the University of Oxford*, ed. R. R. Marett. Oxford: Clarendon Press, 121–169.

———. 1953. *Herodotus. Father of History.* Oxford: Clarendon Press.

Nachtergael, G. 1975. "Le Catalogue des vaisseaux et la liste des théorodoques de Delphes." In *Le monde grec. Hommage à C. Préaux* Bruxelles: Éditions de l'Université de Bruxelles, 44–55.

Nagy, G. 1990. *Pindar's Homer: The Lyric Possesion of an Epic Past.* Baltimore: Johns Hopkins University Press.

———. 1992. "Homeric Questions." *Transactions of the American Philological Association* 122: 17–60.

Naso, A. 2000. "Etruscan and Italic Artefacts from the Aegean." In *Ancient Italy in Its Mediterranean Setting: Studies in Honour of Ellen Macnamara*, ed. D. Ridgway et al. London: Accordia Research Institute, 193–209.

———. 2001. "Reflexe des griechischen Wunders in Etrurien." In *Gab es das Griechische Wunder? Griechenland zwischen dem Ende des 6. und der Mitte des 5. Jahrhunderts v. Chr.*, ed. D. Papenfuss and V. M. Strocka. Mainz: von Zabern, 317–325.

Nazarčuk, V. I. 2010. "Black-Figured Pottery." In *The Lower City of Olbia (Sector NGS) in the 6th Century BC to the 4th Century AD*, ed. N. A. Lejpunskaja et al. Vols. 1–2. Aarhus: Aarhus University Press, 143–170.

Neer, R. T. 2003. "Framing and Gift: The Siphnian Treasury at Delphi and the Politics of Public Art." In *The Cultures within Greek Culture: Contact, Conflict, Collaboration*, ed. C. Dougherty and L. Kurke. Cambridge: Cambridge University Press, 129–149.

Negbi, O. 1992. "Early Phoenician Presence in the Mediterranean Islands: A Reappraisal." *AJA* 96: 599–615.

Nenci, G. 1954. *Hecataei Milesii Fragmenta, Biblioteca di Studi Superiori.* Vol. 22. Florence: La Nuova Italia.

———. 1990. "L'Occidente 'barbarico.'" In *Hérodote et les peuples non grecs. Entretiens sur l'Antiquité classique: Vandoeuvres-Genève, 22–26 Août 1988*, ed. G. Nenci and O. Reverdin. Genève: Fondation Hardt 35, 301–319.

———. 1991. "Filottete in Sicilia." In *Épéios et Philoctète en Italie: donées archéologiques et traditions légendaires. Actes du colloque, Lille, 1987*, ed. J. De La Genière. Naples: Cahiers du Centre Jean Bérard 16, 1311–135.

Nestle, W. 1908. *Herodots Verständnis zur Philosophie und Sophistik.* Stuttgart: Schöntal.

Nielsen, T. H. 1996. "Arkadia. City-Ethnics and Tribalism." In *Introduction to an Inventory of Greek Poleis, Acts of the Copenhagen Polis Centre 3, Historisk-Filosofiske Meddelelser 74*, ed. H. M. Hansen. Kæbenhavn: Kongelige danske Videnskabernes Selskab, 117–163.

———. 1997. "Triphylia. An Experiment in Ethnic Construction and Political Organisation." In *Yet More Studies in the Ancient Greek Polis, Papers from the Copenhagen Polis Centre 4*, ed. T. H. Nielsen. Historia Einzelschriften 117. Stuttgart: Franz Steiner Verlag, 129–162.

———. 1999a. "The Concept of Arkadia: The People, Their Land, and Their Organisation." In *Defining Ancient Arkadia, Acts of the Copenhagen Polis Centre 6, Historisk-Filosofiske Meddelelser 78*, ed. T. H. Nielsen and J. Roy. Kæbenhavn: Kongelige danske Videnskabernes Selskab, 16–79.

———. 1999b. *Defining Ancient Arkadia, Acts of the Copenhagen Polis Centre 6, Historisk-Filosofiske Meddelelser 78.* Kæbenhavn: Kongelige danske Videnskabernes Selskab.

———. 2000. "The Concept of Arcadia—the People, Their Land and Their Organization." In *Defining Ancient Arcadia. Symposium, April 1–4, 1998, Acts of the*

Copenhage Polis Centre 6, ed. T. H. Nielsen and J. Roy. Kæbenhavn: Kongelige danske Videnskabernes Selskab, 16–80.

———. 2007. *Olympia and the Classical Hellenic City-Culture, Historiske-Filosofiske Meddelelser 96.* Kæbenhavn: Det Kongelige danske Videnskabernes Selskab.

Niemeyer, H. G. 1990. "The Phoenicians in the Mediterranean: A Non-Greek Model of Expansion and Settlement in Antiquity." In *Greek Colonists and Native Populations,* ed. J.-P. Descoeudres. Oxford: Clarendon Press, 469–489.

Nippel, W. 2002. "The Construction of the 'Other.'" In *Greeks and Barbarians,* ed. T. Harrison. Edinburgh: Edinburgh University Press, 278–310.

Niutta, F. 1977. "Le fonti letterarie ed epigrafiche." In *Locri Epizefirii,* ed. M. Barra Bagnasco. Florence: Sansoni, 253–355.

Nocita, M. 2000. "I delfini di Olbia: considerazioni storiche ed epigrafiche." *Annali dell'Istituto Italiano di Numismatica* 47: 217–230.

Noonan, Th. S. 1973. "The Grain Trade of the Northern Black Sea in Antiquity." *American Journal of Philology* 94: 231–242.

Norden, E. 1922. *Die germanische Urgeschichte in Tacitus Germania.* Leipzig: Teubner.

Norton, R. E. 2008. "Wilamowitz at War." *Journal of the Classical Tradition* 15, no. 1: 74–97.

Ober, J. 2003. "Postscript: Culture, Thin Coherence, and the Persistence of Politics." In *The Cultures within Greek Culture: Contact, Conflict, Collaboration,* ed. C. Dougherty and L. Kurke. Cambridge: Cambridge University Press, 237–255.

Ogden, D. 1997. *The Crooked Kings of Ancient Greece.* London: Duckworth.

Okhotnikov, S. B. 2001. "Settlements in the Lower Reaches of the Dneister 6th–3rd Centuries BC." In *North Pontic Archaeology: Recent Discoveries and Studies.* ed. G. R. Tsetskhladze. Colloquia Pontica 6. Leiden: Brill, 91–117.

Onyshkevych, L. 2002. "Interpreting the Berezan Bone Graffito." In *Oikistes: Studies in Constitutions, Colonies, and Military Power in the Ancient World. Offered in Honor of A. J. Graham,* ed. V. B. Gorman and E. W. Robinson. Leiden: Brill, 161–179.

Oppenheim, A. L. 1960. "The City of Assur in 714 B.C." *Journal of Near Eastern Studies* 19, no. 2 (April): 133–147.

Orsi, P. 1911. "Locri Epizephyrii." *Notizie degli Scavi di Antichità:* 3–76.

———. 1912. "Locri Epizephyrii." *Notizie degli Scavi di Antichità:* 3–56.

———. 1917. "Locri Epizephyrii. Campagne di Scavo nella Necropolis Lucifero Negli Anni 1914 e 1915." *Notizie degli Scavi di Antichità:* 101–167.

Osborne, C. 1987. *Rethinking Early Greek Philosophy. Hippolytus of Rome and the Presocratics.* London: Duckworth.

———. 2006. "Was There an Eleatic Revolution in Philosophy?" In *Rethinking Revolutions through Ancient Greece,* ed. S. Goldhill and R. Osborne. Cambridge: Cambridge University Press, 218–245.

Osborne, C. 2004. *Presocratic Philosophy.* Oxford: Oxford University Press.

Osborne, R. 1996. *Greece in the Making: 1200–479 BC.* London: Routledge.

———. 1998a. *Archaic and Classical Greek Art.* Oxford: Oxford University Press.

———. 1998b. "Early Greek Colonization? The Nature of Greek Settlement in the West." In *Archaic Greece: New Approaches and New Evidence,* ed. N. Fisher and H. Van Wees. London: Duckworth/ Classical Press of Wales, 251–270.

———. 2000. "An Other View: An Essay on Political History." In *Not the Classical Ideal: Athens and the Construction of the Other in Greek Art,* ed. B. Cohen. Leiden: Brill, 21–43.

———. 2004a. "Homer's Society." In *The Cambridge Companion to Homer*, ed. R. Fowler. Cambridge: Cambridge University Press, 206–218.

———. 2004b. "Images of a Warrior. On a Group of Athenian Vases and their Public." In *Greek Vases: Images, Contexts and Controversies*, ed. C. Marconi. Leiden: Brill, 41–54.

———. 2005. "Ordering Women in Hesiod's Catalogue." In *The Hesiodic Catalogue of Women: Constructions and Reconstructions*, ed. R. Hunter. Cambridge: Cambridge University Press, 5–25.

———. 2006. "Introduction." In *Rethinking Revolutions through Ancient Greece*, ed. S. Goldhill and R. Osborne. Cambridge: Cambridge University Press, 1–9.

———. 2007a. "Landscape, Ethnicity, and the Polis." Unpublished paper.

———. 2007b. "What Travelled with Greek Pottery?" *Mediterranean Historical Review* 221: 85–95.

———. 2008. "Reciprocal Strategies: Imperialism, Barbarism and Trade in Archaic and Classical Olbia." In *Meetings of Cultures—Between Conflicts and Coexistence*, ed. P. Guldager Bilde and J. H. Petersen. Aarhus: Aarhus University Press, 333–346.

Osborne, R., and B. Cunliffe, eds. 2005. *Mediterranean Urbanization 800–600BC*. Oxford: Oxford University Press.

Osanna, M. 1992. *Chorai coloniali da Taranto a Locri: documentazione archeologica e ricostruzione storica*. Rome: Istituto Poligrafico e Zecca della Stato.

Owen, S. 2000. "New Light on Thracian Thasos: A Reinterpretation of the 'Cave of Pan.'" *JHS* 120: 139–143.

———. 2003. "Of Dogs and Men: Archilochos, Archaeology and the Greek Settlement of Thasos." *Proceedings of the Cambridge Philological Society* 49: 1–18.

———. 2006. "Mortuary Display and Cultural Contact: A Cemetery at Kastri on Thasos." *Oxford Journal of Archaeology* 25: 257–270.

Pacciarelli, M. 1989–1990. "Richerche nel Promontorio del Poro e Consideraioni sugli insediamenti del Primo Ferro in Calabria Meridionale." *Rivista Storica Calabrese*, N.S.: 10–11, 33–35.

———. 1999. *Torre Galli: La necropoli della prima età del ferro: Scavi Paolo Orsi, 1922–23*. Soveria Mannelli: Rubbettino.

Page, D. 1955. *Sappho and Alcaeus*. Oxford: Clarendon Press.

———. 1959. *History and the Homeric Iliad*. Berkeley: University of California.

———. 1973. *Folktales in Homer's Odyssey*. Cambridge, Mass.: Harvard University Press.

Palagia, O., ed. 2006. *Greek Sculpture: Function, Materials, and Techniques in the Archaic and Classical Periods*. Cambridge: Cambridge University Press.

Papadodima, E. 2010. "The Greek/Barbarian Interaction in Euripides' Andromache, Orestes, Heracleidae: A Reassessment of Greek Attitudes to Foreigners." *Digressus* 10: 1–42.

Papadopoulos, J. K. 2002. "Minting Identity: Coinage, Ideology and the Economics of Colonization in Akhaian Magna Graecia." *CAJ* 12, no. 1: 21–55.

———. 2003. "The Achaian Vapheio Cup and Its Afterlife in Archaic South Italy." *Oxford Journal of Archaeology* 4: 411–428.

Papataxiarchis, E. 2010. "Reconfiguring Greek Ethnography in a Changing World." *Journal of Mediterranean Studies* 18, no. 2: 419–430.

Parke, H. W. 1939. *A History of the Delphic Oracle*. Oxford: Oxford University Press.

———. 1984. "Croesus and Delphi." *Greek, Roman and Byzantine Studies* 25: 209–232.

———. 1985. *The Oracles of Apollo in Asia Minor.* London: Croom Helm.

Parke, H. W., and D. E. W. Wormell. 1956. *The Delphic Oracle.* Oxford: Blackwell.

Parra, M. 1998. "Il teatro in Locri tra spettacoli o culto: per una revisione dei culti." *Annali della Scuola Normale Superiore di Pisa* 4, no. 3: 303–322.

Parry, M. 1971. *The Making of Homeric Verse: The Collected Papers of Milman Parry / Edited by Adam Parry.* Oxford: Clarendon Press.

Partida, E. 2000. *The Treasuries at Delphi: An Architectural Study.* Jonsered: Paul Åströms Förlag.

Patzek, B. 1996. "Griechen und Phöniker in homerischer Zeit. Fernhandel und der orientalische Einfluss auf die frühgriechische Kultur." *Münstersche Beiträge zur Antiken Handelsgeschichte* 15, no. 2: 1–32.

Payen, P. 1997. *Les îles nomades: conquérir et résister dans l'Enquête d'Hérodote.* Paris: Ecole des Hautes Etudes en Sciences Sociales.

Payne, H., ed. 1940. *Perachora I.* Oxford: Clarendon Press.

———. 1950. *Archaic Marble Sculpture from the Acropolis: A Photographic Catalogue.* London: Cresset Press.

Pearson, L. 1939. *Early Ionian Historians.* Oxford: Clarendon Press.

Pédech, P. 1976. *La géographie des Grecs.* Paris: Presses Universitaires de France.

Pedley, J. G. 2005. *Sanctuaries and the Sacred in the Ancient Greek World.* Cambridge: Cambridge University Press.

Pelling, C. B. R. 1997. "East Is East and West Is West—Or Are They? National Stereotypes in Herodotus." *Histos* 1: Http://Www.Dur.Ac.Uk/Classics/Histos/1997.

———. 2000. "Fun with Fragments." In *Athenaeus and his World: Reading Greek Culture in the Roman Empire,* ed. D. Braund and J. Wilkins. Exeter: Exeter University Press, 1–90.

Pembroke, S. 1967. "Women in Charge: Function of Alternatives in Early Greek Tradition and Ancient Ideas of Matriarchy." *Journal of the Warburg and Courtauld Institutes* 30: 1–30.

———. 1970. "Locres et Tarante: Le rôle des femmes dans la fondation de deux colonies grecques." *Annales. Economies, Sociétés, Civilisations* 25: 1240–1270.

Pendlebury, J. D. S. 1930. *Aegyptiaca. A Catalogue of Egyptian Objects in the Aegean Area.* Cambridge: Cambridge University Press.

Penkova, E. 2003. "Orphic Graffito on a Bone Plate from Olbia." *Thracia* 15: 605–617.

Penny, H. G. 2002. *Objects of Culture: Ethnology and Ethnographic Museums in Imperial Germany.* Chapel Hill: University of North Carolina Press.

Penny, H. G., and M. Bunzl. 2003. *Worldly Provincialism: German Anthropology in the Age of Empire.* Ann Arbor: University of Michigan Press.

Petersen, J. H. n.d. "Greek or Native? A Case Study of Burial Customs in the Northern and Western Black Sea Region-Olbia and Apollonia Pontika." Http://Www.Pontos.Dk/E_Pub/JHP_Stockholm-Foredrag.Pdf.

———. 2010. *Cultural Interactions and Social Strategies on the Pontic Shores. Burial Customs in the Northern Black Sea Area C. 550–270 BC.* Aarhus: Aarhus University Press.

Pfeijffer, I. L. 1999. *Three Aeginetan Odes of Pindar. A Commentary on Nemean V, Nemean III, and Pythian VIII.* Leiden: Brill.

Pfuhl, E. 1923. *Malerei und Zeichnung der Griechen I.* Munich: F. Bruckmann.

Philipp, H. K. 1992. "Le caratteristiche delle relazioni fra il sanctuario di Olimpia e la Magna Grecia." *AttiTaranto* 31: 29–51.

———. 1994. "Olympia, die Peloponnes und die Westgriechen." *JDAI* 109: 77–92.

Phillips, E. D. 1953. "Odysseus in Italy." *JHS* 73: 53–67.

———. 1955. "The Legend of Aristeas: Fact and Fancy in Early Greek Notions of East Russia." *Artibus Asiae* 18, no. 2: 161–177.

Phinney, J. 2004. "Ethnic Identity, Psychology of." In *International Encyclopaedia of the Social & Behavioural Science*, ed. N. Smelser and P. Baltes. Amsterdam: Elsevier Science, 4821–4824.

Pikoulas, Y. A. 1999. "The Road-Network of Arcadia." In *Defining Ancient Arcadia. Symposium, April 1–4, 1998*, ed. T. H. Nielsen and J. Roy. Acts of the Copenhagen Polis Centre 6. København: Kongelige danske Videnskabernes Selskab, 248–320.

Pinney, G. F. 1983. "Achilles Lord of Scythia." In *Ancient Greek Art and Iconography*, ed. W. G. Moon. Madison: University of Wisconsin Press, 127–147.

———. 1984. "For the Heroes Are at Hand." *JHS* 104: 181–183.

Pirenne-Delforge, V. 1994. *L'Aphrodite grecque*. Kernos Supplement 4; Athènes-Lièges: Centre international d'Étude de la Religion grecque antique.

———. 2007. "Something to Do with Aphrodite: Ta Aphrodisia and the Sacred." In *Blackwell Companion to Greek Religion*, ed. D. Ogden. London: Blackwell, 311–323.

———. 2009. "Review of: Budin, S. 2008 The Myth of Sacred Prostitution in Antiquity, New York, Cambridge University Press." BMCR 2009.04.28, available at http://bmcr.brynmawr.edu/2009/http://bmcr.brynmawr.edu/2009/2009-04-28.html

Plassart, A. 1913. "Les Archers D'athenes." *Revue des études grecques* 26: 151–213.

Posamentir, R. 2006. "The Greeks in Berezan and Naukratis: A Similar Story?" In *Naukratis: Greek Diversity in Egypt. Studies on East Greek Pottery and Exchange in the Eastern Mediterranean*, ed. A. Villing and U. Schlotzhauer. London: British Museum Press, 159–167.

Powell, A., and S. Hodkinson, eds. 2002. *Sparta: Beyond the Mirage*. London: Classical Press of Wales and Duckworth.

Powell, B. 1997. "Homer and Writing." In *A New Companion to Homer*, ed. I. Morris and B. Powell. Leiden: Brill, 3–33.

Prag, J. 2006. "Poenus Plane Est—But Who Were the 'Punickes'?" *Papers of the British School at Rome* 74: 1–37.

Procelli, A. M. 1993. *Ripostigli di Bronzi della Sicilia nel Museo Archeologico di Siracusa*. Palermo: Accademia Nazionale di Scienze, Lettere e Arti.

———. 1996. "Appunti sulla distribuzione delle anfore commerciali nella Sicilia arcaica." *Kokalos* 42: 91–137.

Prückner, H. 1968. *Die Lokrischen Tonreliefs*. Mainz am Rhein: von Zabern.

Pu, M. 2005. *Enemies of Civilization: Attitudes toward Foreigners in Ancient Mesopotamia, Egypt, and China*. Albany: State University of New York Press.

Puelma, M. 1977. "Die Selbstbeschreibung des Chores in Alkmans grossem Partheneion-Fragment." *Museum Helveticum* 34: 28–33.

Purcell, N. 2003. "The Boundless Sea of Unlikeness? On Defining the Mediterranean." *Mediterranean Historical Review* 18, no. 2: 9–29.

Qureshi, S. 2011, *Peoples on Parade: Exhibitions, Empire, and Anthropology in Nineteenth-Century Britain*. Chicago: University of Chicago Press.

Raaflaub, K. A. 1998. "A Historian's Headache: How to Read 'Homeric Society'?" In *Archaic Greece: New Approaches and New Evidence*, ed. N. Fisher and H. Van Wees. London: Classical Press of Wales and Duckworth, 169–195.

———. 2004. "Archaic Greek Aristocrats as Carriers of Cultural interaction." In *Commerce and Monetary Systems in the Ancient World: Means of Transmission and Cultural Interaction. Proceedings of the Fifth Annual Symposium of the Assyrian and Babylonian Intellectual Heritage Project Held in Innsbruck, Austria, October 3rd–8th, 2002*, ed. R. Rollinger and C. Ulf. Stuttgart: Franz Steiner Verlag, 197–217.

Raaflaub, K. A., and R. J. A. Talbert, eds. 2010. *Geography and Ethnography: Perceptions of the World in Pre-Modern Societies*. Chichester: Wiley-Blackwell.

Race, W. H. 1997. *Pindar*. Vols. 1–2. Cambridge, Mass.: Harvard University Press.

Raeck, W. 1981. *Zum Barbarenbild in der Kunst Athens im 6. und 5. Jahrhundert v. Chr.* Bonn: Habelt.

Ramin, J. 1979. *Mythologie et géographie*. Paris: Les Belles Lettres.

Rausch, M. 2004. "Neben-und Miteinander in archaischer Zeit: Die Beziehungen von Italikern und Etruskern zum Griechischen Poseidonia." In *Greek Identity in the Western Mediterranean*. Mnemosyne, supp. 246 , ed. K. Lomas. Leiden: Brill, 229–257.

Read, C. H., and O. M. Dalton. 1898. "Works of Art from Benin City." *Journal of the Anthropological Institute of Great Britain & Ireland* 28: 362–383.

Reade, J. 1979. "Ideology and Propaganda in Assyrian Art." In *Power and Propaganda: A Symposium on Ancient Empires*, ed. M. T. Larsen. Mesopotamia 7. Copenhagen: Akademisk, 329–343.

Redfield, J. 1983. "Odysseus: The Economic Man." In *Approaches to Homer*, ed. C. Rubino and C. Shelmerdine. Austin: University of Texas Press, 218–247.

———. 1985. "Herodotus the Tourist." *Classical Philology* 80: 97–118.

———. 2003. *The Locrian Maidens: Love and Death in Greek Italy*. Princeton: Princeton University Press.

Renfrew, C., and J. Cherry, eds. 1986. *Peer Polity interaction and Socio-Political Change*. Cambridge: Cambridge University Press.

Rhodes, P. J. 1994. "In Defence of the Greek Historians." *Greece and Rome* 41: 156–171.

Ridgway, D. 1990. "The First Western Greeks and Their Neighbours 1935–1985." In *Greek Colonists and Native Populations*, ed. J.-P. Descoeudres. Oxford: Clarendon Press, 469–489.

———. 1995. "Archaeology in Sardinia and Southern Italy 1989–1994." *Archaeological Reports*: 75–96.

———. 1996. "Nestor's Cup and the Etruscans." *Oxford Journal of Archaeology* 15: 325–344.

Ridgway, D., F. R. Serra Ridgway, M. Pearce, E. Herring, R. D. Whitehouse, and J. B. Wilkins, eds. 2000a. *Ancient Italy in Its Mediterranean Setting: Studies in Honour of Ellen Macnamara*. London: Accordia Research Institute.

———. 2000b. "The First Western Greeks Revisited." In *Ancient Italy in Its Mediterranean Setting. Studies in Honour of Ellen Macnamara*, ed. D. Ridgway et al. London: Accordia Research Institute, 179–193.

———. 2004. "Euboeans and Others along the Tyrrhenian Seaboard in the 8th Century B.C." In *Greek Identity in the Western Mediterranean*. Mnemosyne, supp. 246, ed. K. Lomas. Leiden: Brill, 15–33.

Risch, E. 1947. "Namensdeutungen und Worterklärungen bei den ältesten griechischen Dichtern." In *Eumusia: Festgabe für Ernst Howald zum Sechzigsten Geburtstag am 20. April 1947*. Zurich: E. Rentsch, 72–91.

Roaf, M. 1974. "The Subject Peoples on the Base of the Statue of Darius." *Cahiers de la Délégation archéologique français en Iran* 4: 73–160.

———. 1983. "Sculptures and Sculptors at Persepolis." *Iran* 21: 1–164.

Robert, L. 1980. *A travers l'Asie mineure. Poètes et prosateurs, monnaies grecques, voyagers et géographie*. Paris: de Boccard.

Roberts, R. 1899. *Longinus' On the Sublime*. Cambridge: Cambridge University Press.

Robertson, K. C. S. I. 1898. "Káfiristan and Its People." *Journal of the Anthropological Institute of Great Britain & Ireland* 28: 75–90.

Rodger, N. A. M. 2004. *The Safeguard of the Sea: A Naval History of Britain 660–1649*. London: Penguin.

Rohde, E. 1900. *Der griechische roman und seine vorläufer*. 2nd ed. Leipzig: Breitkopf & Härtel.

Rolle, R. 1989. *The World of the Scythians*. London: Batsford.

Rollinger, R., and W. F. M. Henkelman. 2008. "New Observations on 'Greeks' in the Achaemenid Empire According to Cuneiform Texts from Babylonia and Persepolis." In *Organisation des pouvoirs et contacts culturels dans les pays de L'empire achéménide. Actes du colloque organisè au College de France par la Chaire d'histoire et civilisation du monde achéménie et l'empire d'Alexandre et le Réseau international d'études et de recherches achéménides*, ed. P. Briant and M. Chauveau. Paris: Éditions de Boccard, 331–352.

Romm, J. S. 1989. "Herodotus and Mythic Geography: The Case of the Hyperboreans." *Transactions of the American Philological Association* 119: 97–113.

———. 1992. *The Edges of the Earth in Ancient Thought: Geography, Exploration, and Fiction*. Princeton: Princeton University Press.

———. 1998. *Herodotus*. New Haven: Yale University Press.

———. 2010. "Greek Theories of Global Structure." In *Geography and Ethnography. Perceptions of the World in Pre-Modern Societies*, ed. K. A. Raaflaub and R. J. A. Talbert. Chichester: Wiley-Blackwell, 215–235.

Ronconi, L. 1997. "La terra chiamata Italia." In *Il dinamismo della colonizzazione greca: Atti della tavolla rotunda Espansione e colonizzazione greca di età arcaica: metodolgie e problemi a confronto (Venezia, 10–11/11/1995)*, ed. C. Antonetti. Napoli: Loffredo, 109–119.

Rood, T. 1999. "Thucydides' Persian Wars." In *The Limits of Historiography: Genre and Narrative in Ancient Historical Texts*, ed. C. S. Kraus. Leiden: Brill, 141–169.

———. 2006. "Herodotus and Foreign Lands." In *The Cambridge Companion to Herodotus*, ed. C. Dewald and J. Marincola. Cambridge: Cambridge University Press, 290–306.

Root, M. C. 1979. *The King and Kingship in Achaemenid Art: Essays on the Creation of an Iconography of Empire*. Acta Iranica 19. Leiden: Brill.

———. 1991. "From the Heart: Powerful Persianisms in the Art of the Western Empire." In *Achaemenid History VI: Asia Minor and Egypt: Old Cultures in a New Empire*, ed. H. Sancisi-Weerdenberg and A. Kuhrt. Leiden: Nederlands instituut Voor Het Nabije Oosten, 1–29.

————. 2011. "Embracing Ambiguity in the World of Athens and Persia." In *Cultural Identity in the Ancient Mediterranean*, ed. E. S. Gruen. Los Angeles: Getty Research Institute, 86–95.

Ross, S. A. 2005. "Barbarophonos: Language and Panhellenism in the Iliad." *Classical Philology* 100: 299–316.

Rostovtzeff, M. 1922. *Iranians and Greeks in South Russia.* Oxford: Oxford University Press.

Rouse, W. H. D. 1902. *Greek Votive Offerings: An Essay in the History of Greek Religion.* Cambridge: Cambridge University Press.

Roux, G. 1976. *Delphes, son oracle et ses dieux.* Paris: Les Belles Lettres.

Rowe, J. H. 1965. "The Renaissance Foundations of Anthropology." *American Anthropologist, New Series*, 67, no. 1 (February): 1–20.

Rudhardt, J. 2002. "The Greek Attitude to Foreign Religions." In *Greeks and Barbarians*, ed. T. Harrison. Edinburgh: Edinburgh University Press, 172–185.

Rusjaeva, A. S. 2003. "The Main Development of the Western Temenos of Olbia in the Pontos." In *The Cauldron of Ariantas. Studies Presented to A. N. Ščeglov on the Occasion of his 70th Birthday*, ed. P. Guldager Bilde et al. Aarhus: Aarhus University Press, 93–117.

————. 2010. "Graffiti." In *The Lower City of Olbia (Sector NGS) in the 6th Century BC to the 4th century AD*, ed. N. A. Lejpunskaja et al. Vols. 1–2. Aarhus: Aarhus University Press, 499–518.

Russell, F. S. 1999. *Information Gathering in Classical Greece.* Ann Arbor: University of Michigan Press.

Russo, J., M. Fernández-Galiano, and A. Heubeck. 1992. *A Commentary on Homer's Odyssey.* Vol. II, Books XVII–XXIV. Oxford: Clarendon Press.

Russo, R. 1996. "Athena Alata sul Timpone della Motta Francavilla Marittima." *Annali della Scuola Normale Superiore di Pisa* 4, no. 1: 523–539.

Rusyayeva, A. S. 1999. "The Penetration of Greeks in the Ukrainian Wooded Steppe in the Archaic Period." *VDI* 1: 84–97.

————. 2007. "Religious Interactions between Olbia and Scythia." In *Classical Olbia and the Scythian World: From the Sixth Century BC to the Second Century AD*, ed. D. Braund and S. D. Kryzhitskiy. Proceedings of the British Academy 142. Oxford: Oxford University Press, 93–103.

Rutherford, I. 2001. *Pindar's Paens. A Reading of the Fragments with a Survey of the Genre.* Oxford: Oxford University Press.

————. 2002. "Interference or Translationese? Some Patterns in Lycian-Greek Bilingualsim." In *Bilingualism in Ancient Society: Language Contact and the Written Word*, ed. J. N. Adams, M. Janse, and S. Swain. Oxford: Oxford University Press, 197–219.

Rutherford, I., and J. Elsner, eds. 2005. *Pilgrimage in Graeco-Roman and Early Christian Antiquity.* Oxford: Oxford University Press.

Rutter, N., ed. 2001. *Historia Numorum: Italy.* London: British Museum Press.

————. 2000. "Coin Types and Identity: Greek Cities in Sicily." In *Sicily from Aeneas to Augustus*, ed. C. Smith and J. Serrati. Edinburgh: Edinburgh University Press, 73–84.

Saatsoglou-Paliadeli, C. 1993. "Aspects of Ancient Macedonian Costume." *JHS* 113: 122–147.

Sabbione, C. 1977. "L'area Locrese," In Il commercio greco nel Tirreno in èta arcaica. *Atti Seminario in Memoria di Mario Napoli*. Salerno: Istituto di storia antica e archeologica Facoltà di Lettere e Filosofia, Universià degli Studi di Salerno, 15–21.

———. 1981. Reggio e Metauros nell'VIII–VII sec. a.C.' *Annuario* 59: 257–289.

———. 1982. "Le aree di colonizzazione di Crotone e Locri Epizefiri nell'VIII e VII sec. a.C." *Annuario* 60: 251–299.

———. 1986. "La colonizzazione greca: Metauros e Myla." *AttiTaranto* 26: 221–236.

Said, E. W. 1978. *Orientalism*. London: Routledge & Kegan Paul.

———. 1993. *Culture and Imperialism*. London: Chatto & Windus.

Sale, W. 1961. "The Hyperborean Maidens on Delos." *Harvard Theological Review* 54, no. 2: 75–89.

Salmon, J. B. 1984. *Wealthy Corinth: A History of the City to 338 BC*. Oxford: Clarendon Press.

Salvador, J. C. 1996. ΘALIA: *un estudio del léxico vegetal en Pindaro*. Zaragoza: Gorfi.

Salvadore, M. 1987. *Il nome, la Persona. Saggio sull' etimologia antica*. Genova: Dipartimento di Archeologia, Filologia Classica e loro tradizioni in epoca cristiana, medivale e umanistica.

Sancisi-Weerdenburg, H. 2001. "Yauna by the Sea and across the Sea." In *Ancient Perceptions of Greek Ethnicity*, ed. I. Malkin. Cambridge, Mass.: Harvard University Press, 323–346.

Sauneron, S., and J. Yoyotte. 1952. "La campagne nubienne de Psammétique II et sa signification historique." *Bulletin de l'institut Français d'archeologie Orientale* 50: 157–207.

Schäfer, C. 1996. *Xenophanes von Kolophon: ein Vorsokratiker zwischen Mythos und Philosophie*. Stuttgart & Leipzig: B. G. Teubner.

Scheer, T. S. 2011. "Ways of Becoming Arcadian: Arcadian Foundation Myths in the Mediterranean." In *Cultural Identity in the Ancient Mediterranean*, ed. E. S. Gruen. Los Angeles: Getty Research Institute, 11–25.

Schein, S. 1996. *Reading the Odyssey*. Princeton: Princeton University Press.

Schepens, G. 1997. "Jacoby's FGrHist: Problems, Methods, Prospects." In *Collecting Fragments = Fragmente Sammeln*, ed. G. W. Most. Göttingen: Vandenhoeck & Ruprecht, 144–173.

———. 2006a. "Il carteggio Jacoby-Meyer. Un piano inedito per la Struttura dei FGrHist." In *Aspetti dell'opera di Felix Jacoby. Seminari Arnaldo Momigliano, Scuola Normale Superiore Pisa 18–19 Dicembre 2002, Pisa*, ed. C. Ampolo. Pisa: Ed. della Normale, 357–381.

———. 2006b. "Storiografia e letteratura antiquaria. La scelte di Felix Jacoby." In *Aspetti dell'opera di Felix Jacoby. Seminari Arnaldo Momigliano, Scuola Normale Superiore Pisa 18–19 Dicembre 2002, Pisa*, ed. C. Ampolo. Pisa: Ed. della Normale, 149–171.

———. 2007. "History and Historia: Inquiry in the Greek Historians." In *A Companion to Greek and Roman Historiography*, ed. J. Marincola. Oxford: Blackwell, 39–55.

———. 2010. "Die Debatte über die Struktur der 'Fragmente der griechischen Historiker.'" *Kilo* 92: 427–461.

Schliemann, H., and W. Dörpfeld. 1885. *Tiryns*. New York: Charles Scribner's Sons.

Schmidt, E. F. 1953. *Persepolis I: Structures, Reliefs, Inscriptions*. Chicago: University of Chicago Press.

————. 1970. *Persepolis III: The Royal Tombs and Other Monuments*. Chicago: University of Chicago Press.

Schoppa, H. 1933. *Die Darstellung der Perser in der griechischen Kunst bis zum Beginn des Hellenismus*. Heidelberg: Coburg.

Schwabl, H. 1962. "Das Bild der fremden Welt bei den frühen Griechen." In *Grecs et Barbares, Entretiens sur l'antiquité classique: Vandoeuvres-Genève, 4–9 Septembre 1961*, ed. H. Schwabl. Genève: Fondation Hardt 8, 1–36.

Schweitzer, B. 1955. "Zum Krater des Aristonothos," *Mitteilungen des Deutschen Archäologischen Instituts Römische Abteilung* 62: 78–106.

Scott, J. 2010. "On Earth as in Heaven: The Apocalyptic Vision of World Geography from Urzeit to Endzeit According to the Book of Jubliees." In *Geography and Ethnography. Perceptions of the World in Pre-Modern Societies*, ed. K. A. Raaflaub and R. J. A. Talbert. Chichester: Wiley-Blackwell, 182–196.

Scott, M. 2010. *Delphi and Olympia. The Spatial Politics of Panhellenism in the Archaic and Classical Periods*. Cambridge: Cambridge University Press.

Seaford, R. 2004. *Money and the Early Greek Mind: Homer, Philosophy, Tragedy*. Cambridge: Cambridge University Press.

Segal, C. 1986. *Pindar's Mythmaking. The Fourth Pythian Ode*. Princeton: Princeton University Press.

————. 1994. *Singers, Heroes, and Gods in the Odyssey*. Ithaca, N.Y.: Cornell University Press.

Sekerskaya, N. M. 2001. "Nikonion." In *North Pontic Archaeology. Recent Discoveries and Studies*, ed. G. R. Tsetskhladze. Colloquia Pontica 6. Leiden: Brill, 67–91.

Seltman, C. T. 1924. *Athens: Its History and Coinage before the Persian Invasion*. Cambridge: Cambridge University Press.

Serra Ridgway, F. 1990. "Etruscans, Greeks, Carthaginians: The Sanctuary at Pyrgi." In *Greek Colonists and Native Populations*, ed. J.-P. Descoeudres. Oxford: Clarendon Press, 511–530.

Settis, S. 1965. "Fonte letterari per la storia e la topografia di Medma." *Athenaeum* 43: 114–141.

Sewell, W. H. 1999. "The Concepts of Culture." In *Beyond the Cultural Turn: New Directions in the Study of Society and Culture*, ed. V. E. Bonnell and L. Hunt. Berkeley: University of California Press, 35–61.

Shanks, M. 1999. *Art and the Early Greek State: An Interpretative Archaeology*. Cambridge: Cambridge University Press.

Shapiro, H. A. 1983. "Amazons, Thracians, and Scythians." *Greek, Roman and Byzantine Studies* 24: 105–114.

————. 1993. "Hipparchos and the Rhapsodes." In *Cultural Poetics in Archaic Greece: Cult, Performance, Politics*, ed. C. Dougherty and L. Kurke. Cambridge: Cambridge University Press, 92–107.

————. 2000. "Modest Athletes and Liberated Women: Etruscans on Attic Black-Figure Vases." In *Not the Classical Ideal: Athens and the Construction of the Other in Greek Art*, ed. B. Cohen. Leiden: Brill, 313–338.

————. 2007. *The Cambridge Companion to Archaic Greece*. Cambridge: Cambridge University Press.

Shaw, B. D. 1982/1983. "Eaters of Flesh, Drinkers of Milk: The Ancient Mediterranean Ideology of the Pastoral Nomad." *Ancient Society* 13/14: 5–31.

Shaw, M. C. 2000. "The Sculpture from the Sanctuary." In *The Greek Sanctuary, Kommos IV*, ed. J. W. Shaw and M. C. Shaw. Princeton: Princeton University Press, 135–209.

Shepherd, G. 1999. "Fibulae and Females: Intermarriage in the Western Greek Colonies." In *Ancient Greece: West and East*, ed. G. Tsetskhladze. Leiden: Brill, 267–300.

Shimron, B. 1989. *Politics and Belief in Herodotus*. Stuttgart: Franz Steiner Verlag.

Shipley, G. 2005. "Little Boxes on the Hillside: Greek Town Planning, Hippodamos, and Polis Ideology." In *The Imaginary Polis*, ed. H. M. Hansen. Copenhagen: Kgl. danske Videnskabernes Selskab, 335–403.

Short, J. P. 2003. "Everyman's Colonial Library: Imperialism and Working-Class Readers in Leipzig, 1890–1914." *German History* 21, no. 4: 445–475.

Shrimpton, G. S. 1997. *History and Memory in Ancient Greece*. Montreal: McGill-Queen's University Press.

———. 2003. "Herodotus' Intellectual Context—A Review Article." *Ancient History Bulletin* 17: 149–157.

Siapkas, J. 2003. *Heterological Ethnicity: Conceptualizing Identities in Ancient Greece*. Boreas: Uppsala Studies in Ancient Mediterranean & Near Eastern Civilizations 27. Uppsala: Uppsala University.

Sikes, E. E. 1914. *The Anthropology of the Greeks*. London: David Nutt.

Silk, M. 2007. "Pindar's Poetry as Poetry: A Literary Commentary on Olympian 12." In *Pindar's Poetry, Patrons, and Festivals: From Archaic Greece to the Roman Empire*, ed. S. Hornblower and C. Morgan. Oxford: Oxford University Press, 177–199.

Simon, E. 1970. "Aphrodite Pandemos auf attischen Münzen." *Schweizerische Numismatische Rundschau* 49: 15–18.

Sinn, U. 1987. "Aphaia und die 'Aigineten,' zur Rolle des Aphaiaheiligtums im religiösen und gesellschaftlichen Lebe der Insel Aigina." *Ath. Mitt.* 102: 131–167.

Skinner, J. E. 2007. "The Metal Small-Finds at San Salvatore." In *Bova Marina Archaeological Project. Preliminary Report, 2007 Season*, ed. J. Robb. Cambridge: Cambridge University Press, 76–81.

———. 2010. "Fish Heads and Mussel-Shells: Visualizing Greek Identity." In *Intentionale Geschichte: Spinning Time in Ancient Greece*, ed. L. Foxhall and H.-J. Gehrken Luraghi. Stuttgart: Franz Steiner Verlag, 137–160.

Skinner, M. B. 2005. "Nossis Thêlyglôssos: The Private Text and the Public Book." In *Women Poets in Ancient Greece and Rome*, ed. E. Greene. Norman: University of Oklahoma Press, 112–138.

Skinner, Q. 2002a. "Meaning and Understanding in the History of Ideas." In *Visions of Politics*, ed. Q. Skinner. Vol. 1. Cambridge: Cambridge University Press, 57–89.

———. 2002b. *Visions of Politics*. Vol. 1. Cambridge: Cambridge University Press.

Skon-Jedele, N. J. 1994. *"Aigyptiaka": A Catalogue of Egyptian and Egyptianizing Objects Excavated from Greek Archaeological Sites, Ca. 1100–525 B.C., with Historical Commentary*. Ph.D. dissertation, University of Pennsylvania.

Skorupski, J. 1976. *Symbols and Theory. A Philosophical Study of Theories of Religion in Social Anthropology*. Cambridge: Cambridge University Press.

Small, A. 2004. "Some Greek Inscriptions on Native Vases from South East Italy." In *Greek Identity in the Western Mediterranean*. Mnemosyne, supp. 246, ed. K. Lomas. Leiden: Brill, 267–285.

Smelik, K. A. D., and E. A. Hemelrijk. 1984. "Who Knows What Monsters Demented Egypt Worships." *Aufstieg und Niedergang der römischen Welt* 174: 1852–2000.

Smith, A. D. 1991. *National Identity*. London: Penguin.

Smith, W. 1854. *Dictionary of Greek and Roman Geography*. London: Walton & Maberly.

Smith, W. D. 2005. "Colonialism and the Culture of Respectability." In *Germany's Colonial Pasts*, ed. E. Ames, M. Klotz, and L. Wildenthal. Lincoln and London: University of Nebraska Press, 3–20.

Snodgrass, A. M. 1971. *The Dark Age of Greece*. Edinburgh: Edinburgh University Press.

———. 1980. *Archaic Greece. The Age of Experiment*. London: Dent.

———. 1982. "The Historical Significance of Fortification in Archaic Greece." In *La fortification dans l'histoire du monde grec. Actes du colloque international. La fortification et sa place dans l'histoire politique, culturelle et sociale du monde grec, Valbonne, décembre 1982*, ed. P. Leriche and H. Tréziny. Paris: Éditions du centre national de la recherche scientifique, 125–133.

———. 1986. "Interaction by Design: The Greek City State." In *Peer Polity Interaction and Socio-Political Change*, ed. C. Renfrew and J. Cherry. Cambridge: Cambridge University Press, 47–58.

———. 1998. *Homer and the Artists: Text and Picture in Early Greek Art*. Cambridge: Cambridge University Press.

———. 2000. "Prehistoric Italy: A View from the Sea." In *Ancient Italy in its Mediterranean Setting. Studies in Honour of Ellen Macnamara*, ed. D. Ridgway et al. London: Accordia Research Institute, 171–179.

———. 2005. "Sanctuary, Shared Cult and Hellenicity: An Archaeological Angle." *Ancient West and East* 42: 432–437.

Snowden, F. 1970. *Blacks in Antiquity: Ethiopians in the Greco-Roman Experience*. Cambridge, Mass.: Harvard University Press.

———. 1991. *Before Colour Prejudice: The Ancient View of Blacks*. Cambridge, Mass.: Harvard University Press.

———. 1997. "Greeks and Ethiopians." In *Greeks and Barbarians: Essays on the Interactions between Greeks and Non-Greeks in Antiquity and the Consequences for Eurocentrism*, ed. J. E. Coleman and C. A. Walz. Bethesda, Md.: CDL Press, 103–126.

Soden, W. V. 1959. "Die Eremboi der Odyssee und die Irrfahrt des Menelaos." *Wiener Studien* 72: 26–28.

Solovyov, S. L. 1999. *Ancient Berezan: The Architecture, History and Culture of the First Greek Colony in the Northern Black Sea*. Colloquia Pontica 4. Leiden: Brill.

———. 2001. "The Archaeological Excavation on the Berezan Settlement." In *North Pontic Archaeology. Recent Discoveries and Studies*, ed. G. R. Tsetskhladze. Colloquia Pontica 6. Leiden: Brill, 117–143.

———. 2007. "Ancient Greek Pioneering in the Northern Black Sea Coastal Plain the Seventh Century B.C." In *The Black Sea: Past, Present and Future: Proceedings of the International, Interdisciplinary Conference, Istanbul, October 2004*, ed. G. Erkut and S. Mitchell. Ankara: British Institute at Ankara.

Sommer, M. 2005. *Die Phönizier. Handelsherren zwischen Orient und Okzident* Stuttgart: Kröner.

———. 2007. "Networks of Commerce and Knowledge in the Iron Age: The Case of the Phoenicians." *Mediterranean Historical Review* 22, no. 1: 97–111.

Sorabji, R. 2006. *Ancient and Modern Insights about Individuality, Life and Death*. Oxford: Clarendon Press.

Sourvinou-inwood, C. 1974. "The Votum of 477/6 B.C. and the Foundation Legend of Locri Epizephyrii." *Classical Quarterly* 24, no. 2: 186–198.

———. 1978. "Persephone and Aphrodite at Locri: A Model for Personality Definitions in Greek Religion." *JHS* 98: 101–121.

———. 1991. *"Reading" Greek Culture: Texts and Images, Rituals and Myths*. Oxford: Clarendon Press.

———. 1997. "The Hesiodic Myth of the Five Races and the Tolerance of Plurality in Greek Mythology." In *Greek Offerings: Essays on Greek Art in Honour of John Boardman*, ed. O. Palagia. Oxbow Books: Oxford, 1–23.

———. 2002. "Greek Perceptions of Ethnicity and the Ethnicity of the Macedonians." In *Identità e prassi storica nel Mediterraneo Greco*, ed. L. Moscati Castelnuovo. Milano: Edizioni ET, 173–205.

———. 2003. "Herodotus and Others on Pelasgians: Some Perceptions of Ethnicity." In *Herodotus and his World: Essays from a Conference in Memory of George Forrest*, ed. P. Derow and R. Parker. Oxford: Oxford University Press, 103–144.

———. 2005. *Hylas, the Nymphs, Dionysos and Others: Myth, Ritual, Ethnicity*. Stockholm: Paul Åström.

Sparks, K. L. 1998. *Ethnicity and Identity in Ancient Israel: Prolegomena to the Study of Ethnic Sentiments and their Expression in the Hebrew Bible*. Winona Lake, Ind.: Eisenbrauns.

Sparkes, B. 1997. "Some Greek Images of Others." In *The Cultural Life of Images: Visual Representation in Archaeology*, ed. B. Molyneaux. London: Routledge, 130–158.

Spawforth, A. 1985. "The World of the Panhellenion. I. Athens and Eleusis." *Journal of Roman Studies* 75: 78–104.

———. 1986. "The World of the Panhellenion. II. The Dorian Cities." *Journal of Roman Studies* 76: 88–105.

———. 2001. "Shades of Greekness: A Lydian Case Study." In *Ancient Perceptions of Greek Ethnicity*, ed. I. Malkin. Cambridge, Mass.: Harvard University Press, 375–400.

Spears, R. 2002. "Four Degrees of Stereotype Formation: Differentiation by any means Necessary." In Stereotypes as Explanations: The Formation of Meaningful Beliefs about Social Groups, eds. C. McGarty, V.Y. Yzerbyt, and R. Spears. London: Cambridge University Press, 127–156.

Speleers, L. 1948. *Catalogue des intailles et empreintes orientales des Musées Royaux du Cintquantenaire*, Supplément. Brussels: Vromant.

Spivey, N. J. 1997. *Etruscan Art*. London: Thames & Hudson.

———. 2007. "Volcanic Landscape with Craters." *Greece & Rome* 53, no. 1: 229–254.

Stadter, P. 1992. "Herodotus and the Athenian Archê." *Annali della Scuola Normale di Pisa, Classe di Lettere e Filosofia* Ser. 33, 22: 781–809.

———. 2006. "Herodotus and the Cities of Mainland Greece." In *The Cambridge Companion to Herodotus*, ed. C. Dewald and J. Marincola. Cambridge: Cambridge University Press, 242–257.

Stansbury O'Donnell, M. D. 1999. *Pictorial Narrative in Ancient Greek Art*. Cambridge: Cambridge University Press.

Stark, M. T. 1998a. "Technical Choices and Social Boundaries in Material Culture Patterning: An introduction." In *The Archaeology of Social Boundaries*, ed. M. T. Stark. Washington, D.C.: Smithsonian Institution Press, 1–11.

———, ed. 1998b. *The Archaeology of Social Boundaries*. Washington, D.C.: Smithsonian Institution Press.

Steadman-Jones, R. 2007. *Colonialism and Grammatical Representation*. Oxford: Blackwell.

Steier, A. 1927. "Lotos." *RE* 13: 1515–1532.

Stevenson, M. G. 1989. "Sourdoughs and Cheechakos: The Formation of Identity-Signalling Social Groups." *Journal of Anthropological Archaeology* 8: 270–312.

Stewart, A. 1995. "Imagining the Other: Amazons and Ethnicity in Fifth Century Athens." *Poetics Today* 16: 571–597.

Stray, C. 1998. *Classics Transformed: Schools, Universities and Society in England, 1830–1960*. Oxford: Clarendon Press.

Strogatz, S. 2001. "Exploring Complex Networks." *Nature* 410: 269–276.

Stucky, R. A. 1982 "Überlegungen zum "Perserreiter." *Antike Kunst* 25: 97–101.

Studniczka, F. S. 1891. "Ein Denkmal des Sieges bei Marathon." *JDAI* 61: 239–249.

Stuurman, S. 2008. "Herodotus and Sima Qian: History and the Anthropological Turn in Ancient Greece and Han China." *Journal of World History* 19, no. 1: 1–40.

Summerer, L. 2007. "Picturing Persian Victory: The Painted Battle Scene on the Munich Wood." *Ancient Civilizations from Scythia to Siberia* 13: 3–30.

———. 2009. "From Tatarli to Munich: The Recovery of a Painted Wooden tomb Chamber in Phrygia." In *The Achaemenid Impact on Local Populations and Cultures in Anatolia*, ed. I. Delemen, D. Casabonne, Ş. Karagöz, and O. Tekin. Istanbul: Türk Eskicag Bilimleri Enstitusu Yayinlari, 129–156.

Tallis, N. 2005. "Transport and Warfare." In *Forgotten Empire. The World of Ancient Persia*, ed. J. Curtis and N. Tallis. London: British Museum Press, 210–235.

Tarrant, H. 1990. "The Distribution of Early Greek Thinkers and the Question of 'Alien influences.'" In *Greek Colonists and Native Populations*, ed. J.-P. Descoeudres. Oxford: Clarendon Press, 621–628.

Tausend, K. 2006. *Verkehrswege der Argolis: Rekonstruktion und historische Bedeutung* Stuttgart: Franz Steiner Verlag.

Taylor, T. 1994. "Thracians, Scythians, and Dacians." In *The Oxford Illustrated Prehistory of Europe*, ed. B. Cunliffe. Oxford: Oxford University Press, 373–410.

Thomas, E. M. 1969. *The Harmless People*. Harmondsworth: Penguin Books.

Thomas, H., and F. H. Stubbings. 1982. "Lands and Peoples in Homer." In *A Companion to Homer*, ed. A. J. B. Wace and F. H. Stubbings. London: Macmillan, 283–310.

Thomas, N. 1999. "The Case of the Misplaced Ponchos: Speculations Concerning the History of Cloth in Polynesia." *Journal of Material Culture* 4: 5–20.

Thomas, R. F. 1982. *Lands and Peoples in Roman Poetry*. Cambridge: Cambridge Philological Society.

Thomas, R. 1989. *Oral Tradition and Written Record in Classical Athens*. Cambridge: Cambridge University Press.

———. 1992. *Literacy and Orality in Ancient Greece*. Cambridge: Cambridge University Press.

———. 2000. *Herodotus in Context: Ethnography, Science and the Art of Persuasion*. Cambridge: Cambridge University Press.

———. 2001. "Ethnicity, Genealogy, and Hellenism in Herodotus." In *Ancient Perceptions of Greek Ethnicity*, ed. I. Malkin. Cambridge, Mass.: Harvard University Press, 213–233.

Tilley, C. 1994. *A Phenomenology of Landscape: Places, Paths and Monuments.* Oxford: Berg.

Tod, M. N. 1964. *A Selection of Greek Historical Inscriptions.* Oxford: Clarendon Press.

Tomaschek, W. 1888–1889. "Kritik der ältesten Nachrichten über den skythischen Norden." *Sitzungsberichte der Wiener Akademie der Wissenschaften* CXVI–VII: 1–70.

Torelli, M. 1993. "Spina e la sua storia." In Spina. Storia di una città tra Greci ed Etruschi, eds. F. Berti and P.G. Guzzo. Ferrara: Ferrara Arte, 53–69.

———. 1996. "The Encounter with the Etruscans." In *The Greek World: Art and Civilisation in Magna Graecia and Sicily,* ed. G. P. Carratelli. New York: Rizzoli, 567–577.

Tourraix, A., and E. Geny. 2000. *Le mirage grec: l'Orient du mythe et de l'épopée.* Franche-Comté: Presses University.

Tozzi, P. 1963–1967. "Studi su Ecateo di Mileto I–V." *Athenaeum* 41–45: n.p.

Trüdinger, K. 1918. *Studien zur Geschichte der griechisch-römischen Ethnographie.* Basel: E. Birkhäuser.

True, M. 1995. "The Murder of Rhesos on a Chalcidian Neck-Amphora by the Inscription Painter." In *The Ages of Homer. A Tribute to Emily Townsend Vermeule,* ed. J. B. Carter and S. Morris. Austin: University of Texas, 415–429.

Tsetskhladze, G., ed. 1994. *The Archaeology of Greek Colonisation. Essays Dedicated to Sir John Boardman.* Oxford University Committee for Archaeology Monograph 40. Oxford: Committeee for Archaeology.

———. 1998a. "Greek Colonisation of the Black Sea Area: Stages, Models, and Native Population." In *Greek Colonisation of the Black Sea Area. Historical Interpretation of Archaeology,* ed. G. Tsetskhladze. Stuttgart: Franz Steiner, 9–68.

———, ed. 1998b. *Greek Colonisation of the Black Sea Area. Historical Interpretation of Archaeology.* Historia Einzelschriften 121. Stuttgart: Franz Steiner Verlag.

———. 1999. "Ancient Greeks West and East." *Mnemosyne* supp. 196.

———. 2001. "Introduction. North Pontic Classical Archaeology: An Historical Essay." In *North Pontic Archaeology. Recent Discoveries and Studies,* ed. G. R. Tsetskhladze. Colloquia Pontica 6. Leiden: Brill, Ix–1.

———. 2002. "Ionians Abroad." In *Greek Settlements in the Eastern Mediterranean and the Black Sea,* ed. G. R. Tsetskhladze and A. M. Snodgrass. BAR International Series 1062. Oxford: Oxbow, 81–96.

———. 2004. "On the Earliest Greek Colonial Architecture in the Pontus." In *Pontus and the Outside World: Studies in Black Sea History, Historiography, and Archaeology,* ed. C. J. Tuplin. Leiden: Brill, 225–279.

———. 2006. *Greek Colonisation: An Account of Greek Colonies and Other Settlements Overseas.* Vol. 1. Leiden/Boston: Brill.

Tsetskhladze, G. R., and A. M. Snodgrass, eds. 2002. *Greek Settlements in the Eastern Mediterranean and the Black Sea.* Oxford: Oxbow.

Tsetskhladze, G., S. L. Solovyov, and J. Boardman, eds. 1999. *Ancient Berezan. The Architecture, History and Culture of the First Greek Colony in the Northern Black Sea.* Colloquia Pontica 4. Leiden: Brill.

Tsiafakis, D. 2000. "The Allure and Repulsion of the Thracians in the Art of Classical Athens." In *Not the Classical Ideal: Athens and the Construction of the Other in Greek Art,* ed. B. Cohen. Leiden: Brill, 364–390.

Tunkina, I. V. 2003. "The Formation of a Russian Science of Classical Antiquities of Southern Russia in the 18th and 19th Century." In *The Cauldron of Ariantas.*

Studies Presented to A. N. Ščeglov on the Occasion of His 70th Birthday, ed. P. Guldager Bilde et al. Aarhus: Aarhus University Press, 303–365.

———. 2007. "New Data on the Panhellenic Achilles' Sanctuary on the Tendra Spit Excavations of 1824." In *Une koinè pontique: cités grecques, sociétés indigènes et empires mondiaux sur le littoral nord de la mer Noire (VIIe s. a.C. –IIIe s. p.C.)*, ed. A. Bresson et al. Bordeaux: Ausonius, 225–241.

Tuplin, C. J. 1999. "'Greek Racism?' Observations on the Character and Limits of Greek Ethnic Prejudice." In *Ancient Greeks West & East*, ed. G. R. Tsetskhladze. Leiden: Brill, 47–77.

———, ed. 2004. *Pontus and the Outside World: Studies in Black Sea History, Historiography, and Archaeology*. Leiden: Brill.

———, ed. 2007a. *Persian Responses: Political and Cultural Interaction Withinwthe Achaemenid Empire*. Swansea: Classical Press of Wales.

———, 2007b. "Racism in Classical Antiquity? Three Opinions." *Ancient West and East* 6: 327–338.

———. 2010. "The Historical Significance of the Tatarli tomb-Chamber." In *The Return of the Colours*, ed. L. Summerer and A. Von Kienlin. Istanbul: Yapi Kredi Yayinlari, 186–195.

———. 2011. "The Limits of Persianization: Some Reflections on Cultural Links in the Persian Empire." In *Cultural Identity in the Ancient Mediterranean*, ed. E. S. Gruen. Los Angeles: Getty Research Institute, 150–182.

Turnbull, C. M. 1972. *The Mountain People*. New York: Simon & Schuster.

Tylor, E. B. 1891. *Primitive Culture: Researches into the Development of Mythology, Philosophy, Religion, Language, Art, and Custom*. London: John Murray.

Tyrell, W. B. 1980. "A View of the Amazons." *Classical Bulletin* 57: 1–5.

———. 1984. *Amazons: A Study of Athenian Myth-Making*. Baltimore: Johns Hopkins University Press.

Tythacott, L. 2003. *Surrealism and the Exotic*. London: Routledge.

Ustinova, Y. 2005. "Snake-Limbed and Tendril-Limbed Goddesses in the Art and Mythology of the Mediterranean and Black Sea." In *Scythians and Greeks: Cultural Interactions in Scythia, Athens and the Early Roman Empire Sixth Century BC—first century AD*, ed. D. Braund. Exeter: University of Exeter Press, 64–79.

Vachtina, M. J. 2003. "Archaic Buildings of Porthmion." In *The Cauldron of Ariantas. Studies Presented to A. N. Ščeglov on the Occasion of his 70th Birthday*, ed. P. Guldager Bilde et al. Aarhus: Aarhus University Press, 37–55.

Vallet, G. 1958. *Rhégion et Zancle. Histoire, commerce et civilisation des cités chalcidiennes du détroit de Messine*. Paris: de Boccard.

Van Berchem, F. 1967. "Sanctuaires d'Hercule Melqart." *Syria* 44: 73–109, 307–326.

Van Compernolle, R. 1992. "Lo stanziamento di apoikoi greci presso Capo Zefirio (Capo Bruzzano) nell'ultimo terzo dell'VIII secolo a.C." *Annpisa* 22: 761–780.

Van Der Eijk, P. J., ed. 2005. *Hippocrates in Context: Papers Read at the XIth International Hippocrates Colloquim, University of Newcastle upon Tyne, August 27–31, 2002*. Leiden: Brill.

Van Dommelen, P. 1995. "Colonial Constructs: Colonialism and Archaeology in the Mediterranean." *World Archaeology* 28, no. 3: 305–323.

———. 2002. "Ambiguous Matters: Colonialism and Local Identities in Punic Sardinia." In *The Archaeology of Colonialism*, ed. C. L. Lyons and J. K. Papadopoulos. Los Angeles: Getty Research Institute, 121–147.

————. 2005. "Urban Foundations? Colonial Settlement and Urbanization in the Western Mediterranean." In *Mediterranean Urbanization 800–600 BC*, ed. R. Osborne and B. Cunliffe. Oxford: Oxford University Press, 143–168.

Van Dommelen, P., and C. G. Bellard, eds. 2008. *Rural Landscapes of the Punic World.* Monographs in Mediterranean Archaeology 11. London: Equinox.

Van Dommelen, P., and A. B. Knapp. 2011a. "Material Connections: Mobility, Materiality and Mediterranean Identities." In *Material Connections in the Ancient Mediterranean: Mobility, Materiality and Identity.* London and New York: Routledge, 1–18.

————, eds. 2011b. *Material Connections in the Ancient Mediterranean. Mobility, Materiality and Identity.* London and New York: Routledge.

Van Straten, F. 2000. "Votives and Votaries in the Greek Sanctuaries." In *Greek Religion*, ed. R. Buxton. Oxford: Oxford University Press, 191–227.

Vanchugov, V. P. 2001. "The Demographic Situation in the North-Western Part of the Black Sea Region in the 9th–7th Centuries BC." In *North Pontic Archaeology: Recent Discoveries and Studies*, ed. G. R. Tsetskhladze. Colloquia Pontica 6. Leiden: Brill, 45–53.

Vannicelli, P. 1989. "Έλληνες in Omero." *RFIC* 117: 34–48.

————. 1993. *Erodoto e la Storia dell' alto e Medico Arcaismo.* Roma: Gruppo Editoriale Internazionale.

Vasunia, P. 2001. *The Gift of the Nile: Hellenizing Egypt from Aeschylus to Alexander.* Berkeley: University of California Press.

Vercoutter, J., J. Leclant, F. M. Snowden, and J. Desanges. 1991. *L'image du noir dans l'art occidental. i, des pharaons à la chute de l'empire romain.* Paris: Gallimard.

Vermeule, E. T. 1971. "Kadmos and the Dragon." In *Studies Presented to George M. A. Hanfmann*, ed. D. G. Mitten, J. G. Pedley, and J. A. Scott. Mainz am Rhein: Zabern, 177–188.

Vernant, J. P. 1982. *The Origins of Greek Thought.* London: Methuen.

Versnel, H. 1990. "What's Sauce for the Goose is Sauce for the Gander: Myth and Ritual, Old and New." In *Approaches to Greek Myth*, ed. L. Edmunds. Baltimore: Johns Hopkins University Press, 23–90.

Vidal-Naquet, P. 1996. "Land and Sacrifice in the Odyssey: A Study of Religious and Mythical Meanings." In *Reading the Odyssey: Selected Interpretative Essays*, ed. S. L. Schein. Princeton: Princeton University Press, 33–55.

Vidal-Naquet, P., and A. Szegedy-Maszak. 1998. *The Black Hunter: Forms of Thought and Forms of Society in the Greek World.* Trans. Andrew Szegedy-Maszak. Baltimore: Johns Hopkins University Press.

Villing, A., and U. Schlotzhauer. 2006a. "Naukratis and the Eastern Mediterranean: Past, Present and Future." In *Naukratis: Greek Diversity in Egypt. Studies on East Greek Pottery and Exchange in the Eastern Mediterranean*, ed. A. Villing and U. Schlotzhauer. London: British Museum Press, 1–22.

————, eds. 2006b. *Naukratis: Greek Diversity in Egypt. Studies on East Greek Pottery and Exchange in the Eastern Mediterranean.* London: British Museum Press.

Vinogradov, J. G. 1997. "Die Stele des Leoxos, Molpagores´ Sohn, aus Olbia und die Skythisch-Griechischen Beziehungen im frühen 5. Jh. v.Chr." In *Pontische Studien. Kleine Schriften zur Geschichte und Epigraphik des Schwarzmeerraumes*, ed. J. G. Vinogradov and H. Heinen. Mainz: Philipp von Zabern, 230–241.

Vinogradov, J. G., and S. D. Kryžickij. 1995. "Olbia." In *Eine Altergriechische Stadt im Nordwestlichen Schwarzmeeraum.* Leiden: Brill.

Visonà, P. 2009. "University of Colorado/University of Kentucky Excavations at Monte Palazzi, Passo Croceferrata Grotteria, Calabria: The 2005, 2007, and 2008 Field Seasons." *Journal of Fasti Online*. as found at: Www.Fastionline.Org/Php/ Download.Php?File=FOLDER-It-2010-188.Pdf (accessed on 7/6/2010).

———. 2010. "Controlling the *Chora*. Archaeological investigations at Monte Palazzi, a Mountain Fort of Locri Epizephyrii." In *Grecs et indigènes de la Catalogne à la mer Noire. Actes des rencontres Ramses 2006–2008*. Aix-en-Provence: Centre Camille Jullian, 595–601.

Visser, E. 1997. *Homers Katalog der Schiffe*. Stuttgart: B. G. Teubner.

Vivante, P. 1982. *The Epithets of Homer. A Study in Poetic Values*. Newhaven: Yale University Press.

Vlassopoulos, K. 2007a. "Beyond and Below the Polis: Networks, Associations and the Writing of Greek History." *Mediterranean Historical Review* 22: 11–22.

———. 2007b. *Unthinking the Greek Polis: Ancient History beyond Eurocentrism*. Cambridge: Cambridge University Press.

Von Bothmer, D. 1957. *Amazons in Greek Art*. Oxford: Clarendon Press.

Von Roques de Maumont, H. 1958. *Antike Reiterstandbilder*. Berlin: W. de Gruyter.

Von Sydow, E. 1930. "Masques-Janus du Cross-River (Cameroun)." Documents 6: 321–328.

Von Wilamowitz-Moellendorf, U. 1923. "Staat und Gesellschaft der Griechen." In *Staat und Gesellschaft der Griechen und Römer bis Ausgang des Mittelalters*, ed. U. Von Wilamowitz-Moellendorf, J. Kroymayer, and A. Heisenberg. 2nd ed. Leipzig and Berlin: B. G. Teubner, 1–214.

Vos, M. F. 1963. *Scythian Archers in Archaic Attic Vase-Painting*. Groningen: Wolters.

Wade-Gery, H. T. 1951. "Miltiades." *JHS* 71: 121–121.

Walbank, F. W. 1951. "The Problem of Greek Nationality." *Phoenix* 5: 41–60.

Wallace-Hadrill, A. 2008. *Rome's Cultural Revolution*. Cambridge: Cambridge University Press.

Walter-Karydi, E. 1973. *Samische Gefässe des 6. Jahrhunderts v. Chr.* Samos VI.1. Bonn: In Kommission bei Rudolf Habelt.

Wathelet, P. 1974. "Les Phéniciens dans la composition formulaire de l'épopée grecque." *Revue Belge de philologie et d'histoire* 52: 5–14.

———. 1983. "Les Phéniciens et la tradition homérique." In *Studia Phoenicia*, ed. E. Lipiński, E. Gubel, and B. Servais-Soyez. Leuven: Peeters, 235–243.

Watson, J. 2011. "Rethinking the Sanctuary of Aphaia." In *Aegina: Contexts for Choral Lyric Poetry. Myth, History, and Identity in the Fifth Century BC*, ed. D. Fearn. Oxford: Oxford University Press, 79–113.

Watts, D. J. 1999. *Small Worlds: The Dynamics of Networks between Order and Randomness*. Princeton, N.J.: Princeton University Press.

Watts, D. J., and S. Strogatz. 1998. "Collective Dynamics of 'Small-World' Networks." *Nature* 3934 (June): 440–442.

Webb, V. 1978. *Archaic Greek Faience: Miniature Scent Bottles and Related Objects from East Greece, 650–500 B.C.* Warminster: Aris & Phillips.

Weigui, F. 2001. "Yi, Yang, Xi, Wai and Other Terms: The Transition from 'Barbarian' to 'Foreigner' in Nineteenth-Century China." In *New Terms for New Ideas: Western Knowledge and Lexical Change in Late Imperial China*, ed. M. Lackner, I. Amelung, and J. Kurtz. Leiden: Brill, 95–124.

Welwei, K. W. 1974. *Unfreie in Antiken Kriegsdienst.* Wiesbaden: Steiner.

West, M. L. 1965. "Alcmanica." *Classical Quarterly* 15: 188–202.

———. 1971a. *Early Greek Philosophy and the Orient.* Oxford: Clarendon Press.

———. 1971b. "Stesichorus," *Classical Quarterly* 21: 302–314.

———. 1985. *The Hesiodic Catalogue of Women: Its Nature, Structure and Origins.* Oxford: Clarendon Press.

———. 1993. *Greek Lyric Poetry: The Poems and Fragments of the Greek Iambic, Elegiac, and Melic Poets Excluding Pindar and Bacchylides Down to 450 BC.* Oxford: Oxford University Press.

———. 1997. *The East Face of Helicon: West Asiatic Elements in Greek Poetry and Myth.* Oxford: Oxford University Press.

West, S. 1988. "Books I–IV." In *A Commentary on Homer's Odyssey.* Vol. 1, *Introduction and Books I–VIII,* ed. A. Heubeck, S. West, and J. B. Hainsworth. Oxford: Clarendon Press, 51–245.

———. 1991. "Herodotus' Portrait of Hecataeus." *JHS* 111: 144–160.

———. 1997. "Alternative Arabia: A Note on 'Prometheus Vinctus.'" *JHS* 48: 374–379.

———. 2002. "Scythians." In *Brill's Companion to Herodotus,* ed. E. Bakker, I. De Jong, and H. Van Wees. Leiden: Brill, 437–457.

———. 2004. "Herodotus on Aristeas." In *Pontus and the Outside World: Studies in Black Sea History, Historiography, and Archaeology,* ed. C. J. Tuplin. Leiden: Brill, 43–67.

———. 2007. "Herodotus and Olbia." In *Classical Olbia and the Scythian World: From the Sixth Century BC to the Second Century AD,* ed. D. Braund and S. D. Kryzhitskiy. Proceedings of the British Academy 142. Oxford: Oxford University Press, 79–92.

White, D. 1984. The Extramural Sanctuary of Demeter and Persephone at Cyrene. Final Reports 1. Background and Introduction to the Excavations. Philadelphia: University of Pennsylvaniá, Tripoli: Libyan Department of Antiquities.

White, R. 1991. *The Middle Ground: Indians, Empires, and Republics in the Great Lakes Region, 1650–1815.* Cambridge: Cambridge University Press.

Whitehouse, D. 1984. "Immigrant Communities in the Classical Polis: Some Principles For a Synoptic Treatment." *L'Antiquité classique* 53: 47–59.

Whitehouse, R. D., and J. B. Wilkins. 1989. "Greeks and Natives in South-East Italy: Approaches to the Archaeological Evidence." In *Comparative Studies in Archaeology,* ed. T. C. Champion. *Centre and Periphery.* London: Unwin Hyman, 102–126.

Will, E. 1955. "Réflexions et hypotheses sur les origins du monnayage." *Revue numismatique* 7: 9–10.

———. 1973. "La grande Grèce, mileau d'échanges. reflexions méthodologiques." *Economia e Società nella Magna Grecia:* 21–67.

Willcock, J.S.M. 1995. Victory Odes. Pindar. Cambridge: Cambridge University Press.

Willetts, R. F. 1955. *Aristocratic Society in Ancient Crete.* London: Routledge & Kegan Paul.

Willi, A. 2008. *Sikelismos. Sprache, Litteratur und Gesellschaft im griechischen Sizilien* 8.-5. Jh. v. Chr. Basel: Schwabe.

Williams, D., and A. Villing. 2006. "Carian Mercenaries at Naukratis?" In *Naukratis: Greek Diversity in Egypt: Studies on East Greek Pottery and Exchange in the Eastern Mediterranean,* ed. A. Villing and U. Schlotzhauer. London: British Museum Press, 47–48.

Williamson, G. 2005. "Aspects of Identity." In *Coinage and Identity in the Roman Provinces,* ed. C. Howgego, V. Heuchert, and A. Burnett. Oxford: Oxford University Press, 19–29.

Willis, P., and M. Trondman. 2000. "Manifesto for Ethnography." *Ethnography* (July 2000): 5–16.

Wilson, P. 2003. "The Sound of Cultural Conflict: Kritias and the Culture of Mousikê in Athens." In *The Cultures within Greek Culture*, ed. C. Dougherty and L. Kurke. Contact, Conflict, Collaboration. Cambridge: Cambridge University Press, 181–206.

Winter, F. 1893. "Archaische Reiterbilder von der Akropolis." *JDAI* 8: 135–172.

Winter, I. J. 1995. "Homer's Phoenicians: History, Ethnography, or Literary Trope?" In *The Ages of Homer: A Tribute to Emily Townsend Vermeule*, ed. J. P. Carter and S. P. Morris. Austin: University of Texas Press, 247–271.

Wolf, E. R. 1982. *Europe and the People without History*. Berkeley and Los Angeles: University of California Press.

Woodbury, L. E. 1980. "Strepsiades' Understanding: Five Notes on the 'Clouds.'" *Phoenix* 342: 108–127.

Woodhead, A. G. 1962. *The Greeks in the West*. London: Thames & Hudson.

Woolf, G. 1994. "Power and the Spread of Writing in the West." In *Literacy and Power in the Ancient World*, ed. A. Bowman and G. Woolf. Cambridge: Cambridge University Press, 84–98.

———. 2009. "Cruptorix and His Kind: Talking Ethnicity on the Middle Ground." In *Ethnic Constructs in Antiquity: The Role of Power and Tradition*, ed. T. Derks and N. Roymans. Amsterdam: Amsterdam University Press, 207–218.

———. 2010. *Tales of the Barbarians: Ethnography and Empire in the Roman West*. Chichester, U.K.: Wiley-Blackwell.

Xenakis, D., and D. Chryssochou. 2001. *The Emerging Euro-Mediterranean System*. Manchester: Manchester University Press.

Yoon, D. 2006. "2006 Field Survey." In *Bova Marina Archaeological Project: Preliminary Report 2006 Season*, ed. J. Robb. Cambridge: Cambridge University Press, 9–12.

Young, R. J. C. 1995. *Colonial Desire: Hybridity in Theory, Culture and Race*. London: Routledge.

———. 2001. *Postcolonialism. A Historical Introduction*. Oxford: Oxford University Press.

Zaccagnini, C. 1982. "The Enemy in Neo-Assyrian Royal Inscriptions: The Ethnographic Description." In *Mesopotamien und seine Nachbarn*, eds. H. Nissen and J. Renger. Berlin: D. Reimer, 409–424.

Zacharia, K. 2008. "Herodotus' Four Markers of Greek Identity." In *Hellenisms: Culture, Identity, and Ethnicity from Antiquity to Modernity*, ed. K. Zacharia. Aldershot, U.K.: Ashgate, 21–36.

Zaikov, A. V. 2004. "Alcman and the Image of the Scythian Steed." In *Pontus and the Outside World: Studies in Black Sea History, Historiography, and Archaeology*, ed. C. J. Tuplin. Leiden: Brill, 69–85.

Zambrini, A. 2006. "Aspetti dell'etnografia in Jacoby." In *Aspetti dell'opera di Felix Jacoby. Seminari Arnaldo Momigliano, Scuola Normale Superiore Pisa 18–19 Dicembre 2002, Pisa*, ed. C. Ampolo. Pisa: Ed. della Normale, 189–201.

Zantop, S. 1997. *Colonial Fantasies: Conquest, Family, and Nation in Precolonial Germany, 1770–1870*. Durham, N.C., and London: Duke University Press.

Page numbers in **bold** type indicate illustrations.

barbarian, barbarians, 3n1, 4, 8, 249
    encounter with, 20, 234n3. *See also*
        Persian Wars
    speech, 119. *See also barbaraphonous*
    stereotypes, 10, 50, 54, 89, 115, 173,
        239, 248
barbitos (stringed instrument), 91
Barth, Fredrik, 24n93
Basilicata, 177, 189n162
Bataille, Georges, 42, 43, 247
Battos, 136n121, 138
Behistun. *See* Bisitun
Beikush, 166
Bellerophon, 79
Berezan, **154**, 155. *See also* Northern
        Pontic Region
    economy and trade, 155–158
    interactions with local populations,
        155–157, 161
    landscape setting, 155
    settlement of, 155n110, 157, 158, 161
    settlers move to Olbia, 158
Berlin Society for Anthropology,
        Ethnology and Prehistory
        (BGAEU), 37
Bes, 99
Bhabha, Homi K., 28–29, 116
Bickerman, Elias, 125–126, 127
bilingualism, 151, 152n4, 155
Bisitun (Bhagasthana), 12n41
Black Sea, 135, 162, 165, 166, 174
Boardman, John, 103, 104–105
Boas, Franz, 40
Boeotia, Boeotians, 87, 114, 120, 253
bone plaques, 169
Borysthenes, river (Dnieper), 164, 171
Borysthenes, 164, 175. *See also* Olbia
Borysthenites, 164
bothroi (pits), 202
Bousiris, 103–104, **105**
Bowra, Cecil M., 65, 66, 67, 71
Braudel, Fernand, 48, 139
Braund, David, 165
Brettia, 176n102
Bug, river (Hypanis), 153, 155, 157
Burkert, Walter, 59n3, 102, 147n168
Busiris. *See* Bousiris

cabotage, 157
Cadmus, 67n44, 87
Calabria, Southern, 47, 175–211, 247
    evidence for contact and interaction
        between Iron Age populations,
        182–185
    evidence for knowledge of foreign
        peoples, 193nn177–178, 193–196
    the historical sources and their
        interpretation, 186–189
    networks of trade/association,
        177–178, 180–181
    reputation in antiquity, 185–186
    settlement history, 181–183, 186,
        188–189
    topography, 178, **179**, 180
    tracing interconnections in myth and
        ritual, 189–192
    the view from Olympia, 192–193
Callippidae (Hellenic-Scyths), 166
Callistratus, 175
Cambridge Ritual School, 40
Cambles (Lydian king), 95
Cambyses, madness of, 16
Cameroon, masks from, 43
Campania, 8, 9, 177, 197n192
Campi di Bova, 204
Canale-Janchina, 182, 184
Candaules (Lydian king), 90, 92
Caria, Carians, 54, 120, 249
Carthage, Carthaginians, 56, 148n170
"Casa Marafioti" (temple), 199
Castellace, 182
catalogues. *See also* genealogy *and* lists
    competing versions, 122
    in epic, 121–123
    as performance ethnography, 123
    politics of, 124
categories, essentialist, 19
Cavafy, Constantine, P., 26
centaurs, 81
Cerveteri, 143
Charon of Lampsacus, 129, 130, 131
charter myths, 124, 130, 138–139, 166,
    172. *See also* myth
Chersonesus, colonization of, 84
Chios, 93, 127, 157, 183, 193, 242

Cyclopes, 55, 65, 66. *See also*
    Polyphemos
    as thinking about culture, 61, 143–**144**
    and Early Iron Age, 61
    ethnographic description in Homer,
        60
    skilled craftsmen, 62
Cyllene, 92
cylinder seals, Achaemenid Persian, 13
Cyme, 251
Cyprus, 86, 87, 95, 97n180, 99
Cyrene, 18, 95, 105–106, 130, 136, 137, 138
    coin depicting eponymous nymph
        tending silphium, **137**
    sanctuary of Demeter and Perse-
        phone at, 209
Cyrus the Great, 94
Cyzicus, 107, 135

Daidalos, 87
Darius, 15–16
Davidson, James, 21
Delos, 229–230
Delphi, 47, 98, 128, 192, 211, 214, **220**,
        226, 253
    and colonization, 221–222
    foreign dedications at, 219–221
    oracle at, 211 (*see also* oracles, Pytho
        and Pythia)
Delphos, 98, 230
Dench, Emma, 13–14
de Polignac, François, 190, 192, 211
diaitetes (judge), 218
dialects, 151
Diels, Hermann, 36
difference
    between Greek and non-Greek, 19,
        26, 27
    between Greeks, 27, 134–140,
        199–204
    conceptualized via genealogy, 125,
        186–187, 241
    explained via epic paradigms, 52
    intellectual engagement with, 112, 134,
        151, 175, 192, 202–204, 222, 234
digressions, 130–131, 177, 241, 244n38
Dio Chrysostom, 175

Dionysius, 102, 103, 170, 202
Dionysius of Miletus, 32–33, 34
Dionysius of Syracuse, 186
Dionysius II of Syracuse, 203
Dioscuri, 200
disciplines, formation of, 36–38, 41–42
    permeability of boundaries, 43
discourse, 8, 175n101
    colonialist, 50, 116. *See also*
        colonialism
    different modes of, 32, 243, 244
    elite, 17, 146
    ethnographic, 8, 10, 46, 49, 233, 235,
        236, 236, 244n42, 252, 254, 255
    identity, 17, 27, 28–29, 44, 45, 107, 114,
        118, 122, 127, 151–152 172, 184, 186,
        193, 172, 215, 233, 248, 253, 256
    of professionalism, 39
    scientific, 17, 241
    of wonder, 38
Documents, 42–43
Dodona, 229
dolphins, 168, 169n75
    as coinage, 168
Dorian, Dorians, 95, 200, 249
    architectural styles, 199 (*see also*
        architecture)
    dress, 147
Dougherty, Carol, 52, 61, 142
doves, 203
Ducetius (Sicel leader), 186
dugouts. *See* pit-dwellings *and* Northern
    Pontic Region

Egypt, Egyptians, 10, 12, 16, 46, 47, 86,
        95, 96, 99–106, 142, 213, 220, 238
    accent parodied, 105
    early interest in, 99–100, 240
    knowledge of arrived at through
        trade, 99–100, 157
    as skilled doctors, 101
    scientific scrutiny of, 101
    See also Bousiris
Eleusis, 143
Eos (Dawn), 98, 167
Epeios (architect of Trojan horse), 190
Ephesus, 157, 225n296

epinicia (praise poetry), 16, 132–134
    links with Greek coinage, 136–139
    purpose of, 132
    role of floral and vegetal imagery in,
        137–138
Epirus, 120
epithets, 92, 97, 106, 112–115, 122, 124
    as descriptive labels, 112
    in Homeric *Catalogue of Ships*, 112–115
    metrical considerations, 113–114
    orality of, 112–115
    as stereotypes, 115
Erechtheion, 77
Eridanus, 63
Erskine, Andrew, 125–126, 127
ethnicity, 27, 125 (*see also* identity)
    essentialized conceptions of, 24
    and material culture, 161n36, 162n39,
        182–183, 198–199, 200, 208–209
Ethiopia, Ethiopians, 15, 85, 95–99, 123,
        133, 167, 184
    on coins, 98, 230
    and Delphi, 230
    earliest representations of, 97
    led by Memmon, 98, 104, 105
    liminality of, 95
    physiognomy of, 96
    piety of, 230
    in vase-painting, 96–97, 98, 142, 193
ethnic portraits, 120
ethnics (on coins), 134–135
ethnics, collective, 189
ethnocentricism, 46, 50, 72, 119, 239
ethnogenesis, Greek, 3n1, 4, 18, 44
    attempts to pinpoint, 19–20, 250
ethnography, ancient
    conventional view of, 3, 6, 7, 52, 140,
        234, 255, 256
    idealized notions of, 3n2, 11, 17, 117,
        120, 131, 140, 234, 235, 254
    Jacoby's definition of, 5n11, 18, 19, 32,
        34, 256
    origins of, 3, 4, 43–44, 46, 233
    other views of, 8n28
    in painted marble, 76, **77**, 78
    and power relations, 46–47, 142, 235,
        248, 254 (*see also* power)

problems arising from a restricted
    definition of, 5, 7, 246
redefining of, 5–8, 14–19, 42–44, 49,
    117, 131
relationship to *historiê*, 5, 131, 243–247
relationship to identity, 17–18, 24, 25,
    28, 29, 44, 47, 49, 52, 131, 234, 246
relationship to material and
    sub-literary evidence, 4, 8, 9, 10,
    14–19, 49, 131, 141
seen as a specifically Greek invention,
    6
of speech, 54, 239
textualization of, 233
unwritten, 57, 71–72, 140–145
    See also interest, ethnographic
Ethnography, journal of, 43
ethnography, modern
    as practice, 5, 6
    current approaches to, 6, 7
    first usage, 5n10
    influence on Jacoby, 36–41
    stereotypical view of, 5
ethnological satire, 67
Etruria, Etruscans, 8, 9, 126, 143, 193,
    202, 224–226
etymology, 129, 187
Euboea, 99, 125, 143, 144, 177, 183n133,
    184, 229
Eumaios, 88
Eurocentricism, 35, 243
Eurybates (a companion of Odysseus),
    96
Eurytanians, 7, 230n314
Euxine, 133
evolution, 4
    of historiography, 4, 32, 34, 44, 148,
        241
    theories of, 35
    towards enlightenment, 237
exchange, 4, 47, 48, 50, 57, 87, 139, 146,
    147, 169, 170, 183, 184, 194, 211

Felsina (Etruria), 225
fictive kinship, 125. See also kinship
figured pottery, 44, 48, 160
fish heads, 135

Fornara, Charles, 244
Fragmenta Historicorum Graecorum, 31
    See also Müller, Carl and Theodore
Fragmentary Greek Historians,
    alternative formats of, 33
    discrete reordering of, 31
    projected structure of, 31
        See also historiê, Historiography,
        Great *and* Jacoby
fragmentation, Hellenic, 28, 254
fragments, 14, 47, 71, 79, 106, 115, 122,
    237, 238
    classification of, 5
Francavilla Marittima, 190
François Vase, 72
frankincense, 147
Freud, Sigmund, his influence on
    Lévi-Strauss, 45

Gaia (Earth), 211
Gandhara, 12
Gelonus (eponym of Scythian Geloni), 171
genealogy, 30, 31, 122. *See also* catalogues
    and lists
    Hellenic, 26n101, 27, 124–125, 214,
        218–219. *See also* Amphiktyonic
    heroic, 122
    a heuristic tool, 124
    a means of conceptualizing difference,
        125, 241 (*see also Nostoi and* Nostos
        genealogical ethnography)
    Italic, 186–187
    objects of consumption, 122
    Scythian, 170–171
genre, 3
    attempts to define, 5n11 (ethnography)
    canonization of, 254
    invention of, 4 (*see also* Great
        Historiography)
Germany, Germans
    enthusiasm for foreign cultures, 37–38
    notions of race and identity, 35–36
    philhellenism of, 35n131
    processes of disciplinary formation
        within, 37, 38
        See also colonialism, imperialism
        and museums

Gernet, Louis, 45
Geryon (giant), 171, 187
Gikandi, Simon, 248
gods. *See individual gods*
Golden Age primitivism, 56, 61, 72
Goldhill, Simon, 236, 249
Golden Bough, The, 40
gorytus (bow case-quiver), 72, 78, 82,
    172, 175n100
Greek identity, 3
    approaches to, 19–30
    assumptions regarding, 18, 246
    in eastern Mediterranean and Black
        Sea, 25
    emergence of, 3, 4, 19–20, 26, 50, 125,
        211–217, 234
    as monolithic, 25, 41, 50, 133
    plurality of, 24, 25, 44, 134, 151, 152
    in western Mediterranean, 25
    role in archaeological studies, 23
griffins, 65n34, 67, 159n25
Gruen, Erich, 21–22,
Gunter, Ann, 100, 213
Gyges (Lydian king), 90, 91, 92

Hall, Edith, 17, 21, 26n102, 50, 53–54, 55,
    115, 117, 120, 239, 243
Hall, Jonathan, 26, 125, 214, 218, 243
Hall, Stuart, 23
    on diasporic experience and cultural
        hybridity, 252
    on identities, 23, 131
Harrison, Thomas, 22n81, 178n108,
    218n263, 248
Hartog, François, 21, 51–52, 53, 60, 142,
    164, 244
Hebrus, river, 83
Hecataeus of Miletus, 32, 34, 99, 107,
    128, 129, 165, 166, 167, 240, 242,
    247
Hedreen, Guy, 167
Heidelberg Painter, 104, **105**
Heinen, Heinz, 251
Hellanicus, 107, 127, 130, 131, 187, 243
Hellanodikai ("Judges of the Hellenes"),
    218
Hellen, 214

role in Delian and Delphic propaganda, 63–64, 229
as steppe nomads, 63
Hyperoche (Hyperborean woman), 229

Iapygians, 176
Ibycus of Rhegion, 132
ideology, royal, 10, (Egypt), 11 (Assyrian), 12 (Persian)
  and power, 46, 142
identity, identities
  "aggregative", 21, 29, 251
  based on shared knowledge, 120
  conceived as bounded and homogenous, 4n6, 25, 50, 133, 151, 161, 250, 256
  construction of, 17, 49, 120, 122, 131, 139, 148, 211, 251
  cultural, 24, 26, 27, 28, 131
  diasporic. See Hall, Stuart
  ethnic, 24, 161, 162
  and invented tradition, 131
  and lifestyle, 55
  and material culture, 161n36, 198–199n196
  modern preoccupation with, 21
  oppositional, 3, 133, 151
Iliad. See Homer
Ik (Ugandan tribe), 7
imagined centre, 211, 212, 216, 253. See also Delphi, Olympia, Panhellenic festivals and sanctuaries
"imagined communities", 252
imaginaire, 52, 74, 78, 111, 114, 140, 148, 255
Immerwahr, Henry R., 246
imperialism
  and ethnography/anthropology, 5, 36
  and Herodotus, 248
  modern, 5, 36, 243, 248
  Persian, 4, 12, 168, 245
information, flow of, 47, 56, 78, 139
interest, ethnographic
  all-pervasive, 8, 134, 235, 243, 245
  development of, 3, 4, 50, 73
  and epithets, 117
  as exhibited by non-Greeks, 8–14, 184

and Greek coins, 134–140, 196–198
Greek, 8, 9, 10, 13, 28, 78, 148, 246
in origins, 131
relationship to Greek identity and culture, 14, 134, 139–140, 148, 251, 256
  See also ethnography, ancient and ethnography, modern
intermarriage, 62, 106n228, 152n4, 155, 161, 168, 174, 213, 224
inventories, 223
Iolkos, 124
Ionia, Ionians, 33, 95, 135, 157, 158, 234, 237, 239, 250
  dress, 147
  inquiry, 11, 66, 99, 101, 109, 148, 165, 167
  servility, 239, 245
Ionian Enlightenment, 68, 240. See also Ionia
Ionian Sea, 178, **179**
Issedones, 64, 65, 67, 70
Ister, river (Danube), 79n91, 123n61, 167, 230
Italia, 176n102, 180, 187n155
Italos (eponym of Italia), 187
Ivantchik, Askold (also Ivanchik), 66, 72, 75, 76

Jacoby, Felix, 4n4, 5n11, 18, 30–34, 42, 243, 256
  his concept of Kultur, 40–41
  on Herodotus and Athens, 239
  his intellectual and cultural milieu, 34–42
  his legacy and achievements, 30, 34
  the secrets of his workshop, 30–34
Justin's epitome of Pompeius Trogus, 202

Kafiristan, Kafirs, 37
Kalapodi, 202n215, 253
Kaplan, Philip, 221n227
kidaris ("Scythian" cap), 74nn74–75, 82, 194
Kim, Hyun .J., 3n1
kinship, 20, 26, 125, 152, 250
Kirk, Geoffrey, 113

Periodos Ges, 32. *See also* Hecataeus
periodization, 4, 238
Persephone, 201, 209
Persepolis, 12
Perserie, 147
Persia, Persians, 72, 76, 78, 220, 234
  and Athens, 245
  in Persian art, 78
  representation of foreign peoples,
    12–13
Persian Rider, 76, 77–78, 174
Persian Wars, 3, 4, 20, 51, 57, 98, 124,
    243, 250
Peucetios (eponym of Picenes), 187
Phaeacians, 61–62, 88n132, 129,
    144
Phasis, river (Rioni), 124
Pherekydes of Athens, 62, 79, 103, 186
Philoctetes, 189, 190n163
Phineus, 68
Phocylides, 119
Phoenicia, Phoenicians, 86–89, 99,
    129, 142
  early contact with, 86–87, 250
  in Homer, 61, 88–89, 117
  Phoenician cargoes, 145, 183
  settlement overseas, 87
Phrygia, Phrygians, 13, 85, 118
  stereotypes, 118
pinakes, Locrian, 200–201, 203n217
Pindar, 15, 44, 49, 57, 62, 63, 67, 70, 71,
    95, 106, 119, 124, 132, 133, 134, 136,
    138, 147, 199, 213, 247, 251
  Isthmian 5, 132–133
  Isthmian 9, 119
  Olympian 3, 229
  Pythian 4, 106
  Pythian 5, 138
  Pythian 6, 13
  Pythian 9, 138
Pinney, Gloria, 167, 173n95, 174n97
Piraeus, 57, 118, 235
Pisistratus, 84, 196
pit-dwellings, 162–163 (*see also* Northern
    Pontic Region)
Pithekoussai, 57, 125, 184n141
Plataea, 251

play, of ideas, 68, 78, 92, 141, 174, 189,
    193, 198, 243, 249
  of meaning, 18, 195, 249
poetic anthropology. *See* Hartog *and*
    anthropology
polarities, 98, 248, 249
  in archaeological discourse, 161, 174,
    207
  attempts to locate in Homer's *Iliad*, 53
  and identity, 8, 26, 44, 51, 73, 152, 208,
    250
  and Leoxus stele, 173–174
  in the *Odyssey*, 60
Polyphemos, 51, 60, 62, 69, 238. *See
    also* Cyclopes
  blinding of, 143–**144**
Porthion, 163
Poseidon, 97
positioning, 29
  in relation to others, 29, 59, 133, 211,
    249, 252, 253, 256
  and the past, 131, 211, 253, 256
postcolonial thought, 6, 19, 101n207, 116,
    222, 248, 255
Potters' Quarter, Athens, 104, 160, 193
power, 46, 47, 142, 149, 210, 222, 235,
    243, 248, 254
practice, notions of, 6n20
Presocratics, 67, 122, 169, 240
professionalization, of Classics and
    Anthropology, 41. *See also*
    discourses of professionalism
promanteia, 219
prose, 3, 30
  emergence of, 44, 235–237
  links to catalogue poetry, 124. *See also*
    periegetic accounts
  its primacy examined, 235
  and stereotypes, 118
  studies in, 3, 5, 8, 13, 16
prostitution, sacred, 201–204
  profane and banal, 89n137, 94
Protagoras, 240, 241
proverbs, 15n53, 17, 71n63, 123n55, 249
  and Lydia, 90–91
  and Nineveh, 119
  and Phoenicians, 89

Tethys (wife of Ocean), 101
Thales, 101, 240
Thamyras (Thracian bard), 84
Thasos, 84, 85, 86, 87, 88n130, 163,
    197n192
Thebes, Boeotian, 87, 132–133
    chariots from, 147
Thebes, Egyptian, 10, 100, 102
Theron of Acragas, 123, 229
Thessaly, Thessalians, 107, 169, 243
    and Hellenic genealogy, 214 (see also
      Amphiktyonic genealogy *and*
      genealogy)
    proverbial bumpkins, 119
Theseus, 79
Thomas, Rosalind, 241, 244
thought-worlds, 17, 240n22. *See also*
    imaginaire
Thrace, Thracians
    "beer-sucking", 85
    contact with, 84–85, 146
    costume, 78, 86
    in Homer, 83, 146
    part of a pan-Mediterranean *koiné*, 84
    physiognomy of, 85
    "top-knotted", 83, 115, 184
    in vase-painting, 84, 86, 140, 142
Thucydides, 7, 16, 186, 198, 230n314
Thutmose IV (Pharaoh), 10
Timpone della Motta, 190, 191–192, 211,
    242
Tmolus, Mt. (Lydia), 91
Torrebians, 95
trade, 9n31, 26, 44, 47, 48, 66n43, 101,
    128
    involving prestige items, 84, 86, 88,
      100, 145, 196
    mute, 56
    and Phaeacians, 61
    and Phoenicians, 61, 86n122, 89
    problematized, 68n48
    riverine, 155, 160, 181
    as a source of information and ideas,
      78, 93, 96, 97, 98, 99n194, 100,
      145–148, 155–157, 159–160, 183n136,
      184, 187, 194
    in wine, 69n53, 145, 146, 147, 159, 187

travelers' tales, 57, 71, 96, 100, 142, 148,
    102, 219
treasury, treasuries, 213 (*see also*
    sanctuaries, Panhellenic)
    belonging to Caere and Spina, 225
    in Egypt, 101
    Sybarite, 192 (*see also* Sybaris)
Troy, Trojans, 54, 55, 60n10, 79, 83, 113,
    250
Trojan horse, 190
Trojan War, 76, 98n185, 100n202, 167,
    182n121, 189. *See also* Troy, Trojans
tryphê (luxury), 89–90
tunny fish, 135
turbans, 93n162, 94, 194
Tylor, Edward, 40
Tyrrhenia, Tyrrhenians. *See* Etruria
Tyrrhenian Sea, 178, **179**

ultraviolet analysis, 76
uraeus, 104, **105**
Urartu, 11
U-shaped Stoa, 199
utopias, 61, 72, 123

van Dommelen, Peter, 116
vase-painting, 93, 140–145, 175
Vernant, Jean-Pierre, 45, 73
Vidal-Naquet, Pierre, 62n19, 73
Virchow, Rudolf, 37, 38n145
Visonà, Paolo, 207
visual ethnographies, 17
    approaches to, 140–141
    and collective identities, 141
    partial treatment to date, 140
Vlassopoulos, Kostas, 18nn62, 64,
    35n132, 46n177, 49n189, 57n226,
    217n261, 221n276, 234n4, 244n40
Volk, usage of, 41
Völkerschauen, 38
votives, votive offerings, 202, 213
    to Achilles, 166
    to Apollo Ietros, 168
    at Centocamere, Locri, 201
    at Delphi, 225
    inscription honouring Ammon, 102
    at Olympia, 224–226

at the sanctuary of Demeter and
Persephone at Cyrene, 209
shield from Tiryns, 80

wagons used as houses, 46, 68, 69, 71
West, Stephanie, 164
White Island (Leuke), **154**, 167
Wilamowitz Moellendorff, Ulrich von,
35
Jacoby's mentor, 35
views on race and identity, 35–36n135
Winter, Irene, 88–89
Witoulia (from *witoulos*, "calf"), 187

Xanthus the Lydian, 15, 86, 95
Xenocrates (Acragantine charioteer), 136
Xenokles (potter), 93
Xenophanes of Colophon, 85, 89–90,
96, 97, 147, 240

Yanamamo (Amazonian tribe), 7

Zaleucus of Locri, 199
Zambrini, Andrea, 5n11, 32n119, 33n124,
34n127, 256
Zeus, 60, 171, 225
Zeus Ammon, 106, 139